PROFESSIONAL
MICROSOFT® SQL SERVER® 2012 REPORTING SERVICES

W9-AHA-222

PROFESSIONAL

Microsoft® SQL Server® 2012
Reporting Services

PROFESSIONAL

Microsoft® SQL Server® 2012 Reporting Services

Paul Turley,
Robert M. Bruckner,
Thiago Silva,
Ken Withee, and Grant Paisley

WILEY

John Wiley & Sons, Inc.

Professional Microsoft® SQL Server® 2012 Reporting Services

Published by
John Wiley & Sons, Inc.
10475 Crosspoint Boulevard
Indianapolis, IN 46256
www.wiley.com

ISBN: 978-1-118-10111-7

ISBN: 978-1-118-22379-6 (ebk)

ISBN: 978-1-118-23713-7 (ebk)

ISBN: 978-1-118-26210-8 (ebk)

Manufactured in the United States of America

10 9 8 7 6 5 4 3 2 1

For general information on our other products and services please contact our Customer Care Department within the United States at (877) 762-2974, outside the United States at (317) 572-3993 or fax (317) 572-4002.

Wiley publishes in a variety of print and electronic formats and by print-on-demand. Some material included with standard print versions of this book may not be included in e-books or in print-on-demand. If this book refers to media such as a CD or DVD that is not included in the version you purchased, you may download this material at http://booksupport.wiley.com. For more information about Wiley products, visit www.wiley.com.

Library of Congress Control Number: 2012933621

This book is dedicated to my wonderful wife, Sherri, for her love and endless support. To my dad, Mark, and to the most incredible young people on the planet; Krista, Sara, Rachael, and Josh.

— PAUL TURLEY

Dedicated to my parents.

— ROBERT M. BRUCKNER

I dedicate this book to my beautiful wife, Michelle, who still loves me and encourages me, after all these years; to my children, Gabriella, Joshua, and Olivia, who brighten my life with their smiles and unconditional hugs; and to my mother Lucia who keeps believing that I am a rockstar.

— THIAGO SILVA

I dedicate this book to my wife and best friend, Rosemarie Withee.

— KEN WITHEE

I dedicate this book to my wife Sue, who still loves me after all these years; to my teenage kids, Megan, Lisa, and Zoe, who have turned out even better than I could have hoped; and to mum and dad who gave me the opportunity and encouragement to always do and learn new things.

— GRANT PAISLEY

ABOUT THE AUTHORS

PAUL TURLEY is a Mentor with SolidQ, a Microsoft MVP, solution architect, teacher and presenter. He speaks at industry conferences and authors several publications on BI, data visualization, and reporting. He blogs at SQLServerBIBlog.com. He has been developing business database solutions since 1991 for companies like Microsoft, Disney, Nike, and Hewlett-Packard. He has been a Microsoft Certified Trainer since 1996 and holds several industry certifications, including MCTS and MCITP for BI, MCSD, MCDBA, MSF Practitioner, and IT Project+.

Paul has authored and coauthored several books and courses on databases, business intelligence, and application development technologies. His books include *SQL Server Reporting Services Recipes for Designing Expert Reports, Professional SQL Server 2008 Reporting Services, Professional SQL Server 2005 Reporting Services, Professional SQL Server Reporting Services (SQL Server 2000), Beginning T-SQL with SQL Server 2005 and 2008, Beginning Transact-SQL with SQL Server 2000 and 2005, Beginning SQL Server 2005 Administration, Beginning Access 2002 VBA, Data Warehousing with SQL Server 2000 Analysis Services,* and *Professional Access 2000 Programming* — all from Wrox. He is also the lead author for *SQL Server 2005 Integration Services Step by Step from Microsoft Press.*

ROBERT M. BRUCKNER, is a principal software architect and developer with the Microsoft SQL Server division. Robert is responsible for the technical architecture of SQL Server Reporting Services including Power View. One of Robert's core areas has been the design and development of the scalable report processing engine, utilized by Reporting Services and Power View. Power View is an enhancement of Reporting Services 2012, enabling end-users to easily and interactively visualize data, quickly gain analytical insights, and simply have fun exploring data!

Prior to joining Microsoft in 2003, Robert researched, designed, and implemented database and business intelligence systems as a system architect at T-Mobile Austria, and as a researcher at Vienna University of Technology, Austria. Robert holds Master and PhD degrees with highest distinctions in Computer Science from Vienna University of Technology, and holds several patents.

Anyone good with a search engine can find thousands of Robert's past postings on public newsgroups and MSDN forums sharing his insights, tips, tricks, and expert advice related to Reporting Services and other SQL Server technologies. Robert has co-authored books on SQL Server Reporting Services as well as Analysis Services. Robert regularly presents at industry conferences and also maintains a popular blog at: http://blogs.msdn.com/robertbruckner. In his spare time, Robert enjoys mountain biking, skiing, and reading.

THIAGO SILVA is an MCPD and an architect and consultant for Credera. Thiago has been developing custom .NET and Reporting Services since the early days of .NET and SQL Server 2000. He is a part of the Microsoft practice within Credera, a Dallas-based consulting firm, delivering Microsoft solutions to clients that include several Fortune 500 companies. He has worked as a consultant for the last eight years and as a software engineer and web developer prior to that. Thiago is co-author of the previous edition of this book, *Professional SQL Server 2008 Reporting Services,* and he was a contributor in the book *Microsoft SQL Server Reporting Recipes for Designing Expert Reports.* Thiago has been featured on the tech podcast ".NET Rocks!", and he is a member of the DFW .NET user groups and community. He occasionally writes articles on his tech blog "Silvaware," found at `http://silvaware.net`. Thiago holds a BBA in Information and Operations Management with a focus on Information Systems from Texas A&M University. He holds MCAD, MCPD, and MCTS titles for web development using ASP.NET 2, 3.5, and 4.

KEN WITHEE is President of Portal Integrators LLC (`www.portalint.com`), a software development company focused on developing world class business applications for the SharePoint platform. He lives with his wife Rosemarie in Seattle, Washington, and is the author or coauthor of several books including *Microsoft Office 365 For Dummies* (Wiley, 2011), *SharePoint 2010 Development For Dummies* (Wiley, 2011), *Professional Microsoft Project Server 2010* (Wrox, 2012), *Microsoft Business Intelligence For Dummies* (Wiley, 2010), *Professional Microsoft SQL Server 2012 Reporting Services* (Wrox, 2012), and *Professional Microsoft SQL Server 2008 Reporting Services* (Wrox, 2008). Ken has also written a number of other published works in a variety of journals and magazines.

Ken earned a Master of Science degree in Computer Science studying under Dr. Edward Lank at San Francisco State University. Their work has been published in the LNCS journals and was the focus of a presentation at the IASTED conference in Phoenix. Their work has also been presented at various other Human Computer Interaction conferences throughout the world.

Ken has more than 12 years of professional computer and management experience working with a vast range of technologies. He is a Microsoft Certified Technology Specialist and is certified in SharePoint, SQL Server, and .NET.

GRANT PAISLEY is an SQL Server MVP and founder of Angry Koala, a Microsoft Business Intelligence consultancy based in Sydney, Australia. Grant is president of the SQL Server Usergroup Sydney and is an internationally recognized speaker who has spoken at TechEd USA, Australia, and even China. His passion about BI, in particular with visualization of data, resulted in Grant creating `http://reportsurfer.com`, a community reporting site. Grant was also a contributing author for *SQL Server 2008 Analysis Services with MD* and *Microsoft SQL Server Reporting Services Recipes.* If you don't see him on stage presenting, you might see him on the water kite surfing in Hawai'i or mountain biking in Whistler.

CREDITS

ACKNOWLEDGMENTS

Thanks to:

My wonderful family for their enduring support and occasional tolerance for my over-commitment to books, papers, projects, and events. To my wife Sherri who says "Honey, I love you, but if you bring home one more piece of conference swag, you'll sleep in the garage."

...the Reporting Services and SQL Server BI product teams at Microsoft; Thierry, Sean, Carolyn, Lukasz, Ariel, Robert, and many others who have been open and available for the past nine years of books, projects, and support. Thank you for letting me play a small role in your quest to avail these fantastic technologies to people who use them to deliver information and make important things happen all over the world. Thanks to Mark, Chuck, Denny, Carl, John, and the SQL CAT team.

...the Microsoft MVP organization for building an unbelievable network of dedicated professionals. To the SQL Server PASS organization who have nurtured a respected and trusted community. To Arnie and the Oregon SQL team for being my "homies." Thanks to all the PASS chapter directors and SQL Saturday organizers everywhere.

...everyone at SolidQ for building a stellar organization, unlike any other. I'm proud to be counted among so many trusted friends and professionals.

A heartfelt thanks to the editorial and management team at Wiley; especially Bob and Kelly. How you maintain your sanity trying to manage those who write books in our "spare" time is beyond my comprehension. Thank you for your enduring patience and perseverance. Thank you to my co-authors and reviewers; Robert, Ken, Grant, Thiago, Joe, Chris, Nigel, and Glyn who have endured endless nights and weekends, reviews, and rewrites. Just one more revision and we should be done, guys! Thank you all for making this book happen.

I have a profound respect for those who write "those other" books, and who I consider to be peers and co-contributors to a vibrant industry. Thank you Stacia, Teo, and Brian for keeping the bar high and for your contributions to the industry.

— PAUL TURLEY

Robert would like to thank in particular Paul Turley and Bob Elliott for great collaboration throughout this project, drawing from the experience of several seasoned Reporting Services experts, and collecting proven best practices from large-scale customer deployments of Reporting Services. Furthermore, Robert would like to express a big "thank you" to all co-authors contributing to this book, to Kelly Talbot for great editorial work, and to technical reviewers for ensuring accuracy.

— ROBERT M. BRUCKNER

ACKNOWLEDGMENTS

Thanks to Thierry D'Hers, Robert Bruckner, and the Reporting Services product team for their guidance and technical assistance during the authoring of this book.

Thanks to Paul Turley for continuing to give me the opportunity to be a part of this book project, and for Kelly Talbot and Bob Elliot's support and patience during the writing and editorial process.

Finally, thanks to my wife and kids, who have put up with my long hours and weekend nights spent during the writing of this book. I appreciate their love and encouragement and could not have done this without them.

— THIAGO SILVA

I would like to acknowledge my grandma Tiny Withee who turns 99 this year and is still going strong. I would also like to acknowledge my wife Rosemarie Withee, mother Maggie Blair, father Ken Withee, sister Kate Henneinke, and parents-in-law Alfonso and Lourdes Supetran and family.

An extraordinary amount of thanks goes to my co-authors; Paul Turley, Robert Bruckner, Thiago Silva, and Grant Paisley. Special thanks to Bob Elliott, Kelly Talbot, Gayle Johnson, Joe Salvatore, Chris Albrektson, Nigel Sammy, and the rest of the Wrox team for making this book a reality.

— KEN WITHEE

Thank you to the Angry Koala Team, Glyn Llewellyn who picks up the reins in my absence and helped in the writing of my chapters; Colin McGowan, David Lean, Geoff Orr, Mark Fitzpatrick, Lesley Llewellyn, Peter Orgill, and Praveen Chand, who through their professionalism and enthusiasm for BI, are the backbone to my success. Thanks to my good friend Paul Turley for opportunity and support during authoring; Kelly and the team at Wrox for their invaluable role in getting the book into production. And finally my family Sue, Megan, Lisa, and Zoe that I love but rarely say so. Oh and I nearly forgot: "Megan is awesome" — actually you all are!

— GRANT PAISLEY

CONTENTS

PART V: SOLUTION PATTERNS

CHAPTER 15: MANAGING REPORT PROJECTS 463

PART VIII: APPENDIXES

FOREWORD

Fifteen years ago, in January 1997, our company, Panorama Software, was acquired by Microsoft during its entry into the business intelligence space. That was a long time ago. In fact, it was so long ago, I'm not sure that business intelligence was even called BI. Back then our mission and strategy were simple, accompanied by the short but effective slogan "OLAP for the masses." For the most part that mission hasn't changed over the years. We've simply focused on different aspects of the product that would deliver us the "masses."

In the early years, our focus and mission were to ensure that our technology was easy to use, didn't require much consulting (relative to what was required at the time in the market), and yes, was cheap. The idea was to make the technology accessible to as many companies as possible. The other element of the strategy was to make the solution a platform play and build a healthy ecosystem around our BI offering.

Indeed, in the early years we set out to build a server with strong capabilities, with a rich set of APIs and query language (MDX). We also built a thriving ecosystem of partners.

Results were seen quickly. The SQL OLAP Server, later known as SQL Server Analysis Services, became the most widely used OLAP Server in the world, a title the product still holds today.

Witnessing the market adoption of and reaction to the Analysis Services server, we began our second act by offering something new and innovative for reporting solutions: SQL Server Reporting Services. Its adoption surpassed our wildest expectations. Overnight our user base grew by tens of millions of report consumers, who got their reports and insights from their IT departments. Just like that, we took a giant step forward in reaching the masses we were after.

As more and more companies have begun using BI solutions, user sophistication has evolved. Our users suddenly felt the power and value BI offers, and they wanted more of it. However, they discovered that their IT departments could not address their demand, and they became a bottleneck.

Viewing the problem as both an inhibitor and an opportunity to expand our reach and continue our mission of providing "BI for the masses," we developed a set of tools. PowerPivot was released in 2010, followed by Power View in 2012. They aimed to help information workers build their own BI solutions with what we called "managed self-service BI." The self-service concept is easy to grasp: Build a tool that can be used by any information worker who has access to data so that he can build his own BI solution. The managed aspect is more fundamental. Even though we want to empower end users, IT wants to do so in a controlled and safe fashion. IT wants to ensure that all critical data and apps are properly backed up, that the data is not stale, and that it is clear how the data is used and by whom.

The change from developing a first-class platform for developers and IT pros to developing a first-class solution for information workers required a significant change in how we design and build our software. It required us to simplify the offering, reducing the technical knowledge users must have. It required us to invest a lot in smart defaults so that users would not need to undergo training to learn the product. It required a whole new level of interactivity of performance, with instant response times, because users are impatient. We needed to assume that the users would experiment with their data set. This is unlike a professional BI project, which has a well-defined set of requirements that developers must meet. In the self-service scenario, the user simply experiments with the data and discovers insights on his own. This leads us to one of our most important design points: have fun. The only way a user will take the time to discover insights on his own is if he has fun with the data.

What I really like about *Professional SQL Server 2012 Reporting Services* is that it's a perfect reflection of the Microsoft BI journey through the eyes of the Reporting Services product line, from the early days of managed and operational to the latest addition of self-service reporting. This book was written by experts who built the product and have implemented it at customers' sites. Together they have more than 40 years of business intelligence experience.

I call this book the encyclopedia of SQL Server Reporting Services. All the chapters have been updated with the latest information to ensure accuracy and compatibility with the latest version of SQL Server 2012. The book includes a new section that reflects the addition of Power View with PowerPivot. You'll learn how to best use the two together to reflect the latest management capabilities of Reporting Services in SharePoint.

I hope you will enjoy reading this book and using SQL Server Reporting Services 2012 as much as we, the product team, have enjoyed building the product.

—ARIEL NETZ
Partner Group Program Manager
SQL Server Reporting Services
Microsoft

INTRODUCTION

Reporting Services is a report design and enterprise-class information delivery tool that has aged and matured for more than nine years now. And this book has grown along with the product. We first started writing *Professional Microsoft SQL Server Reporting Services* before the product was released, back in 2003. After four new versions of Reporting Services, there have been four editions of this book.

We have learned a lot about report writing and report solution development from our experience with SSRS and other reporting tools, and we share the benefit of that experience in this book. Not only do we show you how to use this technology and tools to design reports as they were intended to be used, but we also share the best practices and lessons we have learned along the way. The authors have spent tens of thousands of hours using these tools to solve business problems for organizations in many different industries and businesses.

WHO THIS BOOK IS FOR

Some books are written specifically for beginners, and others are for serious developers and advanced report designers. We've made it a point to address the needs of the many without sacrificing the needs of the few. We wanted to write a book that would meet the needs of a broad audience, along with specific solutions for report designers, developers, administrators, and business professionals. Our goal is for this book to be a comprehensive guide and valuable reference. To meet this objective, we've divided this book into parts — "mini-books," if you will. Depending on your needs, you may spend more time focusing on the material in one of these parts and using the others for reference. This book is written for the novice report designer and the expert interested in learning to use advanced functionality. For the application developer, we cover programming in reports and custom applications that integrate reports. You also learn about report server administration and security issues.

We've come to know more about the people who use Reporting Services in various ways. The following sections describe people in different roles and the parts of the book that address their needs. We've given these people names to make the examples more realistic. Use these examples as a guide to find the role that best describes your needs and the ways in which you will use Reporting Services.

Report Designer

Mary works in the financial group for a company that provides consumer services. She is a computer-savvy worker who possesses a wide range of office skills. She has worked in this group for several years and could easily do her boss's job. She understands her company's business processes, financial reporting practices, invoicing, and billing systems. She's not a computer genius, but she knows her way around word processing, spreadsheets, e-mail, and simple database reporting. Mary started using Microsoft Access a few years ago. She used the wizards to create some simple reports from data exported from the HR and customer billing systems. After a while, she learned how to write queries and build Access reports without the wizards, with custom formatting, groups, and summaries. She has used other reporting tools to report on the data in the company's data warehouse and some operational databases. She has designed several reports with charts and pivots to analyze sales trends and profitability. Her company recently standardized the use of Reporting Services.

Mary's focus is on out-of-the-box reporting — designing and deploying reports as easily as possible using the tools readily available within the product. She might end up designing standard server-based reports that users will access from a central report server via the corporate intranet. She may also want to create her own ad hoc client-side reports from data models created by an administrator or more advanced designer.

The following parts of the book will be of most interest to Mary:

➤ Part I, "Getting Started"

➤ Part II, "Report Design"

➤ Part III, "Business Intelligence Reporting"

➤ Part IV, "Enabling User Reporting"

Application Developer

Joe has been writing database applications for several years. A few years ago he began using Microsoft .NET programming tools and landed a programming position in the company's Information Technology group. Joe has designed many of the company's web sites and portals using the Visual Basic .NET and C# programming languages. Most of the reports Joe has created were written from scratch as custom web pages. He has worked a little with a few specialized reporting applications. He wants to add reporting capabilities to some of the company's custom business applications.

As far as Joe is concerned, writing simple reports is for others to do. He's more concerned with adding functionality to a solution rather than dealing with business questions and aesthetic qualities of reports. His focus will likely be to add filtering, custom formatting, and conditional logic using program code and query scripts. He will also design his reports so that they fit into applications as an integrated part of a solution. He may also want to create customized management utilities to automate report server maintenance routines.

Joe understands that Reporting Services offers many flexible options for integrating reports into different application interfaces. He may want to build reports into a custom Windows desktop application, web application, SharePoint Portal, or mobile device application.

Joe will be most interested in these parts:

➤ Part II, "Report Design"

➤ Part III, "Business Intelligence Reporting"

➤ Part V, "Solution Patterns"

➤ Part VII, "Reporting Services Custom Programming"

Systems Engineer or DBA

Bob is a network engineer and database administrator. He is more concerned with the security and stability of the corporate servers than with the aesthetics and features of each report. He will want to make sure that the report managers, designers, developers, and users are organized into roles and that the report server is appropriately secured. Bob will install and configure options on the report server. He will schedule maintenance tasks, optimize the database and queries, and provide ongoing maintenance and disaster recovery.

Bob will find these parts most useful:

➤ Part I, "Getting Started"

➤ Part V, "Solution Patterns"

➤ Part VI, "Administering Reporting Services"

Business Leader

As a business owner, corporate executive, or project manager, you may be the consumer of a reporting solution or the director of the development effort. Perhaps you have enlisted the services of a business intelligence consulting firm to architect a decision-support system to help run your business. You need to be informed about your options and understand the capabilities of the products and technologies used to create your solution. This book helps you understand these features and the choices necessary to put them into practice. The implementers of this solution will look to you for business requirements and feature choices. Chapters 1 and 4 are a good place to start. Part III, "Business Intelligence Reporting," may be of particular interest to you because it is a guide for the types of reporting scenarios applied to your business analytics. Part V, "Solution Patterns," discusses how to define and manage reporting solutions and business requirements and specifications. This will serve as a communication medium between you, business users, and your report designers.

WHAT THIS BOOK COVERS

This book is divided into seven parts:

➤ Part I, "Getting Started"

➤ Part II, "Report Design"

➤ Part III, "Business Intelligence Reporting"

➤ Part IV, "Enabling User Reporting"

➤ Part V, "Solution Patterns"

➤ Part VI, "Administering Reporting Services"

➤ Part VII, "Reporting Services Custom Programming"

Part I: Getting Started

Chapter 1, "Introducing Reporting Services," describes the capabilities and features of Reporting Services. You learn about its extensible architecture, which makes it a powerful and flexible addition to nearly all existing business systems. This chapter builds a foundation of understanding upon which you will learn to design, deploy, manage, and perhaps customize business intelligence and reporting solutions. You learn about report user profiles and report application and solution types. The new report design tools for SQL Server 2012 are introduced. These include the new SQL Server Data Tools Report Designer and Report Builder.

Chapter 2, "Reporting Services Installation and Architecture," helps you install Reporting Services and explains the architecture of a complete reporting solution. This chapter guides you through the steps to set up your development environment and plan your enterprise deployment. This helps you understand the core services and technologies that Reporting Services uses. By learning how the product works and how the components interact, you will be better prepared to design and maintain a scalable solution.

Chapter 3, "Configuring SharePoint Integration," is for you if you plan to integrate Reporting Services with SharePoint. You learn how to install and configure all the integrated components. You can skip this chapter if you plan to use Reporting Services in Native deployment mode, without SharePoint.

Part II: Report Design

Designing reports can be as simple as running a wizard, or it can be a highly complex development process that defines advanced features. You learn how reports actually process and render data, and how to use parameters and expressions to define creative report solutions.

Chapter 4, "Basic Report Design," starts with the fundamentals and teaches you how to create basic reports using simple design tools. You learn the essentials of what you need to get started building basic reports using the Report Wizard and common Report Designer features. You're introduced to the fundamental building blocks of report design: report items and report layout properties. This chapter describes the two report design tools used to create standard reports. Report Builder is for users who want a simple, straightforward tool for designing basic reports. The SQL Server Data Tools help you manage report projects and design reports in the Microsoft Visual Studio development environment.

Chapter 5, "Report Layout and Formatting," addresses different report design layouts and the components used to assemble a report. This chapter describes the report body, headers, footers, and page-formatting properties. You learn about the capabilities of each report item and the data range components that are used to organize and present data. After you explore the basics, you learn about grouping data, lists, and data regions; using tables and matrix reports; defining drill-through reports; and using charts. You also learn how to write expressions and custom code to extend formatting and apply business logic, and how to design reports for mobile devices.

Chapter 6, "Designing Data Access," reveals that reports are based on a data source and that Reporting Services may be used to present data from many different data sources. You learn to define stand-alone and shared data sources, queries, and datasets and to use parameters to filter data at the database and at the Report Server. You learn to use new parameter features introduced in the latest version of the product. This chapter is a primer on T-SQL queries and stored procedures. You also learn how to build reports using Analysis Services and the MDX Query Builder. Query examples are also provided for Oracle PL/SQL, Sybase, and Access SQL dialects.

Chapter 7, "Advanced Report Design," helps you take design elements to the next level by showing you how to creatively use data groups and combinations of report items. Calculations and conditional formatting may be added by using simple programming code. Whether you are an application developer or a report designer, this chapter contains important information to help you design reports to meet your users' requirements and raise the bar with compelling report features.

Chapter 8, "Chart Reports," focuses on simple and advanced charting visuals. You learn how to group and aggregate values in a variety of chart presentations. This chapter is a guide for the types of charts you can use to present different types of data in different scenarios. We also expose several hard-to-find chart features and properties that are useful when you create more advanced visual reports.

Part III: Business Intelligence Reporting

Chapter 9, "BI Semantic Models," covers a new topic and set of capabilities introduced in SQL Server 2012. This chapter explains these options and technologies in simple terms, clarifying the choices and best solutions.

Chapter 10, "Reporting with Analysis Services," discusses the advantages and unique challenges of reporting on multidimensional cubes and databases. You learn the fundamentals of MDX query design and consuming cube data in the report designer.

Chapter 11, "OLAP Reporting Advanced Techniques," addresses the design techniques and unique best practices for reporting on multidimensional cube data. You learn how to create MDX queries with parameters, calculations, and aggregations. You also learn to apply advanced report design patterns and techniques to build a dynamic cube browser.

Part IV: Enabling User Reporting

Chapter 12, "Tabular Models," covers semantic modeling using PowerPivot and enterprise-scale tabular models in SQL Server 2012. You learn about the basic use and application of tabular models used to perform in-memory aggregation, modeling data from different sources, defining relationships, and performing calculations using DAX, hierarchies, and KPIs.

Chapter 13, "Visual Analytics with Power View," describes Power View, a simple yet powerful user reporting tool used to visualize information in a semantic model. You learn how to browse information to answer key business questions and gain insight from a set of data. Power View users who understand a semantic model and the core mechanics of the tool can create compelling reports and attractive business presentations in a tactile and interactive reporting interface.

Chapter 14, "Report Builder Solution Strategies," is a guide to using the Report Builder design tool, which can be used to enable user self-service reporting scenarios. It helps users help themselves after the necessary preparation and planning. You learn how to teach users to utilize this tool to consume data available to them for reporting. You also learn how to support users and train them to use this tool to answer question and build their own reports using shared components such as shared data sources, shared datasets, and report parts.

Part V: Solution Patterns

Chapter 15, "Managing Report Projects," helps you plan and manage report projects of varying sizes and scales. You learn how to maintain small-scale report projects with one or a few report designers and large-scale, formal projects with a team of developers and report designers. We discuss strategies for using Report Builder in SharePoint to manage business user reports and SQL Server Data Tools with integrated version control and team collaboration.

Chapter 16, "Report Solution Patterns and Recipes," covers design patterns we've learned from years of solution design. We separate reality and theory, and discuss the best practices and techniques that work for others in the industry. We also discuss how to establish the standards and practices adapted for the needs and requirements of your users and business.

Part VI: Administering Reporting Services (via tracking grid)

Report server administration has an important job: keeping data secure and available to the right users. Server-side reports can be configured and secured to optimize performance and to provide the right information to the appropriate user communities. Chapters 13 and 14 teach you how to use all the tools necessary to configure and manage your Report Server.

Chapter 17, "Content Management," teaches you how to use management tools and Reporting Services features to publish reports and manage execution and delivery. You learn to create automated scripts and custom solutions to manage all the Report Server content. You revisit the stages of report execution from an administrator's point of view and learn how to optimize them. You also learn how to automate report delivery and server management.

Chapter 18, "Integrating Reports with SharePoint," helps you understand how Reporting Services and SharePoint are used together to create business solutions. Whether you choose to configure Reporting Services in SharePoint integrated or Native deployment mode, you can embed report content using web parts. You also learn how to take advantage of Integrated mode features to make reporting a seamless part of the team collaboration culture in your business.

Chapter 19, "Native Mode Server Administration," is a comprehensive administrator's guide. You explore the related considerations for reporting requirements and deployment scenarios for Reporting Services. You learn about the configuration tools and utilities, backup and restore procedures, and how to monitor a Reporting Services instance for issues and optimal performance.

Part VII: Reporting Services Custom Programming

Practically all the built-in functionality in Reporting Services can be automated and performed through custom program code. This includes report rendering and the core services of the reporting environment: data access, rendering formats, security, and delivery.

Chapter 20, "Integrating Reports into Custom Applications," shows you that Reporting Services is a flexible reporting tool that can be easily incorporated into different applications. In this chapter, you learn to use URLs to access reports from document and web page links and use the Reporting Services Web service to programmatically render reports. You also use the `ReportViewer` controls to embed reports into custom Windows Forms and ASP.NET Web Forms applications. You learn to display reports in web portals using SharePoint web parts and other techniques. You can use programmatic rendering, URL, or the `ReportViewer` controls to create custom report viewers and parameter interfaces. Examples are provided in C# and VB.NET.

Chapter 21, "Using Embedded and Referenced Code," shows you techniques for adding custom logic to your reports using application code contained within a report or in an externally referenced assembly component. Using either of these techniques, you can use programming techniques to add custom behaviors and to enable advanced reporting features.

Chapter 22, "Extending Reporting Services," is written for serious application developers using object-oriented programming techniques, with examples in C# and VB.NET. You learn how to create custom libraries and extensions to add functionality to reports and Report Server features. These extensions may be used to access unique data sources, to render reports to specific formats, to authenticate users, and to deliver reports outside of the default methods provided with the product.

Appendixes

The appendixes describe T-SQL syntax, variables, and functions and MDX language functions and reference.

WHAT YOU NEED TO USE THIS BOOK

The hardware and software requirements for designing and running SQL Server 2012 and Reporting Services are such that they will run on most newer business grade computers. Some features and the capabilities integrated with SharePoint will require a more advanced configuration including software and more capable hardware. Custom programming examples require that you install any edition of Visual Studio 2010.

The requirements for SQL Server 2012 specified by Microsoft may be found online in the MSDN library located at: `http://msdn.microsoft.com/en-us/library/ms143506.aspx`. Setting up and configuring a SharePoint BI environment can be a complex process that requires specific hardware capabilities. The requirements specified by Microsoft for SharePoint, PowerPivot, Power View, and Reporting Services running in SharePoint Integrated mode may be found at: `http://msdn.microsoft.com/en-us/library/ee210640.aspx`.

➤ The Developer or Enterprise Editions are recommended for all the advanced capabilities covered in the book. You can download an evaluation version of SQL Server from Microsoft at www.microsoft.com/sql.

➤ Report design examples that use standard Reporting Services reports will work with any edition of SQL Server 2012 and will run on a computer meeting the minimum computer requirements.

➤ Chapter 11 and some examples used in other chapters require an installation of SQL Server Analysis Services in multidimensional storage mode. This is an optional part of the SQL Server setup and is installed with a full installation of SQL Server.

➤ Chapters that cover SharePoint integration and Power View require a SharePoint 2010 Enterprise installation, which includes Chapters 13 and 14.

➤ Examples of custom programming performed outside of the report designer will require a separate installation of Visual Studio 2010. This includes the material in Chapters 20, 21, and 22.

➤ The sample databases used in the examples and exercises are available to download from www.wrox.com along with the sample projects for this book. Additional resources may be available.

➤ The complete source code for the samples is available for download from our web site at www.wrox.com. For programming examples, versions are available in both Visual Basic .NET and C#.

An effective method for simulating a multi-server server environment is to use virtual machine images. Microsoft has made virtual images available at times with pre-configured server installations for testing and evaluating their tools. These often contain time-limited-use software. Refer to the book support materials at www.wrox.com for current and updated information.

CONVENTIONS

To help you get the most from the text and keep track of what's happening, we've used a number of conventions throughout the book.

 Boxes with a warning icon like this one hold important, not-to-be-forgotten information that is directly relevant to the surrounding text.

 The pencil icon indicates notes, tips, hints, tricks, and asides to the current discussion.

As for styles in the text:

➤ We *highlight* new terms and important words when we introduce them.

➤ We show keystrokes like this: Ctrl+A.

➤   We show filenames, URLs, and code within the text like so: `persistence.properties`.

➤   We present code in two different ways:

```
We use a monofont type with no highlighting for most code examples.
We use bold to emphasize code that is particularly important in the present context
or to show changes from a previous code snippet.
```

SOURCE CODE

As you work through the examples in this book, you may choose to either type in all the code manually or use the source code files that accompany the book. All the source code used in this book is available for download at `www.wrox.com`. When at the site, simply locate the book's title (use the Search box or one of the title lists) and click the Download Code link on the book's detail page to obtain all the source code for the book. Code that is included on the web site is highlighted by the following icon:

**Available for
download on
Wrox.com**

Listings include the filename in the title. If it is just a code snippet, you'll find the filename in a code note such as this:

Code snippet filename

 Because many books have similar titles, you may find it easiest to search by ISBN; this book's ISBN is 978-1-118-10111-7.

After you download the code, just decompress it with your favorite compression tool. Alternatively, you can go to the main Wrox code download page at `www.wrox.com/dynamic/books/download.aspx` to see the code available for this book and all other Wrox books.

ERRATA

We make every effort to ensure that there are no errors in the text or code. However, no one is perfect, and mistakes do occur. If you find an error in one of our books, such as a spelling mistake or faulty piece of code, we would be grateful for your feedback. By sending in errata, you may save another reader hours of frustration. At the same time, you will help us provide even higher-quality information.

To find the errata page for this book, go to www.wrox.com and locate the title using the Search box or one of the title lists. Then, on the book details page, click the Book Errata link. On this page, you can view all errata that have been submitted for this book and posted by Wrox editors. A complete book list, including links to each book's errata, is also available at www.wrox.com/misc-pages/booklist.shtml.

If you don't spot "your" error on the Book Errata page, go to www.wrox.com/contact/techsupport.shtml and complete the form there to send us the error you found. We'll check the information and, if appropriate, post a message to the book's errata page and fix the problem in subsequent editions of the book.

P2P.WROX.COM

For author and peer discussion, join the P2P forums at p2p.wrox.com. The forums are a Web-based system for you to post messages relating to Wrox books and related technologies and to interact with other readers and technology users. The forums offer a subscription feature that e-mails you when new posts are made to the forums concerning your chosen topics of interest. Wrox authors, editors, other industry experts, and your fellow readers are present on these forums.

At http://p2p.wrox.com, you will find a number of different forums that will help you not only as you read this book, but also as you develop your own applications. To join the forums, follow these steps:

1. Go to http://p2p.wrox.com and click the Register link.

2. Read the terms of use, and then click Agree.

3. Complete the required information to join, as well as any optional information you want to provide, and click Submit.

4. You will receive an e-mail with information describing how to verify your account and complete the joining process.

> *You can read messages in the forums without joining P2P, but to post your own messages, you must join.*

After you join, you can post new messages and respond to messages that other users post. You can read messages at any time on the Web. If you want to receive new messages from a particular forum, click the Subscribe to this Forum icon by the forum name in the forum listing.

For more information about how to use the Wrox P2P, read the P2P FAQs for answers to questions about how the forum software works, as well as many common questions specific to P2P and Wrox books. To read the FAQs, click the FAQ link on any P2P page.

PART I
Getting Started

1

Introducing Reporting Services

WHAT'S IN THIS CHAPTER?

➤ Understanding report designer roles and the tools used to design reports

➤ Understanding dashboards, reports and applications

➤ Examining Business Intelligence solutions

➤ Discovering multidimensional and tabular semantic models

You're holding this book, trying to decide if it will help you solve a problem or teach you essential skills to create reports with Reporting Services. If you and I were having this conversation in person, I'd ask you to tell me what you need. I teach classes and travel to companies to create report and BI solutions, and at the beginning of every class or consulting engagement, I ask what the student or client needs. What are the requirements? What questions does your report need to answer? What's not working? What needs to be fixed, and what will it take to build a solution to help you reach your goals? So, I ask you, what do you need? Why are you reading a book about Reporting Services? Do you have a specific problem to resolve, or do you just need to develop some basic report design skills? Do you need to build an entire reporting solution? Who are the users of these reports? Are they department workers, business managers, or financial analysts? Maybe your user is the CEO of a major corporation or other business executives who need to know if the company is on the right track. Maybe you need to create reports for your own business to make sure it's profitable and achieving its goals. Whether you are creating an invoice to sell arts and crafts out of your garage or a BI dashboard to help manage a multinational corporation, the reports you will create are important. Therefore, you need to make sure they deliver accurate information and are designed correctly, using industry best practices. That's a big responsibility.

Whatever your needs, we'll cover all these bases and address each topic thoroughly. I've enlisted some of my most trusted associates to share their experiences.

This chapter is a high-level introduction to the concepts and capabilities of this powerful reporting tool and the data analysis platform of Microsoft SQL Server 2012. It introduces common reporting scenarios, beginning with the most basic and then moving to the more advanced. In subsequent chapters, you will explore these capabilities in depth and learn how to use them in your own reporting solutions.

SQL Server Reporting Services has grown to become the de facto industry standard reporting tool by which others are measured. It is a foundation upon which you can construct complete report, scorecard, and dashboard solutions for business users. Today, it does everything from simple ad hoc data reporting to delivering enterprise-ready integrated reporting into business portals and custom applications.

Not long ago, the information technology (IT) group for a large financial services company wanted to make sure that they were using the best reporting tool on the market. They decided to hire a consulting company to evaluate every major reporting product and give them an unbiased analysis. I was lucky to land this assignment. We worked with the client to identify about 50 points of evaluation criteria. Then I contacted all the major vendors, installed evaluation copies and explored features, and spoke with other customers and with those who specialized in using these various products. It really helped us see the industry from a broad perspective and was a valuable learning experience. There are some respectable products on the market, and all have their strengths, but I can honestly say that Microsoft has a unique and special platform. As a consultant, contractor to Microsoft, and Microsoft SQL Server MVP, I have had the opportunity to work alongside the Reporting Services product team for many years. They have a vision, and they're passionate about their product. I have a great deal of respect for the fine people who continue to develop and improve Reporting Services, version after version.

WHO USES REPORTING SERVICES?

Business users fit into a few categories when we consider how they use reports. Some are report consumers only. They're happy to use reports that have been written and published for them. Others prefer to create their own reports using business tools they understand and use for other things, as Excel is used for planning and financial analysis. Maybe they just want to browse information to look for trends and to understand how the business is measuring up against their goals. Still other business users want to use more sophisticated tools to create powerful reports. A typical information technology group at most large organizations has three common roles: system administrators, application developers, and project managers. Usually everyone else in the department supports these roles. Where does the report designer fit in the organization? Good question. Honestly, I don't have a simple answer. The fact is that people who design business reports don't come from a common pool of IT professionals. In fact, many people who spend the majority of their time creating reports are part of the business community and are not your typical hard-core computer geeks.

Microsoft has a long history of building highly technical products that appeal to the technical community. In more recent years, Microsoft has begun to enhance its product culture for more suit-and-tie-wearing folks who talk about things such as business performance management strategy and market share rather than remote procedure calls and polymorphic object inheritance. If you're a business-type person, you probably don't care about integrating your reports into custom applications and web sites or writing complex programming logic to make them sing and dance. Some of us live for that. What you may care about is giving your savvy business user the ability to drag and drop report parts from the gallery to visualize important key metrics to see what products are performing well in their sales territory. However, to enable that experience, a certain degree of technical expertise is necessary.

Over the years, I've taken inventory of the people who consider themselves report designers. They generally fall into one of two camps — business-focused or technology-focused. There has been a significant shift toward more accessible reporting tools for those who have less technical aptitude. The following roles represent the majority and describe some of the trends we're seeing as the industry continues to evolve.

Business Information Workers

People in this role have strong computer skills, but they don't spend their time writing code and using programming tools. Their primary interest is exploring information and finding answers, rather than designing complex reports. If you're an information worker (IW), you need easy-to-use tools to browse data and create simple reports quickly and with less technical expertise. IWs typically create a report to answer a specific question or address a particular need, and then they may discard the report or save it to a personal area for reuse. They tend to create a separate report for each task and may or may not share these reports with others who have similar needs. This is by far the largest and fastest-growing group of report tool users in the industry.

Business Managers

If you're a business manager, you're primarily interested in your own domain of the business. Managers need reports to support specific processes to address their analytical needs and to help them make informed decisions. Like information workers, they have little interest in the implementation details or technology used to make it work. As information workers, managers may create their own reports to analyze the productivity of their team or area of responsibility.

Software Developers

To achieve advanced reporting features, software developers write complex queries and custom programming code to process business rules and give reports conditional formatting and behavior. Developers typically feel right at home with the report design environment because it's similar to familiar programming tools. However, report design is not the same as application development. Designing a report can be faster and easier in some ways than developing software. Advanced report design can involve writing code and even developing custom components.

System Administrators

If you are a system administrator, you are typically concerned with the setup and ongoing maintenance of servers and the infrastructure to keep reporting solutions available and working. Administrators typically spend their time and energy managing security and optimizing the system for efficiency. Reporting Services has an administrative component that is especially important in large-scale implementations.

In smaller organizations, the same person may play the role of system administrator, developer, and report designer. Reports can also be created to help monitor system usage and maintenance statistics to make a system administrator's job easier.

Reporting Services meets the needs of information workers and technology professionals with different report design and data browsing tools. Report Builder is simple, focused, and familiar, with a user interface similar to Microsoft Office applications. A more advanced report designer, called SQL Server Data Tools (SSDT), is available to application developers and other technical professionals. It is integrated into the Visual Studio solution design environment shell.

DASHBOARDS, REPORTS, AND APPLICATIONS

From a software perspective, a computer system can present data to a user in different ways. Most legacy reporting systems ran on the client desktop computer.

Just recently we've seen a major shift toward self-service reporting. Many different tools have been developed to provide the right balance between simplicity and capability. It's taken a few years for the dust to settle on all these tools and for the best options to emerge. Most business leaders want a simple dashboard interface that answers key business questions, or a tool they can use to browse a simplified view or semantic model without having to design reports and write queries. This led Microsoft to take two different approaches. First, it created a streamlined report design tool, Report Builder, that makes it easier for less-technical users to design powerful reports using the conventional report definition architecture. Second, it developed a separate visualization tool, Power View, that leverages the Reporting Services architecture but offers a design and user experience that is separate from conventional reports. To manage expectations, we'll omit the Power View tool from of our discussions and treat it as separate from the rest of Reporting Services. You'll read about tabular models and Power View in Chapters 12 and 13.

Quite a few years ago we saw a shift from client-based processing toward applications that ran on web servers. This has proven to be an effective way to make systems available to a large number of people. When Reporting Services was first released, it was available only as a server-based solution, with reports delivered almost exclusively through the web browser — and this is primarily how SQL Server Reporting Services (SSRS) reports are used today. However, the capabilities don't stop there. Reporting Services lets you run reports in a variety of modes and applications. If we've learned anything from the past 20 years of computer system evolution, it's that centralized server-based solutions and client-side applications each offer unique advantages and trade-offs in terms of features, capabilities, interactive user experience, and scalability.

It's important to note that you can install the product and then design and use reports without a lot of fuss and technical expertise. Later in this book, we will discuss how Reporting Services can be used in more advanced and creative ways.

Blurring the Line Between Applications and Reports

With Reporting Services, you can integrate reports into applications in such a way that users may not be able to tell the difference between the report content and the application interface. With a little bit of programming code, reporting features can be extended to look and act much like applications. When do reports start replacing application functionality? What, exactly, is the difference between a report, a dashboard, and a scorecard? The lines have become quite blurred. Your task is to decide which tool best meets your needs. Many intranet sites run on web portals, rather than custom-programmed web sites, and Reporting Services naturally plays well in practically any web portal environment. In particular, Reporting Services has native integration with Microsoft SharePoint Server.

The exciting news is that you now have a tool that can do some incredible things. As my favorite superhero's uncle said, "With great power comes great responsibility." If you are a simple report designer with simple needs, the good news is that using Reporting Services to design simple reports is, well, simple. If you are a software developer and you intend to use this powerful framework to explore the vast reaches of this impressive technology, welcome to the wonderful world of creative custom reporting.

After years of experience with this product, I've learned an important lesson on this topic. They say that to a hammer, everything looks like a nail. Likewise, to a programmer, a lot of challenges may look like an opportunity to write program code. That may be the right solution under certain conditions. But often, the most effective solution is to simply use a feature already baked into the product — and implement that feature as it was designed to work. I often have this conversation with programmers after they have spent hours writing a complicated solution to a simple problem. My father often advised me to follow the well-known KISS principle: "Keep it simple, stupid." The last part was just to make the phrase memorable, and he meant it in the most affectionate way (at least, I'm pretty sure he did).

Launching Reports from an Application

Hyperlinks and application shortcuts can easily be added to documents and custom applications. Much of the standard report-viewing environment may be controlled using parameters passed to the report server in the URL. Reports may be designed to prompt users for parameter values used to filter data and to modify the report format and output. These parameters may also be incorporated into a URL string. This way, one hyperlink displays a report with one set of data, and another hyperlink displays the same report with different data. Parameters can even be used to change display attributes such as font sizes and colors, and to hide and show content.

User Interaction

In the past, many reports were nothing more than a list of values with totals. Now reports can be a starting point that can guide users to the information they need to make decisions. Report elements such as text labels, column headers, and chart data points can be used to navigate to different report sections and new reports. Because navigation links may be data-driven and dynamically created based on program logic, report links may also be used to navigate into business applications. Imagine using your reports to launch programs and to navigate to document libraries and online content!

As the user clicks items or data points in the report, content and the layout of a report can change based on parameter values set in the background. Summary headers may be used to expand and collapse detail sections, giving users the ability to drill down to more specific information, as shown in Figure 1-1.

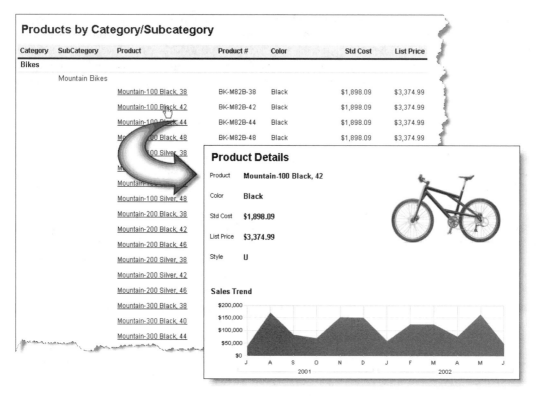

FIGURE 1-1

Integrating Reports and Applications

One of the reasons that Reporting Services integrates so easily with modern web applications is that it natively supports Hypertext Markup Language (HTML), the standard markup language used to create web pages. Techniques may be used to incorporate reports into a web application in a variety of ways:

➤ Hyperlinking to navigate the web browser window to a report

➤ Hyperlinking to open reports in a separate web browser window, with control over report display and browser features

➤ Embedding reports into a page using a frame, IFrame, or ReportViewer web control

➤ Programmatically feeding report content to an Active Server Page (ASP or ASPX) using server-side custom code

➤ Programmatically writing reports to files available for download from a web site

➤ Using a web part to embed reports into a SharePoint Web portal

➤ Fully integrating the report server in SharePoint Integration mode

There are a lot of creative ways to integrate reports into a web or desktop application. These techniques range from simple, requiring a little HTML script, to complex, custom methods. And if it's not enough to be able to embed reports into custom web pages, it's also possible to use custom program code to embed additional content into reports. Imagine the possibilities. Actually, you don't have to imagine anything. Just keep reading!

SharePoint integrated mode allows all your reports and report administration to be managed completely within SharePoint. If you choose to manage the report server separately from your SharePoint portal, you can still use SharePoint web parts to navigate folders and reports and to view reports hosted on the report server running in Reporting Services Native mode.

The ReportViewer control or embedded web browser may be used to view server-based reports in a form. These reports are still managed on the report server and maintain all the security settings and configuration options defined by an administrator. Queries and data access are still performed on the server. The other option is to embed these reports directly into the client-side application. The Windows Forms ReportViewer controls can act as a lightweight report-rendering engine. This means that reports built into a custom application can run independently from the report server.

ENTERPRISE REPORTING

Delivering reports to the masses requires a capable reporting environment. Rather than bringing data from source databases to the desktop for processing, Reporting Services processes queries and then renders reports on the report server. Because it uses Windows Services, shared server-based components, and HTTP web services, all the processing occurs in an efficient and secure environment. Standard data-source connection providers for SQL Server and other enterprise-class databases promote efficient use of server resources. In simple terms, this means that many users can run reports at the same time while consuming minimal server resources.

A business intelligence solution integrates data from multiple sources into a data warehouse, data mart, or semantic data model. Complex analysis solutions often require tabular or multidimensional data structures. If you're not familiar with the terms "OLAP," "tabular," and "semantic model," this might at first be a little confusing. A quick history lesson will clear that up. In the late '90s Microsoft released a product that came with SQL Server 7.0, called "OLAP Services." This was their multidimensional database technology that performed online analytical processing, storing data in cubes and dimensions, rather than tables. In SQL Server 2000, OLAP Services became Analysis Services. Multidimensional (OLAP) databases store data in a pre-grouped and pre-aggregated format on disk so the data is available quickly for reporting and browsing. In SQL Server 2012, Microsoft rebranded their analytical database technologies as "Business Intelligence Semantic Models" or "BISM." They offer two technologies under the BISM umbrella; multidimensional (OLAP) and tabular models, which store and process analytic functions in-memory. In some cases, tabular models are easier to design and may be more efficient and faster for reporting and analysis. The chapters in Part III help you understand the advantages of BI data sources and how reports are designed to work with analytic data and semantic models.

The Reporting Services report server exposes its functionality in the same way that a standard ASP.NET web site is hosted for users. Reports may be accessed from anywhere within or outside of the corporate firewall and are still available only to selected users. In SharePoint integrated mode, reports are available to users through document libraries and are secured and managed within the SharePoint server environment. In Native or nonintegrated server mode, reports are managed through a web application called *Report Manager*. Reports can also be exposed in custom-developed web applications using practically any set of web technologies or development tools.

SOLUTION TYPES

An impressive aspect of Reporting Services is that there are so many different ways to implement reports into a business environment. However, giving people a lot of choices doesn't necessarily solve their problems. In fact, providing users with too many options can just be confusing and overwhelming. As report system designers, our job is to provide the right kind of solution for our users that is simple, uncluttered, and easy to use. Reporting Services has become such a multifaceted platform that we often must clarify what we mean when talking about "Reporting Services reports." Part V, "Solution Patterns," gives you prescriptive guidance about how to create and manage reporting solutions using best practices and solution patterns.

The majority of new Reporting Services implementations for most organizations use the de facto Web-based Report Manager interface or are integrated into a company SharePoint site. Other options to integrate reports into custom applications or web pages may be used to meet specific business needs but are less common. In reality, reports can be integrated into a variety of custom solutions with relative ease. Here are some software solutions that might incorporate reports:

➤ Out-of-the-box, server-based reporting features, using reports created by report designers and deployed to a central web server.

➤ Reports integrated into web applications using URL links to open in a web browser window.

➤ Reports integrated into SharePoint Services applications using SharePoint web parts.

➤ Custom-built application features that render reports using programming code. Reports can be displayed within a desktop or web application or may be saved to a file for later viewing.

➤ Interactive data visualizations using the Power View visualization tool for data exposed through a tabular semantic model.

Simple Report Design

If you need to create common report types to summarize or output information contained in a database, Reporting Services offers some great tools that make this easy to do. For example, suppose you have a record of customers and the products they have purchased. You want to produce a list of customers that contains the number of transactions and the total amount the customers have spent. You can use the Report Wizard to produce a table report that includes this information. If you want to compare the sales for each customer, day-to-day, over a period of time, you can use the Report Wizard to generate a line chart report to view the sales trend. The point is that common report types can be easy to create with tools and features that don't require users to know a lot about complicated things like programming, writing queries, and building expressions.

Categorically, report solutions may be created by information technology staff or business users; a variety of tools have been created to support the needs of each group. After a brief explanation, Table 1-1, shown later, summarizes the report designer options we've seen in the current and past product version.

Managing a fully scaled corporate BI solution can be complex and expensive. Fortunately, all the components of a working solution can be scaled down to a single server if necessary. Small and midscale reporting solutions may use a single, multipurpose database serving as an operational data store and a reporting data structure. As the solution matures, the eventual separation of these databases is almost inevitable. A small-scale data mart, populated from operational databases at regular intervals, will provide a simpler data source for reporting that doesn't compete with users and applications for system resources.

Simple reports are easy to design and deploy for short-term use. With a little planning and discipline, you can design reports to meet future requirements. Properly designed, your reports can include advanced features that meet simple needs now and more sophisticated needs in the future.

The five chapters in Part II, "Report Design," begin with the fundamentals of basic report design and then progressively demonstrate how to add more advanced functionality.

IT-Designed Reports

When Reporting Services was first released, the report design experience was optimized for programmers and application developers who were accustomed to using Visual Studio, a product designed to help technically inclined programmers create custom software. When the product team completed the first-generation product, they immediately went to work on a set of tools to enable business users to design their own reports. This offering came to the market in stages with subsequent product releases. A brief understanding of this history will help you better appreciate how we arrived at the current set of tools and capabilities.

For the more technically inclined, the report design experience in the Visual Studio shell, called the SQL Server Data Tools (SSDT), is both familiar and powerful (see Figure 1-2).

 In previous versions of SQL Server, the Visual Studio-based design tool was called "Business Intelligence Development Studio" (or BIDS for short). If you hear one of us SSRS old-timers refer to this tool by the former name, you can assume that we're talking about SSDT. It's going to take me a while to get use to this change and to start using the new name.

Simple reports are fairly easy to design, and advanced capabilities are possible using a variety of tools that will make most application developers feel right at home. Like other Visual Studio solutions, report definition files are placed in folders that can be managed as a single deployment unit. Reports, data sources, shared datasets, and all other design elements can be managed with integrated version control in the SSDT shell.

Many technical experts use either Report Builder or SSDT to design their reports. Both tools include a simple Report Wizard that can lead you through designing common reports. Table, grouped, matrix, and chart reports are relatively easy to build just by following the Wizard prompts and setting a few properties.

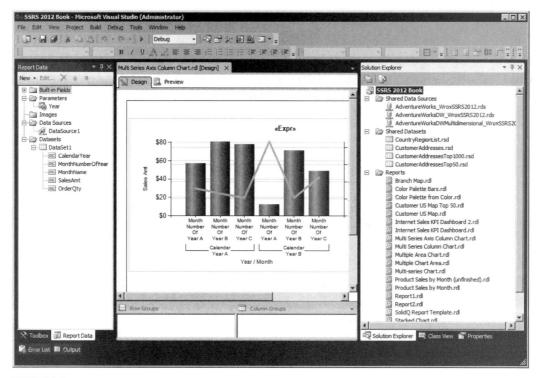

FIGURE 1-2

User-Designed Reports

SQL Server 2012 brings us full circle with two capable self-service design tools. Self-service reporting has been on the minds of many people in the industry for a long time. For Microsoft, the quest to create the perfect easy-to-use BI tool has produced several different products, each with its own unique capabilities. Under the Reporting Services umbrella, two ad hoc reporting tools serve different needs. The current incarnation of Report Builder is based on the mature report definition architecture we've seen progress over the past eight years. Report Builder reports can span the spectrum from simple to complex, with many design options. The Power View visualization report tool introduces an exciting and dynamic data browsing and exploration experience. Power View reports are based on a tabular semantic data model and are surfaced in an intuitive SharePoint-based interactive designer, as shown in Figure 1-3.

The SharePoint environment provides a rich content management and presentation interface for a variety of reports and content types. Figure 1-4 shows the PowerPivot Gallery, with thumbnail previews of Power View reports and PowerPivot workbooks.

Chapters 12 and 13 cover the Power View tool and tabular models for users and for those charged with supporting and enabling this capability in their organization.

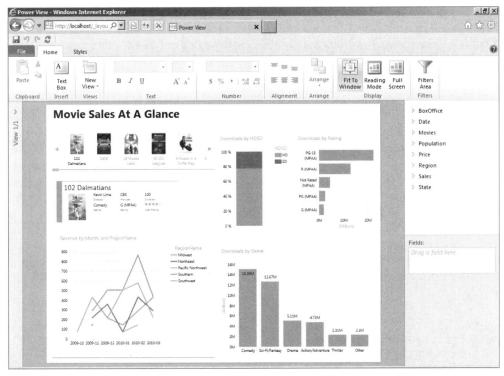

FIGURE 1-3

FIGURE 1-4

The first generation of self-service reporting in SSRS was a step toward the robust capabilities in the current product. Report Builder 1.0 was a basic tool introduced with SSRS 2005 that produced a simple but proprietary report with limited capabilities. It was a great tool for its time that allowed users to simply drag and drop data entities and fields from a semantic data model to produce simple reports. Today, the latest version of Report Builder creates reports that are entirely cross-compatible with SSDT and that can be enhanced with advanced features. Consider Report Builder 1.0 yesterday's news. If you're using it now, I strongly suggest making the transition to the newer tool set.

The 2008 product version introduced Report Builder 2.0, a tool that is equally useful for business users and technical professionals. For user-focused designers, Report Builder 2.0 was simple and elegant. Incremental product improvements over the past few versions have made out-of-the-box report design even easier in Report Builder. Users can design their own queries or simply use data source and dataset objects that have been prepared for them by corporate IT so that they can drag and drop items or use simple design wizards to produce reports. In Report Builder, each report is managed as a single document that can be deployed directly to a folder on the report server or in the SharePoint document library. The version number has been dropped from the Report Builder name; now it is simply differentiated from previous versions by the version of SQL Server that installs it. Figure 1-5 shows the current version of Report Builder (installed with SQL Server 2012) with a map report in design view.

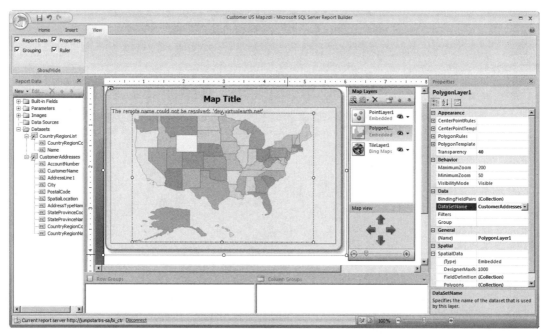

FIGURE 1-5

Table 1-1 summarizes the report design tools available in the past and current product versions.

TABLE 1-1: Report Designer and Visualization Options

REPORT DESIGNER	BACKGROUND	STATUS
SQL Server Data Tools (SSDT)	Implementation of the Visual Studio shell typically used by IT professionals to design reports with a project and team focus. Currently uses the Visual Studio 2010 shell.	Supported.
Report Builder 1.0	Released with SSRS 2005 and supported in SSRS 2008 and 2008 R2.	Limited support. Ongoing use is discouraged.
Report Builder 2.0	Released with SSRS 2008.	Supported for SSRS 2008.
Report Builder 3.0	Released with SSRS 2008 R2.	Supported for SSRS 2008 and 2008 R2.
Report Builder	Released with SSRS 2012.	Supported for SSRS 2008 R2 and 2012.
Power View Visualization	Released with SSRS 2012. Requires SharePoint Enterprise.	Interactive Power View reports are unique and are not cross-compatible with Report Builder or SSDT.

Server-Based Reports

Reports can run on a server or in a stand-alone application on the client computer. It is important to note that Reporting Services is designed and optimized for server-based reporting first. The client-side option, called Local Mode, is possible with some custom programming and takes a little more effort and expertise to implement. For the remainder of this chapter, the discussion is limited to server-based reporting.

It's important to understand the difference between SQL Server Reporting Services and a desktop reporting tool such as Microsoft Access. Reporting Services isn't an application you would typically install on any desktop computer; rather, it is designed for business use. It requires Microsoft SQL Server, a serious business-class relational database management tool. Likewise, reports may be integrated into SharePoint Services to be managed, secured, and administered alongside other shared corporate documents and assets.

For this and other reasons, Reporting Services runs on a server instead of a desktop computer. Whether used in a small business or a huge corporation, Reporting Services is scalable and adaptable for use by a handful or thousands of users and reporting on large sets of data stored in a variety of database platforms. But just because Reporting Services is a business-sized product doesn't mean that reports have to be complicated or difficult to design. Businesses need not host their own servers and can utilize Azure Reporting, Microsoft's cloud-based report server offering.

Report users need to be connected to a network, or perhaps the Internet, with connectivity to the report server. When a report is selected for viewing from a folder on the report server or the SharePoint library, it is displayed as a web page in the user's web browser. Optionally, the same report can be displayed in a number of different formats, including Word, Excel, and Adobe PDF, or as a PNG, JPEG, GIF, or TIFF image. Reports may be saved to files in these and other formats for offline viewing. Reports may also be scheduled for automatic delivery by the report server by e-mail or may be saved to files. These features are standard and require only simple configuration settings and minor user interaction.

BUSINESS INTELLIGENCE REPORTING SOLUTIONS

A business intelligence (BI) solution is the foundation upon which a capable business reporting platform can be constructed. Depending on your needs and business environment, this may simply entail designing a new database. Just because you need to analyze business data doesn't necessarily mean that you need to build a full-scale BI solution. However, if you need to aggregate large volumes of data to analyze business performance with key metrics and trends, relational databases designed for transaction processing may no longer serve this purpose. Understanding these core concepts and investing in BI before report design will often reduce costs and enable you to create an enduring reporting platform for your business users and leaders.

With the current set of Microsoft reporting and BI technologies (namely, SQL Server and SharePoint), you have some choices. These are discussed in appropriate detail in later chapters. Simply put, the data source for a report could be the relational database used to manage transactional data, a data mart, or a data warehouse stored in a relational database management system (such as SQL Server or Oracle). For better performance and flexible analysis over a large volume of data, data can be stored in a semantic model. This can be either a multidimensional structure (often called a cube) or a tabular semantic model that performs aggregations and calculations in-memory. Figure 1-6 illustrates the relative complexity and maturity of a BI solution.

To say that the scope of a reporting or BI solution is relative to the size of a business would be a gross generalization. In some cases, small businesses manage large data volumes, and sometimes big organizations have simple needs. The point is that as your data grows, so does the need to store, manage, and analyze it in the best way.

A BI solution enables business leaders to use the right tools to proactively make informed decisions about their business. Sophisticated reporting and analytics allow information workers and leaders to look beyond the history of their business data. By examining the past and present, you can spot trends and patterns. You can use reliable business analytics to forecast future trends, to plan for improved business processes, and to make informed decisions.

Once upon a time, businesses ran reports to keep track of simple things such as sales totals, invoices, inventory, and production runs. As an industry, we had reached a point where we were quite proficient at gathering and storing data. Most businesses had gigabytes or terabytes of data to report on.

What we (as an industry) were less proficient at was transforming that data back into useful and actionable information. Today, we compete on a global scale. Businesses must be efficient, competitive, and adaptable. Large corporations merge, acquire, outsource, downsize, and realign their strategies more often than ever before. Today's business leaders must be adaptable and prepared to react to industry trends and opportunities in order to thrive.

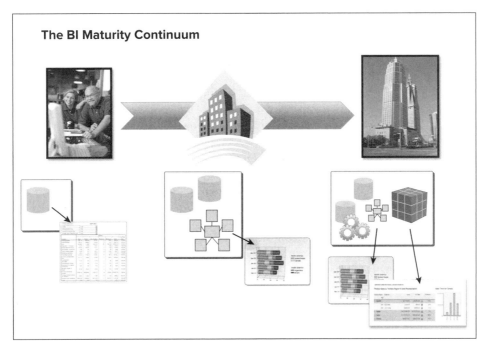

FIGURE 1-6

As a result of this demanding environment, yesterday's static reporting applications have given way to BI solutions. BI is more than the ability to "go get" data. It involves mechanisms that put high-level intelligence in front of leaders in the form of self-service report tools, dashboards, and business scorecards. It proactively alerts users when important events occur and when thresholds are exceeded.

At first, a simple reporting application may use data from a data source or two, but eventually reports may be based on multiple data sources. Sustainable BI solutions are designed around consistent and reliable data sources engineered specifically for reporting. Data is transformed from multiple sources into a central repository using data transformation packages and then may be processed into a semantic model (multidimensional OLAP cube or tabular model). Reports may use a relational data mart, data warehouse, or semantic model. A variety of reports can be created to support business leaders and the decisions they need to make about important business processes. These decision-support reports may take on the form of charts, detail summaries, dynamic drill-down and drill-through reports, dashboards, and business scorecards.

Report Data Sources

Every report has at least one data source and query or reference to the entities that return data values, called a *dataset*. Operational data stores are often the most complex databases. Some packaged systems have databases with thousands of tables. As the dependence on databases and data-driven computer systems increases, most organizations cross a threshold in three areas:

➤ The complexity of each database grows to accommodate more complex processes.

➤ The volume of the data increases.

➤ The number of different databases increases to handle different business data that management needs.

Aside from sheer complexity, it's not uncommon for even midsized companies to store terabytes of data. Storage space is fairly inexpensive when compared with equally capable systems just a few years ago. There may be great value in tracking orders, shipments, calls, cases, and customers, but all this adds up over time. Recording all this activity means that you have a lot of data on hand for reporting. Putting data into a database is the easy part. Getting intelligent, useful information back out — there's the challenge! Finally, different systems are used to manage the same types of data in different ways. For example, a customer relationship management system tracks sales leads and potential customers for a marketing organization differently than an order management system does to support the sales team. In each of these two systems, you may track something called a "customer," but in these systems, the definition may vary. Perhaps a "customer" may represent a consumer, contact, or company in one system, and a lead, vendor, or reseller in another system. Larger companies may have similar records duplicated across other systems such as enterprise resource planning, human resources management, benefits, vendor management, accounting, and payables and receivables systems.

At some point, most solution designers conclude that to obtain valuable reporting metrics from all these operational data sources, they will have to be consolidated into a central, simplified data store specifically designed to support business reporting requirements. A *data warehouse system* is a central data store used to standardize the data extracted from these complex and specialized data sources. It typically makes use of the same relational database technologies used to house the operational data stores, but it does so in a protected, Read Only environment to keep reporting simple and straightforward.

A data warehouse or data mart is a simplified data structure built using relational database technology, designed specifically for reporting. Reports based on these data sources are easier to design and may perform better than reports designed using transactional, operational data stores. Many businesses need to do more than just list transactional records on reports and add up the totals. Simple data aggregation can be performed with large sets of data from a data warehouse, but deep analysis requires special data storage technology and a more capable mathematical and statistical reporting engine.

Analytic Data Sources and Self-Service BI

Once reports were little more than transaction records printed on paper, called ledgers, journals, and lists. As the need for more useful information arose, so did the sophistication of reporting. Today, reports serve as more than just a method to dump records to the printed page. Users need to gain insight and knowledge about their business. Dynamic reports allow users to interact and investigate trends in their business environments, rather than just view static lists. As the sophistication of the business users increases, so does the complexity of the data and the reporting medium. The general trend is from a historical perspective to the future. The more accurate and reliable data you have about the past and present, with appropriate reporting models, you can use this to forecast and predict trends and future activities.

As the requirements grow, so does the need for more complex data. In a midsized business with moderate data reporting needs and a few data sources, a small data mart or warehouse may serve as a complete BI reporting solution. However, in a larger, sophisticated business environment, a comprehensive data extract, transform, and load (ETL) solution; data warehouse; and business intelligence semantic model may be used to feed the appetite for deeper reporting and analysis. Semantic models open the door to high-level analytics using simple, user-enabling self-service reporting and data-browsing tools.

Similar to Analysis Services multidimensional cubes, tabular models can be used to aggregate large volumes of business data. OLAP cubes and models are also much easier for users to explore and browse using self-service reporting tools. BISM tabular models are based on the same in-memory aggregation technology as Microsoft's PowerPivot add-in for Excel. PowerPivot models can be created with the PowerPivot add-in for Excel and published to SharePoint to be shared and hosted as report data sources. Excel may be used to browse these models using pivot tables and charts. In addition to ad hoc reporting and cube browsing, standard Reporting Services reports may be used to report on cube data using a special query language called *Multidimensional Expressions* (MDX).

Self-service BI solutions put the power of data analysis in the hands of business users. Enabling effective analysis has required information technology groups, already stressed by resource constraints, to design enterprise BI solutions that require specialized skills and extensive planning. Recent innovations in self-service BI tools such as Microsoft PowerPivot, tabular models, and Power View have bridged this gap. Tabular semantic models can serve up and aggregate large volumes of business data for browsing and reporting, with the added benefit of being completely server-hosted and secure. The tabular model technology actually utilizes the Analysis Services storage engine. The entire model is loaded into the server memory to aggregate and return results very quickly.

Tabular and multidimensional semantic models each offer unique strengths for efficient analytic reporting, and Reporting Services may use any of these options as report data sources.

Complexity and Report Performance

System performance is often one of the most significant drivers of an effective BI solution. As an organization's reporting needs become more sophisticated and the data's complexity and volume increase, the cost is usually measured first in performance. Queries take longer to run and compete for resources on the report and database servers. In this case, IT professionals typically react by recognizing the value of and need for a simplified database. Whether this is to be a truly enterprise-ready data warehouse, a departmental data mart, or a simple "reporting structure," the basic concept is usually the same — simplify the database design to focus on reporting requirements.

As mentioned, some performance and advanced analytical requirements may also drive the solution's maturity to include OLAP cubes. This doesn't necessarily mean that all the reports designed against other data sources must be updated. A variety of reports may work just fine with an operational data source or relational data warehouse. But other, more sophisticated reports require specialized data sources (such as OLAP cubes) to perform well.

I recall a consulting assignment in which I developed reports with complex financial formulas using the original database structure as the report data source. The T-SQL queries were complex and difficult to debug. The client was thrilled when one of the more complicated reports took only 45 minutes to run instead of the 90 minutes it took before we "optimized" the query. After transforming the same data into a simplified data mart structure, it took less than 3 minutes to run the same report. With an OLAP cube in Analysis Services, the same report ran in just a few seconds. Needless to say, the "acceptable" 45-minute report rendering time was no longer acceptable after the users found out that they could run the same report in a few seconds!

One important consideration in this equation is that the cost of a data-warehouse design or an OLAP database can be low compared to poor report performance and unnecessarily long report development cycles. SQL Server Analysis Services is an impressive and compelling technology with tremendous value for even small and midsized businesses. If you have not explored this option and you need to do reporting beyond the basics, we urge you to take a serious look at this impressive tool set so that you can appreciate its value.

CUSTOMIZING THE REPORTING EXPERIENCE

Reports may be delivered in a variety of ways (not just when a user navigates to a report in real time). Reports may be automatically rendered to the server cache so that they open quickly and don't burden data sources. They may be delivered via e-mail and to file shares on a regular schedule. Using data-driven subscriptions, reports may be "broadcast" to a large audience during off-hours. Each user may receive a copy of the report rendered in a different format or with data filtered differently. You will learn to plan for, manage, and configure these features.

You will learn how to optimize, back up, and recover the Report Server database, web service, and Windows service. You also will learn how to use the management utilities, configuration files, and logs to customize the server environment and prevent and diagnose problems.

SUMMARY

This chapter provided a context for the rest of the book and introduced the concepts, skills, and capabilities you will learn about in subsequent chapters.

The chapters in Part I give you the direction you need to get started with Reporting Services by installing the tools and configuring them in your environment. You will learn how to set up Reporting Services in native mode and integrated with SharePoint 2010.

The five chapters in Part II take you, step-by-step, from a novice report designer to a report rock star. The discussion of basic report design has you use wizards and simple tools to create typical business reports such as tables, a matrix, lists, and simple charts. You'll learn how to lay out and format each report using recommended techniques. You'll design queries for SQL Server and other data sources, and learn the basics of T-SQL to create filtered and parameterized datasets. The discussion of advanced report design covers the more compelling features and creative ways to make reports come to life with dynamic formatting and actions. We've dedicated a full chapter to chart report design to cover more of the useful and advanced visual chart capabilities.

Parts III and IV cover many of the new BI innovations introduced in SQL Server 2012 and SharePoint 2010: semantic tabular models and the Power View visual experience. These parts also cover reporting on multidimensional cubes and MDX queries. Whether you are using Reporting Services with SharePoint or in native mode, you will learn to use Report Builder and a self-service reporting tool to empower business users to answer important business questions using easy-to-use browsing and design tools.

The SQL Server BI and reporting platform gives you many tools and options that can be a bit overwhelming. Part V provides you with prescriptive guidance that helps you benefit from our many years of solution design work and successful reporting projects. We have outlined a number of best practices for report solution architectures, designs, and custom programming techniques.

Report server administration and content management are covered at length in Part VI. You will see how to integrate Reporting Services with SharePoint and manage a native report server, as well as monitor and optimize for reliable, secure, and optimal performance.

Part VII is for the programmer who wants to integrate reports into a custom solution and for the advanced report designer who can use custom program code within report design. You will learn how to extend the capabilities of reports with expressions and custom functions and extend applications by adding reporting capabilities.

2
Reporting Services Installation and Architecture

WHAT'S IN THIS CHAPTER?

➤   Installing a report server

➤   Building an enterprise deployment

➤   Using tools to manage the reporting life cycle

➤   Exploring report server architecture

➤   Leveraging reporting services extensions

To gain familiarity with Reporting Services, developers and administrators often perform a basic installation to a personal computer or development server. Although the basic installation glosses over many of the choices critical in an enterprise deployment, it provides an environment in which features and the installation process itself can be explored. Such an environment is ideal for performing the exercises and tutorials found in Books Online and within this book.

This chapter guides you through a basic installation of SQL Server 2012 Reporting Services. Then you will review some important considerations for an enterprise deployment.

You will explore how features in Reporting Services are implemented and exposed. This information is foundational for both administrators and developers. Subsequent chapters build off concepts explored here.

The reporting life cycle gives you the context within which Reporting Services is employed. You will explore the various applications and utilities associated with Reporting Services.

Following this, you will dig a little deeper into Reporting Services itself by examining the architecture of the Reporting Services Windows service, its components, and supporting databases. By the end of the chapter, you will have a solid understanding of how all these pieces come together to deliver Reporting Services' functionality.

This chapter covers the following topics:

➤   Basic installation

➤   Enterprise deployment considerations

➤   Reporting life cycle

➤   Reporting Services tools

➤   Reporting Services Windows service

➤   Reporting Services processors and extensions

➤   Reporting Services application databases

THE BASIC INSTALLATION

To understand the installation of Reporting Services, it is important to have some knowledge of its components. In SQL Server 2012, Reporting Services offers two modes:

➤   Native mode

➤   SharePoint Integrated mode

At its core, Reporting Services is a Windows service that relies on a pair of databases hosted by an instance of the SQL Server Database Engine. Note that in SharePoint integrated mode, Reporting Services in SQL Server 2012 runs as a SharePoint shared service. This chapter is primarily focused on Reporting Services Native mode installations. Chapter 3 covers details of and differences in SharePoint Integrated mode-specific installation and configuration topics.

Interaction with the Reporting Services service is provided through applications such as Report Manager in Native mode, hosted by Reporting Services, the Reporting Services Add-in in SharePoint mode, and other applications such as the Business Intelligence Development Studio, installed on client systems. These applications, the service, and the Reporting Services databases are introduced in this chapter as well.

With the basic installation of Native mode, server-side and client-side components are installed on a single system. The Reporting Services databases are also installed to a local instance of the SQL Server Database Engine. With no dependencies on other systems, the basic installation is often referred to as a stand-alone installation.

The basic installation typically makes use of the Developer or Evaluation editions of the SQL Server software. Both editions provide access to the full range of Reporting Services features. With the Evaluation edition, the software is free but restricted to 180 days of use. With the Developer edition, the software is provided at a significantly reduced cost but is restricted to use in nonproduction environments only. These editions can be obtained through the Microsoft site, subscription services, or software vendors.

In addition to providing access to the full suite of Reporting Services features at a reduced cost or no cost, both editions support a wider range of operating systems than other production-ready versions of SQL Server. The operating systems supported include Windows Server 2008, Windows Server 2008 R2, and various editions of Windows 7 and Windows Vista.

Additional system requirements include 1 GB of memory and a 1.4 GHz (32-bit or 64-bit) processor. The basic installation also requires at least 6 GB of free hard drive space, plus additional space for the system updates and SQL Server samples.

SQL Server 2012 is supported in virtual machine environments running on the Hyper-V role in Windows Server 2008 SP2 or later, in Standard, Enterprise, and Datacenter editions.

Installing Reporting Services

Before performing the Reporting Services installation, it's a good idea to be certain your system is up-to-date with the latest service packs. You also need to be a member of the local Administrators group on the system on which you intend to perform the installation or be prepared to run the setup application using the credentials of an account that is a member of the local Administrators group.

To start the installation, access the installation media for SQL Server 2012 Evaluation or Developer Edition. This may be a DVD or installation files accessible on a local drive or file share. It is important that the media be accessed from the system on which you intend to install the Reporting Services software. Start the setup application by launching SETUP.EXE, located at the root of the installation media.

First the setup application checks your system for the Microsoft .NET Framework 3.5 SP1 and Windows Installer 4.5. If these are not present, the setup application initiates their installation.

The installation of the Windows Installer (presented as a hotfix) is quite fast, but the .NET Framework can take significantly longer than the minute or two indicated by the setup dialog. The steps for the installation of these components are not shown here but are typical of Microsoft software installations. If either the .NET Framework or Windows Installer is installed by the setup application, your system may require a reboot. Upon restart, you need to relaunch the SQL Server 2012 setup application.

The setup application displays the SQL Server Installation Center, as shown in Figure 2-1. The Installation Center is divided into several pages, each providing access to documentation and tools supporting various aspects of the installation process.

For the purposes of the basic installation, proceed to the Installation page by clicking the appropriate link on the left side of the Installation Center form. On the Installation page, shown in Figure 2-2, select the option "New SQL Server stand-alone installation or add features to an existing installation." This launches the SQL Server Setup Wizard.

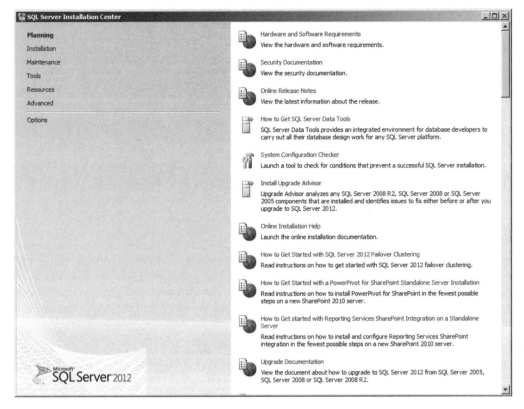

FIGURE 2-1

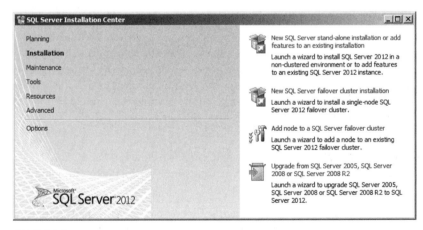

FIGURE 2-2

The first step the SQL Server Setup Wizard performs is to compare your system against a set of "setup support" rules. These rules determine whether the system configuration prerequisites for installation are met. When the analysis is complete, the Wizard shows summary information.

If violations are present, you see the list of rules, identifying which ones require attention. If there are no violations, you can click the Show Details button to see this list, which is shown in Figure 2-3.

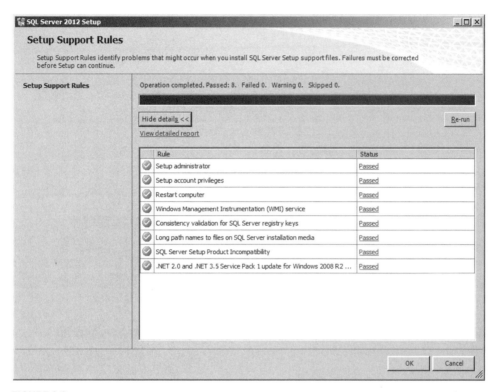

FIGURE 2-3

Clicking the "View detailed report" link on the Setup Support Rules page opens a new window with a detailed report containing recommendations for addressing any warnings or violations, as shown in Figure 2-4. After reviewing this report, you can close this window.

On the Setup Support Rules page of the SQL Server Setup Wizard, click the OK button to go to the Product Key page, shown in Figure 2-5. You can select one of the free editions of SQL Server or enter a product key for one of the other editions. Select the Evaluation edition or enter the product key of the Developer edition to proceed.

Click the Next button to proceed to the License Terms page, shown in Figure 2-6. Carefully read the terms of the product license. To continue with the installation, check the box labeled "I accept the license terms." The check box for feature usage data determines whether high-level information about hardware and SQL Server component usage is sent to Microsoft to help improve the product. You can read the privacy statement by clicking on the hyperlink. Examples of feature usage are whether Reporting Services is installed, and whether the operating system is 32 or 64 bit. The usage data collection is very small and not granular. It does not count how often a feature area is used, just whether it is used at all.

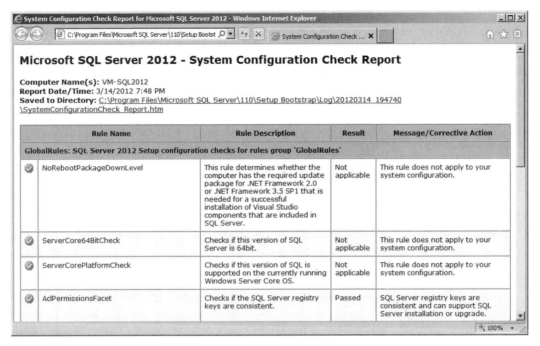

FIGURE 2-4

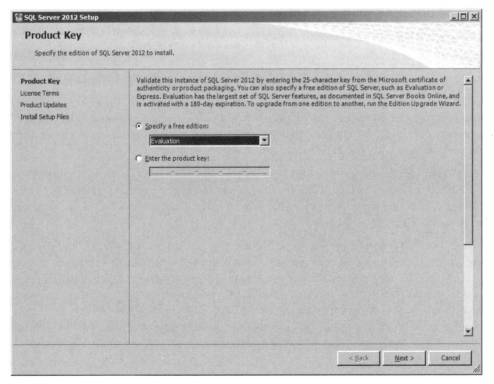

FIGURE 2-5

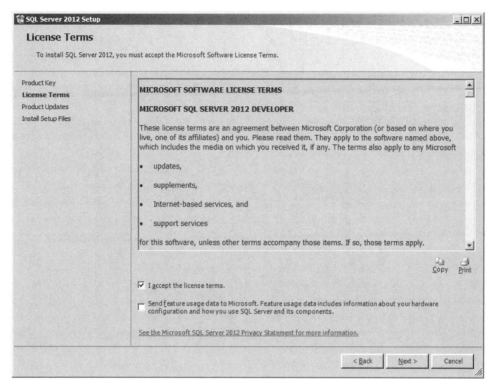

FIGURE 2-6

Click the Next button to go to the Install Setup Files page, shown in Figure 2-7. This page informs you that files will be installed for the purposes of the setup process. When this process is complete, the wizard proceeds to the next page.

As soon as the support files are installed, the Wizard proceeds to another Setup Support Rules page to confirm the system configuration against a different set of rules. As before, you can click the "View detailed report" link to obtain additional information. You should review all warnings and address all violations before proceeding.

Click the Next button to proceed to the Setup Role page, within which you select a SQL Server Feature Installation, as shown in Figure 2-8.

Click the Next button to proceed to the Feature Selection page, within which you select the SQL Server products and features to install, as shown in Figure 2-9. For the basic installation, select the Reporting Services and Database Engine Services features. In addition, select Business Intelligence Development Studio, Client Tools Connectivity, Books Online Components, and Management Tools, both Complete and Basic. If you want to install other components, such as Analysis Services, you can select these as well.

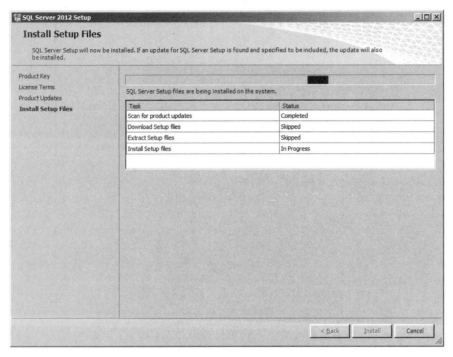

FIGURE 2-7

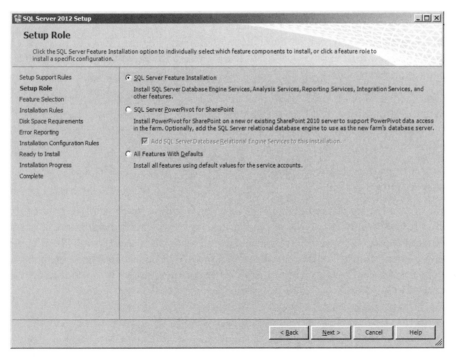

FIGURE 2-8

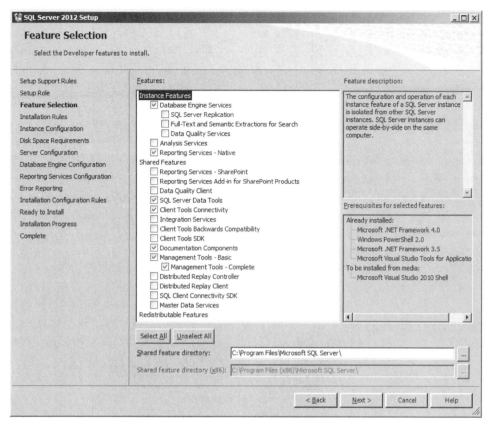

FIGURE 2-9

The Feature Selection page also allows you to modify the path to which shared components will be installed. For the basic installation, typically this is left at the default location. If you have a compelling reason to change this location, click the button next to the displayed path, and select an appropriate alternative location.

Click the Next button to go to the Instance Configuration page, shown in Figure 2-10. Here you identify the instance name for the Database Engine and Reporting Services instances selected on the previous page. Other SQL Server instances that are already installed on the system are listed in the bottom half of the page. If a default instance is not already installed, you can choose to perform this installation to a default instance; otherwise, you need to provide an appropriate instance name.

When naming an instance, it's important to keep in mind that the name is not case-sensitive and must be unique on the system. The name must also be no longer than 16 characters and may include letters, numbers, underscores (_), and the dollar sign ($). The first character must be a letter, and the instance name must not be one of the 174 setup reserved words listed in Books Online. In addition, it is recommended that the instance name not be one of the 235 ODBC reserved words, also listed in Books Online.

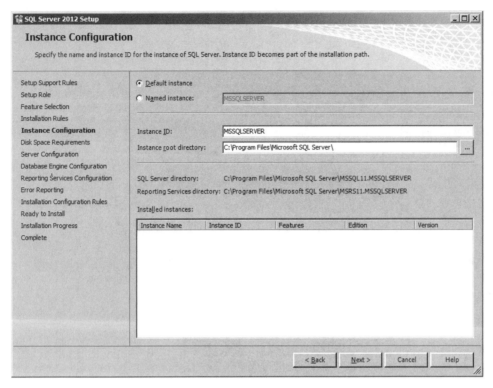

FIGURE 2-10

The Instance Configuration page also allows you to alter the path to which the instance-specific components will be installed. As before, typically this is left to the default location. If you have a compelling reason to change this location, click the button at the end of the path, and select an appropriate alternative location.

The Instance Configuration page also allows you to enter an installation ID other than the instance name. The instance ID is used to identify installation directories and registry keys for the SQL Server instance. In general, you should not alter the instance ID without a compelling reason to do so.

Click the Next button to proceed to the Disk Space Requirements page, shown in Figure 2-11. Here you can review the amount of space consumed by the various components of the installation.

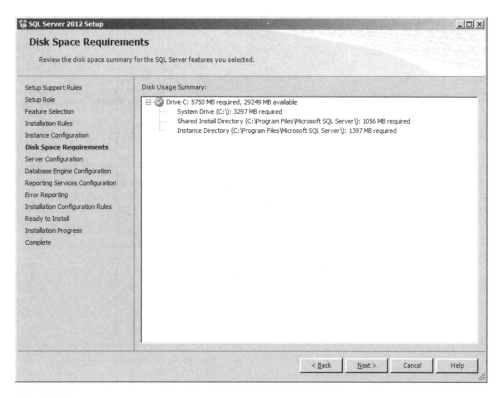

FIGURE 2-11

Click Next to go to the Server Configuration page. This page contains two tabs — Service Accounts and Collation. Service Accounts is the default.

On the Service Accounts tab, shown in Figure 2-12, select the service account to be used for each service to be installed. For the basic installation, it is generally recommended that you use the local service or (generated) network service accounts for the Database Engine and Reporting Services Windows service. As described in Chapter 19, you can change the service account after the installation.

On the Collation tab, shown in Figure 2-13, you can alter the collation to be used for the Database Engine instance. The default selection is determined by the locale configured with the local operating system. As with other options, it is generally recommended that you not alter the collation unless you have a compelling reason to do so.

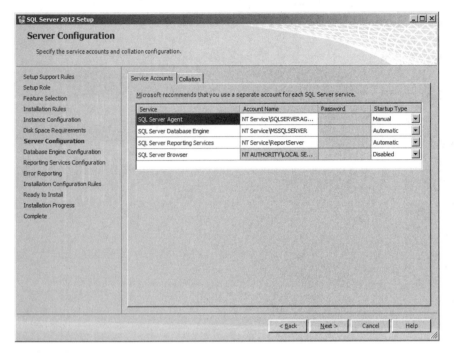

FIGURE 2-12

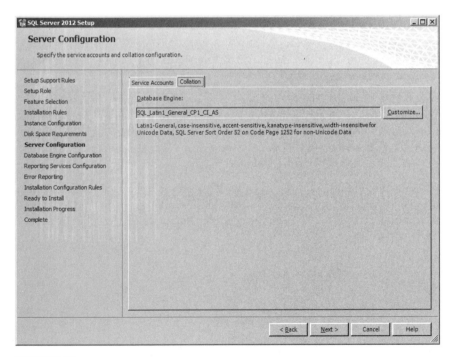

FIGURE 2-13

Click the Next button to proceed to the Database Engine Configuration page. This page allows you to configure the instance of the SQL Server Database Engine you are installing with Reporting Services. It is divided into three tabs: Server Configuration, Data Directories, and FILESTREAM.

On the Server Configuration tab, shown in Figure 2-14, click the Add Current User button so that you will be set up as an administrator of the Database Engine instance. Leave all other options on this tab as they are, unless you have a compelling reason to change them.

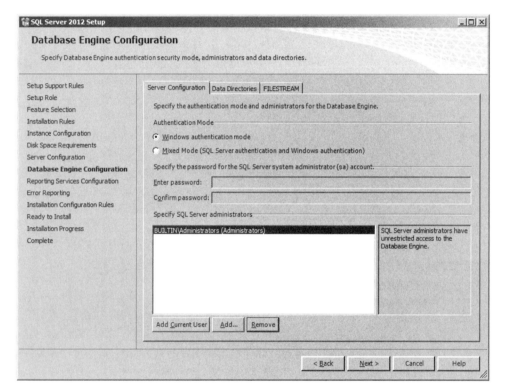

FIGURE 2-14

On the Data Directories tab, shown in Figure 2-15, you can alter various paths used by the Database Engine instance. Again, unless you have a compelling reason to make changes, leave the settings as they are configured by default.

On the FILESTREAM tab, shown in Figure 2-16, select the "Enable FILESTREAM for Transact-SQL access" option. This is required for the sample databases, which you will install later. If you forget to set this during installation, you will need to alter the FILESTREAM properties of the SQL Server Database Engine service using the SQL Server Configuration Manager and update the configuration option "filestream access level" with an appropriate value using `sp_configure`. Additional details of these steps for configuring the database engine can be found in Books Online.

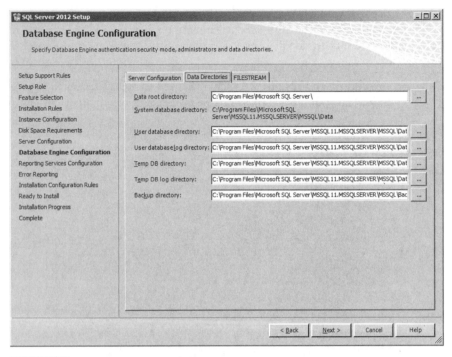

FIGURE 2-15

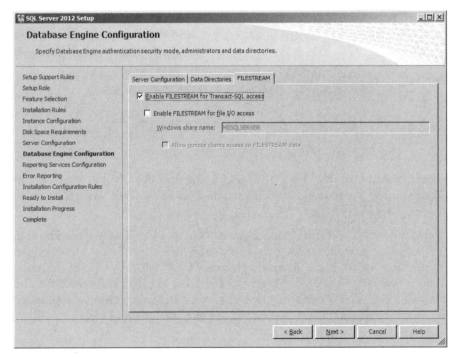

FIGURE 2-16

Click the Next button to go to the Reporting Services Configuration page, shown in Figure 2-17. On this page, you can select from one of three Reporting Services installation options. The various options are discussed in the second half of this chapter. For most basic installations, you should select the "Install and configure" option under Reporting Services Native Mode. The remaining instructions assume that you have selected this option.

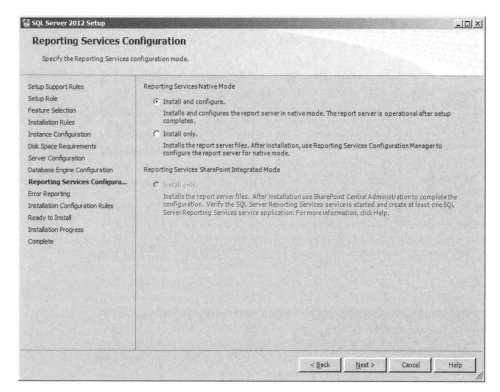

FIGURE 2-17

Click the Next button to proceed to the Error Reporting page, shown in Figure 2-18. Select whichever options align with your willingness to participate in this program. Although you are encouraged to participate, the options you select will not affect the installation.

Click the Next button to go to the Installation Configuration Rules page, shown in Figure 2-19. These rules check that everything is in order before proceeding with the installation given the options you have selected. As before, the "View detailed report" link opens a separate report.

Click the Next button to go to the Ready to Install page, shown in Figure 2-20. Carefully review the options you have selected. If you will be repeating this installation on other systems, consider copying the path of the INI file listed at the bottom of the page. The INI file can be used for future command-line installations, as described in the "Command-Line Installation" section later in this chapter.

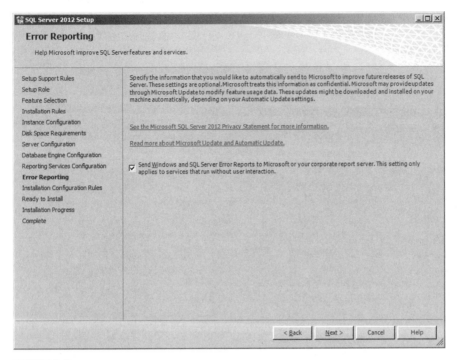

FIGURE 2-18

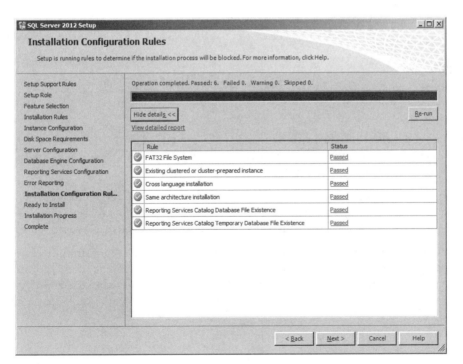

FIGURE 2-19

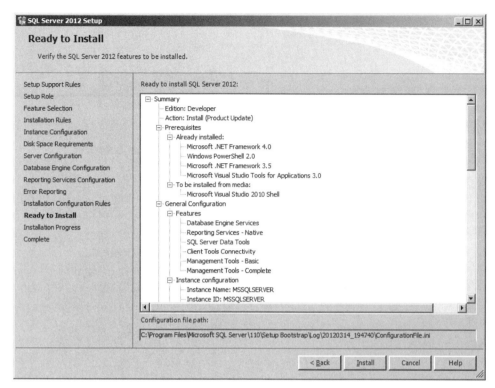

FIGURE 2-20

Click the Install button to start the software installation. The installation process can take quite a bit of time to complete. During this time, an Installation Progress page appears, as shown in Figure 2-21. Upon completion, a summary of the installation process is presented.

Click the Close button to complete the Wizard and return to the Installation Center. You can now close the Installation Center or use the "Search for product updates" option on the Installation Center's Installation page to look for any SQL Server hotfixes or service packs.

With the installation completed, your final step should be to verify the installation. Open Internet Explorer, and enter one of the following URLs:

➤ If you installed a default instance, enter **http://localhost/reports**.

➤ If you installed a named instance, enter **http://localhost/reports_*instancename***, with the appropriate substitution.

The URL may take a while to completely resolve upon this first use, but it should return a screen like the one shown in Figure 2-22 that indicates the service is working properly. If you do not see the tabs (New Folder, New Data Source, Report Builder, Folder Settings, Upload File, Details View), as shown in the figure, or if you get an error message that the user has insufficient permissions, try launching Internet Explorer as Administrator.

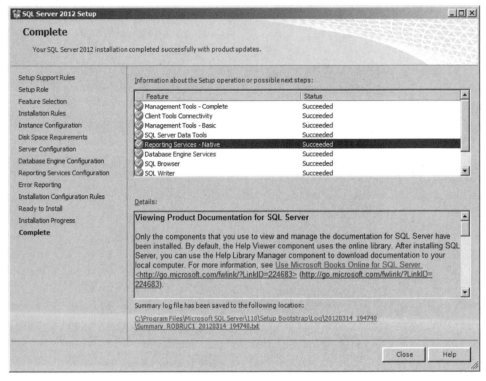

FIGURE 2-21

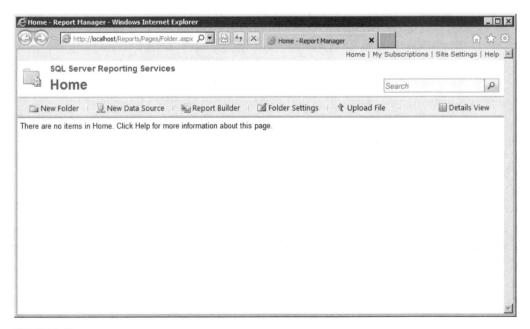

FIGURE 2-22

Installing the Reporting Services Samples and SQL Server Sample Databases

With the Reporting Services software installed, it's now time to install the Reporting Services samples and SQL Server sample databases. These are used throughout this book and in various tutorials available through Books Online.

The Reporting Services samples consist of various applications, extensions, models, reports, and scripts. These samples can help you learn about various aspects of Reporting Services or, in some cases, serve as a starting point for production applications.

The sample databases included as downloads with the book primarily consist of two databases containing data related to a fictional bicycle manufacturer, Adventure Works Cycles. The sample database AdventureWorks_WroxSSRS2012 contains structures typical of a transactional system, whereas the sample database AdventureWorksDW_WroxSSRS2012 contains structures typical of an analytical system. Together, these will help you gain familiarity with both operational and analytical reporting.

The Reporting Services samples and sample databases are available on the Wrox book web site at www.wrox.com. For each sample database and the Reporting Services samples, you need to download an installation file appropriate to your hardware platform.

Before starting the sample installations, verify that the SQL Server Database Engine and Reporting Services are running. Then launch each downloaded MSI and follow the instructions provided to install the samples.

THE ENTERPRISE DEPLOYMENT

As stated at the start of this chapter, the basic installation sidesteps many of the considerations important to an enterprise deployment of Reporting Services. This is done to avoid overwhelming you so early in the game. But when it's time to start planning how Reporting Services will be installed, configured, and distributed within your enterprise environment, you should carefully consider the following topics:

➤ SQL Server editions

➤ Named instances

➤ Topology

➤ Modes

➤ Installation options

➤ Command-line installation

SQL Server Editions

SQL Server 2012 comes in several editions, the following of which include Reporting Services:

➤ Enterprise

➤ Business Intelligence

➤ Standard

➤ Developer

➤ Evaluation

➤ Web

➤ Express with Advanced Services

Enterprise, Business Intelligence, Standard, and Web editions are the only editions supported in a production environment. The Business Intelligence and Enterprise editions provide access to the full set of features available with Reporting Services and run on 32-bit and x64 64-bit platforms. The Standard and Web editions provide access to a reduced feature set. They cost less than the Enterprise and Business Intelligence editions, and may be more appropriate for smaller installations.

The Developer and Evaluation editions provide access to the same features available through the Enterprise edition. The Developer edition is inexpensive and is intended for development and testing environments only. The Evaluation edition is free but expires after 180 days. These two editions support a wider range of operating systems than either the Enterprise or Standard edition.

The Web edition supports a reduced feature set, even more so than the Standard edition, and reduced capacity as may be appropriate for small-scale or Web-based deployments.

Finally, the Express with Advanced Services edition is a highly restricted edition of SQL Server with limited support for Reporting Services. This edition is freely available, but its limitations make it unlikely to be used for anything other than highly specialized needs. The Express with Advanced Services edition is available on 32-bit and x64-bit platforms.

For precise system requirements and features available with each of these editions, consult SQL Server Books Online. Table 2-1 is a limited comparison of core feature and hardware differences relevant to Reporting Services. For the operating systems supported, refer to the details within Books Online.

TABLE 2-1

FEATURE	ENTERPRISE, BUSINESS INTELLIGENCE EVALUATION, DEVELOPER	STANDARD	WEB	EXPRESS ADVANCED
Reporting Services Windows service	Yes	Yes	Yes	Yes
SharePoint Integrated mode	Yes	Yes		
Scale-out topologies	Yes			
Report Data Alerts	Yes			
Power View	Yes			
Role-based security	Yes	Yes	Yes, limited	Yes, limited

FEATURE	ENTERPRISE, BUSINESS INTELLIGENCE EVALUATION, DEVELOPER	STANDARD	WEB	EXPRESS ADVANCED
Custom security extensions	Yes	Yes	Yes	Yes
Export to Word, Excel, PDF, and images	Yes	Yes	Yes	Yes
Remote and nonrelational data sources	Yes	Yes		
Data source, delivery, and rendering extensibility	Yes	Yes		
Report delivery	Yes	Yes		
Report history, scheduling, subscription, and caching	Yes	Yes		
Data-driven subscriptions	Yes			
SSDT Report Designer	Yes	Yes	Yes	Yes
Report Builder	Yes	Yes		
Report Manager	Yes	Yes	Yes	Yes
Server memory (minimum)	1 GB	512 MB	512 MB	256 MB (32-bit) 512 MB (64-bit)
Server memory (recommended)	2+ GB	2+ GB	2+ GB	1+ GB
Server memory (maximum utilized)	Unlimited	64 GB	64 GB	4 GB
Supported CPU architectures	32-bit 64-bit	32-bit 64-bit	32-bit 64-bit	32-bit 64-bit
Maximum number of CPU cores used by a single Reporting Services instance	Unlimited	16 cores	16 cores	4 cores
CPU speed (minimum)	1.4 GHz	1.4 GHz	1.4 GHz	1.4 GHz
CPU speed (recommended)	2.0+ GHz	2.0+ GHz	2.0+ GHz	2.0+ GHz

Named Instances

More than one instance of Reporting Services can be installed on a single server. Each instance runs independently of the others and may be a different version and/or edition. Each has its own Windows service, its own code base, and its own pair of Reporting Services databases with which it interacts. These databases may be housed on separate SQL Server Database Engine instances or on a shared instance, so long as each database is assigned a unique name.

To distinguish between the Reporting Services instances on a server, each is assigned a name, unique on that system. This is called the *instance name*, and an instance with a name assigned to it is called a *named instance*.

In addition to named instances, one instance on a given server may be assigned no instance name. This is called the *default instance*. When only one instance is installed to a server, it is often a default instance.

Multiple instances on a single server, whether all named or a combination of named instances and a default instance, can be practical for supporting the migration of a Reporting Services instance from SQL Server 2008 or SQL Server 2008 R2 to SQL Server 2012 when server hardware is limited. Multiple instances can also be a convenient way to minimize the licensing requirements associated with a deployment. That said, historically it has been recommended that a single Reporting Services instance, whether named or default, should be deployed to a production server for the optimal allocation of resources and overall stability.

Topology

Topology refers to how Reporting Services components are distributed among servers while presenting users with unified access to the service's features. The emphasis is on the Reporting Services Windows service and the Reporting Services databases, as opposed to the client tools. Reporting Services provides support for two generalized topologies: standard and scale-outs.

In a standard topology, the Reporting Services Windows service is installed on a system. It interacts with a pair of Reporting Services databases hosted locally or remotely and dedicated for use by this one instance of Reporting Services. The basic installation performed at the beginning of this chapter is an example of a standard topology.

With a scale-out topology, in Native mode, multiple instances of the Reporting Services Windows service are installed across various servers. In SharePoint Integrated mode, the Reporting Services service runs as a shared service on multiple nodes of the SharePoint farm.

In both types of scale-out topologies, these Reporting Services instances share a pair of Reporting Services databases. By sharing these databases, each server (called a *node*) hosting the Reporting Services service has access to the same content and security configuration as the other nodes within the scale-out topology. If load-balancing hardware or software is available on the network, some or all of the nodes in the topology can be presented to end users as a single resource, but with greater and more flexible capacity than is available through a standard deployment. Other nodes within the scale-out topology can be configured to be dedicated to scheduled processing, removing this burden from other nodes in the environment.

As you are deciding between a standard and scale-out topology, it is important to note that scale-outs are supported with only the Enterprise edition of the product. Setting up the scale-out requires additional configuration following the standard installation.

Finally, if you are considering a scale-out topology in pursuit of higher availability, you might want to consider implementing the Reporting Services databases on a failover cluster. It's important to keep in mind that although the SQL Server Database Engine supports failover clustering, and Reporting Services can interact with databases hosted on a cluster, the Reporting Services service itself does not have any clustering capabilities.

Modes

Reporting Services runs in one of two modes: Native or SharePoint Integrated. In Native mode, Reporting Services manages its content using its own internal, or "native," functionality.

Reporting Services deployments using Enterprise, Developer, Evaluation, or Standard editions can run in SharePoint Integrated mode. In this mode, content management is handled through SharePoint. Native content management interfaces, such as Report Manager, are inaccessible. Chapter 3 discusses SharePoint Integrated mode in detail.

SharePoint Integrated mode is an appealing option for many organizations that want to leverage SharePoint as their enterprise content-management solution, or that use new capabilities such as Power View analysis and visualizations, and alerting for reports. However, Integrated mode has some limitations, such as the lack of support for linked reports.

For organizations that want to run Reporting Services in Native mode but still want to display Reporting Services content through SharePoint, the Reporting Services web parts provide an alternative to SharePoint Integrated mode. Chapter 18 discusses these web parts.

Installation Options

During installation, you are presented with three Reporting Services configuration options. You can install Reporting Services in Native mode using a default configuration, in SharePoint Integrated mode also using a default configuration, or in a minimally configured mode called a *files only* installation.

The Native with default configuration option is available only if you are installing Reporting Services and the Database Engine as part of the same installation process. These installation options leave Reporting Services in an operational state following the completion of the setup process, although not all Reporting Services features (such as the unattended execution account and e-mail delivery) are configured upon completion. If you are installing Reporting Services using SharePoint Integrated mode, additional steps must be performed for configuration to be completed, as outlined in Chapter 3.

For enterprise deployments, the "Native mode - Install only" installation is the option most frequently used. With the install only option, the server components are installed but not configured. Following installation, you are required to use the Reporting Services Configuration tool to configure the Reporting Services databases and URLs for the Reporting Services Web service and Report Manager before the service can be made operational. These steps are discussed in Chapter 19.

Command-Line Installation

For large-scale enterprise deployments, command-line installations using script files, as opposed to the interface-driven installation performed at the beginning of this chapter, are encouraged. By using a common script file across installations in your organization, you can achieve greater consistency between installations.

To start the command-line installation, launch the SETUP.EXE application from the command line using the /CONFIGURATIONFILE parameter. The /CONFIGURATIONFILE parameter requires the path of the script file containing the installation instructions. This file can be created using a text editor using information in Books Online or through an interactive setup, as mentioned in the first section of this chapter. If you create the file through an interactive setup, you need to review its parameter settings and make appropriate modifications.

The following is the call to SETUP.EXE for a command-line installation:

```
SETUP.EXE /CONFIGURATIONFILE=c:\temp\configuration.ini
```

And the following are the contents of the INI file instructing SETUP to install a default instance of Reporting Services using a files-only configuration:

Available for download on Wrox.com

```
[SQLSERVER2012]
QUIET=True
ACTION=Install
FEATURES=RS
INSTANCENAME=MSSQLSERVER
RSINSTALLMODE=FilesOnlyMode
RSSVCACCOUNT="NT AUTHORITY\NETWORK SERVICE"
RSSVCSTARTUPTYPE=MANUAL
```

Code snippet 101117 codedownload0201.txt

THE REPORTING LIFE CYCLE

The reporting life cycle is often described as consisting of three phases. A report is designed and developed in the authoring phase, made accessible to end users in the management phase, and placed in the hands of end users in the delivery phase. These three phases are illustrated in Figure 2-23 and discussed in the following sections.

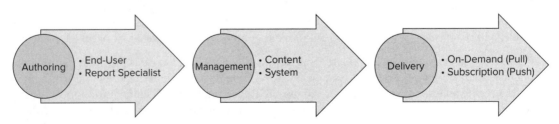

FIGURE 2-23

Authoring

The *authoring phase* of the reporting life cycle starts with gathering requirements through formal and informal processes. These requirements then drive the design of queries that provide data for the report. Data is integrated with charts, tables, matrices, or other presentation elements to form the basic report. Formatting and layout adjustments are then applied to produce a draft report that is validated for accuracy and consistency with the requirements before being published to a centralized management system in preparation for end-user consumption.

Report authoring is handled by two general classes of workers:

End-user authors develop reports as a secondary part of their job. These folks typically belong to the non-IT part of an organization and tend to require less technical, more user-friendly report authoring tools. These tools present data in a manner that is easy to interpret and incorporate into the report design. They make report layout and formatting a relatively simple or even automatic task.

Reporting specialists focus on report development as a primary part of their job. These folks often reside within the IT department. Reporting specialists demand precise control over query and report design. Their authoring tools tend to be more technical, providing access to the complete array of features available through the reporting system.

Of course, not every report author falls neatly into one of these groups. The end-user author and the reporting specialist represent two ends of a spectrum, with many authors leaning toward one end or the other. A variety of report development tools are needed to address the full range of needs along this spectrum.

Management

In the *management phase* of the reporting life cycle, published reports are organized, secured, and configured for end-user access. Resources employed by multiple reports and specialized features, such as subscription delivery and caching, are configured. These activities are collectively referred to as *content management* and are often handled to some degree by both authors and administrators.

The report management system itself requires configuration and ongoing maintenance to ensure its continued operation. System management activities are often the exclusive domain of administrators.

Delivery

After it is deployed and configured, a report is ready for end-user consumption in the *delivery phase* of the reporting life cycle. End users may view reports on demand or may request that reports be delivered to them on a predefined schedule. These are called the *pull* and *push* methods of report delivery, respectively. The key to successful report delivery is flexibility.

REPORTING SERVICES TOOLS

Reporting Services supports the full reporting life cycle. This support is provided through a collection of tools that come with Reporting Services, as shown in Table 2-2.

TABLE 2-2

AUTHORING	MANAGEMENT	DELIVERY
Report Designer	Report Manager	Report Manager
Power View	SharePoint reports library	Power View
Report Builder	Reporting Services Configuration Manager	SharePoint libraries and web parts
Third-party authoring tools	SQL Server management applications	Report Viewer control
	Command-line utilities	Reporting Services Web service
		Subscriptions

Report Designer

Report Designer exposes the full range of available report-development features, giving report specialists precise control over their reports. The application is accessible through the SQL Server Data Tools (SSDT), which is a collection of specialized designers available through Visual Studio. SSDT is installed with SQL Server and integrates with existing installations of Visual Studio. If Visual Studio 2010 was not installed previously, SQL Server setup installs a Visual Studio shell from which SSDT will be run.

Report Designer is divided into two tabs: Design and Preview. Each of these tabs provides access to interfaces supporting query development, report layout and formatting, and validation. Wizards and dialogs accessible through Report Designer provide support for the development of highly customized, sophisticated reports. In the following chapters, you will gain deep exposure to these features.

Power View

Power View enables end users to author their own highly interactive reports and visualizations, and to gain insights into their data.

Power View is Reporting Services' new reporting tool introduced in SQL Server 2012. Power View targets data consumers and helps them visually explore their data, answer ad hoc questions with ease, and present and collaborate with others in a SharePoint environment. Power View is a thin browser experience and is working against a BI Semantic Model. The BI Semantic Model is available on the client through the Excel-based Power Pivot modeling tool, or on the server through the Analysis Services Tabular project with SQL Server 2012. Chapter 9 covers BI Semantic Models in more detail.

Report Builder

Report Builder is a report designer with capabilities similar to those in the SSDT Report Designer, but it sports more of a Microsoft Office look and feel. It is available as a stand-alone download without a report server and as part of a server installation.

Third-Party Authoring Tools

Reporting Services reports are recorded as XML documents. The particular flavor of XML used by Reporting Services is known as *Report Definition Language (RDL)*. Report authoring tools provide graphical interfaces for report development, shielding authors from the gory details of assembling the underlying RDL document.

Because RDL is an open standard, third parties have developed their own report-authoring tools generating RDL documents that are consumable with Reporting Services.

Report Manager

Report Manager is primarily a content-management tool that provides access to reports and other items through an intuitive, folder-based navigational structure. Because it is securable and easy to navigate, Report Manager often serves double duty as a report delivery application. Use of Report Manager is covered in Chapter 17.

It is important to note that Report Manager is available only with Reporting Services instances running in Native mode. For instances running in SharePoint Integrated mode, content management and report display functionality are provided through SharePoint. For more information, refer to Chapter 3.

SharePoint Libraries and Web Parts

For Reporting Services instances running in SharePoint Integrated mode, reports and other Reporting Services items are presented as part of standard SharePoint libraries and are managed as SharePoint content. The Report Viewer web part, installed during the setup of SharePoint integration, allows reports from instances in this mode to be presented through SharePoint.

Access to Reporting Services content through SharePoint is not the exclusive domain of instances running in SharePoint Integrated mode. Native-mode instances can also present content using an older version of Reporting Services SharePoint 2.0 web parts. The Report Explorer 2.0 and Report Viewer 2.0 web parts allow Report Manager and rendered reports from Native-mode instances to be displayed within a SharePoint site. Chapter 18 provides more details on integrating reports with SharePoint.

Reporting Services Configuration Manager

The Reporting Services Configuration Manager lets you access system-critical settings. In addition, the tool provides support for certain administrative tasks, such as creating the Reporting Services application database and backing up and restoring encryption keys. Chapter 19 covers these tasks and the use of the Reporting Services Configuration Manager to perform them.

SQL Server Management Applications

Because Reporting Services is a member of the SQL Server product suite, it is supported through the standard SQL Server management applications. SQL Server Management Studio allows you to perform several administrative tasks, including managing shared schedules and roles. Configuration of the Reporting Services Windows service is supported through the SQL Server Configuration Manager, although some of this functionality is redundant with the Reporting Services Configuration Manager. The use of SQL Server Management Studio for various management tasks is addressed in Chapters 17 and 19.

Command-Line Utilities

To assist with the automation of management tasks, Reporting Services comes with a series of command-line utilities. Table 2-3 describes each utility and its default location.

TABLE 2-3

UTILITY	DESCRIPTION	DEFAULT LOCATION
Rs.exe	Executes VB.NET scripts, automating administrative tasks. This tool may be used with Reporting Services installations not running in SharePoint Integrated mode.	`<drive>:\Program Files\Microsoft SQL Server\110\Tools\Binn\ rs.exe`
Rsconfig.exe	Modifies connection information for the Reporting Services database and sets the default execution account used by Reporting Services to connect to data sources when no credentials are provided.	`<drive>:\Program Files\Microsoft SQL Server\110\Tools\Binn\ rsconfig.exe`
Rskeymgmt.exe	Manages the encryption keys used by Reporting Services. It is also used to join a Reporting Services installation with another Reporting Services installation to form a "scale-out" deployment.	`<drive>:\Program Files\Microsoft SQL Server\110\Tools\Binn\ rskeymgmt.exe`

HTML Viewer

Web browsers, such as Microsoft Internet Explorer, are the most popular tools for viewing Reporting Services reports. In most cases, when a report is rendered to HTML, Reporting Services adds JavaScript to provide several interactive features, including a toolbar, document maps, fixed table headers, and table sorting. Collectively, these script-based features are called the *HTML Viewer.*

To ensure compatibility with the HTML Viewer, it is recommended that you use the latest version of Internet Explorer. Currently, Microsoft guarantees full HTML Viewer functionality in Internet Explorer versions 8.0 and 9.0 with up-to-date service packs and scripting enabled.

Other web browsers can be used to view Reporting Services reports rendered to HTML, such as Firefox, Chrome, and Safari. Refer to Books Online for details on which features are supported by which browsers, if you plan to distribute reports to users employing browsers other than current versions of Internet Explorer.

Report Viewer Control

The *Report Viewer control* lets you display Reporting Services reports within custom applications. The Report Viewer control is actually two controls — one for use in web applications, and the other for Windows Forms applications. Each supports the same functionality.

 Don't confuse the Report Viewer control with the SharePoint Report Viewer web part and the Report Viewer 2.0 web part used to support the display of Reporting Services content within SharePoint.

The Report Viewer control runs in one of two modes. In the default Remote Processing mode, reports are rendered by a Reporting Services instance and displayed through the control. This is the preferred mode, because the full feature set of Reporting Services is available, and the processing power of the Reporting Services server can be employed.

In situations in which a Reporting Services server is unavailable or data must be retrieved directly through the client system, the Report Viewer control can be run in Local Processing mode. In this mode, the application retrieves data and couples it with the report definition to produce a rendered report on the host system without the support of a Reporting Services server. Not all Reporting Services features are available when the control is executed in Local Processing mode.

Integrating reports with custom applications through the Report Viewer control is covered in detail in Chapter 20.

Reporting Services Web Service

To support specialized application integration needs, Reporting Services offers a web service through which reports can be both managed and delivered. As described in Table 2-4, the web service has several endpoints that provide access to various programmatic classes.

TABLE 2-4

ENDPOINT	DESCRIPTION
ReportExecution2005	Provides programmatic access to Reporting Services report processing and rendering functionality. Available in both Native and SharePoint Integrated modes, although different URLs are used.
ReportService2010	Provides programmatic access to Reporting Services report management functionality. Available in both Native and SharePoint Integrated modes.
ReportService Authentication	Provides support for user authentication when Reporting Services runs in SharePoint Integrated mode and SharePoint is configured for forms authentication.

Chapter 20 covers the use of the Reporting Services Web service. Complete documentation of each endpoint is provided through Books Online.

A special feature of the Reporting Services Web service is *URL access*, in which a rendered report is retrieved through a relatively simple call to a URL. Parameters and rendering options are supplied in the URL's query string to affect the resulting report. URL access is also addressed in Chapter 20.

Subscriptions

Subscriptions allow you to put reports into the hands of your users based on a predefined schedule or following an event, such as the update of data. Reporting Services supports two types of subscriptions:

Standard subscriptions render a report in a specific format with predefined parameter values and deliver them to a single, preset location. This type of subscription meets the needs of many report consumers, giving them sufficient freedom to determine how, when, and where they will view reports.

Data-driven subscriptions support even more flexibility, and are better suited for managing delivery of reports to a large number of users with varying needs. These subscriptions are established with a reference to a custom relational table holding a record for each report recipient. Each record in the table may specify rendering and delivery options as well as report parameter values. Through data-driven subscriptions, a single subscription can be tailored to the specific needs of many individual consumers.

By default, subscription delivery is limited to e-mail transmittal or file share drop-off. Additional delivery options are supported through the integration of custom delivery extensions, as discussed in Chapter 22.

REPORTING SERVICES WINDOWS SERVICE

The preceding section looked at the applications through which authors, administrators, and end users interact with Reporting Services. This section covers the basic architecture of the Reporting Services service itself.

In Native mode, the service is a Windows service. For SharePoint Integrated mode, SQL Server 2012 provides deeper integration with SharePoint than previous product versions; the service runs as a shared service directly as part of SharePoint. For more details, refer to Chapter 3.

Interaction with the service takes place through HTTP and WMI interfaces. The HTTP interfaces provide access to Reporting Services' core report management and delivery functionality, and the WMI interface provides direct access to service management functionality in Native mode. SharePoint integrated mode in SSRS 2012 integrates its service configuration directly into the SharePoint configuration pages. External configuration files and application databases support the service. Figure 2-24 shows these interfaces and features.

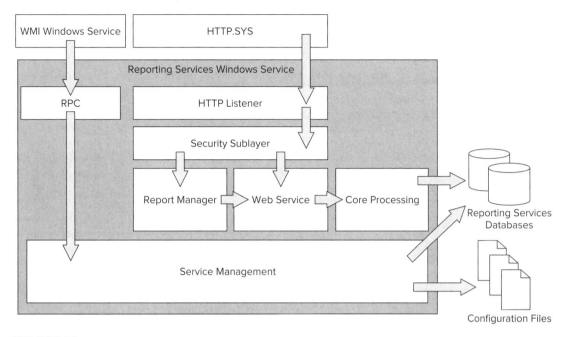

FIGURE 2-24

The following sections explore these aspects of the Reporting Services Windows service:

➤ HTTP.SYS and the HTTP Listener

➤ The security sublayer

➤ Report Manager and the web service

➤ Core processing

➤ Service management

➤ Configuration files

➤ WMI and the RPC interface

HTTP.SYS and the HTTP Listener

When an HTTP request is sent to the Reporting Services server in Native mode, the request is first received by the server operating system through the HTTP.SYS driver. HTTP.SYS is responsible for managing a connection with the requestor and routing HTTP communications to the appropriate application on the server.

URL reservations recorded in the Registry by Reporting Services provide the instructions HTTP. SYS requires to route communications to Reporting Services. The HTTP Listener feature of the

Reporting Services Windows service receives the rerouted requests from HTTP.SYS and engages either the Report Manager or the web service application it hosts.

Reporting Services in Native mode does not use Internet Information Server (IIS), Microsoft's web server. This simplifies the installation and management requirements for Reporting Services.

Although Reporting Services does not depend on or interact with IIS, you can still run IIS on the Reporting Services server if you have some other need for it. So long as URL reservations recorded by the two do not conflict, both Reporting Services and IIS can even communicate over the same TCP ports.

 The one exception is that IIS 5.1 and Reporting Services cannot share TCP ports on 32-bit Windows XP. If you have this configuration, you need to alter the URL reservations to use different TCP port numbers. You can alter the Reporting Services reservations using the Reporting Services Configuration Manager, as described in Chapter 19.

The Security Sublayer

As requests are received, the HTTP Listener hands them over to the Reporting Services security sublayer. The sublayer is responsible for determining the requestor's identity and then determining if the user has the required rights for the request to be fulfilled. These steps are called *authentication* and *authorization*.

Reporting Services in SharePoint Integrated mode plugs into the SharePoint site authentication mechanisms; see Chapter 3 for more details.

The Reporting Services security sublayer is implemented through a component called a *security extension*. The extension handles the mechanics of authentication and authorization and exposes a standard set of interfaces for Reporting Services to call. Various security extensions can be used with Reporting Services, but Reporting Services deployment can be configured to use only one at a time.

Reporting Services in Native mode comes preconfigured with the Windows-integrated security extension. This extension authenticates users based on their Windows credentials and supports four mechanisms for exchanging credentials, called *authentication types*:

Kerberos is the preferred mechanism for authentication if the feature is supported within the domain. Kerberos is highly secure. If delegation and impersonation are enabled, Kerberos can be used to allow Reporting Services to impersonate the end user when querying an external data source.

NTLM employs a challenge-response mechanism to authenticate end users. This is a secure but limited method of authentication in that impersonation and delegation are not supported.

The Negotiate authentication type is the default authentication type of the Windows Integrated Security extension. With this authentication type, Kerberos is used if available. Otherwise, NTLM is used.

Basic authentication is the least secure of the authentication types. With Basic authentication, user credentials are passed between the client and Reporting Services in plaintext. If you are using Basic authentication, you should consider implementing a Secure Socket Layer (SSL) certificate to encrypt your HTTP communications.

The default Windows Integrated Security extension is not ideal for all situations. Delivering reports over the Internet and integrating Reporting Services functionality with applications employing custom security mechanisms are two common scenarios within which Windows Integrated authentication may not be an option. In these and other scenarios, custom security extensions may be developed and employed by Reporting Services. Custom extensions are addressed in Chapter 22.

Regardless of whether the default or a custom security extension is used, as soon as identity is established, the user's rights to perform a requested action must be verified. (Closer to the actual sequence of events, the user is authenticated, and the request is passed directly or indirectly to the web service, which then calls back to the security extension for authorization.) Like many other Microsoft products, authorization in Reporting Services is based on role assignments. As roles are created, the rights to perform system- and item-level tasks are assigned to a role. Users are then made members of a role, providing the linkage required to determine whether a user is authorized to perform a requested task.

Report Manager and the Web Service

All requests sent via HTTP are targeted to the Report Manager or web service applications. The functionality of these applications is outlined in the "Reporting Services Tools" section.

What's important in the context of this discussion is to understand that both ASP.NET applications — Report Manager and the Reporting Services web service — are hosted from within the Reporting Services Windows service (with no dependencies on IIS, as discussed a moment ago). Both operate in their own application domains. This allows the Windows service to manage these as independent applications (despite Report Manager's functional dependency on the web service). The benefit is that problems within an application domain can be isolated. The Windows service can respond by starting a new instance of the application domain while dissolving the problem instance of the application domain.

Core Processing

Reporting Services' core processing features — scheduling, subscription management, delivery, and report processing — are performed by a collection of components hosted within the Reporting Services service. Although not based on ASP.NET, these components are managed as a separate application domain within the service. The "Reporting Services Processors and Extensions" section explores these components in more detail.

Service Management

Much goes on within Reporting Services. To ensure that resources are available and the service is working properly, a collection of internal service management features is implemented. Although not truly a single entity, these can be thought of collectively as a service management sublayer.

One critical feature of the sublayer is application domain management. As mentioned, Report Manager, the web service, and core processing features are hosted within the Reporting Services

Windows service as three separate application domains. Occasionally, problems within these arise. The service management sublayer's application-domain management feature monitors for these problems and recycles the affected application domains. This helps ensure the overall stability of the Reporting Services Windows service.

Another critical feature of this sublayer is memory management. Report processing can be memory-intensive. The Reporting Services service monitors memory pressure and responds, if needed, by temporarily moving portions of large requests out of memory to disk, while small requests proceed unaffected. Much of this is achieved through dynamic memory allocation and the use of disk caching in memory-constrained situations. The Reporting Services memory management model is outlined in Chapter 19.

Configuration Files

Reporting Services' internal and external features are controlled by collections of parameters recorded in configuration files. *Configuration files* are XML documents that follow a prescribed structure containing information governing the behavior of various components of the Reporting Services Windows service. Table 2-5 lists the most critical of these configuration files.

TABLE 2-5

CONFIGURATION FILE	DESCRIPTION	DEFAULT LOCATION
Reporting ServicesService .exe.config	Contains settings affecting tracing and logging by the Reporting Services Windows service.	`<drive>:\Program Files\ Microsoft SQL Server\ MSRS11.<instancename>\Reporting Services\ReportServer\Bin`
RSReportServer .config	Contains settings affecting numerous aspects of Reporting Services. This is the primary configuration file for Reporting Services functionality.	`<drive>:\Program Files\ Microsoft SQL Server\ MSRS11.<instancename>\Reporting Services\ReportServer`
RSSrvPolicy.config	Contains settings regulating code access security policies for the Reporting Services extensions.	`<drive>:\Program Files\ Microsoft SQL Server\ MSRS11.<instancename>\Reporting Services\ReportServer`
RSMgrPolicy.config	Contains settings regulating code access security policies for Report Manager.	`<drive>:\Program Files\ Microsoft SQL Server\ MSRS11.<instancename>\Reporting Services\ReportManager`

WMI and the RPC Interface

Microsoft's Windows Management Instrumentation (WMI) technology lets you consistently manage devices and applications running on Windows platforms. The Reporting Services Windows service exposes itself to WMI by registering two classes with the local WMI Windows service. These classes expose properties and methods that the WMI service makes available to administrative applications.

The first of the two classes registered by Reporting Services, MSReportServer_Instance, provides basic information about the Reporting Services installation, including edition, version, and mode.

The second class, MSReportServer_ConfigurationSetting, provides access to many of the settings in the RSReportServer.config configuration file and exposes a host of methods supporting critical administrative tasks. Administrative interfaces such as the Reporting Services Configuration tool leverage this provider for their functionality.

> *Developers can also take advantage of these and other WMI interfaces. The chief difficulty is making sense of the namespace organization within WMI. The WMI Code Creator utility, available from the Microsoft web site, is an excellent tool for exploring the WMI namespaces and the properties and methods exposed through each.*

A remote procedure call (RPC) interface provided by the Reporting Services service acts as a bridge between the WMI and Reporting Services Windows service. Through this bridge, calls against the registered classes received by the WMI service are relayed to Reporting Services.

REPORTING SERVICES PROCESSORS AND EXTENSIONS

In the "Reporting Services Tools" section, you looked inside the Reporting Services Windows service. The service's core processing features were introduced as an application domain whose functionality is provided through a collection of components. You will now explore those components to gain a deeper understanding of just how Reporting Services delivers its primary functionality and where that functionality can be extended.

Before jumping into the specific components, you should be aware of the difference between extensions and processors. *Processors* are the coordinators and facilitators in Reporting Services' component architecture. They call the extensions as needed and provide mechanisms for data exchange between them (see Figure 2-25). Although configuration settings may alter their behavior, processors cannot be extended through custom code.

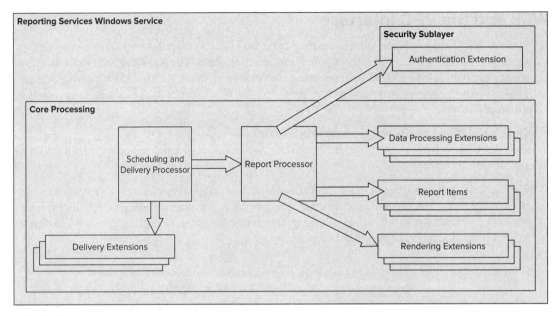

FIGURE 2-25

Extensions are components registered with Reporting Services to provide specific functionality. They expose standardized interfaces, which provide the mechanism by which Reporting Services engages them.

With these concepts in mind, let's now take a look at the following:

➤ The Report Processor

➤ Data processing extensions

➤ Report items

➤ Rendering extensions

➤ The Scheduling and Delivery Processor

➤ Delivery extensions

The security extension was discussed in the earlier section "*The Security Sublayer.*"

The Report Processor

The Report Processor combines data and layout instructions to produce a report. Following the arrival of a request for a report, the processor does the following:

1. Calls the security extension to authorize the request

2. Retrieves the report definition from the Reporting Services database

3. Communicates data retrieval instructions in the report definition to the data processing extensions

4. Combines data returned from the data processing extensions with layout instructions, using report processing extensions if needed to produce an intermediate format report

5. Passes the intermediate format report to the appropriate rendering extension to produce the final report

6. Returns the final report to the requestor

End users can't view the intermediate format report, but it can be rendered to any of the formats supported by Reporting Services. To reduce the time and resource expense of producing a final report, the intermediate format report can be stored (cached) for reuse. This provides a way to skip Steps 2, 3, and 4, allowing a report to be returned with less time and resource consumption. Reporting Services supports three forms of caching:

➤ Report session caching

➤ Report execution caching

➤ Snapshots

Report Session Caching

When an end user connects to Reporting Services, a session is established. Requests from an end user are made within the context of a specific session until that session expires.

During a session, users often request that the same report be rendered multiple times, possibly in differing formats. Reporting Services anticipates this by storing the intermediate format report in its Session cache. The cached copy is recorded with Session identifiers so that when an end user repeats a request for a report as part of his or her session, the cached copy can be leveraged. This feature of Reporting Services, known as *report session caching*, is always enabled.

If you change report parameter selections and those parameter values are used in dataset queries, an additional cache for the changed datasets is created in the report session.

Report Execution Caching

Why tie cached reports to a session? Why not make them available to all users requesting the same report? The reason has to do with security.

Reports are populated by data retrieved from external data sources. Connections to those data sources are established using credentials. The credentials used depend on the report's configuration or the shared data source it uses.

If data is retrieved using the requestor's credentials, the report may contain data appropriate only to that specific user. The intermediate report contains this data so that if it is cached and made available to another requestor, that user may be exposed to data that he or she otherwise should not see.

For this reason, only reports that do not use the requestor's credentials to retrieve data from external data sources can be configured for report execution caching. With report execution caching, the intermediate report generated from a report request is cached for some period of time and is used to render reports for other users until the cached copy expires.

Snapshots

With both report session and report execution caching, the end user requests a report, and the Report Processor checks for a cached copy. If none exists, the Report Processor must assemble the intermediate format report, store it in a cache for subsequent requests, and then render the requested final report. Later requests may take advantage of the cached copy, but the first request does not have this option. This can lead to an inconsistent end-user experience.

To address this issue, snapshots are scheduled to populate the cache before an end-user request. Snapshots are recorded in the same intermediate format and have the same security requirements as report execution caching.

Data Processing Extensions

As mentioned, the Report Processor reads data retrieval instructions from the report definition, but hands over the work of establishing connections and retrieving data from external sources to the data processing extensions. These extensions expose a data reader interface back to the Report Processor, allowing data to flow through them to the Report Processor and into the intermediate report.

Multiple data source extensions can be in use on the Report Server and even employed from within a single report. Reporting Services includes several data extensions, providing support for the following data sources:

- ➤ Microsoft SQL Server
- ➤ Microsoft SQL Server Analysis Services
- ➤ OLE DB data sources
- ➤ ODBC data sources
- ➤ Oracle
- ➤ XML data sources
- ➤ SAP NetWeaver BI
- ➤ Hyperion Essbase
- ➤ Teradata

It's important to note that the SAP NetWeaver BI, Hyperion Essbase, and Teradata extensions require the separate installation of client components or .NET data providers. If you need to use these data processing extensions, refer to Books Online for details on how to make these fully operational.

If access to other data sources is required, you can implement a custom data processing extension and register it with Reporting Services. This topic is addressed in Chapter 22.

Alternatively, you may be able to use a standard .NET or OLE DB data provider to obtain the data access you require. As mentioned a moment ago, data processing extensions expose a standard data reader interface. This interface is based on .NET specifications, which are themselves not that far removed from interfaces exposed by some OLE DB providers. As a result, many .NET and OLE DB data providers can be registered and used by Reporting Services in place of a formal data processing extension. Books Online provides details on the registration of data providers for use with Reporting Services.

Report Items

The Report Processor can generate tables, matrices, charts, and various other report items. These standard report items meet the needs of most report authors. Still, sometimes other report items are required. In these situations, additional report items can be registered with Reporting Services.

Typically, these report items are purchased from third-party vendors, such as barcode and chart controls. Custom report items can be developed as well.

Report items, whether purchased or custom, consist of both design and runtime components that must be registered with the Report Designer and Reporting Services, respectively. Both expose standard interfaces allowing the Report Designer or the Report Processor to interact with them appropriately.

Rendering Extensions

After the intermediate format report has been generated (or retrieved from cache) by the Report Processor, it is delivered to a rendering extension for translation to the end-user requested format. Reporting Services comes standard with seven rendering extensions, as described in Table 2-6. Each supports one or more report formats. Custom rendering extensions are also supported, although Microsoft does not encourage their development. Custom rendering extensions typically involve a large development cost.

TABLE 2-6

RENDERING EXTENSION	FORMATS SUPPORTED
HTML	HTML 4.0 (default)
	MHTML
CSV	Excel-optimized CSV (default)
	CSV-compliant CSV
XML	XML
Image	TIFF (default)
	BMP
	EMF
	GIF
	JPEG
	PNG
	WMF
PDF	PDF 1.3
Excel	Excel (XLSX)
Word	Word (DOCX)

Parameters affecting how each rendering extension generates the final report are known as *device information settings*. Default settings for each rendering extension can be set in the `rsreportserver.config` file. These can be overridden as part of a specific request to deliver the report in the precise format required.

It is important to note that the Report Processor does not simply hand over the intermediate format report to a rendering extension. Instead, the processor engages the rendering extension, which, in return, accesses the intermediate report through the Rendering Object Model (ROM) exposed by the Report Processor.

The ROM has retained the same basic structure since the release of Reporting Services 2008 and has many benefits. The most significant of these is improved consistency between online and print versions of a report and reduced memory consumption during rendering.

The HTML Rendering Extension

HTML is highly accessible and generally is a good format for interactive reports. For these reasons, HTML 4.0 is the default rendering format for Reporting Services reports.

The downside of HTML is that web pages have never been very good for printing. The HTML Viewer, a JavaScript-based application embedded in most HTML-rendered reports discussed toward the start of this chapter, provides client-side printing that overcomes some of the challenges experienced when printing from a web browser. (Client-side printing is accessed through the HTML Viewer toolbar.)

The HTML rendering extension can be instructed to return MIME HTML (MHTML) as an alternative to the HTML 4.0 default. With MHTML, images, style sheets, and other referenced items are embedded in the HTML document. This allows a report to be delivered without dependencies on external resources. This can be useful in certain scenarios, such as delivering a report to a user by e-mail.

 Not all e-mail products support MHTML, so check with your user community before selecting this format for e-mail delivery.

The CSV-Rendering Extension

The *comma-separated values (CSV)-rendering extension* renders the data portion of a report to a comma-delimited flat-file format accessible by spreadsheets and other applications.

The CSV-rendering extension operates in two modes. In the default, Excel-optimized mode, each data region of the report is rendered as a separate block of comma-delimited values. In CSV-compliant mode, the extension produces a single, uniform block of data accessible to a wider range of applications.

The XML-Rendering Extension

XML is another format commonly used to render reports. The *XML-rendering extension* incorporates both data and layout information in the XML it generates.

One of the most powerful features of the XML-rendering extension is its ability to accept an XSLT document. XSLT documents provide instructions for converting XML to other text-based formats. These formats may include HTML, CSV, XML, or a custom file format. The Reporting Services team recommends that you attempt to leverage the XML-rendering format with XSLT for specialized rendering needs before you attempt to implement a custom rendering extension.

The Image-Rendering Extension

Through the *image-rendering extension*, reports are published to one of seven image formats. Tagged Image File Format (TIFF) is the default. TIFF is widely used for storing document images. Many fax programs use TIFF as their transfer standard, and many organizations use it for document archives.

The PDF-Rendering Extension

Reporting Services comes with a rendering extension for Adobe's Portable Document Format (PDF). PDF is one of the most popular formats for document sharing over the Internet. It produces clean, easy-to-read documents with exceptional printing capabilities. In addition, PDF documents are not easily altered.

Although they are not as interactive as an HTML report with the HTML Viewer, PDFs do support document maps. This functionality enables the creation of a table of contents-like feature, which is invaluable with large reports. Adobe Acrobat Reader 8.0 or higher is required for viewing the PDF documents produced by Reporting Services. This application is available for free download from the Adobe web site.

When possible, the PDF rendering extension embeds the subset of each font that is needed to display the report in the PDF file. Fonts that are used in the report must be installed on the report server. When the report server generates a report in PDF format, it uses the information stored in the font referenced by the report to create character mappings within the PDF file. If the referenced font is not installed on the report server, the resulting PDF file might not contain the correct mappings and might not display correctly when viewed.

The Excel-Rendering Extension

Rendering reports to Excel is another option that Reporting Services supports. Rendering to Excel is highly useful if the end user needs to perform additional analysis on the data.

Reporting Services in SQL Server 2012 by default produces Excel OOXML format (XLSX). The original Excel renderer producing BIFF8-based format for Excel 97 and above is still available, but it is hidden in `rsReportServer.config` by default.

Not all report elements translate well to Excel. Rectangles, subreports, the report body, and data regions are rendered as a range of Excel cells. Text boxes, images, and charts must be rendered within one Excel cell, which might be merged, depending on the layout of the rest of the report.

It is a good idea to review your reports rendered to this format prior to publication to end users if Excel rendering is a critical requirement. Reporting Services Books Online provides details on how each report feature is handled when rendered to Excel.

The Word-Rendering Extension

This extension renders reports in Microsoft Word format with many of the same features and limitations as rendering in PDF. Unlike PDF, the Word format allows reports to be more easily edited by the end user following rendering.

Reporting Services in SQL Server 2012 by default produces Word OOXML format (DOCX). The original Word renderer producing Word 97 format is still available, but it is hidden in `rsReportServer.config` by default.

The Scheduling and Delivery Processor

The Scheduling and Delivery Processor's primary function is to send requests for subscribed reports to the Report Processor, accept the returned report, and engage the delivery extensions for subscription delivery. The processor also generates snapshots.

The processor works by periodically reviewing the contents of tables within one of the Reporting Services application databases. These tables are populated through on-demand events, through programmatic execution of the Reporting Services Web service's `FireEvent` method, or through schedules configured through Reporting Services. Schedules themselves are jobs created by Reporting Services but executed by the SQL Server SQL Agent Windows service. Reporting Services handles the details of setting up and configuring these jobs when you create a schedule, but the use of schedules creates a dependency on this additional Windows service.

Delivery Extensions

The Scheduling and Delivery Processor calls the delivery extensions to send reports to subscribers. Reporting Services comes with delivery extensions for e-mail and file share delivery. If running in SharePoint Integrated mode, Reporting Services also supports the SharePoint delivery extension for delivery of content to a SharePoint site.

As with other extensions discussed in this chapter, custom delivery extensions can be assembled and registered for use by Reporting Services. Books Online provides sample code for a custom delivery extension, sending reports directly to a printer.

REPORTING SERVICES APPLICATION DATABASES

This chapter has often referred to the two Reporting Services application databases: ReportServer and ReportServerTempDB. These databases store report definitions, snapshots, cache, security information, and much more. Although it is strongly recommended that you not directly access these databases, it is important to understand their basic structure and role within the Reporting Services architecture.

 When run in SharePoint Integrated mode, Reporting Services stores content and settings in the SharePoint content and configuration databases. These databases are the domain of the SharePoint application and therefore are not discussed here. As with the Reporting Services databases, it is recommended that you not directly access those databases.

ReportServer

The ReportServer database is the main store for data in Reporting Services. It contains all report definitions, report models, data sources, schedules, security information, and snapshots. Because of this, it is critical that the database be backed up regularly. Chapter 19 discusses backup and recovery to the application databases.

Table 2-7 lists some of the tables and their related functions.

TABLE 2-7

FUNCTIONAL AREA	TABLE NAME	WHAT IT CONTAINS
Resources	Catalog	Report definitions, folder locations, and data source information
	DataSource	Individual data source information
Security	Users	Username and security ID (SID) information for authorized users
	Policies	A list of references to different security policies
	PolicyUserRole	An association of users/groups, roles, and policies
	Roles	A list of defined roles and the tasks they can perform
Snapshots	SnapshotData	Information used to run an individual snapshot, including query parameters and snapshot dependencies
	ChunkData	The report snapshots
	History	A reference between stored snapshots and the date they were captured
Scheduling	Schedule	Information for different report execution and subscription delivery schedules
	ReportSchedule	An association between a given report, its execution schedule, and the action to take
	Subscriptions	A list of individual subscriptions, including the owner, parameters, and delivery extension
	Notifications	Subscription notification information such as date processed, last run time, and delivery extension
	Event	Temporary storage location for event notifications
	ActiveSubscriptions	Subscription success/failure information
	RunningJobs	The currently executing scheduled processes

continues

TABLE 2-7 *(continued)*

FUNCTIONAL AREA	TABLE NAME	WHAT IT CONTAINS
Administration	ConfigurationInfo	Reporting Services configuration information, which should be administered through prescribed interfaces and not by directly editing this table's data
	Keys	A list of public and private keys for data encryption
	ExecutionLogStorage	A list of reports that have been executed and critical metadata about the event

ReportServerTempDB

The ReportServerTempDB database stores temporary Reporting Services information. This includes both session and cache data.

Reporting Services do not function properly without the ReportServerTempDB database. Still, there is no need to back up the database, because all data within it is temporary. If the database is lost, you can simply rebuild it. Rebuilding this database is covered in Chapter 19.

Table 2-8 lists some of the tables and their related functions.

TABLE 2-8

TABLE NAME	DESCRIPTION
ChunkData	Stores report definition and data for session cached reports and cached instances
ExecutionCache	Stores execution information, including time-out for cached instances
PersistedStream	Stores session-level rendered output for an individual user
SessionData	Persists individual user session-level information, including report paths and time-outs for given session information
SessionLock	Temporary storage to handle locking of session data
SnapshotData	Stores a temporary snapshot

SUMMARY

The purpose of this chapter was to help you get a basic installation of Reporting Services in Native mode up and running so that you can explore the product as you progress through this book. Although it was highly useful, this installation ignored many of the issues considered during an enterprise deployment. To help you plan your enterprise deployment, each of these issues was introduced.

This chapter also toured the Reporting Services Native mode architecture. Through this chapter, you explored the following:

➤ The reporting life cycle as a three-phase process. Reports are authored by end users and reporting specialists, managed as part of a centralized reporting system, and ultimately delivered to end users through various means.

➤ The numerous applications provided by Reporting Services in support of the reporting life cycle. These include but are not limited to Report Builder, Report Designer, Report Manager, the Reporting Services Configuration tool, HTML Viewer, the Reporting Services Web service, and subscriptions.

➤ The structure of the Windows service as well as the components (processors, extensions, and databases) the service uses to provide its functionality.

The knowledge you have obtained in this chapter will provide a solid foundation for your detailed exploration of topics in the following chapters.

3

Configuring SharePoint Integration

➤ Understanding the SharePoint technologies

➤ Getting PowerPivot going in SharePoint

➤ Installing Reporting Services in Integrated mode

➤ Understanding the Reporting Services settings in SharePoint

➤ Native and Integrated mode topologies for SharePoint

This chapter explores the integration of SQL Server 2012 Reporting Services with the SharePoint technologies. In recent years, SharePoint has become a web-portal centerpiece for collaboration and information sharing. As a result, Microsoft has tightly integrated its reporting solution with the SharePoint technologies.

Integrating SQL Server 2012 Reporting Services and SharePoint allows a user to navigate to his or her intranet portal. There the user has instant access to company information, as well as personalized business reports and key performance indicators (KPIs). The reports can be embedded directly into web portal pages for seamless integration for the user. In addition, the exciting new Power View technology can be used to explore data in an ad hoc fashion.

SQL Server 2012 Reporting Services can be installed in either Native mode or SharePoint Integrated mode. In Native mode, a user interacts with Reporting Services using two web parts (Report Explorer and Report Viewer). In Integrated mode, SharePoint takes over all the duties of Report Manager. It also adds SharePoint document management values such as a consistent and friendly user experience, versioning, security trimming, alerts, enterprise search, and, when properly configured, the meeting of regulatory compliance requirements, to name just a few. Viewing reports in Integrated mode and Native mode using web parts is explored in detail in Chapter 18.

In a real-world situation, a number of servers would be used to host the SharePoint and SQL Server environments. What I have seen as a standard production enterprise-level implementation is a SharePoint farm that breaks out application servers and the servers running SQL Server. For the sake of simplicity and to make the examples in this chapter easier for the home user to follow, we will install everything on one Windows Server machine.

THE SHAREPOINT TECHNOLOGIES

The SharePoint technologies are made up of SharePoint Foundation and SharePoint Server. SharePoint Foundation is a framework built on the .NET framework and is included with Windows Server 2008. SharePoint Server, on the other hand, is a finished product built on top of the SharePoint Foundation framework and thus requires its own licensing. Figure 3-1 shows how SharePoint Foundation is built on .NET and ASP.NET and SharePoint Server is built on SharePoint Foundation. Also shown is the fact that both SharePoint Foundation and SharePoint Server use SQL Server to store configuration and content databases.

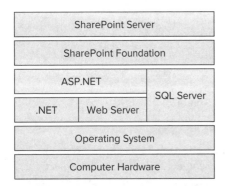

FIGURE 3-1

SharePoint sites are Web-based applications that provide a single point of entry for information across an enterprise. Better yet, sites can be created without any programming. Microsoft SharePoint sites can be created by anyone with sufficient permissions. The functionality is made available using nothing more than a web browser.

SharePoint Foundation

SharePoint Foundation is included with Windows Server 2008 and provides a simple portal solution with minimal overhead. SharePoint Foundation does not include as many components as SharePoint Server and is designed for basic communication and collaboration within an organization. As a result, customization is generally required to meet specific business needs. SharePoint Foundation is built on the .NET framework and thus provides endless customization options for .NET developers.

SharePoint Server

SharePoint Server is a Microsoft product that was built as a finished product and extends SharePoint Foundation with a great deal of functionality. Some of the key features found in SharePoint Server include Excel Services, the Business Intelligence Center, and PowerPivot. SharePoint Server is released in two versions: Standard Edition and Enterprise Edition. Table 3-1 lists the functionality provided, out-of-the-box, by the three versions of SharePoint (the information is from the Microsoft SharePoint web site).

TABLE 3-1

SHAREPOINT FOUNDATION	SHAREPOINT SERVER STANDARD EDITION	SHAREPOINT SERVER ENTERPRISE EDITION
Accessibility	Ask Me About	Access Services
Blogs	Audience Targeting	Advanced Content Processing
Browser-Based Customizations	Basic Sorting	Advanced Sorting
Business Connectivity Services	Best Bets	Business Data Integration with the Office Client
Business Data Connectivity Services	Business Connectivity Services Profile Page	Business Data Web Parts
Claims-Based Authentication	Click Through Relevancy	Business Intelligence Center
Client Object Model (OM)	Colleague Suggestions	Calculated KPIs
Configuration Wizards	Colleagues Network	Chart Web Parts
Connections to Microsoft Office Clients	Compliance Everywhere	Contextual Search
Connections to Office Communication Server and Exchange	Content Organizer	Dashboards
Cross-Browser Support	Document Sets	Data Connection Library
Developer Dashboard	Duplicate Detection	Decomposition Tree
Discussions	Enterprise Scale Search	Deep Refinement
Event Receivers	Enterprise Wikis	Excel Services
External Data Column	Federated Search	Excel Services and PowerPivot for SharePoint
External Lists	Improved Governance	Extensible Search Platform

continues

TABLE 3-1 *(continued)*

SHAREPOINT FOUNDATION	SHAREPOINT SERVER STANDARD EDITION	SHAREPOINT SERVER ENTERPRISE EDITION
High-Availability Architecture	Keyword Suggestions	Extreme Scale Search
Improved Backup and Restore	Managed Metadata Service	InfoPath Forms Services
Improved Setup and Configuration	Memberships	PerformancePoint Services
Language Integrated Query (LINQ) for SharePoint	Metadata-Driven Navigation	Rich Web Indexing
Large List Scalability and Management	Metadata-Driven Refinement	Similar Results
Managed Accounts	Mobile Search Experience	Thumbnails and Previews
Mobile Connectivity	Multistage Disposition	Tunable Relevance with Multiple Rank Profiles
Multilingual User Interface	My Content	Visio Services
Multi-Tenancy	My Newsfeed	Visual Best Bets
Out-of-the-Box Web Parts	My Profile	(Includes all Foundation and Standard features as well)
Patch Management	Note Board	
Permissions Management	Organization Browser	
Photos and Presence	People and Expertise Search	
Quota Templates	Phonetic and Nickname Search	
Read-Only Database Support	Query Suggestions, "Did you mean?", and Related Queries	
Remote Blog Storage (SQL Feature)	Ratings	
REST and ATOM Data Feeds	Recent Activities	
Ribbon and Dialog Framework	Recent Authored Content	
Sandboxed Solutions	Relevancy Tuning	
SharePoint Designer	Rich Media Management	
SharePoint Health Analyzer	Search Scopes	

SHAREPOINT FOUNDATION	SHAREPOINT SERVER STANDARD EDITION	SHAREPOINT SERVER ENTERPRISE EDITION
SharePoint Lists	Secure Store Service	
SharePoint Ribbon	Shared Content Types	
SharePoint Service Architecture	SharePoint 2010 Search Connector Framework	
SharePoint Timer Jobs	Status Updates	
SharePoint Workspace	Tag Clouds	
Silverlight Web Part	Tag Profiles	
Site Search	Tags	
Solution Packages	Tags and Notes Tool	
Streamlined Central Administration	Unique Document IDs	
Support for Office Web Apps	Web Analytics	
Unattached Content Database Recovery	Windows 7 Search	
Usage Reporting and Logging	Word Automation Services	
Visual Studio 2010 SharePoint Developer Tools	Workflow Templates	
Visual Upgrade	(Includes all Foundation features as well)	
Web Parts		
Wikis		
Windows 7 Support		
Windows PowerShell Support		
Workflow		
Workflow Models		

SharePoint Web Parts

A fundamental SharePoint concept is the web part. Web parts can be thought of as modular elements containing functionality that is added to the user interface. Typically, web parts display specific information and can be moved around the web page. For example, SharePoint comes with web parts that can display images and list files. They have a consistent format, with a customizable title bar and a web part drop-down menu available in the upper-right corner. The web parts used for Reporting Services are covered in detail in Chapter 18.

INSTALLATION AND CONFIGURATION

Configuring Report Services in SharePoint Integrated mode creates a tightly coupled technology that provides a seamless, user-friendly experience. To achieve Integrated mode in SQL Server 2008, an administrator had to use the separate configuration utilities that are part of the SQL Server product. This created confusion since an administrator also had to be extremely familiar with SQL Server configuration in order to configure SharePoint integration. In SQL Server 2012, after installation, all configuration is completed from within SharePoint. There is no need to access the SQL Server configuration utilities, as was required in SQL Server 2008. In addition, the Reporting Services Add-In for SharePoint can be installed directly from the SQL Server installation media. In previous versions of SQL Server this was a separate download and configuration. All in all, SharePoint integration with SharePoint has greatly improved in SQL Server 2012. To get the most out of Reporting Services and the new and exciting technology known as Power View (see Chapter 13), you will also be required to install PowerPivot for SharePoint (which is covered in this chapter).

To integrate SQL Server 2012 with SharePoint, be sure you have installed Service Pack (SP) 1 for SharePoint.

To follow along during the installation, you need a clean and fully patched 64-bit version of Windows Server 2008 with SP2 or Windows Server 2008 R2. These are the only operating systems that SharePoint supports.

Installing SharePoint Server 2010

To get your environment up and running as quickly as possible, you will want to install SharePoint Server 2010, but hold off on configuring it until later in the process.

1. Install the SharePoint 2010 prerequisites. You can do so from the SharePoint installation media, as shown in Figure 3-2.

2. When the prerequisites are installed, you are ready to install SharePoint. Before you begin, be sure to reboot the machine so that the SharePoint installation will recognize that all the prerequisites have been installed. Click the link Install SharePoint Server to begin the installation.

If SharePoint complains about not having certain components, it is possible that not all the prerequisites installed correctly. Rerun the prerequisites installation from the SharePoint media as described in Step 1 and then reboot again.

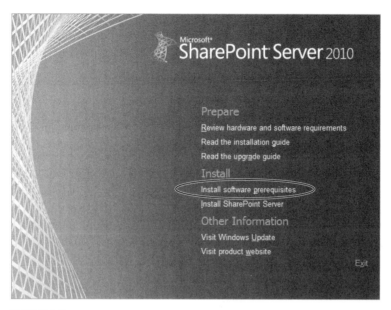

FIGURE 3-2

3. The SharePoint installation wizard asks for a product key. Enter either the key provided for your organization or the key you received when you downloaded the SharePoint trial.

4. Accept the terms set forth by Microsoft, and click Next.

5. The next screen is very important. Be sure to select the Server Farm installation, as shown in Figure 3-3, so that the installation does not automatically install an embedded version of SQL Server 2008.

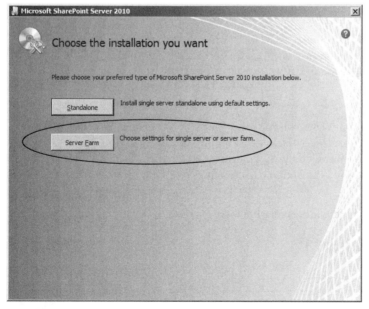

FIGURE 3-3

6. Select Complete, as shown in Figure 3-4, to install all the SharePoint components on this server, except for the SQL Server 2008 Express edition. You will use SQL Server 2012 to hold all the SharePoint configuration and content databases.

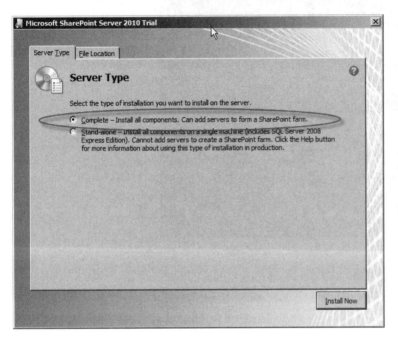

FIGURE 3-4

7. Click the Install Now button to begin the installation.

 By default, after installation SharePoint has a radio button selected to automatically configure SharePoint. Be sure not to just click Finished after installation without deselecting the Automatically configure SharePoint radio button.

8. When the installation is complete, you have the option of automatically configuring SharePoint. It is very important to deselect this option, because you do not want to configure SharePoint until you have installed the SQL Server integrated components later in the chapter. After you have deselected the option to automatically configure SharePoint, click Close, as shown in Figure 3-5.

9. Click Exit to close the SharePoint installation media screen.

Installing Service Pack (SP) 1

The SQL Server 2012 product requires SP1 be installed in your SharePoint environment. You do so by first downloading the installation media and then installing the service pack:

If you have downloaded SharePoint Server 2010 with SP1 already included you can bypass this step.

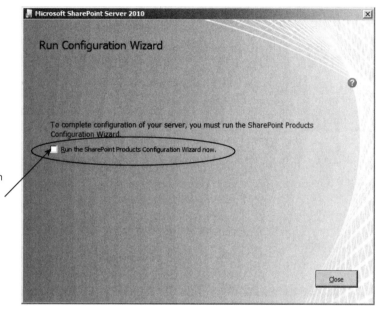

Do not run the configuration wizard at this time. We will run it later once we install some of the integration components.

FIGURE 3-5

1. Download the SP1 executable by opening your web browser and navigating to the Microsoft download center at www.microsoft.com/download/en/default.aspx.

2. In the download center search box, enter "SharePoint 2010 SP1" and look for "Service Pack 1 for Microsoft SharePoint Server 2010."

3. Download the executable to the computer where SharePoint is installed, and double-click the file to begin the installation.

4. Accept the Microsoft agreement, and click Continue to begin installing the service pack.

5. When the service pack has finished installing, you receive a simple message stating that the installation is complete. Click OK.

Installing and Configuring PowerPivot for SharePoint

Now that SharePoint and Service Pack 1 are installed, you are ready to install some of the integrated components that come with SQL Server 2012. The first step is to install PowerPivot. You will also configure your SharePoint farm to work with the SQL Server 2012 integrated components.

Note that you will need to provide a valid domain account in order to install PowerPivot for SharePoint. If the development server you are using is not already part of a domain, you will need to create a development domain environment.

1. Launch the SQL Server 2012 media to begin installing PowerPivot for SharePoint.

2. On the Installation tab, select "New SQL Server stand-alone installation or add features to an existing installation."

3. The installation checks for support files and rules and provides a report. Click OK to continue.

4. Enter your product key and click Next.

5. Agree to the terms of the license and click Next.

6. Keep the default, which will provide you with the most recent product updates. Then click Next.

7. The setup scans for product updates and downloads and installs any updated software before proceeding.

8. On the Setup Role screen, shown in Figure 3-6, select "SQL Server PowerPivot for SharePoint" and select the checkbox to add the database relational engine to this instance. Click Next to continue.

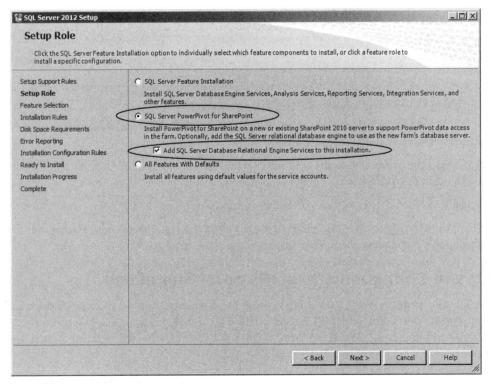

FIGURE 3-6

9.   On the Feature Selection page, keep the defaults, and click Next to continue.

10. The setup runs a set of tests to determine if the installation can proceed. When the screen shows that the tests have passed, click Next to continue.

11. On the Instance Configuration screen, choose to keep the default POWERPIVOT instance, and click Next to continue.

12. The installation calculates the disk space requirements and confirms that the machine has enough disk space to continue the installation. Click Next to continue.

13. Enter the domain service accounts for the SQL Server Analysis Services service, Database Engine service, and Analysis Services administrator. Because you are installing everything on a single box to gain familiarity with the product, you will use the same account for each credential. You can also click Add Current User if you are logged in as the same domain account you will use to test the functionality of SQL Server 2012.

14. After you have entered the user information, you are asked if you want to submit feedback to Microsoft. Click Next to continue.

15. The installation wizard runs checks to make sure everything is ready to be installed on the server. Click Next to continue.

16. The wizard shows you an overview of the installation that will happen, as shown in Figure 3-7. Click Install to begin the installation.

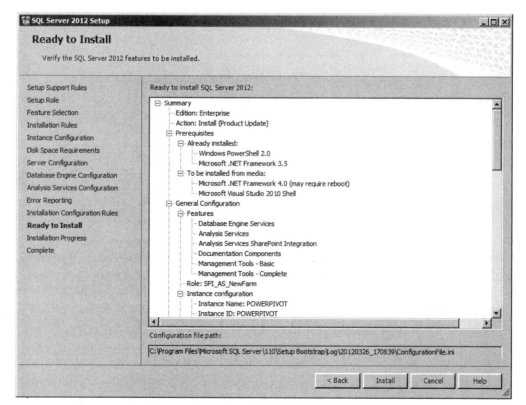

FIGURE 3-7

17. When the installation is complete, you receive a status report, as shown in Figure 3-8. From the status page you can click the link "Please launch the PowerPivot Configuration Tool to configure the server." to begin configuring PowerPivot for SharePoint, as shown in Figure 3-8.

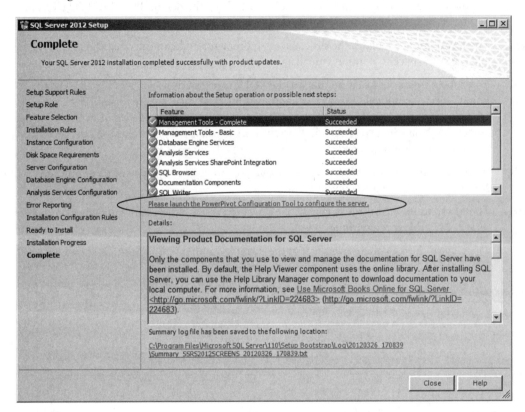

FIGURE 3-8

18. The PowerPivot configuration utility is new in SQL Server 2012. It performs all of the necessary configuration for integration with SharePoint. Click the button labeled "Configure or Repair PowerPivot for SharePoint" to begin the configuration. The PowerPivot Configuration Tool guides you through the configuration steps for SharePoint integration, as shown in Figure 3-9.

19. Enter the account username and password, and then enter the database server name if it is not already prepopulated. Finally, enter a passphrase for this installation of PowerPivot. Click the Validate button to validate the information you have entered. The passphrase is extremely important to remember for your SharePoint farm. When you need to alter the farm (such as adding a new server) you will need to enter the passphrase.

20. When the information has been validated, click Run to configure your SharePoint farm for PowerPivot. You see a status window as the configuration takes place, as shown in Figure 3-10.

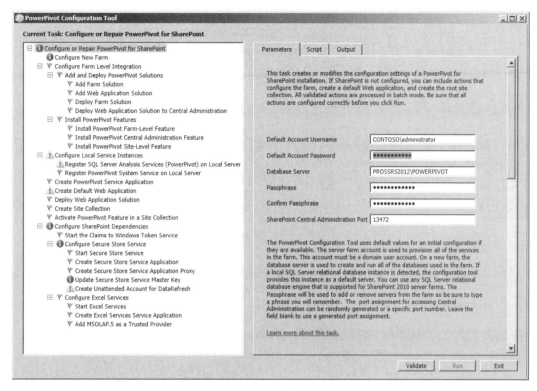

FIGURE 3-9

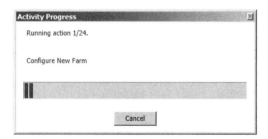

FIGURE 3-10

21. When the configuration is complete, a pop-up window lets you know the tasks have finished successfully. Click OK, and then click Exit to close the PowerPivot configuration window.

Installing and Configuring Reporting Services for SharePoint

Now that PowerPivot for SharePoint has been installed and the configuration utility has configured your farm, you are ready to install the Reporting Services for SharePoint components. You will also install a SQL Server Analysis Services (SSAS) instance in VertiPaq mode, which will be used to support Power View reports (see Chapter 13). To install and configure Reporting Services for SharePoint as well as SSAS for Power View, follow these steps:

1. You already ran the SQL Server installation media to install PowerPivot for SharePoint, but you need to run it again to install the Reporting Services components and also SSAS in VertiPaq mode. Start the SQL Server installation media, and then click the Installation tab.

2. Choose "New SQL Server stand-alone installation or add features to an existing installation."

3. On the Installation Type screen, confirm that the radio button "Perform a new installation of SQL Server" is selected. You will notice that the POWERPIVOT instance you installed in the preceding section is shown as well. You do not want to add features to this instance; you want to install a new instance for Reporting Services.

4. Enter the product key, and click Next.

5. Accept the terms of the licensing agreement, and click Next.

6. On the Setup Role page, confirm that the radio button SQL Server Feature Installation is selected, and click Next.

7. On the Feature Selection page, select Analysis Services, Reporting Services - SharePoint, and Reporting Services Add-in for SharePoint Products, as shown in Figure 3-11. Click Next to continue.

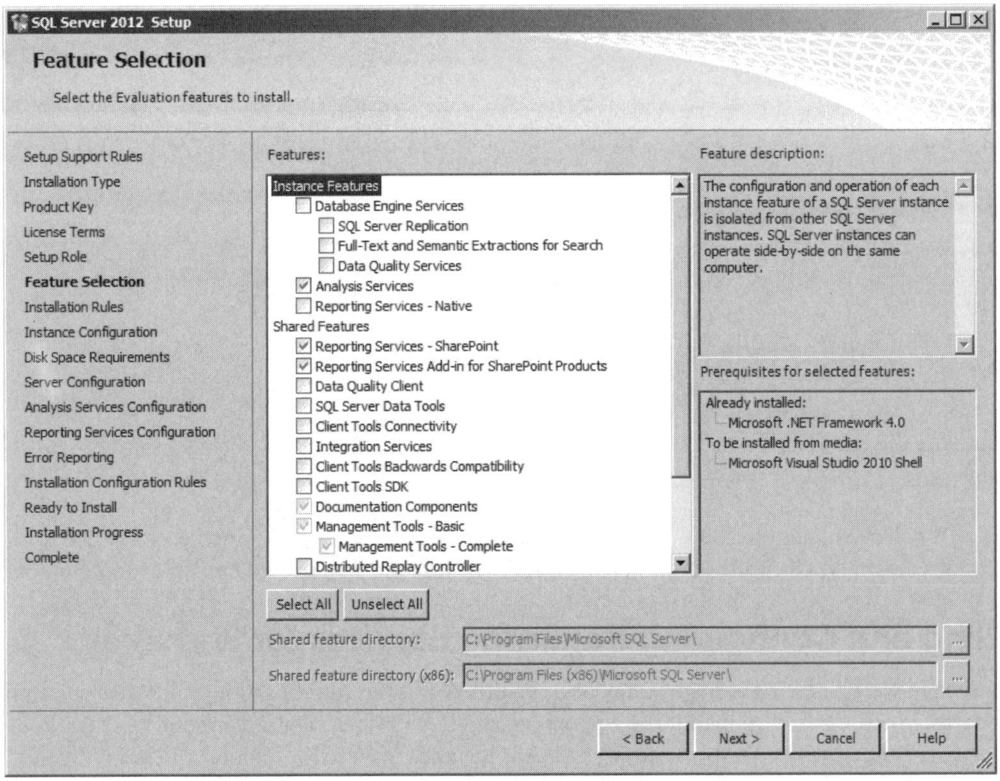

FIGURE 3-11

8. On the Instance Configuration screen, shown in Figure 3-12, select the radio button to create a Default Instance. You can also provide a named instance, but in this example you will use the default instance. Click Next to continue.

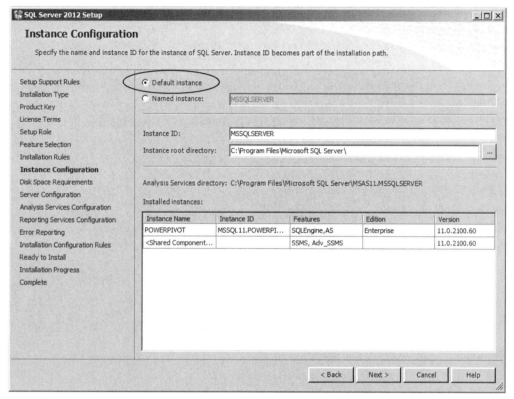

FIGURE 3-12

9. After reviewing the disk space requirements screen, click Next.

10. Enter the administrative account for SQL Server Analysis Services. Note that this should be a domain account. In this example you will continue to use the same account for all services for the sake of simplicity and understanding the technology. Your administrative account is part of the CONTOSO domain and is called administrator, as shown in Figure 3-13. After you have entered the credentials, click Next to continue.

11. On the Analysis Services Configuration screen, be sure you have selected the radio button for Tabular mode, and then add the administrative user. Because I am logged in as my sample CONTOSO\administrator account, I can simply click the button to add the current user. Click Next to continue.

12. Notice that on the Reporting Services Configuration screen, the only option is to Install Only for SharePoint Integrated mode. The Native mode installation options for Reporting Services are unavailable because you did not choose Native mode on the feature selection screen. After Reporting Services for SharePoint is installed in Integrated mode, you will use Central Administration, which is the management application for SharePoint, to configure Reporting Services. Click Next to continue.

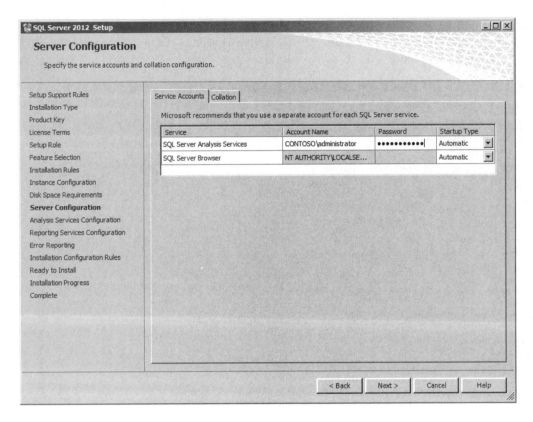

FIGURE 3-13

13. Decide if you want to submit feedback to Microsoft, and then click Next on the Error Reporting screen.

14. The installation runs some tests and provides you with a simple report. Click Next on the Installation Configuration Rules screen to continue.

15. You see a summary of the installation, as shown in Figure 3-14. Click Install to begin the installation process.

16. When the installation is complete, you receive a report letting you know that everything installed correctly, as shown in Figure 3-15. Click Close to complete the installation process.

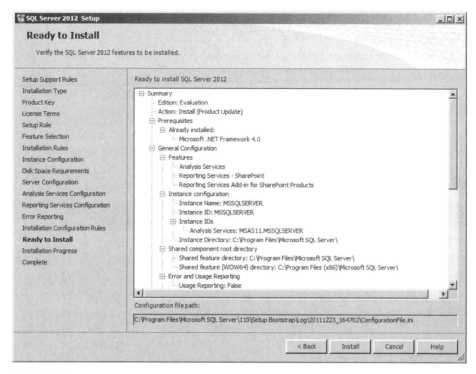

FIGURE 3-14

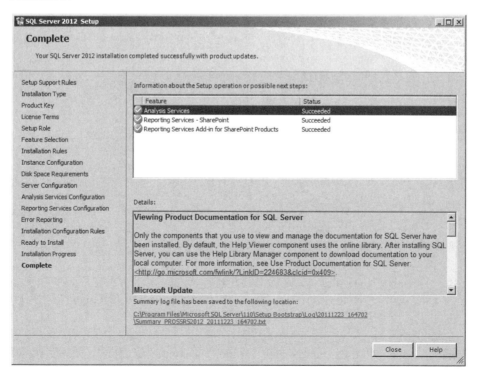

FIGURE 3-15

Now that Reporting Services is installed in SharePoint Integrated mode, you need to create a Reporting Services service application in your SharePoint environment. To do so, follow these steps:

1. Open Central Administration by navigating to Start ⇨ All Programs ⇨ Microsoft SharePoint 2010 Products ⇨ SharePoint 2010 Central Administration.

2. Click the Application Management tab on the left, and then click Manage Service Applications, located in the Service Applications section.

3. In the ribbon at the top of the screen, click New. From the drop-down menu, select SQL Server Reporting Services Service Application, as shown in Figure 3-16.

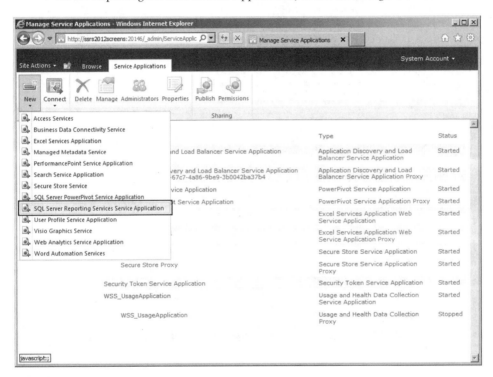

FIGURE 3-16

4. Enter a name for the service application, and then choose to create a new App Pool that the service application will run under. You could use an existing App Pool, but it is best practice to separate the Reporting Services service application from other service applications such as Excel Services. Separating the Reporting Services service into its own App Pool achieves process isolation, which creates an additional security layer to the SQL Server reporting data.

5. Enter a database server to hold the Reporting Services database. Earlier in the chapter you created a named instance called POWERPIVOT that you used to store the SharePoint configuration and content databases. You will use this instance again for the Reporting Services database in this example.

6. Make sure that Windows Authentication is selected, and also choose to associate the service application with the default SharePoint site. The completed configuration is shown in Figures 3-17 and 3-18.

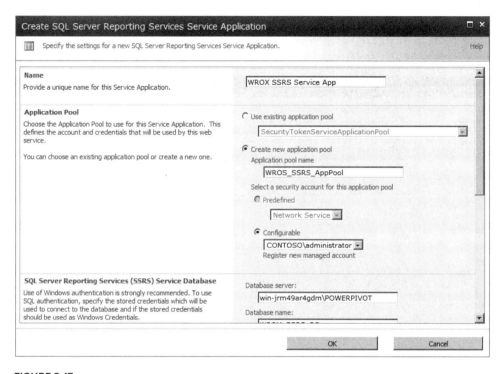

FIGURE 3-17

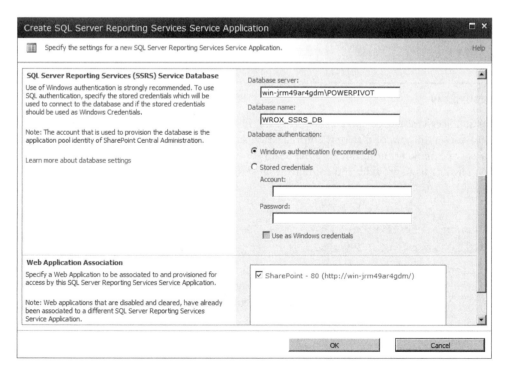

FIGURE 3-18

7. After the service application has been created, you see the status screen shown in Figure 3-19. Click OK to close it. You see the Reporting Services service application you created. You are now ready to begin using Reporting Services in SharePoint Integrated mode.

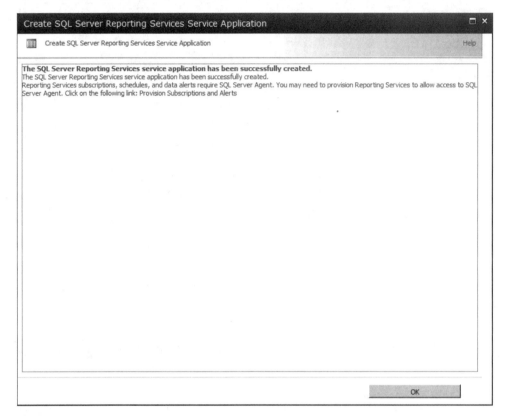

FIGURE 3-19

The Reporting Services service application provides the integration with Reporting Services and, as a result, provides a number of different configuration screens. You can access the configuration section of the service application by clicking the SSRS service application you just created. The service application settings page provides the configuration settings shown in Table 3-2.

TABLE 3-2

CONFIGURATION SECTION	DESCRIPTION
System Settings	Defines the overall system settings for the Reporting Services service application. Includes configuration items such as the report settings, session settings, logging settings, security settings, and client settings.
Manage Jobs	Lets you view and delete running reporting jobs.
Key Management	Lets you view and manage encryption keys, including the ability to back up, restore, change, and delete keys.

CONFIGURATION SECTION	DESCRIPTION
Execution Account	Lets you set credentials for data sources where a logged-in user will not be executing the report. It is best practice to maintain a unique account for this execution account and provide only the minimum credentials required to access the needed data sources.
E-mail Settings	Reporting Services can deliver reports using e-mail. The settings on this page let you configure e-mail so that reports, processing notifications, and alerts can be sent to end users through e-mail. Using this screen, you can instruct Reporting Services to use an SMTP server and then provide the outgoing server information and FROM information. The FROM information is who the e-mail will appear to be coming from to end users.
Provision Subscriptions and Alerts	For subscriptions, alerts, and scheduled reports to work with SQL Server 2012 and SharePoint, you must have the SQL Server Agent running, and Reporting Services must have access to it. A detailed description of this feature can be found in Microsoft's TechNet library: `http://msdn.microsoft.com/en-us/library/hh231725(v=sql.110).aspx`.

SharePoint Site Settings

When SSRS is installed in Integrated mode, a new section called Reporting Services is created in the SharePoint Site Settings, as shown in Figure 3-20. The new section allows the administrator to manage the server's shared schedules, manage the site's reporting services settings, and manage data alerts.

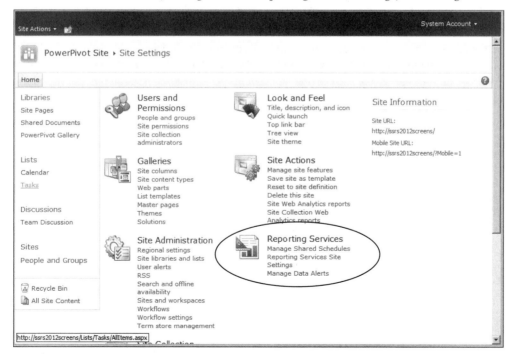

FIGURE 3-20

Table 3-3 describes the configuration of each of these features.

TABLE 3-3

CONFIGURATION SECTION	DESCRIPTION
Manage Shared Schedules	Provides an interface for adding and managing scheduled reports. In addition, you can pause currently running schedules and start selected schedules on an ad hoc basis.
Reporting Services Site Settings	Allows you to configure settings for the SharePoint site, including allowing client-side printing, showing detailed error messages on remote computers, and enabling accessibility metadata in the HTML of the generated reports.
Manage Data Alerts	Provides an interface for administrators to view and manage the alerts set on reports by users. Using this screen, an administrator can both view and delete alerts. In addition, all the alerts for a specific report or all the alerts for a specific user can be viewed.

ARCHITECTURE

When SQL Server 2012 Reporting Services is installed in Native mode, it runs in its own completely separate database. It uses an application called Report Manager to manage the database and does not share any database elements with the SharePoint environment. In this situation the SharePoint environment is simply a viewer of the reports. As described in Chapter 18, the Report Viewer web part and the Report Explorer web part are used to view and explore the report server. The architecture of Reporting Services in Native mode was covered in Chapter 2.

When Reporting Services is installed in Integrated mode, the integration is achieved through tightly coupled data sharing among the Reporting Services databases and the SharePoint databases. In this configuration SharePoint becomes the primary mechanism for displaying, managing, and securing not only reports and models but data sources as well.

In the simplest form, everything can be installed on one server. To review, the following components are used in Integrated mode:

➤ SharePoint (object model)

➤ SQL Server Engine (hosting SharePoint databases)

➤ SQL Server Engine (hosting report server databases)

➤ SQL Server Analysis Services (VertiPaq)

➤ SharePoint databases

➤ SQL Server Reporting Services databases

➤ SQL Server Reporting Services SharePoint add-in

When you install SharePoint under the stand-alone configuration, SQL Server 2008 Express Edition is used. SharePoint can be installed in an Advanced configuration, in which case the SQL Server engine in SQL Server 2012 can be used to host its content and configuration databases.

The SharePoint Service Application architecture (new in SharePoint 2010) allows you to distribute the load of different services to different physical machines. The consumers of the service in your SharePoint farm do not care where the service is physically located. An example of this distribution might be putting the PowerPivot service on a different server from the Reporting Services service and then putting the Excel service on yet another server. This allows you to mix and match services and physical hardware, depending on what you have available and what your load requirements will be for each service.

The distribution can continue as the organization's needs multiply. A very large organization usually has several servers that host various pieces of the SharePoint and Reporting Services scenario. A common approach is to distribute SharePoint among application servers and Web front-end servers. Generally, a large, failsafe SQL Server cluster is used to host the multiple configuration and content databases of the SharePoint farm. There is also a computer that hosts the Reporting Services service and another server for the PowerPivot service.

Each of these scenarios breaks apart the pieces to gain stability and performance. In every scenario, however, the underlying architecture remains the same. The SharePoint database takes control of the Reporting Services objects. The objects are stored in the SharePoint databases but are synced with the Reporting Services database to improve report rendering performance.

One of the key benefits of SharePoint is that it provides users with a single access point to store all their business documents. A SharePoint site could be set up for the executive leadership team that includes all documents they require on a daily basis. With Reporting Services in SharePoint Integrated mode, reports are also stored in these same document libraries and are easily accessed and managed. One of the main benefits of storing the reports in the SharePoint libraries is that end users only have to go to their specific SharePoint site to obtain all their business documents, including their reports. The world of modern information workers has become increasingly chaotic in a digital sense. Microsoft has made great strides in consolidating this chaos into a single point of reference with the SharePoint site.

SUMMARY

SharePoint is a technology that organizations have come to rely on for their intranet, extranet, and Internet web sites. Integrating SQL Server 2012 Reporting Services and the SharePoint technologies is a natural fit and provides an attractive solution for delivering reports to end users throughout the organization. As Microsoft continues to add and integrate functionality with SharePoint, the installation process grows in complexity.

This chapter looked at the following topics:

➤ The SharePoint technologies in general, including Windows SharePoint Services and Microsoft Office SharePoint Server, and SQL Server Engine (hosting SharePoint databases)

➤ Installing PowerPivot for SharePoint, including configuring the SharePoint farm from the PowerPivot configuration screen

➤ Installing and configuring SQL Server Reporting Services for SharePoint, including creating the Reporting Services Service Application in Central Administration

➤ The Reporting Services section of the Site Settings screen in SharePoint 2010

➤ The architecture of SQL Server Reporting Services integration with SharePoint

PART II
Report Design

Basic Report Design

WHAT'S IN THIS CHAPTER?

- ➤ Understanding the basic building blocks of report design
- ➤ How to design a report using the Matrix Wizard to learn the essential components
- ➤ A tour of the Report Builder design tool
- ➤ How to design a simple report using manual design steps to learn basic report structure

It's time to jump in and design a report! This chapter is designed to guide you through the steps necessary to design a basic report, first using the Matrix Wizard and then again using manual steps that will help you understand the components and design process a little at a time. The purpose of this first exercise is to demonstrate high-level report design without getting into the nuts and bolts of the process. We'll cover all the nuances and details later, but in this quick tour, you'll see how to create a simple report in a few easy steps.

WHAT GOOD ARE WIZARDS, ANYWAY?

I go back and forth on using the Report Wizard when I teach report design classes. I decided not to use it in this chapter, as I have in the past. The Report Wizard is handy if you want to throw together a quick report. If you know how to create a report manually, you'll be able to use the Report Wizard on your own, and you don't need me to hold your hand through the process. I figured that you probably didn't buy this book so that you could learn how to run a wizard, so I chose not to waste your time with this step. We will, however, use wizards to create a matrix data region.

In this quick tutorial, you will create a simple report, and I'll point out some of the essential components as we go. In later chapters, we'll slow down a little and discuss some of the finer points as we explore some of the same components in greater depth.

Building Blocks

Reports are assembled from basic components. Did you ever play with Legos? I did. I'm not talking about the kits with all the special pieces to make the star destroyer or pirate ship, but just a bucket of regular blocks. I'd use the standard-shaped blocks to create really tall buildings. By adding the flat pieces and the round ones that spin, I'd make helicopters with big, long rotor blades that would spin around until my little brother would break them apart. I'd chase him around the house until our mother would send us both to our rooms after we cleaned up the mess. Building reports is like making Lego helicopters.

Every report has three essential components, as shown in Figure 4-1. It has a data source to connect to the database or provider, a dataset to contain the query or command information used to return a set of records, and at least one data region to consume and visualize the data from the dataset. More-sophisticated reports might have several of these components. Each of these components can be created either individually or together using various dialogs and wizards. Every design should start with a clear understanding of the requirements, so let's outline them before moving forward with the report design.

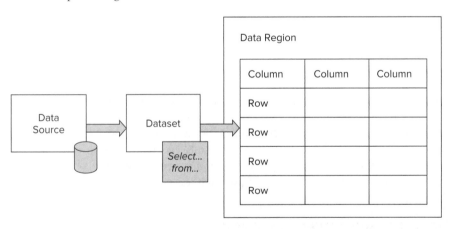

FIGURE 4-1

➤ **Data source** — The data for this report is stored in the AdventureWorksDW_WroxSSRS2012database located on our local development server. This is a SQL Server database that the report will access using the SQL Server data provider.

➤ **Dataset** — The dataset for the report uses a view object stored in the database. The vSales-ByTimeAndTerritory view contains a query that returns product sales records and returns the columns: CalendarYear, Month, MonthNumberOfYear, TerritoryGroup, Country, OrderQuantity, and SalesAmount. Each of these columns or fields includes values that can be used to display, group, sort, or aggregate into totals.

➤ **Data region** — This is a matrix report with header records grouped across both rows and columns. Sales records are grouped by the calendar year in the column headings, and by the product category on the row headings. A matrix data region is like a pivot table in Excel that has cells at the intersect points between each of the column and row group headings. We want the cells to contain the sum of all retail sales for the corresponding year and category that the cell represents. In reality, this report actually has two nested data regions, so the first group can be split across pages. Let's not worry about how that works right now. We'll cover it in more detail in a later chapter.

Following Along?

People have different learning styles. Some learn by reading and looking at examples. Others learn by following the steps and working through the entire process. We didn't write this book to adhere exclusively to either of these approaches. In fact, we've made it a point to provide short walk-through exercises that you can follow if you choose, but you may also learn by simply reading through the steps. This chapter in particular is written to show you each step in detail so that you can follow along. If you've done this before, you may choose to skim through these steps to get a quick refresher and then move on to more-advanced content. It's up to you.

If you like, you can download all the finished report examples from the Wrox site. However, if you're new to report design, I strongly recommend that you take the time to follow the steps in this chapter and build a new set of reports from beginning to end.

Let's Get Started

First, you need to know how your environment is set up. When Reporting Services was installed or configured, it was set up for either Native mode or SharePoint Integrated mode. This has little consequence for the report design environment, but it does change how you get started using Reporting Services. I'll give you two sets of instructions for the first couple of steps, but your experience will be the same either way, after you get into the Report Builder design tool.

1. Open Report Builder and create a new report:

    a. If you are using Reporting Services integrated with SharePoint Services 2010, open a web browser and navigate to your SharePoint site and then to a document library.

        Creating a new report is like adding a new Word or Excel document to the library. Figure 4-2 shows a document library with the New Document menu selection.

    b. If Reporting Services is not integrated with SharePoint, open a web browser and navigate to your Report Manager site.

        By default Report Manager is located at `http://<server name>/Reports`, where `<server name>` is the name of the web server hosting Reporting Services. If you have a complete Reporting Services instance installed on your local computer with default settings, you can use the address `http://LocalHost/Reports`. Figure 4-3 shows the Report Builder option in the Report Manager web interface.

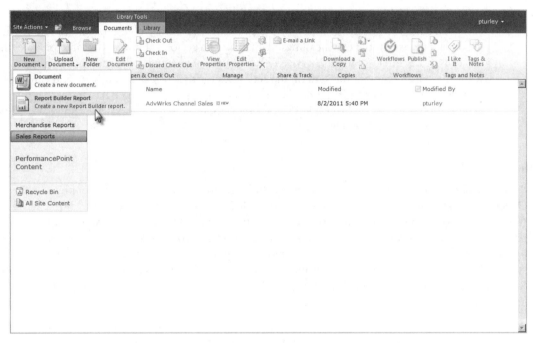

FIGURE 4-2

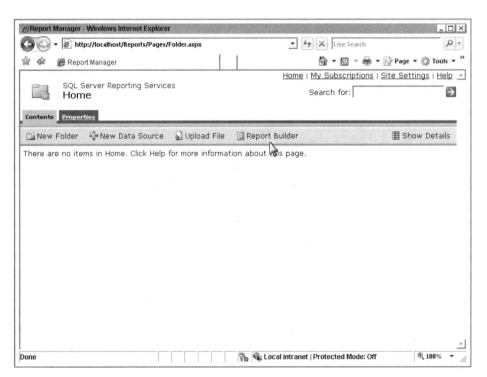

FIGURE 4-3

2. Create a new report in Report Builder:

a. To create a new report in SharePoint Integrated mode, click the Documents drop-down button on the ribbon bar and choose New Report.

b. In Non-integrated mode, click the toolbar button labeled Report Builder. Either of these actions takes you to the same point — opening Reporting Builder. Now that we're on the same page, instructions after this point will be the same, regardless of the configuration option.

Report Builder opens with a dialog window asking how you want to create the report, as shown in Figure 4-4. Choose Blank Report.

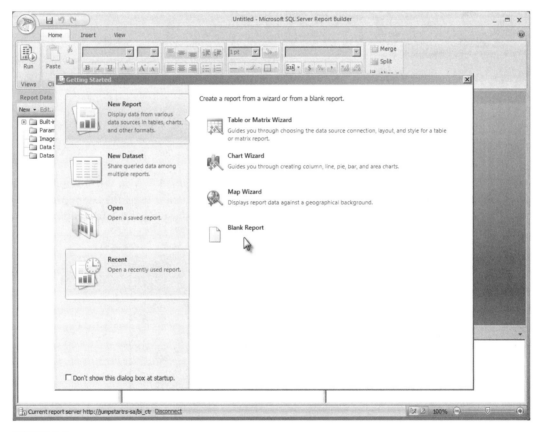

FIGURE 4-4

In the future, you will have shared data sources already saved to the server, and you will simply choose the one that will connect to the appropriate data source. This time around, you'll build a new data source to connect to the AdventureWorksDW_ WroxSSRS2012database on the local server. The Report Data pane is displayed on the left side of the report designer. It's a tree view containing the items Built-in Fields, Parameters, Images, Data Sources, and Datasets.

3. Right-click Data Sources and choose Add Data Source from the menu, as shown in Figure 4-5.

FIGURE 4-5

4. This opens Data Source Properties window, shown in Figure 4-6. You are prompted for the data source name, whether to use a shared or embedded data source, the connection type, and a connection string. I like to use the name of the database for the data source name. In the Name box, enter **AdventureWorksDW_WroxSSRS2012**.

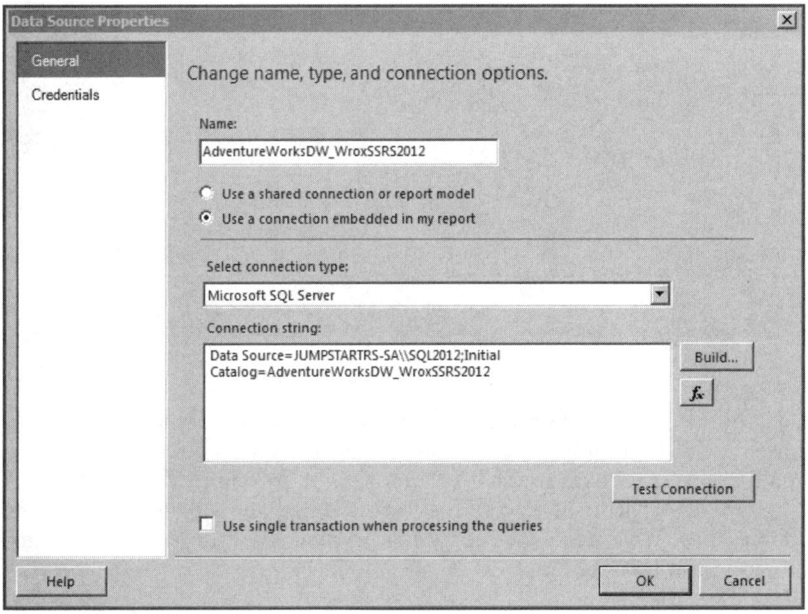

FIGURE 4-6

5. Select Use a connection embedded in my report.

6. For the connection type, be sure Microsoft SQL Server is selected.

7. Under some conditions you might enter a connection string manually, but in this case you will use another dialog window to build the connection string, so click the Build button. This opens the Connection Properties dialog, shown in Figure 4-7, which prompts you for the database server and connection information.

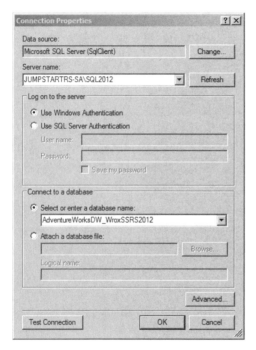

FIGURE 4-7

8. Enter the name of the database server in the Server name box.

If you are using the default SQL Server instance on your local development machine, you can enter **LocalHost**. This will be the case if you installed SQL Server on your local development computer and then added the Adventure Works sample databases.

Note that in later examples you may see the server name, a period, or the text (local). All these are valid techniques for referencing the local SQL Server database server.

If you are using a database server on your business network, you must obtain this information from your system administrator. In my case, the database server is named JUMPSTARTRS-SA, and the SQL Server instance is named SQL2012.

Because this is the first time you've referred to the sample database we'll be using throughout the report design chapters, I'll remind you that the right version of the Adventure Works sample must be installed.

9. In the section titled Log on to the server, leave the default selection set to Use Windows Authentication.

10. In the section titled Connect to database, drop down the list and select the AdventureWorksDW_WroxSSRS2012 database.

11. Click OK to close the Connection Properties dialog.

    Like shared data sources, shared datasets can be saved to the server for later use. Again, since we're just getting started, you'll create a new dataset embedded into the report.

12. In the Report Data pane, right-click Datasets and choose Add Dataset. The Dataset Properties dialog appears, as shown in Figure 4-8.

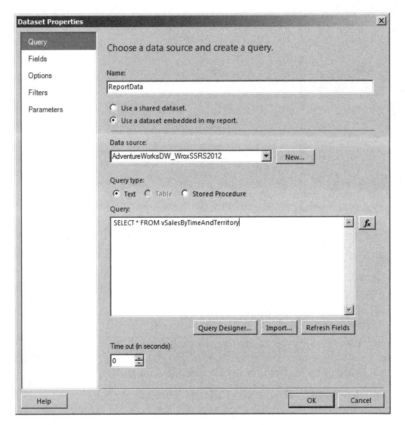

FIGURE 4-8

13. Name the dataset **ReportData**.

    Dataset names can't include spaces or special characters. As a rule, just use a simple name, using mixed-case characters, as in "ReportData." There's no need to overcomplicate dataset names. Additional datasets are used to fill parameter lists and to supply data to other parts of the report.

14. Select the option Use a dataset embedded in my report.

15. Using the drop-down list, select the data source you just created.

You have a database view that will query and return the data you need for this report. You can treat a view much like a table and use Structured Query Language (SQL) to select rows from it. You'll use a simple query to return all rows and all columns that the view is designed to provide.

16. Type this text into the Query box:

```
SELECT * FROM vSalesByTimeAndTerritory
```

17. Click OK to close the Dataset Properties dialog. The report designer window shows a blank report with a textbox in the report header, as shown in Figure 4-9. You provide a header title and then create the matrix.

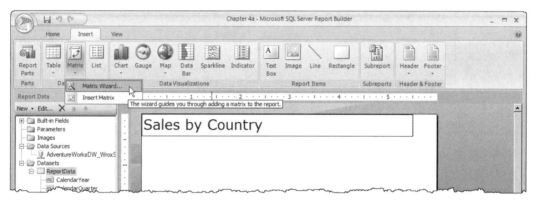

FIGURE 4-9

18. Place the cursor in the textbox where you see the text Click to add title. Type the text **Sales by Country**.

19. On the Insert tab, click the arrow below the Matrix icon and select Matrix Wizard. This action opens a window titled New Table or Matrix, as shown in Figure 4-10. You use this mini wizard dialog to add fields to areas of the matrix data region, and to choose properties and styling features.

20. On the Arrange Fields page, you add fields to the different headings to group values in the report. You can either drag and drop field names from the Available fields list or select a field and use the group label buttons to move a field to the appropriate group box under Displayed fields.

21. Add the `CalendarYear` field to the `Row groups`.

22. Add `MonthName` to the `Row groups`.

23. Add `SalesTerritoryCountry` to the `Column groups`.

24. Add `SalesAmt` and `OrderQty` to `Values`.

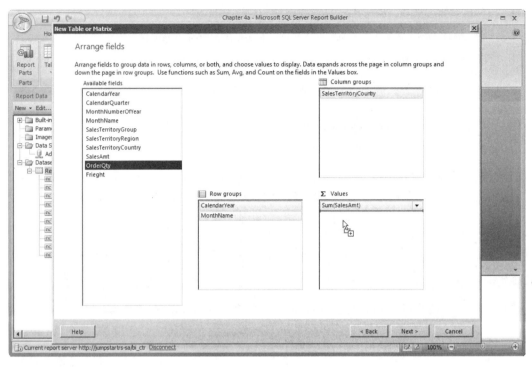

FIGURE 4-10

25. Make sure your selections match those shown in Figure 4-10 (including the OrderQty field added under SalesAmt), and click Next to move to the next page.

26. For the Choose Matrix Style, you may choose any option you like. I have selected the Forest style.

27. On the last page of the wizard, enter Sales by Territory for the report name. Click Finish to complete the report wizard and view the new report in the designer. At this point, the report is actually usable, but we will do a little housekeeping before calling it done. Let's take a quick look at the output before we clean things up.

On the ribbon bar, the leftmost button in the View group toggles between Design and Preview modes.

28. Click the Run icon to preview the report with data. The green "spinny" icon tells you that the report server is working as the report renders data. After a few seconds you should see the report filled with data, similar to Figure 4-11.

29. On the next page, select any style that tickles your fancy. Click the Finish button to complete the wizard and add the new matrix to the report body.

30. On the left of the ribbon, click the Run button to preview the report.

The last step is to clean things up just a little. The numeric cells in the matrix have unformatted values that could be a little easier to read. This part's easy:

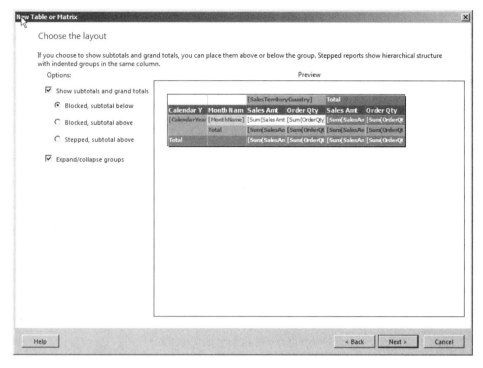

FIGURE 4-11

31. Use the ribbon button to switch back to Design view.

32. Click the column header for the SalesAmt field.

33. In the ribbon bar, use the icons and controls in the Number group to format the cell as Currency (you can either use the dollar sign icon or the drop-down list).

The two rightmost icons in the Number group are used to add or remove decimal places.

34. Click the icon on the right twice to move the decimal point two positions. This rounds the value displayed in these cells to a whole number.

35. Click the column header for the OrderQty field.

36. In the ribbon bar, use the icons and controls in the Number group to format the cell with a thousand separator and no decimal positions.

By switching between design and preview (using the Design/Run button), you can experiment with these formatting properties and get the results you want.

37. Repeat the same steps for the Sales Amt and Order Qty columns in the Total section to the right, as shown in Figure 4-12.

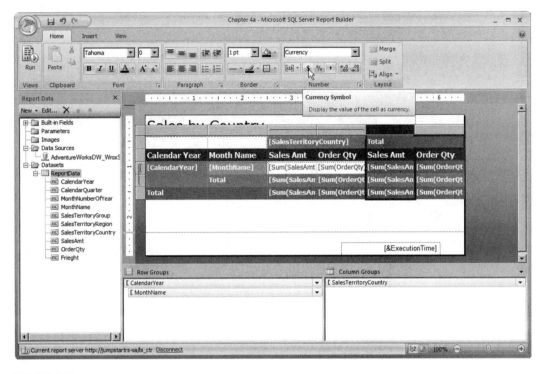

FIGURE 4-12

38. Click the Run button again to preview the report.

39. When you're done reviewing the report, switch back to Design.

40. Click the Report Builder button and then choose Save as. Optionally, you can navigate to any folder or library and save the report anywhere you like. Enter the name **Sales by Territory Matrix (wizard)**. This saves a copy of the report to the report server or SharePoint document library, depending on how your report server is configured.

41. Run the report and compare your results to Figure 4-13. Use the drill-down expand and collapse buttons (the plus and minus icons) displayed next to each year to view the detail rows for each month within that year.

You may notice that the months are out of order. This is expected. We'll take care of this in the next exercise when you build the matrix manually.

42. Reach over your shoulder and pat yourself on the back for a job well done!

Congratulations on creating your first report. If this isn't your first Reporting Services report, you can save that last step for your first victory when we cover more advanced report design later in the book. With a working report in front of you, this is a good opportunity to take a closer look at the design environment.

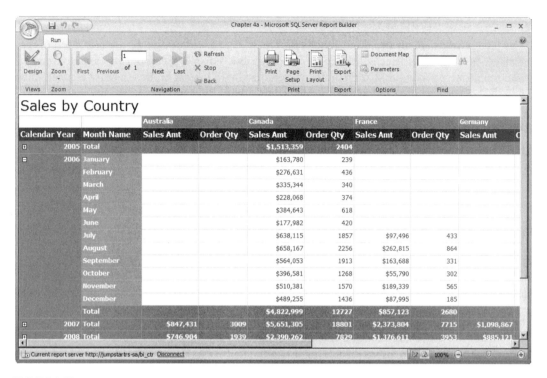

FIGURE 4-13

Touring Report Builder

Now that you've had some brief experience with the Report Builder design environment, it's only fitting that we take a more comprehensive look at the environment where you'll be spending a lot of your time. Many of the report design features in Report Builder are the same as or very similar to the SSDT or Visual Studio report designer, but it's a more sleek and uncomplicated interface. To create a new report, you can either use the Report Wizard or manually build a data region and a dataset to supply its data. The basic theme in Report Builder is simplicity. Although I do a lot of report design work in Visual Studio projects, I often prefer to start designing new reports with Report Builder because it's so convenient and easy to use.

Report Builder 2.0, for use with Reporting Services in SQL Server 2008, was actually the first generation of this business user-friendly report design application. The first Report Builder tool (which many people now call Report Builder 1.0) was an acquired product. Although it had some useful functionality, the product team decided to build a new application rather than continuing to extend the existing code base. Report Builder 2.0 was developed while the Microsoft Office product team was working on the Office 2007 suite. As you may know, this is when they refactored all the Office application menus and toolbars. Now tabs and ribbons are part of the Microsoft Office user interface, replacing the old drop-down menus found in earlier Microsoft applications. Subsequently, Report Builder 2.0 and the new version have this same look and feel.

Office Tabs and Ribbons

Large icon buttons are arranged on ribbons that may be accessed using tabs along the top of the interface. When a tab is selected, the corresponding ribbon displays icon buttons and commands related to different activities. Commands are organized into logical groups that are enabled only when the appropriate object is selected or when you are in the appropriate designer mode.

Home Tab

The Home tab, shown in Figure 4-14, is the starting point in the Report Designer. It contains common layout and formatting features for designing reports.

FIGURE 4-14

The formatting commands on the Home tab ribbon work with multiple selected items. To select multiple items, draw a marquee box around a group of items while holding down the left mouse button, or click individual items while holding down the Shift or Ctrl key. Note that most report item properties may also be set using a custom Properties dialog that appears after right-clicking an item, but this option doesn't work with multiple selected items. Using the Properties window or ribbon commands does work with multiple selected items.

On the Home tab, you will find the following groups and commands:

➤ **Views** — This group contains one icon button that toggles between Run and Preview depending on the current designer view. Similar controls are located in the bottom, right-hand side of the designer window status bar, next to the zoom slider control.

➤ **Clipboard** — This group contains common Windows Clipboard features such as Copy, Cut, and Paste. The Clipboard is an essential tool in report design and is used often for duplicating captions and expressions. You can use the Clipboard with objects such as report items and images, in addition to text values that you might want to cut, copy, or paste using the Windows Clipboard.

➤ **Font** — The items in this group correspond to the font-related properties for textboxes. Using the command buttons on the ribbon typically is much faster than setting all the individual properties for each object in the Properties window.

➤ **Paragraph** — The Paragraph settings affect textboxes or the text selected within a textbox. Be careful to note the difference between these two options. When one or more textbox items are selected, the textbox is displayed with selection handles along the rectangular border. To select all or part of the text within a textbox, the text is highlighted.

➤ **Border** — The Border commands allow you to quickly set the border style, weight, and color for the top, left, right, and bottom borders of any object. Using the ribbon commands to set an outside border for an item actually sets all these individual properties. Keep in mind that nearly all items have border properties and may contain child items that also have borders. For example, setting the borders for a table does not set the borders for all the cells within the table. If you need to fine-tune borders, you may find it useful to set the borders for the entire table, rows, columns, or a range of cells and then adjust the borders for individual cells afterward.

➤ **Number** — The options in this group are for formatting selected values. These commands are similar to other Office applications like Excel. These settings are used to specify formatting for numeric and date type values.

➤ **Layout** — These commands allow you to easily format multiple report items by aligning the edges or centers of all items selected. When this option is used with a group of items, all items are aligned with the first selected item.

Insert Tab

The Insert tab and corresponding ribbon, shown in Figure 4-15, contain report design components that you can place on the report body to visualize data or format the report layout. Items in the Data Regions, Report Items, and Subreports groups are added to the top-left corner of the report body when the ribbon button is clicked. Note that this behavior differs from the Visual Studio report design Toolbox items. In the other report designer, items are dragged or drawn onto the report body.

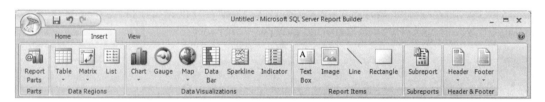

FIGURE 4-15

These items are organized into the following groups:

➤ **Parts** — The Report Parts button is used to show or hide the Report Part Gallery pane to search for and add report parts to a report.

➤ **Data Regions** — The data regions consume data from a dataset and visualize it into rows, columns, chart items, and gauges. Data regions are actually report items, but they are different from standard report items, because they consume whole sets of data rather than just individual values.

To add a data region to the report in Design view, click the ribbon button for the appropriate data region. The data region is added to the top-left corner of the report body. Click the item to show the repositioning handle, and then drag and drop the data region to the right place on the report.

➤ **Data Visualizations** — This group contains report items and data regions that present data visually. These items include charts, gauges, maps, data bars, sparklines and indicators. Like the items in the Data Regions group, these items may be inserted into the report body in the design window.

➤ **Report Items** — Report items may be visual elements used to enhance the report layout, such as lines and rectangles. Some report items are designed to display or visualize a specific value or aggregated value from a dataset, such as a textbox or image.

Report items are added to the report body in the same manner as data regions. Often, you will want to place a report item into a data region or other report item so that it becomes a container.

➤ **Subreports** — This group contains only one item — a subreport. This is a special report item that allows you to place an existing report within this report body. If a subreport is placed directly on the report body, it is rendered once, at that location, within the report. If it is placed within a data region, a separate instance of the subreport is rendered for each row or column of the data region. Subreports can be filtered based on a field value to define master/detail relationships between datasets based on separate data sources.

➤ **Header & Footer** — This group is used to enable or disable page headers and footers for the report. Unlike the other items in the Insert table, headers and footers are not "added" to the report body but are designated as sections of the report.

View Tab

The View tab and ribbon, shown in Figure 4-16, includes the Show/Hide group. Checkboxes in this group are used to enable design panes and features in the report designer. These include the Report Data pane, Grouping Lists pane, Properties pane, and the Ruler.

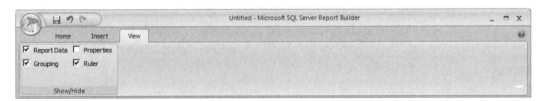

FIGURE 4-16

The View tab also contains a group to show or hide utility panes and rulers. The Data pane, displayed on the left side of the Report Designer, is used to manage built-in fields, parameters, images, data sources, datasets, and dataset fields. This pane replaces the Data tab in earlier versions of the Report Designer that contained some of these options.

The grouping pane is displayed at the bottom of the Report Designer. It shows the row and column groups associated with the currently selected data range object. You can drag fields into the row and column list boxes to create data groups. Each group is displayed with a set of tools to enable adding, editing, and deleting a group. The drop-down button displayed on each group item enables a drop-down menu with additional group management options.

The Properties pane is used to browse and change nearly all the properties for the currently selected design object. This is the traditional method used to manage property values. Although it duplicates some property settings that may be set using more convenient methods, it provides a consistent interface for managing all properties without the need to use different methods to access them.

Report Builder Menu

Figure 4-17 shows the Report Builder menu and the Recent Documents list.

FIGURE 4-17

When a report is previewed, the Run tab and ribbon are displayed with several feature groups and corresponding icons:

➤ The Views group includes the Design button, which is used to return to the report designer.

➤ The Zoom group and button are used to change the magnification of the report preview.

➤ The Navigation group includes several buttons. The First, Previous, Next, and Last buttons provide a convenient way to navigate through the report pages, and the Page textbox allows you to navigate to a specific page. The Refresh button forces a requery of all data sources and rerenders the report. The Stop button suspends report execution and stops the queries and report from running. The Back button navigates to a previous report when using a drill-through report action.

➤ The Print group contains client-side printer controls.

➤ The Export button allows a report to be rendered into selected formats and to be exported to a separate file.

➤ The Options button allows you to hide and show optional toolbars in the report preview interface, including a document map (if the previewed report contains document map settings) and the parameters selection pane.

➤ The Find group includes a Search textbox and corresponding button used to find a string of text within the body of the rendered report.

You can switch back to design view using the Run/Design button on the left side of the Home tab ribbon. You can also always toggle between report design and preview using the smaller icons in the status bar, to the left of the zoom slider control.

While the report is previewed and the Run tab options are visible, a smaller pane is displayed between the ribbon and the report. It contains a link to change user credentials and the View Report button. Click this button after making parameter selections to execute the report with these selections.

Viewing and Setting Properties

You can set properties for different objects in the Designer using three different methods. The first and most convenient method is to use the Home tab on the ribbon. For simple report items, such as a textbox, just click the report item, and then use the ribbon commands to make changes. You can also choose multiple objects of the same type. This is easy to do with the properties font size, color, background color, and so on.

Another method is to use the Properties pane to display all the properties for a selected object or group of objects. With more than one object selected, properties with common values are displayed and can be set as a group.

The final method is to right-click the object and then use the object-specific Properties dialog. This window typically displays specific properties and has an interface designed to manage the selected object. This technique cannot, however, be used to change properties for multiple objects at one time.

Data Sources

When you define a data source in Report Builder, you have the option to use shared data sources that have been deployed to the report server. The data source selection dialog is displayed when you design a report manually and in the New Table or Matrix wizard. When using the report or report item wizard or when creating a dataset, you can select a deployed data source, browse to a data source file in the local file system, or create a new data source using the corresponding buttons in this interface.

Keep in mind that when prompted for a data source file location, you may use a traditional file path or report server URL. If you are using SharePoint Integrated mode, you may also have the option to provide the URL for data sources located in a SharePoint data connection library.

Server Reports

Report Builder allows business users to create reports directly on the server without using the local file system. With permissions granted to the user, any report can be opened directly in Report

Builder using the standard Open dialog. To open a report on the server, local, or network file system, click the Report Builder button in the top-left corner and choose Open from the menu. You can navigate to a folder using the most recent items or other folder shortcuts on the Open Report dialog window.

MANUAL REPORT DESIGN

You've had the nickel tour. We created a matrix report and looked at the results. Now we'll slow down a bit and step through the process without the aid of the report wizard. Since we'll be covering all the steps to create more-advanced reports in later chapters, we'll actually leverage part of this report to show you how to design the matrix data region manually.

Because you have already saved a copy of the report to your report server, you can use that as a starting point for a new report. If you still have that report open in Report Builder, we'll get started in a moment. If you've already closed Report Builder, you can navigate to the saved report in the document library or Report Manager folder (depending on whether you are using Reporting Services integrated with SharePoint). Hover the mouse pointer over the report name until the drop-down list appears. Click the drop-down arrow to display the context menu, and select Edit in Report Builder. This opens the report in the Report Builder design window. Now we're ready to begin.

One of the things I've learned about document management in Windows is that when I open a document intending to save a copy, it's a good idea to save the copy right away. This way, I don't make changes and then accidently save them on top of the original document. Let's take care of that task right now to avoid an "Oh, crud" moment later:

1. Click the Report Builder button and select Save As. Give the new report a name similar to the first one, such as **Sales by Territory Matrix (manual)**. Now you can make all the mistakes you want, and it won't affect the original report.

2. Select the matrix data region. This can be tricky until you do it a few times. Click anywhere within the matrix region. Doing so selects one of the cells (actually, the textbox in the cell).

3. Near the top-left corner of the matrix, a selection handle appears. It's a small icon with a four-pointed arrow. Right-click that and select Delete Tablix.

Now you add a new matrix and build it from scratch. Report items and data regions are added to a report in Report Builder from the ribbon groups on the Insert tab.

Building a Matrix

To add a matrix to the report, follow these steps:

1. Select the Insert tab and locate the Matrix icon.

2. Drop down the list and select Insert Matrix, as shown in Figure 4-18. (Note: do not select the Matrix Wizard menu option.)

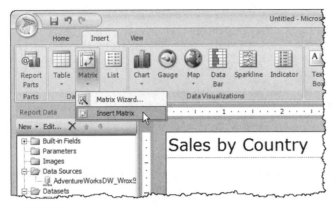

FIGURE 4-18

3. Use the modified mouse pointer to point to the top-left position on the report, below the title text, and click to place the new matrix. There should be plenty of white space below and to the right of the pointer before you let go, as shown in Figure 4-19.

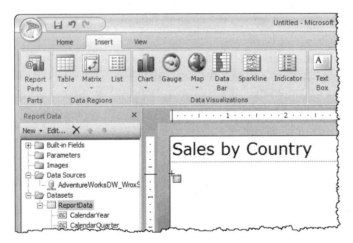

FIGURE 4-19

When you add a List, Table, or Matrix to a report, in actuality you are adding a data region object called a Tablix that has certain properties preset to match your selection. Earlier product versions had separate data region controls, each with unique features and idiosyncrasies. Our good friends on the Reporting Services product team decided that the List, Table, and Matrix all had enough in common that they should be combined into one supercontrol they called the Tablix. When they first told me of their plans, I thought it was a joke, but I'm quite happy with the result. The Tablix provides a great deal of flexibility for custom reports. Sometimes it gets me in trouble when I get lost in its recesses and caverns of properties and element tags. But never fear, it's quite easy to use the main out-of-the-box features.

The matrix begins to take shape as you add fields to it. Note the axis field drop zones below the report designer. One is labeled Row groups, and the other is labeled Column groups.

On the left side of the design window, locate the Report Data pane, which lists the Parameters, Data Sources, and Datasets.

1. Expand the fields list for the dataset.

2. Drag and drop the `SalesTerritoryCountry` field to the column header in the matrix, as shown in Figure 4-20.

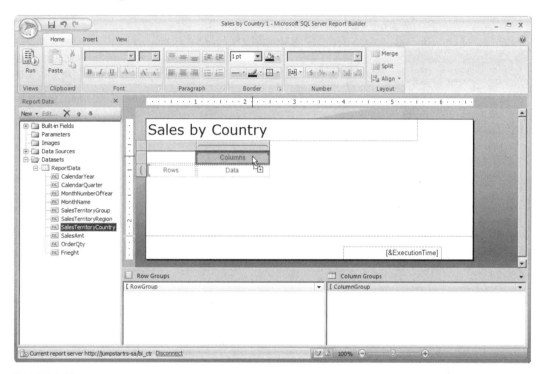

FIGURE 4-20

3. Drag and drop the `CalendarYear` field to the row header cell on the left side of the matrix.

4. Drag the `MonthName` field, but don't drop it until you're sure the pointer is in the right position. Place the mouse cursor over the new `CalendarYear` cell, and move to the right, over the cell. A vertical bar is displayed between the row header and detail cells. Drop the field at this location to insert a new header cell for the `MonthName` to the right of the `CalendarYear`.

In the first exercise, I told you we would fix the month-sorting issue. The records returned from the dataset aren't ordered by month, so they need to be sorted in the matrix definition. The dataset contains a field for this purpose. When a field is added to the row or column group list, the report designer assumes that the group should also sort values using the same field. This is usually the case, but there are common exceptions. With the matrix selected, the group pane appears at the bottom of the report designer window.

1. The second row group is defined for the `MonthName`. Click the down arrow on the right of the row group to display the menu shown in Figure 4-21, and then select Group Properties.

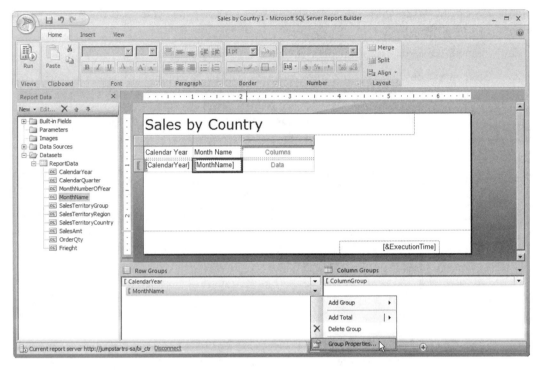

FIGURE 4-21

2. The Group Properties dialog opens (see Figure 4-22). Drop down the Sort by list and select the MonthNumberOfYear field.

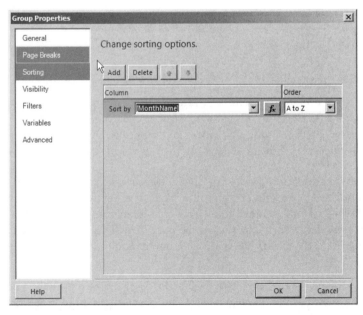

FIGURE 4-22

3. Click OK to close this dialog and save this change.

Numeric fields are commonly called "measures," and we're including two measure fields. They're the values that get repeated for every combination of group header labels. Measures also get added up and totaled in most cases. That's the definition and purpose of a measure field — it measures stuff. The group header and sort fields group and sort detail values.

4. Drag the SalesAmt field to the detail cell on the right side of the double broken line (that's the third column), as shown in Figure 4-23. The details row is the second row.

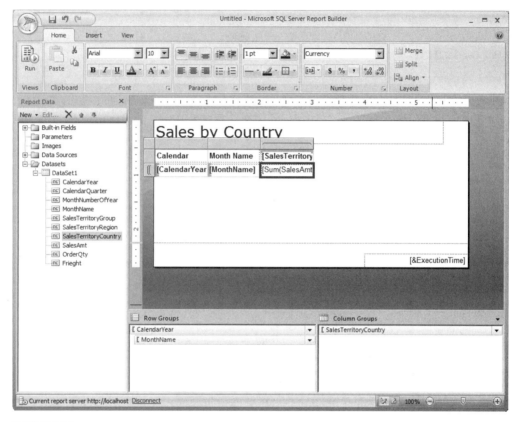

FIGURE 4-23

5. Select the row and column header cells (all the cells except the new SalesAmt) by holding down the Ctrl key while clicking each cell.

6. Use the font controls on the Home ribbon to set the text for all these header cells to use a bold font.

In the Wizard-created report, you added the OrderQty field to the matrix as well. We've already covered these basics, so to keep things simple, I'll forgo this addition. I encourage you to play with this design by adding fields and changing the fonts, colors, and formatting. That's how I learn. But before you make changes, I suggest that you save a copy of the report so that you can return to a working version if you get into trouble.

Let's take a look at the report at this point. Click the Run button on the Home ribbon to preview the report. The results are shown in Figure 4-24.

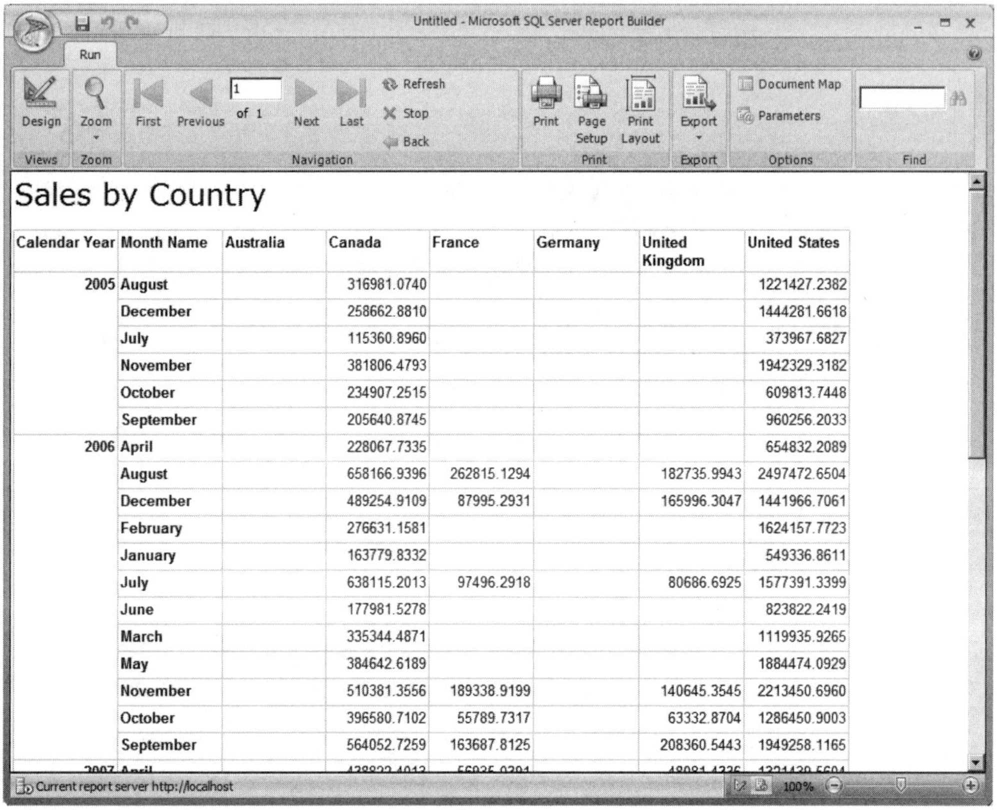

FIGURE 4-24

Note that the `SalesAmt` field values in all the detail cells are unformatted. By default these currency values are displayed with four decimal positions and with no thousands separator.

Wrapping It Up

The remainder of the design experience should be much like the preceding exercise. The first time around, the Matrix Wizard took care of many additional details we haven't added to this report, such as the group headers, footers, and totals, and styling. By contrast, when you design the report manually, you get to do all that work yourself.

As you discovered in the preceding exercise, when you add numeric fields to a data region, these values aren't automatically formatted. You can run the report and see that these fields return the correct values, but it won't be very pretty. Because we performed the formatting earlier, let's go straight to formatting these cells. There are at least three different ways to format a field value in the report designer. In the preceding exercise, you used the ribbon bar controls. We'll cover formatting in greater depth in Chapter 5. In the following chapters you'll learn that all the user interface controls in the visual report design tools set property strings in the report definition document. This is one of the reasons that there are often different ways to set properties and obtain the same result in the design. The following technique doesn't use a sophisticated dialog window or user interface; it just lets you set the format string. We'll keep this simple for now. You'll learn more about working with properties and format strings in Chapter 5. The following short example gives you a taste of one technique:

1. Above the ribbon bar, select the View tab.

2. Check the box labeled Properties.

   The Properties window appears on the right side of the report designer, as shown in Figure 4-25. This window is a common feature in Microsoft development and design tools. It shows you all the properties for a selected object and allows you to change them. Some objects have just a few properties, and others may have dozens or even hundreds. You can use the Properties window toolbar to group and sort the properties list to make it easier to find what you're looking for.

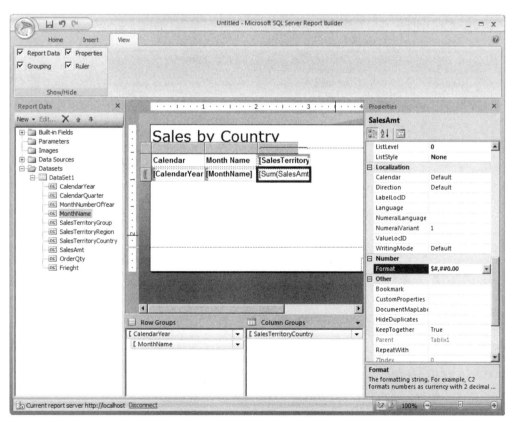

FIGURE 4-25

3. Click the `SalesAmt` cell to set focus to the textbox in this cell.

4. In the Properties window, locate the Format property.

5. Place the cursor in the box to the right of the word Format, and enter **$#,##0.00**.

That's about as far as I'd like to go with this simple exercise. You can do much more with this report by adding group totals and styling features. Those features are covered in later chapters.

Running and Saving the Report

To appreciate your work, click the Run button and take a look at the finished product (see Figure 4-26). Now the cells are formatted correctly (for U.S. dollars, at least).

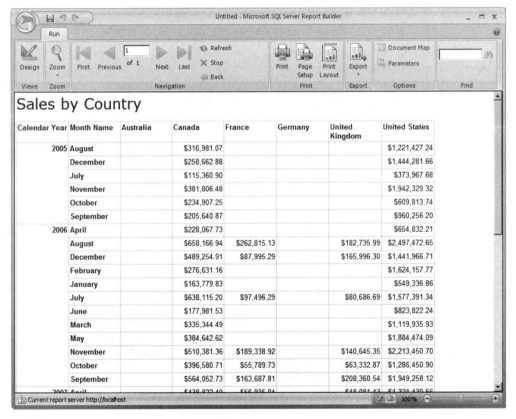

FIGURE 4-26

SUMMARY

When constructing a house, you must first lay a foundation and then start with the basic building blocks. In this chapter, you saw some examples and learned to use the essential components of common reports. You learned to create a foundation with a data source and dataset to obtain data from a database.

Using the common data range items and report items — the textbox, table, matrix, and chart — you can visualize a range of data by aggregating a grouping on meaningful field values. You learned to add totals and sorting to a table. You also learned to do some basic formatting to the table and matrix layout.

Reporting Services is highly extensible, and reports can be integrated into different types of applications. This chapter is a starting point for report design. In the following chapters, you will apply these and other techniques to create more advanced and compelling report solutions to solve business problems and to enable users and business leaders to be more effective and to make informed decisions.

5

Report Layout and Formatting

WHAT'S IN THIS CHAPTER?

➤ Basic report layout types, including the table, matrix, list, and chart reports

➤ Page layout options for table, matrix, list, chart, dashboard, and composite reports

➤ Report navigation features

➤ Formatting properties for visually enhancing various reports

➤ Pagination control

➤ Characteristics of different rendering formats

This chapter is about report design options and the elements you will use to assemble more complex reports. It's not a tutorial or exercise to show you specifically *how* to design specific reports with these features. It's an introduction to *what* you can do and *where* to find the details when you're ready to add these features. You'll read about the design components and techniques used in many common professional business reports. Building on the basic report and dataset design skills you acquired in Chapter 4, you'll learn how to add features to enhance the presentation and functionality of your reports.

I learned long ago that Reporting Services is designed to allow you to resolve certain problems using a specific approach or method. You'll see common examples of the features and capabilities inherent in Reporting Services reports. With an understanding of what the product was architected and optimized to do (as opposed to what it isn't designed to do so well), you can save yourself a lot of energy. You have numerous options for presenting information in a report. One of the most important factors in report design is understanding these options and providing an appropriate report layout to meet the needs of your users and their business requirements.

Some industries have been presenting data the same way for a long time. I think this is the case for a variety of reasons. The primary reason is that many of us started out using restrictive tools that provided only limited options. Another reason is that the business community has become accustomed to doing things the same way for a long time, even if there might be a better way. I've become a firm believer in getting the requirements at the beginning of a project. This way, we know up front what kind of reports we are designing, and what a report should and shouldn't do.

For some of your users, the reports you create will be their lifeline to important business information. The manner in which you present data may affect business decisions and how people do their jobs. When I start a report project or a new set of reports, I try to carefully consider these factors. I take the time to show users and business leaders a selection of report layout options. Then we discuss the pros and cons of each option to decide which are most appropriate and valuable to the people who will be using them. Your challenge as a report designer is to find the best way to present information to business users so that it's logical, makes sense, and is appealing and readable. The right format for your business users may be different for someone in a different industry, culture, or discipline.

I learned an important lesson a few years ago when I was asked to design a set of reports for a large commercial airplane manufacturer. The users were all structural and aerospace engineers, and they had been using the same static, monospaced, spreadsheet-like reports for ages. I decided to add some flair to the new reports by using charts and graphics. I made them colorful and attractive. I made a point to use different font sizes and weights. I added background shading and borders. Proud of the updated design, I created a standard report template with the company colors and logo in the report header, as I had for clients in the past. When the users saw the first report, they immediately shot it down and complained about the "fluff" and "pretty pictures." In their rigid engineering world, data was a serious matter and shouldn't be dressed up. At the request of our project sponsor, I took out the graphics and embellishments and changed all the text to one size of Courier New. They were elated with the design.

 There are several places in this chapter that mention the functionality of SQL Server 2000 or SQL Server 2005. If you are upgrading from SQL Server 2005 to SQL Server 2012, these differences will be of particular interest to you.

REPORT LAYOUT TYPES

Report layout can be boiled down to a few simple design patterns. These simple styles also can be combined with others to form composite reports and more advanced layouts to visualize data. This section offers a quick review of the report layout types, followed by some examples.

Table Reports

This style of report has actually been around for thousands of years. They may not have been reports in the modern sense, but when you think about it, some common reports are really little more than "lists of stuff" organized into rows and columns. Ever since early merchants began trading seashells or precious gems for beaver pelts or goat cheese, someone was recording the transaction in some kind of list, be it on papyrus, stone tablets, or a tablet computer.

Ever since VisiCalc, the predecessor to Lotus 123 and then Microsoft Excel (which was released in 1981), the tabular spreadsheet format has become the way many computer users are accustomed to viewing business data. For decades, the only printed reports available from mainframe and midrange computer systems were greenbar reports printed on pin-fed, fan-folded "greenbar" paper in classic spreadsheet style. Whether it's a spreadsheet, grid, ledger, or table, the notion of laying out information in rows and columns will be around for a long time.

A table is not just a flat list of records. In addition to the repeating detail rows, data can be grouped on various fields, and each group can have headers, footers, breaks, and subtotals. Table reports have a finite number of columns, typically representing the fields in a database table.

Matrix Reports

Table reports can be fine for logging detailed transactions and lists, but business reporting is often about summarizing information for analysis and providing context to all the numbers and listed items. This is often best done by rolling up the details along groups and hierarchies, then viewing the aggregate totals, rather than the details. A matrix, cross-tab, or pivot report aggregates data along a grid's x-axis and y-axis to form a summarized table, as shown in Figure 5-1. The most unique characteristic of a matrix is that columns are not static but are based on grouped values. Both rows and column groups may be multilevel hierarchies, and there may be an infinite number of grouped members on rows and columns.

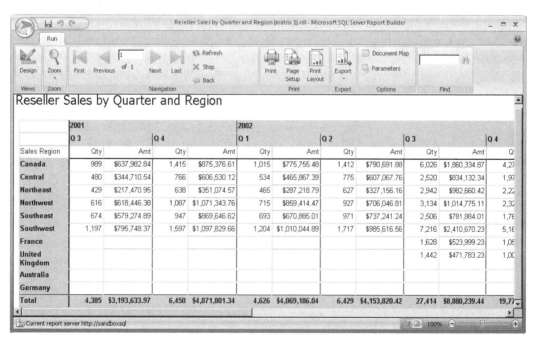

FIGURE 5-1

A matrix is most useful for viewing aggregated values along two different dimensional hierarchies, such as time and geography. For example, a product sales summary report might show aggregated sales with years and months on the columns axis, and the customers' countries and regions along the rows axis. At the intersection of each member along each axis, a cell displays the summarized product sales for that time and geography. For example, a single cell might represent the total sales for April 2008 in Berlin, Germany.

Ever since the table and matrix overhaul made with the 2008 product, designing table and matrix reports has been very similar. Because both of these report styles use the tablix report item under the covers, the option to design a table, matrix, or list report simply applies a set of templated properties to a tablix object. Regardless of what the designer does behind the scenes, you still select one of these specific report items to place in the report body. The only significant difference between a table and a matrix is that the columns of a matrix are dynamically generated from grouped values.

List Reports

A list report consists of a single rectangular detail area that repeats for every record or group value in the underlying dataset. This is useful to create reports with free-form layout, like an invoice, where a single record contains a lot of detail. If you think about it, a list is a simplified table of sorts, with no headers and only one column and one detail row. The main purpose of the list data region is to contain other related data regions and report items and to repeat them for a group of values. A chart, table, matrix, and any combination of textboxes or images can be repeated as a group for every record or distinct group value returned by a query.

Unlike a table or matrix, a list is always used as a container for other report items and cannot be used to visualize data on its own. In the designer, the list requires a little more manual effort. Dragging and dropping a field from the Report Data pane does not bind the list to the dataset as it does when you do the same thing in a table or matrix. You must view list's properties and set the DatsetName property, and then you can drag fields or set data binding properties for data regions contained within the list.

In Reporting Services for SQL Server 2000 and 2005, the table, matrix, and list data regions were separate and distinct components. Since its re-architecting in SSRS 2008, these three items are now variations of a data region object called the tablix. When you add any of these data regions to a report, the designer creates a tablix data region with certain properties preset. Now, all three items support common settings and behaviors. By adding or removing groups and manipulating certain properties, you can actually convert a list into a table, a table into a matrix, and so forth. To the novice user, this may seem to be useless, if not confusing, nonsensible information. But to the Rembrandts and Warhols of the report design community, it opens doors of opportunity for unique design patterns and yet-undiscovered capabilities. Stay tuned, and you'll see what I'm alluding to.

Chart Reports

Many business users now expect to see data visualized in summary form so that they can quickly and easily understand it. A chart can convey trends and comparisons in a concise form, helping users make sense of data that could otherwise be complicated and difficult to understand when presented in just a numeric table or matrix format. Chart reports are no longer an exception but are very much the rule for expressing aggregated data values for comparison and trending. Column and line charts have become a natural medium to visualize a series of data in a meaningful and intuitive way. We've grown accustomed to seeing charts on the stocks page of the newspaper and on the homepage of our news portal site, showing gas prices and housing market data. And, of course, we expect to see charts in the executive board room, used to explain the latest widget sales trends. They are typically useful in cases where you have large volumes of data that have been gathered over a span of time, or when you have a range of values to be aggregated across multiple categories or groups of distinct values.

For a given report, should you choose to use a chart or a textual data region (such as a table or matrix)? Sometimes the best answer is both — the chart to show summary data and the tablix for details.

The nice thing about charts is that they provide visual context for many different kinds of data. When used appropriately, the right chart types can tell a complex and important story with little explanation. Your challenge is to choose the right types of charts to visualize data in the most meaningful way for your users. In addition to the typical set of column, bar, line, point, and pie charts, you have a huge array of specialized chart types at your disposal.

Gauge Reports and Dashboards

The term *dashboard* describes a lot of different tools and report styles, but the essential concept is quite clear. Think of the dashboard in your car. Its purpose is not to provide a deep and detailed analysis of your car's performance. If it did, more accidents would occur because of distracted drivers. A dashboard's purpose is to provide a glance at important metrics. All you really need to know is if your speed is in an acceptable range, if the engine is revving too little or too much, if the oil and coolant levels are sufficient, and if you have enough gas to get to the office for that meeting in 10 minutes.

Dashboard reports are the same — they give you important information at a glance. Everyone knows how to read a simple gauge, so as mechanical equipment has been replaced with computers why not use the same gauge visualizations as those we're accustomed to using in a control room or on the machines on the production floor? Actually, several tangible gauge-type metaphors are appropriate in business. The great thing about using these components in certain business situations is that when a business user sees a thermometer, VU meter, dial, or partially full cylinder, he immediately understands its meaning. Figure 5-2 shows a dashboard-style report with gauges, indicators, and sparklines.

Maps and Spatial Reports

The map report item has the capability to visualize data in several different ways. Maps may consist of multiple layers with different map information. Geographic shapes and boundary information may be imported from shape files or stored as SQL Server spatial data. Geographic points and lines may be plotted over other maps layers. The map report item also integrates with Bing Maps to visualize point and boundary information over political, traffic, and satellite map imagery.

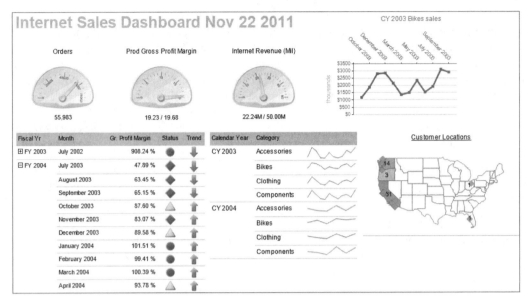

FIGURE 5-2

Defining Table Groups

Groups are used throughout Reporting Services and are useful in many ways. A significant change was made with the 2008 version of Reporting Services in how groups are created and managed. When any part of the table is selected in the designer, the grouping pane at the bottom of the design window displays field wells for the Row Groups and Column Groups. Fields can be dragged to a position in the field well list. To modify or manage a group, or to add group totals, hover the mouse pointer over a group name and use the drop-down list to access the group menu.

The purpose of this chapter is to give you a high-level view of the capabilities and common report design patterns. I don't want to get bogged down in details. This is not a hands-on exercise. I'll ask you to follow along in later chapters. For now, just kick back and observe as I show you some simple design steps.

Group Expressions and Options

This is where a lot of the magic happens in most reports. Defining field group expressions is a fundamental skill, necessary for using the advanced capabilities of several next-generation report items and regions such as composite charts, sparklines, data bars, KPI indicator sets, and geospatial map reports. If you have mastered the nuances of grouping, you're well on your way to the big time — the upper echelon of report designers who are called in when no one else can figure things out. The application of groups is a little different in each report item, but the concept is universal.

By dragging and dropping fields into the Row Groups list, as shown in Figure 5-3, you automatically add group definitions to a table (or any other implementation of a tablix). If you drag a field to the Column Groups list, a column group is defined for a matrix. The Group Properties dialog, shown in Figure 5-4, is used in every data region to define group expressions.

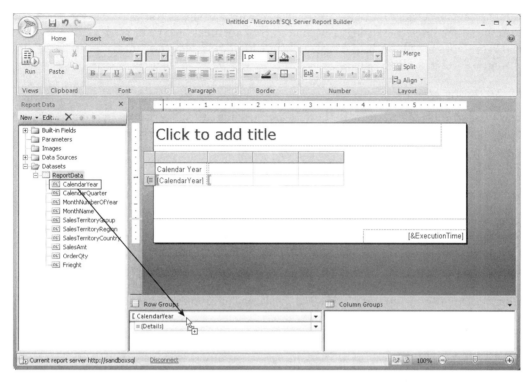

FIGURE 5-3

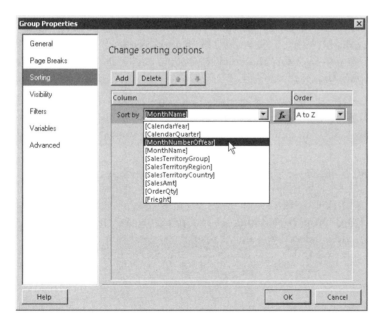

FIGURE 5-4

Several useful and advanced features are associated with a group, as you can see in the pages available in the Group Properties dialog. You can control page breaks before or after a group, use conditional expressions to hide or show items and data within the group, filter the data within the group, and control sorting of group values.

Sorting Group Values

It is always advisable to make sure that values are sorted in the right order when grouping them. If the data in the dataset query explicitly returns values in the correct order, sorting the group isn't necessary. The logic used to sort a list in the same order as the dataset introduces some (but often minimal) overhead for smaller result sets. If in doubt, sort. If you want to streamline the execution as much as possible, sort data in the query and don't do it here.

Sometimes it's necessary to sort on a different field than the values displayed in the report. This is especially useful when display values aren't in alphabetic or numeric order. For example, data grouped on the Calendar Month should be sorted on the month number of the calendar year, not the month name. Otherwise, the months would be listed as "April," "August," "December," "February," and so on. The Date dimension table in our sample data warehouse database, AdventureWorksDW_WroxSSRS2012, contains a `MonthNumberOfYear` column to be used for this reason. Setting the group to sort on this field displays months in the proper order even if the month name is displayed in the group header.

Formatting Table Values

Values in a table are formatted using the properties of constituent report items. Because each cell contains a textbox, property settings are applied to each textbox rather than to the container, including the background color, foreground color, font style, and size, weight, and number formatting.

To format a cell or textbox, select the textbox by clicking it, or click the border so that you see the selection handles. Clicking within a textbox more than once places the cursor there. To select the textbox, click off and then back onto the textbox.

In Report Builder, the styling properties of a selected textbox, and many other properties can be set using buttons and icons on the ribbon. Many of the same properties can be set using toolbar buttons in the SQL Server Data Tools (SSDT) design environment. Figure 5-5 shows the background fill selector.

Text formatting can be set in different ways. Using the ribbon or toolbar buttons, as we did in Chapter 4, is convenient and useful for setting most formatting options. To access even more properties and capabilities, right-click a textbox and choose Text Box Properties, as shown in Figure 5-6, to reveal the Text Box Properties dialog, shown in Figure 5-7. It shows a list of property categories on the left side. Selecting Number displays several numeric formatting options. In this example, I selected Currency and checked the box to include a thousands separator.

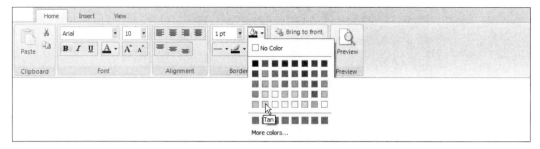

FIGURE 5-5

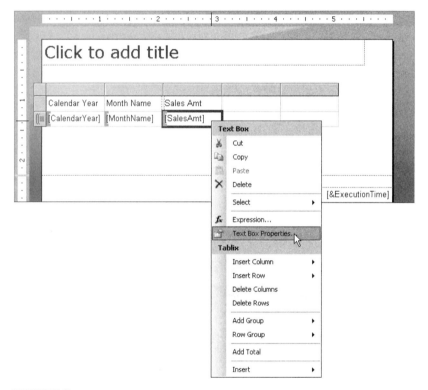

FIGURE 5-6

When the table is added to the report body, it contains three blank columns. Adding row groups creates new columns, and dragging a field directly to the table occupies one of the empty columns. Unused table columns should be deleted. To remove more than one column at a time, drag the mouse pointer across all the blank column headers, right-click, and choose Delete Columns, as shown in Figure 5-8.

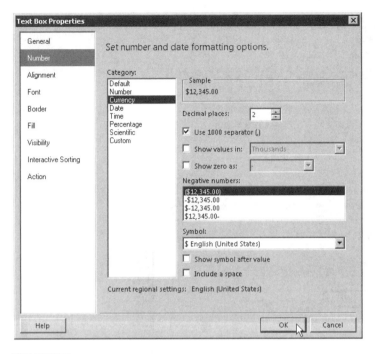

FIGURE 5-7

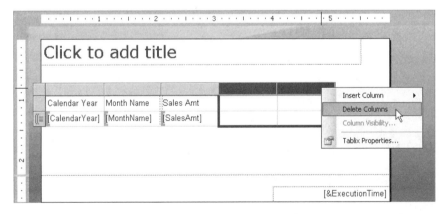

FIGURE 5-8

If we stopped here, this would be a nice little table report that would show all the details grouped by the year and then the month. Typically, you will use a table's details row to present the dataset's individual rows. However, grouping the table's detail rows reduces the report's length by summarizing detail rows into aggregate groups. If I group the detail rows on a field, such as

`SalesTerritoryRegion`, the Sales Amount for all detail rows is summed for each unique field value. To add a detail row group, click the down arrow next to the Details group in the Row Groups pane, and choose Group Properties.

In the Group Properties dialog, you can use the Add button to add a group expression and select the field for the group, as shown in Figure 5-9. Repeat the same step on the Sorting page to sort and group on the same field.

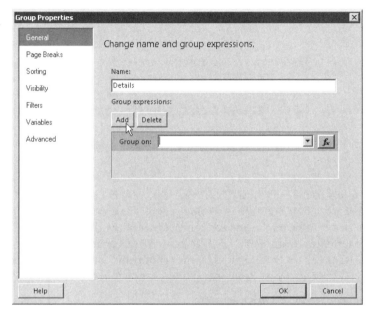

FIGURE 5-9

When you define a group in this manner, the field isn't automatically added to the table, so you have to add it yourself. You can add a column by dropping the `SalesTerritoryRegion` field into the table between the `MonthName` and `SalesAmt` columns.

An important principle to keep in mind is that a dataset should usually return data at the same level of detail as you will present in the report. However, you may not always have control over the specific data returned from certain data sources. In the example, rows are returned from a view called by the dataset, and they are rolled up by the `SalesTerritoryRegion` field.

Two different design methods may be used to add totals to the end of a group break. If you right-click a numeric cell and choose Add Total, a subtotal is added for the group above the details. You can also add a group at any level you like by clicking the down arrow for the group in the Row Group pane and choosing Add Total. The summary group may be added above or below the group.

To view the report in Report Builder, click the Preview button on the Home ribbon. To view the report in SSDT, click the Preview tab. The report preview is shown in Figure 5-10.

Calendar Year	Month Name	Sales Territory Region	Sales Amt
2001	August	Canada	$316,981.07
		Central	$252,715.02
		Northeast	$71,552.89
		Northwest	$296,069.69
		Southeast	$301,907.49
		Southwest	$299,182.15
			$1,538,408.31
	December	Canada	$258,662.88
		Central	$197,792.58
		Northeast	$159,194.19
		Northwest	$348,122.13
		Southeast	$252,006.38
		Southwest	$487,166.39
			$1,702,944.54

FIGURE 5-10

Interactive Sort

The interactive sort feature was added to the table in the 2005 product version and now works much the same way in the new and improved tablix. Interactive sorting is applied after the groups are processed, so the entire report doesn't need to be rerendered each time a user clicks the column header to reorder column values. This is actually a feature of a textbox located in a header. To add interactive sorting for the `SalesRegionTerritory` field, right-click the cell for this column header and choose Textbox Properties. The resulting Text Box Properties dialog is shown in Figure 5-11.

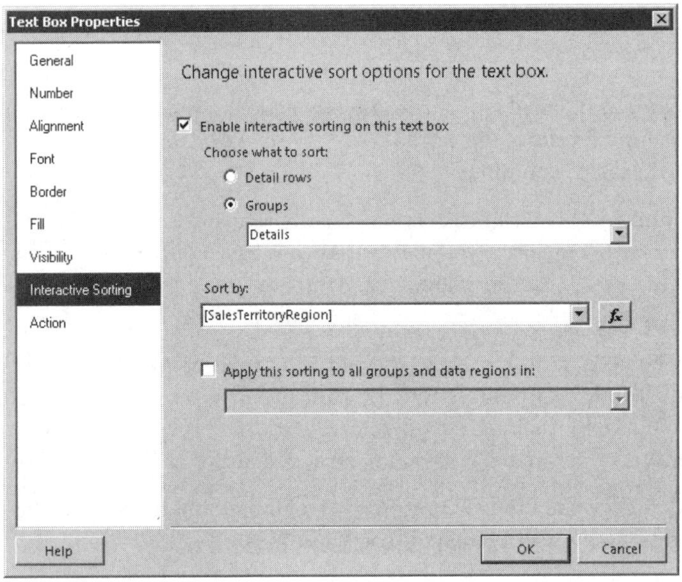

FIGURE 5-11

On the Interactive Sorting page of this dialog, I chose the group name and Sort by field. Because the details are grouped, I chose the Details group, which, as you recall, is grouped on the `SalesTerritoryRegion` field. Rows within this group are sorted within their parent group. In other words, when a user clicks the column header textbox, the `SalesTerritoryRegion` rows are resorted in either ascending or descending order, and the `CalendarYear`, `MonthName`, and heading values remain the same. Figure 5-12 shows a preview of the report. Before the column is resorted, a pair of up and down arrows is displayed. Hovering the mouse pointer over these arrows changes the mouse pointer to indicate that each is a hyperlink.

Calendar Year	Month Name	Sales Territory Region	Sales Amt
2001	August	Southwest	$299,182.15
		Southeast	$301,907.49
		Northwest	$296,069.69
		Northeast	$71,552.89
		Central	$252,715.02
		Canada	$316,981.07
			$1,538,408.31
	December	Southwest	$487,166.39
		Southeast	$252,006.38
		Northwest	$348,122.13
		Northeast	$159,194.19
		Central	$197,792.58
		Canada	$258,662.88
			$1,702,944.54

FIGURE 5-12

Adding Page Breaks

By default, page breaks are added when repeated data fills the available space for a page. You can add page breaks explicitly before or after a tablix region. You can also add page breaks before or after a group value changes. To force a break for the entire table, display the Tablix Properties dialog. There are a few different ways to open this dialog. My preference is to click anywhere within a table, list, or matrix and then right-click the top-left gray selection handle and choose Tablix Properties, as shown in Figure 5-13.

FIGURE 5-13

Use the "Page break options" section on the General page, as shown in Figure 5-14.

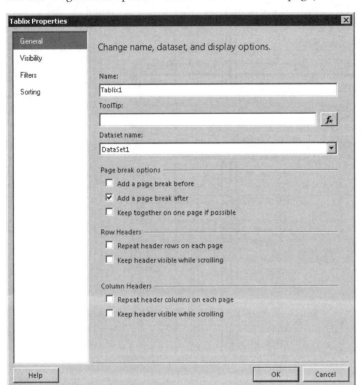

FIGURE 5-14

You can also control page breaks at the group level. It is a common reporting requirement to break before or after a group header or subtotals displayed in a footer row. Show the Tablix Group Properties dialog, and then use the Page Breaks page to set the page break options for the group. It's often a good idea to repeat header information at the top of each printed page. You do this using the Repeat header rows on each page option in the Tablix Properties dialog.

Creating Drill-Down Reports and Dynamic Visibility

You can create a dynamic reporting experience by hiding and showing report elements. Various techniques may be used to show and hide fields, groups, rows, columns, and entire data regions using conditional expressions and toggle items. All report items and group definitions have a Visibility property that can be set either permanently or conditionally.

A common use of the Visibility property is to create drill-down reports, where table or matrix group headers are used to toggle, or expand and collapse, details. Typically, a plus (+) or minus (–) icon is displayed next to the toggle item row or column header. Figure 5-15 shows a drill-down report with toggle items set for a table's group header rows.

Creating a drill-down report is a simple matter of hiding a group and setting its ToggleItem property to refer to a report item, usually a textbox, in a higher-level group. In our sample report, records are grouped by Calendar Year and then Sales Territory Region. The properties for the latter group are set using the group pane in the lower part of the Design window, as shown in Figure 5-16.

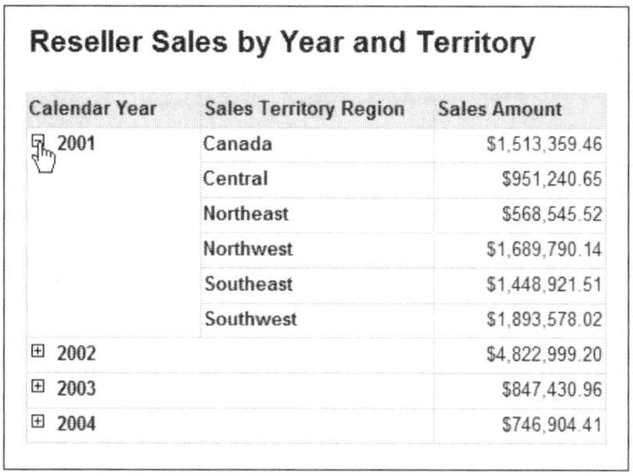

FIGURE 5-15

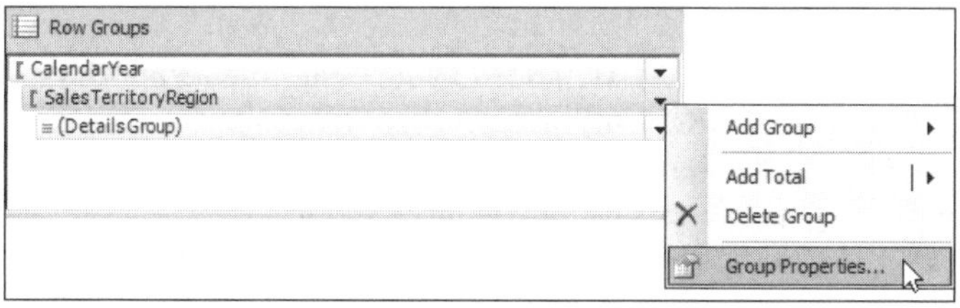

FIGURE 5-16

In the Visibility page of the Group Properties dialog, set the display options to hide the group contents, check the box labeled "Display can be toggled by this report item," and then select the textbox bound to the `CalendarYear` field, as shown in Figure 5-17. Note that this textbox may not always have the same name as the field to which it is bound. Click OK to save these property changes.

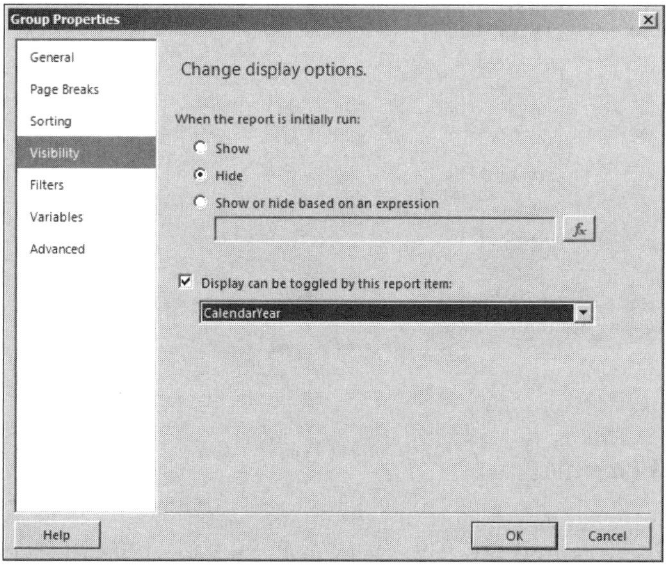

FIGURE 5-17

Dynamic visibility can also be used to hide and show areas of a report based on parameters or field threshold values. With a little creativity and some basic programming skills, you can do some interesting things.

Formatting Report Data

Nearly as important as the data displayed on the report are the layout and visual elements that make the data readable. For reports to be functional, data must be presented in a format that makes sense to the user and that conforms to a standard that is both readable and visually appealing. Reports may be static in design, or certain elements can be set to dynamically adapt to user requests. Report elements can be designed to change or to appear only under specific conditions.

All formatting features are based on property settings. Static formatting involves the use of several properties, such as background color to apply shading, the font, font size, font weight, style, foreground color, and borders.

In Report Builder, formatting properties are applied to selected items using the Format ribbon. In SSDT, you can apply formatting using the Report Format toolbar.

Background colors, font sizes, font weights, and borders are added using either the formatting options on the Report Builder Home ribbon or the Report Formatting toolbar in SSDT. The ribbon and toolbar buttons are used to set properties that can also be changed using the Properties window. Figure 5-18 shows the same report with these properties changed on the group footer rows for the `SalesTerritoryRegion` and `CalendarYear` groups. This makes the report easier to read and helps the user visually separate each group section with the corresponding details and totals.

Reseller Sales by Year and Territory

Calendar Year	Sales Territory Region	Sales Amount
⊞ 2001	Total	$8,065,435.31
⊟ 2002	Canada	$4,822,999.20
	Central	$2,625,639.72
	France	$857,123.18
	Northeast	$2,443,901.73
	Northwest	$3,471,099.54
	Southeast	$2,815,903.10
	Southwest	$6,266,005.43
	United Kingdom	$841,757.76
	Total	$24,144,429.65
⊞ 2003	Total	$32,202,669.43
⊞ 2004	Total	$16,038,062.60
Total		$80,450,596.98

FIGURE 5-18

Introduction to Dynamic Formatting

You've seen how a report can be formatted using simple features and properties. Totals can be added to groups; sections can be made to expand or collapse using drill-down toggle items; values can be formatted; and areas of the report can be dressed up using borders, shading, font sizes, font weights, and colors.

Expressions are the heart and soul of dynamic reports. You can design simple reports without special coding, but if you want to take your reports to the next level, you need to learn some simple programming. You will learn later how to use expressions to incorporate more advanced report design techniques. Here, I just want to give you a taste of the kinds of things you can do.

As the reports grow and evolve in a business, often different reports are just variations of other reports. You can define unique behaviors, such as dynamic sorting, filtering, or visual subsets of report data, by using a single report to include all the features. Then you can use expressions to modify the report's behavior and to enable or disable certain features.

Chapter 16 demonstrates a table report designed for use by different groups of users. A parameter is used to specify the fields and columns displayed in the report. Using this dynamic formatting technique, you can create one report to meet the reporting requirements of multiple users.

DESIGNING MULTICOLUMN REPORTS

Table reports can be designed to display continuous data in snaking columns. To be clear, this style of report is different from a conventional report with a single table containing several columns. The entire table content flows into two or more columns within the report, from the top down and then into the next column, in a snaking fashion.

To create a multicolumn report, add a table to the report body that occupies a fraction of the report width, allowing for column margin spacing. The `Columns` and `ColumnSpacing` properties are set for the `Report` object in the Properties window. For example, a report with two columns should contain a table that is less than one-half of the report width plus the `ColumnSpacing`. Use the following formula to calculate the width of a multicolumn report:

```
Report Width = (Body Width x # Columns) + (ColumnSpacing x # Margins between
columns) + Left Margin + Right Margin
```

To be honest, this is not my favorite feature, and it isn't a design I choose to use very often. Reporting Services does a lot of things well, but this isn't one of them. Multicolumn reports are not supported in some of the more common rendering formats, such as HTML. A multicolumn report works well only when rendered as an image or PDF file. In short, don't use this feature unless you really need to. And if you do, test the design thoroughly before investing a lot of effort.

DESIGNING GAUGE REPORTS

A dashboard report is composed of different report items that provide quick status information at a glance. A recent addition to Report Services, and a simple and compelling new visualization tool, is the gauge report item.

The scale and pointers both have minimum and maximum value properties that can be set to either fixed or variable values using expressions and field values. A gauge can have multiple pointers using a common scale or multiple scales.

Although there are two distinct types of gauges (radial and linear), several varieties are possible when you adjust various properties. The Select Gauge Type dialog is displayed when you add a gauge to a report. Making any of the selections shown in Figure 5-19 adds a new radial or linear gauge with properties based on one of these templates.

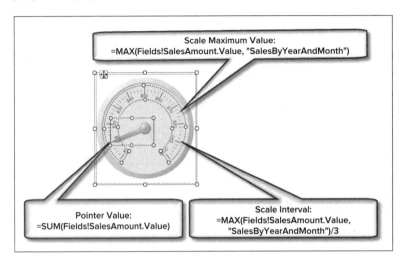

FIGURE 5-19

Although gauge design is simple in principle, gauge reports typically require the use of design techniques we'll cover in subsequent chapters. Each gauge consists of a scale and a pointer. The pointer is set to a field expression that shows the current value for a selected month and year. Gauges are versatile and can include scale ranges, markers, titles, and labels. Using the properties of these gauge features, you can reproduce most any type of linear or radial visual you've seen on a control panel or mechanical measuring device.

Figure 5-19 shows one of the gauges in the dashboard, with callouts to show the values of three significant properties (which are set using field expressions). You can see that the pointer represents the sum of the SalesAmount field value; the scale maximum value is the Max, or highest monthly value, for the year; and the scale interval is one-third of this range so that it doesn't become crowded with several very large numbers. You'll learn more about using expressions and working with parameterized and grouped dataset queries in the following chapters, all of which are used to feed data to a simple gauge item like this one.

Browser Compatibility

You should design a solution to meet the needs of the least capable user or application platform. The optimal design for the Web has always been a moving target. When you design reports, if you view them only in the latest version of Internet Explorer, you may be unaware of incompatibilities or design issues for other browsers. Creating solutions independent of the client platform for a diverse audience will always be challenging, with a certain degree of unpredictability.

Reporting Services renders to HTML 4.0 by default, which works in most of the standard web browsers. However, the interpretation of this standard is subtle. You can find guidance about supported web browsers for Reporting Services reports, development and management tools at `http://msdn.microsoft.com/en-us/library/ms156511%28v=SQL.110%29.aspx`.

Reports with interactive design elements such as drill down and autohide sections, for example, generate client-side JavaScript. This script runs in the user's browser to produce effects and interactive functionality. Theoretically, pages containing many JavaScript functions should run in newer versions of Internet Explorer and other browsers. In a report, scripted features include documentation maps, bookmarks, and show/hide features (used for drill-down reports). On the standard report toolbar, scripted features let you zoom, search, refresh, export, and request help.

Another variable to consider when using HTML is the font typeface and size. If you make it a point to use common fonts, this usually is not an issue. However, the user's configuration isn't always predictable. Font files on the user's computer can be uninstalled or deleted, and default font sizes can be changed in the browser. A popular solution for unpredictable HTML results is to use a proprietary document format typically read in a downloadable viewer. Rendering reports to an Adobe Portable Document Format (PDF) document ensures that reports are displayed and printed consistently.

Offline Viewing

Reporting Services can render reports in three different forms of HTML, including HTML 4.0 for desktop browsers, HTML 3.2 for mobile devices, and a MIME-encoded HTML called *MHTML* (or *web archive*). MHTML is a more recent standard that encapsulates content that normally would be linked to separate files, typically graphics, into a single document. Using this format simplifies web content rendering for portability, but it isn't supported in all browsers (including Pocket Internet Explorer). Even when using standard HTML format, most report files are self-contained with the exception of any graphics. If all the content is contained in one file, it will be easier to download and view offline. If your users consistently use Internet Explorer or a browser you have tested thoroughly, consider rendering reports in MHTML to preserve embedded graphics content. If you don't have that kind of control over the user's environment, PDF document rendering may be the best choice.

Rendering Format Limits and Considerations

A significant design goal of Reporting Services is its ability to render reports into a variety of formats. This offers a great deal of flexibility and opportunity for reports to meet specific business requirements and to be integrated into a variety of business solutions. It's important to understand that each rendering format has certain capabilities and restrictions. I hear from consulting clients on a regular basis who ask when a rendering limitation will be "fixed" or enhanced. Although the product team does their best to enhance each rendering extension within reason, we simply have to accept the architectural characteristics of the different viewers and applications used to view reports. My response (often echoed from similar questions posed to the product team) is that each renderer generally uses the capabilities of the related viewer. Here are some examples:

➤ PDF- and image-rendered reports don't support drill-down and drill-through features. This is simply not possible.

➤ Subreports often don't work well with Excel rendering. Although several enhancements were made to the Excel renderer because of its popularity, you can still expect these reports to behave differently than HTML at times. In HTML rendering, items can be placed at any axis point in the report body. The Excel renderer has to define rows and columns for the resulting worksheet and then output report items to an exact grid. This means that textboxes and other items that are slightly misaligned at design time may end up in the same column in the resulting report.

➤ HTML-rendered reports can have pages of differing lengths. HTML is not considered a pixel-perfect print format. Also, because of the different ways in which an HTML browser handles tables, borders, or margins, the report layout may not be ideal for page printing. If you want to print a report, render it to PDF or use the client-side printing capability in the Report Manager.

➤ Many improvements have been made to the Excel rendering extension over the years; the product team has done some impressive things with Excel rendering. Several interactive features are supported, such as drill down, links, and sorting. Due to Excel's two-dimensional form factor, all report items must be aligned and grouped into discrete rows and columns, and some cells are merged to make room for larger items. This means that some items may be moved around to fit the grid format. All expressions and calculations performed in the report are rendered to static values in the resulting workbook. Charts and other advanced visuals are rendered as images.

➤ The current version of Reporting Services supports the Microsoft Word 2007/2010 formats as well as Word 2003 when the Microsoft Office Compatibility Pack is installed. Word rendering is quite accurate compared with HTML and image formats. Word does not support some of the interactive features.

SUMMARY

Like constructing a house or building, when designing reports you must first lay a foundation and start with the basic building blocks. In this chapter, you saw some examples and learned to use the essential constructs of common reports. You learned to create a data source and dataset to obtain data from a database. You will learn more about consuming data from different data sources and how to filter and manipulate that data as it flows to your reports.

Using the common data region items and report items — namely, the textbox, table, matrix, and chart — you can visualize a range of data by aggregating a grouping on meaningful field values. You learned how to add totals, fixed sorting, and interactive sorting to a table. You also learned how to do some basic formatting to the table and matrix layout.

You learned about report rendering and formatting options and how reports can be read on mobile devices, third-party viewers, and different web browsers. Reporting Services is highly extensible, and reports can be integrated into different types of applications.

This chapter was a starting point for report design. In the following chapters, you will apply these and other techniques to create more advanced and compelling report solutions to solve business problems, and to enable users and business leaders to be more effective and to make informed decisions.

Designing Data Access

WHAT'S IN THIS CHAPTER?

- ➤ Installing a report server

- ➤ Building an enterprise deployment

- ➤ Using tools for managing reporting life cycle

- ➤ Exploring report server architecture

- ➤ Leveraging reporting services extensions

In Chapter 4, you used Report Builder to design basic reports. When it comes to accessing data for reports, there are generally two schools of thought. You can use capable tools to allow advanced report designers to design complex queries and enable creative report functionality. Or you can use uncomplicated tools to keep the design experience for business users simple and error-free. Needless to say, trade-offs exist on either side of this equation. This is one of the most significant reasons that there are two different report design applications.

Report Builder is a great tool for designing reports, but it doesn't help you very much with designing anything but simple queries. At the PASS (Professional Association for SQL Server) Global Summit a few years ago, I attended a session where one of the other SQL Server MVPs introduced Report Builder 2.0. He explained that it was a great report design tool but it fell short in the query design category. After conversations with the Reporting Services product team members who designed and created it and numerous consulting engagements with clients who had self-service reporting initiatives, my perspective changed. Report Builder is right-sized for business users, making it an ideal choice for those who will use database objects that have been prepared for them by their corporate IT staff. You'll read more about how to plan for and design self-service report design solutions for business users in Chapter 14. By contrast, the SQL Server Data Tools (SSDT) report designer leverages query design tools that get installed with the SQL Server client tools. These tools give more-advanced users a great deal of functionality and capabilities that are usually appropriate for application developers and IT professionals. As an IT professional and tenured report designer, I often prefer to use Report Builder in many cases. If I need to build complex queries, I step out of Report Builder and use the SQL Server Management Studio query design tools. For me, this is the best of both worlds.

Table 6-1 summarizes the options for designing queries for SQL Server data sources with the design tools available for SQL Server and Reporting Services.

TABLE 6-1

OPTION	SUMMARY	PROS	CONS
Report Builder Query Designer	Easy to use. The user selects from lists of tables and fields.	Good interface for novice users. Requires little or no SQL knowledge.	Limited functionality for advanced queries. Not preferred by most advanced SQL users.
SSDT graphical SQL query designer	Integrated query builder interface from SQL Server client tools.	Powerful designer. Familiar to users who have used SQL Server tools and Microsoft Access SQL Server projects.	Available only if SSDT and SQL Server client tools are installed.
SQL Server Management Studio query window	Free-forum text query editor with advanced debugging capabilities.	Includes keyword color coding and IntelliSense autocompletion. Preferred by advanced users.	Not integrated with report designer. Requires copy/paste to and from report designer.

To demonstrate the full report design experience, this chapter uses examples from the SSDT, but I'll also show some examples with Report Builder. The differences between the two report designers in most cases are minor enough that it really shouldn't make a difference; you should be able to use either.

A big part of the report design process is query design. In nearly all cases, your reports are based on a data source of some kind. Therefore, the first order of business when designing a report is to create a connection and define the queries to retrieve the report data. This chapter discusses the essential first step of report design — consuming data. Although this is usually simple and straightforward, you must consider several options when designing data sources and queries. Although SQL Server Reporting Services is packaged with the SQL Server database product, it may be used with other database products as data sources. This chapter discusses the following topics:

➤ Creating stand-alone and shared data sources

➤ Designing queries and datasets

➤ Grouping and filtering data in a T-SQL query

➤ Using parameters to filter data at the database

➤ Using parameters to filter data at the Report Server

➤ Obtaining data from other data sources

Almost every report has at least one data source. The simplest reports have a single data source to provide data for a single dataset. The data source defines a connection as a string of text stored either in the report definition file or in a separate shared data source file that can be shared among several reports. This connection information may include security credentials. The dataset defines a query expression or a reference to query objects stored in the database. The dataset is also contained within the report definition. Figure 6-1 shows how data flows to the report. The data source lets you connect to the database, and the dataset contains a query expression that populates the report with data.

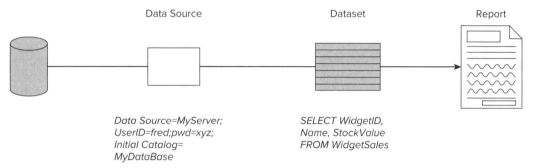

FIGURE 6-1

More-complex reports may require multiple datasets to provide data for different data ranges or items in the report or to feed values to parameter value selection lists. Datasets can be based on query expressions from the same data source, as shown in Figure 6-2.

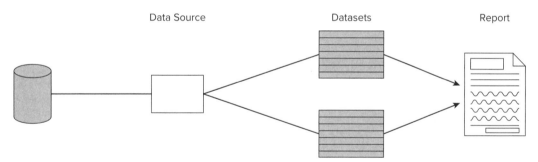

FIGURE 6-2

Multiple datasets can get their data from multiple data sources. This model would enable a report to have parameter selection values to be obtained from a local database and report data to be obtained from a central data store. In some cases, data regions, subreports, and various report items might obtain data from multiple sources through associated datasets, as shown in Figure 6-3.

As you can see, almost anything is possible in terms of combining data sources and datasets. Data sources can be practically any database product or any data source you can query by means of standard connection libraries or drivers. Reporting Services consumes data using the .NET data providers, which support common database platforms such as SQL Server, Analysis Services, Oracle, Sybase, Teradata, SAP, DB2, and all OLE DB providers. These include almost any database product that supports ODBC access or a capable ISAM driver. Datasets in Reporting Services are always read-only, so you usually don't need to specify cursor types or locking options. Reports can be designed to use data from operational line-of-business databases and databases designed specifically for reporting and data analysis.

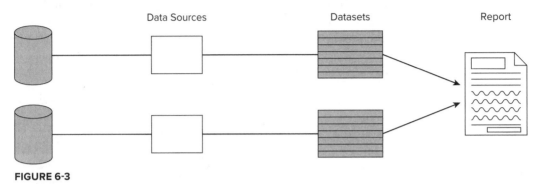

FIGURE 6-3

BUSINESS INTELLIGENCE REPORTING

When you design any kind of business solution, it's always a good idea to step back and look at the big picture. Maintaining a solution-level perspective usually helps ensure that your report design efforts will continue to solve changing business problems. With an intelligently designed reporting application, the introduction of future requirements is less likely to render the whole solution obsolete.

One of the most important considerations with a reporting solution is the structure of the data used for reporting. Nearly all business goes through a similar cycle of data evolution. At the beginning, the data structure is simple. Reports are often based on a few simple tables in a single relational database used to manage day-to-day operations and for simple reporting. As time goes on, multiple data sources are introduced, each housing specialized data to support various business processes. Because business decisions are made based on information from multiple sources, this data must be consolidated. As users and applications compete for access to databases, using transactional data sources may no longer be feasible. As a result, data marts and data warehouses may become necessary to simplify the data used in reports. A query used to bring together data from complex data structures can be complicated, slow, and difficult to manage.

Along with the volume and complexity of business data, reporting requirements also expand, making it more and more difficult to squeeze out meaningful reporting metrics from traditional data sources. Relational databases and T-SQL queries may be used to group, aggregate, and perform calculations, but these queries can be slow and complicated. The next step in the process may be to store data in a multidimensional data structure designed specifically for data analysis. Microsoft SQL Server Analysis Services contains an Online Analytical Processing (OLAP) storage engine that can significantly improve performance and support for self-service reports and reports with complex calculations. Analysis Services supports both multidimensional cubes and tabular semantic models.

An exhaustive discussion of business intelligence (BI) data sources is beyond the scope of this book, but these are important considerations. Chapter 11 will show you how to use traditional multidimensional, OLAP data sources in reports. Chapter 12 introduces the new generation of semantic model design and discusses designing reports to use these data structures as sources. Briefly, the general choices for report data sources are as follows:

➤ Operational, transactional database with data stored in normalized table structures using a relational database product such as SQL Server or Oracle

➤ Relational data mart or data warehouse using simplified fact/dimension star schemas

➤ Semantic multidimensional OLAP cubes or tabular models such as SQL Server Analysis Services

➤ A nontraditional data source such as an XML web service or Atom Data Feed

We work with a lot of companies, large and small, to build enterprise reporting solutions. Typically, the best way to build a business reporting solution is to make sure that reports don't use live application databases for their data sources. If you can simplify how data is stored and optimize a decision-support database used only for reporting, life will be much simpler. I realize that may be a big undertaking. Often the person charged with designing reports has been directed to use a specific data source, and it may be completely outside the scope of a person in that role to build a utopian BI solution. However, if you have the tools, the skills, and the time to "do it right," designing a full-fledged BI solution with a relational data mart and OLAP cubes can make the reporting part of the equation much easier and faster (both to design reports and for users to run).

Although there is much to consider, depending on the size and scope of the data and business reporting needs, Figure 6-4 shows the general layout of a fully evolved corporate reporting environment. Due to the relative complexity of the data stored in the operational databases, on the left side of the diagram, operational reports typically are static and simple in design, based on unstructured data. Data is organized as it moves through transformation packages and into a data warehouse and OLAP cubes, where the data is structured and simplified. This affords the opportunity to design more complex and useful reports that run quickly and produce reliable results. Reports on the right side of the figure require less effort to design and debug because of the efficiency of hierarchal data structures.

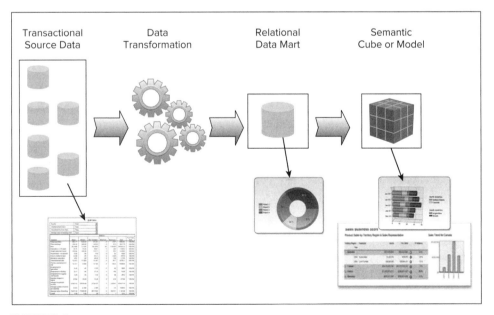

FIGURE 6-4

The examples in this chapter use a relational data warehouse. Chapter 10 demonstrates reports using data from a multidimensional cube.

REPORTING FOR RELATIONAL DATA

Now you'll take a closer look at how queries are created and how data is provided for a report. At this point, it's important to understand the basic building blocks of reports. The discussion begins with some of these fundamentals. You will go through several short walk-through exercises so that you can see and experience how it works.

A query or command statement that produces a set of report data is called a dataset. Within the report design tool, this is called both a "dataset" and a "data set." I would argue that the first is more correct than the latter, but it's probably not a point worthy of a street brawl or even a simple argument.

By the way, the term "dataset" in Reporting Services has nothing in common with a programming object in the ADO.NET namespace with the same name. Why does the term dataset mean two different things in different Microsoft technologies? As a "green" community, we believe in recycling. Since we ran out of new words in the English language a long time ago, so we're now recycling names.

Data and Query Basics

Reporting Services can obtain data from a variety of data sources. Nearly all relational database products are queried using a form of Structured Query Language (SQL), which means that a query created for one database product (say, IBM DB2) may be somewhat portable to a different data source (perhaps Oracle, MySQL, Sybase, or Microsoft SQL Server). Most database products implement a form of SQL conforming to the ANSI SQL standard. Microsoft SQL Server, for example, conforms to the ANSI 92 SQL standard, and other products may conform to other revisions (such as ANSI 89 SQL or ANSI 99 SQL). Beyond the most fundamental SQL statements, most dialects of SQL are not completely interchangeable and require some understanding of their individual idiosyncrasies.

Other specialized database products may use a different query language. Microsoft SQL Server Analysis Services is a data storage and analysis product that uses multidimensional cube structures to organize complex data for business intelligence and decision-support systems.

The main point here is that you can use whatever query language your database product understands. Reporting Services provides a Query Editor designed especially for T-SQL and a generic editor that accommodates other query languages or SQL dialects.

Data Sources

A data source contains the connection information for a dataset. Data sources can be created for a specific report dataset or can be shared among different reports. Because most reports get data from a common data source, it often makes sense to create a shared data source. Using shared data sources has a few advantages. Even if you don't have several reports that need to share a central data source, it takes no additional effort to create a shared data source. This may be advantageous in this case because the data source is managed separately from each report and can be easily updated if necessary. Then, as you add new reports, the shared data source will already be established and deployed to the Report Server.

There are three different ways to create a data source in a SSDT/Visual Studio report project:

➤ From the Add Item template, launched from the Project context menu

➤ In the Report Wizard

➤ When defining a dataset

Let's look at each of these options in detail.

Creating a Data Source from the Project Add Item Template

You can add a new shared data source to a project and then use that data source in any report in the project. To do this, in the Solution Explorer right-click Reports and choose Add ➪ Add New Item. The options in this dialog include Report Wizard, Report, and Data Source. Selecting the Data Source option creates a shared data source.

Using this technique brings up the Shared Data Source Properties dialog. Although the layout of this dialog is slightly different from the Wizard pages described in the following section, the functionality is the same.

Creating a Data Source in the Report Wizard

The following steps will help you get started with data sources and datasets. In this exercise, you will run the Report Wizard in a SSDT report project and then define the data source and dataset properties for a new report. The exercise will continue in the following sections to help you develop some basic T-SQL query language skills and then use parameters and filtering in a report design. If any of these topics are not new to you, you should be able to quickly skip ahead to later material that will be more educational for you. Keep in mind that there is more than one way to use the report designer to create most objects. Rather than using the Report Wizard, you can use the Report Data pane on the left side of the designer to add a data source or dataset using the same (or nearly the same) dialog boxes you will see in this section.

The Report Wizard is launched from a report project in SSDT. From the Solution Explorer, right-click the Reports folder and choose Add Report to launch the Report Wizard. On the first page in the Wizard you select an existing shared data source or create a new one, as shown in Figure 6-5. Name the data source AdventureWorksDW_WroxSSRS2012. You can name a data source anything you like, but I typically use the actual name of the database for which the data source provides connectivity. If you are accustomed to prefixing or post fixing standard object names, knock yourself out. Keep in mind that data source names cannot contain spaces or some special characters.

For this SQL Server database, leave the data source Type property as Microsoft SQL Server. Click the Edit button to build a connection string. This opens the Connection Properties dialog, shown in Figure 6-6.

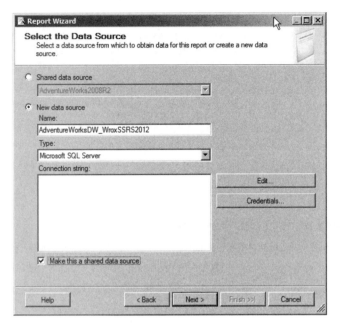

FIGURE 6-5

Note that this dialog might look a little different if you select a different option in the Type drop-down list. Although many of these options do correspond to standard data providers (and may include .NET native providers, OLE DB data providers, and ODBC drivers), these are actually data processing extensions that were installed with, or added to, the Reporting Services configuration. For example, selecting the SQL Server Analysis Services type results in a dialog window that is unique to Analysis Services connections.

Whether you use the Report Wizard or add a new data source directly from the Project Add Items dialog or the Data Sources folder in the Solution Explorer, the interface is the same. The only significant difference is whether you click OK to save the data source or Next to move to the next page in the wizard.

A word of caution about this dialog: You can either type or select from a list of database servers in the Server name drop-down list. If you choose to use the

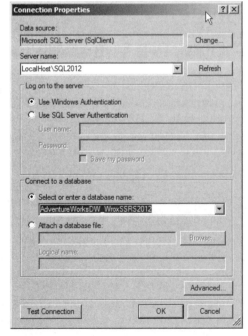

FIGURE 6-6

drop-down option, rather than typing the server name, a process runs that searches all available servers on your network. This can be time-consuming, so if you are on a large corporate network, you might want to type your database server name. If the database server is a default instance, simply type the server name or address. If it is a named instance, type the server name or address followed by a backslash and the instance name.

If your development database is the default instance on your development computer, you can simply type **LocalHost**, (**local**), or a period to have the local database server name automatically discovered by the data provider.

If you are working with a local development database server installed on the same computer, type **LocalHost**. Otherwise, enter the name of the database server. Note that in my examples, I have a named instance of SQL Server called SQL2012 on my local database server. Yours will most likely be a default instance or you may have a different server name.

In the next step, choose the security authentication method the database server will use to check security credentials. SQL Server may be configured to use Integrated Windows Authentication or both SQL Server Security and Integrated Windows Security. In a development environment, integrated security is a simple choice.

Finally, select or type the database name. Click the OK button to close this dialog and enter the new information into the Connection String property, as shown in Figure 6-7.

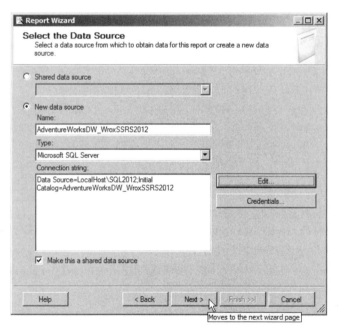

FIGURE 6-7

Click the Next button to move to the page titled Design the Query, shown in Figure 6-8. You can enter a query in one of three ways. You can type directly into the Query String box in this page of the Report Wizard, use the generic Query Builder window to enter the query text, or use the graphical query designer to generate the query text.

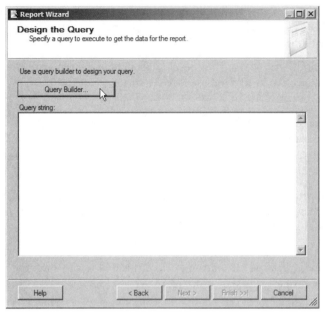

FIGURE 6-8

Click the Query Builder button. This opens the Query Designer window, shown in Figure 6-9. After you use the Query Designer to enter or design a query, the resulting script is placed in the Query string box in this page of the Report Wizard.

This Designer window has two views: the generic Query window and the Graphical Query Builder. You can toggle between these two modes using the Edit As Text button on the toolbar in the upper-left corner. You used the graphical builder in the preceding chapter, so I won't repeat the same exercise here. This is a useful tool. I continue to use the Graphical Query Builder, especially when I am less familiar with the source database or I need to quickly throw together a query for prototyping. However, if you're not careful, it can promote poor query design.

With some experience and familiarity with a database, you may choose to just type the query text into the Query String box. We'll come back to this in a moment. Go ahead and leave the Query Designer open in preparation for the rest of the exercise.

After you enter a query, you click OK on the Dataset Properties dialog. This generates the field definitions for the dataset, allowing you to design the report.

Creating a Data Source When Defining a Dataset

If you create a new report without using the Report Wizard, data sources are selected or created using the Report Data pane when creating a dataset. When you place the first data range object on the report body, the Data Source Properties dialog appears. It leads you through the process of defining a data source and dataset without using the Report Wizard. Regardless of the method used, a data source is simply a connection string saved into the report definition or shared data source file.

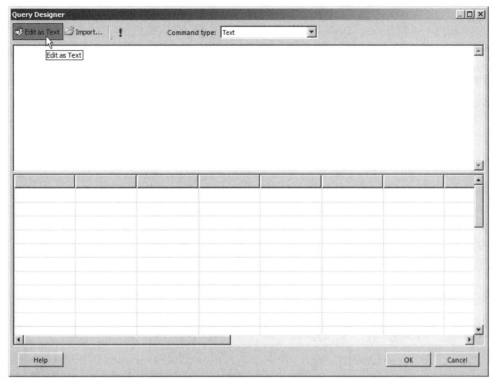

FIGURE 6-9

Data Sources and Query Languages

The examples in this chapter are based on versions of the Adventure Works sample databases we have prepared for this book and use the native SQL Server and Analysis Services client data providers. When creating a data source, if you choose any data provider other than SQL Server, queries must be written in the query language appropriate for that product. For most relational database products, this is a dialect of SQL. For example, Oracle uses a version of SQL called PL/SQL, and Microsoft Access uses Access SQL. Some providers require unique types of query expressions or scripting code specifically designed for that data source environment.

When defining a dataset's query expression, the Designer displays one of the two similar query windows. If you are using the SQL Server data provider, the T-SQL Query Designer appears. In the case of another data provider that uses another query language or dialect of SQL, a generic Query window is displayed.

To query cube structures in Analysis Services (which is an OLAP database engine), a specialized expression language called Multidimensional Expressions (MDX) is used. The current implementation of Reporting Services supports MDX queries. Unlike the Cube Browser in Analysis Services and other specialized multidimensional data query tools, reports are based on data that is flattened to two-dimensional structures and represented as rows and columns like a SQL query.

If you have not used MDX with OLAP cubes, you might find it interesting to contrast this language with more familiar SQL queries. In this sample MDX query expression for the Adventure Works DW Multidimensional_WroxSSRS2012 OLAP database, measures and KPI values (from a key performance indicator, defined in the Adventure Works cube) are returned on the columns axis, and dimension hierarchy members are on the rows axis:

```
SELECT
  {
      [Measures].[Reseller Sales Amount]
    , [Measures].[Reseller Gross Profit Margin]
    , KPIGoal("Channel Revenue")
    , KPIStatus("Channel Revenue")
  } ON Columns,
  (
      [Date].[Calendar].[Calendar Year]
    , [Sales Territory].[Sales Territory].[Region]
  ) ON Rows
FROM [Adventure Works]
;
```

This example is offered merely to pique your interest. You will learn how to design datasets and reports for SQL Server Analysis Services in Chapter 10.

T-SQL Query Design

If you are using SQL Server as the report data source, queries are written using T-SQL. For some reports, writing the query is a simple matter of using the graphical query designer to create a basic report. However, most business reports require a little more than just drag-and-drop queries, so some basic T-SQL skills are essential for report design.

This section takes you through some of the basics and even demonstrates some intermediate-level grouping and filtering techniques. If you are new to T-SQL and will be using SQL Server for your report data sources, you may need to acquire some basic SQL skills before moving forward.

Serious query design is performed in SQL Server Management Studio. You will use Management Studio to design queries and then paste the text into the Reporting Services Query Designer.

In the following exercise, you will design a series of T-SQL queries, progressively adding features, and then use this for a report dataset. You will use the generic Query Designer in the Reporting Services report design environment and the Query Designer in SQL Server Management Studio. You'll begin where you left off — with a data source that provides a connection to the AdventureWorksDW_WroxSSRS2012 relational data warehouse.

Leave the Report Designer open, and then open SQL Server Management Studio. When prompted, connect to the relational database engine on your local server, as shown in Figure 6-10.

FIGURE 6-10

Using the Object Explorer on the left side of the window, expand Databases, and then select the AdventureWorksDW_WroxSSRS2012 database. In the toolbar, click the New Query button, as shown in Figure 6-11.

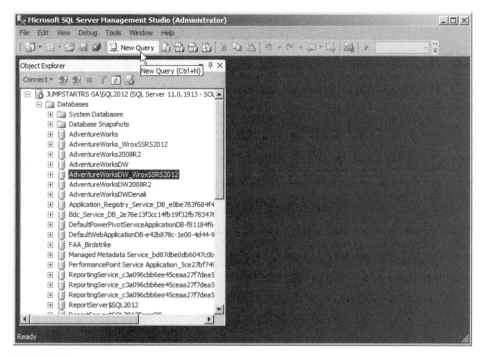

FIGURE 6-11

Data Warehouse Star Schema

In case you've never worked with a data warehouse star schema, let's take a moment to discuss some simple concepts. In a book on data warehouse design, the following information would occupy one of several chapters (in much greater detail, of course).

The purpose of a database of this type is to simplify data for reporting. Records are organized into two categories of tables. The numeric values that feed summarized or aggregated data point values are called measures or business facts. These exist in Fact tables (often prefixed with Fact). The Dimension tables (often prefixed with Dim) contain attributes used to organize and describe these business facts. The dimensional attributes can be used to form multilevel hierarchies. (In other words, the date dimension is often used to group measure data by periods in a hierarchy, such as the year, quarter, and month.) That's it — the ten-cent tour of data warehouse dimensional design! In summary, for our purposes, the Dimension-table attribute columns will be used to group, order, and organize records, and the measure columns, from a fact table, are used as aggregated numeric reporting metrics.

A new Query window opens in the Management Studio design pane. The Management Studio Query Designer includes IntelliSense code completion features that help with query design. If you write queries correctly, the Designer suggests object names and completes the query script as you type. To take advantage of this useful functionality, write the query's structure first.

Type the following text into the query pane:

```
SELECT

FROM

ORDER BY

;
```

This is the essential structure of a T-SQL query. Each of these language clauses is followed by a database object name used to return data from the query.

You can use the Object Explorer to see the table and column names you will use. You can drag these from the tree view into the Query pane, or you can type them. This query will use columns from the `DimDate`, `FactResellerSales`, and `DimSalesTerritory` tables.

The completed FROM clause should match the following added text:

```
SELECT

FROM
    DimDate D INNER JOIN FactResellerSales F ON D.DateKey = F.OrderDateKey
    INNER JOIN DimSalesTerritory ST ON F.SalesTerritoryKey = ST.SalesTerritoryKey

ORDER BY

;
```

Rather than memorizing the database object names and typing the whole thing by hand, however, let the Designer do the work for you.

Begin typing the first table name. Magic things happen! Notice that when you type the first few characters, a list of object names appears, and the characters you type are matched against the items in the list. You can also use the keyboard's up and down arrow keys to find an item nearby in the list. As soon as the `DimDate` table is selected, as shown in Figure 6-12, press the Tab key.

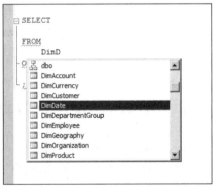

FIGURE 6-12

Rather than continuing to use long object names such as `DimDate`, I've defined object aliases. By preceding the table name `DimDate` with the letter D, from now on I can simply use the letter D to represent this table name.

Now fill in the SELECT clause by listing the columns separated by commas.

The ORDER BY clause is similar but includes only the dimension table columns. The fact table values (`OrderQuantity` and `SalesAmount`) will be aggregated in the report, so I don't care about the order of these values in the query result set. Since I want the report to be grouped by the dimension attributes `CalendarYear`, `CalendarQuarter`, `SalesTerritoryCountry`, and `SalesTerritoryRegion`, sorting records in this order will assist the report design.

The completed query is ready for testing. Verify that your query matches the following text, and then click the Execute button on the Management Studio toolbar.

```
SELECT
    D.CalendarYear, D.CalendarQuarter, ST.SalesTerritoryCountry
    , ST.SalesTerritoryRegion
    , F.OrderQuantity, F.SalesAmount
FROM
    DimDate D INNER JOIN FactResellerSales F ON D.DateKey = F.OrderDateKey
    INNER JOIN DimSalesTerritory ST ON F.SalesTerritoryKey = ST.SalesTerritoryKey
ORDER BY
    D.CalendarYear, D.CalendarQuarter, ST.SalesTerritoryCountry
    , ST.SalesTerritoryRegion
;
```

The query results should look like those shown in Figure 6-13.

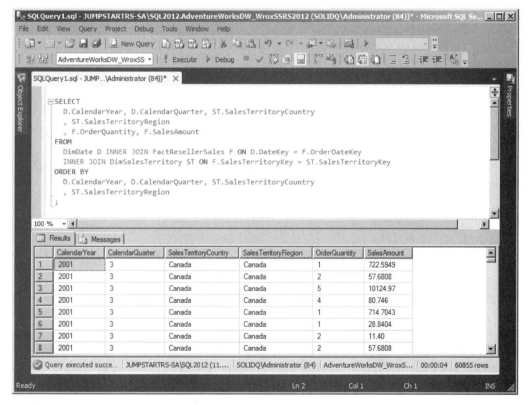

FIGURE 6-13

Note the record count in the lower-right corner of the Query results pane. I'll return to this topic. For now, just note that the query returns 60,855 rows.

The following examples will work in either SSDT or Report Builder. Keep in mind that there are subtle differences between the two designer interfaces, but their functionality is very similar.

Highlight and copy the query text from the Management Studio Query Designer window. Now switch back to the Report Designer, and paste the query text into the Dataset Properties or Query Design window. Click OK to close the Query Design window (if you were using it), and then click OK to close the Dataset Properties window. Figure 6-14 shows the query script pasted into the Dataset Properties window. If using the Report Wizard, the same script could be pasted into the Query String box.

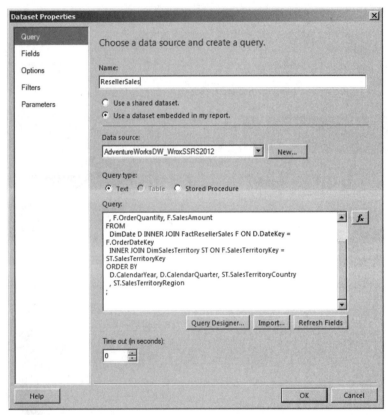

FIGURE 6-14

Figure 6-15 shows the report design after this dataset has been created. The Report Data pane in SSDT or the Data pane in Report Builder displays the available field for the newly added dataset.

To build the report, add a matrix from the Insert menu or toolbox. Move the matrix down the report body to make room for a title.

Drag the Report Name from the Built-in Fields list into the top of the report body.

Drag fields from the dataset into the matrix column and row group header cells. Drag the `CalendarYear` and `CalendarQuarter` fields into the column

FIGURE 6-15

headers. Drag the `SalesTerritoryCountry` and `SalesTerritoryRegion` fields into the row headers, to match Figure 6-16.

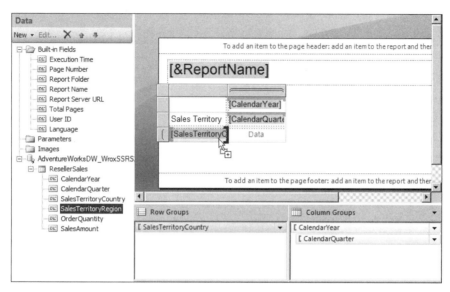

FIGURE 6-16

Drag the `SalesAmount` field into the Data cell. Right-click the cell, and format the number as currency.

Click the Preview button on the ribbon or choose the Preview tab in the Report Design window to view the report. Remember that you haven't done any formatting, so it should look similar to Figure 6-17.

If your groups are sorted differently than mine, that's okay. The group sorting expression can be removed or changed. With the exception of a little beautification effort, this report design is pretty much done.

Or is it? Think about it. The query returns more than 60,000 rows of raw data that has aggregated into 10 rows and 12 columns in this matrix report. In a production environment, the results of this query would be streamed across the corporate network from the database server to the Report Server, only to be grouped and summed into only 120 cells. This is not a particularly efficient solution. When designing a report, always consider the scalability of your design. Imagine if there were 100 times the volume of data. That's 6 million rows. This would be grossly inefficient!

For the rest of the query examples, you will make simple changes to the base query just defined. You can simply edit the dataset with these changes. Of course, you also can make modifications in the Management Studio Query Designer and then copy and paste the changes into the report dataset.

Since the results will be grouped in the report, if you can group the data in the query, you save the report rendering engine from having to do dual duty. You also can send a lot less data over the network. Grouping in the query does add some complexity to the SQL statement, but it reduces this complexity elsewhere.

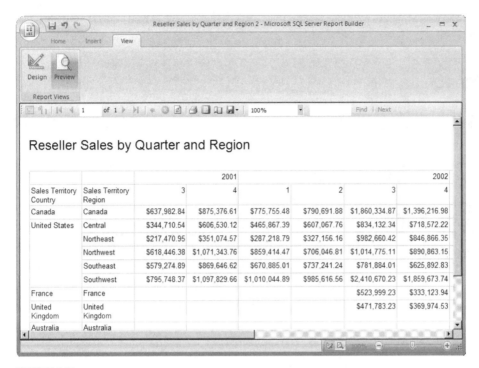

FIGURE 6-17

The grouped version of this query looks like this:

```
SELECT
      D.CalendarYear
    , D.CalendarQuarter
    , ST.SalesTerritoryCountry
    , ST.SalesTerritoryRegion
    , SUM(F.OrderQuantity) AS OrderQuantity
    , SUM(F.SalesAmount) AS SalesAmount
FROM
    DimDate D INNER JOIN FactResellerSales F ON D.DateKey = F.OrderDateKey
    INNER JOIN DimSalesTerritory ST ON F.SalesTerritoryKey = ST.SalesTerritoryKey
GROUP BY
      D.CalendarYear
    , D.CalendarQuarter
    , ST.SalesTerritoryCountry
    , ST.SalesTerritoryRegion
ORDER BY
      D.CalendarYear
    , D.CalendarQuarter
    , ST.SalesTerritoryCountry
    , ST.SalesTerritoryRegion
    ;
```

Even though this query is now more complex, you'll notice that it's a little easier to read. At some point in the process of adding more and more appendages to a query, try to clean it up and make it easier to read. I can't emphasize how important it is to make sure that your query scripts are well organized and easy for you and others to read. Use tabs, returns, and spaces liberally. Placing delimiting commas at the beginning, rather than the end, of each line makes the lines easier to read and easier to remark out or remove without breaking the query.

This T-SQL language pattern is relatively simple as long as you adhere to some basic rules. Every column in the SELECT list must either be included in the GROUP BY list or be passed to an aggregate function. In the example, the two measure fields are aggregated using the SUM function. The output from a function doesn't naturally return a column name, so it's common to define an alias using the AS keyword. This example actually defines the column aliases using the original column names, which is perfectly acceptable. You will typically want to set the ORDER BY list to match the GROUP BY list.

This query design is very "copy-and-pasteable." In other words, as soon as you get this working in one query, it's pretty easy to duplicate the pattern in subsequent queries and reports.

Executing this query in the Management Studio Query Designer produces only 96 rows. This means that the result set is less than 1/600th of the size, with exactly the same report results! Imagine how much faster this report might run if you had proportionally more data.

FILTERING TECHNIQUES

When retrieving report data from a data source, it's important to consider the most efficient way to filter report data based on the user's selection criteria. Many databases contain large amounts of data. Therefore, it is always important to retrieve just the right amount of data required for reporting. Sometimes a report is used only to view data for a narrow range of values. At other times, the user may specify different criteria, causing the report to render a varied range of related values.

In the case of a narrow range of possible values, it makes more sense to retrieve only the associated data. However, if users specify different criteria during a session — causing the data source to be queried multiple times — it could prove to be slow and an inefficient use of resources.

In Figure 6-18, parameters presented to the data source cause data to be filtered and return only the data for a single rendering of the report. The dataset represents the database server's result set on the client side (the Report Server). As shown in the figure, this is a small volume of data, because it has already been filtered at the database.

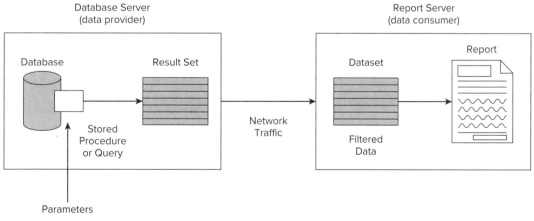

FIGURE 6-18

Passing selection criteria parameters at the database object level means that network traffic can be greatly reduced and that the report is rendered more efficiently. However, if the user will be providing different parameter values to render several views of the same report within a session, the database will be queried repeatedly. This might result in longer overall wait times. Much of the same data will move across the network multiple times. In Figure 6-19, a larger volume of data is returned from the database server since it is unfiltered. Filtering then occurs by using report parameters on the Report Server against the cached set of records on the Report Server.

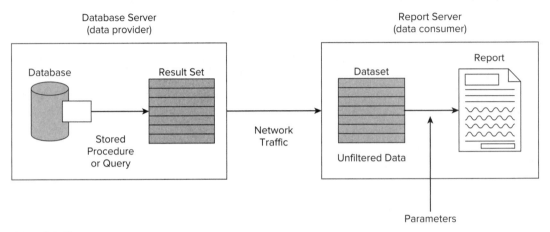

FIGURE 6-19

If all the data necessary for each query to be executed in a user's session is obtained in one result set, a greater volume of network traffic for a single execution will result. However, this may reduce subsequent report rendering times.

Selection parameters can be applied to data at the report level rather than at the data source. Because all the data is cached (held in memory), reports render much faster. This technique can reduce the overall network traffic and rendering time. The report can also be configured so that the cached data is saved to disk, usually for a specific period of time. This technique is presented in Chapter 17.

You certainly don't want to retrieve unnecessary data from the data source, so a combination of these two techniques may be the appropriate solution, depending on specific reporting needs. For example, if you are a regional sales manager and you want sales summaries for each of the territories within your region, you may begin your session by retrieving all the regional sales data for a range of dates. For each territory report, this data is simply filtered down to the territory level. If these were long-running report queries, it might actually be more efficient to retrieve all the sales data for the date range and then filter the sales regions on the Report Server.

Filtering a Query

You filter records in the query by adding a WHERE clause. Make the following changes to the query:

```sql
SELECT
     D.CalendarYear
   , D.CalendarQuarter
```

```
    , ST.SalesTerritoryCountry
    , ST.SalesTerritoryRegion
    , F.OrderQuantity, F.SalesAmount
FROM
    DimDate D INNER JOIN FactResellerSales F ON D.DateKey = F.OrderDateKey
    INNER JOIN DimSalesTerritory ST ON F.SalesTerritoryKey = ST.SalesTerritoryKey
WHERE
    D.CalendarYear = 2003
ORDER BY
      D.CalendarYear
    , D.CalendarQuarter
    , ST.SalesTerritoryCountry
    , ST.SalesTerritoryRegion
;
```

Before rows are returned from the database server, candidate rows are scanned, and only qualifying rows are returned when the `CalendarYear` value is `2003`. Execute the report, and note that only the 2003 calendar year and related quarters are displayed in the matrix.

Parameter Concepts

Using parameters in report design isn't complicated, but until you have a chance to do some creative things with them in both queries and report expressions, you might not fully appreciate their power. This section starts by explaining how parameters are defined in simple queries and reports. Then it explains how you might need to use (and define) parameters in more complex reports.

You may contend with two (and possibly three, depending on your query technique) different types of parameters in report design: dataset parameters and report parameters. Dataset parameters can be derived from database objects, such as stored procedures and user-defined functions, or they can be derived from a parameterized query statement. As shown in Figure 6-20, the design process can have three different layers where you can encounter parameters.

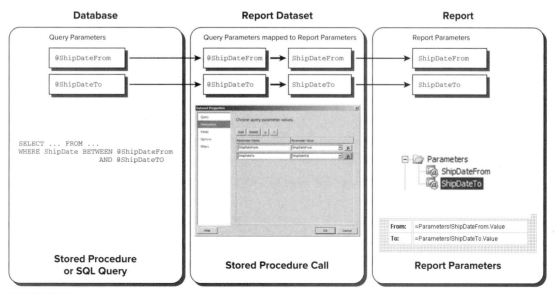

FIGURE 6-20

Most commonly, report parameters are derived from parameters defined in an ad hoc query or SQL stored procedure. But you don't have to have a parameterized query to use parameters in a report, as you'll see in a later example.

When SQL Server is used as the data source, parameters are defined in the SQL syntax by prefixing the names with a single @ symbol. In a stored procedure, these parameters are defined first and then are used in the procedure body much as they would be used in an ad hoc query. The Report Designer automatically parses the query and generates corresponding report parameters. The third section of Figure 6-20 shows the report parameters of the Dataset Properties dialog open with the two derived parameters. If you use the Graphical Query Builder or generic Query Designer to write a T-SQL statement, the Report Designer resolves dataset parameters and database object parameters and prompts for the parameter values when running the query. Dataset parameters are mapped to report parameters in the Dataset Properties dialog. You can access this dialog when editing the dataset in the Report Data pane of the Report Designer.

For most basic queries, the Report Designer populates this dialog and matches the parameters for you. But if have created a complex or unusual dataset query, you may need to match the dataset and report parameters manually. Parameter resolution is performed when you test a query in the Query Designer, click the Refresh Fields button, or close the Dataset Properties dialog.

Let's step out of this exercise for a moment to show a different example. The following query contains two parameters used to specify a range of date values for filtering a Date type field:

```
SELECT
     D.CalendarYear
   , D.CalendarQuarter
   , D.MonthNumberOfYear
   , D.FullDateAlternateKey AS OrderDate
   , ST.SalesTerritoryCountry
   , ST.SalesTerritoryRegion
   , SUM(F.OrderQuantity) AS OrderQuantity
   , SUM(F.SalesAmount) AS SalesAmount
FROM
   DimDate D INNER JOIN FactResellerSales F ON D.DateKey = F.OrderDateKey
   INNER JOIN DimSalesTerritory ST ON F.SalesTerritoryKey = ST.SalesTerritoryKey
WHERE
   D.FullDateAlternateKey BETWEEN @ShipDateFrom AND @ShipDateTo
GROUP BY
   D.CalendarYear
   , D.CalendarQuarter
   , D.MonthNumberOfYear
   , D.FullDateAlternateKey
   , ST.SalesTerritoryCountry
   , ST.SalesTerritoryRegion
ORDER BY
     D.CalendarYear
   , D.CalendarQuarter
   , D.MonthNumberOfYear
   , D.FullDateAlternateKey
   , ST.SalesTerritoryCountry
   , ST.SalesTerritoryRegion
 ;
```

For each of these two parameters, the `Data Type` has been set to `Date/Time` in the Report Parameter Properties dialog, as shown in Figure 6-21.

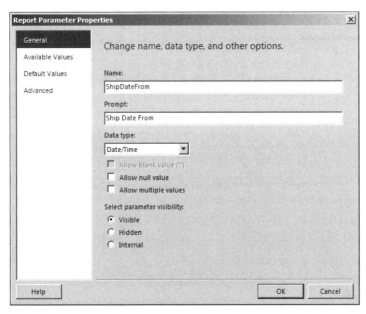

FIGURE 6-21

When the report is run, the result is that a date picker control is used to select a date, as shown in Figure 6-22. The user clicks the calendar icon next to the textbox to reveal the calendar drop-down; uses the controls to select a year, month, and date; and then clicks the View Report button on the parameter bar.

FIGURE 6-22

Filtering Data with Query Parameters

Parameters are often used to filter data at the data source. Whether or not the data is to be filtered within the report, filtering at least some of the data within the database is an essential technique for most report solutions. If you have created parameterized stored procedures in SQL Server, you are already familiar with this pattern. The technique applies to stored procedures and query expressions that use similar syntax. Let's start with a simple ad hoc query expression and then move on to creating a stored procedure.

Query parameters begin with the @ symbol and must conform to the naming convention standards for T-SQL identifiers. The name should not contain spaces or certain punctuation characters and can't begin with a numeral; for simplicity, just use letters. In stored procedures, parameters must be declared before they are used. In an ad hoc query, simply make up parameter names when you need them. In the WHERE part of our sample SQL statement, use a parameter to represent a variable value, as follows:

```
SELECT
    D.CalendarYear
  , D.CalendarQuarter
  , ST.SalesTerritoryCountry
  , ST.SalesTerritoryRegion
  , F.OrderQuantity
  , F.SalesAmount
FROM
  DimDate D INNER JOIN FactResellerSales F ON D.DateKey = F.OrderDateKey
  INNER JOIN DimSalesTerritory ST ON F.SalesTerritoryKey = ST.SalesTerritoryKey
WHERE
  D.CalendarYear = @Year
ORDER BY
    D.CalendarYear
  , D.CalendarQuarter
  , ST.SalesTerritoryCountry
  , ST.SalesTerritoryRegion
;
```

To test this query, you must execute it in the Report Designer's Query Editor, because Management Studio doesn't know what to do with the parameter. If you execute this query and enter 2003 when prompted for the Year parameter, the original 60,855 rows are reduced to 26,758. Aside from letting the user see only the data he or she wanted, this certainly wouldn't hurt performance.

Now, let's combine filtering with grouping records and see what happens. Add the GROUP BY clause from the earlier example, and then execute this query in the Report Designer Query Editor. Enter 2003 for the Year parameter. Voilà! Only 36 rows are returned.

```
SELECT
    D.CalendarYear
  , D.CalendarQuarter
  , ST.SalesTerritoryCountry
  , ST.SalesTerritoryRegion
  , SUM(F.OrderQuantity) AS OrderQuantity
  , SUM(F.SalesAmount) AS SalesAmount
FROM
  DimDate D INNER JOIN FactResellerSales F ON D.DateKey = F.OrderDateKey
  INNER JOIN DimSalesTerritory ST ON F.SalesTerritoryKey = ST.SalesTerritoryKey
WHERE
  D.CalendarYear = @Year
GROUP BY
    D.CalendarYear
  , D.CalendarQuarter
  , ST.SalesTerritoryCountry
  , ST.SalesTerritoryRegion
ORDER BY
    D.CalendarYear
```

```
    , D.CalendarQuarter
    , ST.SalesTerritoryCountry
    , ST.SalesTerritoryRegion
  ;
```

Over time, reports tend to grow and expand. Users will inevitably ask for more fields, more totals, and other features. Allowing the requirements to evolve in this manner can make your reports unruly and difficult to support — especially when you have different people involved in this haphazard and incremental style of design. Writing well-designed queries will go a long way toward achieving efficient, maintainable reports. Carefully consider whether functionality should be built into the query or report design. Often, handling business challenges in the query makes report design easier.

Creating a Parameter List

When you run this report, you are prompted to type a parameter value into the parameter bar area above the report. Although this works, it's not very convenient. You can provide a list of values for the user to select from by modifying the properties of the Year parameter. You can create a list of available values by adding them in the Available Value page of the Parameter Properties dialog, or you can use a query to return a list of available values.

To create a query-driven list, first create a new dataset called YearList under the same data source as the previous dataset. Enter the following T-SQL statement, and verify that it returns a list of calendar year values:

```
SELECT DISTINCT CalendarYear
FROM DimDate
ORDER BY CalendarYear
```

Figure 6-23 shows the Dataset Properties dialog for this new dataset query.

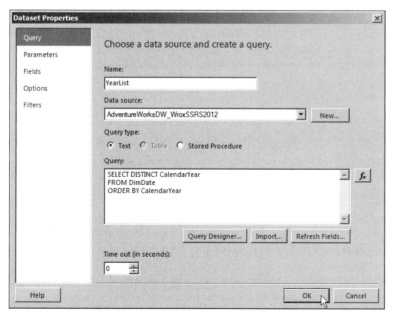

FIGURE 6-23

To set up the parameter list, right-click the `Year` parameter in the Report Data pane and choose Parameter Properties. Select the Available Values page of the Report Parameter Properties dialog, and select the radio button labeled "Get values from a query." Select the new dataset and the `CalendarYear` field for both the `Value` field and `Label` field properties. Verify that this page looks like Figure 6-24, and then click OK.

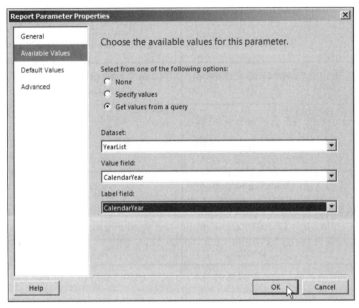

FIGURE 6-24

You can build a simple table report to view the results of the query. A sample report is provided in the Chapter 6 sample project.

Now, preview the report. Select a year from the drop-down list, and click View Report to see the results. You'll see that only sales records from the selected year are included in the results.

Multivalue Parameters

You can configure parameters so that a user can select a combination of values. This is easy to do using the Report Parameter Properties dialog.

Modify the `Year` parameter by right-clicking it in the Report Data pane and selecting Parameter Properties. Check "Allow multiple values" in the resulting Report Parameter Properties dialog, as shown in Figure 6-25, and click OK.

Changing this setting changes the behavior of the parameter drop-down list, but it doesn't enable the SQL Server database engine to deal with the changes. A simple modification is required in the query syntax. Making the report parameter multivalued changes it to an array type object. When the report parameter value is mapped to the corresponding query parameter value (which is not an array), the value is converted into a string value containing a comma-separated list. Both T-SQL and MDX contain parsing functions that know how to deal with comma-delimited values. In T-SQL, the `IN` function matches a field value against items in such a list.

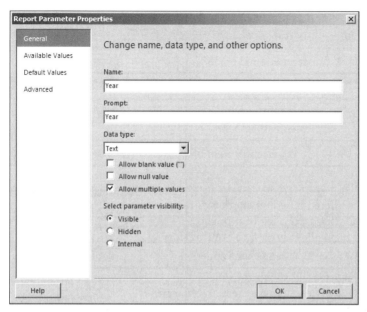

FIGURE 6-25

Modify the main dataset query by making the following change in the WHERE clause. Replace the equals sign with the IN function, and place parentheses around the @Year parameter reference.

```
SELECT
      D.CalendarYear
    , D.CalendarQuarter
    , ST.SalesTerritoryCountry
    , ST.SalesTerritoryRegion
    , SUM(F.OrderQuantity) AS OrderQuantity
    , SUM(F.SalesAmount) AS SalesAmount
FROM
    DimDate D INNER JOIN FactResellerSales F ON D.DateKey = F.OrderDateKey
    INNER JOIN DimSalesTerritory ST ON F.SalesTerritoryKey = ST.SalesTerritoryKey
WHERE
    D.CalendarYear IN ( @Year )
GROUP BY
      D.CalendarYear
    , D.CalendarQuarter
    , ST.SalesTerritoryCountry
    , ST.SalesTerritoryRegion
ORDER BY
      D.CalendarYear
    , D.CalendarQuarter
    , ST.SalesTerritoryCountry
    , ST.SalesTerritoryRegion
;
```

Now run the query. You should see that the Year parameter drop-down list contains items with check-boxes next to them, as shown in Figure 6-26. Select any combination of Year values, and then click the View Report button to test the report. Records should be filtered for the set of years you've selected.

FIGURE 6-26

Cascading Parameters

A parameter can depend on another parameter so that the list of available values for a parameter is filtered based on another parameter selection. For example, if you offer users a list of product categories and another list of product subcategories, the subcategory list would show only subcategories for a selected category.

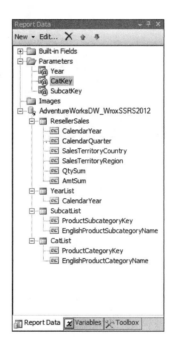

The Report Data pane shown in Figure 6-27 shows the objects defined in the finished report. As you can see, parameters are defined for the user to select the product category (named `CatKey` in this example) and the product subcategory (named `SubcatKey`). A dataset query corresponds to each parameter. These are named `CatList` and `SubcatList`, respectively. (I like to give parameters names that are similar to the fields.)

The most logical way to define these objects is to work backward through the process from the user's perspective. In other words, a user selects a product category to see a filtered list of subcategories. After he or she selects a subcategory, the report is filtered based on the subcategory selection. To design this, you would add the subcategory filtering to the main dataset query and then create the filtered subcategory query and corresponding parameter. Finally, you would define the category query and parameter. The following steps take you through creating each of these objects and the filtering mechanism in the main dataset query:

FIGURE 6-27

1. Right-click the main report dataset and choose Query. Your dataset may be named `Dataset1`. It's renamed `ResellerSales` in this example. Note that if you rename a dataset after using it, you must update the `DatasetName` of any affected data range or report items used in the report.

2. Modify the `FROM` and `WHERE` clauses to match the following query script:

```
SELECT
    D.CalendarYear
, D.CalendarQuarter
, ST.SalesTerritoryCountry
, ST.SalesTerritoryRegion
, SUM(F.OrderQuantity) AS OrderQuantity
, SUM(F.SalesAmount) AS SalesAmount
FROM
    DimDate D INNER JOIN FactResellerSales F ON D.DateKey = F.OrderDateKey
```

```
        INNER JOIN DimSalesTerritory ST ON F.SalesTerritoryKey = ST.SalesTerritoryKey
        INNER JOIN DimProduct P ON F.ProductKey = P.ProductKey
    WHERE
        D.CalendarYear = @Year AND P.ProductSubcategoryKey = @SubcatKey
    GROUP BY
          D.CalendarYear
        , D.CalendarQuarter
        , ST.SalesTerritoryCountry
        , ST.SalesTerritoryRegion
    ORDER BY
          D.CalendarYear
        , D.CalendarQuarter
        , ST.SalesTerritoryCountry
        , ST.SalesTerritoryRegion
    ;
```

3. Now for the subcategory list query. Right-click the AdventureWorksDW_WroxSSRS2012 data source and add a new query named SubcatList. Use the Query Builder or manually enter this query text:

```
SELECT      ProductSubcategoryKey, EnglishProductSubcategoryName
FROM        DimProductSubcategory
WHERE       ProductCategoryKey = @CatKey
ORDER BY    EnglishProductSubcategoryName
```

When you closed the Dataset Properties dialog after making changes to the main dataset, the referenced SubcatKey parameter was automatically generated and added to the list of available parameters.

4. Right-click the SubcatKey parameter and select Parameter Properties from the menu. The Report Parameter Properties dialog appears, as shown in Figure 6-28.

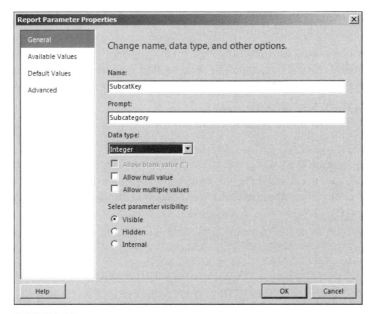

FIGURE 6-28

5. Change the Prompt to a friendly name for this parameter. Your users don't need to see the cryptic parameter name. Change the Data type to Integer.

6. Choose the Available Values page, and select "Get values from a query." Three drop-down lists are displayed, as shown in Figure 6-29.

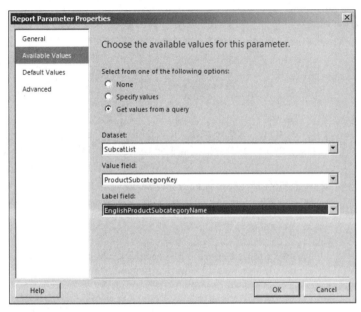

FIGURE 6-29

➤ From the Dataset list, select the name of the dataset that returns product subcategory values. It should be named `SubcatList`.

➤ From the Value field list, select the `ProductSubcategoryKey` field. This field contains numeric key values that will be used to filter the main query after the user selects a subcategory.

➤ From the Label field list, select `EnglishProductSubcategoryName`. This is the friendly value the user will see in the parameter list. Click OK to close the Report Parameter Properties dialog.

7. Right-click the AdventureWorksDW_WroxSSRS2012 data source and add a new query named `CatList`. Either use the Query Builder or manually enter the following for the query text. Then click OK to close the Dataset Properties dialog.

```
SELECT     ProductCategoryKey, EnglishProductCategoryName
FROM       DimProductCategory
ORDER BY   EnglishProductCategoryName
```

8. In the Report Data pane, right-click the `CatKey` parameter and select Parameter Properties from the menu. The Report Parameter Properties dialog is displayed.

9. As with the main report dataset, when you closed the Dataset Properties dialog after making changes to the `SubcatList` dataset, the referenced `CatKey` parameter was automatically generated and added to the list of available parameters.

10. Right-click the `CatKey` parameter and select Parameter Properties from the menu. The Report Parameter Properties dialog is displayed, as shown in Figure 6-30.

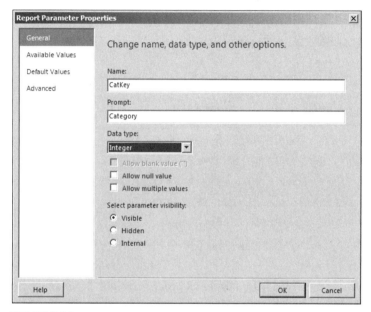

FIGURE 6-30

11. Change the Prompt to a friendly name for this parameter. Your users don't need to see the cryptic parameter name. Change the Data type to Integer. Choose the Available Values page, and select "Get values from a query." Three drop-down lists are displayed, as shown in Figure 6-31.

> ➤ From the Dataset list, select the name of the dataset that returns product subcategory values. It should be named `CatList`.

> ➤ From the Value field list, select the `ProductCategoryKey` field. This is the field containing numeric key values that will be used to filter the main query after the user selects a category.

> ➤ From the Label field list, select `EnglishProductCategoryName`. This is the friendly value the user will see in the parameter list.

12. Click OK to close the Report Parameter Properties dialog.

13. The last thing to do is to make sure the parameters are in the right order. Referring to Figure 6-27, verify that the `CatKey` parameter is listed before the `SubcatKey` parameter. You can rearrange parameters using the up and down arrows in this pane's toolbar. If everything checks out, you should be ready to test the report.

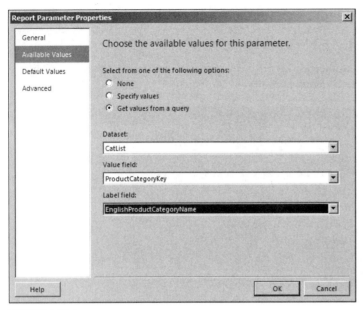

FIGURE 6-31

Preview the report. Because the `Year` parameter was left over from the previous example, make sure it has a valid selection.

The Category parameter list is displayed with a list of all product categories, as shown in Figure 6-32. Note that the Subcategory list is disabled and empty.

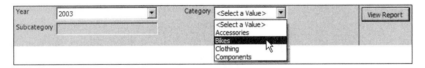

FIGURE 6-32

When you choose a category, the Subcategory list becomes available, with a list of values filtered by the previous category selection, as shown in Figure 6-33. Select a subcategory, and then click the View Report button.

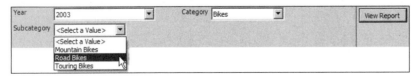

FIGURE 6-33

The report should run with results filtered for the selected product subcategory. As you can see, multiple parameters may be used to coordinate filtered parameters or to narrow down the report's results. In Chapters 10 and 11, you will see how to use parameters with expressions to design even more interesting report behaviors and to build creative solutions.

Report Parameters

In addition to report parameters derived from dataset parameters, you can explicitly add report parameters of your own. These report parameters (that do not have corresponding query parameters) can be added to support additional report functionality, such as hiding and showing report sections, page numbers, and dynamic formatting.

The following example demonstrates some simple report parameters used to dynamically set values on the report. Later we'll apply this technique to more practical report features. This example is intended to demonstrate two simple report parameters for academic purposes.

1. Create a new report without using the Wizard. You can use the Start "pearl" button in Report Builder. Or, in SSDT, you can right-click the Solution Explorer and select Add ➪ Add New Item.

2. Select Report from the report item templates in the Add New Item dialog. Do not specify a dataset for the new report.

3. Report parameters are added in the Report Data pane. Right-click Parameters and add a report parameter named `ReportTitle`.

4. Click OK to save the parameter, and then repeat Step 3 to add a report parameter named `TextColor`. For this parameter, use the Available Value page to add a list of simple color values such as Red, Blue, Yellow, and Black. The Value and Label for each of the items should be the same. Click OK to save this parameter.

5. Drag and drop the two parameters onto the report body. This creates a textbox for each. Click in the second textbox and insert text before `[@TextColor]`, as shown in Figure 6-34. You can also change the font size and weight for these textboxes.

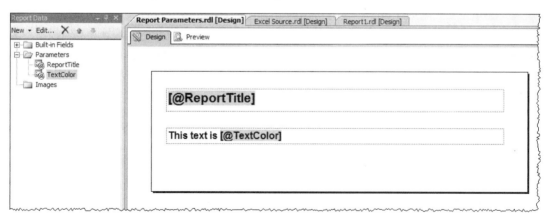

FIGURE 6-34

Chapter 7 discusses the use of expressions. Using an expression to set properties is easy, though. You've actually been doing this just by dragging and dropping fields and parameters into the Report Designer.

6. With the Property Pane visible, click the second textbox, find the `Color` property, and then either type or use the Expression Builder to set the property to an expression. Set the `Color` property for the second textbox to use the following expression:

```
=Parameters!TextColor.Value
```

Now preview the report and notice what happens. The parameter bar prompts you to enter a report title and select a color. When you click the View Report button, the first textbox displays the text entered into the `ReportTitle` parameter, and the second textbox displays not only the specific color name but also the text, as shown in Figure 6-35.

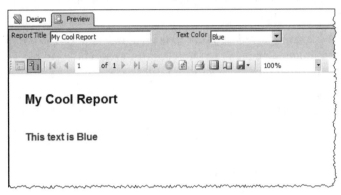

FIGURE 6-35

Because this book is printed in black and white, to clarify, the text "This text is Blue" is blue.

As you can see, this is an effective way to feed values to the report to be used in expressions. Chapter 7 expands on this technique to provide filtering and dynamic formatting.

Using Stored Procedures

Using stored procedures rather than verbose T-SQL queries in a report offers several advantages. Complex queries can be stored as reusable database objects. Stored procedures can run more efficiently and provide greater security and control.

The following T-SQL script is used to create a stored procedure in SQL Server Management Studio. After it is created, the procedure is simply referenced and executed by name from the report.

```
CREATE PROCEDURE spGet_ResellerSalesByRegion
  @ShipDateFrom Date
 ,@ShipDateTo   Date
AS
SELECT
  D.CalendarYear
  , D.CalendarQuarter
  , D.MonthNumberOfYear
  , D.DateKey
  , ST.SalesTerritoryCountry
  , ST.SalesTerritoryRegion
  , F.OrderQuantity
  , F.SalesAmount
FROM
  DimDate D INNER JOIN FactResellerSales F ON D.DateKey = F.OrderDateKey
  INNER JOIN DimSalesTerritory ST ON F.SalesTerritoryKey = ST.SalesTerritoryKey
WHERE
  D.FullDateAlternateKey BETWEEN @ShipDateFrom AND @ShipDateTo
ORDER BY
```

```
    D.CalendarYear
    , D.CalendarQuarter
    , D.MonthNumberOfYear
    , D.DateKey
    , ST.SalesTerritoryCountry
    , ST.SalesTerritoryRegion
;
```

The best way to go about querying a data source depends mainly on your requirements. Refer to the earlier discussion about filtering techniques where processing parameters (on the database server, the client, or both) affects the performance, efficiency, and flexibility of your reporting solution. Handling parameters on the database server is almost always more efficient. Processing parameters on the client gives you the flexibility of handling a wider range of records and query options without needing to go back to the database every time you need to render the report.

Using a parameterized stored procedure typically provides the most efficient means of filtering data, because it returns only the data matching your criteria. Stored procedures are compiled to native-processor instructions on the database server. When any kind of query is processed, SQL Server creates an execution plan, which defines the specific instructions the server uses to retrieve data. In the case of a stored procedure, the execution plan is prepared the first time it is executed, and then it is cached on the database server. In subsequent executions, results are returned faster, because some of the work has already been done.

Filtering Data with Report Parameters

So far you've only filtered data at the database level. In cases in which users may be using the same report in one sitting to view data for different criteria, it may be more effective to retrieve a larger result set from the data source and then filter the report data on the Report Server.

As you've seen, parameters defined in a query or stored procedure that serves as a report dataset are pulled into the report as report parameters. You can also define your own parameters and use expressions to filter data at the report level.

Using the report from the previous query filtering exercise, suppose that you want to return records for all subcategory values from the database and then filter by SubcatKey on the Report Server. Why would you want to return more records from the database server than those displayed in the report? This may seem inefficient at first, but perhaps not if you consider the bigger picture. If you have a long-running query and you anticipate that a user will run the report multiple times with different parameter values, it may actually be more efficient to get all the data at the beginning of the user's session. Query results can be cached on the server for a user's session or for all users. After it has been deployed to the server, a report can be configured to cache data for a period of time, for the benefit of other users.

The first change to make is to remove the query filter for the SubcatKey parameter. This query continues to filter results for the product subcategory using the Year parameter.

You must also add the ProductSubcategoryKey column to the SELECT column list. You didn't have to return this column when you used it for filtering in the query. To use this field for dataset filtering, it must now be returned:

```
SELECT
    D.CalendarYear
```

```
    , D.CalendarQuarter
    , ST.SalesTerritoryCountry
    , ST.SalesTerritoryRegion
    , P.ProductSubcategoryKey
    , SUM(F.OrderQuantity) AS OrderQuantity
    , SUM(F.SalesAmount) AS SalesAmount
FROM
    DimDate D INNER JOIN FactResellerSales F ON D.DateKey = F.OrderDateKey
    INNER JOIN DimSalesTerritory ST ON F.SalesTerritoryKey = ST.SalesTerritoryKey
    INNER JOIN DimProduct P ON F.ProductKey = P.ProductKey
WHERE
    D.CalendarYear IN ( @Year )
GROUP BY
      D.CalendarYear
    , D.CalendarQuarter
    , ST.SalesTerritoryCountry
    , ST.SalesTerritoryRegion
    , P.ProductSubcategoryKey
ORDER BY
      D.CalendarYear
    , D.CalendarQuarter
    , ST.SalesTerritoryCountry
    , ST.SalesTerritoryRegion
    , P.ProductSubcategoryKey
;
```

The SubcatKey parameter remains in the report definition even though it's been removed from the query.

In the Report Data pane, right-click the main dataset and choose Dataset Properties. In the Dataset Properties dialog, select the Filters page, as shown in Figure 6-36. Click the Add button to define a new filter expression for the dataset. Select the ProductSubcategoryKey field in the Expression drop-down list. Next to the Value textbox, click the Expression button (labeled f_x).

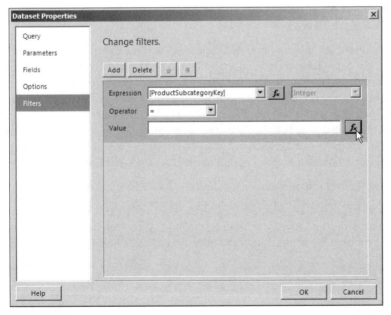

FIGURE 6-36

Clicking this button in any dialog opens the Expression window, allowing you to build an expression using fields, built-in objects, and parameters in the report.

To create an expression that references the `SubcatKey` parameter value, choose Parameters in the Category list. In the Values list on the right side of the dialog, double-click the `SubcatKey` parameter to insert the expression into the Expression box at the top.

You can also type text directly into this window. Verify that your expression looks like Figure 6-37, and then click the OK button to accept these changes.

FIGURE 6-37

If you've worked with previous versions of Reporting Services, you'll notice that expressions now appear in a different format. The Value box shown in Figure 6-38 shows a token for the `SubcatKey` parameter that corresponds to the complete expression you generated in the Expression Editor dialog. Click OK to accept these changes.

This report should behave just like it did before, with one important difference. If you run the report once with a set of parameter values, it will take as long to run and render the report as it has before. However, if you choose a different subcategory value from the parameter drop-down list and then rerun the report, it should run faster than before. This may not be as apparent with a small set of data, but in production, with much larger data volumes, this design change would have a significant impact on performance.

Let's review how dataset filtering works. The `Year` parameter filters data at the database. The resulting data is cached in memory on the Report Server, where the subcategory filter further limits results.

You could easily extend the design of this report using more complex items, sorting, and grouping. The dataset query could also be replaced with a stored procedure. With these building blocks, you now can create efficient reports that move the appropriate volume of data across network connections and allow users to use filtering criteria without needing to requery the entire dataset.

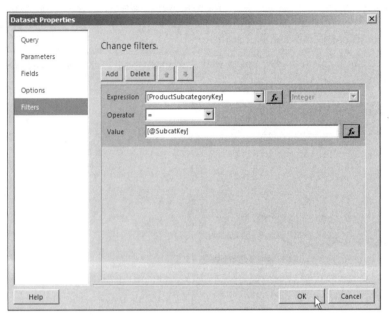

FIGURE 6-38

USING OTHER DATA SOURCES

After using Reporting Services with SQL Server databases and then later with others, I realized that I had become a bit spoiled. It's true that you can use practically any standard database product as a data source for reports; you won't have the assistance of the Graphical Query Builder and other automated features of the Report Designer. Nevertheless, Reporting Services can work with the language syntax and features of most databases; you just need to do some of the easy stuff yourself. This section showcases a few different products we've used as data sources. One point to keep in mind is that the compatibilities and behaviors are influenced by a number of factors, including the features and capabilities of the data provider or database driver you are using. Many database product vendors don't develop their own data providers. Therefore, a data source's capabilities and behaviors vary not only between different versions of a product, but also by the native or third-party provider you have installed.

The technique demonstrated a little later in this chapter with an Access query (in the section "Building a Query in a String Expression") is a universal pattern that applies to all database products. I strongly recommend that you consider this technique, because it will be useful to you at some point, regardless of the data source you use for reporting.

Microsoft Access

Microsoft Access is built on top of the JET Database Engine, with data stored in a single MDB file. This is simple and convenient for small, portable databases. However, Microsoft continues to take steps to replace JET databases with SQL Server and the desktop implementations of SQL. As a desktop application, Access may also be used as a front end to SQL databases. If you have the luxury of building a new database solution, it may be best to use one of these newer products in place of older Access databases. But if you have existing solutions based on older Access databases, it likely will be easier to continue working with them in their present form.

Two standard data providers may be used to connect to Access databases. The JET 4.0 .NET OLE DB provider is newer and should be a little more efficient than using the older Access ODBC driver. The data provider rarely is a performance bottleneck, so this is probably a moot point. The OLE DB provider is easier to use and doesn't require a separate ODBC data source name (DSN) to be configured. One of the nice features of the new data provider is that it accepts Transact-SQL and translates it into Access-specific syntax. Although Access SQL and Transact-SQL are

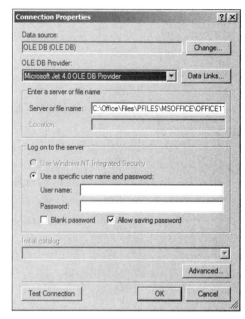

FIGURE 6-39

very close, they have some subtle differences. This feature enables the Report Designer to use the Transact-SQL Graphical Query Builder when a dataset uses a JET data source.

Figure 6-39 shows the Connection Properties dialog used when defining an Access database connection using the JET OLE DB provider.

Note that the default security credentials used with an unsecured Access database are the Admin user with a blank password. Even if you provide this information and check the Blank Password box, the dialog doesn't show these values. This is because the data provider knows to use default credentials when the database hasn't been secured.

The connection string and credentials are shown in Figures 6-40 and 6-41, respectively. Select the Credentials tab to view or modify the user authentication information.

Access has some minor quirks that you should be aware of. Any file-based data source can present a challenge for Reporting Services, because the service must have the necessary security access to open the database file. If the MDB file is on the Report Server, this shouldn't be a concern, but if the file is on another network share, it may be. If you get file-sharing errors, make sure that Reporting Services runs using a network account that has privileges to open the Access database file and its containing folder.

Parameterized Access queries have always presented a challenge in custom code, outside of simple Access forms applications. The JET database engine has difficulty resolving parameter values passed into queries and may report errors even if the values are passed using the correct data type and format. For example, the following Access query defines and then uses two parameters to filter order records in the Northwind sample database:

```
PARAMETERS [ShipDateFrom] DateTime, [ShipDateTo] DateTime;
SELECT Orders.ShippedDate
  , Orders.OrderID
```

```
    , [Order Subtotals].Subtotal
    , Format([ShippedDate],"yyyy") AS [Year]
FROM Orders INNER JOIN [Order Subtotals]
    ON Orders.OrderID = [Order Subtotals].OrderID
WHERE (((Orders.ShippedDate) Is Not Null AND (Orders.ShippedDate)
    BETWEEN [ShipDateFrom] AND [ShipDateTo]));
```

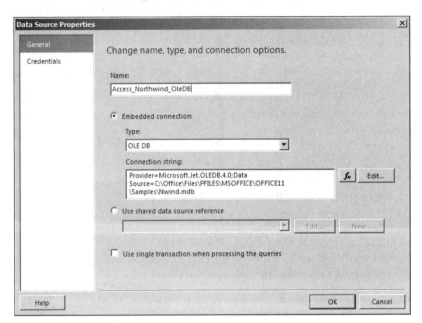

FIGURE 6-40

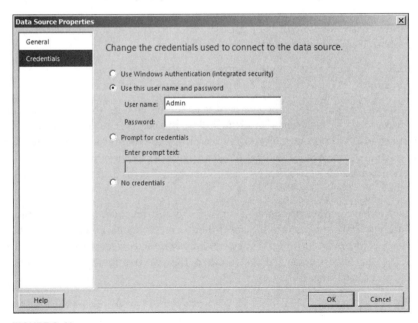

FIGURE 6-41

Even when the `ShipDateFrom` and `ShipDateTo` query parameters are mapped correctly to corresponding report parameters, the report runs with an error. If you are connecting via the JET OLE DB provider, it reports this error:

```
No value given for one or more required parameters.
```

If the Access ODBC driver is used, the native JET error is reported:

```
Too few parameters. Expected 2.
```

The easiest way I've found to work around the Access query parameterization issue is to build the query string using an expression rather than relying on this feature. It's not hard to do. The first step is to define the parameters in your report. When the report parameters are in place, they can be referenced in the dataset query expression. There is no need to define the parameters or any other properties of the dataset, because this will be handled in the expression.

Building a Query in a String Expression

This technique typically can be used when other options, such as using the Graphical Query Builder and defining query parameters, won't work in the Designer. Any expression may be used to build a text string and can include Visual Basic functions and custom code. The resulting string is simply presented to the database engine through the connection's data provider. No other parsing or processing is performed. The query expression must be entered using the generic Query Designer window for the dataset.

```
="SELECT Orders.ShippedDate, Orders.OrderID, [Order Subtotals].Subtotal,
ShippedDate "
  + "FROM Orders INNER JOIN [Order Subtotals] ON Orders.OrderID = [Order
Subtotals].OrderID "
  +
"WHERE Orders.ShippedDate Is Not Null AND Orders.ShippedDate BETWEEN #" +
Parameters!ShipDateFrom.Value + "# AND #" + Parameters!ShipDateTo.Value + "#"
```

Because this is a Visual Basic expression, double quotes are used to encapsulate literal text. Line breaks cannot be used without terminating and concatenating the string using the + or & character. Parameter values are concatenated into the query string with appropriate delimiters. The two parameter expressions refer to the parameters I defined in the report.

Note that this is an Access SQL query, rather than T-SQL. The pound character (#) is used to delimit dates, rather than single quotes.

Some variations of this technique can be useful to meet specific needs. Rather than building the entire query string in the dataset designer, you can call a custom Visual Basic function to do the work in programming code. Parameters could be passed to this function that returns the entire query.

An unfortunate side effect of using this expression query technique is that the dataset designer does not allow you to execute the query. If you need to make any changes to the query expression that will update the fields available to the report, you must convert the query back to a SQL expression (by removing the = and ' characters), execute the query, and update the Fields list using the Refresh button. Another option is to manually edit the Fields list.

I recommend that you paste the expression into Notepad, modify the expression in the dataset designer to update the Fields list, and then paste the expression back into the designer. This will save effort and give you an "undo" option if things don't go well.

Microsoft Excel

As a quick-and-easy data source, Excel is a great tool. I am continually amazed by the proliferation of Excel spreadsheets as production enterprise databases used in large businesses. Even at Microsoft, this practice is commonplace. I think this is mainly because business data comes from business people, and business people use Excel. I'll leave the data management and consolidation discussion for another time. The fact remains that a lot of important data exists in Excel files, and you can create reports to view this data as you would with any database system.

Figure 6-42 shows an Excel data source example. When connecting to Excel, you use the simple OLE DB connection type and then build a connection string that includes the JET OLE DB provider and the full path to the Excel document file. This currently works with XLS files and newer XLSX files.

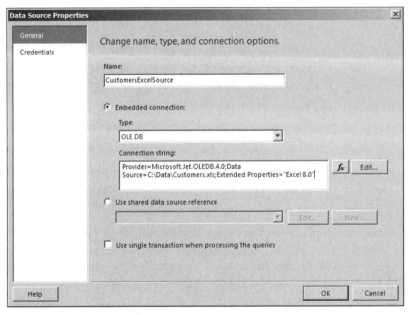

FIGURE 6-42

The dataset query text uses a simplified version of the SQL query language. The data provider treats a `Worksheet` object as if it were a table and `Worksheet` columns like table columns. The worksheet name is enclosed in square brackets and is followed by a dollar sign. The column names are derived from column header text in the first row, and any text containing spaces or other disallowed characters must be enclosed in square brackets:

```
SELECT
    CustomerID
```

```
      , CustomerName
      , [Street Address]
      , City
      , State
      , [Zip Code]
      , Phone
FROM [Sheet1$]
```

Oracle P/L SQL

Connecting reports to an Oracle database is quite easy. Depending on the version of Oracle and the Oracle client software, you can use the ODBC, Simple OLEDB, or native Oracle Client data providers. The native Oracle Client provider is preferred and is simple to use. When creating a data source, choose the Microsoft OLE DB Provider for Oracle; enter the server name and username and password required to log in to the Oracle database server.

Oracle PL/SQL is an ANSI-compliant dialect that is similar to Transact-SQL in most regards. Newer implementations use the ANSI join syntax rather than the =, *=, and =* syntax in the WHERE clause to denote joins. This style was popular until just a few years ago and is still used by many Oracle SQL query designers.

Oracle has a handful of data types that are equivalent to T-SQL types. Since Reporting Services uses the .NET data types used in Visual Basic .NET expressions, it's advisable to explicitly convert field values when they are used in expressions. Use the Visual Basic conversion functions (CStr(), CDbl(), CInt(), CDate(), CBool(), and so on) liberally.

The syntax for PL/SQL variables and parameters is quite different from T-SQL. Rather than being prefixed with an @, these items are prefixed with a colon (:). Variables used in a PL/SQL script may be assigned a value when they are declared. T-SQL doesn't allow this. Here is a brief example of a parameterized PL/SQL expression:

```
SELECT
      SL.STORE_CODE
    , SL.LOCATION_NAME
    , SL.TELEPHONE_NUMBER AS LOCATION_PHONE
FROM STORE_LOCATION SL
  INNER JOIN REGION R ON R.LOCATION_ID = SL.LOCATION_ID
WHERE SL.STORE_CODE = :STORE_CD
```

Testing for equality with a numeric type works as you would expect. However, character type comparisons may be performed using the LIKE operator. String concatenation is performed using double pipe symbol characters, rather than the plus sign used in T-SQL:

```
SELECT
      SL.STORE_CODE
    , SL.LOCATION_NAME
    , SL.TELEPHONE_NUMBER AS LOCATION_PHONE
FROM STORE_LOCATION SL
  INNER JOIN REGION R ON R.LOCATION_ID = SL.LOCATION_ID
WHERE SL. LOCATION_NAME LIKE '%' || UPPER(:STORE_NM) || '%'
```

Sybase Adaptive Server

Adaptive Server's query language is most similar to SQL Server because these products share some history. Like SQL Server, Sybase databases can implement stored procedures for modularized, more efficient query processing. Overall, I've found Adaptive Server to be fairly easy to use with Reporting Services, but it may require a little extra effort to prepare SQL queries. Simple queries can be written using the generic Query Designer. Stored procedures are executed using a string expression similar to the following example:

```
="spMonthEndSalesByCust
'" + Parameters!MonthEndDateMonth.Value, Parameters!monthEndDateYear.Value + "'"
```

Report parameters have some known minor data type incompatibilities. In particular, you may find it easier to use string-type parameters for dates rather than the native Date type. If you use date or numeric parameters, you may need to convert them in the query expression. Since SQL queries and stored procedure calls are assembled as a string expression, parameters need not be converted into explicit types. Type conversion is performed by the database engine.

The Report Server and development computer need to have the Sybase ASE OLE DB Provider installed and configured correctly. This enables you to create connections using the Microsoft Simple OLE DB Provider with the installed Sybase client components.

Federating Data Sources

I see this question on the Reporting Services MSDN forum occasionally. A user wants to combine data from multiple data sources or from different databases and join the unified data into a single report data region. Today this can be done using semantic models, which are discussed in Chapter 9. You can do this in a few different ways, but some of these options are more ideal than others.

It's true that you can combine the data from multiple data sources into a single report, but each data region gets its data from a single dataset. This means that to group data in a table, matrix, list, or chart, the data must come from a single query fed by one data source. Before you get too excited about this architectural restriction, you need to understand the bigger picture and then plan accordingly. You have a few ways to work with Reporting Services to combine data from more than one data source. These options include defining a linked server to connect and unify a foreign database connection from SQL Server, and using the OPENDATASOURCE or OPENROWSET system functions in a query. These functions enable you to specify remote databases and tables in a query. If the Report Designer has appropriate permissions to access remote objects, tables from different servers can be specified in the query. But the data is actually combined at the data source hosting the query before being returned to the Report Server. Because these queries can be complex to write and debug, it's often a good idea to create views or stored procedures on the database server to contain the script, rather than to promote the use of ad hoc federated queries in reports. Keep in mind that federating data inevitably comes with some added cost of query performance, increased network traffic, and security compromises.

The need to perform federated data source reporting is often a symptom of a greater business need that should be addressed at the solution level. When it becomes necessary to combine data from multiple sources for reporting and data analysis, this should help define the requirement for a central data warehouse with data fed from different sources at scheduled intervals.

BEST PRACTICES

➤ Use shared data sources to reuse the connection information. Data sources are not rede-
ployed to the server by default to preserve server settings. Remove the report and data source
file from the Report Server and redeploy to update connection information and certain report
metadata.

➤ When using complex query expressions, keep a copy of the last working query script in a
separate query tool window or in Notepad.

➤ When using an expression for a dataset (such as `="SELECT..."`), if changes are made to the
query expression, you may need to remove the string encapsulation characters from the text
to run the query. Make a point to execute the query and click the Refresh toolbar button
to update the report fields definition. After the fields metadata has been updated, make any
changes you like to the query text.

➤ Filter records in the query or stored procedure to reduce network traffic and reduce Report
Server processing overhead. Filter data in the report to reuse the same result set in an
improved response time for longer, interactive report sessions.

➤ Plan ahead and filter data consistently in the dataset, report item, or group.

➤ In MDX queries, add and configure parameters before making any manual changes to MDX
script. You cannot modify or view the query using the graphical MDX query designer after
making manual changes. Chapter 9 covers these options in greater detail.

SUMMARY

Defining data sources and datasets to manage data source queries is the starting point for almost
any data-driven report. It's essential to understand basic data storage and query architecture to
achieve the best design. Data can be filtered within the database server or in the report. Making the
correct choice and finding the best combination of these options will improve performance and provide flexibility with the least amount of overhead.

Defining shared data sources in your projects makes it much easier to maintain data connections for
all your reports as a group. Changing the database location or security credentials becomes a much
simpler proposition. The datasets for your reports define queries for retrieving data and may be used
as the source for the report and repeatable data regions or to provide data values for report parameters. Shared datasets can reduce the cost of writing queries and filtering logic in a similar way.

An ad hoc query expression is stored in the report within the report definition. A database view or
stored procedure is stored in the database on the database server. Using these database objects is
an effective way to process parameters and filter data before sending it to the report. Using a report
filter lets you reuse the data you've already retrieved. A combination of these parameterized filtering
techniques may be an optimal solution for more complex reporting needs.

By applying the skills and techniques you've learned in this chapter, you can start designing more
powerful and useful reports that consume and visualize the right data in the most appropriate way.

7

Advanced Report Design

WHAT'S IN THIS CHAPTER?

➤ Adding report and page headers and footers

➤ Using aggregate functions

➤ Adding group totals

➤ Creating report templates

➤ Creating composite reports

➤ Embedded formatting

➤ Designing master/detail reports

➤ Designing subreports

➤ Navigating reports and using actions

➤ Reporting on recursive data

The real power behind Reporting Services is its ability to creatively use data groups and combinations of report items and data regions. You can add calculations and conditional formatting by using simple programming code. Whether you are an application developer or a business report designer, this chapter contains important information to help you design reports to meet your users' requirements and to raise the bar with compelling report features.

This chapter covers the following topics:

➤ Advanced data grouping features

➤ Headers and aggregation

➤ Lists and data regions

➤ Links and drill-through reports

➤ Using custom code to extend formatting and apply business logic

➤ Advanced charting features

HEADERS AND FOOTERS

Page headers and footers can be configured so that they are displayed and printed on all pages or omitted from the first and/or last page. Unlike many other reporting tools, there is no designated report header or footer. This is because the report body acts as a header or footer, depending on where you place data region items. If you were to place a table an inch below the top of the report body, this would give you a report header 1 inch tall. And because there is no set limit to the number of data regions or other items you can add to a report (and you can force page breaks at any location), all the space above, below, and between these items is essentially header and footer space.

You have a lot of flexibility when displaying header and footer content. In addition to the standard report and page headers and footers, data region sections can be repeated on each page, creating additional page header and footer content. Figure 7-1 shows a table report with each of the header and footer areas labeled.

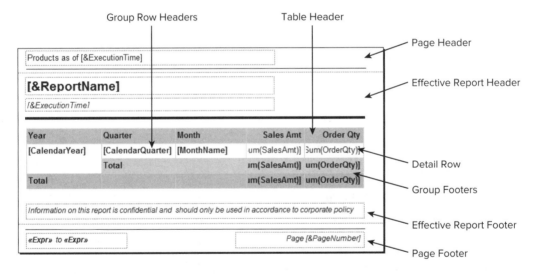

FIGURE 7-1

To make this report easier to view, I've shortened the page height on this report to 5 inches. Figure 7-2 shows the first rendered page of this report.

Note the page header containing the date at the top of this page, the repeated table header, and the table footer showing the continuation of the CategoryName group and then the page footer with the page number and page count.

In earlier versions of Reporting Services, you were restricted from placing fields in the page headers and footers. These areas were added to the final report output after the data was processed and before the rendering extension applied pagination. This restriction is no longer in place. As you can see, I am referring to the `CalendarYear` field in the page footer. You also have access to several resources, such as global variables, parameters, and report items.

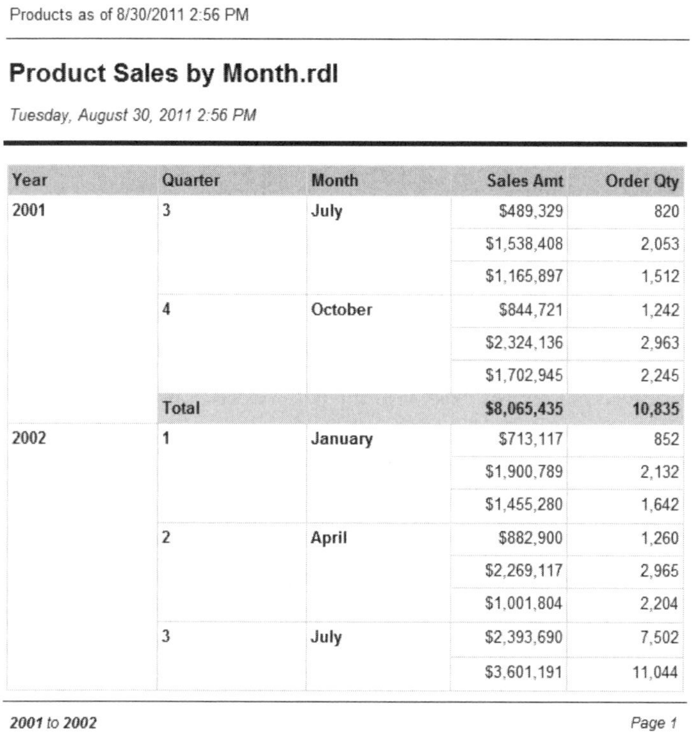

Products as of 8/30/2011 2:56 PM

Product Sales by Month.rdl

Tuesday, August 30, 2011 2:56 PM

Year	Quarter	Month	Sales Amt	Order Qty
2001	3	July	$489,329	820
			$1,538,408	2,053
			$1,165,897	1,512
	4	October	$844,721	1,242
			$2,324,136	2,963
			$1,702,945	2,245
	Total		$8,065,435	10,835
2002	1	January	$713,117	852
			$1,900,789	2,132
			$1,455,280	1,642
	2	April	$882,900	1,260
			$2,269,117	2,965
			$1,001,804	2,204
	3	July	$2,393,690	7,502
			$3,601,191	11,044

2001 to 2002   *Page 1*

FIGURE 7-2

The following are the steps used to design this report if you want to build it from scratch. The report in Design view is shown in Figure 7-3. You can also review the finished report in the Chapter 7 sample project and follow these steps to review the design:

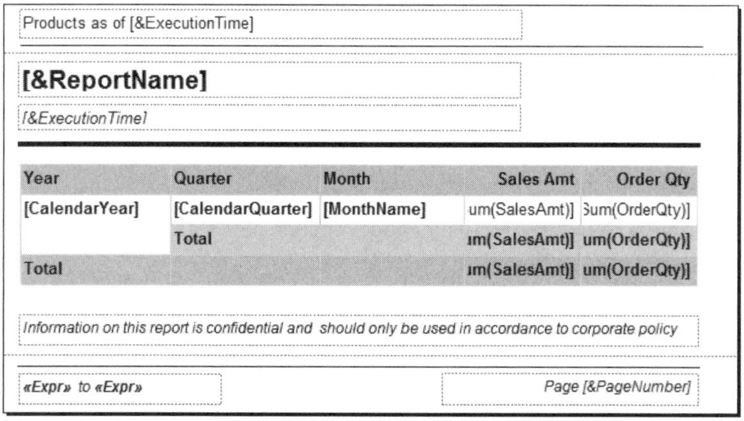

Products as of [&ExecutionTime]

[&ReportName]

[&ExecutionTime]

Year	Quarter	Month	Sales Amt	Order Qty
[CalendarYear]	[CalendarQuarter]	[MonthName]	um(SalesAmt)]	Sum(OrderQty)]
	Total		im(SalesAmt)]	um(OrderQty)]
Total			im(SalesAmt)]	um(OrderQty)]

Information on this report is confidential and should only be used in accordance to corporate policy

«Expr» to «Expr»   *Page [&PageNumber]*

FIGURE 7-3

1. Start with a new blank report. Add a data source to connect to the AdventureWorksDW_
    WroxSSRS2012 database.

2. Enable the page header and footer by selecting Report ⇨ Add Page Header and Report ⇨
    Add Page Footer while the report is open in Design view. Using the report properties, you
    can optionally omit the page header or footer from the first or last page of the report.

3. Now that the page header and footer are visible in the Report Designer, drag the Report
    Name built-in field from the Report Data pane into the header area. Drag the Execution
    Time built-in field to the page header, click in the new textbox, and then add the text
    Products as of and a space before the ExecutionTime field expression.

4. Add a line, and place it immediately below this textbox in the page header. Resize the page
    header area as needed.

5. Add a table to the report body about an inch or 2.5 cm from the top.

6. When prompted, create an embedded dataset based on the data source, and use the following
    query for the command text:

    ```
    SELECT * FROM vResellerSalesProdTerrDate
    ```

7. Close and save the Dataset Properties dialog.

8. From the Report Data pane, expand the dataset, and drag the MonthName field to the detail
    cell in the first column of the table.

9. Using the Row Groups pane below the report design window, edit the (Details) group
    properties, as shown in Figure 7-4.

FIGURE 7-4

10. Add a group using the MonthName field. See Figure 7-5.

11. On the Sorting page, sort the group by the MonthNumberOfYear field. Close the Group
    Properties dialog. See Figure 7-6.

12. Drag the CalendarYear field above the (Details) group to define a new top-level row group.

13. Drag and drop the CalendarQuarter field below the CalendarYear group to create a second
    row group.

14. Drag the SalesAmt and OrderQty fields into the detail cells to the right of the MonthName
    cell. Compare your report to Figures 7-5 and 7-6.

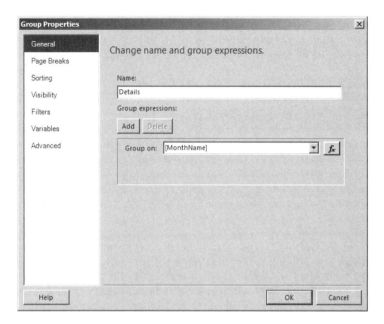

FIGURE 7-5

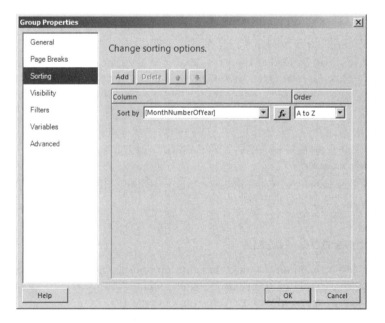

FIGURE 7-6

15. Totals are added from the Row Groups pane. Click the down arrow on the `CalendarYear` group and add a total after the group. Do the same for the `CalendarQuarter` group. Click the down arrow and choose Add Total ⇨ After, as shown in Figure 7-7.

FIGURE 7-7

The rest of the table design is up to you. Set the Format properties for the `SalesAmt` and `OrderQty` columns, as we did in Chapter 4. Change the font weight, background color, and add borders to the table rows and cells to suit your taste. Rather than giving specific directions, I encourage you to experiment with these attributes to find the best presentation. You can refer to Figure 7-3 or look at the finished report from the book downloads to match the style and formatting. I used a combination of `LightBlue` and `LightSteelBlue` for the table header and group total row background colors.

16. After the table in the report body, add a textbox with some static text: **Information on this report is confidential and should only be used in accordance to corporate policy**. This will serve as the report footer and will be displayed only once — on the last page, below the table.

The `CalendarYear` range I added to the left side of the page footer is an example that we will cover in greater detail later. You can omit this for now. You can add a variety of expressions and text to a page header or footer. Expressions and custom code are covered at length in Chapter 21.

17. From the list of Built-in fields in the Report Data pane, drag and drop the `PageNumber` to the right side of the page footer. Place the cursor to the left of the `PageNumber` placeholder and type **Page** followed by a space.

18. Add a horizontal line above the page number textbox spanning the width of the page footer. Compare the finished report to Figure 7-3.

Aggregate Functions and Totals

So far you've seen that if you drop a numeric field into a group or table footer cell, an expression is added applying the `SUM()` aggregate function. The Designer assumes that you will want to sum these values, but this function can be replaced with one of several others.

Reporting Services supports several aggregate functions, similar to those supported by the T-SQL query language (see Table 7-1). Each aggregate function accepts one or two arguments. The first is the field reference or expression to aggregate. The second, optional argument is the name of a dataset, report item, or group name to indicate the scope of the aggregation. If not provided, the scope of the current data region or group is assumed. For example, suppose a table contains two nested groups based on the Category and Subcategory fields. If you were to drag the `SalesAmount` field into the Subcategory group footer, the `SUM(SalesAmount)` expression would return the sum of all `SalesAmount` values within the scope of each distinct Subcategory group range.

TABLE 7-1

FUNCTION	DESCRIPTION
`AVG()`	The average of all non-null values.
`COUNT()`	The count of values.
`COUNTDISTINCT()`	The count of distinct values.
`COUNTROWS()`	The count of all rows.
`FIRST()`	Returns the first value for a range of values.
`LAST()`	Returns the last value for a range of values.
`MAX()`	Returns the greatest value for a range of values.
`MIN()`	Returns the least value for a range of values.
`STDEV()`	Returns the standard deviation.
`STDEVP()`	Returns the population standard deviation.
`SUM()`	Returns a sum of all values.
`VAR()`	Returns the variance of all values.
`VARP()`	Returns the population variance of all values.

In addition to the aggregate functions, some special-purpose functions behave in a similar way to aggregates but have special features for reports, as shown in Table 7-2.

TABLE 7-2

FUNCTION	DESCRIPTION
`LEVEL()`	Returns an integer value for the group level within a recursive hierarchy. The group name is required.
`ROWNUMBER()`	Returns the row number for a group or range.
`RUNNINGVALUE()`	Returns an accumulative aggregation up to this row.

Examples of aggregate function expressions and recursive levels are found in the following sections for table and matrix report items. Refer to Chapter 21 to learn more about expressions and custom code.

Adding Totals to a Table or Matrix Report

Because the matrix and table data regions are both based on the tablix data region, design techniques work the same way for both of these report types. Adding a total to a row group adds a new row that applies an aggregate function to all the members of *that* group. The same applies to a total added to a matrix column group. If you think about this, you're actually adding a total that applies to the *parent* of the group. Consider this example: Suppose columns are grouped by quarter and then by year. If you were to add a total to the Quarter column group, the total would be for all the quarters adding into the year. This means that a total applied to the topmost group will always return the grand total for all records in the data region. We've included a report with the samples to help make this point. Figure 7-8 shows a simple example.

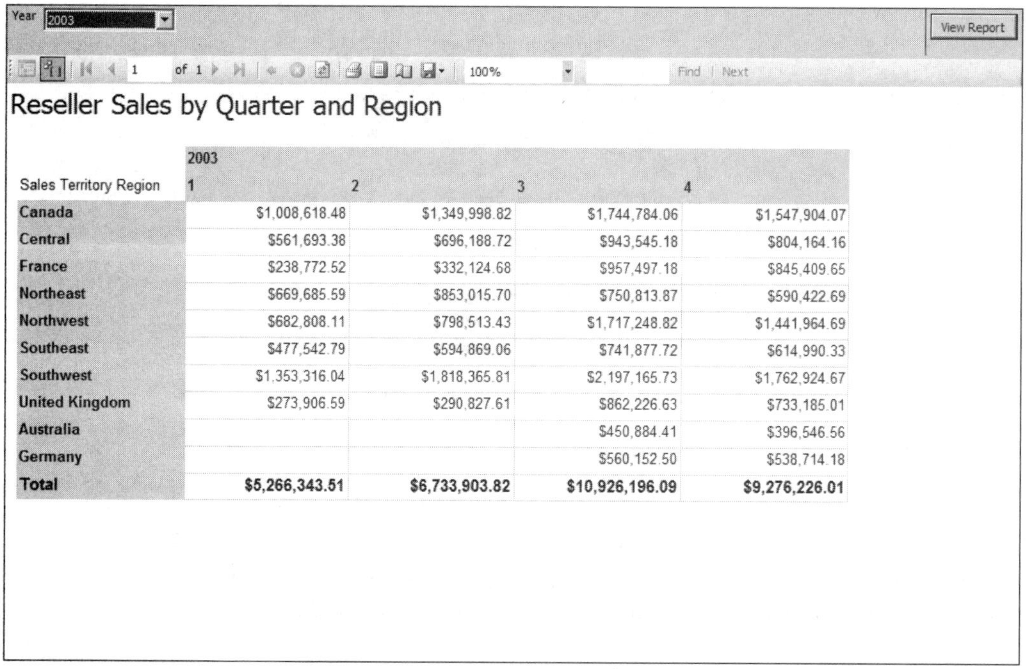

Sales Territory Region	2003			
	1	2	3	4
Canada	$1,008,618.48	$1,349,998.82	$1,744,784.06	$1,547,904.07
Central	$561,693.38	$696,188.72	$943,545.18	$804,164.16
France	$238,772.52	$332,124.68	$957,497.18	$845,409.65
Northeast	$669,685.59	$853,015.70	$750,813.87	$590,422.69
Northwest	$682,808.11	$798,513.43	$1,717,248.82	$1,441,964.69
Southeast	$477,542.79	$594,869.06	$741,877.72	$614,990.33
Southwest	$1,353,316.04	$1,818,365.81	$2,197,165.73	$1,762,924.67
United Kingdom	$273,906.59	$290,827.61	$862,226.63	$733,185.01
Australia			$450,884.41	$396,546.56
Germany			$560,152.50	$538,714.18
Total	**$5,266,343.51**	**$6,733,903.82**	**$10,926,196.09**	**$9,276,226.01**

FIGURE 7-8

Adding a total to a group displays total values for all fields in the data area of the matrix. Because this matrix contains only the SalesAmount field, this is the value that is totaled. If the objective is to define a total for all CalendarYear group values (the top-level column group), this will essentially be a grand total for all rows. Defining a total for a group at a lower level would create a subtotal break. Totals can be placed before or after group values. For a column group, adding totals after the group inserts a total column to the right of the group. Inserting a total before the group places totals to the left of the group columns.

In the earlier exercise, you added a total to the row group. Totals can also be added using the right-click menu for a group header cell. Figure 7-9 shows how this is done for a matrix column group header.

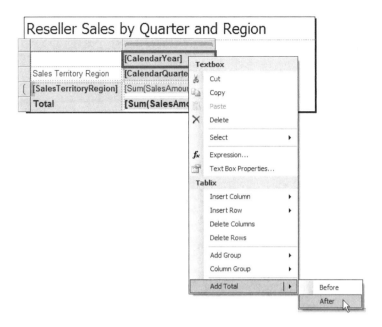

FIGURE 7-9

The new column is added to the right of the CalendarYear and the associated cells. By default, group totals are aggregated like the data cells in the same group, using a sum in this case. Because each total cell has its own expression, different aggregate functions can be used in each cell or total. For example, the expression [Sum(SalesAmount)] could be modified to use the AVG() function. In Figure 7-10, detail cells are summed, and the column total cells are averaged. Figure 7-11 previews the report after this design change.

	[CalendarYear]	Avg Amt
Sales Territory Region	[CalendarQuarter]	
[SalesTerritoryRegion]	[Sum(SalesAmount)]	[Avg(SalesAmo
Total	**[Sum(SalesAmount)]**	**[Avg(SalesAr**

FIGURE 7-10

Groups, headers, footers, and totals are all related design elements that can take a simple report to the next level and provide significant value. In the book download samples, we've included another version of this report for you to analyze. It demonstrates a more complex matrix report with row and column totals at a few more levels.

Groups are an essential design concept and a number of more advanced capabilities have been added as Reporting Services has evolved through newer versions. At the group level, you can now conditionally control things like page breaks and page numbers. After you've mastered the basics, go back and take a close look at the group properties in the Properties Window. There you will find several useful features. For more specific examples of these and other related group features, check out the sample downloads on the Wrox.com site for the book titled "Microsoft SQL Server Reporting Services Recipes for Designing Expert Reports."

Reseller Sales by Quarter and Region

Sales Territory Region	2003 1	2	3	4	Avg Amt
Canada	$1,008,618.48	$1,349,998.82	$1,744,784.06	$1,547,904.07	$1,412,826.36
Central	$561,693.38	$696,188.72	$943,545.18	$804,164.16	$751,397.86
France	$238,772.52	$332,124.68	$957,497.18	$845,409.65	$593,451.01
Northeast	$669,685.59	$853,015.70	$750,813.87	$590,422.69	$715,984.46
Northwest	$682,808.11	$798,513.43	$1,717,248.82	$1,441,964.69	$1,160,133.76
Southeast	$477,542.79	$594,869.06	$741,877.72	$614,990.33	$607,319.97
Southwest	$1,353,316.04	$1,818,365.81	$2,197,165.73	$1,762,924.67	$1,782,943.06
United Kingdom	$273,906.59	$290,827.61	$862,226.63	$733,185.01	$540,036.46
Australia			$450,884.41	$396,546.56	$423,715.48
Germany			$560,152.50	$538,714.18	$549,433.34
Total	$5,266,343.51	$6,733,903.82	$10,926,196.09	$9,276,226.01	$894,518.60

FIGURE 7-11

CREATING REPORT TEMPLATES

When you choose to create a report from the Solution Explorer or File menu in SSDT, the new RDL file is actually copied from a selected template. A template is really nothing more than a partially completed report file. You can add your own report templates to the SSDT report project template items folder. The default installation path for this folder is `C:\Program Files (x86)\Microsoft Visual Studio 10.0\Common7\IDE\PrivateAssemblies\ProjectItems\ReportProject`.

Simply design a report with any settings, items, and formatting you want to use as a starting point for new reports, and save the RDL file to this location.

 On new consulting projects, I typically create a new report with page headers and footers, built-in fields such as page numbers, standard titles, borders, colors, and background images to match the client's UI standards. I add the company logo and save a portrait and landscape page orientation version of the report to the templates folder. I typically don't add a dataset or any data-bound data region items to the template.

Figure 7-12 shows a simple example. This report contains a page header and footer with tiled background images and some standard built-in fields and titles. The report header contains our company logo image and a textbox with the formatted report execution date and time. The report page size height and width properties are set for a portrait and landscape version of this file.

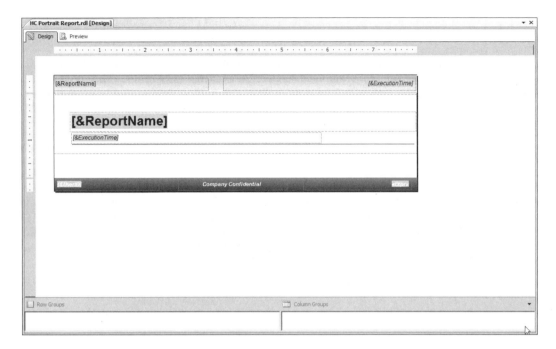

FIGURE 7-12

To make these templates available for future report design, copy them to the project template items folder. To use the templates, right-click the Reports folder in Solution Explorer and choose Add ➪ New Item. When the Add New Item dialog opens, the new report templates are available as a starting point for all new reports.

CREATING COMPOSITE REPORTS

This section shows you how to build more capable reporting interfaces by combining data regions and other report items.

As a product like Reporting Services matures, it will inevitably become easier to use. Compared to prior versions, it's much easier to design a report by simply dragging and dropping objects onto the design surface. To design more advanced reports, you often need to work with objects at a lower level and to understand their core architecture, rather than relying so much on the simplified design tools.

Before you begin building bigger, better, and more sophisticated reports, let's go back to the basics and take a closer look at a few of the fundamental report design components in more detail.

Anatomy of a Textbox

The textbox is one of the most fundamental and common report items. Generally, all text and data values are displayed using textboxes. The cells of a table and matrix contain individual textboxes. In addition to the text displayed, several useful properties manage the placement, style, and presentation of data. The `Font`, `Color`, `BackGroundColor`, and `BackGroundImage` properties make it possible to dress up your report data with tremendous flexibility.

The `BorderStyle` properties of a textbox are similar to those of other report items (such as a rectangle, list, table, and matrix). Once you have mastered the textbox properties, you should be able to use these other items in much the same way. With a table, group separation lines are created by setting the border properties for textboxes in header and footer rows (typically by selecting the entire row and setting the textbox properties as a group).

Three property groups are used for borders. In the Properties window, these groups are expanded using the plus sign (+) icon to reveal individual properties. The group summary text can actually be manipulated without expanding the properties, but it's usually easier to work with specific property values. The `BorderColor`, `BorderStyle`, and `BorderWidth` properties each contain a `Default` value that applies to individual properties (`Left`, `Right`, `Top`, and `Bottom`) that have not otherwise been set. This provides a means to set general properties and then override the exceptions. By default, a textbox has a black `BorderColor` and a 1-point `BorderWidth`, with the `BoderStyle` set to `None`. To add a border to all four sides, simply set the Default `BorderStyle` to `Solid`. Beyond this, you may use individual properties to add more creative border effects. Figure 7-13 shows a textbox with border styles.

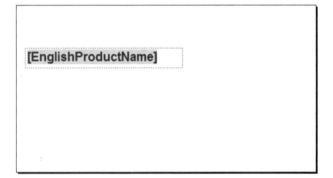

FIGURE 7-13

Padding and Indenting

Most report items support padding properties, which are used to offset the placement of text and other related content within the item. Padding is specified in points. A unit of measure from the printing industry, a *PostScript point* is 1/72nd of an inch, or approximately 1/28th of a centimeter.

Figure 7-14 shows the four padding properties, in the Padding group of the Properties pane, applied to all textbox items. The Padding properties provide an offset between

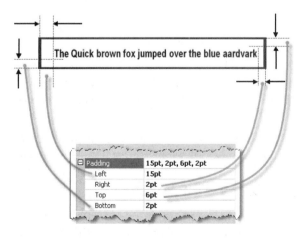

FIGURE 7-14

textbox borders and the contained text. This can be used to indent text and provide an appropriate balance of white space.

Three similar properties provide more flexibility for text indentation. You can use the `HangingIndent`, `LeftIndent`, and `RightIndent` properties to control paragraph-style text in rich-formatted textboxes. These properties also enable the new Word rendering extension to apply hanging, static text indentations.

Embedded Formatting

This feature allows the text in a textbox to be structured and formatted, much like a document or web page. Textboxes support two modes: a single-value expression or a range of text containing multiple expression placeholders.

To format a range of text, simply highlight the text in the textbox and use the toolbar or Properties window to set properties for the selected text. Figure 7-15 shows a range of highlighted text with the `HangingIndent` and `LeftIndent` properties set to 18 points and 12 points, respectively. Note that certain keywords and phrases within the text are also set using bold and italic. Some title text has also been isolated with bold and larger fonts.

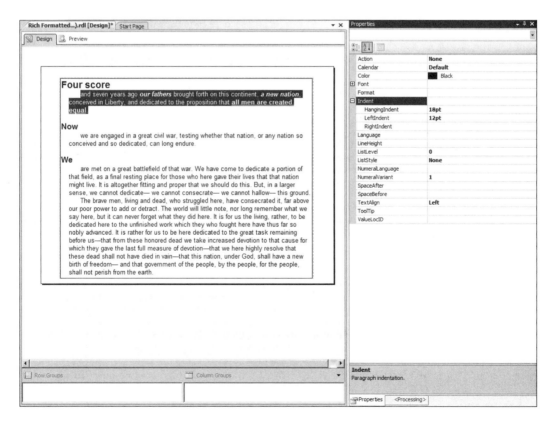

FIGURE 7-15

Embedded HTML Formatting

Another option is to embed simple HTML tags within text. This provides a great deal of flexibility for using expressions or custom code to return formatted text. The HTML tags listed in Table 7-3 are supported.

TABLE 7-3

TAG	DESCRIPTION
`<A>`	Anchor. For example: `<A href="http://www.somesite.com"> Click Here</A>`
`<FONT>`	Sets font attributes for a group of text. Used with the attributes `color`, `face`, `point size`, `size`, and `weight`. For example: `<FONT color="Blue" face="Arial" size="6">Hello</FONT>`
`<H1>`, `<H2>`, `<H3>`, `<H4>`, ...	Headings.
`<SPAN>`	Used to set text attributes for a range of text within a paragraph.
`<DIV>`	Used to set text attributes for a block of text.
`<P>`	Paragraph break.
` `	Line break.
`<LI>`	List new line.
`<B>`	Bold.
`<I>`	Italic.
`<U>`	Underscore.
`<S>`	Strikeout.
`<OL>`	Ordered list.
`<UL>`	Unordered list.

Figure 7-16 shows a textbox with text containing embedded HTML tags. This text can also be stored in a database table and bound to the textbox using a `Dataset` field.

When you use static text, rather than text fed from a dataset, you must set one more property — `MarkupType`. Highlight the text containing the embedded HTML tags, right-click, and choose Text Properties. In the Text Properties dialog, on the General page, set the Markup type property to the selection shown in Figure 7-17, "HTML - Interpret HTML tags as styles."

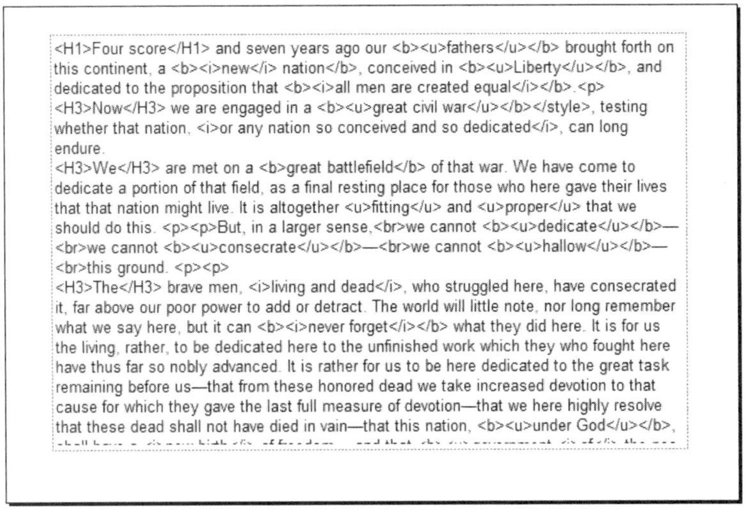
<H1>Four score</H1> and seven years ago our <b><u>fathers</u></b> brought forth on this continent, a <b><i>new</i> nation</b>, conceived in <b><u>Liberty</u></b>, and dedicated to the proposition that <b><i>all men are created equal</i></b>.<p>
<H3>Now</H3> we are engaged in a <b><u>great civil war</u></b></style>, testing whether that nation, <i>or any nation so conceived and so dedicated</i>, can long endure.
<H3>We</H3> are met on a <b>great battlefield</b> of that war. We have come to dedicate a portion of that field, as a final resting place for those who here gave their lives that that nation might live. It is altogether <u>fitting</u> and <u>proper</u> that we should do this. <p><p>But, in a larger sense,
we cannot <b><u>dedicate</u></b>—
we cannot <b><u>consecrate</u></b>—
we cannot <b><u>hallow</u></b>—
this ground. <p><p>
<H3>The</H3> brave men, <i>living and dead</i>, who struggled here, have consecrated it, far above our poor power to add or detract. The world will little note, nor long remember what we say here, but it can <b><i>never forget</i></b> what they did here. It is for us the living, rather, to be dedicated here to the unfinished work which they who fought here have thus far so nobly advanced. It is rather for us to be here dedicated to the great task remaining before us—that from these honored dead we take increased devotion to that cause for which they gave the last full measure of devotion—that we here highly resolve that these dead shall not have died in vain—that this nation, <b><u>under God</u></b>,

FIGURE 7-16

Text Properties
General
Action
Alignment
Font
Change markup options.
Tooltip:
Markup type
None - Plain text only
HTML - Interpret HTML tags as styles
Help
OK
Cancel

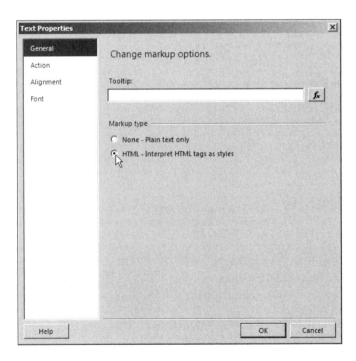

FIGURE 7-17

Figure 7-18 shows the output for the rendered report.

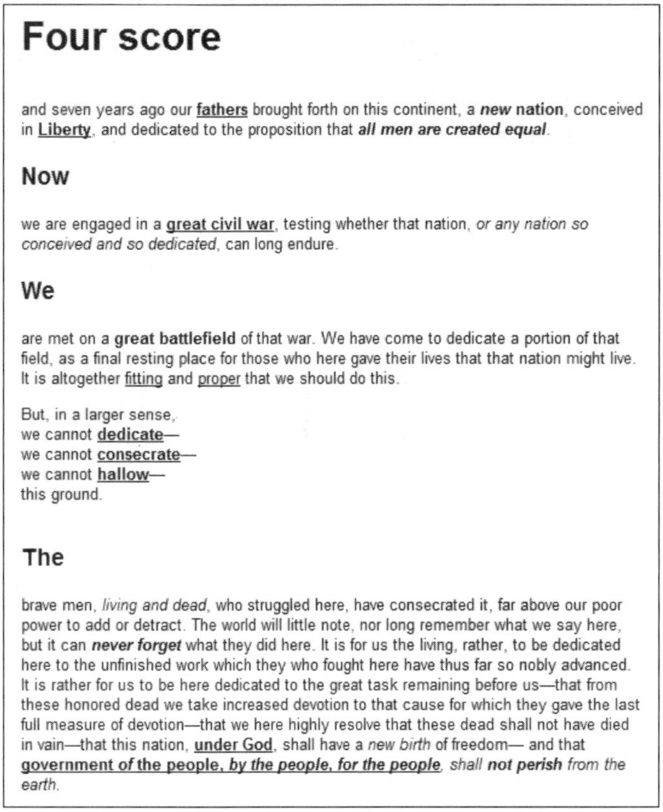

FIGURE 7-18

Designing Master/Detail Reports

Most data can be expressed in a hierarchal fashion. Whether data is stored in related tables in a relational database, as dimensional hierarchies in a cube structure, or as separate spreadsheets or files, this information can usually be organized into different levels. This is often a natural way to present information for reporting. Common examples of master/detail data include invoices and line items, customers and orders, regions and sales, categories and products, colors and sizes, and managers and workers.

The best way to organize this data in a master/detail report depends largely on how your users want to see the data visualized. For each master record, details may be presented in a rigid tabular or spreadsheet-like form or in free-forum layout with elements of different sizes and shapes placed at various locations within a repeating section. And, of course, details may also be expressed visually using charts, icons, and gauges.

The last consideration for master/detail report design is whether the data source for the master records and detail records can be combined into a single data stream. If records exist in different tables in the same database, this is a simple matter of joining tables using a query. If the records can't be combined in a query or view, the two result sets should expose the fields necessary to join them, and a subreport can be used. This section about composite reports explores techniques for combining data ranges to filter a single dataset and then uses subreports to combine two separate data sources.

Groups and Dataset Scope

One of the fundamental reasons that composite reports work — and are relatively easy to construct — is the principle of dataset scope. The term *scope* refers to the portion of data from a dataset that is available within a group. When a data region, such as a table, list, or matrix, is rendered, the data is sectioned into the subranges according to a group definition. Any report items or data region items placed in a grouped area, header, or footer are visible only to the data currently in scope. This means that if a table, for example, has a group based on the ProductCategory field and another table is placed in the group header, a table is rendered for each distinct ProductCategory value. Each table instance "sees" a range of detail records filtered by this group value. This can be an incredibly powerful feature, because there is no stated limit on how many items can be embedded within a group; nor is there a limit on group levels and nested embedded data regions. With that said, we have found it impractical to embed several data regions to create overly complex reports.

In this section, we will apply this principle of group embedded data regions for each data region container. This includes the list, table, and matrix.

Using a List to Combine Report Items and Data Regions

The list item is the simplest of all data regions. Like the table and matrix, a list is an implementation of the tablix report item with certain properties preset to provide the list behavior. It contains one cell with no headers or footers, and, instead of a textbox, it contains an embedded rectangle item. This allows other report items to be dragged and dropped anywhere within the list area.

 We've created a report called Product Cost and List Price — List. You can open and review this report in the Chapter 7 project as you learn how it was created.

One list visually represents one group, and the body of the list is simply repeated for each underlying data row. Using the properties for the list, it is associated with a dataset. After you place a list item on the report, fields dragged from a dataset in the Report Data pane bind the list to the dataset and create data-bound textboxes. Figure 7-19 shows formatted textboxes used for labels and values, and a line used as a row separator. The textbox on the right contains an expression to calculate a product's profit margin by subtracting the StandardCost from the ListPrice field values.

Like most report items, you may set properties for the list using the standard Properties window or the custom Properties dialog.

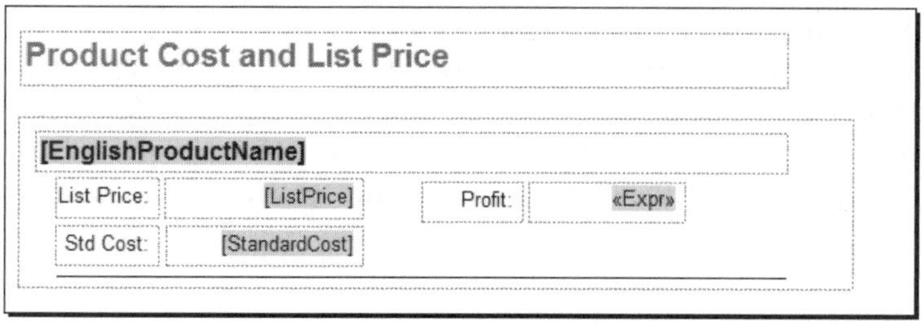

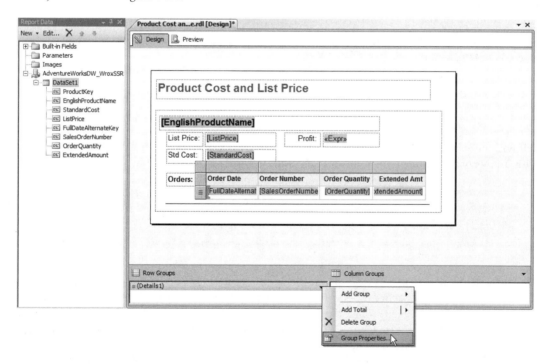

FIGURE 7-19

We've already defined a dataset for this report. The `DataSetName` property for the list was set when we dragged a field from this dataset into the list item in the Report Designer. We'll set the Grouping in the next step.

Note that a list contains a details group by default, but this needs to be set up to group on a distinct field value. This is usually a field with redundant values so that each group contains multiple detail rows.

Click the drop-down list on the (Details1) Row Groups and choose Group Properties from the menu, as shown in Figure 7-20.

FIGURE 7-20

In the Group Properties dialog, shown in Figure 7-21, add a group expression, and select the `EnglishProductName` field in the "Group on" row. Click OK to save this setting.

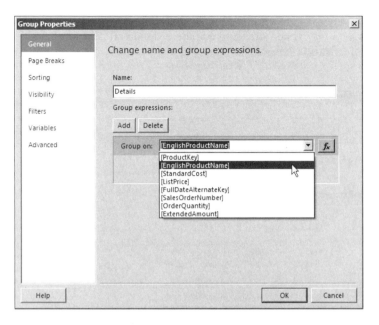

FIGURE 7-21

Figure 7-22 shows what the report looks like in preview.

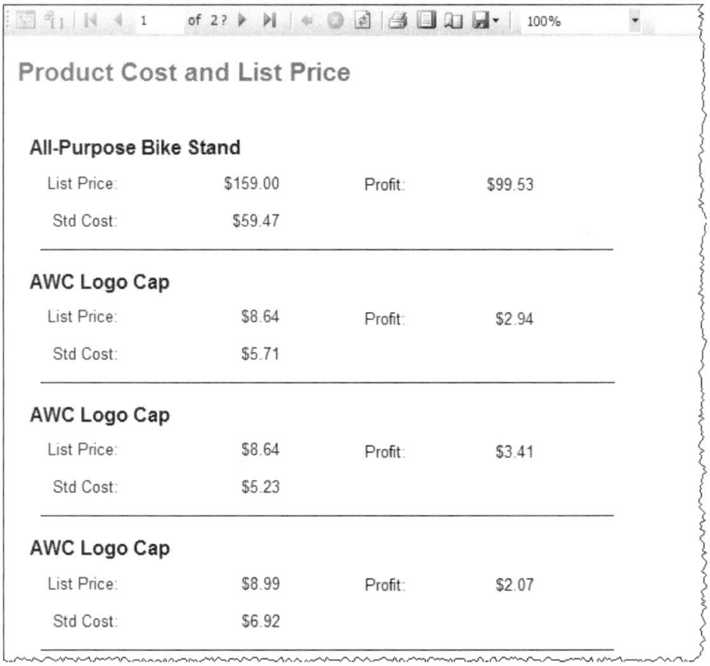

FIGURE 7-22

For each product, I want to see the related orders. To do this, I expand the list height to make some room, and add a table within the list area. Then I drag appropriate order detail fields to the table. Figure 7-23 shows this table and the fields we've added.

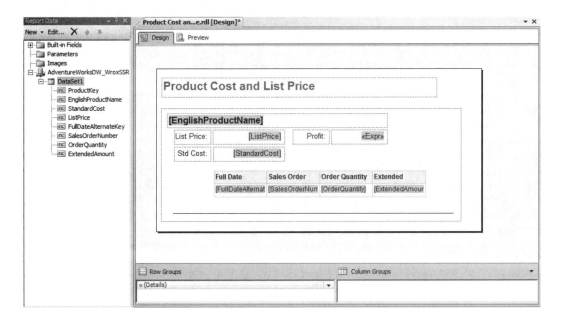

FIGURE 7-23

A finished copy of the following report in the sample project is named Product Cost and List Price — Embedded Table.

When previewed, this report shows order detail in a table below each product-detail section, as shown in Figure 7-24.

To demonstrate how the list can be used as a container for other data range items, we've added a chart item to the list in place of the table. Because the list contains a detail group that returns only one record at a time and the chart is configured to recognize this parent group, the chart has visibility to this level of detail. In other words, each instance of the chart sees only one product record.

Data fields (or data point fields) are dropped into or selected in the drop zone at the top of the chart. If a pie chart has a Series Axis expression (drop zone to the right), multiple pie slices are rendered for each distinct group value. Because this chart has no series value, two fields will result in two slices: one for the StandardCost and another for the ListPrice field value. You'll learn more about configuring this chart later in this chapter.

Figure 7-25 shows the finished sample report, named Product Cost and List Price — Embedded Chart.

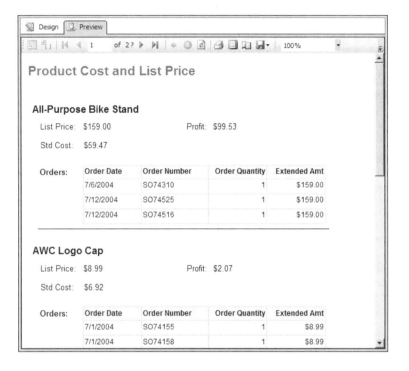

FIGURE 7-24

FIGURE 7-25

Figure 7-26 shows this report in preview. Each row of the report displays a pie chart with the calculated profit as a percentage of the ListPrice field value.

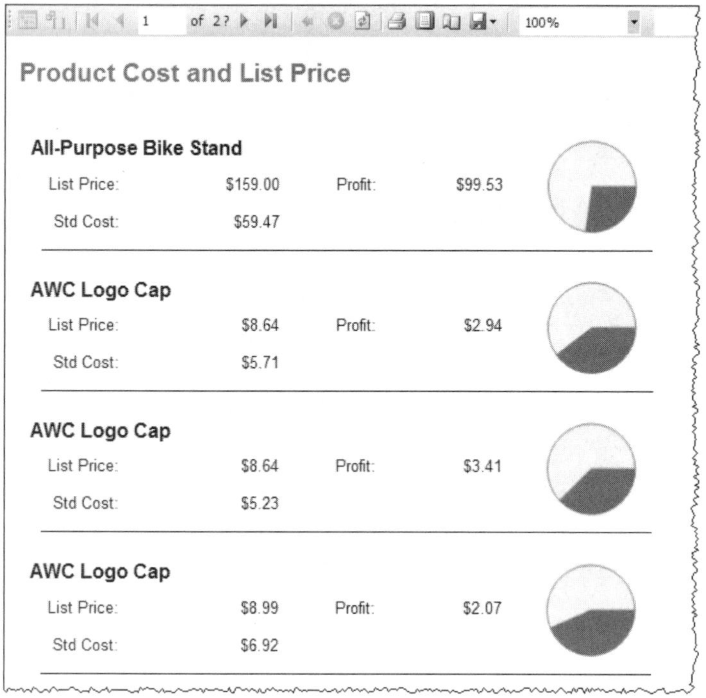

FIGURE 7-26

Now the best of both worlds: the sample report named Product Cost and List Price — Embedded Table and Chart contains both the table and the chart. Figure 7-27 shows it in preview.

The list item works well when repeating graphical items such as images and charts. Although the list offers a great deal of flexibility, it can require quite a lot of detail work if used for complex columnar reports and those with multiple levels of grouping. Consider using a table instead of a list when all the data fits into rows and columns.

The next couple of reports, showing a chart embedded in a table and a matrix, are created using the same basic pattern, so we need not go over the design details. These are included in the sample project. The report shown in Figure 7-28 is a table report grouped on Fiscal Year and then Fiscal Quarter. You cannot have an embedded object within a details group, so we removed the details group in the Row Groups pane. The chart is dragged into an empty cell. With the details group removed, the SalesAmount and the embedded chart are in the scope of the lowest-level table group (which is the Fiscal Quarter).

As you can see, the chart category axis is grouping on the product category field with a single data point based on the sales quantity field. Each instance of the table shows the isolated sales quantities across each product category for a specific fiscal quarter.

FIGURE 7-27

FIGURE 7-28

A chart can also be placed in a matrix group in the same manner. The Product Category Sales Profile by Year and Region report (shown in Figure 7-29) has a column group defined on the `SalesTerritoryGroup` field. Because columns are rendered for each distinct group value, the chart is repeated in each column group, and the scope of the chart is for a combination of fiscal quarter and sales territory group.

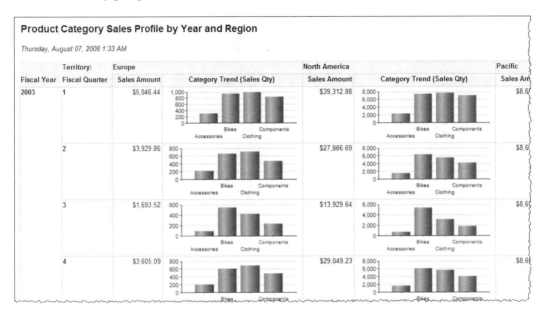

FIGURE 7-29

In summary, data region objects (such as charts, tables, and matrices) can be embedded within other data region groups, as long as the data is served from a single dataset.

DESIGNING SUBREPORTS

The concept of a subreport isn't new. In fact, most reporting tools offer this feature, and the Reporting Services implementation of subreports is not much different from tools such as Microsoft Access and Crystal Reports. Before getting into the details of subreport design, let's review some basic guidelines.

When I started using Reporting Services to design reports with nested groups and data regions, my first impulse was to use subreports. This seemed like the best approach because I could design simple, modular reports and then put them together. The programming world promotes the notion of reusable objects. However, the downside of this approach is that subreports can create some challenges for the report rendering engine, resulting in formatting issues and poorer performance. In SQL Server 2000 and 2005, subreports didn't render in Excel. Improvements have been made for Excel rendering, but I'm not quite ready to dismiss my bias and recommend the use of subreports in all cases. When using subreports, carefully test the report to be sure that it will render in the target format.

The bottom line is that subreports are useful for implementing a variety of design patterns, but they are not a cure-all. If you can design a report by embedding data regions into a list, table, or matrix, you may get better results than if you use a subreport to do the same thing.

A *subreport* is a stand-alone report that is embedded into another report. It can be independent, with its own dataset, or, using parameters, you can link the contents of a subreport to data in the main report.

There are some limitations to the content and formatting that can be rendered within a subreport. For example, a multicolumn report may not be possible within a subreport (depending on the rendering format used). If you plan to use multiple columns in a subreport, test your report with the rendering formats you plan to use.

Subreports generally have two uses. The first is for embedding one instance of a separate report into the body of another report with an unassociated data source. The other scenario involves using the subreport as a custom data region to display repeated master and detail records in the body of the main report. From a design standpoint, this makes perfect sense. Using a subreport allows you to separate two related datasets and perhaps even data sources, linked as you would join tables in a SQL query. It allows you to reuse an existing report so that you don't have to redesign functionality you've already created. However, there may be a significant downside. If the master report will consume more than just a few records, this means that the subreport must execute its query and render the content many times. For large volumes of data, this can prove to be an inefficient solution. Carefully reconsider the use of subreports with large result sets. It may be more efficient to construct one larger report with a more complex query and multiple levels of grouping, rather than assume the cost of executing a query many times. I rarely use subreports in standard reporting scenarios. If I do, the main report is limited to one or a few records.

A subreport can be linked to the main report using a correlated parameter and field reference so that it can be used like a data region, but this is not essential. A subreport could be used to show aggregated values unrelated to groupings or content in the rest of the report.

Creating a subreport is like creating any other report. You simply create a report and then add it to another report as a subreport. If you intend to use the main report and subreport as a Master/Detail view of related data, the subreport should expose a parameter that can be *linked* to a field in the main report. In the following walk-through, you'll build a simple report that lists products and exposes a subcategory parameter. The main report will list categories and subcategories, and the product list report will then be used as a data region, like a table or list in previous examples.

Federating Data with a Subreport

When the data source for a master data region is different from the data source for detail records, using a subreport can be just the ticket for creating a master/detail report. The following example combines report data from two different data sources.

In the sample project, you will find two reports named Product Details and Product Orders Subreport. The Product Details report contains a list whose data source is the data-warehouse database: AdventureWorksDW_WroxSSRS2012. The Product Orders Subreport contains a table with a data source based on the OLTP database: Adventure Works DW Multidimensional_WroxSSRS2012. Records in the DimProduct table, located in the AdventureWorksDW_WroxSSRS2012 database, can be related using the `ProductAlternateKey` column. This contains `ProductNumber` values from the Product table in the AdventureWorksDW_WroxSSRS2012 database.

Figure 7-30 shows the Product Orders Subreport in the Designer. This report is simply a table bound to the following query. The data source for this dataset is the AdventureWorksDW_WroxSSRS2012 transactional database.

```
SELECT
     Sales.SalesOrderDetail.ProductID
   , Production.Product.ProductNumber
   , Sales.SalesOrderDetail.OrderQty
   , Sales.SalesOrderDetail.LineTotal
   , Sales.SalesOrderHeader.OrderDate
FROM
     Sales.SalesOrderDetail
     INNER JOIN Sales.SalesOrderHeader
     ON Sales.SalesOrderDetail.SalesOrderID = Sales.SalesOrderHeader.SalesOrderID
     INNER JOIN Production.Product ON Sales.SalesOrderDetail.ProductID =
Production.Product.ProductID
WHERE
     Product.ProductNumber = @ProductNumber
ORDER BY Sales.SalesOrderHeader.OrderDate
```

The actual query in the sample report limits records to a small date range to keep the number of records manageable. This isn't relevant to the example, so I've simplified the query script shown here.

Note the `ProductNumber` parameter, which will be passed from the master report. Each instance of this report will be filtered for a specific product.

The master report is shown in Figure 7-31. This report contains a list data region that is bound to the following query and whose data source is the AdventureWorksDW_WroxSSRS2012 data warehouse database:

```
SELECT
     ProductKey
   , ProductAlternateKey
   , EnglishProductName
   , StandardCost
   , ListPrice
FROM   DimProduct
WHERE  (StandardCost IS NOT NULL) AND (ListPrice IS NOT NULL)
ORDER BY EnglishProductName
```

The WHERE clause criterion is included to simplify the example; it may be omitted in production.

The details group for the list is set to the `EnglishProductName` field. This satisfies the requirement that, for a data range to contain a nested data range object, it must have a group defined. You create the subreport by dragging and dropping the Product Orders Subreport report from the Solution Explorer into the list area.

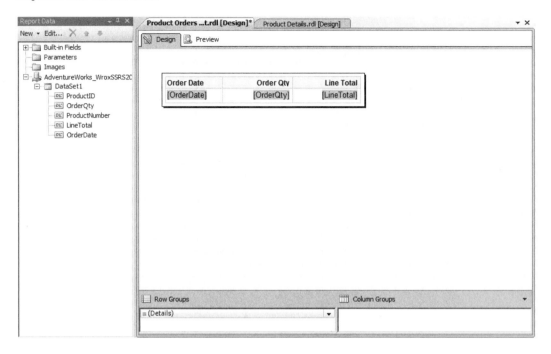

FIGURE 7-30

Note that regardless of the dimensions of a subreport at design time, when dropped into a containing report, it always appears as a square area that usually takes up more design space than necessary (which also expands the dimensions of its container). After resizing the subreport, I also had to resize the list to appear as it does in Figure 7-31.

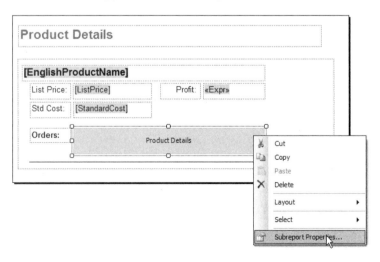

FIGURE 7-31

Right-click the subreport and choose Subreport Properties to set the parameter/field mapping, as shown in Figure 7-31. The Subreport Properties dialog, shown in Figure 7-32, is used to map a field in the container report to a parameter in the subreport.

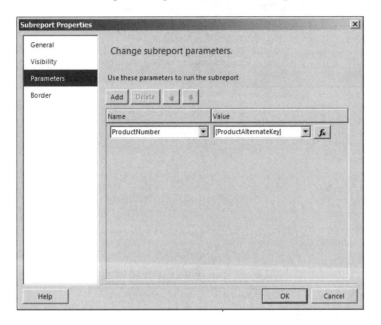

FIGURE 7-32

Navigate to the Parameters page, and then click Add to define a parameter mapping. Under the Name column, select the ProductNumber parameter. Under the Value column, select the ProductAlternateKey field. Click OK to save these changes and close the Subreport Properties dialog.

This completes the report design. Using lists and subreports typically makes the design process more ad hoc and artful than when you use more rigid tables. Go back and check the size and placement of items so that they fit neatly within the subreport space. You often have to go through a few iterations of preview and layout to make the appropriate adjustments.

At this point, you should be able to preview the report and see the nested table/subreport, as shown in Figure 7-33.

Execution and Resource Implications

There is no doubt that subreports enable you to do some things you can't do with any other report design technique. But to help you appreciate the ugly side of subreports, let's run a trace using SQL Server Profiler to compare the embedded table report we just created to this subreport. Let's see how many queries run on the server and how individual connections are required. We'll start the Profiler trace and then run the Product Cost and List Price — Embedded Table report.

Figure 7-34 shows the trace results. As you can see, after the initial session start-up, only one query runs. (Each query will have a BatchStarting and BatchCompleted event.)

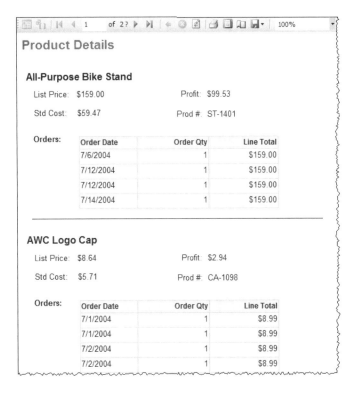

FIGURE 7-33

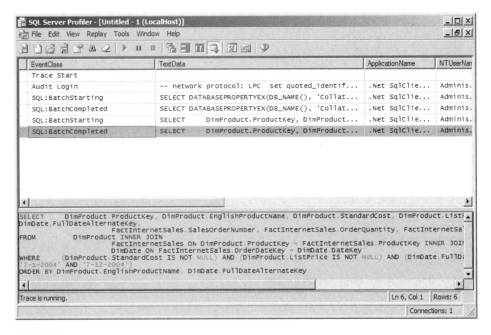

FIGURE 7-34

Contrast this with the subreport. We'll start a new trace and then run the subreport. Figure 7-35 shows the trace results in SQL Server Profiler. Note the height of the vertical scroll bar; this is only the last page of a very long set of trace results. The entire trace screen capture would be 12 pages long! To save a tree or two, imagine what this would look like. Then suppose that after this report were put into production for a few years and business expanded, it was run for a thousand products. Never assume that data volumes will always be small or that users will always make reasonable parameter selections before running a report.

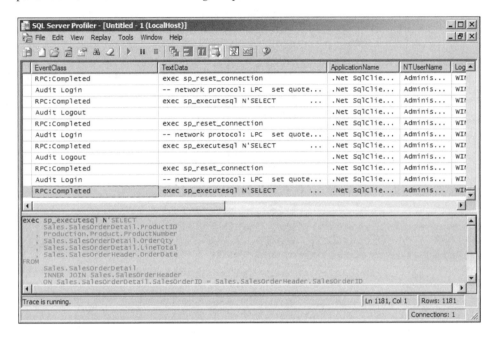

FIGURE 7-35

The Profiler trace for this report recorded 294 individual query executions (once for the master query, returning products in the AdventureWorksDW_WroxSSRS2012 database, and then once for each of the corresponding product orders in the AdventureWorks_WroxSSRS2012 database). For each query, a connection is open, an execution plan is prepared and run, and the connection is reset — 294 times. Although the .NET native SQL Server client and the database engine optimize this process by recycling connections and query execution plans, the overall result certainly is not as efficient as a report running on a single query.

In the final analysis, if you must coordinate data in a master/detail fashion, you generally have three options:

➤ Stage the data into one physical database.

➤ Create a federated view on the server using a linked server or OPENROWSET query.

➤ Create a subreport like the one you just examined.

In any case, try to keep the number of master records to a minimum by using a static filter or parameter in the WHERE clause. If you can source the data for the report's master and detail area from a single query and you can't limit the scope of the master records, avoid using a subreport, and use an embedded data range instead.

NAVIGATING REPORTS

Reports of yesterday were static, designed for print. At best, they could be previewed on a screen. To find important information, users had to browse through each page until they found the information they were looking for. Today, you have several options to provide dynamic navigation to important information — in the same report or to content in another report or an external resource.

Creating a Document Map

The *document map* is a simple navigation feature that allows the user to find a group label or item value in the report by using a tree displayed along the left side of the report. It's sort of like a table of contents for report items that you can use to quickly navigate to a specific area of a large report. You typically will want to include only group-level fields in the document map rather than including the detail rows.

 The document map is limited to the HTML, Excel, and PDF rendering formats. In the Excel and HTML formats, the document map may not survive when you save report files to an older document format, such as Pocket Excel on an older Windows Mobile device.

The sample report provided in the Chapter 7 project is Products by Category and SubCategory (Doc Map). We've added the CategoryName and SubCategoryName groupings to the document map. In the Group Properties dialog for the Category row group (see Figure 7-36), on the Advanced page, set the Document map property using the drop-down list to the ProductCategoryName field.

Be careful to specify the document map label property only for items you want to include in the document map. For example, if you specify this property for a grouping (as is done here), don't do the same for a textbox containing the same value. Otherwise, you will see the same value appear twice in the document map.

Figure 7-37 shows a report with a document map. The report name is the top-level item in the document map, followed by the product category and subcategory names.

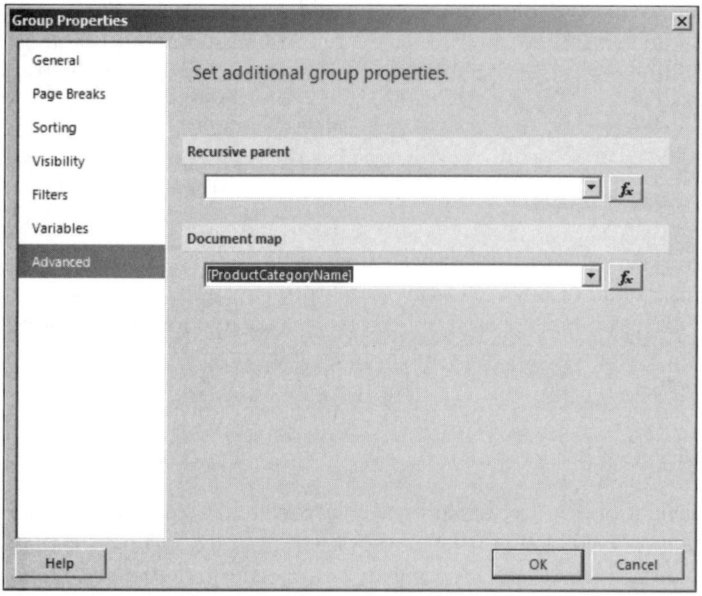

FIGURE 7-36

FIGURE 7-37

You can show or hide the document map using the leftmost icon in the Report Designer's Preview or the Report View toolbar in the Report Manager or SharePoint Report Viewer web part after the report is deployed to the server.

My experience has been that the drill-down and document map features usually don't work well together because they duplicate some functionality. Use the document map to navigate to a visible area of the report.

Links and Drill-Through Reports

Links and drill-through reports are powerful features that enable a textbox or image to be used as a link to another report by passing parameter values to the target report. The target report can consist of a specific record or multiple records, depending on the parameters passed to the target report. The following example uses the Products by Category report in the sample project. The Product Name textbox is used to link to a report that will display the details of a single product record. The Product Details report, shown in Figure 7-38, is simple. It contains only textboxes and an image bound to fields of a dataset based on the Products table. This report accepts a `ProductID` parameter to filter the records and narrow down to the record requested.

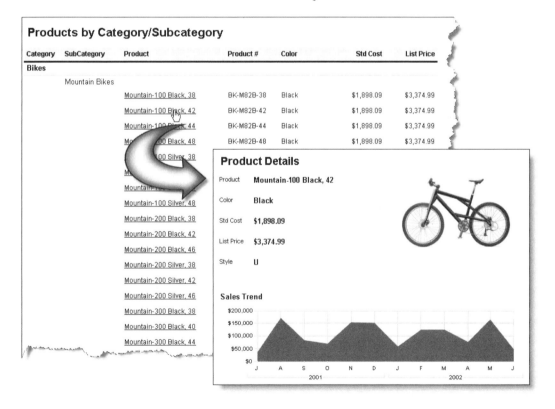

FIGURE 7-38

Any textbox or image item can be used for intrareport or interreport navigation, for navigation to external resources such as web pages and documents, and to send e-mail. You enable all these features using navigation properties you can specify in the Textbox Properties or Image Properties dialog. First, open the Text Box Properties dialog by right-clicking the textbox and selecting Properties. In the Text Box Properties dialog, use the Actions page to set the drill-through destination and any parameters you would like to pass.

Figure 7-39 shows the Text Box Properties dialog Action page for the Products_Details — Table with Groupings and Drillthrough report in the sample project.

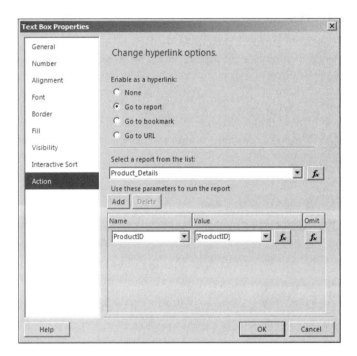

FIGURE 7-39

Note the navigation target selections under the "Enable as a hyperlink" option list. When you choose "Go to report," the report selection drop-down is enabled, listing all reports in the project. A report selected from this list must be deployed to the same folder on the Report Server as the source report. A drill-through report typically is used to open the report to a filtered record or result set based on the value in this textbox. (Remember that the user clicked this textbox to open the target report.) The typical pattern is to show a user-friendly caption in the textbox (the product name in this case) and then pass a key value to the report parameter to uniquely identify records to filter in the target report. In this case, the ProductID value is passed.

To enable this behavior, add a parameter reference that will be used in the target report to filter the dataset records. All parameters in the target report are listed in the Name column. In the Value column, select a field in the source report to map to the parameter. A new feature is apparent in the rightmost column. An expression may be used to specify a condition in which the parameter is not passed to the target report. Expressions are short pieces of VB.NET code, and can be used to call custom code functions and even code libraries referenced as .NET assemblies. You'll see how to do this in Chapter 21.

By default, drill-through reports are displayed in the same browser window as the source report. There are a few techniques for opening the report in a secondary window, but none are out-of-the-box features. My favorite technique is to use the "Go to URL" navigation option and open the target report using a URL request. Although this is a little more involved, it provides a great deal of flexibility.

To navigate to a report in a separate web browser window, call a JavaScript function to create a pop-up window using any browser window modifications you like. The function call script, report folder path, report name, and filtering parameters are concatenated using an expression. Here are two examples. The first is simple and opens the report in a browser window in default view:

```
="JavaScript:void window.open('http://localhost/reportserver?/Sales Reports/
Product Sales Report');"
```

The second, somewhat more elaborate example adds report parameters, hides the report viewer toolbar, and customizes the browser window size and features:

```
="JavaScript:void window.open('http://localhost/reportserver?/Sales Reports/
Product Sales Report&rc:Toolbar=False&ProductID=" & Fields!ProductID.Value &
"', '_blank', 'toolbar=0,scrollbars=0,status=0,location=0,menubar=0,resizable=0,
directories=0,width=600,height=500,left=550,top=550');"
```

The report name can be parameterized and modified using custom expressions. Expressions and custom code are discussed at length in Chapter 21, but these short examples give you an idea of the kinds of customizations possible with custom code and expressions.

Navigating to a Bookmark

A *bookmark* is a textbox or image in a report that can be used as a navigational link. If you want to allow the user to click an item and navigate to another item, assign a bookmark value to each target item. To enable navigation to a bookmark, set the "Go to bookmark" property to the target bookmark.

Using bookmarks to navigate within a report is easy. Each report item has a `BookMark` property that can be assigned a unique value. After adding bookmarks to any target items, use the "Go to bookmark" selection list to select the target bookmark in the properties for the source item. This allows the user to navigate to items within the same report.

Navigating to a URL

You can use the "Go to URL" option to navigate to practically any report or document content on your Report Server; files, folders, and applications in your intranet environment; or the World Wide Web. With some creativity, this may be used as a powerful, interactive navigation feature. It can also be set to an expression that uses links stored in a database, custom code, or any other value. It's more accurate to say that any URI (Uniform Resource Identifier) can be used, because a web request is not limited to a web page or document. With some creative programming, queries, and expressions, you can design your reports to navigate to a web page, document, e-mail address, Web Service request, or custom web application, directed by data or custom expressions.

Reporting Services does not make any attempt to validate a URL passed in an expression. If a malformed URL is used, the Report Server returns an error. There is no easy way to trap this error or prevent it from occurring. The most effective way to handle this issue is to validate the URL string before passing it to the "Go to URL" property.

REPORTING ON RECURSIVE RELATIONSHIPS

Representing recursive hierarchies has always been a pain for reporting and often is a challenge to effectively model in relational database systems. Examples of this type of relationship (usually facilitated through a self-join) can be found in the DimEmployee table of the AdventureWorksDW_WroxSSRS2012 sample database. Most reporting tools were designed to work with data organized in traditional multitable relationships. Fortunately, our friends at Microsoft built recursive support into the reporting engine to deal with this common challenge. A classic example of a recursive relationship (where child records are related to a parent record contained in the same table) is the employee/manager relationship. The Employee table contains a primary key, EmployeeID, that uniquely identifies each employee record. ManagerID is a foreign key that depends on the EmployeeID attribute of the same table. It contains the EmployeeID value for the employee's manager. The only record that wouldn't have a ManagerID would be the president of the company or any such employee who doesn't have a boss.

Representing the hierarchy through a query would be difficult. However, defining the dataset for such a report is simple. You just expose the primary key, foreign key, employee name, and any other values you want to include on the report.

To see how this works, follow these steps:

1. Create a new report, and define a dataset using the AdventureWorksDW_WroxSSRS2012 shared data source. The Dataset query is simple and includes both the primary key and a recursive foreign key. The ParentEmployeeKey for each employee contains the EmployeeKey value for that employee's supervisor or manager.

```
SELECT    EmployeeKey, ParentEmployeeKey, LastName, Title
FROM      DimEmployee
WHERE     Status = 'Current'
```

2. Add a table data region to the report body, and drag the LastName and Title fields to the detail row. For demonstration purposes, we've also dragged the EmployeeKey and ParentEmployeeKey fields.

3. Insert a column named Org Level in the table. (We'll get to this in a moment.)

4. Edit the (Details) group properties using the drop-down button for this item in the Row Groups pane, as shown in Figure 7-40.

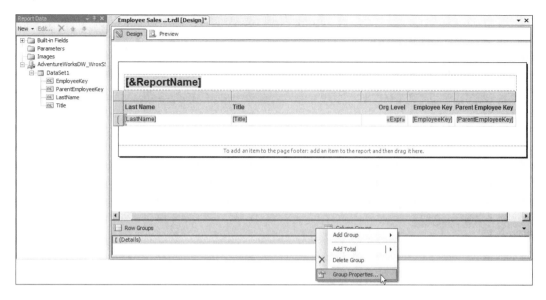

FIGURE 7-40

This action opens the Group Properties dialog, shown in Figure 7-41. To define a recursive group, you must set two properties. First, the group must be based on the unique identifier for the child records. This is typically a key value and must be related to the unique identifier for parent records — usually a parent key column in the table. Second, the Recursive parent property is set to relate the parent key to the table's primary key.

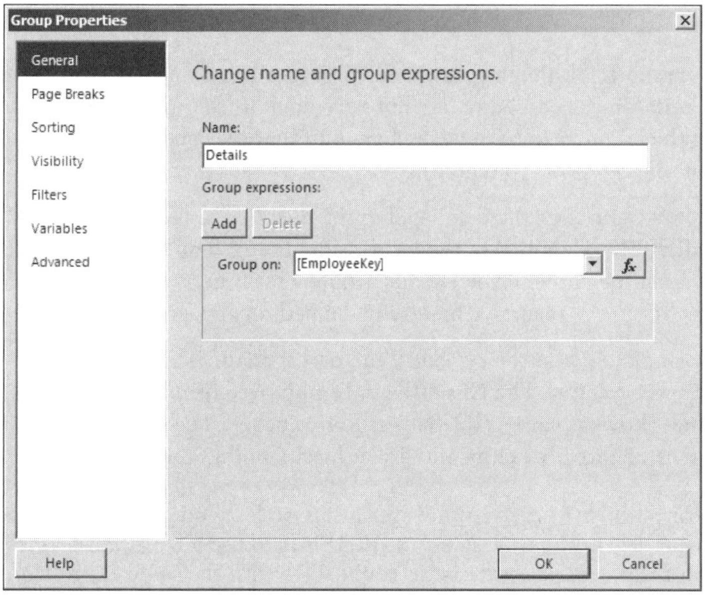

FIGURE 7-41

5. Use the General page to set the group expression to the EmployeeKey field.

6. Move to the Advanced page on this dialog, and set the Recursive parent property to the ParentEmployeeKey field, as shown in Figure 7-42.

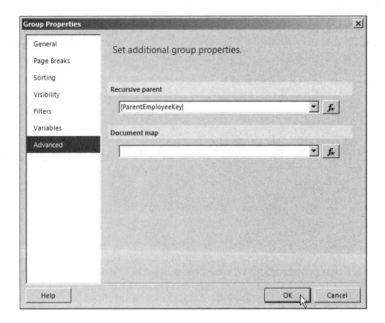

FIGURE 7-42

7. Go ahead and preview the report. Although the records are actually arranged according to each employee's pecking order in the company, it's not very obvious that this recursive hierarchy report is really working. You need to make a change so that the report lets you visualize the employee hierarchy (who reports to whom).

8. Switch back to Design view. Right-click the detail cell in the new Org Level column and select Expression. Type =LEVEL("**Details**") in the Expression dialog. This expression calls the LEVEL function, passing in the name of the Details group. This function returns an integer value for a row's position within the recursive hierarchy defined for this group.

9. Click OK on the Expression dialog, and then preview the report again. This time, you see numbers in the Org Level column. The CEO (the only employee record without a ParentEmployeeKey value) shows up at level 0. This is Ken Sanchez. The employees who report to Mr. Sanchez are listed directly below and are at level 1 within the hierarchy.

You're not done. The report still isn't very visually appealing, so let's indent each employee's name according to his or her level. The easiest way to do this is to use a little math to set the Left Padding property for the LastName textbox. You'll start with the same expression as before. Padding is set using PostScript points. A point is about 1/72nd of an inch, and there are about 2.83 millimeters to a point. Because this is such a small unit of measure, we'll indent our employee names by 20 points per level.

10. Right-click the `LastName` textbox and choose Textbox Properties.

11. In the Text Box Properties dialog, move to the Alignment page. Under the Padding options section, click the Expression button (labeled fx) next to the Left property box.

12. In the Expression dialog, type the following text:

=((LEVEL("Details") * 20) + 2).ToString & "pt"

13. Verify that your design environment looks like Figure 7-43.

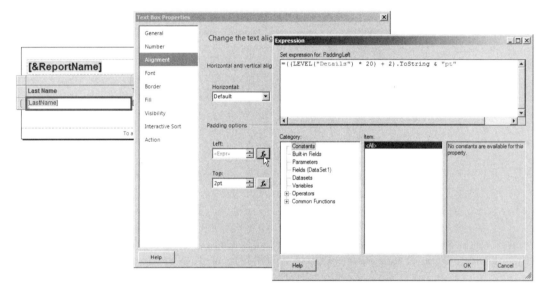

FIGURE 7-43

14. Click OK in the Expression Editor window, and then click OK to close the Text Box Properties dialog.

15. Preview the report. Now you see each employee name indented according to his or her position in the organization. You can verify these results by noting the level value in the `Org Level` column and the correspondence between the `EmployeeKey` and `ParentEmployeeKey` column values.

Don't be concerned if your results don't match Figure 7-44 exactly. The employee data has been modified in various versions of the sample databases. The point of this exercise is to see the hierarchal relationship between various employee records.

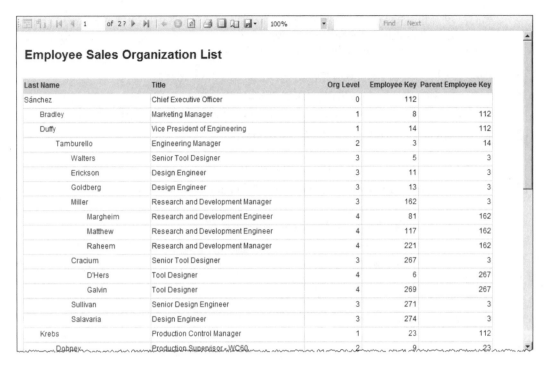

FIGURE 7-44

SUMMARY

Building on the basic design concepts and building blocks you learned in the previous chapters, you have raised the bar and created more powerful and compelling reports using a variety of design techniques.

You can define report page headers and footers in a report template, where you can reuse the design in all your new reports. You can add built-in fields and summary information to page headers and footers to display and print useful information such as the report name, execution date and time, page numbers, and the report user. These provide important context information if the report is printed or archived.

The essential design patterns for composite reports include the use of embedded data regions and subreports. Report elements, including complex data regions, can be nested in a list, table, or matrix to create more sophisticated interface paradigms. Subreports can provide this same functionality when a master/detail report must coordinate related information managed in different data sources. Report navigation features take reporting beyond static, passive data browsing. Document maps, as well as drill-down and drill-through techniques, allow users to interact with reports to create a dynamic information analysis and discovery experience.

Expressions and custom programming take report design to new heights by allowing a single report to deliver more functionality, behaving more like a multifunction business application than a traditional report.

8

Chart Reports

WHAT'S IN THIS CHAPTER?

➤ Chart types and design approaches

➤ Anatomy of a chart

➤ Chart objects and collection hierarchy

➤ Creating a multiseries chart

➤ Multiple chart areas

➤ Useful properties and settings

A chart data region is based on a dataset just like any other data region. It uses groups, query parameters, and filters in much the same way as a table, list, or matrix. Of course, the difference is that a chart consumes the data and then visualizes the grouped aggregate values in the form of bars, columns, lines, points, bubbles, or slices.

Before we get into the details, let's cover the simple method of chart design. After you add a chart to the report, you see a simple chart design user interface. Using the Chart Data window, you select the type of chart you want and then add fields to define a category and a field for the series value. Then — badda boom, badda bing — you have a working chart. Easy, right? Designing simple charts is a fairly easy task, but adding features and customizing a chart can require a lot more effort.

After placing the chart in the report body, you can drag fields from the Dataset window directly onto the chart design surface. At the minimum, a chart should have one aggregated field for the value and one grouped field for the category. The category and series groups represent the x-axis and y-axis in bar, column, line, area, and point charts.

With each version of Reporting Services, the charting capabilities keep getting better and more powerful. There's both good news and bad whenever a product grows and becomes more capable. The good news is that you have a great deal of flexibility and power and can create just about any chart style or format you can imagine within the broad confines of the 58 chart types the product supports. With all this flexibility comes the potential for a good deal of complexity. All told, the chart data region and its constituent objects support approximately 150 to 200 individual properties. Some of these properties apply to only certain chart types. But no matter how you look at it, that's a lot of properties to dig through and keep track of! However, with a little experience and a basic understanding of how the chart objects are organized, this task is not as daunting as it may seem.

Ever since Microsoft acquired the code base for Dundas Software's .NET charting components and added newer versions along the way, it has done a remarkable job of simplifying the design interface. You can take chart design as far as you need to. The necessary effort to design charts may range from simple to tedious. Having been down this road many times, I recommend that after you familiarize yourself with charting basics, you approach the design with some specific objectives. Otherwise, you're likely to get lost in the interface.

The purpose of a chart is to highlight important information and let it tell a story. Different report types can effectively convey comparisons or trends, but it's important to use the right chart for your data. Before we move on, I want to make an important point. If you work in a field where specialized visualizations are useful and appropriate, you may find some of the more abstract and special-purpose charts of great value. But for day-to-day business reporting, it's common to use just a handful of traditional charts to visualize business metrics. So, even though Polar, Stock, and Funnel charts look cool, they may not help you convey an effective message. In business, 99 percent of the industry uses about 5 percent of the available chart types.

CHART TYPES

Some of the more common chart types (such as column, bar, line, and area) can be used for different views of the same data. Pie charts present a more simplified view and work well with fewer category values. Other charts are more specialized and may be appropriate for multivalue data points, range values, and variances. All the chart types support dynamic capabilities, such as actions and tooltips. Using these features in report design, a chart user can get more information and details by hovering over or clicking a range, point, or area of the chart.

Column Charts

Figure 8-1 shows a simple column chart. The horizontal x-axis series values are product categories, and the vertical y-axis values represent annual sales revenue. You can modify several visual elements to alter the color, shading, borders, text, formatting, labeling, and value placement. Figure 8-1 shows the default property settings.

Figure 8-2 shows the same chart with default three-dimensional (3D) modeling.

This view is boxy and uses space inefficiently without lending more value to the data presentation. You can use 3D modeling to show data in a more interesting presentation, but this can also be distracting and less effective for analysis. Figure 8-3 shows a more extreme 3D view of the same data with perspective. This chart is set up with a fairly extreme 3D and perspective view to show you what can be done. This type of view tends to distort the values, and the clustering (stacking the columns along the z-axis — the third axis in a 3D coordinate system) can hide some columns from view.

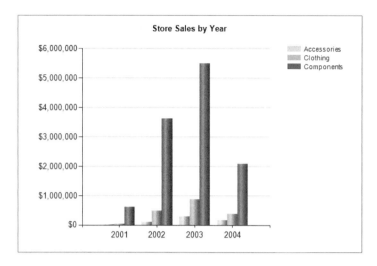

FIGURE 8-1

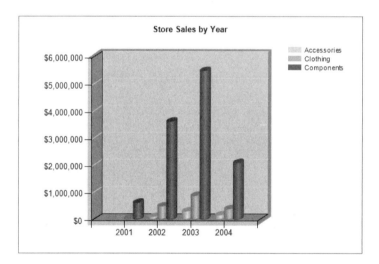

FIGURE 8-2

As a rule, keep chart visual effects to a minimum. Effects are the trim, not the substance, of the data message, so don't let them get in the way. If in doubt, reduce or eliminate an unnecessary effect. You have control over several 3D properties to generate more realistic representation of the chart data. Be careful to maintain the appropriate balance between artistry and accuracy. Note that it's difficult to quantify and distinguish the difference in height between the front-right column and the right-most column in the back. The degree to which it makes sense to use these features depends largely on the chart's purpose. Is it sufficient to demonstrate that one data point is less than or greater than another, or do these points need to be strictly measurable? This type of view can be effective for making an impact, but a flatter view is usually more appropriate to maintain accuracy.

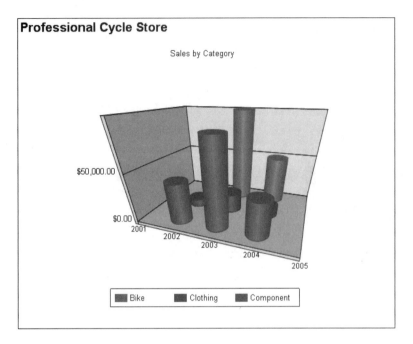

FIGURE 8-3

Figure 8-4 is a 3D view with cylindrical columns arranged in a clustered formation. When used correctly and in moderation, this 3D chart adds a sense of realism while remaining readable.

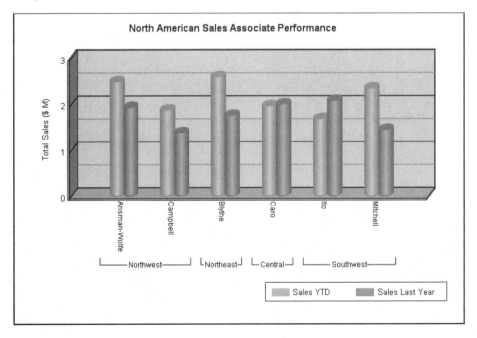

FIGURE 8-4

Stacked Charts

Column and bar charts can have their bars stacked, as shown in Figure 8-5. This appends the different colored bars (for a like series value) into one bar with multiple colored bands. This may be an appropriate method for showing the accumulation of all values within the series point. The individual values are displayed in a different color as a percentage of the bar. In essence, each bar becomes like a linear pie chart.

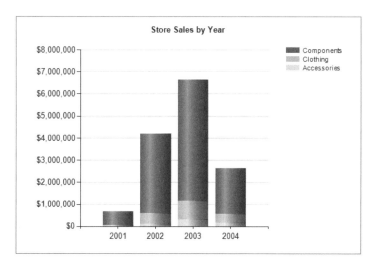

FIGURE 8-5

To emphasize the proportion of like values rather than the comparative accumulation, the 100 percent stacked view (not pictured) makes all the bars in the chart the same length rather than depicting the sum of all the values in the bar.

Area and Line Charts

An *area chart*, shown in Figure 8-6, plots the values of each point and then draws a line from point to point to show the progression of values along the series. This is an effective method for analyzing trends and works well when values tend to climb, decline, or remain level in the series. This type of chart is accurate when data exists for all category values on the x-axis. It typically doesn't work well to express a series of values that are not in a relatively uniform plane.

A *line chart* is a variation of an area chart using a line or ribbon rather than a solid area. The line chart works better than the area chart for comparing multiple categories for a series of values,

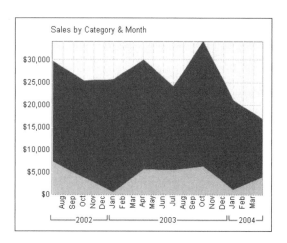

FIGURE 8-6

because one layer may obscure another in the area view. In the preceding example, the area chart works because of how the values are sorted. Larger values are in the background, and other points in the foreground are smaller, and the trend increases back to front.

Pie and Doughnut Charts

A pie chart is an excellent tool for comparing proportional values. Display options for a pie chart include exploded and 3D views. The 3D pie chart pictured in Figure 8-7 shows that there are three different grouped values. Point labels displayed over each slice provide specifics where the chart visual just gives proportions, and using both can add value in the right types of report scenarios. I call this piece "Pac-Man Gets a Root Canal."

The purpose of a chart is to tell a complete story about the data and it's important to label it clearly so we know what the groups represent. Group values can be titled using point labels, call-out labels, or in a legend.

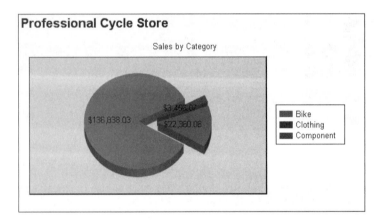

FIGURE 8-7

A *doughnut chart* is a pie chart with a hole. When a pie chart has several smaller slices, the doughnut chart can be easier to read and provides a variation on an age-old chart theme. Figure 8-8 is the same as Figure 8-7, but without the exploded view and with a legend showing the series labels.

Pie charts traditionally are used to show multiple slices representing their percentage of the whole. In the usual form, data values grouped on another axis result in slices automatically generated with the same style settings and contrasting colors from a standard color palette. The Designer provides eight color palettes. Sometimes data may need to be presented as a percentage value, or you might have two values and need to express one as a percentage of the other. You can do this by adding multiple value groups to the chart, with each representing a specific slice. Figure 8-9 shows only two values. In this example, values in the dataset exist for Bike Sales and Total Sales. Using an expression or a calculation in the query, subtracting Bike Sales from the total provides a value for Other Sales.

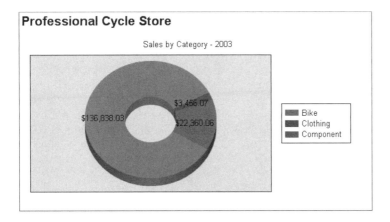

FIGURE 8-8

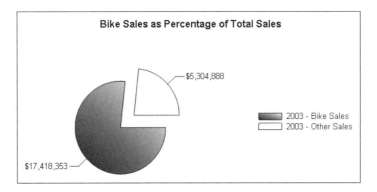

FIGURE 8-9

I created a specific group for these two values. Another advantage of using this approach is that you can set the color and styles for each slice independently.

Bubble and Stock Charts

Bubble charts are essentially a point plotted in a grid representing three dimensions. The value of the z-axis is expressed by the size of the bubble. Imagine that the bubble exists in a 3D plane and appears larger if it is closer to you. Actually, the bubble can be a circle, square, triangle, diamond, or cross shape. This also means that a combination of shapes can be used to represent different data elements in the same chart space.

In Figure 8-10, employees' vacation and sick hours are plotted above their names. The number of vacation hours is represented by the bubble's vertical distance from the 0 baseline, and the number of sick hours is represented by the size of the bubble.

Figure 8-11 is a stock chart. For each product, a line is plotted to span a range of values. Each line has a large tick mark to indicate the position of a value within the high/low range. In this example, the beginning of the range (the lowest point of the line) is the standard cost of the product. The tick mark represents the last receipt cost, and the high range of the line is the list price.

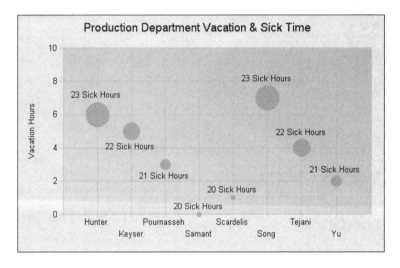

FIGURE 8-10

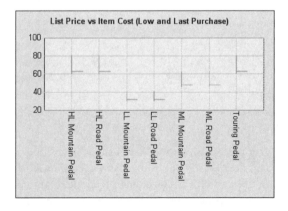

FIGURE 8-11

Chart Type Summary

Twelve general chart types are available, as described in Table 8-1.

TABLE 8-1

CHART TYPE	DESCRIPTION	BEST USE
Column	A classic vertical bar chart with columns representing values along the y-axis. Like-valued items along the x-axis are grouped, and bars representing the same x-axis values in each group have the same colors or patterns. Series values may also be grouped and subgrouped. Columns can have point labels, and the colored bars may be labeled using a legend. Columns may be arranged side by side (along the x-axis) or in front of one another (along the z-axis.) Columns may appear to be extruded from their base using a rectangular or circular (cylindrical) shape.	Discrete group values on the Category (x) axis. Also effective with linear time-series periods broken into discrete buckets (such as days, weeks, or months).
Bar	Functionally the same as a column chart turned 90 degrees. It has the advantage of more accurately depicting value comparisons for layouts in which you have more available horizontal space.	Used only with discrete group values, not for linear series groups.
Line	Like the area chart, but the charted area isn't filled. This type of chart is useful for comparing multiple series (along the z-axis) without obscuring trend lines behind a series.	Time-series and linear interval category groups (time, dates, and progressive numeric values).
Area	Like a column chart with a trend line drawn from one point to the next in the series. This type of chart is appropriate for a series of values that tend to progress over a relatively even plane that describes a "level," "up," or "down" trend. It is inappropriate for series values that tend to jump around. The solid shading of the charted area depicts a volume of data values.	Time-series and linear interval category groups.
Pie	The classic pie chart is an excellent tool for comparing relative values. Unlike bar, column, line, and area charts, the aggregate value isn't quantified. Users understand pie charts because they put comparative values into a proportional context and can drive quick decision support at a glance. Pie chart views can be exploded to visually separate each slice. Consider using a column or bar chart when more accurate comparisons are needed.	Use only for discrete category groups and never for linear series values. However, may be used for discrete bucket values. Typically, use pie charts with no more than 10 to 15 slices.

continues

TABLE 8-1 *(continued)*

CHART TYPE	DESCRIPTION	BEST USE
Doughnut	A doughnut is a pie with a hole in the middle. It's more effective as a bold marketing visual. A 3D doughnut rendering may expose smaller slices more clearly than a pie chart because each slice has four sides rather than three.	Use with 3-D effect for conveying a bold statement and not for accurately measuring business metrics. Typically, limit slices to 10 or 15.
Scatter	Plots several points in a range (both x and y) to show trends and variations in value. The result is more like a cloudy band of points rather than a specific aggregated point or line.	Used with dozens to hundreds of data points when analyzing the general trend is of greater value than seeing a specific point.
Bubble	A technique for charting points on three dimensions. Values are plotted using different-sized points, or bubbles, on a two-dimensional (2D) grid. The size of the bubble indicates the related value along the z-axis.	Appropriate when measuring two different series values along two different linear axes where size represents one value and position represents the other.
Ranges	Range and Gantt charts are often used to visualize project phases and the progress of stages in a process along a linear series.	Used when each data item (project, commodity, unit of work) has a beginning and end value on a linear axis.
Stock	This category of charts (sometimes called candlestick or whisker graphs) plots values vertically like a column chart having variable start and end points. For each item along the y-axis series, a vertical line indicates a start and end value for the range. A tick mark in the line can indicate a significant value in that range or an aggregation of the range. This type of chart is useful for showing trading stocks with opening, closing, and purchase values; wholesale, retail, and discount prices; and so on.	A specialized kind of visual for discrete data items that have multiple events along a linear axis, typically multiple start and end values.
Shapes	Shape charts like the funnel and pyramid are effectively a single, stacked column chart. These typically are used to model sales and production against goals, and sales opportunity pipelines.	Used in specific business scenarios where data items progress through ranked stages.

CHART TYPE	DESCRIPTION	BEST USE
Polar	Polar and radar charts plot points from a central hub at different angles and distances in a radial fashion. This kind of visual does have some useful applications, but traditional nonlinear charts, such as a column or bar, are often more suitable.	A specialized visual. Can be used with discrete, nonlinear but related categories. Best used to express that no category exists at the beginning or end of the range.

The Anatomy of a Chart

Much detail work typically is involved in chart design; there are many properties to manage. Figure 8-12 shows the major property groups for charts. Although some charts have a few unique properties and some may not support all properties, generally these properties are shared across all chart types.

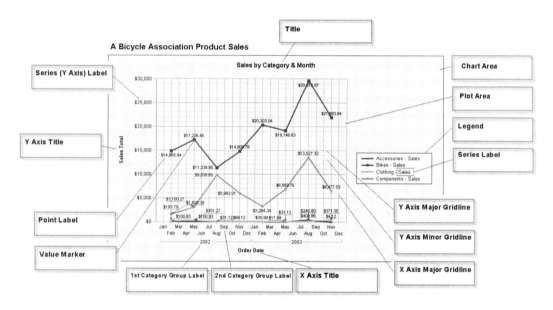

FIGURE 8-12

Chart objects are organized into the following hierarchy. Understanding this structure and the relationships between these objects will save you a lot of time and effort. See Figure 8-13.

The Chart object is really is just a container. The Chart Area does most of the work and contains most of the useful properties. I recommend that you take some time to explore the chart objects in the design interface. Because there are so many different objects, selecting the right object can be tricky at first, but with a little experience, you'll get used to the interface. With a chart open in the designer, show the Properties Window and then click on different areas of the chart to select and view the name of various objects. Use the chart objects hierarchy as a reference as you click different areas to select objects. You can also right-click an object to reveal menu options that will take you to subordinate objects and collections. For example, if you were to right-click on the Chart object, the Properties Window and the right-click menu will let you find the Chart Areas. Taking time to do this now will save you time and effort when you follow the next exercise.

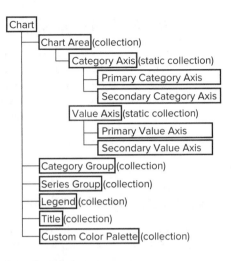

FIGURE 8-13

Note that many of these objects are organized into collections to make them fit neatly into the standard properties windows and design interface. As a rule, you can select an object and set its properties in one of two ways. If you right-click an object in the chart designer, you see a menu item to edit the object's properties. That menu may also include related objects that you can edit. Choosing this menu option opens a custom property page for the object. Choosing an option in a property page to edit another object opens another property page. These are stacked in the order in which they were opened. Some properties are actually object collections. Clicking an ellipsis (...) button for that collection opens a dialog with the object collection and associated properties. In addition to the custom properties pages for each chart-related object, you can edit properties in the standard Properties window.

CREATING A MULTISERIES CHART

In Chapter 5 you learned how to design a basic column chart with one series and axis. Charts can be used to visualize multiple values with different axes and scales. In the following exercise, you will design a chart report with two different series axes that align to a common category axis. One series will show sales currency values on one scale, and the other series will show order quantity values on a different scale within the same chart area. You will also use different chart types to visually separate the two series. Finished copies of all these reports are in the Chapter 8 sample project.

1. In the dataset connected to the AdventureWorksDW_WroxSSRS2012 database, use the following query:

```
SELECT
        CalendarYear, MonthNumberOfYear,
        MonthName, SalesAmt, OrderQty
FROM  vSalesByTimeAndTerritory WHERE CalendarYear = @Year
```

2. Add a 3-D Cylinder column chart to the report body. Doing so opens the Dataset Properties dialog. Select the new shared dataset.

3. Edit the `Year` report parameter. Set the Available Values (Label and Value) to 2002, 2003, 2004, and 2005. Add and set the Default Value to 2007.

4. Select the chart. Use the Chart Data window to add the `SalesAmt` and `OrderQty` fields as values and the `CalendarYear` and `MonthNumberOfYear` fields as category groups. Compare the design to Figure 8-14.

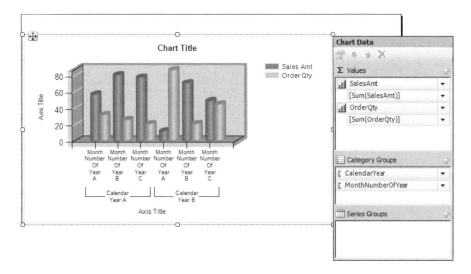

FIGURE 8-14

5. Click to choose the chart area, and then right-click to set the Chart Area Properties.

6. Uncheck Enable 3D, and accept the properties change.

7. Resize the chart to make enough room to display the values.

8. Preview the report shown in Figure 8-15.

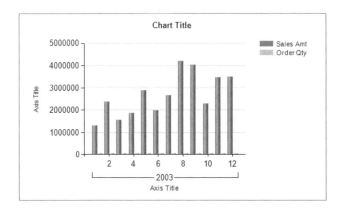

FIGURE 8-15

The chart plots both series values on the same axis. Because the `OrderQty` values are significantly smaller than the `SalesAmt` currency values, those columns are barely visible. The left axis values are an irrelevant scale for the `OrderQty`; this should be rectified.

9. In design view, click any gold `OrderQty` series column. Right-click and choose Series Properties.

10. In the Series Properties dialog, Axis and Chart Area page, change the Vertical Axis to Secondary. Click OK to close the dialog and save the properties.

11. Right-click the `OrderQty` series again, and change the chart type to a line chart.

12. If you like, style the chart by setting the series border width, series axis number formats, and axis titles.

13. Preview the report shown in Figure 8-16.

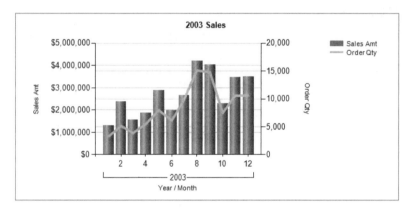

FIGURE 8-16

The chart is functional at this point but there are a few adjustments you can make to tidy things a bit.

14. Edit the chart category group to use the `MonthName` field for the Label.

15. Edit the Horizontal Axis properties. On the Axis Options page, set the Interval to 1. On the Labels page, disable auto-fit and rotate the label text 45 degrees.

16. Move the legend to make more room for the chart area.

17. Use an expression to set the chart title caption to use the `Year` parameter.

18. Preview the report and admire your work.

Using Multiple Chart Areas

Reporting Services charts support multiple chart areas. This powerful feature enables you to place multiple charts, of different types and characteristics, in the same chart container. Each of these chart areas are based on the same dataset, and can be aligned and correlated with a sibling chart in a variety of ways. The following is a simple example.

Using the chart report we have been designing, you will separate the two data fields into different chart areas, arranged vertically. When you align the Category Axis, any changes in the data are consistently reflected in both chart areas.

To make room for the second chart area, increase the chart's height by stretching it vertically. Right-click the chart and choose Add New Chart Area, as shown in Figure 8-17.

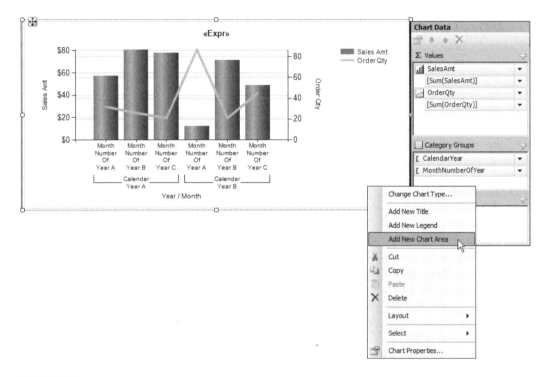

FIGURE 8-17

The new chart area appears as only white space below the original chart until a series axis is assigned to it. Right-click the Cost field in the Chart Data Values pane, and choose Series Properties, as shown in Figure 8-18.

In the corresponding Series Properties dialog, on the Axes and Chart Area page, use the "Change chart area" drop-down list to select the new chart area. Verify your settings with Figure 8-19, and then click OK to close the Series Properties dialog.

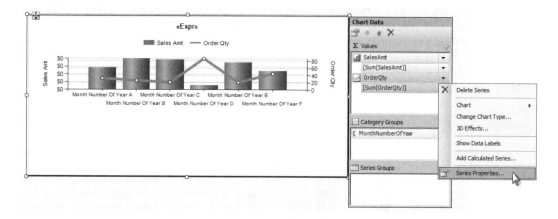

FIGURE 8-18

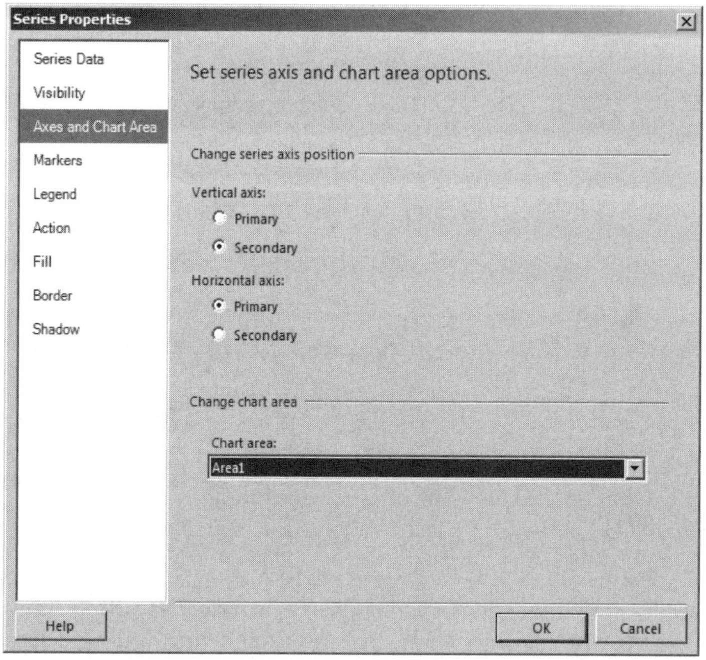

FIGURE 8-19

The finished report, shown in Figure 8-20, shows a chart visual very similar to the previous example. However, the line chart and its axis have been moved to the second chart area.

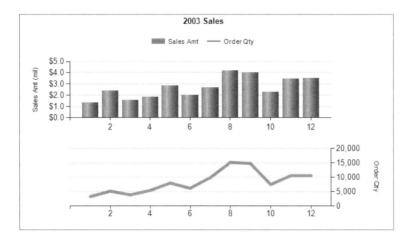

FIGURE 8-20

To set properties for the chart area, right-click the chart in the Designer and choose Chart Area Properties. Selecting the chart area can be a little tricky. I have found it easiest to right-click the second chart area without selecting it first. When you right-click, the designer selects the chart area and displays the appropriate menu option. The Chart Area Properties dialog is shown in Figure 8-21. On the Alignment page, use the "Align with chart area" drop-down list to choose the Default chart area. Click OK to accept this change, and then preview the report.

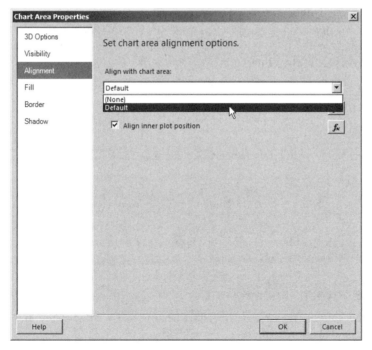

FIGURE 8-21

This last change ensures that the horizontal axis scales always align. Although the two chart areas appear to be separate charts with distinct chart types, they both use the same scale so that data in the two chart areas can be used for comparison.

Useful Properties and Settings

Hundreds of chart design variations exist. After many years of chart report design, I have some favorite features and settings. The following sections describe a few I've collected. For a comprehensive guide to chart styles and updated advanced report tips, refer to *Microsoft SQL Server Reporting Services Recipes*: *For Designing Expert Reports* (Wrox) and the authors' respective blog sites.

Control the Number of Items Displayed on an Axis

Select Chart ➪ Axis.

Interval property - 1 means display every value regardless of whether the text fits when rendering the axis labels.

Manage Axis Text Placement and Rotation

Select Chart ➪ Axis ➪ Labels group/page.

Disable auto-fit and set the rotation angle. Try 45 or experiment with other values.

Manage the Format of Axis Values

Select Chart ➪ Axis ➪ Number group/page.

Choose a format option or use a custom format string such as "#,##0" or "$#,##0.00".

Change the Color and Width of a Series Line

In a line chart, click a series line or series value in the Chart Data window. Change the `Color` and `BorderWidth` properties.

Set a Tooltip for a Chart Value

In the chart designer, click a series value or the item in the Chart Data window Values pane.

Set the `ToolTip` property using an expression.

Using the expression builder, reference fields and concatenate a string value with formatted text and carriage return characters. For example:

```
=Fields!FirstName.Value & " " Fields!LastName.Value & vbCrLf & "Income: "
& Format(Fields!Income.Value, "$#,##0")
```

Control the Width and Gap Between Columns or Bars

In the chart designer, click a series value or the item in the Chart Data window Values pane. In the properties for the chart series, select CustomAttributes ➪ PointWidth.

A value of 1 fills the gap between columns or bars. Less leaves a space, and more causes overlap.

For a Chart with Multiple Chart Areas, Control the Exact Position of Each Chart Area

Chart area size and positions are managed automatically by default. To override this behavior, edit the chart area properties. Set the CustomPosition ⇨ Enabled property to True, and then set the Height, Width, Left, and Top properties. To control the placement of the chart area plotted content, repeat these steps for the `CustomInnerPlotPosition` properties group.

Dynamically Increase a Chart's Size

Edit the Chart properties.

Set the `DynamicWidth` property to expand the size of a column, area, or line report. Use an expression to increase the width based on the number of records or distinct group values. For example:

```
=(1 + COUNT(Fields!Country.Value, "Chart1")) & " in"
```

SUMMARY

The charting capabilities in Reporting Services have improved over the years with new product versions. New chart types provide more options to visualize business data to information workers. Advanced charts provide a more flexible means to deliver actionable information through compelling new features that include multiseries charts and chart areas.

The chart design skills you've learned in this chapter can be extended to specialized chart types and more advanced styles of chart reports based on the same properties and capabilities. Most of the additional properties you'll find in the designer are used to manage the aesthetic qualities of charts, which you can use to customize the style and fine-tune your chart reports.

PART III
Business Intelligence Reporting

BI Semantic Models

➤ Introduction to data modeling

➤ The BI Semantic Model

➤ The conceptual architecture of the BI Semantic Model

➤ Options for building models

Building reports requires some level of understanding the underlying data. This is often expressed as metadata and called a model. The model can be as simple as a flat list of fields returned by a query used in a report, or sophisticated enough to express complex data relationships and calculations.

In this chapter, you will learn about dimensional and relational modeling. You will explore how the BI Semantic Model supports both types of data models as a unified semantic model. You will discover the conceptual layers of the BI Semantic Model. They provide flexibility in how you can create models, richness in how you can express business logic, and scalability in terms of model and organizational sizes.

Furthermore, you will explore the options available for building each layer of the model. You will learn about designing data access and storage, see how to implement business logic in the model, and learn how other tools, such as Excel and Power View, use the model. You also will become familiar with dimensional modeling and relational/tabular modeling, discover the spectrum and needs of BI applications, explore the conceptual architecture of the BI Semantic Model, and understand the model's hybrid nature.

INTRODUCTION TO DATA MODELING

In previous chapters, you started to build your first reports, and then you explored more sophisticated report layouts, visualizations, and expression calculations. The type of data source for your reports can vary, and the chapters so far have focused on connecting to data stored in relational databases.

Many organizations use databases to keep track of the things they are doing to run their business — acquiring raw materials, manufacturing products, receiving orders, delivering services, receiving client payments. Each of these interactions results in one or more data transactions stored in databases.

Databases are often carefully designed and optimized for efficiently processing and storing data transactions. This typically results in structures designed to minimize any redundancy of data stored, often split into small chunks. This structure is frequently called normalized schemas.

Although these underlying database structures are a concept familiar to developers and IT professionals, they are often difficult for business users to understand. At times it can be challenging to use them to answer typical business intelligence questions. For example:

➤ Which product was the best-seller during the past winter season among my most profitable customers?

➤ What was the average quantity in stock for my best-selling products in retail stores during the past month?

➤ If a product was sold out in one retail store, how often was it available in another store within 5 miles?

Transactional databases typically focus on day-to-day operation. Databases frequently use the relational data model. It is a mathematical model defined in terms of predicate logic and set theory.

Answering the business questions just mentioned often requires comparing historical and current data. Transactional databases often don't store historical information, but only reflect the current situation, such as how many products of each type are in stock right now.

The dimensional model is a specialized adaptation of the relational model. It represents data in data warehouses in a way that allows data to be easily summarized using Online Analytical Processing (OLAP) queries. The so-called unified dimensional model (UDM) was originally introduced with SQL Server Analysis Services.

In the dimensional model, a database schema frequently consists of a large table of facts (such as sales transactions) that are described using dimensions and measures.

A dimension provides the context of a fact (such as which products were sold to which customer at what time) and is used in queries to group related facts. Dimensions tend to be discrete and are often hierarchical. For example, a time dimension may include year, quarter, month, day, and hour, and a geographic dimension may include country, state, region, city, and street.

A measure is a quantity describing the fact, such as cost or revenue. Measures are frequently aggregated as facts and grouped by dimensions. In an OLAP query, such as revenue for a particular product during the past year in the United States, all facts associated with those particular dimension values are grouped and aggregated to return the result.

THE BI SEMANTIC MODEL

The BI Semantic Model is a hybrid of the relational data model and the dimensional model. It unifies both types of models under a single BI platform for all BI end-user tools, such as Excel and Power View, newly added in SQL Server 2012.

The model builds on the strengths and success of Analysis Services and expands its reach to a much broader user base. Every UDM becomes a BI Semantic Model, so existing applications and tools built on previous version of Analysis Services and cubes simply keep working. For new applications, you have two options (tabular and dimensional) to build a model, but with a single common BI Semantic Model served to client tools. The model encompasses the capabilities of UDM today and also new interfaces and experiences for the tabular paradigm. One model provides all end-user experiences, such as accessing data from Excel, Reporting Services, and Power View. It is the same model for all tools — no conversions, no separate storage, and no separate security.

PowerPivot for Excel is one way of creating a BI Semantic Model. PowerPivot includes a wizard that you can use to import data from different types of sources. Data is imported into PowerPivot for Excel as tables, which are shown as separate sheets in the PowerPivot window, similar to worksheets in an Excel workbook.

PowerPivot data is stored in an analytical database (the so-called VertiPaq database) inside the Excel workbook, and a local VertiPaq engine loads, queries, and updates the data in that database. You can create relationships between tables in the PowerPivot window. The VertiPaq engine leverages the richness of Analysis Services object models internally, but without imposing dimensional modeling concepts on users.

Any Excel PowerPivot workbooks created with the original PowerPivot add-in for Excel 2010, released with SQL Server 2008 R2, already contain an autogenerated BI Semantic Model. They can be immediately leveraged with the new capabilities in SQL Server 2012, such as Power View.

The BI Semantic Model embraces the relational data model, well understood by developers and professionals, and provides flexibility to meet the needs of a variety of BI applications. The role of the data access layer shown in Figure 9-1 is to mash up and relate data. It integrates data from several sources, including databases, data warehouses, OData feeds, web services such as SQL Azure, spreadsheets, text files, and existing Reporting Services reports rendered as Atom data feeds.

The model offers an expression language to define calculations, map to business entities, extend the data with calculated columns, and enrich the model with metadata. The underlying language is called DAX (Data Analysis Expressions language). It is closely modeled after the Excel formula language, with extensions. For example, the language includes time-based analysis functions to simplify expressing business logic in calculations.

The information is then served to client tools, such as Excel and Power View, as a semantic model that influences and drives a BI tool's automatic behavior. For example, a product sales revenue field's default aggregation is typically defined as "sum," and for rebates the default aggregation may be defined as "average." When the end user chooses any of these fields in an interactive analysis or visualization, the default aggregation is automatically applied in the specific usage context.

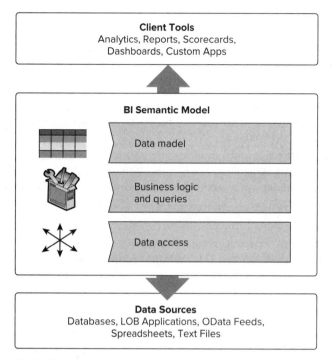

FIGURE 9-1

The BI Semantic Model powers experiences in business user tools as well as a spectrum of BI application scenarios, as shown in Figure 9-2. *Personal BI* focuses on business users who want to perform BI analysis in a flexible, self-service fashion using tools they are familiar with, without requiring advanced skills or the IT department. This empowers business users to create contents in their user context and typically manage them as documents. Business users are familiar with the concepts of granting access and managing document security.

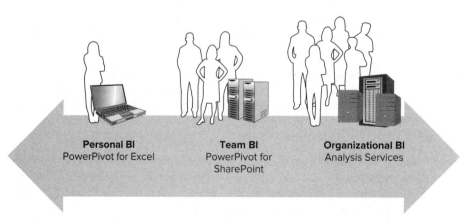

FIGURE 9-2

PowerPivot is a freely downloadable add-in for Excel that provides a modeling experience focused on tables and relationships, with which business users are often familiar. PowerPivot offers very fast performance for hundreds of millions of rows of data directly within Excel. Every PowerPivot workbook contains an automatically generated BI Semantic Model. Models in workbooks can be consumed in Excel as pivot tables, published to SharePoint to be used with Excel Services, or published to a PowerPivot Gallery in SharePoint.

Team BI focuses on collaboration among a workgroup. It may involve server infrastructure, such as SharePoint, to provide a common place for business users and IT departments to publish, share, and collaborate. An Excel PowerPivot workbook published in a SharePoint document library utilizes PowerPivot for SharePoint as an underlying service to expose APIs for model metadata discovery and query execution.

PowerPivot for SharePoint also includes services that integrate with Excel Services to consume and edit spreadsheets with PowerPivot data directly in the browser.

Furthermore, PowerPivot Gallery, shown in Figure 9-3, is a special-purpose SharePoint document library that provides rich preview and document management for the following:

➤   Excel workbooks that contain PowerPivot data, including the ability to specify a schedule for data refresh

➤   Power View reports

➤   Other document types

The PowerPivot Gallery combines an accurate preview of the file contents with facts about document origin. You can discover who created the document and when it was last modified. To create preview images, PowerPivot Gallery uses a snapshot service that can read PowerPivot Excel workbooks, Reporting Services, and Power View reports. If you publish a file that the snapshot service cannot read, no preview image is available for that file.

Organizational BI scenarios typically involve much data and many users. The contents are frequently created and managed by IT departments for business users. PowerPivot models originally created in Excel can be imported and extended using a professional developer-oriented SSDT (SQL Server Data Tools) PowerPivot modeling experience, which provides richer and more advanced capabilities. The underlying modeling technology is still the same, though. An IT department can track usage trends of business user-created PowerPivot workbooks in SharePoint, set up scheduled data refresh, and efficiently move workbooks as needed to dedicated Analysis Services servers. PowerPivot models from Excel, as well as models created in SSDT, can be deployed directly to an Analysis Services server. This provides scalability as models grow to billions of rows and increase in popularity from individual users to workgroups with dozens of users to large organizations with hundreds or thousands of users.

The choices available for how to build models, storage options, and query languages are discussed later in this chapter. Using multidimensional models with Reporting Services is covered in detail in Chapters 10 and 11, and tabular modeling is discussed in Chapter 12.

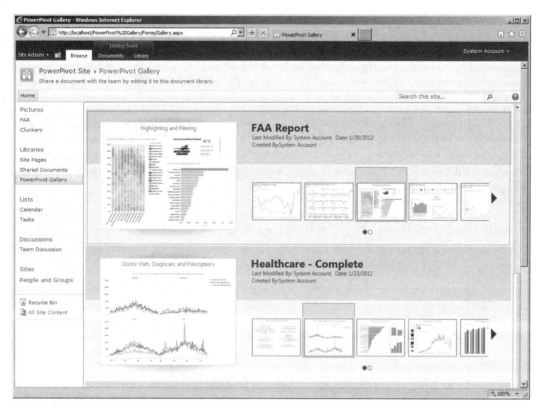

FIGURE 9-3

Conceptual Architecture

The BI Semantic Model supports a variety of data source types, as shown in Figure 9-4. For example, using the PowerPivot add-in for Excel, a business user can easily integrate and mash up data on their own from different sources directly in Excel, and thereby create a tabular model without actively thinking about modeling. The data integration could involve data added manually into Excel worksheets and linked to the model, data from external connections such as databases, data from SQL Azure and Azure Marketplace, data from web services and OData feeds directly from web sites.

In addition, an existing PowerPivot workbook can serve as a data source. For instance, an IT department can publish a model on an Analysis Services server or as a workbook in SharePoint, which business users then can leverage to mash up with their own data. This enables IT departments to provide "certified" data sources and monitor usage to adjust server capacity as needed. This also enables reuse (instead of copying) of modeled data. It also helps avoid issues with multiple copies of data disconnected from original sources that become inconsistent over time and are difficult to manage.

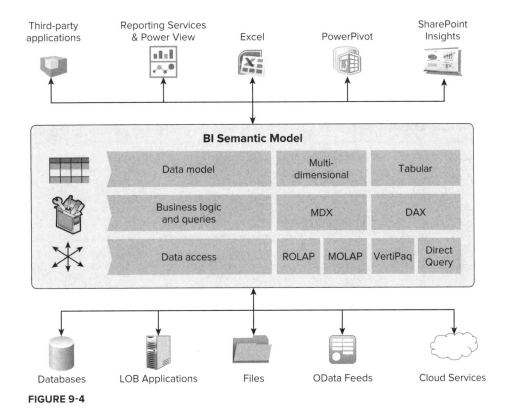

FIGURE 9-4

The BI Semantic Model has three layers:

- ➤ Data model
- ➤ Business logic and queries
- ➤ Data access

Each layer contributes to the hybrid nature of the BI Semantic Model, explained in more detail later in this chapter. First, we'll focus on each layer of the BI Semantic Model.

Data Model

The data model is consumed by applications such as Excel (PivotTable, PivotChart) and Power View to comprehend the model's contents, such as tables, relationships, and other metadata. Figure 9-5 shows a data model, with hidden columns and tables in gray.

There are two ways to build a model: PowerPivot for Excel and SSDT.

Business users may prefer to use PowerPivot for Excel, shown in Figure 9-6, to create models. PowerPivot is focused on tables and relationships and provides a simplified user interface experience for a lower barrier of entry. Power users can still easily create advanced workbook applications that rely on data relationships between tables as in a database, include calculated columns and measures, and aggregate over billions of rows.

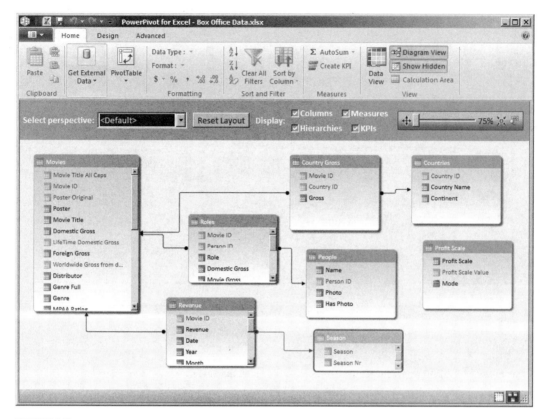

FIGURE 9-5

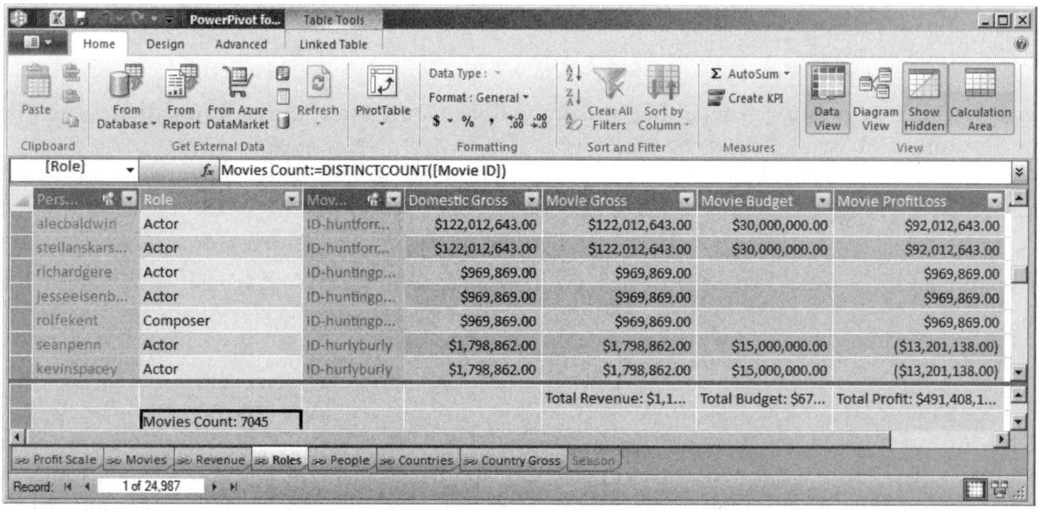

FIGURE 9-6

Developers and professional users may prefer SSDT to create a multidimensional model or a tabular model, and to get access to advanced properties and settings. Besides creating new models, the project types available in SSDT also allow you to import an existing model or cube already deployed on an Analysis Server and import from an Excel PowerPivot workbook (see Figure 9-7).

FIGURE 9-7

Here are some examples of model settings available only in SSDT:

➤ Fine-grained security to set up read, read and refresh, refresh, and administration privileges for particular roles and users

➤ Defining model partitions avoids reloading all rows in a model, but only small partitions. Any table can be partitioned, including dimension tables in tabular models, because everything is a table.

Table 9-1 compares tabular and dimensional model creation options.

TABLE 9-1

TABULAR MODELING	DIMENSIONAL MODELING
A familiar model for many business users. Typically easier to build, with faster time to solution.	A sophisticated model with a steeper learning curve.
It's quick and easy to wrap a model over a raw database or warehouse for reporting and analytics.	Best suited for OLAP-type applications (such as planning, budgeting, and forecasting) that need the more advanced capabilities of the multidimensional model.
Advanced concepts (parent/child, many-to-many) are unavailable natively in the tabular model. You need calculations to simulate these.	Advanced concepts are baked directly into the model and are optimized (parent/child, many-to-many, attribute relationships, key versus name).

Business Logic and Queries

Two languages can be used to express business logic and queries. MDX is a well-established and powerful language for expressing sophisticated business logic. It has achieved broad adoption as a standard, beyond the Analysis Services platform.

DAX is a new expression language inspired by the Excel formula language. DAX is built on top of tabular concepts to lower the barrier of entry to implement business logic. DAX was introduced in the PowerPivot add-in for Excel 2010. It was extended to become a query language in SQL Server 2012 (such as utilized by Power View).

SSDT for SQL Server 2012 offers a multidimensional project type. It expresses business logic in MDX and uses multidimensional OLAP (MOLAP) or relational OLAP (ROLAP) storage, as well as a tabular project type, to use the DAX expression language and VertiPaq or DirectQuery storage modes. Future versions could include additional project types, such as VertiPaq storage in multidimensional projects, or MDX scripts in tabular projects.

It is important to note that regardless of how the model is built, and which language is chosen to express business logic, client tools can use both MDX and DAX to send and execute queries.

Table 9-2 compares the use of DAX and MDX for business logic.

TABLE 9-2

DAX	MDX
DAX is based on Excel formulas and relational concepts. It's typically easy for new users to get started.	MDX is based on understanding multidimensional concepts, which has a higher initial learning curve.
Complex solutions such as row/filter context and calculated measures require a steeper learning curve.	Provides more expressive power than DAX, but complex solutions require a steeper learning curve (CurrentMember concept, calculation scopes, overwrite semantics).

Data Access

The BI Semantic Model offers several storage modes to both cache the data, and occasionally refresh or pass through queries and calculations to the model's underlying data sources.

ROLAP and MOLAP storage are well known and available for multidimensional models. These storage modes are optimized for disk I/O to achieve high performance but also are somewhat rigid.

MOLAP uses disk-based storage with compression (typically a 3x compression ratio) and can scale up to terabytes. MOLAP typically requires aggregation tuning to determine a good trade-off between performance gains and aggregation maintenance costs. Calculations use disk scans with in-memory subcube caching.

ROLAP passes through fact table requests as queries to the original data source. This is supported for most types of relational databases. ROLAP storage is not recommended for large dimension tables.

VertiPaq is an in-memory column-store database technology that is optimized, but not limited, to main memory. VertiPaq achieves very high data compression ratios (typically 10× and, in some real-world scenarios, closer to 100× compression). It does not require any tuning, indexes, or aggregation. It accomplishes very fast performance by executing queries through sophisticated scanning algorithms of compressed data in memory. VertiPaq is the underlying technology and engine that power PowerPivot for Excel, PowerPivot for SharePoint, tabular models in Analysis Server in SQL Server 2012, and the new SQL Server 2012 Column Store Index in the relational database.

Direct Query passes through and translates DAX queries and calculations to the underlying database. This provides up-to-date results in each query execution. The data source is not just used as a row store, but the generated queries leverage database capabilities to execute queries efficiently. Currently in SQL Server 2012, the only type of relational data source that supports Direct Query is the SQL Server database. Another restriction is that only DAX queries, not MDX queries, can be translated for models in Direct Query mode (although it is likely to soon be an update to change that). Power View generates DAX queries, so it can leverage models configured with Direct Query enabled. A primary scenario for Direct Query in SQL Server 2012 is exposing a model (without cached data) directly over a SQL Server database or data warehouse.

Chapter 12 explains tabular model design in more detail, and provides a tutorial using PowerPivot for Excel.

The Hybrid Nature of the BI Semantic Model

It is important to note that regardless of how the data access layer, business logic, or data model are built and designed, client applications interact with one representation of the BI Semantic Model.

For example, a sales model is created with PowerPivot in Excel, is imported to SSDT, is further enhanced, and then is deployed to an Analysis Server to provide scalability for large data volumes:

➤ Data model is tabular

➤ Business logic is DAX

➤ Data access is VertiPaq

For the model in this example, Table 9-3 analyzes how the BI Semantic Model is used when a business user connects when using an Excel PivotTable or PivotChart, when using Power View, and when using Report Builder.

TABLE 9-3

EXCEL PIVOTTABLE, PIVOTCHART	POWER VIEW	REPORT BUILDER
The BI Semantic Model is consumed as a multidimensional model.	Consumed as a tabular model.	Depending on the query designer utilized, may be multidimensional or tabular.
Excel generates MDX queries.	Power View generates DAX queries.	Depending on the query designer utilized, may be MDX or DAX queries.

As a second example, consider a finance model with complex business logic. The model is created with SSDT as a cube and deployed to an Analysis Server:

➤ Data model is multidimensional

➤ Business logic is MDX

➤ Data access is MOLAP

Although the model's underlying internal layers are quite different from the first example, a BI Semantic Model is still exposed. Business users can connect using an Excel PivotTable or PivotChart and Report Builder (see Table 9-4). Power View in SQL Server 2012 won't work, because the multidimensional MOLAP model doesn't yet support DAX queries. They should be supported in the future, however, at which point the promise of a full hybrid model will be fulfilled.

TABLE 9-4

EXCEL PIVOTTABLE, PIVOTCHART	POWER VIEW	REPORT BUILDER
The BI Semantic Model is consumed as a multidimensional model.	Not yet supported in SQL Server 2012. Should be supported in a future update.	The BI semantic model is consumed as a multidimensional model.
Excel generates MDX queries.		MDX is used as the query language.

SUMMARY

This chapter introduced data modeling and the BI Semantic Model. It provided an overview of how client tools such as Excel PivotTable and Power View consume models, and the options available to build models.

This chapter also provided a more detailed explanation of the conceptual layers of the BI Semantic Model, what options exist for each layer, and what application and user needs to consider for the layers of data access and storage, business logic, and data model.

This chapter's overview provides a solid foundation for your detailed exploration of building reports over multidimensional models, as well as building tabular models and using Power View, in the following chapters.

10

Reporting with Analysis Services

WHAT'S IN THIS CHAPTER?

➤ Understanding Analysis Server

➤ Working with Multidimensional Expressions (MDX)

➤ Building queries with the MDX Query Designer

➤ Adding nonadditional measures

➤ When to use the Aggregate function

➤ Creating cube report actions

SQL Server 2012 Analysis Services is used to store and aggregate data. Specifically, it supports decision-support systems, ad hoc reporting, and business data analysis. After it is designed, cube data is easy to navigate to produce complex, business-relevant results for business leaders and information workers.

This chapter introduces some of the basic concepts of OLAP and multidimensional storage systems. You will use the Report Designer to create Multidimensional Expressions (MDX) language queries, both with and without the MDX Graphical Query Builder. You will learn how to build compelling reports using parameters, pivot tables, and KPI indicators in a table or matrix report.

Finally, you will learn to use cube actions and apply best practices and safety checks to your report solutions that use Analysis Services as a data source.

In the following chapter, you will build on this knowledge to create advanced reports that can change their content (rows, columns, and measures) by simply changing report parameter values.

WHY USE ANALYSIS SERVICES FOR REPORTING?

Every year at the Professional Association for SQL Server (PASS) Community Summit, I poll the Reporting Services session attendees and ask who is using Analysis Services or plans to in the near future. Over the past three years, the number of positive respondents has increased significantly, but the overall percentage is still a significant minority — perhaps 25 percent.

A couple of years ago I was pulled aside by one of the research groups within Microsoft Redmond, given a Post-it Note, and asked to write down the definition of business intelligence (BI). Like nearly every other professional in the room, I struggled to come up with a succinct definition. As it turns out, the definition is quite simple:

Business intelligence is *turning data into knowledge.*

To do this, you need easy access to your data. So you must be able to "slice and dice" data without having to know data relationships or SQL syntax. An Analysis Server cube gives you this ability. Do you need to use SQL Server Analysis Services to manage your data for reporting and analytics? This depends on a few factors.

Figure 10-1 shows data storage options for business reporting data. In all but the smallest business environment, the data collected and managed by various business processes is stored in different databases and systems. Getting reliable answers to important business questions from these data sources can be challenging at best. Consolidating this data into a central data store is no simple matter, but the value to the business is significant and often critical.

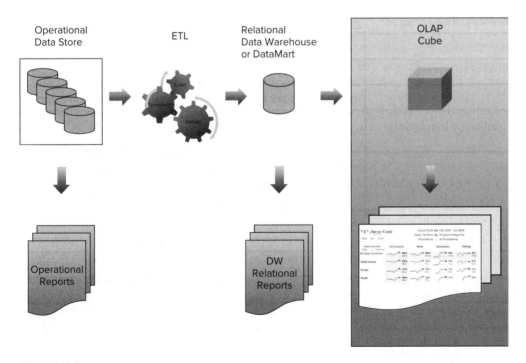

FIGURE 10-1

Data is transformed from multiple data sources, staged, validated, and optimized for reporting. The simplified relational data structures are stored in subject area data marts or a central data warehouse. The data organized in a relational data warehouse structure supports faster queries, and helps report designers create reports without the unnecessary complexity found in most operational database systems that are primarily designed for transactions.

As soon as the necessary effort has been expended to build and populate a data warehouse, taking the next step of creating OLAP cubes on this data is relatively easy.

Making the leap from the operational data store to a relational data warehouse may be sufficient in a small business with unsophisticated reporting needs. However, even for a medium-scale business environment, including Analysis Services in the solution has many advantages. Generally, moving to an OLAP solution enables capabilities in four categories:

➤   Data in a cube is "browseable" without your having to write sophisticated queries. Information is organized into dimensional hierarchies so that report designers can simply drag and drop to design report datasets.

➤   Information workers can design their own reports without understanding the underlying data structure and with no query-writing skills. Users simply select from predefined measures and hierarchies to create queries and design reports.

➤   Sophisticated calculations are built into the cube using calculated members. Users and report designers can select from calculated members as easily as they can use standard measures and other cube members.

➤   Cube-based queries typically run very fast, even when the cube is derived from large sets of data. The improved performance is due primarily to preaggregated values stored in optimized, nonrelational hierarchies in the OLAP data storage engine.

The bottom line is that building an OLAP cube with Analysis Services is generally easy to do if you have a properly designed relational datawarehouse. It's much easier to navigate than a relational database. Cubes enable self-service reporting and effective data exploration. And, sometimes most importantly, cubes can be very fast compared to other data sources and reporting solutions.

If you work for a small company or in an environment with manageable volumes of data, you will likely find significant advantages. Because Analysis Services is already covered under your SQL Server product license, there is little or no cost to build cubes and realize these benefits.

If you work for a large company and work with larger volumes of complex business data, you probably don't need much persuasion to recognize the advantages of using cubes to help solve these challenges. Making the move to OLAP cubes will help you take reporting to the next level while solving performance and query design issues.

A quick note on dimensional modeling: Keep it simple. The design tools make it easy to add lots of attributes to an Analysis Server cube. As a developer or superuser, you might think you are helping your clients by adding all these attributes. Don't do it. Think carefully about what attributes you want to add, and minimize the number of dimensions (ideally, you should use seven to ten). Keep the overall cube simple and therefore easy to use.

USING REPORTING SERVICES WITH ANALYSIS SERVICES DATA

Reporting Services works natively with several Analysis Services capabilities:

➤ **Native support for nonadditive measures and calculations.** Rather than building sophisticated expressions and calculation logic into reports, Reporting Services lets you take advantage of features already built into the Analysis Services cube.

➤ **Analysis Services and the MDX query language support custom formatting defined for measures in the cube.** Reports may be designed to use this formatting without duplicating this effort in the report design.

➤ **Drill-through reports can work for MDX datasets.** With some basic knowledge of MDX member reference formatting and special field properties present in Reporting Services for MDX reports, drill-through reports can be used.

➤ **Cube data may be protected through user role-based security.** This works with no special report provisions if user credentials are provided to data sources using Windows Authentication.

➤ **Summary reports that would normally aggregate a lot of data run much faster with cubes.** Take advantage of this capability by designing summary reports and dashboards with drill-through actions to lower-level, detailed reports.

Most reports that use Analysis Services as a data source are fairly easy to design for two reasons:

➤ The mission of OLAP is to make data easy to use. A properly designed cube simplifies your business data by organizing it into predefined, hierarchical structures with business facts preaggregated and ready to use by dragging and dropping into the MDX Query Designer.

➤ The Report Designer is friendly, with an MDX-based dataset. It automatically generates parameter lists, cascading parameters, and filtering logic. In many ways, designing a report for OLAP is easier than for a relational database because of the simplification applied in the cube, and these enhancements to the Report Designer.

Most OLAP reports are usually simple in design, just because of the nature of the cube. With predefined drill-down paths, and multiple multilevel hierarchies, it should be natural to visualize this information in a matrix or multiaxis chart. Business leaders now expect to see data presented in standard formats, using key performance indicators (KPIs) to present business metrics in dashboards and business scorecards with gauges and iconized graphical indicators. In the following exercises, you will see how using an OLAP data source with dimensional hierarchies, measures, KPIs, calculated members, and related cube elements make business report design simple and manageable.

WORKING WITH MULTIDIMENSIONAL EXPRESSION LANGUAGE

The MDX query language is part of the OLEDB for OLAP specification from Microsoft. The MDX query language is used in several different OLAP products from different vendors such as IBM Cognos, Hyperion EssBase, Business Objects, and, of course, Microsoft SQL Server Analysis

Services. Like SQL, the language varies from product to product, but the concepts and core features are the same — or at least very similar in some categories.

MDX: Simple or Complex?

Most IT professionals who want to learn MDX already know a little or a lot of SQL. They have worked through the process of reporting on transactional databases, migrating to a data warehouse, and building queries on a relational/dimensional model. They now realize the benefits of a truly dimensional storage engine to solve complex business problems. This presents an interesting challenge for most of these people. You see, MDX is a simple query language that sits squarely on the multidimensional foundations of OLAP technologies — all of which exists for the sole purpose of simplifying business data. But if OLAP and MDX are so *simple*, why does the industry perceive them to be so difficult to learn? There's a simple answer. MDX is very different from SQL, but on the surface it looks a lot like SQL. This means that anyone making the transition must struggle through a mental paradigm shift — from two-dimensional (2D), row-set-based thinking to multidimensional, axis-based cell-set thinking. Making this mental transition is not so difficult with a bit of effort, but it's easy to slip back into a SQL mindset if you don't stay in practice. MDX is not really harder than SQL; it is more like the difference between a procedural language and an object-oriented language. Here's the interesting twist: When you're done working with all these cool, multidimensional concepts, you take the output and pound it back into a 2D result so that you can display it on a screen or print it on a sheet of paper.

I'd love to launch into a discourse on sets, axes, tupples, slicers, subcubes, and other nifty OLAP concepts, but this isn't the time or place. This is one of those topics that can't be introduced without sufficient background and an exhaustive set of exercises. So you won't learn everything you need to know about MDX in this short section on Reporting Services. My purpose is to give you some exposure to the kinds of things you can do using this powerful query language for OLAP. For most cube report work, you shouldn't need to know more than some basic commands and functions. However, if you plan to do extensive work with MDX, you should pick up *Professional Microsoft SQL Server Analysis Services 2008 with MDX* (Wrox, 2009) or take a class on MDX for SQL Server Analysis Services. The language and query techniques haven't changed much between SQL Server 2005, 2008, and 2012.

Building Queries with the MDX Query Designer

When you choose the SQL Server Analysis Services data processing provider as you define a report data source, the MDX Query Designer is automatically invoked for any new datasets. Your first objective is to work with dataset results from a query generated by the MDX Query Designer. After exploring this feature, you'll write MDX queries without the aid of the builder.

Here's what I think: The graphical MDX Query Designer generates well-formed, efficient MDX script. If you design all the necessary calculated members into the cube, you shouldn't have to make changes to the report queries. If you do need to write advanced MDX queries, you probably don't need to use the graphical designer anyway. Compared to T-SQL, MDX queries are usually simpler and less verbose, because business rules are resolved in the cube rather than in the query. But regardless of what I think, the MDX Query Designer works the way it does, and you should work with it and take advantage of its capabilities when doing so serves your needs. As a general practice I also utilize MDX Studio, available at `http://mdx.mosha.com/`, to format my custom MDX queries.

Creating a Data Source

Let's start by creating a shared data source for the Adventure Works DW Multidimensional_
WroxSSRS2012 database:

1. On the Solution Explorer for a report project, right-click Shared Data Sources and select
    "Add New Data Source," as shown in Figure 10-2.

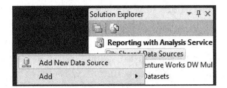

FIGURE 10-2

2. The Data Source Properties dialog opens, as shown in Figure 10-3. Select the Microsoft SQL
    Server Analysis Services data provider from the "Select connection type" drop-down list.

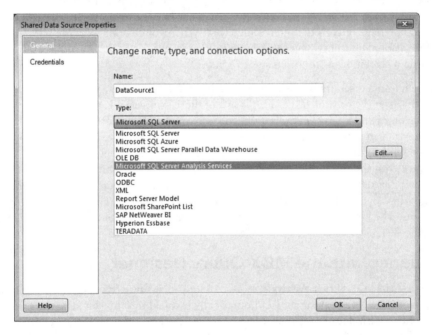

FIGURE 10-3

3. Click the Edit button to the right of the "Connection string" box to open the
    Connection Properties dialog, shown in Figure 10-4.

4. Type **LocalHost** or the name of your Analysis Services server in the "Server name" box.
    From the drop-down list in the "Connect to a database" section, select the Adventure
    Works DW Multidimensional_WroxSSRS2012 OLAP database. Click OK to accept these
    connection settings.

5. Back in the Shared Data Source Properties dialog, change the Name to AdventureWorksDWMultidimensional_WroxSSRS2012, as shown in Figure 10-5. Doing so differentiates between a relational data source and this Analysis Services data source for databases that have the same name or a similar one.

FIGURE 10-4

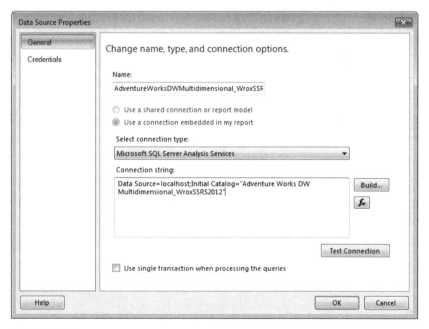

FIGURE 10-5

You can see that a connection string is generated and placed in the Connection string box. Click OK to save the new shared data source then right-click on the new shared data source and select "Deploy."

You will choose this shared data source for all the examples used in this chapter. Because the data source uses the Analysis Services data provider, the Report Designer generates MDX queries rather than the T-SQL queries you've seen in previous examples using the SQL Server data provider.

Building the Dataset Query

Now let's design a report using a KPI defined in the Adventure Works cube. A KPI is a standardized set of related members used to report the state of a business metric. In this case, you want to report the current value, goal, and status of Channel Revenue by product category for a selected calendar year. This section does not step you through every click and keystroke, because you already know how to design reports. This section covers the MDX-specific features and then shows you how to use the report design skills you acquired in previous exercises. Of course, you're also welcome to open the completed report in the Chapter 10 sample project.

1.   To get started, let's create a new dataset. Open Report Builder and select New Data Set tab. Select the shared data source, Adventure Works DW Multidimensional_WroxSSRS2012, and then click Create, as shown in Figure 10-6. Note that if the data set is not available, you need to click the "Browse other data sources" option and navigate to `http://localhost/ReportServer/Data Sources` and open it.

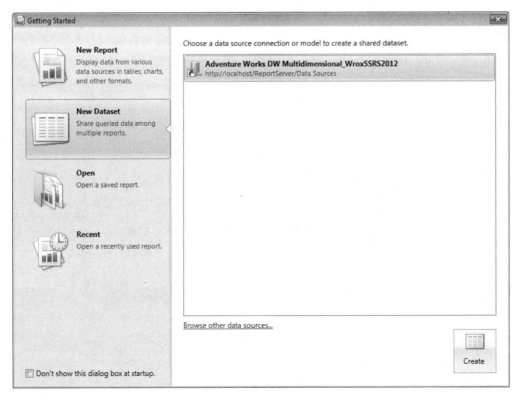

FIGURE 10-6

You see that the MDX Query Designer, shown in Figure 10-7, is used to construct the query using simple drag and drop. I've labeled this figure to point out the important components of this screen. At first, you will use the cube metadata pane to select cube members and then drag them into the cube member drop area (or data pane). I'll refer to other components in this figure as we continue to work with this tool.

 I tend to work from the inside out, dragging in measures and then the dimension members. This may seem a little backward, but it's a logical approach.

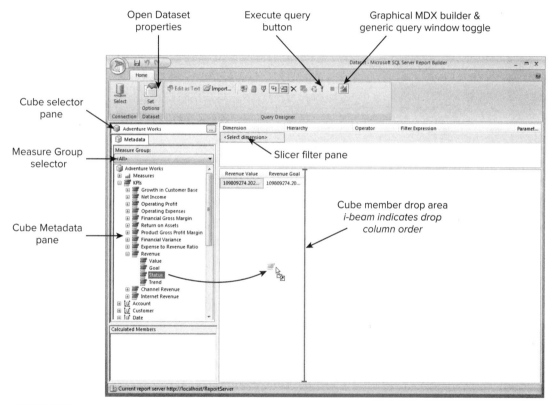

FIGURE 10-7

2. Using the Cube metadata pane, expand the KPIs node and the Channel Revenue KPI. Drag the Value, Goal, and Status members into the data pane. Note that a large I-beam bar indicates the drop position of the current member. Use this to position these members in the proper order.

The metadata pane enables you to explore and select from any member of the cube structure. Figure 10-8 shows various members of the Adventure Works sample cube. In short, measures, calculated members, and KPIs represent numeric values for reporting. All other members are used to group, filter, and provide navigational paths to these values. I've expanded nodes in the metadata pane to demonstrate examples of each of these elements.

Another technique I find useful is to select a specific option from the Measure Group selector. This restricts information to just the Measures and Dimensions that relate to that measure group. For example, you can select Reseller Sales.

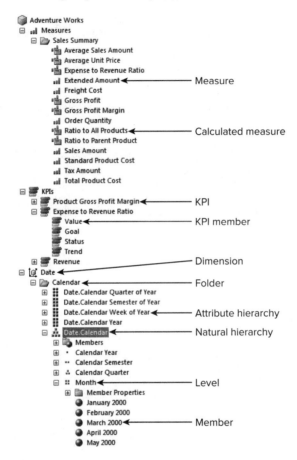

FIGURE 10-8

All cube attributes are organized into subject-specific dimensions. Dimensions have two types of hierarchies — attribute and user. An *attribute hierarchy* is simply a flat collection of dimension members derived from a specific data attribute. A *user hierarchy* has multiple levels of attributes organized into a logical drill-down structure. For the most part, you want to use user hierarchies for all drill-down and structured reporting. As a matter of convention, hierarchies consist of levels and members. Members are just the individual attribute values for a level (such as Years, Quarters, or Months). Note that attribute hierarchy levels typically have the same name as the hierarchy (such as [Date].[CalendarYear].[CalendarYear]), but user hierarchies do not. The user attribute name typically is more explicit (such as [Date].[Calendar].[CalendarYear]). Unless specifically hidden in the cube design, the members of every user hierarchy level correspond to the members of an attribute hierarchy.

3.   After dragging the KPI members to the data pane, expand the Sales Territory dimension. Drag the Sales Territory hierarchy to the left most position in the drop area (also known as the Data pane), as shown in Figure 10-9. The Query Designer parses the hierarchy levels and generates columns for each. The query runs and shows the results grouped by the attribute members, in order of column placement.

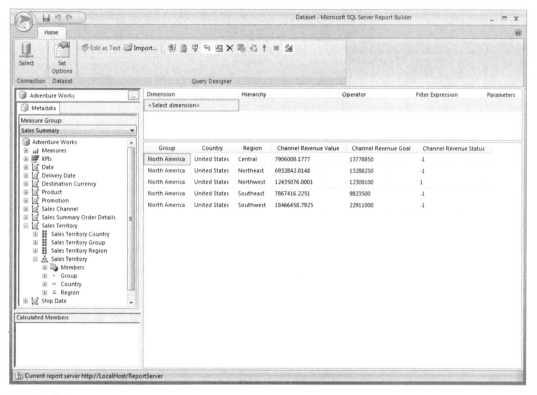

FIGURE 10-9

Using Parameterized Queries

The query created with the previous steps is complete and usable, but returns results for all the cube data. To filter data from a cube, you "slice" the cube to limit the query's scope to certain members of a hierarchy. You do so using the filtering pane of the MDX Query Designer. Follow these steps to add a parameterized filter to the query you just created:

1.   To filter the results, drag the Calendar Year attribute hierarchy into the Filter pane, as shown in Figure 10-10. This parses the hierarchy and places elements into the Dimension, Hierarchy, and Operator columns.

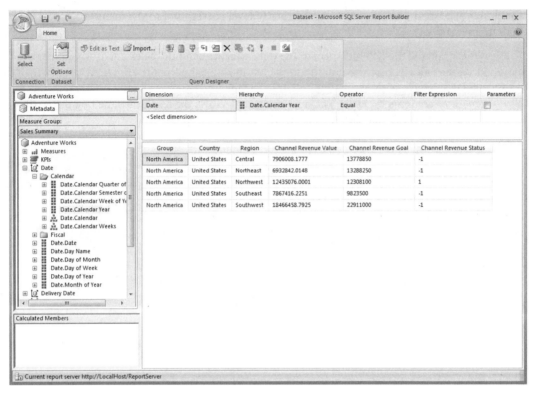

FIGURE 10-10

2. Use the Filter Expression drop-down window to set the default filter member. Note that every hierarchy has an `All` member, which is used to include all members of the hierarchy. Check All Periods to set the filter to include all members. This essentially negates the filter unless you make a different selection.

3. Depending on your screen size, the rightmost column may not be in view. If it isn't, scroll and adjust the columns to view the Parameter column. Check this box to generate a related report parameter for this filter.

Slicing the Cube

The concept of a filter is actually contrary to how OLAP works. We commonly use the term *filter* because most people understand this notion based on their experience with relational database technologies. However, what we've actually defined here is more accurately known as a *slicer*. To limit the results of an OLAP dataset, we won't tell the query engine to scan individual rows, looking for values that match certain criteria. We're actually telling it to "slice off" a portion of the cube, which is already organized into predefined ranges of grouped and sorted attributes. An important distinction between these two conventions is that slicing doesn't toss out the rest of the cube that doesn't meet the WHERE clause criteria (as a true filter would). It sets the context, or `CurrentMember` property, for the specified hierarchy. Members of the hierarchy outside this scope are still accessible to

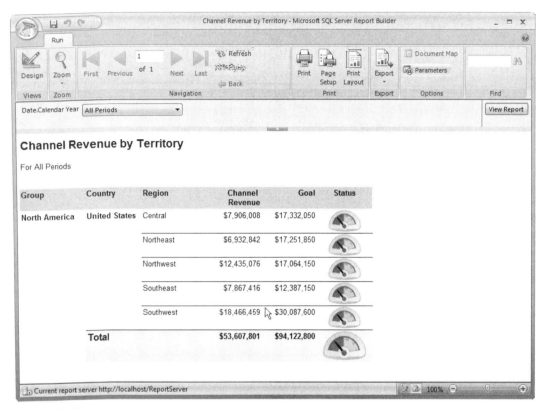

FIGURE 10-13

This is the Channel Revenue by Territory report in the Chapter 10 sample project. We simply defined groups on the sales territory region hierarchy levels and used the fields derived from the Value and Goal KPI members in the table's detail row. To visualize the Status KPI member, we added a radial gauge (180 degrees north) to the detail group and set the properties shown in Table 10-1.

After setting up the detail row textboxes and gauge, we added a total to the Country group and copied and pasted the gauge to the same column cell in the total row. The only change for this gauge is that the pointer value must use an AVG function instead of a SUM function. The gauge shows a red and a lime-green range with the pointer pointing to one of three positions, depending on the Status KPI member value.

You are encouraged to explore some of the standard features that were added as a result of using the MDX Query Designer. The parameter drop-down is completely configured and populated with a hidden dataset to provide Calendar Year values. Items on the list below the All member are indented. Had we used a user hierarchy, all the levels would be indented appropriately to indicate their position within the hierarchy. All parameter lists are automatically generated as multivalue selection lists. Of course, this can be changed in the Report Parameter Properties dialog.

functions and operators that may be used in the query. The default slicer, shown in Figure 10-11, is set to use the `All` member, which returns data for all calendar year members. Of course, users can change this parameter selection when they run the report.

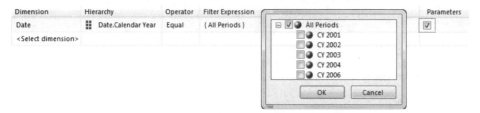

FIGURE 10-11

The Value and Goal KPIs typically are used to return a measure or calculated value. The Status and Trend members are used to simplify the state of the KPI performance based on some scripted logic and to drive a graphical dashboard indicator of some kind. In the case of Channel Revenue, the Status KPI member returns an integer with one of three values to indicate the state of channel revenue. The value –1 indicates poor performance, 0 is marginal, and 1 indicates acceptable or exceptional performance.

4. Click the Dataset Set Options button in the toolbar and add friendly names for three KPIs, as shown in Figure 10-12. Click OK.

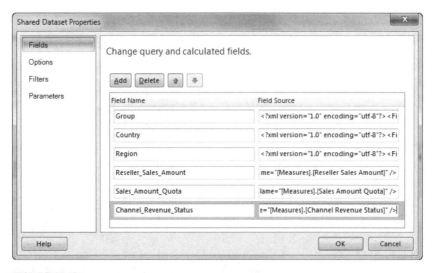

FIGURE 10-12

5. Name the dataset `ChannelRevenueByTerritory.rsd` and save it to `http://LocalHost/ReportServer/Reporting with Analysis Services Datasets/`.

After you create a dataset, designing a report that uses Analysis Services is no different from designing most other reports. Figure 10-13 shows a table report we designed for this dataset.

The majority of reports we create with an Analysis Services data source are this simple. Because the calculation and KPI business logic are designed into the cube, no extra work is necessary when reports are designed. With the Report Builder Designer, information workers can design reports with little or no knowledge of cube design or MDX query scripting. Using practically any MDX-based dataset, reports can be designed with a table, matrix, chart, or combinations of the data ranges and other report items to visualize business information in the most appropriate format.

TABLE 10-1

OBJECT	PROPERTY	VALUE
RadialScale1	MinimumValue	-2
	MaximumValue	2
RadialRange1	FillColor	Red
	FillGradientType	None
	StartValue	-2
	EndValue	0
	StartWidth	60
	EndWidth	60
	Placement	Cross
RadialRange2	FillColor	Lime
	FillGradientType	None
	StartValue	0
	EndValue	2
	StartWidth	60
	EndWidth	60
	Placement	Cross
RadialPointer1	FillColor	Black
	Value	=Sum(Fields!Channel_Revenue_Status.Value)
	MarkerLength	35

Modifying the MDX Query

We're now crossing a bridge, and on the other side is an environment that is a little more complex and delicate than the one we just left. Reporting Services enables you to do a lot of interesting things with MDX and OLAP data sources, but the Query Designer was not engineered for advanced MDX. The authors do a lot of MDX reporting, and we often step into client projects where others have tried to implement complex MDX queries and have failed. Over the past few years, working on these projects, we've discovered what has and hasn't worked, and we've developed techniques for achieving the desired results. One of our most important lessons has been to work with the product and its capabilities. I've had numerous conversations with members of the Reporting Services product team on this topic, and the advice I often receive is "We didn't intend for you to write an MDX query that way, and we don't support that particular technique. You can achieve the same result by doing it this way." I'd like to share some of these techniques with you.

I've not had much luck adding my own parameter logic to a handwritten query. It can be done, but the Query Designer is particular about script changes and intervenes at the most inconvenient times. I recommend that you do the following:

➤ Use the MDX Query Designer to design the original query with the built-in parameter logic and supporting datasets, and then modify the query logic, leaving the parameter logic alone.

Building a Query Using the MDX Designer

Let's start with a copy of the dataset you just completed. The objective is to define three calculated members based on the same KPI members you used. These calculated members don't exist in the cube. Let's assume you don't have permission to modify the cube structure to add them to the cube design. In addition to the Value, Goal, and Status members for the Channel Revenue KPI, you need to see what these values were for the prior year.

1. To get started, from Report Builder open the dataset query ChannelRevenueByTerritory, switch to the generic query view, and then copy the MDX script to the Clipboard.

2. Apparently, the Reporting Services MDX Query Designer was created before carriage returns were invented. Open MDX Studio (or use the online version at `http://mdx.mosha.com`). Paste the query from the Report Designer in the Query window and click Format, and then recopy the query to the Clipboard.

3. Open SQL Server Management Studio, connect to Analysis Services, and then click the New Query button on the toolbar to open a new MDX query.

4. Paste the query from the Report Designer in the Query window.

5. The nested parameter references won't work in Management Studio, so simplify this query to run without them. The easiest way to do this is to divide the first part of the script, up to the ON ROWS expression, from the rest with a few carriage returns. (This example uses only the first part for testing.) To complete the test query, you just need to add a FROM clause with the cube name and terminate this query with a semicolon.

6. Highlight only the first query, and click the Execute button on the toolbar. Your screen should look like Figure 10-14.

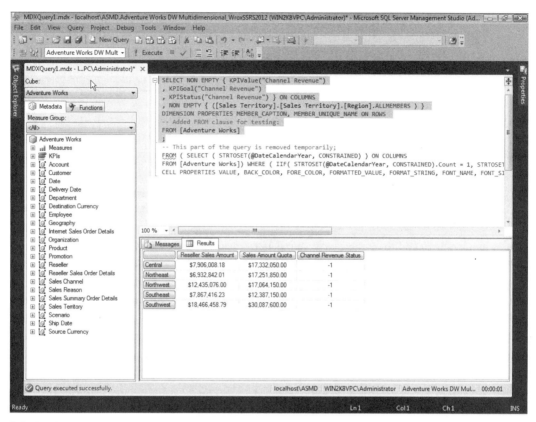

FIGURE 10-14

7. To add the calculated members to the query, type the following into the Query window before the existing script:

```
WITH
  MEMBER Measures.[Last Year Value] AS
    (
      [Date].[Calendar Year].CurrentMember.PrevMember
      ,KPIValue("Channel Revenue")
    )
    ,FORMAT_STRING = "$#,##0.00"
  MEMBER Measures.[Last Year Goal] AS
    (
      [Date].[Calendar Year].CurrentMember.PrevMember
      ,KPIGoal("Channel Revenue")
    )
    ,FORMAT_STRING = "$#,##0.00"
  MEMBER Measures.[Last Year Status] AS
    (
      [Date].[Calendar Year].CurrentMember.PrevMember
      ,KPIStatus("Channel Revenue")
    )
```

To explain the logic for each of these calculated members, we'll examine the first one. A new member named Last Year Value is added to the Measures collection, applying this expression:

```
MEMBER Measures.[Last Year Value] AS
  (
    [Date].[Calendar Year].CurrentMember.PrevMember
    ,KPIValue("Channel Revenue")
  )
  ,FORMAT_STRING = "$#,##0.00"
```

This member returns the Channel Revenue KPI Value for the previous Calendar Year, based on the current member of the Calendar Year hierarchy. If your user selects 2004 for the DateCalendarYear parameter, the WHERE clause uses the parameter to set this as the current member. The PREVMEMBER function causes the expression to return the Channel Revenue KPI Value for Calendar Year 2003. Because the final report query will be parameterized, this functionality is completely dynamic.

8. You want to add these three new members to the query's COLUMNS axis, which will be interpreted as three new fields in the report. Remove the NON EMPTY directive after the SELECT clause. This ensures that all columns will be returned, even if no data is present.

To add the new calculated members to the query, apply the following changes:

```
WITH
  MEMBER Measures.[Last Year Value] AS
    (
      [Date].{Calendar Year}.CurrentMember.PrevMember
      ,KPIValue("Channel Revenue")
    )
    ,FORMAT_STRING = "$#,##0.00"
  MEMBER Measures.[Last Year Goal] AS
    (
      [Date].[Calendar Year].CurrentMember.PrevMember
      ,KPIGoal("Channel Revenue")
    )
    ,FORMAT_STRING = "$#,##0.00"
  MEMBER Measures.[Last Year Status] AS
    (
      [Date].[Calendar Year].CurrentMember.PrevMember
      ,KPIStatus("Channel Revenue")
    )
SELECT
  {
    KPIValue("Channel Revenue")
    ,KPIGoal("Channel Revenue")
    ,KPIStatus("Channel Revenue")
    ,[Last Year Value]
    ,[Last Year Goal]
    ,[Last Year Status]
  } ON COLUMNS
  ,
    {
      [Sales Territory].[Sales Territory].[Region].ALLMEMBERS
    }
  DIMENSION PROPERTIES
    MEMBER_CAPTION
```

```
      ,MEMBER_UNIQUE_NAME
      ON ROWS
-- Added FROM clause for testing:
FROM [Adventure Works]
```

9. Run the query to verify that it works. You should now see six columns in the results. The reason that the new members don't return a value is that the current member of the Calendar Year has not been set. To do this, add a WHERE clause to slice the cube on Calendar Year 2004:

```
WITH
  MEMBER Measures.[Last Year Value] AS
    (
      [Date].[Calendar Year].CurrentMember.PrevMember
     ,KPIValue("Channel Revenue")
    )
   ,FORMAT_STRING = "$#,##0.00"
  MEMBER Measures.[Last Year Goal] AS
    (
      [Date].[Calendar Year].CurrentMember.PrevMember
     ,KPIGoal("Channel Revenue")
    )
   ,FORMAT_STRING = "$#,##0.00"
  MEMBER Measures.[Last Year Status] AS
    (
      [Date].[Calendar Year].CurrentMember.PrevMember
     ,KPIStatus("Channel Revenue")
    )
SELECT
  {
    KPIValue("Channel Revenue")
   ,KPIGoal("Channel Revenue")
   ,KPIStatus("Channel Revenue")
   ,[Last Year Value]
   ,[Last Year Goal]
   ,[Last Year Status]
  } ON COLUMNS
  ,
    {
      [Sales Territory].[Sales Territory].[Region].ALLMEMBERS
    }
  DIMENSION PROPERTIES
    MEMBER_CAPTION
   ,MEMBER_UNIQUE_NAME
    ON ROWS
-- Added FROM clause for testing:
FROM [Adventure Works]
-- Added WHERE clause for testing:
WHERE
  [Date].[Calendar Year].&[2004];
```

10. Apply this change, check your query with the following script, and then run the query. You should now see the 2003 values for the new calculated members. You can check this by making note of the values, using 2003 in the WHERE clause rather than 2004, and then running it again.

11.   To prepare the query for the report, you need to add all the parameter logic from the original query. Comment out the FROM and WHERE lines from the new query, and then remerge the two halves. Your final query should look like this:

```
WITH
  MEMBER Measures.[Last Year Value] AS
    (
       [Date].[Calendar Year].CurrentMember.PrevMember
      ,KPIValue("Channel Revenue")
    )
   ,FORMAT_STRING = "$#,##0.00"
  MEMBER Measures.[Last Year Goal] AS
    (
       [Date].[Calendar Year].CurrentMember.PrevMember
      ,KPIGoal("Channel Revenue")
    )
   ,FORMAT_STRING = "$#,##0.00"
  MEMBER Measures.[Last Year Status] AS
    (
       [Date].[Calendar Year].CurrentMember.PrevMember
      ,KPIStatus("Channel Revenue")
    )
SELECT
  {
    KPIValue("Channel Revenue")
   ,KPIGoal("Channel Revenue")
   ,KPIStatus("Channel Revenue")
   ,[Last Year Value]
   ,[Last Year Goal]
   ,[Last Year Status]
  } ON COLUMNS
  ,
    {[Sales Territory].[Sales Territory].[Region].ALLMEMBERS}
  DIMENSION PROPERTIES
    MEMBER_CAPTION
   ,MEMBER_UNIQUE_NAME
    ON ROWS
-- Added FROM clause for testing:
-- FROM [Adventure Works]
-- Added WHERE clause for testing:
-- WHERE
--   [Date].[Calendar Year].&[2004]


FROM
(
  SELECT
    StrToSet
    (@DateCalendarYear
     ,CONSTRAINED
    ) ON COLUMNS
  FROM [Adventure Works]
)
WHERE
  IIF
  (
```

```
         StrToSet(@DateCalendarYear,CONSTRAINED).Count = 1
         ,StrToSet
         (@DateCalendarYear
          ,CONSTRAINED
          )
         ,[Date].[Calendar Year].CurrentMember
         )
     CELL PROPERTIES
        VALUE
       ,BACK_COLOR
       ,FORE_COLOR
       ,FORMATTED_VALUE
       ,FORMAT_STRING
       ,FONT_NAME
       ,FONT_SIZE
       ,FONT_FLAGS;
```

12. Now you're ready to update the query in the report. Copy the query from the Management Studio Query window, and paste it over all the script in the Report Designer Query window. If you lose the formatting, paste the query into Microsoft Word or WordPad, and then recopy to the Clipboard.

13. Click the Query Parameters toolbar button, and change the parameter value for `DateCalendarYear` to CY 2004. Click OK to return.

14. Click the Execute button to test the query and refresh the field collection, as shown in Figure 10-15. Then Save As `ChannelRevenueByTerritoryOnLastYear.rsd`.

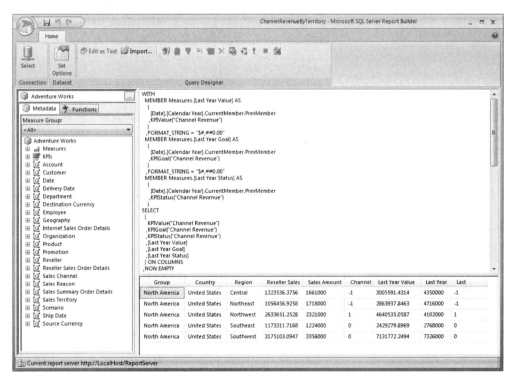

FIGURE 10-15

Report design based on this new shared dataset is pretty straightforward. As you can see in Figure 10-16, the three new calculated members are added to the dataset fields collection. They can be used to add columns to the table using the same drag-and-drop technique you have used before.

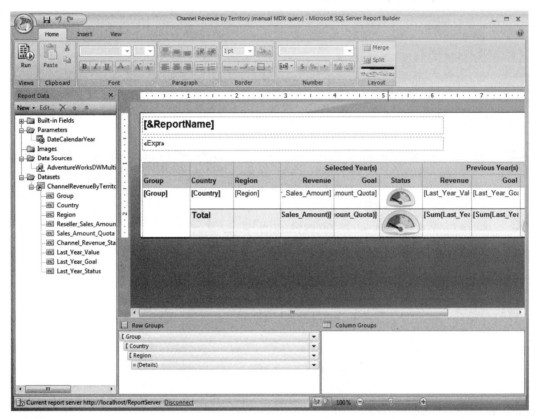

FIGURE 10-16

The gauges can also be copied and pasted from the original Status column. On the new gauge, click the pointer, and then use the smart tag to update the field binding to use the `Last_Year_Status` field.

Figure 10-17 shows this report in preview. A copy of the completed report is also available in the Chapter 10 sample project.

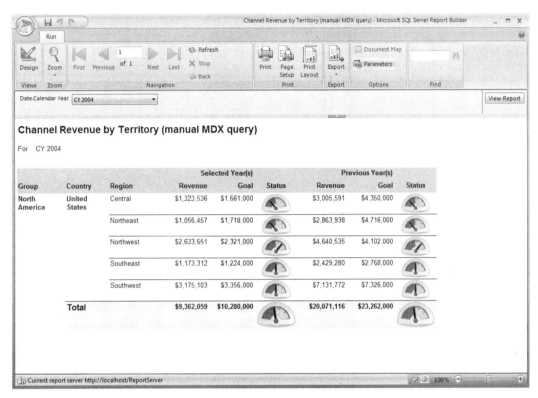

FIGURE 10-17

ADDING NONADDITIVE MEASURES

Often, the values you need to see on reports are calculated using more complex logic than simple sums. Measure values can be based on statistical functions, rolling or weighted averages, or industry-specific standard calculations. Special logic is often required to calculate common metrics such as inventory counts, profit, and ratios. Regardless, these aren't calculations you should have to repeat in every report. One of the advantages of using SQL Server Analysis Services is that all the necessary business logic for reporting and analysis can be designed into the cube. This means that as soon as the business rules are sorted out in the cube design, you simply use the measures, calculated members, and KPIs with full confidence that the results will be accurate and reliable.

Let's use a simple example of an average sales amount calculation. You can use your imagination to extend this scenario to other business cases that would apply to your situation. The Adventure

Works cube contains a measure named Reseller Average Sales Amount. The logic behind this calculation relies on the knowledge of individual transaction sales amounts that are actually not present in the cube. In fact, unless you were to go back to the original data source for these sales records, you couldn't calculate this value yourself. Fortunately, Analysis Services performs some magic when it processes the cube and aggregates this measure value. It figures out which values must be stored in the cube, and which values can be derived at query time. In the case of an average measure, it must store the average at every level of a dimensional hierarchy, because it's not possible to derive an average from a range of average values at a lower level. Although it's interesting to know how Analysis Services performs these aggregations and stores selected values, you can sleep soundly at night knowing that you don't have to worry about it.

Enter Reporting Services. When you drag and drop a field onto a report item or data region at a group level above a detail row, the Report Designer always applies the SUM function to a numeric value. It assumes that you want to roll up individual values into a summed total. This is a helpful assumption most of the time, but not when your measure fields don't sum, or if you want to do something else with them. What if the measure were a standard deviation or a weighted, rolling average? How would you roll this up into a group footer?

It doesn't matter. This is Analysis Services' job, and you should not have to worry about it. Here's a simple example to illustrate the simple solution. Figure 10-18 shows a basic matrix report, named AS Avg Sales in the Chapter 10 sample project. The detail and total value cells were designed by dragging the `Sales_Amount_Quota` and `Reseller_Average_Sales_Amount` fields to the detail area of the matrix. We've made a point to expand the column widths so that you can see the expressions. As you can see, the Designer applied the SUM function to all four of these cells.

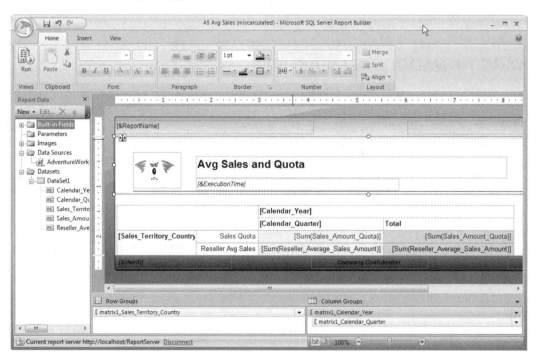

FIGURE 10-18

Figure 10-19 shows the report in preview. We point out one example where the total for two quarterly sales averages is the sum of these values. This is an inaccurate total. (Read on.)

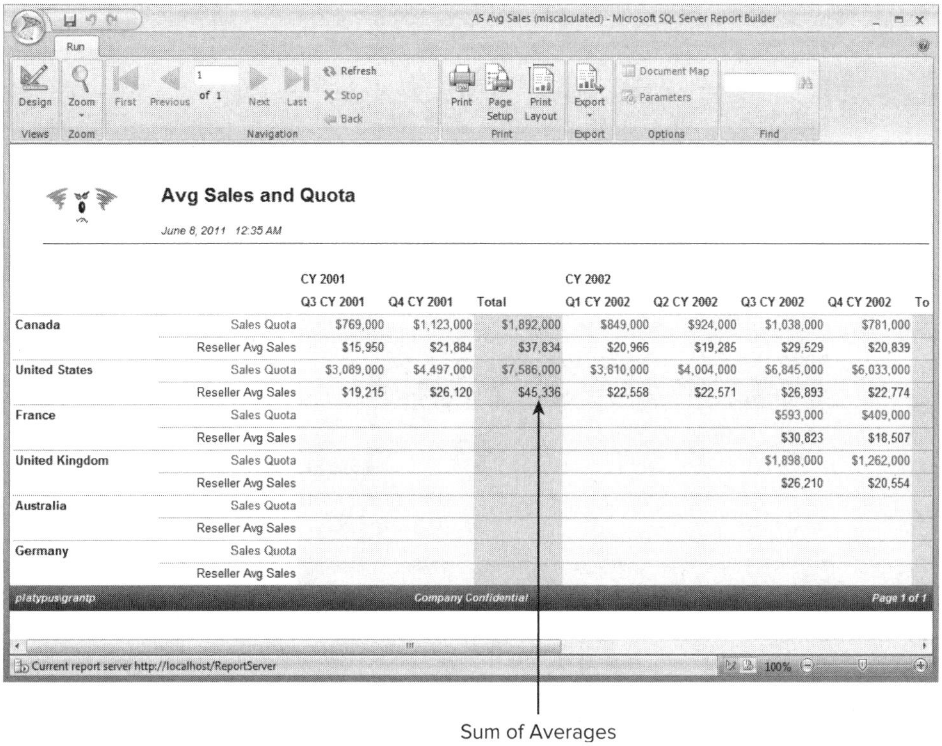

Sum of Averages

FIGURE 10-19

When to Use the Aggregate Function

The solution to this problem is to let Reporting Services know that it should not try to aggregate any values. The measure values for an OLAP query have already been aggregated, and the value at each level represents the appropriate rollup of subordinate levels. This is done by replacing occurrences of SUM with the AGGREGATE function.

Figure 10-20 shows the report with these changes. We have replaced all the SUM function references with AGGREGATE by editing each expression.

Preview the report again to see the results. Note that all the Sales_Amount_Quota total values remain the same, because this is an additive measure and these values were already using the SUM function in the cube. The summed value from the cube (which you see here) and the summed values in the report are the same. However, the Reseller_Average_Sales_Amount totals are different. This is because the calculation returned from the cube in Figure 10-21 is the calculated average rather than the sum of averages you saw in the previous example.

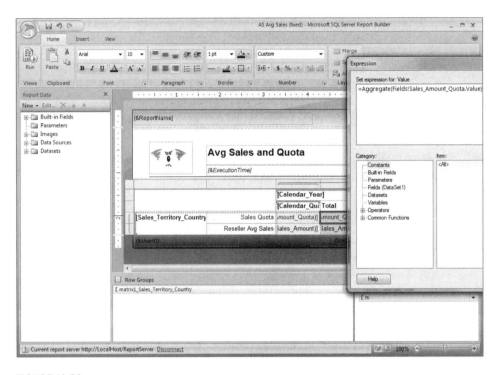

FIGURE 10-20

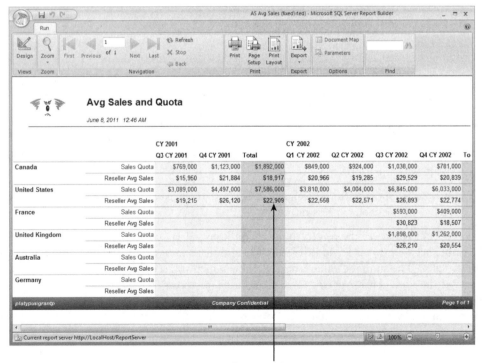

Corrected Average

FIGURE 10-21

MDX PROPERTIES AND CUBE FORMATTING

As you've looked at the MDX queries generated by the MDX Query Designer, you may have noticed several property references in the MDX script under the headings CELL PROPERTIES, DIMENSION PROPERTIES, and CUBE PROPERTIES. This is evidence of one of the most significant differences between Analysis Services and a relational database product such as SQL Server 2012. When you run a T-SQL query for a SQL Server database, the result set contains very little information aside from the column names and values. The data provider and client components use a bit of metadata, such as data types, numeric scales, and string lengths. The formatting of the query results is entirely in the hands of whichever client application is consuming the data.

MDX-based queries provide a mechanism for returning a variety of useful information about different objects returned from a query. Within the cube design, every measure can be formatted, and every calculated member can have font, color, and other styling characteristics associated with it. Dynamic expressions defined in the cube are used to modify these properties based on threshold values or any other logic. This way, profit-related measures are displayed in green, and losses are in red and bold text. These properties are returned through the query results as metadata tags associated with each cell and dimension member. The query script can explicitly request that certain properties be returned.

Reporting Services uses these properties by generating corresponding properties for each field object it derives from an MDX query. These field properties are accessible in the Report Designer Expression dialog. When you select a field, the `Value` property is referenced by default. To see all the available field properties, just back up the cursor to the period following the field name. Figure 10-22 shows an example setting the `Color` property of the textbox used to display the `Sales_Amount_Quota`.

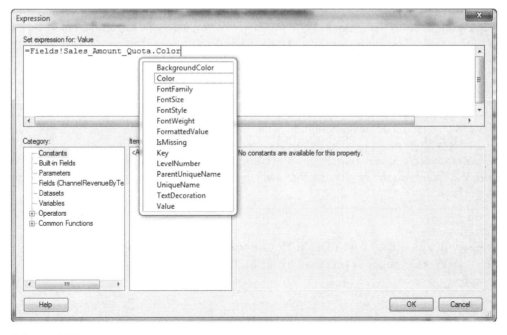

FIGURE 10-22

This is a powerful concept. I had a client who insisted on having specific colors for specific currencies. This technique allows you to set the color in the database/cube, and then the Reporting Services report consumes this information.

Unfortunately, the current version of the Adventure Works DW Multidimensional_ WroxSSRS2012 sample Analysis Services database doesn't implement any dynamic formatting, so I'm unable to easily demonstrate this feature without using a cube you don't have access to.

DRILL-THROUGH REPORTS

As you know, a drill-through report uses a report action to navigate to a second report when the user clicks a report item (often a textbox) that contains a reference value of some kind. The typical scenario for drill-through reports is where a high-level summary report lists dimension members in a data region in a table or matrix. Using the example of a table report showing sales summary information for products, if users were to click a product name, they might expect to see sales details for that product. If a report based on relational tables were used for drill-through, you would expect a key value, such as the ProductID, to be passed from the source report to a parameter in the target report, and used to filter records.

MDX-based reports can play this role as well as any other data source. The difference is in how keys and unique identifiers are defined in a cube. Every dimensional attribute does have a key value, but it might not necessarily correspond to a primary key value in a relational data source. Because attributes are organized into hierarchies, the unique value used to describe an attribute preserves the entire hierarchy lineage through a property called UniqueName. This is the value passed to any parameters generated by the MDX Query Designer. It is considered a best practice to use the same technique for drill-through reports. The value of a dimension member is derived from the MDX Name property for a member by default. For a product, this would just be the product name as it appears on the report. The UniqueName property value is derived from the ProductKey field in the DimProduct table and would look something like this:

```
[Product].[Product].&[470]
```

The example provided in the Chapter 10 sample project consists of a source and target report that you can use as an example of this functionality. The Top 10 Product Internet Sales by Year report contains a table with an action configured for the Product textbox. The Product Sales by Year report has a parameter called Product that filters an MDX query bound to a chart. The source report contains an action defined on the Product textbox, which passes a value using the following expression to the target report:

```
=Fields!Product.UniqueName
```

The target report, Product Sales by Year (MDX drill-through target), contains a query parameter named ProductProduct that was generated by the MDX Query Designer when this report was designed.

Figure 10-23 shows the Action expression settings for the source report product textbox. Note the expression used in the Values column of the parameter mapping. Also note that back on the design surface the product textbox font color is blue. This is a visual clue to the user they can click on a product. Users can't help clicking things that are blue!

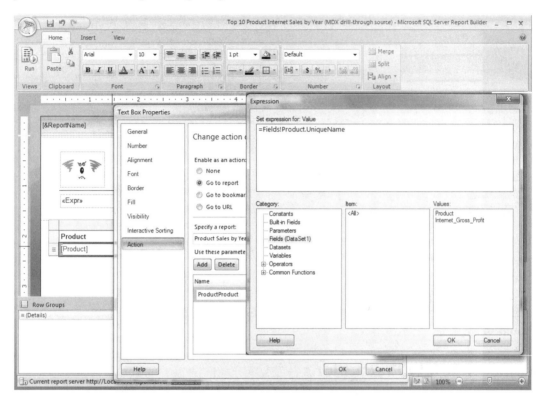

FIGURE 10-23

Drill-through actions are one of the most useful features of Reporting Services. In the next chapter you will use this technique extensively.

Creating Cube Report Actions

Report navigation can also be driven by the cube itself. Cube actions are designed in a cube and exposed as metadata in an MDX query cell-set result. When a compatible cube-browsing client (which includes Excel PivotTables) displays a query result, hotspots are generated for the related cells. The user can choose a drill-through action for the relevant cell and navigate to a report or other target defined by the cube action.

From a report design perspective, designing a report to receive a report action is exactly the same as designing a drill-through target report. You simply create a parameter to filter the results of a query. Figure 10-24 shows the View Map for [City] cube action from an Excel pivot table.

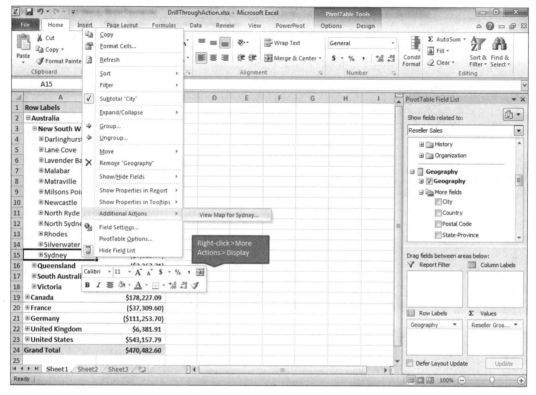

FIGURE 10-24

Parameter Safety Precautions

If a drill-through report, URL, or cube report action is exposed to the Internet or an uncontrolled network environment, precautions should be taken to prevent script injection attacks. Two common safety precautions are used when parameters are passed to an MDX query. The first is implemented by default in the script generated by the MDX Query Designer. Parameters are passed to the function STRTOSET or STRTOMEMBER with the CONSTRAINED optional argument flag. This flag instructs the MDX query processing engine to disallow any dynamic script or function calls in the parameter text. The other provision that you can implement yourself is the URLEscapeFragment function. Passing any MDX object reference to this function MIME-encodes any characters that could be used to embed script. The query processor decodes any valid characters on the receiving end after validating the unaltered text. This sample code returns a properly escaped form of a dimension member reference:

```
UrlEscapeFragment(SetTostr({[Dim].[MyHierarchy].CurrentMember}))
```

BEST PRACTICES AND PROVISIONS

The following are some important considerations for designing reports for Analysis Services. Keep these factors in mind as you create reports:

➤ **Leverage the cube.** Design business rules and calculations into the cube. Report and query design with a comprehensive cube is a simple matter of dragging and dropping members into the Query Designer.

➤ **Allow empty rows.** By default, the MDX Query Designer eliminates rows that have all empty cells. This may impede certain reports, such as charts and matrices. To include all rows, regardless of empty cells, remove the NON EMPTY directive on the rows axis.

➤ **Let the cube manage aggregation.** Replace the SUM or FIRST aggregate functions added by the Report Designer with the AGGREGATE function. This instructs Reporting Services to let the Analysis Services query engine take care of the aggregate values.

➤ **Sorting months.** When you use the Report Wizard to create a table or matrix report, groups are sorted on the same field as the group. Fields such as Months are sorted in alphabetical order. Because the members are already sorted correctly in the cube dimension, this is resolved by removing the Sort expression for the group.

➤ **Cascading parameters.** Autobuilt MDX queries create multiple datasets with interdependent parameters. Removing an unneeded parameter can be challenging. Check each hidden dataset query for references to the parameter, and remove those references or delete the dataset and rebuild it without the parameter.

➤ **Use the Query Designer to create parameters.** Allow the MDX Query Designer to create parameter and filter logic, and then modify the query after making a backup copy.

SUMMARY

SQL Server 2012 Analysis Services is a powerful tool for storing and managing critical business information to support business decisions and analytics. If Analysis Services is used correctly, compelling and useful reports can be created easily using Reporting Services. Business users shouldn't need to understand the MDX language to design day-to-day reports with Report Builder. But with some basic MDX knowledge, BI solution developers can create advanced visualizations and powerful business dashboards that would be slow and difficult to design with a relational data source.

The advantages afforded by Analysis Services and the OLAP query engine are numerous. Queries are lightning-fast, data is simplified and accessible, and business-specific calculations are managed in a central location. Using Reporting Services to design reports for Analysis Services data can create a fast, secure, and reliable BI solution with uniform results across the business enterprise.

11

OLAP Reporting Advanced Techniques

WHAT'S IN THIS CHAPTER?

➤ Dynamically changing report content and navigating hierarchies by changing report parameters

➤ Restricting the number of rows with a parameter

➤ Displaying and allowing users to explore cube metadata

➤ Creating your own OLAP browser in Reporting Services

Years ago, when I attended Tech Ed (Microsoft's annual conference for developers and IT professionals) in Boston, I noticed that the Blue Man Group was in town. I just *had* to see them; they are compelling on stage. This reminds me that when you see blue text in a browser (or report), you are *compelled* to click it. This chapter discusses how you can use this "blue clicking compulsion" to create dynamic and flexible reports that can be navigated simply by clicking blue content.

This chapter describes a series of reports that demonstrate the techniques behind building an OLAP client in SSRS. Along the way you will learn about the following:

➤ Using self-calling drill-through reports to navigate content

➤ Using other reports to collect parameters

➤ Formatting reports to make them easy to navigate

➤ Using cube metadata to drive report content (this will work on any cube)

CUBE DYNAMIC ROWS

I have often observed when I'm creating reports for clients that the reports they want are very similar. The columns stay fairly static, with values such as Amount, Amount Last Year, Growth, Growth Percentage, and Gross Profit. The only difference is the data shown on rows. So two reports could have identical columns, but one has Products on rows and another has Regions.

One of the neat things about Analysis Services is that it lets you move up and down through hierarchies, selecting what you are interested in. In the Product dimension, for instance, you can select Product Category: Bikes or Product Sub-Category: Mountain Bikes. You can even select a single Product Model.

This report uses a parameter that lets you change what hierarchy is displayed on rows and lets you drill up or down within that hierarchy. It also uses a parameter for the measure to display. The final report will behave as shown in Figure 11-1. Simply clicking a hierarchy member allows you to drill down to more and more detail, or similarly drill back up.

Product Categories	Gross Profit
All Products	13 m
Bikes	11 m
Components	1.0 m
Accessories	634 k
Clothing	369 k

Product Categories	Gross Profit
All Products	13 m
Bikes	11 m
Mountain Bikes	5.9 m
Road Bikes	4.4 m
Touring Bikes	217 k

Product Categories	Gross Profit
All Products	13 m
Bikes	11 m
Road Bikes	4.4 m
Road-150 Red, 48	470 k
Road-150 Red, 62	466 k
Road-150 Red, 52	421 k
Road-150 Red, 56	406 k

FIGURE 11-1

The Cube Browser report (an extension of this concept) calls a modified version of the Cube Metadata report. It allows users to dynamically change what measure and hierarchy to display on rows without needing to type a value into the parameter.

Cube Dynamic Rows Anatomy

This report utilizes custom MDX, mainly calculated measures, to present consistent column names to Reporting Services. Therefore, it facilitates dynamically changing rows and the measure by simply changing the parameters.

From SQL Server Data Tools (SSDT), open the report called Cube Dynamic Rows. Figure 11-2 shows the Cube Dynamic Rows Report Data.

Parameters

First, let's look at the parameters.

The string report parameter called `pMeasure` has this default value:

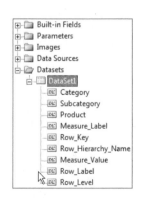

FIGURE 11-2

```
[Measures].[Gross Profit]
```

and these available expression values (label / value):

Gross Profit / = "[Measures].[Gross Profit]"

Sales Amount / = "[Measures].[Sales Amount]"

Amount / = "[Measures].[Amount]"

So this parameter drives the measure value displayed in the report.

The string report parameter called pRowMbr has this default value:

[Product].[Product Categories].[Subcategory].&[1]

This is the "focus" member of the report. In this case it is Product dimension, Product Categories hierarchy, and Subcategory level Mountain Bikes.

Dataset

Open the Query Designer for DataSet1, as shown in Figure 11-3.

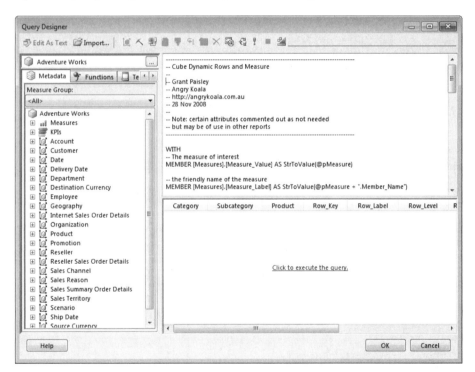

FIGURE 11-3

Here is the MDX query:

```
----------------------------------------------------------------------------------
-- Cube Dynamic Rows and Measure
--
```

```
-- Grant Paisley
-- Angry Koala
-- http://angrykoala.com.au
-- Nov 2011
--
-- Note: certain attributes commented out as not needed
-- but may be of use in other reports
-------------------------------------------------------------------------------

WITH
-- The measure of interest
MEMBER [Measures].[Measure_Value] AS StrToValue(@pMeasure)

-- the friendly name of the measure
MEMBER [Measures].[Measure_Label] AS StrToValue(@pMeasure + ".Member_Name")

MEMBER [Measures].[Row_Key]
    AS StrToValue( @pRowMbr + ".Hierarchy.Currentmember.Uniquename" )
MEMBER [Measures].[Row_Label]
    AS StrToValue( @pRowMbr + ".Hierarchy.CurrentMember.Member_Caption" )

MEMBER [Measures].[Row_Level]
    AS StrToValue( @pRowMbr + ".Hierarchy.CurrentMember.Level.Ordinal" )

--MEMBER [Measures].[Row_Level_Name]
--    AS StrToValue( @pRowMbr + ".Hierarchy.Level.Name" )

MEMBER [Measures].[Row_Hierarchy_Name]
    AS StrToValue( @pRowMbr + ".Hierarchy.Name" )

--MEMBER [Measures].[Row_Hierarchy_UniqueName]
--   AS StrToValue( @pRowMbr + ".Hierarchy.UniqueName" )

MEMBER [Measures].[Row_Dimension_Name]
    AS StrToValue( @pRowMbr + ".Dimension.Name" )

--MEMBER [Measures].[Row_Dimension_UniqueName]
--    AS StrToValue(@pRowMbr + ".Dimension_Unique_Name" )

SELECT NON EMPTY {
 -- display the measure and rowmbr attributes on columns

 [Measures].[Row_Key],
 [Measures].[Row_Label],
 [Measures].[Row_Level],
 --[Measures].[Row_Level_Name],
 [Measures].[Row_Hierarchy_Name],
 --[Measures].[Row_Hierarchy_UniqueName],
 --[Measures].[Row_Dimension_Name],
 --[Measures].[Row_Dimension_UniqueName],

 [Measures].[Measure_Label] ,
 [Measures].[Measure_Value]
```

```
    } ON COLUMNS,

NON EMPTY
    -- if want to display row member parent, self and children
    -- un-comment following code
    --STRTOSET("{" + @pRowMbr + ".parent, "
    --            + @pRowMbr + ", "
    --            + @pRowMbr + ".children}" )

    -- show the current hierarchy member with its ascendants
    -- together with its children on rows
    STRTOSET(
        "{Ascendants(" + @pRowMbr + " ), "
        + @pRowMbr + ".children}"
    )

ON ROWS

FROM [Adventure Works] -- must hard code the cube :(
-- the cube name, together with the paramater default values are the only
-- things required to point this report at a different cube
```

In effect you create a calculated measure for each row member property of interest and display them on columns:

```
[Measures].[Row_Key],
 [Measures].[Row_Label],
 [Measures].[Row_Level],
--[Measures].[Row_Level_Name],
 [Measures].[Row_Hierarchy_Name],
--[Measures].[Row_Hierarchy_UniqueName],
--[Measures].[Row_Dimension_Name],
--[Measures].[Row_Dimension_UniqueName],
```

In additional to the current measure label and value:

```
[Measures].[Measure_Label] ,
[Measures].[Measure_Value]
```

On rows you simply display the "ascendants" of the current member and its children:

```
STRTOSET(
    "{Ascendants(" + @pRowMbr + " ), "
    + @pRowMbr + ".children}"
)
```

If you select the Query Parameters icon from the toolbar you see the following, as shown in Figure 11-4:

➤ pMeasure with a default value of [Measures].[Gross Profit]

➤ pRowMbr with a default value of [Product].[Product Categories].[Subcategory].&[1]

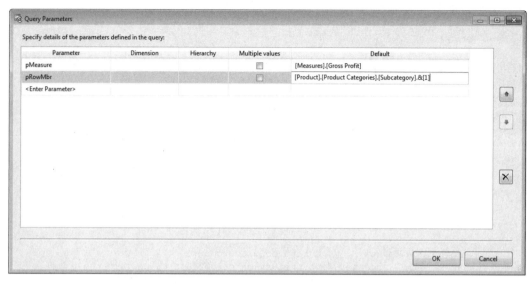

FIGURE 11-4

Execute the query to see the results, as shown in Figure 11-5.

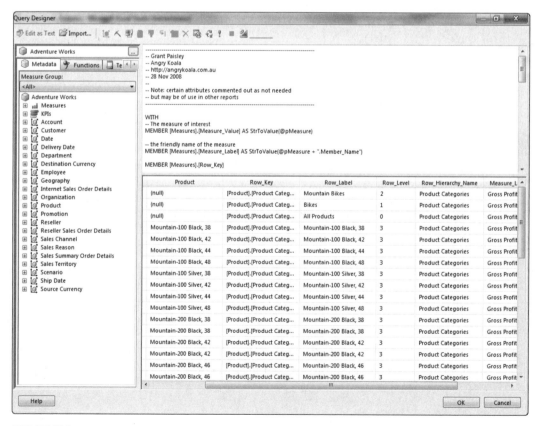

FIGURE 11-5

Matrix Content

So now that you have some data, let's look at how you format the tablix, including a neat trick to better display numbers.

A single table with the detail row shows `Row_Label` and `Measure_Value` data fields.

The first column header displays the name of the current hierarchy as it is set to `[Row_Hierarchy_Name]`.

The second column header shows the name of the current measure as it is set to `[Measure_Label]`.

If you right-click the Details group in the Row Groups pane and select Group Properties, you see it has expression to group on `[Row_Key]`, as shown in Figure 11-6.

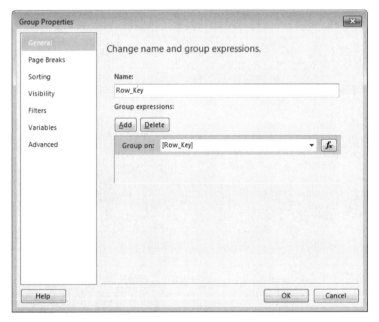

FIGURE 11-6

Go to the Sorting tab. As shown in Figure 11-7, rows are sorted by the `Row_Level` and then `Measure_Value` data fields. This ensures that members are displayed in hierarchy level order (ascending) and then by value (descending).

Formatting the Row Label

Right click on `Row_Label` textbox, select Text Box Properties, select Alignment options, and click the *fx* button in the Padding Options area, as shown in Figure 11-8. You see an expression for the cell's left alignment. This indents the text four characters for each level in the hierarchy:

```
=str( (Fields!Row_Level.Value * 4) + 2 ) + "pt"
```

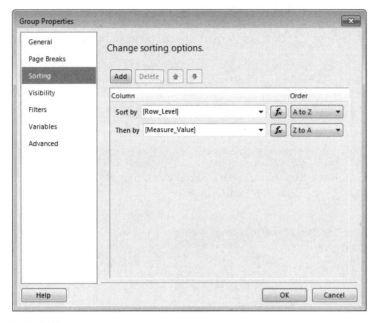

FIGURE 11-7

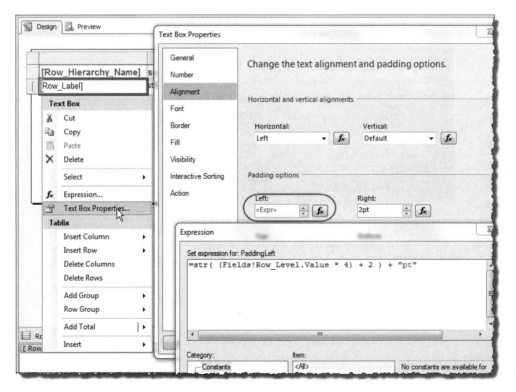

FIGURE 11-8

Highlighting the Current Row

You can highlight the row currently selected to indicate to the user that he or she can select a row by setting its color to blue. (Remember, users can't help clicking something that is blue.)

For both the `Row_Label` and `Measure_Value` cells, in the detail row, set the property `BackgroundColor` to this expression:

```
=iif(Fields!Row_Key.Value=Parameters!pRowMbr.Value,
    "LemonChiffon",
    Nothing
    )
```

This is shown in Figure 11-9.

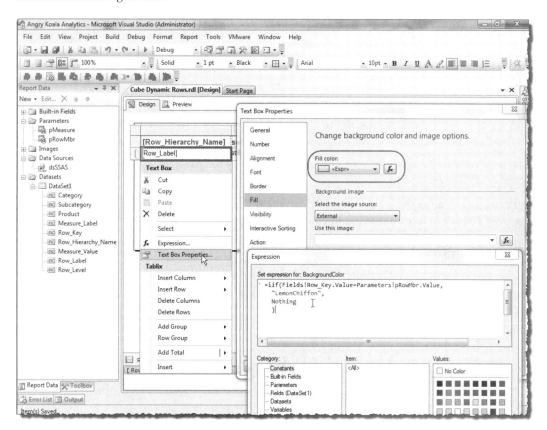

FIGURE 11-9

You also need to set the font color to this expression:

```
=iif(Fields!Row_Key.Value=Parameters!pRowMbr.Value,
"DimGray",
"Blue")
```

Notice that the cell property `BorderColor = LightGray` and `BorderStyle` default has been changed from `Solid` to `None` and that `BorderStyle` is set to `Solid`, as shown in Figure 11-10.

This approach to formatting gives the report a clean look. You don't really need vertical lines, because the data/values in the columns already line up.

FIGURE 11-10

Dynamic Number Formatting

Our last party trick is creating dynamic formatting for the measure value. Select the properties for the `Measure_Value` textbox. You will see it is formatted by the following expression:

```
=iif(last(abs(Fields!Measure_Value.Value)) > 10000000, "#,, m;(#,, m)",
    iif(last(abs(Fields!Measure_Value.Value)) > 1000000,  "#,,.0 m;(#,,.0 m)",
    iif(last(abs(Fields!Measure_Value.Value)) > 10000,    "#, k;(#, k)",
    iif(last(abs(Fields!Measure_Value.Value)) > 1000,     "#,.0 k;(#,.0 k)",
        "#,#;(#,#)"
))))
```

This is a pretty neat trick. Now you can succinctly display values that range from 1 to into the millions without needing extra-wide cells or having so many digits that it's hard to read.

Let's preview this. You now have rows driven by the `pRowMbr` parameter, and for each row, the value for the measure specified in `pMeasure`.

You can test changing the report content by changing the value of the `pMeasures` parameter combo box from Gross Profit to Sales Amount, as shown in Figure 11-11.

Self-Calling Drill-Through Action

To change the focus to another row, you need to create a self-calling drill-through action. Specifically, you create an action that calls the same report, passing through the member unique name of the row that is clicked.

In the Action tab, shown in Figure 11-12, the "Go to report" radio button is enabled, and "Specify a report" is set to the built-in global value `[&ReportName]`. The two parameters (name / value) are as follows:

➤   pRowMbr / [Row_Key]

➤   pMeasure / [@pMeasure]

Select the preview tab, as shown in Figure 11-13, and experiment with drilling up and down the product hierarchy.

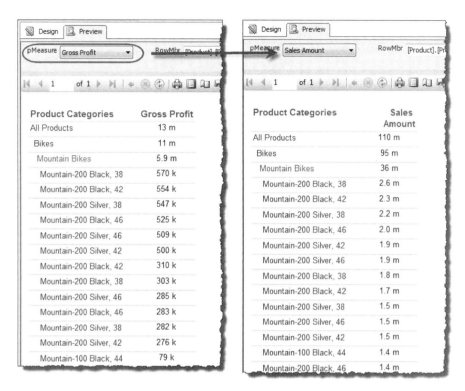

FIGURE 11-11

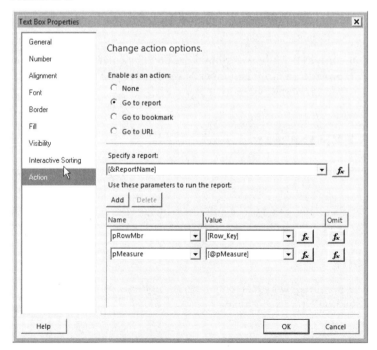

FIGURE 11-12

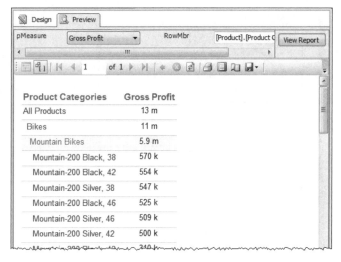

FIGURE 11-13

Cube Dynamic Rows Summary

This report demonstrates the fundamental content presentation and navigation technique employed by Angry Koala Analytics reports. It allows any dimension hierarchy to be displayed on rows and allows you to navigate up and down through that hierarchy.

In the Cube Browser report you will add columns, a filter, and a date. Then you will hook it up to a modified version of the Cube Metadata report, thus allowing the user to change what is displayed in the report.

So effectively you have the start of a mini OLAP browser build in SSRS. By creating linked reports with different parameters, you can provide an infinite number of reports for your users, from a Profit and Loss report to a Salesperson Profitability report.

CUBE DYNAMIC ROWS EXPANDED

This report demonstrates how you can create an even better, user-friendly, way to navigate dimension hierarchy data.

With a quick change to the MDX query and by adding a column group, you can change the Cube Dynamic Rows report to display each hierarchy level in a new column. Figure 11-14 is a preview.

MDX Query Modifications

You add one more measure, `MbrIsAncestor`, which is referenced to highlight all ancestor members (see the "Vizualization Tweaks" section later in this chapter):

```
MEMBER [Measures].[MbrIsAncestor] AS
      StrToValue(
```

```
         "IsAncestor( " +@pRowMbr + ".hierarchy.currentmember, "
                       +@pRowMbr + " )"
       + " or ( " + @pRowMbr + ".hierarchy.currentmember is " +@pRowMbr + " )"
       )
```

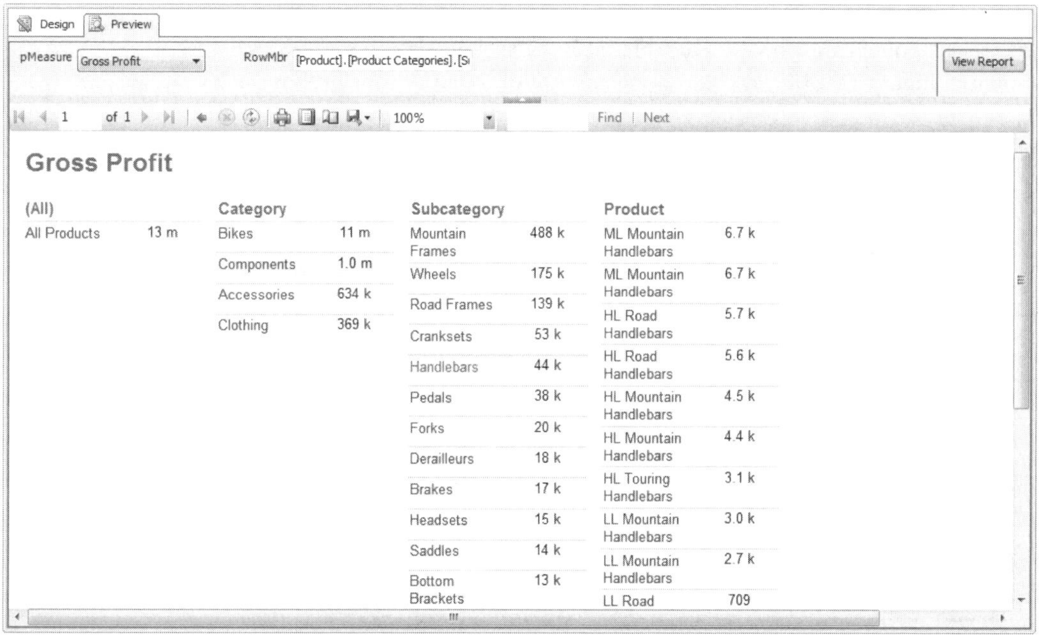

FIGURE 11-14

You change the core part of the query to show the current member (pRowMbr) ancestors. For each ancestor member, you also return its siblings:

```
-- for each ascendant member
-- generate its siblings

STRTOSET(
  "{" +
  GENERATE(
     Ascendants(StrToMember( @pRowMbr) )
     ,StrToValue(@pRowMbr + ".Hierarchy.CurrentMember.Uniquename")
     ,".siblings, "
  )
  + ".siblings,"

-- and add the childern

  + @pRowMbr + ".children"
  + "}"
  )
```

Design Surface Modifications

You now need to make modifications to the design surface to show multiple columns and indicate the navigation path.

Tablix

In essence, you create a new 1 × 1 table/tablix with a single column group based on Row_Level, as shown in Figure 11-15. This creates one column of data per row level in the hierarchy.

The existing tablix (with row group on Row_Key) is pasted into this cell. In other words, we have a table within a table. This gives the desired behavior of one column per hierarchy level and all the members listed within that level in rows, ordered by the current measure value.

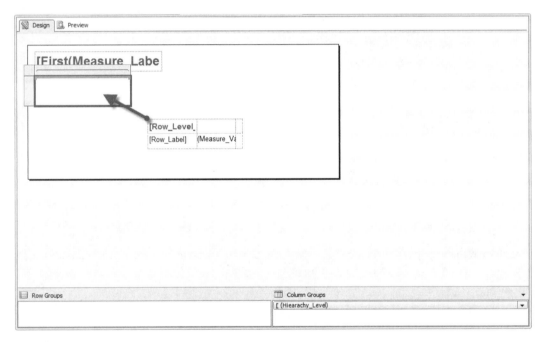

FIGURE 11-15

Visualization Tweaks

First you remove the expression for indenting the RowLabel textbox (each level is now in a new column, not in the same column):

```
=2pt
```

Insert a title textbox above the two tables to display the current measure name:

```
=Fields!Row_Level_Name.Value
```

Display the name of the current row hierarchy level in the header:

```
=Fields!Row_Level_Name.Value
```

Highlight not just the current member in the dimension hierarchy, but all ancestors in the hierarchy. This shows the path selected at each level in the hierarchy. Set the `BackgroundColor` property:

```
=iif(Fields!MbrIsAncestor.Value,
  "LemonChiffon",
  Nothing
  )
```

Summary

You can use this style of report to select members of interest within a hierarchy. This has the added benefit that, for the current measure, only members with data are displayed.

CUBE RESTRICTING ROWS

This report is another step toward the SSRS Cube Browser report that you began in the Cube Dynamic Rows report.

One of the challenges in creating dynamic reports is that the user can accidentally request a huge amount of data. In this report you take a quick look at how to add functionality to restrict the number of rows returned in a report.

Effectively you simply use the TOPCOUNT function in MDX to restrict the number of rows the query returns with a parameter. However, instead of requiring the user to select the parameter with a fiddly option box in the parameters, you can create a table in the report so that the user just clicks the number of rows he or she wants. Figure 11-16 shows the completed report.

Designing the Report

This report utilizes custom MDX and the TOPCOUNT function to restrict the number of rows returned in a query. This technique can by utilized on any query against MDX. For this example you start with the report you created earlier in the Cube Dynamic Rows report.

Essentially you need to make three modifications:

➤   Add a parameter for the number of rows to display.

➤   Modify the MDX query to restrict the number of rows (uses the TOPCOUNT function).

➤   Modify self-calling drill-through actions.

Figure 11-16 shows the final report.

pRowCount Parameter

First you need a new dataset to produce a list of values for the `pRowCount` parameter.

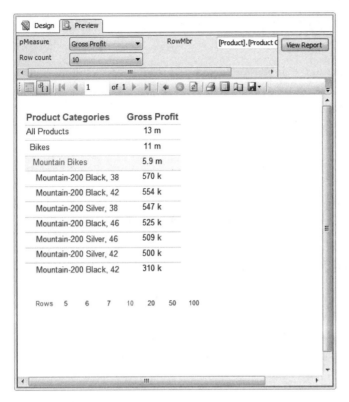

FIGURE 11-16

As shown in Figure 11-17, the following SQL query was used to create a new dataset called CellCount that is based on the shared data source dsAnySQLDB:

```
Select 5 as CellCount union all
select 6 union all
select 7 union all
select 10 union all
select 20 union all
select 50 union all
select 100
```

On the properties of the pRowCount parameter, both the Value and Label fields are set to CellCount, as shown in Figure 11-18.

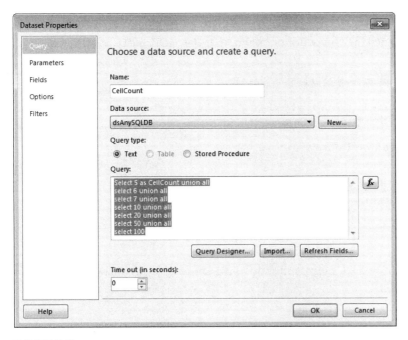

FIGURE 11-17

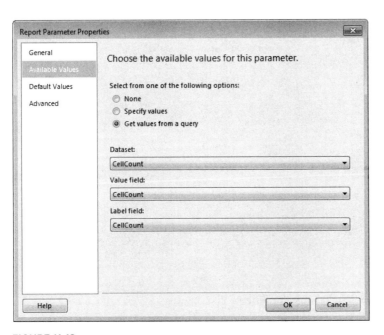

FIGURE 11-18

Restricting the Number of Rows in the MDX Query

Right-click DataSet1 and open the Query Editor. Notice that the MDX query is wrapped with the TOPCOUNT function:

```
-- returns the top n number of rows based on current measure
TOPCOUNT(
    -- show the current hierarchy member with its ascendants
    -- together with its children on rows
    STRTOSET(
        "{Ascendants(" + @pRowMbr + " ), "
        + @pRowMbr + ".children}"
    )
    ,StrToValue(@pRowCount)
    ,[Measures].[Measure_Value]
)

ON ROWS
```

Select the Parameter icon from the toolbar, and see that the pRowCount parameter is set to a default of 6, as shown in Figure 11-19.

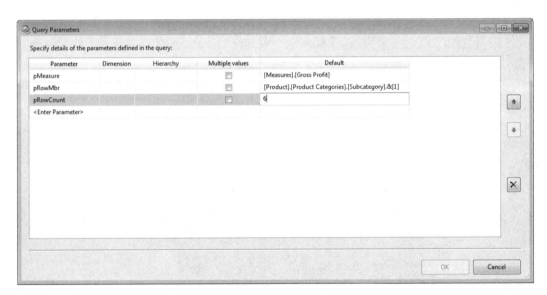

FIGURE 11-19

If you execute the query observer, the results should look like Figure 11-20.

If you preview the report, you'll see that you can now change the number of rows displayed, as shown in Figure 11-21.

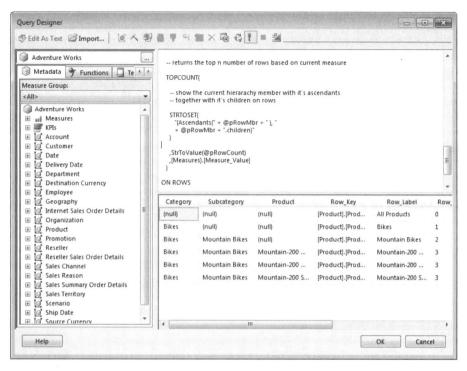

FIGURE 11-20

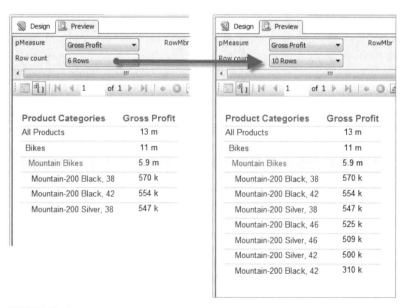

FIGURE 11-21

Adding pRowCount to Self-Calling Drill-Through Report Action

Now that you can control how many rows are returned, you need to add the pRowCount parameter to the row hierarchy self-calling drill-through action.

Open the Row_Label textbox properties. Notice that the pRowCount parameter has been added to the existing action, with a value set to [@pRowCount], as shown in Figure 11-22.

FIGURE 11-22

A Better Way to Interact with a Report Parameter

This report also has a table displaying the available pRowCount values. The current selected number of rows is highlighted in gray. The self-calling drill-through action on the CellCount textbox, as shown in Figure 11-23, now includes the pRowCount parameter and is set to the column value the user clicked ([CellCount]).

Summary

Another step toward the simple SSRS OLAP browser is complete. Already the user can change rows and measures (at least manually) and drill up and down a cube hierarchy. You have added the ability for the user to control the number of rows returned.

The next step is to build a way to directly interrogate the cube structure. You do so in the Cube Metadata report.

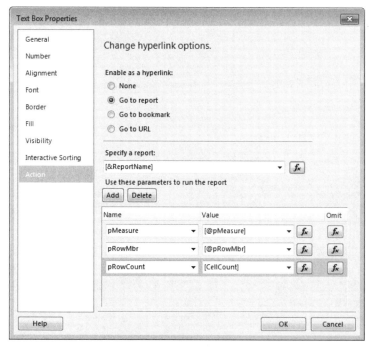

FIGURE 11-23

CUBE METADATA

Wouldn't it be nice to have all your cube documentation up-to-date and available to your users? Wouldn't it be even better if you could create generic reports and, just by creating a linked report in Report Manager and changing a few parameters, generate a completely new report?

So how do you do this? Creating the report in this chapter requires that we combine a few techniques, but first we need to access Analysis Services metadata.

Designing the Report

This solution involves tricking Reporting Services into talking nicely to Analysis Services and taking advantage of the dynamic management views (DMVs) in SQL Server 2012. You use the following DMVs:

➤ MDSCHEMA_CUBES

➤ MDSCHEMA_MEASUREGROUPS

➤ MDSCHEMA_MEASURES

➤ MDSCHEMA_MEASUREGROUP_DIMENSIONS

➤ MDSCHEMA_HIERARCHIES

➤ MDSCHEMA_LEVELS

You might want to explore others (that won't be needed in this report):

➤ DBSCHEMA_CATALOGS

➤ DBSCHEMA_DIMENSIONS

To get the full list of DMVs, run this command:

```
SELECT * FROM $SYSTEM.DBSCHEMA_TABLES
```

Figure 11-24 shows how the finished report will look.

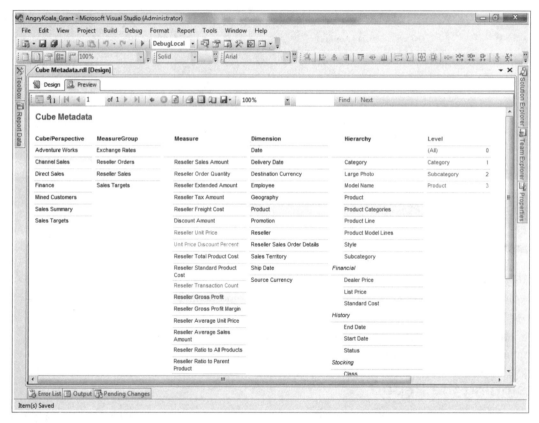

FIGURE 11-24

The following are the steps to list the cubes/perspectives and, after selecting a cube/perspective, displaying the list of related measure groups.

Follow these steps to add the cubes metadata DMV dataset information:

1. Add a dataset, enter the following DMV script as an expression, and click Refresh Fields:

   ```
   SELECT * FROM $System.MDSCHEMA_CUBES WHERE CUBE_SOURCE =1
   ```

2. Name the dataset **Cubes.** Your dataset properties should look those shown in Figure 11-25

3. Insert a table on the design surface and drag the CUBE_NAME column onto it, to list the cubes/perspectives. When you preview this, you see the cube metadata, as shown in Figure 11-26.

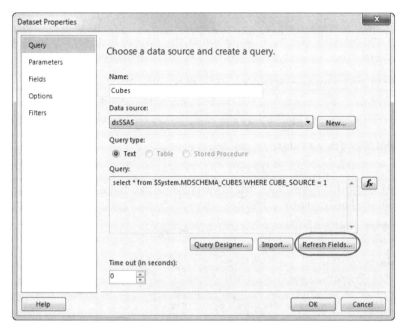

FIGURE 11-25

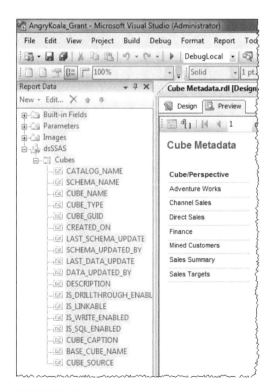

FIGURE 11-26

MeasureGroups

Follow these steps to insert another table to display MeasureGroups, filtered by the selected CUBE_NAME (or perspective) in our first table utilizing a self-calling drill-through action:

1. Create a report parameter called pCube, and set the default value as Channel Sales.

2. Create a new dataset called MeasureGroups, and set the query to the following:

```
SELECT * FROM $System.MDSCHEMA_MEASUREGROUPS
```

3. Add a parameter with this default value:

```
[CUBE_NAME] = [@pCube]
```

4. Add the filter [CUBE_NAME] = [@pCube]. The Dataset Properties dialog shown in Figure 11-27 shows the filter condition.

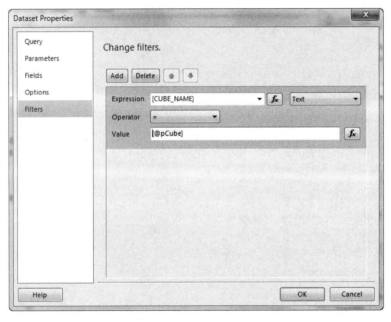

FIGURE 11-27

Finally, you need to "highlight" the currently selected cube and MeasureGroup and add the self-calling drill-through action.

5. For the CUBE_NAME text box in the properties window, set the BackgroundColor expression to the following:

```
=iif(Fields!CUBE_NAME.Value=Parameters!pCube.Value,"LemonChiffon","White")
```

6. Open the CUBE_NAME Text Box Properties dialog. In the Action tab, set the Enable action as a hyperlink radio button to "Go to report." Set "Specify a report" to [&ReportName]. Add the following report parameter name and value, as shown in Figure 11-28.

PARAMETER	VALUE
pCube	[CUBE_NAME]

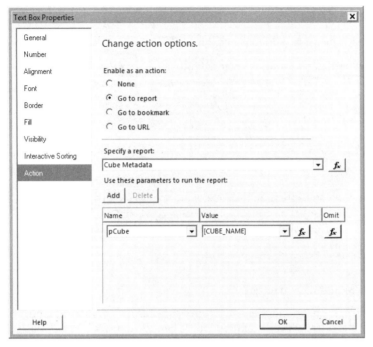

FIGURE 11-28

7. Insert a table on the design surface and drag on the MEASUREGROUP_NAME column, to list the MeasureGroups associated with the selected cube (or Measure Group) and add the filter [CUBE_NAME] = [@pCube], as before.

Preview the report. You can see that clicking a cube (or perspective), to select it, displays the associated MeasureGroups, as shown in Figure 11-29.

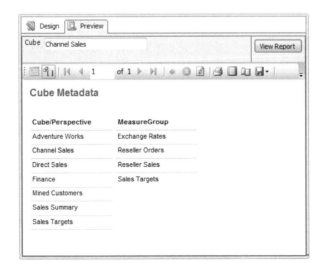

FIGURE 11-29

Adding Other Cube Metadata

Similarly, you can add metadata for measures, dimensions, hierarchies, and levels.

1. Add the following report parameters, and set their default values as shown:

PARAMETER	VALUE
pMeasure	`[Measures].[Reseller Gross Profit]`
pMeasureGroup	`Reseller Sales`
pDimension	`="[Product]"` This must be an expression because of the special meaning of [ ] in SSRS. `[Product]` is a shortcut for the value of a DataSet column, such as `Product.Value`, where you want the dimension unique name, `[Product]`.
pHierarchy	`[Product].[Product Categories]`

2. Enter the following code to add these datasets.

In each case, enter the sample query and then click Refresh Fields (to populate columns from the query). Then replace the query with the expression. When the dataset is saved, you still receive a message that the field could not be updated, but if you click OK, the fields are in fact there.

Measures

```
="SELECT * FROM $System.MDSCHEMA_MEASURES"
+ " WHERE CUBE_NAME = '" & Parameters!pCube.Value & "'"
+ " AND ( MEASUREGROUP_NAME = '" & Parameters!pMeasureGroup.Value & "'"
+ " OR MEASURE_DISPLAY_FOLDER = '" & Parameters!pMeasureGroup.Value & "' )"
```

Example:

```
SELECT * FROM $System.MDSCHEMA_MEASURES
WHERE CUBE_NAME = 'Channel Sales'
AND ( MEASUREGROUP_NAME = 'Reseller Sales'
OR MEASURE_DISPLAY_FOLDER = 'Reseller Sales' )
```

MeasureGroupDimensions

```
="SELECT * FROM $System.MDSCHEMA_MEASUREGROUP_DIMENSIONS "
+ " WHERE CUBE_NAME = '" & Parameters!pCube.Value & "'"
+ " AND MEASUREGROUP_NAME = '" & Parameters!pMeasureGroup.Value & "'"
```

Example:

```
SELECT * FROM $System.MDSCHEMA_MEASUREGROUP_DIMENSIONS
WHERE CUBE_NAME = 'Channel Sales'
AND MEASUREGROUP_NAME = 'Reseller Sales'
```

Hierarchies

```
="SELECT * FROM $System.MDSCHEMA_HIERARCHIES"
+ " WHERE CUBE_NAME = '" & Parameters!pCube.Value & "'"
+ " AND [DIMENSION_UNIQUE_NAME] = '" & Parameters!pDimension.Value & "'"
```

Example:

```
SELECT * FROM $System.MDSCHEMA_HIERARCHIES
 WHERE CUBE_NAME = 'Channel Sales'
 AND [DIMENSION_UNIQUE_NAME] = '[Product]'
```

Levels

```
="SELECT * FROM $System.MDSCHEMA_LEVELS "
+ " WHERE CUBE_NAME = '" & Parameters!pCube.Value & "'"
+ " AND [DIMENSION_UNIQUE_NAME] = '" & Parameters!pDimension.Value & "'"
+ " AND [HIERARCHY_UNIQUE_NAME] = '" & Parameters!pHierarchy.Value & "'"
```

Example:

```
SELECT * FROM $System.MDSCHEMA_LEVELS
WHERE CUBE_NAME = 'Channel Sales'
AND [DIMENSION_UNIQUE_NAME] = '[Product]'
AND [HIERARCHY_UNIQUE_NAME] = '[Product].[Product Categories]'
```

You should see the report data shown in Figure 11-30.

3. Insert a table on the design surface based on each dataset, add an expression to highlight the field when it's selected, and create a self-calling drill-through action.

4. For the Text Box Properties of CUBE_NAME, in the Action page, set the Enable action as a hyperlink radio button to "Go to report," set "Specify a report" to [&ReportName], and add the following Report Parameter names and values:

FIGURE 11-30

PARAMETER	VALUE
pCube	= [@pCube]
pMeasureGroup	= [MEASUREGROUP_NAME]
pMeasure	= [@pMeasure]

5. Now that you have added the extra parameters, go back to the CUBE_NAME Text Box properties and add the following parameters to the Action page:

PARAMETER	VALUE
pMeasureGroup	= [@pMeasureGroup]
pMeasure	= [@pMeasure]

Measures

6. Set the Measure textbox to Gray if the metadata is not visible and you can display additional information with a tooltip. Alternatively, you can add columns to show other metadata.

7. In the Text Box properties of MEASURE_NAME, add a self-calling drill-through action (set "Specify a report" to [&ReportName]) with the following parameter names and values:

PARAMETER	VALUE
pCube	= [@pCube]
pMeasureGroup	= [@pMeasureGroup]
pMeasure	= [MEASURE_UNIQUE_NAME]

The design surface should resemble Figure 11-31 and preview like Figure 11-32.

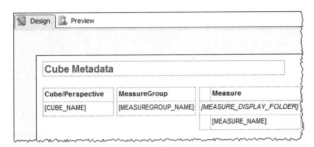

FIGURE 11-31

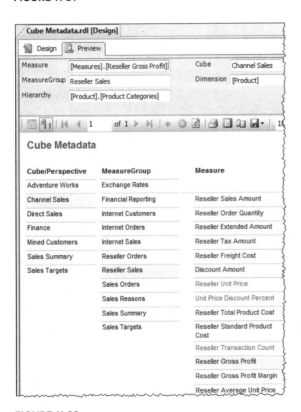

FIGURE 11-32

Dimensions

List the dimensions for the selected `MeasureGroup`, and highlight the current dimension.

8. Add a self-calling drill-through action with the following values:

PARAMETER	VALUE
pCube	= [@pCube]
pMeasureGroup	= [@pMeasureGroup]
pMeasure	= [MEASURE_UNIQUE_NAME]

Hierarchies

9. Add a self-calling (report is `[&ReportName]`) drill-through action with the following parameter names and values:

PARAMETER	VALUE
pCube	= [@pCube]
pDimension	= [@pDimension]

Levels

10. To provide complete information, show the level name and number for the selected hierarchy.

Figures 11-33 and 11-34 show the design surface and preview for Dimensions, Hierarchies, and Levels.

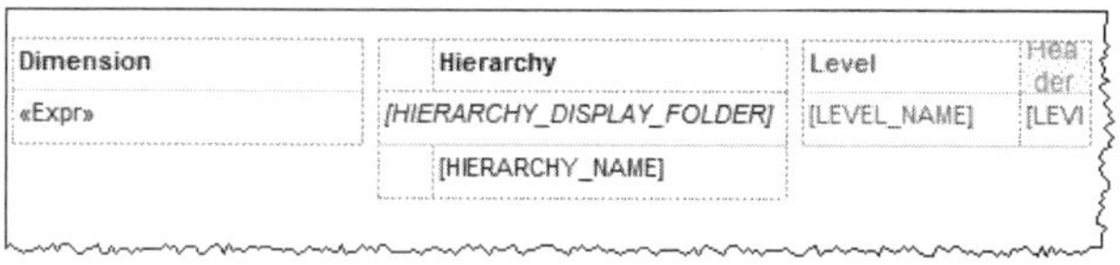

Dimension	Hierarchy	Level	Hea der
«Expr»	[HIERARCHY_DISPLAY_FOLDER]	[LEVEL_NAME]	[LEVI
	[HIERARCHY_NAME]		

FIGURE 11-33

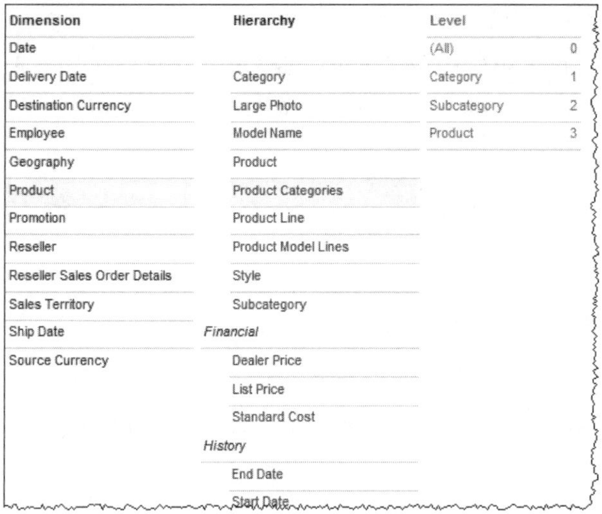

Dimension	Hierarchy	Level	
Date		(All)	0
Delivery Date	Category	Category	1
Destination Currency	Large Photo	Subcategory	2
Employee	Model Name	Product	3
Geography	Product		
Product	Product Categories		
Promotion	Product Line		
Reseller	Product Model Lines		
Reseller Sales Order Details	Style		
Sales Territory	Subcategory		
Ship Date	*Financial*		
Source Currency	Dealer Price		
	List Price		
	Standard Cost		
	History		
	End Date		
	Start Date		

FIGURE 11-34

Final Thoughts

You now have a way to discover information about the structure of your cubes so that, if you also populate the description fields within Analysis Server, you can provide users with up-to-date documentation, such as a measure's meaning. You can also enable users to search for a measure by name, or you can add a help button on a standard report to display details of a dimension or measure.

The Cube Browser and the Angry Koala Cube Browser reports in this book use this report. With some modifications, this will enable users to dynamically change the rows, columns, and filters in their Cube Browser reports.

CUBE BROWSER

You can build a simple, functional OLAP browser in Reporting Services by using some of the advanced reporting techniques described earlier in the chapter:

1. Extend the Cube Dynamic Rows report to include dynamic columns.

2. Add a date filter.

3. Add a dynamic filter.

4. Allow users to change the measure.

5. Link the new report with a modified version of the Cube Metadata report to allow users to do the following:

➤ Select the measure to display

➤ Change the content of rows and columns

➤ Change the filter

With these features, developers or power users can create a report with any combination of Rows, Columns, Filter, Date, and Measure by creating a linked report and setting the parameters appropriately. Also, as soon as a report is running, users can slice and dice their data. If they are using the native reporting services manager, they can also create their own version of a report by simply saving the current report as a favorite in Internet Explorer.

This cube browser report is also *fast*. In a traditional report, when you add parameters in the MDX query window, behind the scenes an MDX query is generated for each parameter. This means that when a report is run, 10 to 20 MDX queries can run before the report is rendered. The Cube Browser Report has only the MDX query to bring back data for the grid (plus a basic SQL union statement to generate a list of numbers for the row count and column count). You go to other supporting reports to collect parameters. Consequently, when you drill up and drill down, the response time is fantastic.

Figure 11-35 shows a Sales report, and Figure 11-36 shows a Profit and Loss report. Both are examples of the same Cube Browser report, just with different parameters.

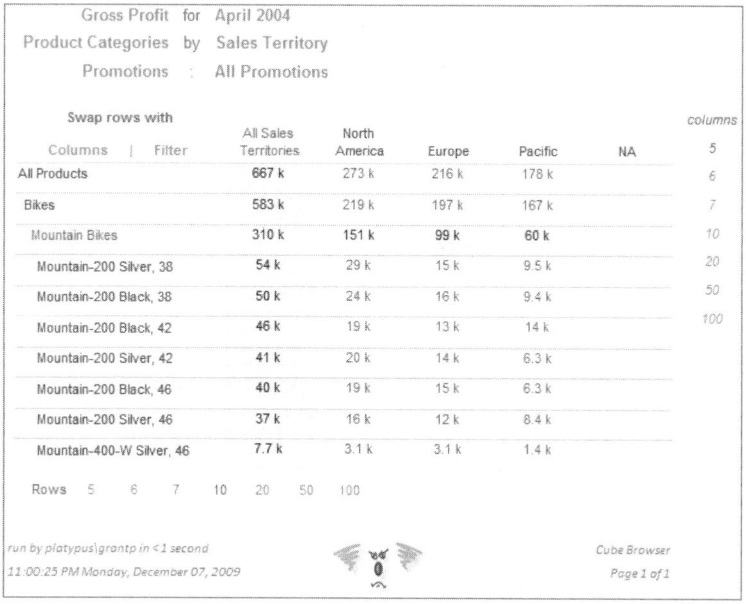

Gross Profit for April 2004						
Product Categories by Sales Territory						
Promotions : All Promotions						
Swap rows with						columns
Columns | Filter	All Sales Territories	North America	Europe	Pacific	NA	5
All Products	667 k	273 k	216 k	178 k		6
Bikes	583 k	219 k	197 k	167 k		7
Mountain Bikes	310 k	151 k	99 k	60 k		10
Mountain-200 Silver, 38	54 k	29 k	15 k	9.5 k		20
Mountain-200 Black, 38	50 k	24 k	16 k	9.4 k		50
Mountain-200 Black, 42	46 k	19 k	13 k	14 k		100
Mountain-200 Silver, 42	41 k	20 k	14 k	6.3 k		
Mountain-200 Black, 46	40 k	19 k	15 k	6.3 k		
Mountain-200 Silver, 46	37 k	16 k	12 k	8.4 k		
Mountain-400-W Silver, 46	7.7 k	3.1 k	3.1 k	1.4 k		
Rows 5 6 7 10 20 50 100						

run by platypus\grantp in <1 second
11:00:25 PM Monday, December 07, 2009

Cube Browser
Page 1 of 1

FIGURE 11-35

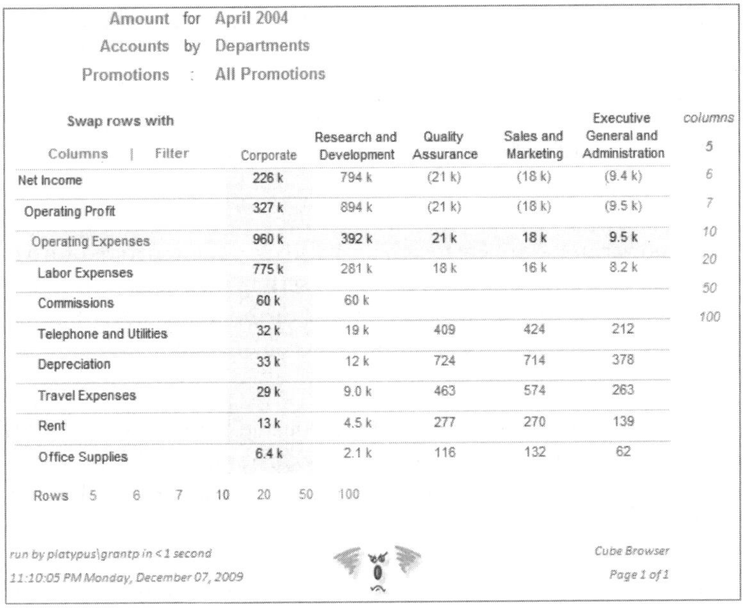

Amount for April 2004
Accounts by Departments
Promotions : All Promotions

Swap rows with
Columns | Filter

	Corporate	Research and Development	Quality Assurance	Sales and Marketing	Executive General and Administration
Net Income	226 k	794 k	(21 k)	(18 k)	(9.4 k)
Operating Profit	327 k	894 k	(21 k)	(18 k)	(9.5 k)
Operating Expenses	960 k	392 k	21 k	18 k	9.5 k
Labor Expenses	775 k	281 k	18 k	16 k	8.2 k
Commissions	60 k	60 k			
Telephone and Utilities	32 k	19 k	409	424	212
Depreciation	33 k	12 k	724	714	378
Travel Expenses	29 k	9.0 k	463	574	263
Rent	13 k	4.5 k	277	270	139
Office Supplies	6.4 k	2.1 k	116	132	62

columns 5 6 7 10 20 50 100

Rows 5 6 7 10 20 50 100

run by platypus\grantp in < 1 second
11:10:05 PM Monday, December 07, 2009

Cube Browser
Page 1 of 1

FIGURE 11-36

Anatomy of the Reports

Rather than going through a step-by-step approach to building the reports in this suite, let's run through the architecture and then the necessary techniques utilized within each report.

The reports are:

- Cube Browser
- Cube Browser Metadata
- Cube Browser Member

First, let's look at the roles of these reports.

Cube Browser

This Cube Browser is the main report and the only one directly visible to your users. You can have multiple linked reports based on this physical report showing different data on rows, columns, and filters by simply creating a linked report and changing the parameters.

The following list explains what users can do in this report and in any linked reports and how to do it. The key action for each item is listed, as are any supporting parameter settings.

- **Change the measure to display.** Click Measure Name in the title to drill through to the Cube Browser Metadata report.

  driver = Measure

➤ **Change what hierarchy to display on rows.** Click Hierarchy Name in the title to drill through to Cube Browser Metadata.

driver = Rows

➤ **Change what hierarchy to display on columns.** Click the Column Hierarchy Name to drill through to Cube Browser Metadata.

driver = Columns

➤ **Change what hierarchy to use for a filter.** Click the Filter Hierarchy Name to drill through to Cube Browser Metadata.

driver = Filter

➤ **Change the Filter value (member).** Click the Filter Member Name to drill through to Cube Browser Member.

driver = Filter

➤ **Change the date period** (it can be year, quarter, month, or day). Click the Date Member in the title to drill through to Cube Browser Member.

driver = Date

➤ **Drill up and down the hierarchy displayed on rows or columns.** Click a row member to drill-to-self with new selection.

➤ **Change the number of rows or columns to display.** Click the row number to drill-to-self with a new selection.

➤ **Swap rows with filter.** Click the Swap Filter textbox to drill-to-self with the `Row` and `Filter` parameters swapped.

➤ **Swap rows and columns.** Click the Swap Column textbox to drill-to-self with the `Row` and `Column` parameters swapped.

Figure 11-37 shows the key navigation paths from the Cube Browser to the Cube Browser Metadata and the Cube Browser Member.

Cube Browser Metadata

The Cube Browser Metadata report is called from the Cube Browser report and returns a measure or hierarchy. Its design is based on the Cube Metadata report and is called when the user wants to do the following:

➤ Change the measure

➤ Select what hierarchy to display on rows or columns

➤ Select what hierarchy to filter by

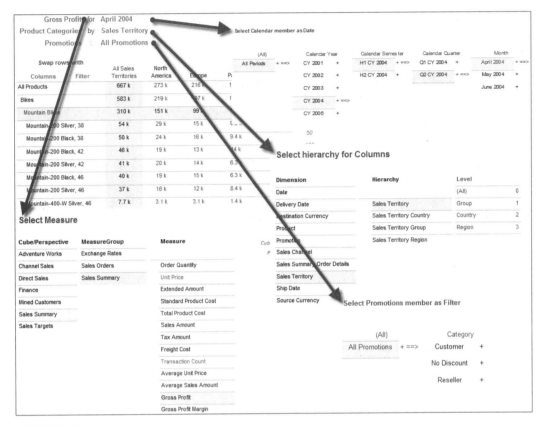

FIGURE 11-37

It therefore has two distinct behaviors. The following list explains what users can do if the driver parameter value is Measure, and how to do it.

➤ **Select a cube/perspective.** Click the MeasureLabel to initiate drill-to-self action to display measures available in the selected cube.

➤ **Select a measure from the cube/perspective.** Click a measure to fire as a drill-back action to the Cube Browser report passing the selected Measure.

The following list explains what users can do if the driver parameter is Row, Column, or Filter, and how to do it. The key action for each item is listed, as are any supporting parameter settings.

➤ **Select a dimension.** Drill-to-self to display hierarchies.

➤ **Choose a hierarchy for a selected dimension.** Drill back to Cube Browser with the selected hierarchy.

driver = Rows, Columns, or Filter

Note that you do not hard-code the report you *drill back* to. One of the parameters is the calling report. It allows this report to be called from different linked reports.

Cube Browser Member

The Cube Browser Member report is called from the Cube Browser report and returns a hierarchy member. It is called when the user wants to do the following:

➤ **Select a period of time to filter the report by** (a specific year, quarter, month, or day).

➤ **Select a member to filter the report by.**

Behind the Scenes

Now let's look at the details and the reports utilized.

Cube Browser

The Cube Browser report is based on the Cube Dynamic Rows report. It uses the same basic concept but extends the idea to columns. Date and dynamic filters are added. To add the date and dynamic filters, you need the following parameters (I have included a sample default value):

➤ `pCube = Sales Summary` (the name of the cube or perspective)

➤ `pMeasureGroup = Sales Summary` (the name of the MeasureGroup)

➤ `pMeasure = [Measures].[Gross Profit]` (the UniqueName of the measure)

➤ `pDateMbr = [Date].[Calendar].[Month].&[2004]&[4]` (the UniqueName of the Date member)

➤ `pRowMbr = [Product].[Product Categories].[Subcategory].&[1]` (the UniqueName of the member from which ascendants and children are shown on rows)

➤ `pRowCount = 10` (the number of rows to show)

➤ `pColMbr = [Sales Territory].[Sales Territory].[All Sales Territories]` (the UniqueName of the member from which ascendants and children are shown on columns)

➤ `pColCount = 5` (the number of columns to show)

➤ `pFilterMbr = [Promotion].[Promotions].[All Promotions]` (the UniqueName of the member acting as filter)

If you open the DataSet1 query and select the parameters icon from the Query Designer Toolbar, you'll see the list of parameters together with their default values, as shown in Figure 11-38.

Here is the required MDX query, including the necessary additions for extra functionality:

```
-----------------------------------------------------------------
-- Cube Browser
--
-- Grant Paisley
-- Angry Koala
-- http://angrykoala.com.au
-- 14 Nov 2011
--
--
```

```
-- Note: certain attributes commented out as not needed
-- but may be of use in other reports
-----------------------------------------------------------------

WITH
-- The measure of interest
MEMBER [Measures].[Measure_Value]
  AS StrToValue(@pMeasure)

-- the friendly name of the measure
MEMBER [Measures].[Measure_Label]
  AS StrToValue(@pMeasure + ".Member_Name")

-- Row metadata
MEMBER [Measures].[Row_Key]
  AS StrToValue( @pRowMbr + ".Hierarchy.Currentmember.Uniquename" )
MEMBER [Measures].[Row_Label]
  AS StrToValue( @pRowMbr + ".Hierarchy.CurrentMember.Member_Caption" )
MEMBER [Measures].[Row_Level]
  AS StrToValue( @pRowMbr + ".Hierarchy.CurrentMember.Level.Ordinal" )
MEMBER [Measures].[Row_Level_Name]
  AS StrToValue( @pRowMbr + ".Hierarchy.Level.Name" )
MEMBER [Measures].[Row_Hierarchy_Name]
  AS StrToValue( @pRowMbr + ".Hierarchy.Name" )
MEMBER [Measures].[Row_Hierarchy_UniqueName]
  AS StrToValue( @pRowMbr + ".Hierarchy.UniqueName" )
MEMBER [Measures].[Row_Dimension_Name]
  AS StrToValue( @pRowMbr + ".Dimension.Name" )
MEMBER [Measures].[Row_Dimension_UniqueName]
  AS StrToValue(@pRowMbr + ".Dimension_Unique_Name" )

-- Column metadata
MEMBER [Measures].[Col_Key]
  AS StrToValue( @pColMbr + ".Hierarchy.Currentmember.Uniquename" )
MEMBER [Measures].[Col_Label]
  AS StrToValue( @pColMbr + ".Hierarchy.CurrentMember.Member_Caption" )
MEMBER [Measures].[Col_Level]
  AS StrToValue( @pColMbr + ".Hierarchy.CurrentMember.Level.Ordinal" )
MEMBER [Measures].[Col_Level_Name]
  AS StrToValue( @pColMbr + ".Hierarchy.Level.Name" )
MEMBER [Measures].[Col_Hierarchy_Name]
  AS StrToValue( @pColMbr + ".Hierarchy.Name" )
MEMBER [Measures].[Col_Hierarchy_UniqueName]
  AS StrToValue( @pColMbr + ".Hierarchy.UniqueName" )
MEMBER [Measures].[Col_Dimension_Name]
  AS StrToValue( @pColMbr + ".Dimension.Name" )
MEMBER [Measures].[Col_Dimension_UniqueName]
  AS StrToValue(@pColMbr + ".Dimension_Unique_Name" )

-- Filter metadata
MEMBER [Measures].[Filter_Key]
  AS StrToValue( @pFilterMbr + ".Hierarchy.Currentmember.Uniquename" )
MEMBER [Measures].[Filter_Label]
  AS StrToValue( @pFilterMbr + ".Hierarchy.CurrentMember.Member_Caption" )
MEMBER [Measures].[Filter_Level]
  AS StrToValue( @pFilterMbr + ".Hierarchy.CurrentMember.Level.Ordinal" )
```

```
MEMBER [Measures].[Filter_Level_Name]
  AS StrToValue( @pFilterMbr + ".Hierarchy.Level.Name" )
MEMBER [Measures].[Filter_Hierarchy_Name]
  AS StrToValue( @pFilterMbr + ".Hierarchy.Name" )
MEMBER [Measures].[Filter_Hierarchy_UniqueName]
  AS StrToValue( @pFilterMbr + ".Hierarchy.UniqueName" )
MEMBER [Measures].[Filter_Dimension_Name]
  AS StrToValue( @pFilterMbr + ".Dimension.Name" )
MEMBER [Measures].[Filter_Dimension_UniqueName]
  AS StrToValue(@pFilterMbr + ".Dimension_Unique_Name" )

-- Date metadata
MEMBER [Measures].[Date_Key]
  AS StrToValue( @pDateMbr + ".Hierarchy.Currentmember.Uniquename" )
MEMBER [Measures].[Date_Label]
  AS StrToValue( @pDateMbr + ".Hierarchy.CurrentMember.Member_Caption" )
MEMBER [Measures].[Date_Level]
  AS StrToValue( @pDateMbr + ".Hierarchy.CurrentMember.Level.Ordinal" )
MEMBER [Measures].[Date_Level_Name]
  AS StrToValue( @pDateMbr + ".Hierarchy.Level.Name" )
MEMBER [Measures].[Date_Hierarchy_Name]
  AS StrToValue( @pDateMbr + ".Hierarchy.Name" )
MEMBER [Measures].[Date_Hierarchy_UniqueName]
  AS StrToValue( @pDateMbr + ".Hierarchy.UniqueName" )
MEMBER [Measures].[Date_Dimension_Name]
  AS StrToValue( @pDateMbr + ".Dimension.Name" )
MEMBER [Measures].[Date_Dimension_UniqueName]
  AS StrToValue(@pDateMbr + ".Dimension_Unique_Name" )




SELECT NON EMPTY {
-- display the measure and rowmbr attributes on columns

[Measures].[Row_Key],
[Measures].[Row_Label],
[Measures].[Row_Level],
[Measures].[Row_Level_Name],
[Measures].[Row_Hierarchy_Name],
[Measures].[Row_Hierarchy_UniqueName],
[Measures].[Row_Dimension_Name],
[Measures].[Row_Dimension_UniqueName],

[Measures].[Col_Key],
[Measures].[Col_Label],
[Measures].[Col_Level],
[Measures].[Col_Level_Name],
[Measures].[Col_Hierarchy_Name],
[Measures].[Col_Hierarchy_UniqueName],
[Measures].[Col_Dimension_Name],
[Measures].[Col_Dimension_UniqueName],

[Measures].[Filter_Key],
[Measures].[Filter_Label],
[Measures].[Filter_Level],
```

```
[Measures].[Filter_Level_Name],
[Measures].[Filter_Hierarchy_Name],
[Measures].[Filter_Hierarchy_UniqueName],
[Measures].[Filter_Dimension_Name],
[Measures].[Filter_Dimension_UniqueName],

[Measures].[Date_Key],
[Measures].[Date_Label],
[Measures].[Date_Level],
[Measures].[Date_Level_Name],
[Measures].[Date_Hierarchy_Name],
[Measures].[Date_Hierarchy_UniqueName],
[Measures].[Date_Dimension_Name],
[Measures].[Date_Dimension_UniqueName],

[Measures].[Measure_Value],
[Measures].[Measure_Label]


} ON COLUMNS,

-- returns the top n number of rows based on current measure

TOPCOUNT(
-- show the current hierarchy member with its ascendants
-- together with its children on rows

STRTOSET(
"{Ascendants(" + @pRowMbr + " ), "
+ @pRowMbr + ".children}"
)

,StrToValue(@pRowCount)
,[Measures].[Measure_Value]
)

* -- cross product

-- returns the top n number of Columns based on current measure

TOPCOUNT(

-- show the current hierarchy member with its ascendants
-- together with its children on Columns

STRTOSET(
"{Ascendants(" + @pColMbr + " ), "
+ @pColMbr + ".children}"
)

,StrToValue(@pColCount)
,[Measures].[Measure_Value]
)


ON ROWS
```

```
FROM [Adventure Works] -- must hard code the cube :(
-- the cube name, together with the default values are the only
-- things required to point this report at a different cube

WHERE STRTOTUPLE( "(" +@pFilterMbr +"," + @pDateMbr + ")" )
```

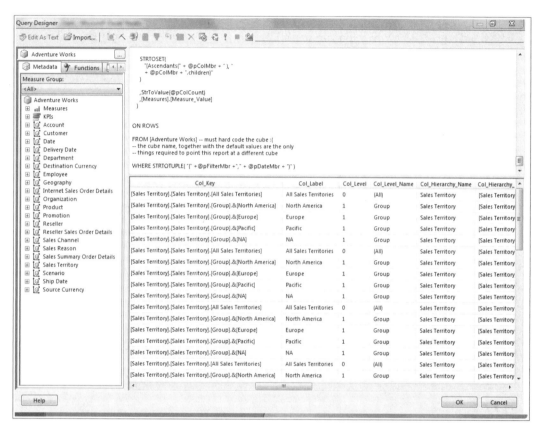

FIGURE 11-38

Much like how you created calculated measures for the metadata on rows, you now get the same metadata for the `Date`, `Filter`, and `Column` members. For each you collect the following:

- ➤ Key
- ➤ Label
- ➤ Level
- ➤ Level_Name
- ➤ Hierarchy_Name
- ➤ Hierarchy_UniqueName
- ➤ Dimension_Name
- ➤ Dimension_UniqueName

Notice that you have done the following:

➤ Added extra measures to display metadata for columns, date, and filter

➤ Created a cross product between rows and columns

➤ Added a tuple in the WHERE clause based on the Date member and the Filter member

As shown in Figure 11-39, when you run the MDX query, you see all the metadata together with the Measure value you want to display: Measure_Value.

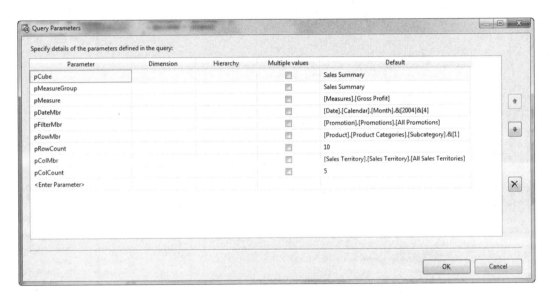

FIGURE 11-39

Report Body

The main tablix, shown in Figure 11-40, is a matrix with:

➤ Columns grouped by Col_Key and displaying Col_Label

➤ Rows grouped by Row_Key and displaying Row_Label

➤ The Measure_Value in the details cell

In the columns, similar to the rows, the group is by Col_Key and sorted by the Col_Level (the level in the hierarchy) and within the level, descending by Measure_Value. You could enhance the report by adding a parameter to control whether sorting is ascending or descending, as shown in Figure 11-41.

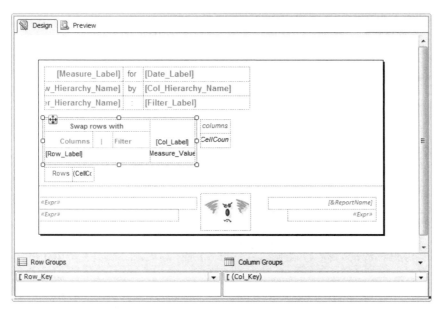

FIGURE 11-40

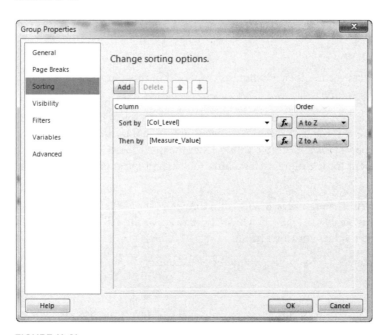

FIGURE 11-41

The Measure_Value textbox is tweaked to highlight the current member (LemonChiffon) for rows and columns.

The BackgroundColor is set as follows:

```
=iif(Fields!Row_Key.Value=Parameters!pRowMbr.Value, "LemonChiffon",
 iif(Fields!Col_Key.Value=Parameters!pColMbr.Value, "LemonChiffon",
 Nothing
 ))
```

Similarly, the font is set to Black if this cell corresponds to the current member; otherwise, it is set to DimGray.

```
=iif(Fields!Row_Key.Value=Parameters!pRowMbr.Value, "Black",
 iif(Fields!Col_Key.Value=Parameters!pColMbr.Value, "Black",
 "DimGray"
 ))
```

On the labels for rows and columns, the same background color is set (LemonChiffon), but the text color is DimGray if they correspond to the current member. Otherwise, it is Blue, indicating that you can click it to drill up and down the hierarchy.

```
=iif(Fields!Row_Key.Value=Parameters!pRowMbr.Value,
 "DimGray",
 "Blue")
```

Restricting Rows and Columns

The parameter pColCount restricts the number of columns displayed in this report.

You use the TOPCOUNT function in MDX to restrict the number of column members returned in the query driven by the parameter pColCount. However, instead of having to select the parameter with a fiddly option box in the parameters, the user just clicks the number of columns he or she wants. The TablixColCount table displays these selectable values from the CellCount dataset. The clickable values are colored Blue except for the numeric matching the current parameter value, and it is DimGray.

Clicking invokes a self-calling drill-through action with all parameters set as their existing values except for pColCount, and that is set [CellCount], which is the value of the cell that is clicked. Figure 11-42 shows the parameter values for this action.

Restricting rows works in the same way, but with parameter pRowCount.

Swap Actions

In the top-left cell of the main tablix is the TablixSwap. It contains two blue cells that allow the user to swap the rows with columns or swap the rows with the filter. Again, all that happens is a self-calling drill-through action takes place. For instance, for the rows and columns swap we set up a tooltip:

```
="Swap rows ("
+ Fields!Row_Hierarchy_Name.Value
+ ") with columns ("
+ Fields!Col_Hierarchy_Name.Value
+ ")"
```

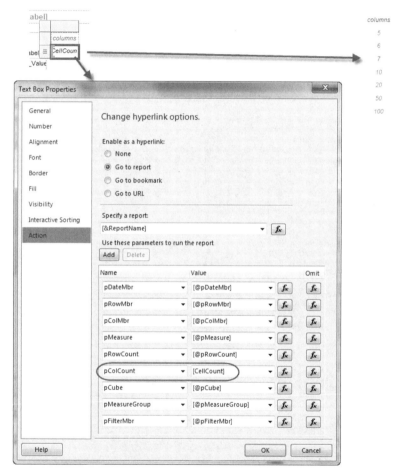

FIGURE 11- 42

We also set up a self-calling drill-through action. Notice the swapping of row and column parameters shown in Figure 11-43.

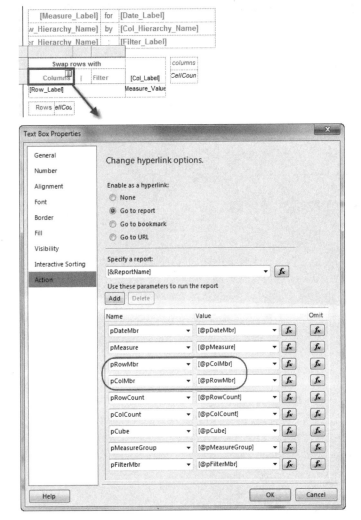

FIGURE 11-43

Titles

The titles in the report work both as titles and as places where users can change what they see in the report.

Changing the Measure (TextboxMeasureName)

The first textbox in the Titles table includes the Measure to display in the report. When the user clicks it, he or she is taken to the Cube Browser Metadata report to select a different measure from the same cube, or even a measure from a different cube. All parameters are passed to the Cube Browser Metadata report, plus the following:

➤ pCallingReport = is set by the report calling this report. This allows drill-through text-box action to return to the calling report.

➤ pDriver = Measure indicates that the user wants to select a cube and measure. Other possible values are Rows, Columns, Date, and Filter.

Figure 11-44 shows the action, and Figure 11-45 shows how to select a measure.

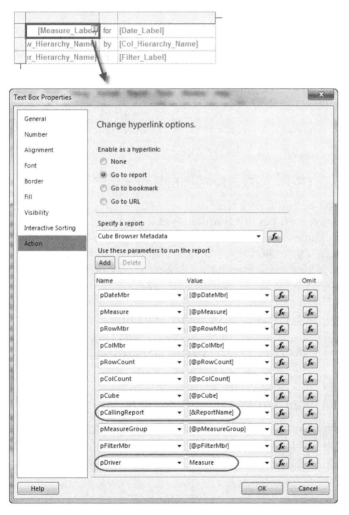

FIGURE 11-44

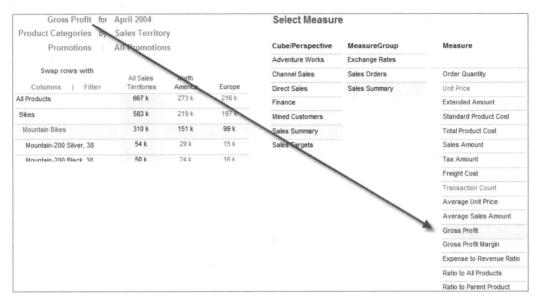

FIGURE 11-45

Changing the Hierarchy on Rows (TextboxRowHierarchyName)

Similarly, if you want to change what is on rows, click the `TextboxRowHierarchyName`. This action calls the same Cube Browser Metadata report, but this time with `pDriver = Rows`. Now the Cube Browser Metadata report displays the Dimensions and Hierarchies for the Measure Group corresponding to the current measure. Figure 11-46 shows `TextboxRowHierarchy` on the design surface and the Action tab of the textbox properties window with the parameter values required to call the Cube Browser Metadata report. Figure 11-47 shows a preview of the result.

Changing the Hierarchy on Columns (TextboxColHierarchyName)

Changing columns works the same way as `TextBoxRowHierarchyName`, except that the `pDriver` parameter is set to `Columns` so that the Cube Browser Metadata report knows to display, and later return, the `pColMbr` parameter.

Changing the Hierarchy for the Filter (TextboxFilterHierarchyName)

Changing the filter also works the same way as `TextBoxRowHierarchyName`, except that the `pDriver` parameter is set to `Filter` so that the Cube Browser Metadata report knows to display, and later return, the `pFilterMbr` parameter.

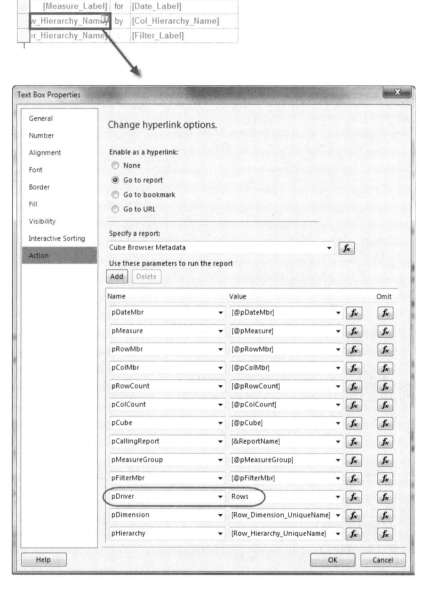

FIGURE 11-46

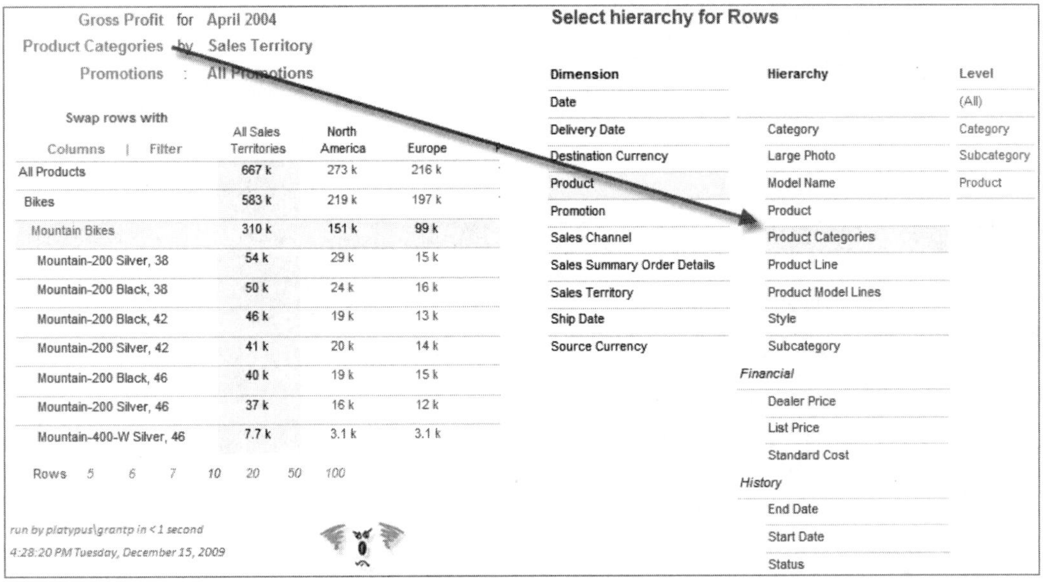

FIGURE 11-47

Changing the Date Member (TextboxDateLabel)

The user can change the period of time the report covers by clicking the `TextboxDateLabel`. This drills through to the Cube Browser Member report, where the user can select another `Date` member in the hierarchy. This can be a year, quarter, month, or even a single day. Figure 11-48 shows the action parameters. This time `pDriver` is set to `Date`. Figure 11-49 shows what the user sees.

Footer Information

To round out the report, we have added some interesting information to the footer:

➤ Who ran it

➤ How long it took to execute

➤ Page numbers in 1 of *n* format

➤ The name of the report

In production we always number our reports using the following format:

p*nnn - meaningful name*

For example, p012 - Channel Sales.

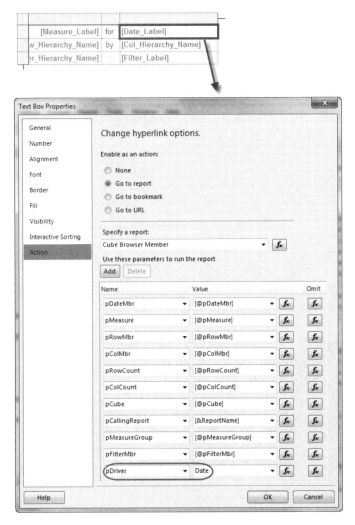

FIGURE 11-48

So in the footer we would display the report's full number and name, but in the title we would strip the number and just leave the report name.

Figure 11-50 shows a formatted footer.

The following is the code for the first textbox, which displays who ran the report and how long it took to run:

```
="run by " & User!UserID + " in " +

IIf(
```

```
System.DateTime.Now.Subtract(Globals!ExecutionTime).TotalSeconds<1,
    "< 1 second",
(

IIf(System.DateTime.Now.Subtract(Globals!ExecutionTime).Hours >0,
    System.DateTime.Now.Subtract(Globals!ExecutionTime).Hours
    & " hour(s), ", "") +

IIf(System.DateTime.Now.Subtract(Globals!ExecutionTime).Minutes >0,
    System.DateTime.Now.Subtract(Globals!ExecutionTime).Minutes
    & " minute(s), ", "") +

IIf(System.DateTime.Now.Subtract(Globals!ExecutionTime).Seconds >0,
    System.DateTime.Now.Subtract(Globals!ExecutionTime).Seconds
    & " second(s)", ""))

)
```

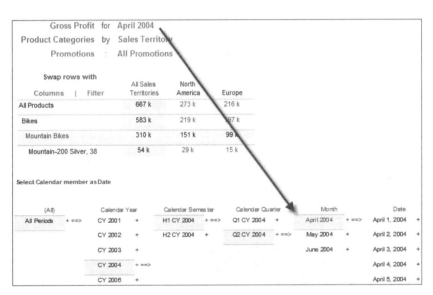

FIGURE 11-49

run by Joey\grantp in < 1 second		Cube Browser
12:24:01 PM Monday, November 14, 2011		Page 1 of 1

FIGURE 11-50

The next textbox shows when the report was run:

```
= FormatDateTime(Globals!ExecutionTime,3)
& " "
& FormatDateTime(Globals!ExecutionTime,1)
```

Then, at the right of the footer comes the report's name:

```
=Globals!ReportName
```

The final textbox holds the page number and total number of pages:

```
= "Page "
& Globals!PageNumber
& " of "
& Globals!TotalPages
```

Now you have a simple OLAP browser. You can create user reports by creating linked reports with different parameters. Interestingly, your users can also configure the report to one they like and then just save it as a favorite in Internet Explorer.

Final Thoughts

This is a great starting point for creating your own variation on an OLAP Cube Browser. For instance, the Angry Koala Cube Surfer report, shown in Figure 11-51, uses the same basic concept as the Cube Browser. But instead of showing a single measure in each data cell, it shows the following:

➤ The measure for the current period (in bold)

➤ The measure for the same period in a comparison period (driven by a lag number — for example, 12 means 12 months, and therefore means the same month last year)

➤ An Australian sparkline (it has a line down under)

Figure 11-51 shows the Cube Surfer comparing the last three periods to the previous periods — six, five, and four (lag = 3).

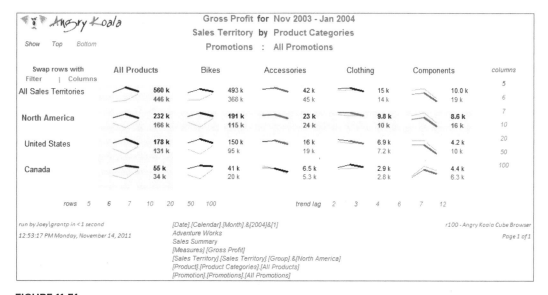

FIGURE 11-51

Figure 11-52 shows the same report with a lag of 12 for a year-on-year comparison.

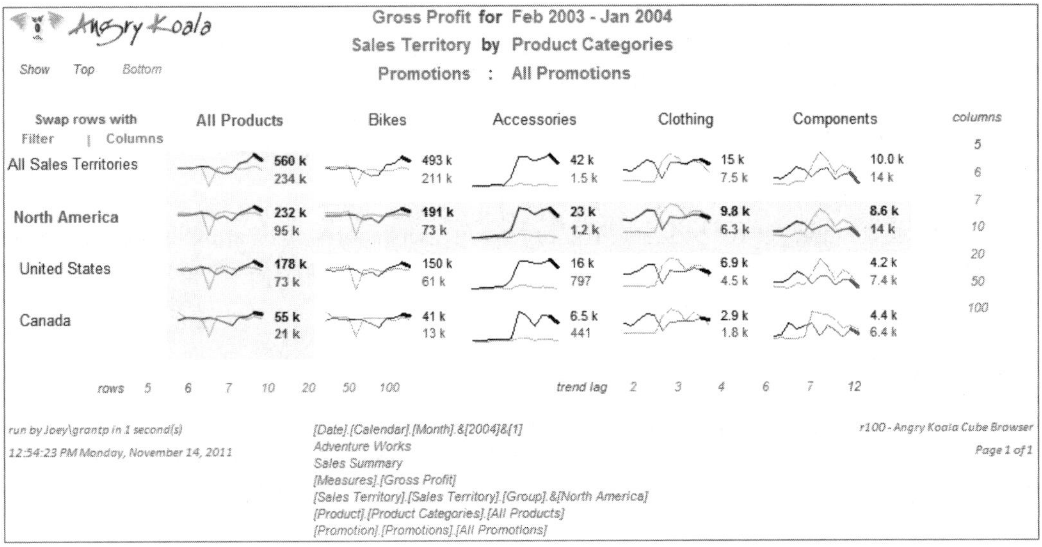

FIGURE 11-52

SUMMARY

In this chapter you have harnessed the power of Analysis Services to create compelling reports with dynamic content. You have learned how to use self-calling drill-through reports to navigate cube hierarchies and create helper reports to collect parameters based on Analysis Services metadata utilizing DMVs. As a result, you will now be well placed to meet, and in many cases exceed, the expectations of your business users.

PART IV
Enabling User Reporting

12

Tabular Models

In Chapter 9 you learned about Microsoft Business Intelligence Semantic Model (BISM). You learned that it is made up of two components: multidimensional mode, which corresponds to the previous unified dimensional model (UDM), and tabular modeling, which is a more recent approach first implemented in the initial release of PowerPivot in SQL Server 2008 R2, with an add-in for Excel as the model development tool.

The Analysis Services team received a lot of positive feedback on PowerPivot. It considered different approaches for how to evolve it and make it available for corporate BI developers, as well as enable the underlying model for Power View for self-service business users performing highly interactive, visual analysis. SQL Server 2012 has two development tools for creating tabular models: an enhanced PowerPivot add-in for Excel and a new tabular development environment in Visual Studio for BI applications. This chapter focuses primarily on PowerPivot for Excel and covers these topics:

➤ Creating a tabular model using PowerPivot for Excel

➤ Enhancing a tabular model by integrating additional data

➤ Creating relationships between tables

➤ Analyzing data in a model through sorting and filtering

➤ Enriching a model by defining custom calculations

INTRODUCTION TO POWERPIVOT

A key aspect of Microsoft's vision behind self-service business intelligence, as implemented in PowerPivot and Power View, is that your analytical data remains connected to its source. Also, it should be easy to update and refine your BI application and model to frequently evolving requirements. Furthermore, you can easily share data in a controlled way, and share visualizations and analyses built from the data.

PowerPivot is made up of two separate components that work together to accomplish this:

➤ PowerPivot for Excel is an Excel add-in that allows business analysts and Excel power users to create and edit tabular models within a tool they already know, Microsoft Office Excel.

➤ PowerPivot for SharePoint extends Microsoft Office SharePoint Server to include the ability to share and manage PowerPivot applications as well as tabular models created with PowerPivot for Excel.

PowerPivot applications are like Excel workbooks, but they include PowerPivot data and metadata embedded in the workbook. This enables PowerPivot workbooks to offer additional functionality over regular Excel workbooks. For example, PowerPivot workbooks can contain tables of hundreds of millions of rows of data; PowerPivot tables are not constrained by Excel tables, which can contain only 1 million rows of data (1,048,576 rows to be exact).

PowerPivot tables can be a source for Excel PivotTables and PivotCharts, as well as a source for Power View (which you'll read more about in Chapter 13) for reporting, analysis, and visualization. PowerPivot can represent relationships between tables and join tables just like a database. Figure 12-1 shows a PowerPivot workbook with multiple tables.

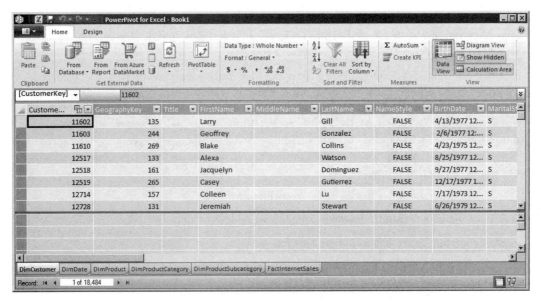

FIGURE 12-1

PowerPivot workbooks can be shared using Microsoft Office SharePoint Server. Workgroup members can then browse and interact with the workbook using the Excel client, a web browser (with Excel Services configured), or Power View. There is also PowerPivot Gallery, shown in Figure 12-2. This is a custom SharePoint document library type that previews workbook contents and provides an entry for creating a Power View analysis and visualization from a workbook, as discussed in Chapter 13.

FIGURE 12-2

PowerPivot workbooks can reference external data sources, for which you schedule automatic data refresh. Although manual data refresh can be accomplished directly within PowerPivot for Excel when the workbook is loaded, automatic data refresh uses PowerPivot for SharePoint and executes unattended on a specified schedule. As shown in Figure 12-3, you could configure an automatic data refresh for your workbook with the latest data every morning at 6.

To summarize, PowerPivot workbooks provide all the capabilities of Excel, plus additional modeling and analytical capabilities, to deliver self-service BI in conjunction with Excel and Reporting Services Power View.

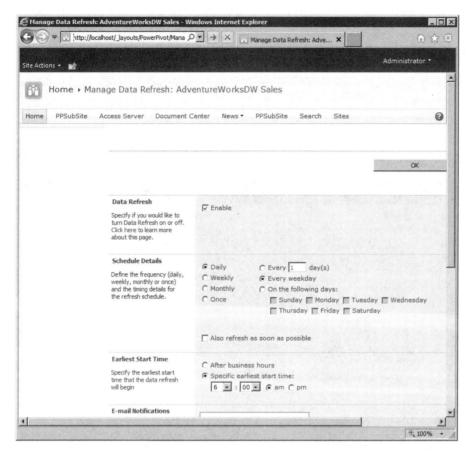

FIGURE 12-3

PowerPivot for Excel

PowerPivot for Excel allows you to integrate data from various types of external data sources, link to existing data inside the workbook, add relationships between data, and enrich data with custom calculations. The data can then be used directly within Excel through features such as PivotTables and PivotCharts. You also can create highly interactive visualizations and analytical presentations with Power View.

PowerPivot for Excel includes the VertiPaq engine, a local version of the Analysis Services in-memory engine in VertiPaq mode that performs calculations and executes queries with high performance.

When you are working with PowerPivot for Excel, the data resides in memory. When you save the workbook, the data and metadata are stored inside the Excel workbook file.

PowerPivot for Excel is a free download on the web that can be found at `http://powerpivot.com`. It has the following prerequisites:

➤ **.NET 3.5 SP1** — This component is automatically available on newer operating systems such as Windows 7. For older operating systems, you need to install .NET 3.5 SP1 before installing Office 2010. You can download .NET 3.5 SP1 from the Microsoft Download center at `www.microsoft.com/download`.

➤ **Excel 2010 and Office Shared Features** — PowerPivot for Excel requires Excel 2010; it won't install with earlier versions of Excel. An important feature of Excel 2010 is support for the 64-bit processor architecture. You have the option to choose a 64-bit or 32-bit installation. If you work with large quantities of data, you should use the 64-bit version. With the 32-bit version of the product, you are limited to a maximum of 2 GB of memory for Excel. PowerPivot for Excel also is limited to a maximum of 2 GB. The processor architecture of the Excel installation has to match the processor architecture of the PowerPivot add-in installation.

The installation of Office Shared Features is required because PowerPivot for Excel is a Visual Studio Tools for Office (VSTO) add-in and requires the VSTO runtime. The latter is installed when Office Shared Features are installed.

> *You must install Office Shared Features either before you install Excel or at the same time as Excel. Otherwise, you have to uninstall Excel and redo the installation.*

➤ **Windows Vista / Windows Server 2008 Platform Update** — If you are running Excel on the Vista or Windows Server 2008 operating system, PowerPivot for Excel requires the platform update described in KB 971644. You can download it at `http://support.microsoft.com/kb/971644`.

After you install these prerequisites and PowerPivot for Excel, start Microsoft Office Excel. A new command called PowerPivot Window appears on the Excel ribbon, as shown in Figure 12-4. This command is the entry point for PowerPivot for Excel. When you click it, the PowerPivot window opens, as shown in Figure 12-5.

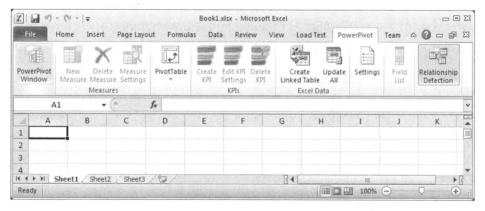

FIGURE 12-4

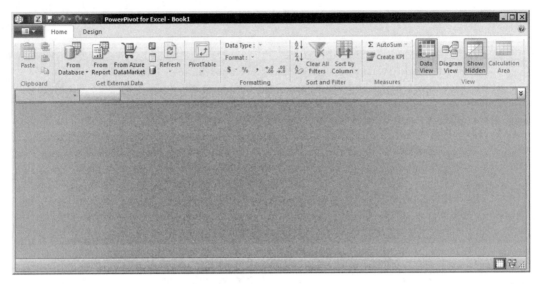

FIGURE 12-5

The PowerPivot Window provides commands to integrate data from various types of external data sources, linking to existing data inside the workbook, adding relationships between data, and enriching data with custom calculations. It provides a "window" into the PowerPivot data that is stored inside the workbook.

The following sections describe some of the key features of PowerPivot for Excel. You will work through a tutorial based on a sample relational database for SQL Server. It is called AdventureWorksDW_WroxSSRS2012 and is available on the Wrox download page for this book.

Setup and Installation

If you haven't installed Excel and PowerPivot for Excel, follow these steps:

1. Install Excel 2010 from the Office 2010 suite, along with the Office Shared Features. As mentioned in the preceding section, it is important to install the Office Shared Features before or at the same time as Excel. If you install on an operating system older than Windows 7, you might need to install additional prerequisites, as explained in the preceding section.

2. Download and install PowerPivot for Excel, which is available at http://powerpivot.com.

3. Install a SQL Server database server from the SQL Server 2012 release.

4. Download the AdventureWorksDW_WroxSSRS2012 sample relational database from the Wrox download site for this book.

5. Connect to your SQL Server relational database server using SQL Server Management Studio, and attach the sample database on your SQL Server instance.

IMPORTING DATA INTO POWERPIVOT

The PowerPivot window provides several ways to import data from various types of data sources, including the following:

➤ Relational data sources such as SQL Server, Oracle, and Teradata via OLE DB providers.

➤ Analysis Services or other PowerPivot workbooks.

➤ Existing reports rendered from Reporting Services.

➤ File-based data from Microsoft Access, Excel, and delimited text files.

➤ Data feeds such as RSS or Atom, SharePoint 2010 lists.

➤ Datasets from Azure DataMarket.

➤ Tables in an Excel worksheet. You can create a PowerPivot table from data on a worksheet in the Excel workbook. This links the PowerPivot table to the Excel table such that if the Excel table is updated, the PowerPivot table is automatically updated as well to match.

➤ Paste data from the Windows clipboard into a PowerPivot table if PowerPivot recognizes the clipboard data as tabular data.

The following steps take you through an example of importing data from a SQL Server database that has the AdventureWorksDW_WroxSSRS2012 relational sample database deployed:

1. Start Microsoft Excel with the PowerPivot add-in installed.

2. Select the PowerPivot tab on the Excel ribbon, and select PowerPivot Window to open the PowerPivot window. Here you see commands for importing data, filtering, sorting, and analyzing data, as well as creating calculations.

3. From the Home tab of the PowerPivot window, within the Get External Data section of the ribbon menu bar, select to import From Database. From the drop-down menu that appears, select From SQL Server, as shown in Figure 12-6.

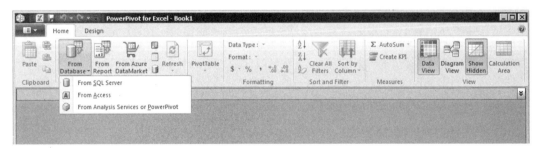

FIGURE 12-6

4. The Table Import Wizard appears, as shown in Figure 12-7. Here you specify how to connect to a Microsoft SQL Server Database. First, you specify the name of the database server instance, on which you deployed the AdventureWorksDW_WroxSSRS2012 sample database. Specify credentials to connect to the database server, and then select AdventureWorksDW_WroxSSRS2012 as database name from the field's drop-down list. Click Next. If you deployed the AdventureWorksDW_WroxSSRS2012 relational database on a SQL Server on your local machine (localhost), you can fill out the import wizard dialog as shown in Figure 12-7.

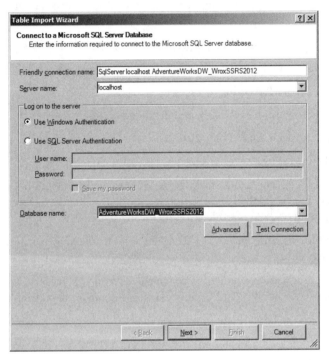

FIGURE 12-7

5. On the Choose How to Import the Data page, choose the "Select from a list of tables and views to choose the data to import" option and in the Select Tables and Views page, shown in Figure 12-8, check the following tables:

➤ DimCustomer

➤ DimDate

➤ DimProduct

➤ DimProductCategory

➤ DimProductSubcategory

➤ FactInternetSales

Editing the names in the Friendly Name column allows you to rename them immediately upon import. You can also rename them after the import is completed, directly in the PowerPivot window.

6. In the same dialog, select DimCustomer table and click the Preview & Filter button. You see the Preview Selected Table dialog for the DimCustomer table, as shown in Figure 12-9. It previews the columns and the first 50 rows of the table. You can apply filters to imported data, as well as deselect columns that you do not want to import if they are not needed for your analysis.

FIGURE 12-8

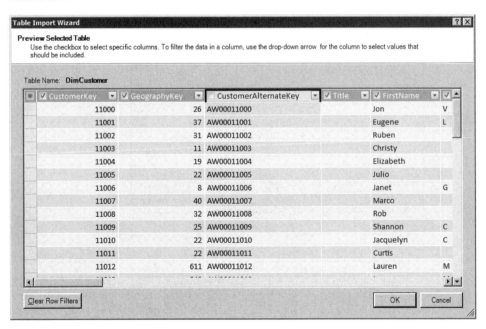

FIGURE 12-9

7. Uncheck the box next to CustomerAlternateKey, as shown in Figure 12-9, and click OK. That field will not be used for the analysis during this tutorial.

8. You are back on the Select Tables and Views page. The Filter Details column shows Applied Filters next to `DimCustomer`. Clicking it shows the filters you have applied.

9. Click the Finish button.

PowerPivot for Excel creates a data store utilizing the VertiPaq engine running in PowerPivot, and retrieves the data from the data source. You see the progress of these operations in the Importing page of the Table Import Wizard.

When importing tables directly, PowerPivot also tries to detect relationships between those tables in the data source system, to add them in the PowerPivot data store.

You can inspect the relationships created by clicking the Details link in the Message column of the import dialog, as shown in Figure 12-10.

If PowerPivot was unable to import relationships, the dialog provides more information on which relationships could not be successfully imported.

FIGURE 12-10

10. Click Close in the import dialog.

The PowerPivot window is now populated with all tables that have been imported. The default view of a model is Data View, where you can see a single table at a time and switch between them using tabs, such as Excel worksheet tabs, as shown in Figure 12-11. For each table, you see the columns of the table and data rows. You can select a cell value, and the Record indicator at the bottom of the window describes which record the cursor is currently positioned on. You can navigate rows within a table using the vertical scrollbar or the arrow buttons next to the Record indicator.

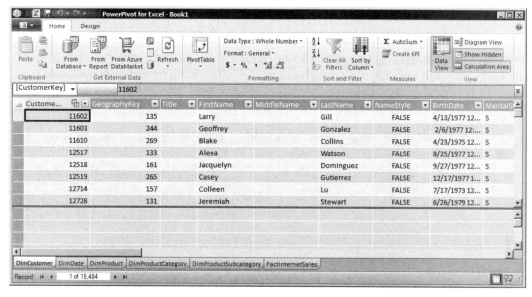

FIGURE 12-11

11. In the PowerPivot ribbon, select Diagram View. Diagram View shows you all the tables in your model and visualizes the relationships between them, as shown in Figure 12-12. This view doesn't show the actual data values in the tables.

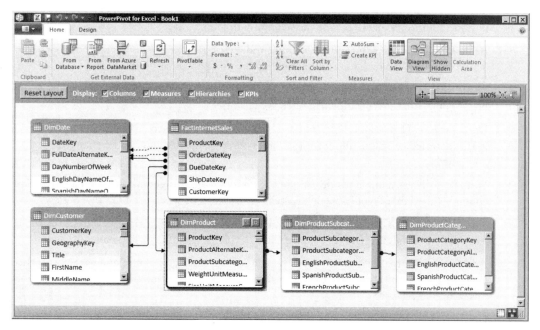

FIGURE 12-12

POWERPIVOT WINDOW

With data imported, we can further enrich and refine the model. Before we do that, though, let's take a look at some of the features of the tabular designer. Figure 12-13 shows the PowerPivot tabular designer after our import is completed. Clicking the button to the left of the Home tab opens the File menu to save, and to toggle between Normal and Advanced mode. Advanced mode provides additional model options that are otherwise hidden in the PowerPivot window.

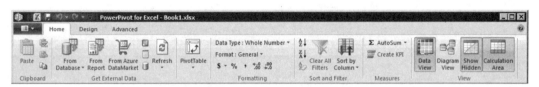

FIGURE 12-13

The Home Tab

The Home tab, shown in Figure 12-13, contains commands that apply to the model you are currently working on. The following is a brief description of its commands:

➤ **Clipboard** — This provides copy and paste actions, including appending rows to PowerPivot tables.

➤ **Get External Data** — This provides various import options: From Database, From Report, Azure DataMarket, Data Feed, Text, Other Sources. You saw these commands in action when you imported data into your model in the preceding section. You can also use them to import (additional) data into the model at any time.

➤ **Refresh** — This command refreshes your model with the current contents of the data sources. You can refresh from all data sources or just from a particular connection.

➤ **PivotTable** — This command creates a new PivotTable (or PivotChart) in the Excel workbook using your current tabular model as the source.

➤ **Data Type** — This command changes the data type of the selected column. The data type is autodetected on importing from the data source originally and can be changed afterwards.

➤ **Format** — These commands determine the textual formatting to apply when a particular column is used in a PivotTable or PivotChart in Excel, or when used in Power View.

➤ **Sort and Filter** — There offer various options that affect sorting and filtering of the table. The section "Analyzing and Enriching Data" explains them in more detail.

➤ **AutoSum** — AutoSum allows you to create a measure using common aggregation functions over the data in the currently selected column. AutoSum is covered later in this chapter in the "Measures" section.

➤ **Create KPI** — This command lets you create key performance indicator (KPI) visualizations for columns in the table.

> ➤ **Data View / Diagram View** — These commands switch between Data View (shown in Figure 12-11) and Diagram View (shown in Figure 12-12).

> ➤ **Show Hidden** — This command toggles whether hidden elements are shown in the designer.

> ➤ **Calculation Area** — This command toggles whether the calculation area below the rows of a table is shown in the tabular designer.

The Design Tab

The Design tab, shown in Figure 12-14, contains commands that affect individual model columns, define calculations, relationships, and table properties. The following is a brief description of its commands:

> ➤ **Add** — This command allows you to add a calculated column to the table. You'll learn about calculated columns later in this chapter.

> ➤ **Delete** — This command deletes the currently selected column or columns.

> ➤ **Freeze** — Freeze Column moves the currently selected columns to the far left of the table and freezes them. Freezing holds the columns in place regardless of the position of the horizontal scroll bar. You generally use this command when you want to see columns that are off the screen in relation to a particular column. The Unfreeze command removes the freeze action on frozen columns. They will scroll along with the rest of the columns when you move the horizontal scroll bar. Note that the Unfreeze command does not move the columns back to their original position.

> ➤ **Width** — This command adjusts the width of the selected table columns.

> ➤ **Insert Function** — This command inserts a new calculated column with a formula.

> ➤ **Calculation Options** — These commands control the calculation mode of the PowerPivot designer. In automatic calculation mode, calculations are updated automatically whenever the data changes. This can have performance implications for very large models with millions of rows or more. In automatic mode, the Calculate Now command is disabled.

> You can use Calculation Options to change to manual calculation mode. In manual mode, the Calculate Now command is enabled, and calculations are updated only when you invoke the Calculate Now command.

> ➤ **Existing Connections** — This command brings up a dialog that lets you interact with all the data connections that are defined in the model. From that dialog you can import more data from an existing connection, edit an existing connection's properties, refresh the source data for a single connection, or delete a connection.

> ➤ **Create Relationship and Manage Relationships** — These commands allow you to work with relationships between tables. You'll learn about relationships in tabular mode later in this chapter.

> ➤ **Table Properties** — This command invokes the Edit Table Properties dialog. Here you can change the definition of the currently selected table, including the field import mapping from the table's data source.

➤ **Mark as Date Table** — The two commands under this menu item allow you to mark the currently selected table as a date table. This means that special date filtering functionality in Excel is enabled.

FIGURE 12-14

The Advanced Tab

The Advanced tab, shown in Figure 12-15, is visible only after PowerPivot switches from normal mode to advanced mode. This can be accomplished by clicking the top-left corner of the PowerPivot window to get to its File menu, which contains options for saving, asking questions, sending feedback, and switching between normal and advanced modes. The following is a brief description of the commands on the Advanced tab:

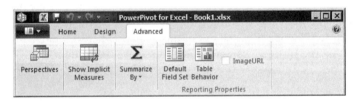

FIGURE 12-15

➤ **Perspectives** — This command brings up the perspectives dialog, which allows you to add or change the perspectives defined in the model. You can think of perspectives as multiple views (like database views) over the same underlying model tables.

➤ **Show Implicit Measures** — This toggles whether implicit measures are shown in the PowerPivot table designer. An implicit measure is generated automatically when a field is added to the Values area of the field list in an Excel PivotTable.

➤ **Summarize By** — This command determines the default aggregation function that reporting client tools, such as PowerPivot and Power View, apply when this column is added to a field list area. For example, you can change the default behavior of using a Sum aggregate to a DistinctCount aggregate. This command is enabled only for columns with numeric values.

➤ **Table Behavior** — This command enables you to change the default behavior of different visualization types and default grouping behavior in client tools, such as Power View, for the current table.

➤ **Default Field Set** — This command brings up the default field set dialog. Here you can specify the columns, measures, and field ordering that define the default field set when visualizing the selected table of your model in Power View. For example, you can define a set of default fields that should be picked when a business user initially selects an entire table to visualize.

➤ **ImageURL** — This command marks the selected column with metadata. Reporting clients such as Power View will treat the column's contents not as a string, but as a URL address of an image resource to download and visualize as an image in a report.

ANALYZING AND ENRICHING DATA

This section describes some basic operations on tables using PowerPivot. Specifically, you'll learn about filtering and sorting, relationships, calculated columns, and measures.

Filtering and Sorting

While importing data, you can apply filters and preview data. After importing data into PowerPivot, you can filter and sort data in a table in the PowerPivot window. For example, you can analyze sales data by following these steps:

1. Switch to the `FactInternetSales` table in the PowerPivot window.

2. Click the drop-down next to the `OrderDateKey` column.

3. Click the checkbox next to Select All to deselect all dates.

4. Click the checkbox next to the date item 20040101, as shown in Figure 12-16, and then click OK. You see that with the filter applied, the sales data has been filtered instantly to 99 rows of orders that happened on that day.

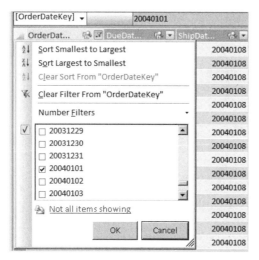

FIGURE 12-16

Figure 12-16 shows the Filter drop-down in the PowerPivot window for a specific table column. Depending on the data type of the underlying field, custom filter options are available.

For example, fields that are whole numbers would show Number Filters with options for conditions such as greater than. For string columns, you would see Text Filters in the Filter drop-down.

With the sales data filtered to 99 rows for that particular date, you can view minimum and maximum sales by order on that date by sorting the `SalesAmount` column following these steps:

5. Select the `SalesAmount` column in the `FactInternetSales` table.

6. Click the Sort Largest to Smallest button, as shown in Figure 12-17.

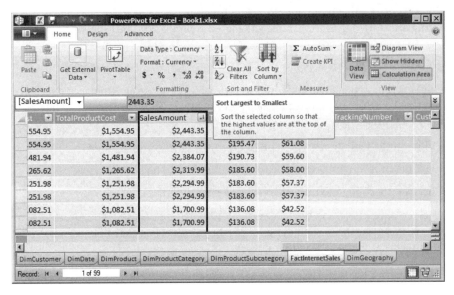

FIGURE 12-17

Sorting is performed over the filtered rows. It is very fast utilizing the VertiPaq engine in PowerPivot, even if the underlying dataset has millions of rows. By sorting, you can see that the maximum sales order on that day was $2,443.35, and the minimum sales order was $2.29.

Finally, on the Home tab, in the Sort and Filter section, select Clear All Filters to see all the data in the model again.

Relationships

An important aspect of the tabular model is relationships between tables. PowerPivot for Excel supports one-to-many relationships. This means that a column value in a specific table can have multiple instances of the value in another table's related column.

The table import wizard detects and understands the relationships that are present in the source data. It creates relationships in your model based on the relationships defined in the source data. In addition, the tabular designer provides ways to add relationships yourself.

If you are working in Data View, the designer indicates columns that participate in relationships with a glyph in the column header next to the column name. Hovering over the glyph provides details of the relationship. For example, hovering over the ProductKey column's glyph indicates "Related to [ProductKey] in table [DimProduct]." in a tooltip window.

Diagram View provides a richer environment for working with relationships. You can see all the relationships in your model simultaneously in Diagram View. You can also work with them in a graphical way. For example, you can create new relationships by dragging and dropping from one column to the other. Follow these steps to add a new column to the model and manually create a relationship between it and an existing table:

1. In the PowerPivot window, go to the Design tab and select Existing Connections. The Existing Connections dialog opens.

2. Click the Open button.

3. If a dialog appears asking for credentials, enter the credentials to reopen the connection to the relational data source. The Choose How to Import the Data page appears. Verify that "Select from a list of tables and views to choose the data to import" option is selected. Click Next.

4. On the Select Tables and Views page, select the DimGeography table.

5. Click Finish and then close the dialog page. The DimGeography table is added to the model, as shown in Figure 12-18. If you view the model in Diagram View, you can see the newly added table. You can also see that it is not connected to any other table in the model.

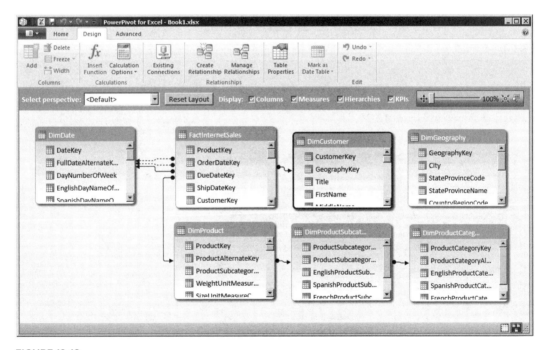

FIGURE 12-18

6. To create a relationship between the newly added DimGeography table and the DimCustomer table, click and drag the GeographyKey field in the customer table and drop it onto the GeographyKey field in the DimGeography table. This creates a relationship between the two tables based on the GeographyKey field, as shown in Figure 12-19.

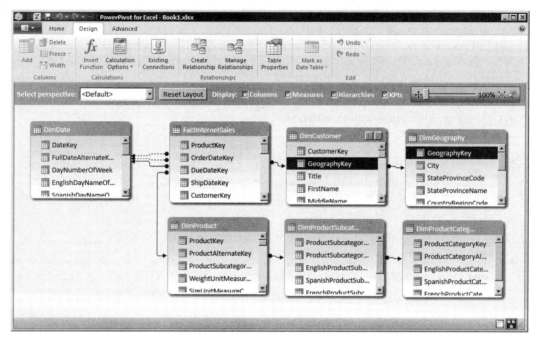

FIGURE 12-19

Alternatively, you can accomplish the same task using the Create Relationship command available on the Design tab. You can manage relationships by selecting Manage Relationships, which opens the dialog shown in Figure 12-20.

Active	Table	Related Lookup Table
Yes	DimCustomer [GeographyKey]	DimGeography [GeographyKey]
Yes	DimProduct [ProductSubcategoryKey]	DimProductSubcategory [ProductSubcate...
Yes	DimProductSubcategory [ProductCategory...	DimProductCategory [ProductCategoryKey]
Yes	FactInternetSales [CustomerKey]	DimCustomer [CustomerKey]
Yes	FactInternetSales [OrderDateKey]	DimDate [DateKey]
No	FactInternetSales [DueDateKey]	DimDate [DateKey]
No	FactInternetSales [ShipDateKey]	DimDate [DateKey]
Yes	FactInternetSales [ProductKey]	DimProduct [ProductKey]

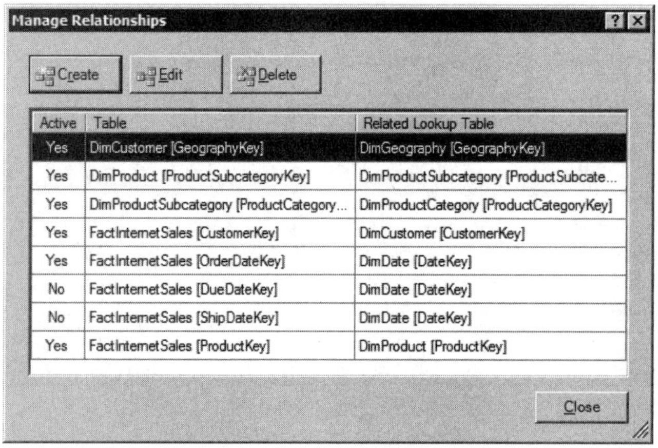

FIGURE 12-20

Relationships are a key part of the tabular model. The calculations that you create with DAX (Data Analysis Expressions) can use relationships to allow calculations that involve columns in different tables. Understanding when and how to create relationships in your model will help you realize your goals when analyzing your business data.

You can add DAX calculations to your model in two ways. The first, calculated columns, allows you to add expressions that define a new column in an existing table. You can refer to columns in the same table in your calculation, and the execution engine uses the value of the column in the current row as the calculation being evaluated. Another way to add calculations to your model is through what are called measures. Measures are calculations that are not done within the context of a table row. Rather, they are evaluated in the contents of the particular cell whose value they are being asked to provide.

Calculated columns and measures are explained in more detail in the following sections.

Calculated Columns

Similar to performing calculations on an Excel worksheet, PowerPivot allows you to create calculated columns and measures within the PowerPivot window using DAX functions. DAX functions are grouped into eight major categories:

- ➤ Date and Time
- ➤ Math and Trig
- ➤ Statistical
- ➤ Text
- ➤ Logical
- ➤ Filter
- ➤ Information
- ➤ Parent/Child

Calculated columns are useful when you need particular data values in your tables but those values are not in the data you have imported. It could be that you want to format data to display in a certain way in your client application. Or you may want to analyze a value that could be calculated from data values that are in the table. Or you may need a calculated column for some other purpose. The following steps show you how to add calculated columns to your model:

1. Switch to Data View in the PowerPivot tabular designer, and select the DimDate table.

2. From the Design tab, select Add Column. The far-right column in the table grid is selected, and the formula bar (located above the table data) goes into editing mode, as shown in Figure 12-21. In editing mode, the formula bar provides help in the form of autocomplete — tooltips that show the arguments expected for the function you are entering. You also can click a column in the table to enter that table's name at the current point in the formula. In addition, you can click the f_x button at the left of the formula bar to select a DAX function name to insert into the formula bar.

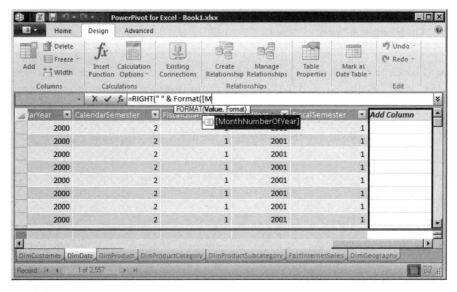

FIGURE 12-21

3. Enter the following DAX expression and press Enter:

```
=RIGHT(" " & Format([MonthNumberOfYear],"#0"),2) & " - " & [EnglishMonthName]
```

You can verify the formula is correctly specified based on the values populating the calculated column (for example, "1 - January").

4. Right-click the newly created column and select Rename column. Enter **DateHeader** for the new column name.

5. Select the `FactInternetSales` table and, in the Design tab, select Add Column.

6. Enter the following DAX expression as the definition of the new calculated column and press Enter:

```
=[SalesAmount] - [TotalProductCost]
```

7. Rename the new column **Profit**.

You now know how to create calculated columns in PowerPivot. The columns you added are available in reporting client tools the same as any column that came from the source date. In this way, calculated columns allow you to customize the data for your model beyond the data you imported. This is a powerful capability of tabular mode.

Measures

Measures, like calculated columns, are defined by a DAX expression. Unlike calculated columns, they cannot refer to a particular column as a value unless an aggregation function has been applied to the column name. The values for measures are calculated on-the-fly at the time they are evaluated in the context that the value is being asked for. This section shows you how to work with measures.

In the PowerPivot window, you work with measures in an area called the Calculation Area. (In the tabular designer in SQL Server Data Tools, the Calculation Area is called the Measure Grid.) The Calculation Area is the grid area below the splitter bar in the lower half of the Data View grid, as shown in Figure 12-22.

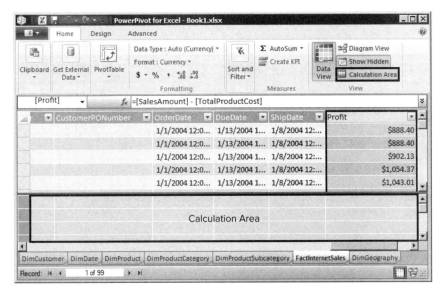

FIGURE 12-22

Follow these steps to create a measure in your model using the AutoSum feature:

1. In Data View, select the `FactInternetSales` table.

2. If the Calculation Area is not visible, right-click the FactInternetSales tab and select Show Calculation Area. Alternatively, go to the Home tab's View section and click the Calculation Area command.

3. Select the `SalesOrderNumber` column.

4. Click the down arrow next to the AutoSum button in the toolbar and select Distinct Count from the drop-down menu, as shown in Figure 12-23.

5. In the formula bar (the narrow bar above the table of data), change the Measure Name property (to the left of the ":=" sign) to **DistinctSalesOrders**. At this point, your newly created measure should look like Figure 12-24. Note that with the measure selected in the Measure Grid, the formula bar shows the formula that defines the measure, but in the Measure Grid you see the value that the formula produces.

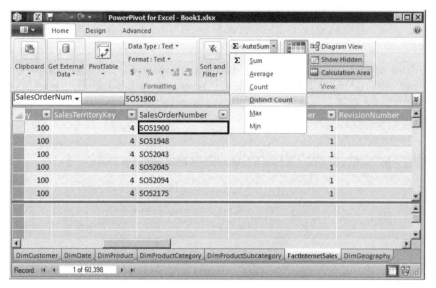

FIGURE 12-23

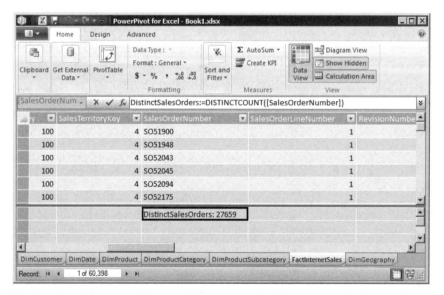

FIGURE 12-24

6. In the Upper portion of the Grid View, select the SalesAmount column of the FactInternetSales table.

7. From the Auto Sum button's drop-down menu, select Sum.

8. In the Properties window, change the newly created measure name from Sum of SalesAmount to InternetSalesAmount.

You have now used the `AutoSum` function to create two measures. As you learn more about DAX, you will be able to create your own DAX measures to do more sophisticated analysis actions.

Browsing the Model

As you work with your tabular model, you may want to work with your tabular model in a client tool to verify it. Chapter 13 shows you how to accomplish this with Power View. You can also explore the model directly in Excel using a PivotTable or PivotChart by using the PivotTable menu on the Home tab, as shown in Figure 12-25.

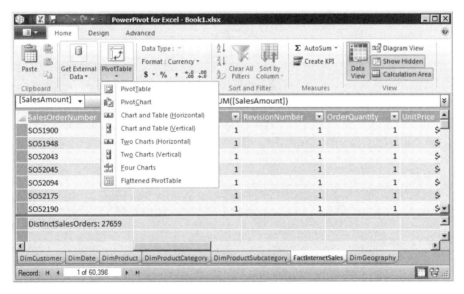

FIGURE 12-25

Figure 12-26 shows a PivotTable connected to the current model. Note that the measures you defined in the preceding section are available as values for analysis. The PivotTable shown in Figure 12-26 uses `DimGeography.CountryRegionCode`, `FactInternetSales.DistinctSalesOrder`, and `FactInternetSales.InternetSalesAmount`, which you created earlier.

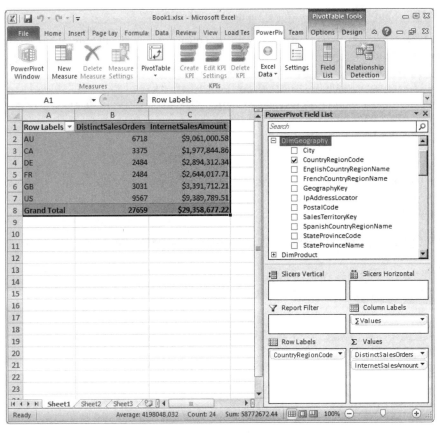

FIGURE 12-26

SUMMARY

This chapter gave you your first taste of working with PowerPivot for Excel, creating a tabular model. You learned about the commands available in the tabular designer and the two main model views, Data View and Diagram View. You walked through a simple scenario that showed the main components that make up a tabular model.

In the next chapter you'll learn about analyzing and visualizing your tabular models with Power View and creating exciting presentations in the process.

13

Visual Analytics with Power View

WHAT'S IN THIS CHAPTER?

➤ Introduction to Power View

➤ Understanding the Power View architecture

➤ Exploring, visualizing, and presenting with Power View

➤ Configuring data source connections

➤ Configuring PowerPivot for SharePoint

➤ Installing Analysis Services in tabular mode

In Chapter 12 you learned how to use PowerPivot for Excel to create tabular models directly in an Excel workbook. In this chapter you learn how to interactively explore, visualize, and present data from workbooks and model databases in Power View.

Power View, a new feature of Reporting Services 2012, provides intuitive ad hoc reporting for business users such as data analysts, business decision makers, and information workers. Power View is a browser-based Silverlight application launched from SharePoint Server 2010 that enables users to present and share insights with others in their organization through interactive presentations. Data has much more impact when it comes from a well-understood, quality-assured source; is shared and available to the people who need it; and is presented in a format that helps people share and explore insights easily. This is what the self-service Microsoft BI platform is about, tightly integrated with Microsoft Office and SharePoint.

SharePoint facilitates building BI portals and dashboards that contain Reporting Services reports (both operational and Power View), Excel Services reports, data-alerting capabilities over reports, and PerformancePoint Services for scorecards and management dashboards.

This chapter covers the following topics:

➤ Understanding Power View's capabilities and architecture

➤ Uploading PowerPivot workbooks to SharePoint

➤ Deploying PowerPivot models to Analysis Services

➤ Creating model connection files in SharePoint for end users

➤ Interactively exploring data in Power View

➤ Creating presentations with Power View

➤ Configuration options for connection files and trade-offs

➤ Installing Analysis Services in Tabular Mode

INTRODUCTION TO POWER VIEW

Power View makes fast, interactive, visual analytics pervasive and accessible to business users and BI professionals. It enables them to easily create and interact with views of data from a Microsoft BI Semantic Model (BISM). They are based on PowerPivot Excel workbooks published in a PowerPivot Gallery in SharePoint, or tabular models deployed to SQL Server 2012 Analysis Services server instances configured for tabular mode.

PowerPivot for Excel was introduced in SQL Server 2008 R2 for Excel 2010. Any workbooks you created with PowerPivot data can be uploaded in SharePoint. Also, you (and anyone else who has read permissions on the workbook file in SharePoint) can easily and quickly build highly interactive visualizations with Power View, connected to your existing Excel PowerPivot workbooks. You can quickly create a variety of visualizations, from tables and matrices to column; bar, line, and bubble charts; and sets of small multiple charts. Figure 13-1 shows multiples in design mode. For every visualization you want to create, you start with a table. You can then easily convert to other visualizations to determine which one best illustrates your data.

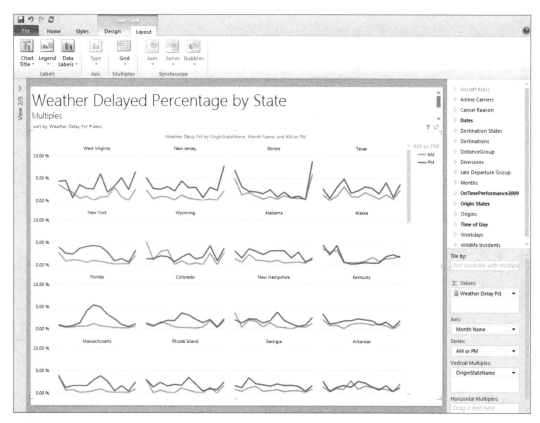

FIGURE 13-1

A Power View report is always presentation-ready. You can't switch between report design and preview modes (as with Report Builder); instead, in each step you work with the real data. You don't need to author queries. Power View does so on your behalf automatically based on the tables and fields you are exploring and underlying meta data in the semantic model (such as data types and relationships between tables).

You explore your data and visualize at the same time. A single report can contain multiple views. All the views are based on the same tabular model. Each view has its own visualizations and filters on each view are for that view only.

Power View has reading and full-screen presentation modes. The field list, ribbon, and other design tools are hidden to focus the attention on data visualizations and presenting, as shown in Figure 13-2.

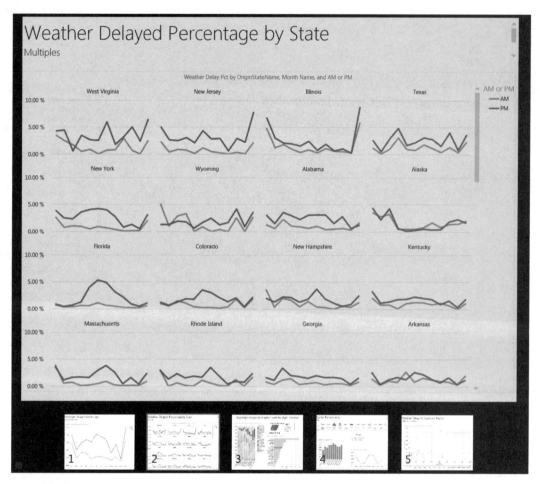

FIGURE 13-2

The report is fully interactive in presentation modes, with the same sorting, filtering, and highlighting capabilities available in other modes.

Power View provides several ways to filter data. Utilizing the meta data in the underlying tabular model, Power View knows the relationships between the different tables and fields in a report. Because of these relationships, you can use visualizations to filter and highlight all other visualizations in the same view, as shown in Figure 13-3, with one of the airlines selected in the chart on the right, its contribution highlighted in the chart on the left, and the data filtered at the right top of the screen.

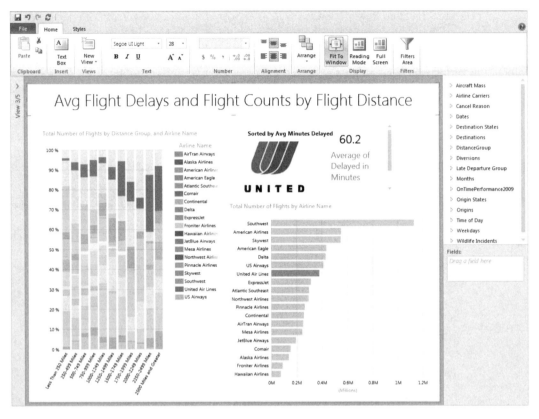

FIGURE 13-3

Alternatively, you can display the filters area and define filters that will apply to an individual visualization or to all the visualizations on a view. You can leave the filter pane visible or hide it before switching to reading or full-screen mode.

You can sort tables, matrices, bar and column charts, and sets of small multiples in Power View. You sort the columns in tables and matrices, the categories or measures in charts, and the multiple field or measures in small multiples. In each case, you can sort in ascending or descending order either on attributes, such as Product Name, or measures, such as Total Sales.

At any point, you can save your reports created with Power View back into SharePoint and share with other users, as shown in Figure 13-4.

You can print directly from Power View, as well as export an interactive version of your Power View report to PowerPoint presentations, as shown in Figure 13-5. Each view in Power View becomes a separate PowerPoint slide.

Interacting with Power View reports exported to PowerPoint is similar to interacting with Power View views in reading and full-screen modes. You can interact with the visualizations and filters that were added to each view, but you cannot create new visualizations or significantly modify the original visual analysis.

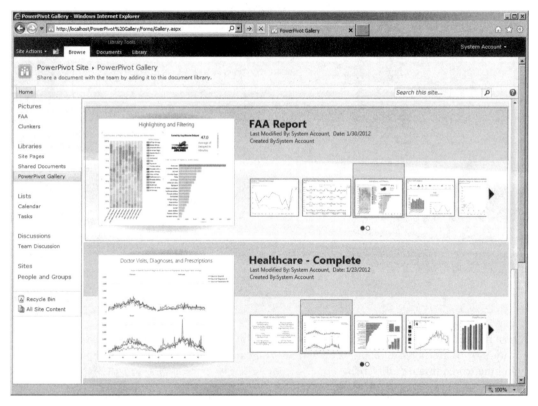

FIGURE 13-4

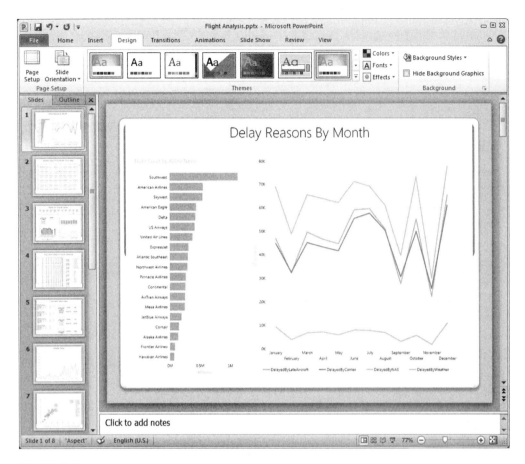

FIGURE 13-5

POWER VIEW ARCHITECTURE

Power View is a feature of SQL Server Reporting Services 2012 in SharePoint Integrated mode. The deployment consists of the following components:

➤ SharePoint Server 2010 with Service Pack 1

➤ SQL Server 2012 Database Engine

➤ SQL Server 2012 Reporting Services and Reporting Services Add-in

➤ Optional: SQL Server 2012 PowerPivot for SharePoint

➤ Optional: SQL Server 2012 Analysis Services stand-alone server instance in tabular mode

Chapter 3 explains step-by-step how to install and configure SharePoint, PowerPivot for SharePoint, and Reporting Services in SharePoint Integrated mode.

If you haven't yet installed a stand-alone Analysis Services server instance in tabular mode, see the "Analysis Services Tabular" subsection of this chapter. After you install these features, you will be able to do the following:

➤ Access PowerPivot workbooks you created in PowerPivot for Excel from SharePoint sites.

➤ Deploy the large sample FAA flight data model provided on the download site for this book.

➤ Build interactive Power View reports based on PowerPivot workbooks in SharePoint.

➤ Create Report Builder reports when you launch Report Builder in SharePoint.

Architecture Overview

Power View is a thin web client that launches in the browser from a published report or a tabular model available in SharePoint. The Power View application is hosted by the Reporting Services add-in for SharePoint on the web front end (WFE). Power View doesn't directly connect to the tabular model. Instead, it uses the Reporting Services service application to authenticate users and connect to a tabular model, as shown by the dotted arrows in Figure 13-6.

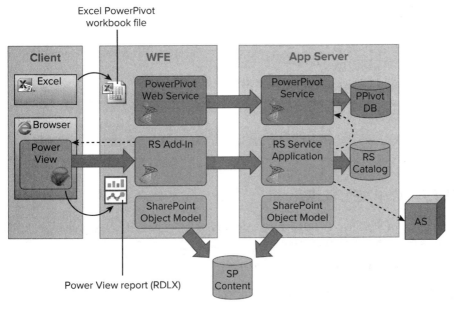

FIGURE 13-6

The tabular model can be an Excel PowerPivot workbook or a tabular model running on a SQL Server 2012 Analysis Services server. When you're working in Power View, you don't need to know the names of servers, or know about logins and permissions. Power View is automatically connected to the tabular model from which you launched Power View.

Power View saves reports with the RDLX file extension to SharePoint. The default click action for an RDLX file in a standard SharePoint document library is to launch Power View in presentation mode for the selected report. When Power View is launched, it connects to the Reporting Services (RS) add-in and the RS service application to load the RDLX report in an in-memory user session.

Reporting Services Add-in

The Reporting Services add-in for SharePoint installs on WFE machines of your SharePoint deployment, as shown in Figure 13-6. The add-in provides services for both RDL and RDLX reports. For Power View specifically, the RS add-in does the following:

➤ Hosts the Power View application (XAP package)

➤ Hosts the Power View page (`AdhocReportDesigner.aspx`) to launch Power View from a model or a published RDLX report

➤ Provides affinity and automatic failover to report server services in the farm for Power View user sessions

Reporting Services Service Application

The Reporting Services service application is the central component of a SharePoint-integrated report server installation. For Power View specifically, the Reporting Services service application provides several services to enable a highly interactive experience in Power View:

➤ Data connections to the semantic model, including impersonation and delegation as configured and needed

➤ Query execution and data processing

➤ Fetching web images hosted in a SharePoint site or document library or on external web server locations

➤ Configurable tracing and error logging for diagnostics and support

All Reporting Services service applications share a catalog database to provide storage for internal meta data used by report server instances in a SharePoint farm.

PowerPivot for SharePoint

PowerPivot for SharePoint adds services and infrastructure to SharePoint to enable users to work with Excel PowerPivot workbooks. PowerPivot for SharePoint installs on top of SharePoint 2010 with SP1. It adds services and functionality to SharePoint to enable collaboration, sharing, and reporting for PowerPivot workbooks. PowerPivot for SharePoint consists of two main components that allow SharePoint to host PowerPivot applications:

➤ **PowerPivot Service** lets you deploy and query PowerPivot workbooks. The service also includes the PowerPivot web service component, which allows applications to connect to PowerPivot workbook data from outside the SharePoint farm. This includes reusing PowerPivot data from one workbook in other workbooks. The PowerPivot service refreshes external connections to data sources to keep the data in a PowerPivot workbook current. You can define a refresh schedule to automatically update data, such as every morning at 7.

➤ **Analysis Services Service in Tabular/VertiPaq mode** is sometimes also called PowerPivot database. It is an Analysis Services database instance running inside the SharePoint farm in tabular mode.

PowerPivot for SharePoint gives you two setup options: a new farm installation and an existing farm installation.

The new server installation installs all the required components for PowerPivot for SharePoint on a single machine. This type of installation takes care of installing and configuring SharePoint for you. Chapter 3 explains the necessary steps to set up and configure PowerPivot for SharePoint.

For complex SharePoint deployment scenarios, such as multi-machine installations and existing SharePoint farm installation, refer to Chapter 21 in *Professional Microsoft SQL Server 2012 Analysis Services with MDX and DAX* (Wrox, 2012) and the MSDN documentation (`http://msdn.microsoft.com/en-us/library/ff487867(v=sql.110).aspx`).

PREPARING A MODEL AND CONNECTION FOR A TUTORIAL

Now that you have installed and configured Reporting Services in SharePoint integrated mode and PowerPivot for SharePoint, you are ready to deploy a sample BI Semantic Model, learn about connection files, and then launch Power View to explore the data, visualize insights, and share presentations of your analysis results.

You start by preparing the model and data connections for the subsequent Power View tutorial. The model database is an Excel PowerPivot workbook, created from publicly available datasets from the Federal Aviation Administration (FAA). The FAA is the national aviation authority of the U.S. and thus regulates and oversees all aspects of civil aviation in the U.S.

The FAA publishes a variety of datasets on airline traffic data, such as flight on-time performance, flight cancellations, and flight incidents with wildlife. The data is published through the Bureau of Transportation Statistics (BTS) at www.bts.gov.

The FAA.XLSX workbook was created by importing the raw datasets into PowerPivot for Excel, detecting and creating relationships between tables, and enriching the data with other datasets and images. The images, referenced from the PowerPivot workbook as image URL paths, are available to download from the Wrox download site next to the PowerPivot FAA sample workbook. However, feel free to create your own airline logo images instead of using the provided clip art images.

Deploying the FAA Flight Data Model

Follow these steps to upload the sample PowerPivot workbook as a new database in an Analysis Services server in tabular mode. If you haven't installed an Analysis Server, refer to the installation and configuration steps in the "Analysis Services Tabular" section of this chapter.

1. Locate the download for the FAA PowerPivot workbook on the Wrox download site for this book.

2. Download and save FAA.XLSX to the default backup folder of your Analysis Server, typically located at C:\Program Files\Microsoft SQL Server\MSAS11.MSSQLSERVER\OLAP\Backup.

3. Select All Programs ➪ Microsoft SQL Server 2012. Launch SQL Server Management Studio as administrator by right-clicking the entry and selecting "Run as administrator."

4. In SQL Server Management Studio, connect to your Analysis Server instance. If you have multiple instances installed, connect to the default instance. Do not connect to local\ PowerPivot, because this is a reserved instance in Analysis Services 2012 that cannot be used to deploy regular databases.

5. When connected, right-click Databases and select Restore from PowerPivot, as shown in Figure 13-7.

6. In the Restore from PowerPivot dialog, specify the location of FAA.XLSX as the backup file, and specify the database name as FAA, as shown in Figure 13-8. Click OK. If you connected to a 32-bit instance of the Analysis Server, you may receive an error that there is not enough memory available, because the database is fairly large and needs substantial memory during the restore process. Sometimes the restore still succeeds despite the error message. You can also try to use a 64-bit instance of the Analysis Server or close applications before you restore the database to ensure sufficient memory.

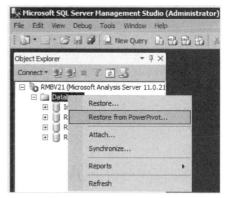

FIGURE 13-7

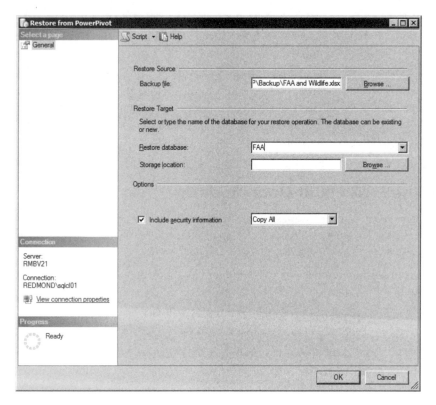

FIGURE 13-8

Creating a SharePoint Image Library for FAA Airline Images

To create a new image library in SharePoint, follow these steps:

1. Log on as a user who has administrator or full control permissions on the SharePoint server.

2. In a browser window, navigate to http://*YourSharePointServer*.

3. In the SharePoint ribbon, select Site Actions ➪ Manage Content and Structure. If this option is not visible, then try to select More Options, filter by Library, select Picture Library, and skip to step 6 below.

4. In the Site Content and Structure page, select New ➪ List from the ribbon.

5. On the next page, click Picture Library, as shown in Figure 13-9.

6. On the Create Picture Library page, specify the name as FAA, and click Create.

7. You should see a new picture library on the home of your SharePoint site, as shown in Figure 13-10.

8. Click the FAA link to navigate to the picture library.

9. Using the SharePoint ribbon, upload all the airline images into the FAA picture library. The result should look similar to Figure 13-11.

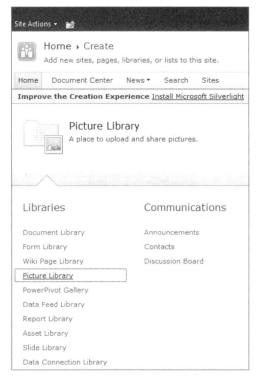

FIGURE 13-9

FIGURE 13-10

FIGURE 13-11

Publishing the FAA Workbook Directly to the PowerPivot Gallery

Chapter 12 introduces PowerPivot for Excel. You can open the FAA workbook using Excel. Due to the workbook's large size, it may take a minute to open and load all the data.

If you haven't installed and configured PowerPivot for SharePoint, refer to the installation and configuration steps in the "Analysis Services Tabular" section of this chapter.

If you receive an error in subsequent steps about exceeding the maximum limit for file size, you can change this setting to publish/upload large PowerPivot workbooks, such as the FAA workbook, by following these steps:

1. On your SharePoint server, launch the SharePoint Central Administration page by selecting Start ⇨ All Programs ⇨ Microsoft SharePoint 2010 Products ⇨ SharePoint 2010 Central Administration.

2. Under the heading Application Management, click the Manage web applications link.

3. Select SharePoint - 80. Then, in the SharePoint ribbon, select General Settings ⇨ General Settings, as shown in Figure 13-12.

FIGURE 13-12

4. In the Web Applications General Settings dialog, navigate to the bottom of the page, to the value "Maximum upload size," and change the value from 200 MB to 2047 MB. Click OK.

5. For the setting to take effect immediately, open a command prompt in administrator mode, type the command `iisreset`, and press Enter to reset the Internet Information Services (IIS) applications.

To publish the FAA workbook from Excel to SharePoint, follow these steps:

1. Switch to your machine with Excel and PowerPivot for Excel.

2. Open the FAA workbook.

3. In Excel, select File ⇨ Save and Send ⇨ Save to SharePoint ⇨ Save As.

4. Enter `http://`*YourSharePointServer*`/PowerPivot Gallery` in the folder path of the Save As dialog, and click Save. If the machine you are running Power View in is using Windows Server 2008 R2 as the operating system, make sure to enable the Desktop Experience feature first, in order to save to SharePoint.

Alternatively, you can upload the FAA workbook directly in SharePoint by following these steps:

1. Open a browser and navigate to `http://`*yourSharePointServer*`/PowerPivot Gallery`.

2. On the SharePoint ribbon, select Documents ➪ Upload Document.

3. In the Upload dialog, browse to the location of the FAA workbook, and click OK to upload.

Creating Data Source Connections for Power View

Power View can connect to data using several different connection options, which are explained in more detail in the section "Configuring Data Source Connections." For the tutorial in this section, you will create two files, which you will use later to create a new Power View report from the published FAA workbook/database.

BI Semantic Model (BISM) Connection File

Following are the steps to set up a BISM connection file:

1. Open a browser and navigate to `http://`*yourSharePointServer*`/`
`Shared Documents`

2. In the SharePoint ribbon, select Documents ➪ New Document ➪ BI Semantic Model Connection, as shown in Figure 13-13.

3. Specify the BISM connection file settings as shown in Figure 13-14. Replace "localhost" with the server and, optionally, the instance name (if you didn't install as the default instance) of your Analysis Server in tabular mode where you uploaded the FAA database in the previous section, such as *MyServer\InstanceName*.

FIGURE 13-13

 If the menu option is missing, either you are logged in as a user who doesn't have permissions to create new contents, or you did not correctly install and configure PowerPivot for SharePoint. In addition, for your current document library, open the Library Tools and go to Library Settings. Select Advanced Settings and enable Allow management of content types, and click OK. In the document library settings, under Content Types, click Add from existing site content types, and add BI Semantic Model Connection.

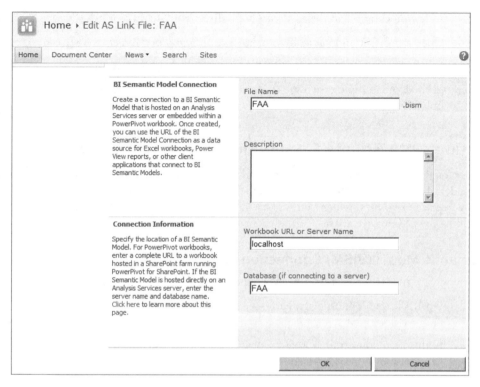

FIGURE 13-14

4. Click OK to create the BISM connection file. You should see a new file in your document library, as shown in Figure 13-15.

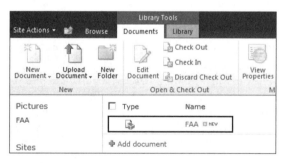

FIGURE 13-15

Report Data Source (RSDS) Connection

Connection strings for semantic models in Report Data Sources can have the following formats:

➤ Connecting to a PowerPivot workbook published in SharePoint by specifying the path of the workbook: `Data Source = http://`*YourSharePointServer*`/PowerPivot Gallery/FAA.xlsx`

➤ Connecting to a tabular model on an Analysis Server by specifying the server name and database name: `Data Source = `*YourASServer*`; Initial Catalog = FAA`

To create an RSDS connection file, follow these steps:

1. In the document library where you just created a BISM connection file, on the SharePoint ribbon, select Documents ➪ New Document ➪ Report Data Source.

2. In the data-source properties page, specify connection settings, as shown in Figure 13-16. Be sure to specify the data-source type as Microsoft BI Semantic Model for Power View. For the connection string, specify the name of your Analysis Server in tabular mode where you uploaded the FAA database in the previous section.

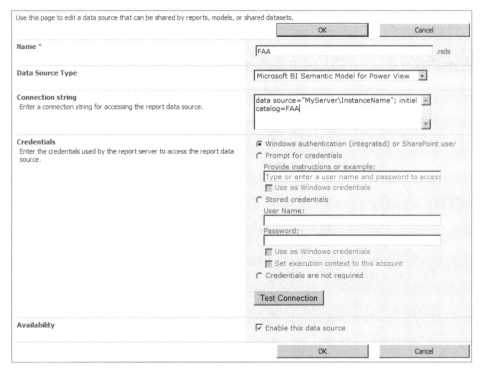

FIGURE 13-16

3. Click Test Connection to verify that the connection can be successfully established.

4. Click OK to create the RSDS file. It should appear as a new file in your document library.

VISUAL ANALYTICS WITH POWER VIEW

Power View makes fast, interactive, visual analytics pervasive and accessible to business users and BI professionals. It enables them to easily create and interact with views of data from a Microsoft BISM, based on PowerPivot Excel workbooks published in a PowerPivot Gallery in SharePoint, or tabular models deployed to SQL Server 2012 Analysis Services server instances configured for tabular mode.

In this section, you learn to interactively explore data in Power View and create compelling presentations.

Getting Started with Power View

Power View runs directly in the browser, using the Silverlight 5 browser plug-in. The first time you start Power View, it asks you to install the latest Silverlight browser plug-in if you don't have it yet.

Creating a New Power View Report

You start a new Power View report from a tabular model in a SharePoint Server 2010 document library or in a PowerPivot Gallery. The model can be one of the following:

➤ An Excel PowerPivot workbook published in a PowerPivot Gallery. You create a new Power View report from a PowerPivot Gallery by clicking the Power View icon shown on the entry of a workbook, as shown in Figure 13-17.

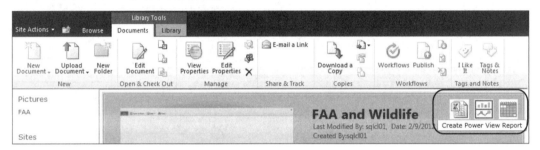

FIGURE 13-17

➤ A shared data source (RSDS) using a Microsoft Business Intelligence Semantic Model data source type. The RSDS can point to either an Excel PowerPivot file or a tabular model deployed on an Analysis Services server. You create a new Power View report from an RSDS in a SharePoint document library by clicking the down arrow next to the RSDS file and selecting Create Power View Report, as shown in Figure 13-18.

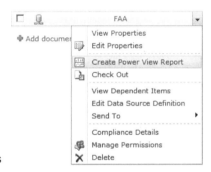

FIGURE 13-18

➤ A BI Semantic Model connection file (.bism) that points to either an Excel PowerPivot file or a tabular model deployed on an Analysis Services server. You create a new Power View report from a BISM connection file in a SharePoint document library by either clicking the file entry or clicking the down arrow next to the BISM file and selecting Create Power View Report, as shown in Figure 13-19.

For more information about RSDS and BISM connection files, see the later section "Configuring Data Source Connections."

The Power View design environment opens, and you see the view where you build your new report from a semantic model, as shown later in Figure 13-22. The Power View design environment has

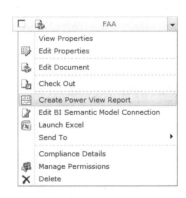

FIGURE 13-19

several main elements, which you will learn about in detail in a moment, in the section "Introduction to the Design Experience."

Opening an Existing Power View Report

When you open reports in a PowerPivot gallery, you can choose to open the report in a specific view by clicking any of the preview images, as shown in Figure 13-20.

FIGURE 13-20

Clicking a preview image of a report in PowerPivot gallery opens the report in reading mode. To open the report in edit mode, click the Edit Report icon in the upper-left corner of the report entry in PowerPivot Gallery.

To open a Power View report published in a regular SharePoint document library, simply click the file entry. To open a report directly in edit mode, click the down arrow next to the report, and then click Edit in Power View, as shown in Figure 13-21.

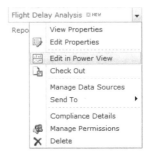

FIGURE 13-21

Introduction to the Design Experience

The Power View design environment consists of several main elements, as shown in Figure 13-22.

Power View has a *ribbon* similar to that in Microsoft Office. The Home, Styles, Design, and Layout tabs are context-sensitive and contain buttons and menus for the most common tasks. The Design and Layout tabs appear only if you create or select a visualization on the *canvas*, and the tab content changes depending on the type of visualization. For example, a chart visualization provides options to modify the chart title and legend and to synchronize chart axes.

Ribbon Area · Filters Area · Field List

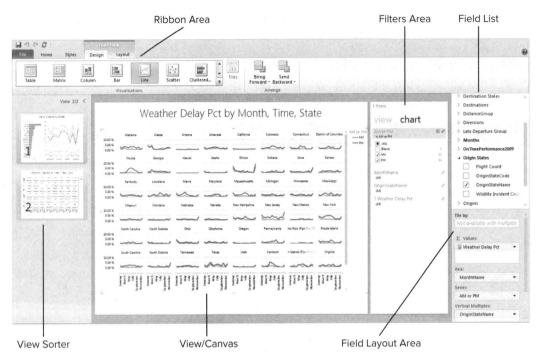

View Sorter · View/Canvas · Field Layout Area

FIGURE 13-22

The canvas, also called *view*, is of fixed size, similar to a PowerPoint slide, but unlike Report Builder. A Power View report can have many views, similar to a PowerPoint presentation consisting of many slides.

A view fits to the window using autofit mode by default. As you resize the browser window, or open panes such as the *filters area*, the view adjusts to fit the remaining window.

You can disable this behavior and use scrollbars to view the different parts of the view. To stop the view from resizing to autofit to the window, deselect the Fit to Window button in the Power View ribbon.

Ribbon options are disabled (grayed out) if a particular action is unavailable based on what you selected in the view. For example, if a table has no measures, you cannot convert it to a chart, and all chart options are disabled on the Design tab.

The pane to the right of the canvas is the *field list*. The top half displays the tables and fields available in the semantic model that your Power View report is based on. The lower half is the *field well* or *layout section*. It displays field grouping and layout options for the selected visualization in the canvas.

Creating a Table Visualization

As you click a field in the field list, Power View draws a table in the view, displaying your actual data and automatically adding column headings. You do not insert an empty table in the view or author a query. As you select more fields, they are added to the table in the view.

When you add a field to the view, you immediately see the actual values in that field — the same values you would see in reading and full-screen modes. Power View always operates with the live data. The columns are formatted according to the field's data type, as defined in the model that the report is based on.

If an existing visualization is selected in the view, clicking a field adds it to that visualization. If not, the new field starts a new table visualization in the view.

For example, assuming you started a new Power View report from the FAA semantic model, go to the field list, expand `Airlines` (representing the Airlines model table), and select the `Airline Name` field. This creates a new table visualization, as shown in Figure 13-23. Airline Name also appears in the field well, shown as one of the fields used in the visualization.

FIGURE 13-23

Measures in a model table are fields marked with a sigma (Σ) symbol in the field list. A measure is a set of numeric values that typically indicate the size, quantity, or scale of something. Measures are defined in the tabular model that your report is based on. You need at least one measure to create a chart data visualization.

You can also use a *nonmeasure* field as a measure. To make use of this functionality in our tutorial, hover the mouse cursor over the `Airlines` `.Flight Count` field in the field list, click the drop-down arrow, and select Add to Table as Sum, as shown in Figure 13-24. The resulting table is shown in Figure 13-25. It also includes an automatic (sub)total aggregation at the

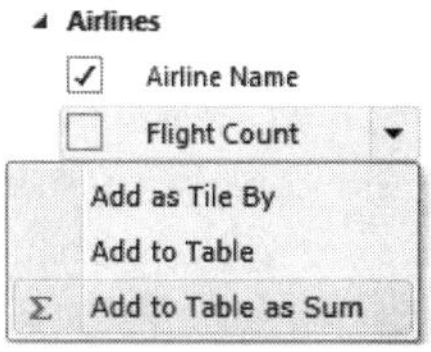

FIGURE 13-24

bottom. Note that you can also change the aggregate function using the field well after a field is added as a measure. For example, if you have a field that cannot be aggregated, such as a Rating field with values from 1 to 5, you could add it to a table and then set the aggregate to Average.

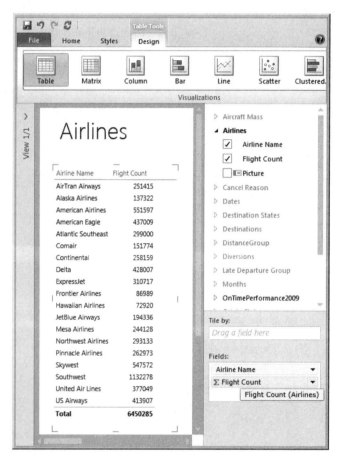

FIGURE 13-25

Converting Visualizations

You can quickly create a variety of visualizations in Power View, from tables and matrices to charts and sets of small multiple charts. For every visualization you want to create, you start with a table, which you can then easily convert to other visualizations, to determine which one best illustrates your data.

To convert a table to other visualizations, ensure that the table is selected in the view, and then click a visualization type in the visualizations gallery on the Table Tools Design tab. Figure 13-26 shows the table with airlines and flight counts created in the previous section, converted into a bar chart.

FIGURE 13-26

Depending on the current fields and data in your table, Power View enables and disables different visualization types to give you the best visualization for that data. To start another visualization on the view, you create another table by clicking a blank part of the view before selecting fields from the fields section of the field list.

Sorting Inside a Chart

In Power View, you can sort data in tables, matrices, and bar and column charts. You can sort individual charts within small multiples. You can sort measures, such as Sales Amount, and nonmeasures, such as Airline Name. Sorting on various types of visualizations is explained in more detail later in this section.

Using the bar chart you created in the previous step, you may notice that by default a chart is sorted in ascending alphabetical order by category unless the model specifies an explicit sort order.

To sort the chart of airlines in ascending order by flight counts, hover the mouse cursor over the top edge of the chart until a floating toolbar appears. The toolbar shows "sort by" in the upper-left corner, and then the name of the currently sorted field (such as `Airline Name`), and then either "asc" for ascending or "desc" for descending.

You can click the field name to sort on a different value. Alternatively, click the drop-down arrow to select a specific field to sort on, as shown in Figure 13-27.

As a next step, click asc to sort in the opposite direction, such that the airline with the highest flight count is shown at the top of the bar chart, as shown in Figure 13-28.

Until now, you have made only six (or fewer) mouse clicks and haven't used the keyboard, from launching Power View from the FAA model to figuring out that Southwest Airlines has the highest flight count recorded in the dataset of the FAA sample workbook database.

Expanding Visualizations

All visualizations have a *pop-out* button in the upper-right corner, except for Tile visualization. When you click the button shown in Figure 13-29, the visualization expands to fill the entire Power View view. If you are in reading or full-screen mode, it expands to fill the entire window. When you click the pop-out icon again, the visualization returns to its original spot in the report.

Filtering in Views

FIGURE 13-27

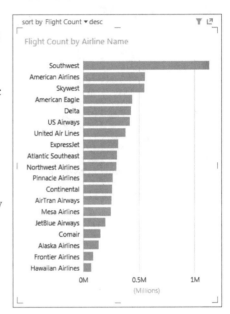

FIGURE 13-28

FIGURE 13-29

Power View provides several ways to filter and highlight data in reports. Based on the meta data in the underlying model, Power View knows the relationships between the different tables and fields in a report. This enables you to use visualizations on a view to automatically filter each other using the underlying relationship information.

You start with building a visualization that analyzes the causes of flight delays:

1. Click an empty area of the current view to ensure that no visualization is selected.

2. In the field list, expand `Months`, and select the `MonthName` field. This creates a new table on the view showing all month names.

3. In the field list, expand `OnTimePerformance2009`, and select the `DelayedByLateAircraft` field.

4. Using the ribbon, convert the table into a column chart. As you resize the column chart, notice how the category axis and numeric y-axis automatically adjust to make optimal use of the visual view port. For example, Figure 13-30 shows a chart too narrow to fit all categories. Only a subset of the categories is visible; you must use a scrollbar to view the others. Figure 13-31 shows a chart that can fit all categories in its view. The category labels automatically adjust to improve readability. Figure 13-32 shows an even wider chart, in which category axis labels appear on two lines to use the available space optimally.

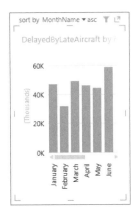

FIGURE 13-30

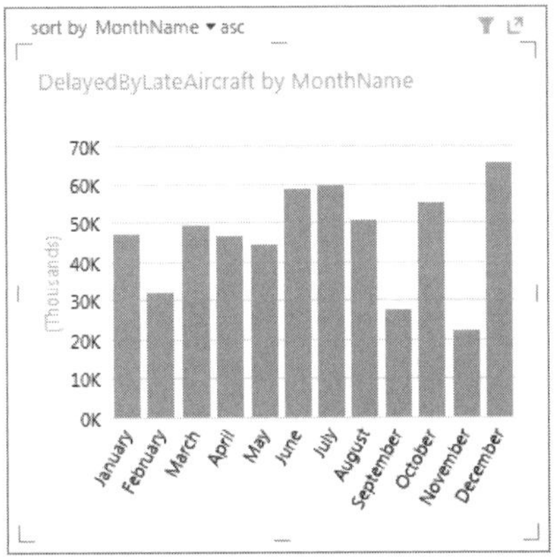

FIGURE 13-31

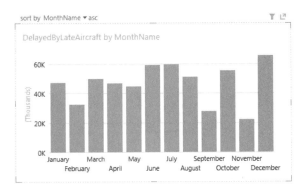

FIGURE 13-32

5. In the field list, select the following additional measures from the `OnTimePerformance2009` table:

➤ `DelayedByCarrier`

➤ `DelayedByNAS` (National Air Space)

➤ `DelayedByWeather`

6. Select the chart, go to Chart Tools Layout in the ribbon, click Chart Title, and select None. Select Legend ⇨ Show Legend at Bottom. Figure 13-33 shows the resulting chart as stacked columns. This type of chart quickly shows the aggregated number of flights. Not surprisingly, the peaks for delays are during the December holiday and summer travel seasons.

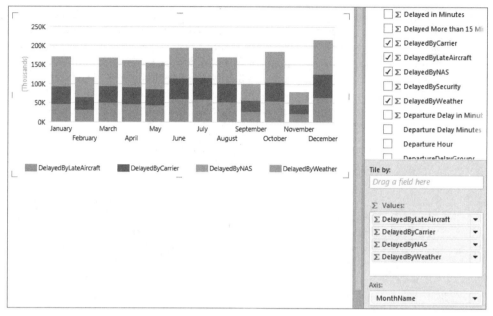

FIGURE 13-33

7. In the ribbon, switch to Chart Tools Design, and select Line to convert the column chart to a line chart, as shown in Figure 13-34. The line chart visualization shows clearly that overall for all carriers, delays due to National Air Space are the most common type of delay, consistently affecting flights' on-time performance.

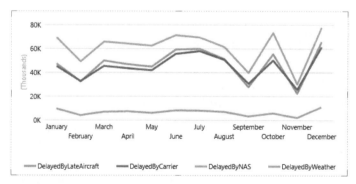

FIGURE 13-34

8. On your current view, locate the bar chart showing flight counts by airline. Click the bar for Southwest, and notice how the line chart with delay reasons automatically updates and filters to just flights by Southwest, as shown in Figure 13-35. The filter is applied with an animation to help you see the differences compared to the general trends for all airlines. In the case of the FAA data for on-time performance during 2009, the most common type of delay for Southwest was a late aircraft, unlike the general trend.

9. You can also perform multiselect for filtering. In the bar chart for flight counts, hold down the Shift or Ctrl key and click additional airline names. This way you select multiple values; with each filter click, the line chart updates automatically, as shown in Figure 13-36.

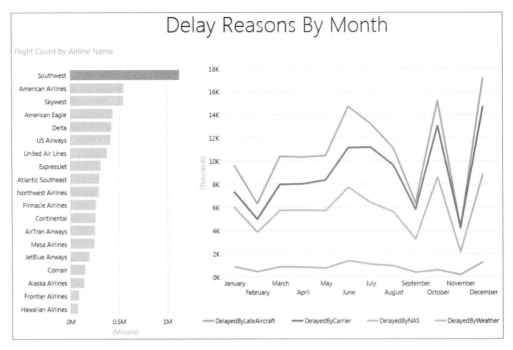

FIGURE 13-35

10. You can clear your chart filter value selection by clicking anywhere in the empty space of the bar chart for flight counts.

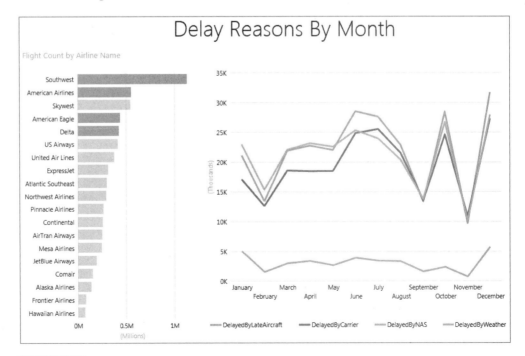

FIGURE 13-36

Multiple Views

You can create a report with multiple views in Power View using the New View menu on the Home tab, as shown in Figure 13-37.

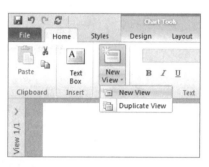

You can click through multiple views in a presentation, similar to PowerPoint. All the views in one report are based on the same model. You can copy and paste from one view to another and duplicate whole views. If you save preview images of the views, an image of each view is displayed in the PowerPivot Gallery.

FIGURE 13-37

To explore the multiple view capability, you create a second view in your report:

1. Using the New View menu shown in Figure 13-37, create a new empty view.

2. In the field list, expand `Months` and select the `MonthName` field.

3. In the field list, expand `OnTimePerformance2009` and select the `Weather Delay Pct` field.

4. Using the ribbon, convert the table into a line chart, as shown in Figure 13-38. Not surprisingly, the chart reveals that weather delays are most common during December and January, due to winter conditions.

FIGURE 13-38

5. In the field list, expand `Time of Day` and select the `AM or PM` field. This automatically puts the field into the chart series. As you can see in the resulting chart shown in Figure 13-39, the underlying model contains an undesired (Blank) value that shows up in the chart as an extra series. You can filter out undesired values using filters for the entire view or on a particular visualization.

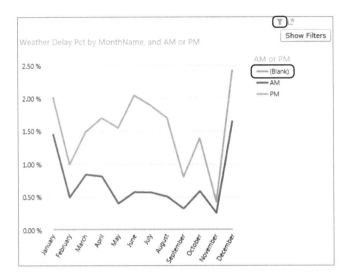

FIGURE 13-39

6. Open the Filters Area for the selected visualization by clicking the filter icon in the chart's floating toolbar, as shown in Figure 13-39.

7. The Filters Area appears and prepopulates with all fields currently used in the selected visualization. Click the AM or PM field within the filter pane. This expands the filter and automatically runs a query in the background to fetch the list of distinct values for the filter, as well as its counts. Select the individual filter values for AM and PM, as shown in Figure 13-40. As you select individual filter values, the chart visualization immediately updates.

FIGURE 13-40

 Each view can have its own filters, but the state of the Filters Area is constant: If the Filters Area is expanded on one view, it is expanded on all views. As you move from view to view, in any mode, the state of the filter on each page persists. For example, if you have a filter for the Airline Name field filtering for one view for Southwest, when you leave the view and then return to it, the filter will still be filtering for Southwest. When you duplicate a view, the filters are duplicated too, along with the state of each filter. Saving the report also saves the state of each filter.

8. Minimize the Filters Area by clicking the arrow shown in Figure 13-41.

FIGURE 13-41

9. In the field list, expand `Origin States` and select the `OriginStateName` field. This changes the visualization into a small multiple (also known as a Trellis chart), as shown in Figure 13-42. Notice that the chart multiples are automatically synchronized, on both the category axis and the value axis. This helps you visually compare and grasp information quickly, such as seeing that a higher percentage of flights in the afternoon are affected by weather delays than flights in the morning.

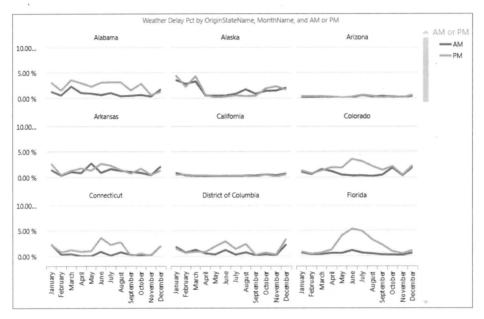

FIGURE 13-42

10. Set the number of multiples to display across and down by going to the Chart Tools Layout ribbon, clicking the Grid button, and selecting the desired layout, as shown in Figure 13-43.

11. Expand the View Sorter by clicking the arrow icon next to the View pane, as shown in Figure 13-44. You can navigate between views by simply clicking the thumbnail picture of a view. You can create a new view, duplicate a view, or delete a view using the down-arrow menu on a given view, as shown in Figure 13-44. You can reorder views using drag-and-drop within the View Sorter area.

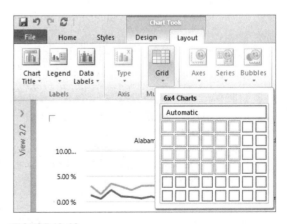

FIGURE 13-43

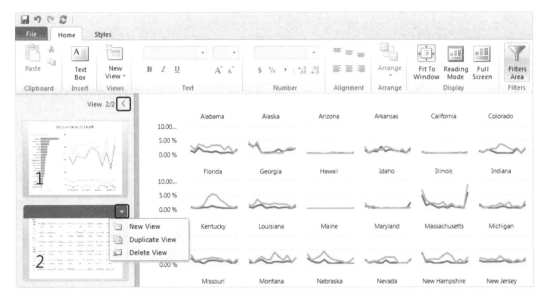

FIGURE 13-44

Saving Reports

You save a Power View report to the same SharePoint site and location as the model from which you launched Power View:

1. To save the report you have created so far, go to the Power View File menu, shown in Figure 13-45, and choose Save or Save As.

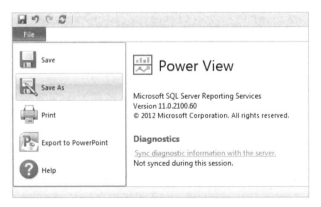

FIGURE 13-45

2. The first time you save the report, the default location is the folder where the model is located. To save it to a different location, browse to that location. For example, in the dialog, navigate to the root of your SharePoint site, select PowerPivot Gallery as the save location, and specify a report name, as shown in Figure 13-46. By default, the check box to save preview images is selected. For privacy reasons you may want to deselect it and not save preview images.

FIGURE 13-46

View preview images are the images that Power View displays in the View pane in design mode. They are snapshots of a view. They are not real-time images, but they do refresh frequently. When you save a Power View report, by default these images are saved with the report. They are then displayed in the PowerPivot Gallery in SharePoint, just as Microsoft Excel worksheets are displayed. See Figure 13-47.

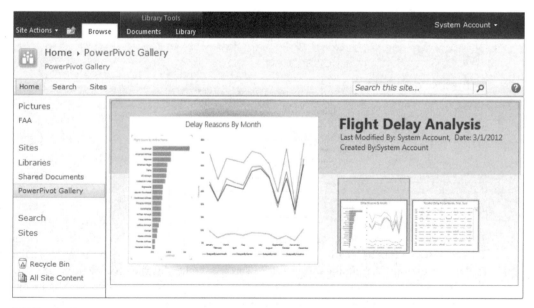

FIGURE 13-47

The first time you save a file, or when you save as, you have the option not to save preview images. Consider not saving them if they display information you consider potentially sensitive. Keep in mind that the PowerPivot Gallery Carousel view displays images that are large enough to be readable. Views without preview images are shown with a watermark icon and a label, "Preview not available."

Also, if you open and view the views in a report that has preview images saved with it, when you save the report you are saving the updated preview images. To avoid this, disable the option to save preview images.

Power View creates files in the RDLX file format. Currently you can open reports in RDLX file format only with Power View, not with Report Builder. Similarly, you can open and edit reports in RDL file format with Report Builder, but not in Power View.

Permissions for Power View

Power View uses SharePoint permissions to control access to Power View reports. If you have adequate permissions for a SharePoint folder, you can open a Power View report in edit or reading mode. You can modify the report in edit mode as much as you want, but to save your changes, you need Add Items permissions for the destination library or folder, or Edit Items permissions to overwrite an existing document.

Visualizations and Interactivity

Power View can create a variety of visualizations, from tables, cross-tabs (matrices), cards, and tiles to charts and sets of small multiple charts. For every visualization you want to create, you start with a table, which you can then easily convert to other visualizations to determine which one best illustrates your data. To create a table, you click a table or field in the field list, or you drag a field from the field list to the view. For optimal performance, Power View does not fetch all data in a table at one time. It fetches more data as you scroll.

In this section, you convert tables to several types of visualizations. You also learn about synchronizing chart axes and several other capabilities.

Tile Visualizations

Tiles are containers with a dynamic navigation strip to help visualize master-detail relationships. You can convert a table or matrix to tiles to present tabular data interactively. As you navigate through values in the navigation strip, related information appears in data visualizations that you add to the container. All content in the container is automatically filtered by the selected value.

To create tile visualizations, you can continue with the report created in the previous subsection by following these steps:

1. Create a new empty view in your report.

2. In the field list, expand `DistanceGroup` and select the `Distance Group` field.

3. In the field list, expand `OnTimePerformance2009` and select the `OnTime Pct` and `Delayed by Carrier Pct` fields.

4. Using the ribbon, convert the table into a column chart, as shown in Figure 13-48. The chart reveals that with increasing flight distance, the percentage of on-time flights overall decreases slightly. Flights delayed by the airline carrier tend to increase with flight distance, whereas other factors for delays are mostly independent of flight distance.

5. In the field list, expand `Airlines` and drag the `Picture` field to the "Tile by" area in the field well, as shown in Figure 13-49.

After you have created a set of tiles, you can switch between two navigation styles using the ribbon's Tile Tools Design tab:

➤ A tab strip that displays values at the top of the tile container, as shown in Figure 13-50

➤ A cover flow that display values at the bottom of the tile container, as shown in Figure 13-51

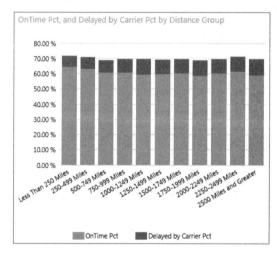

FIGURE 13-48

FIGURE 13-49

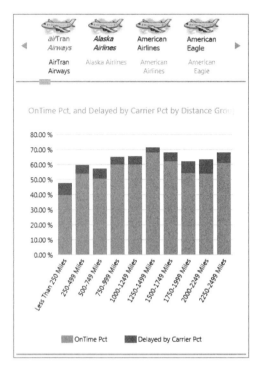

FIGURE 13-50

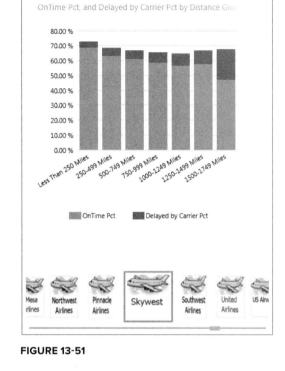

FIGURE 13-51

As you navigate the tiles shown in Figures 13-50 and 13-51, you realize that some carriers don't offer long-distance flights (such as SkyWest and ExpressJet). Carriers also exhibit differences in on-time performance.

By default, Power View does not automatically synchronize the horizontal and vertical chart axes, series, and bubble size in charts in a tiles container. For each chart, it sets these scales based on the values in the chart on each individual tile. This makes each chart easy to read.

However, to simplify comparing chart values across multiple tiles, you can synchronize chart scales by following these steps:

6. Select the chart inside the tiles container. In the ribbon, select Chart Tools Layout, click the Axes drop-down, and select Same across all tiles for the horizontal and vertical axes, as shown in Figure 13-52.

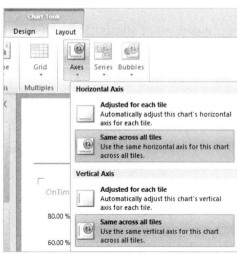

FIGURE 13-52

Synchronizing a chart category axis, such as flight distance, means that every category value is present for every chart, even if a value does not exist in a specific chart. As shown in Figure 13-53, Hawaiian Airlines has either short-distance or long-distance flights. Hawaii consists of several small islands close together (short-distance flights) and is far from the North American continent (long-distance flights).

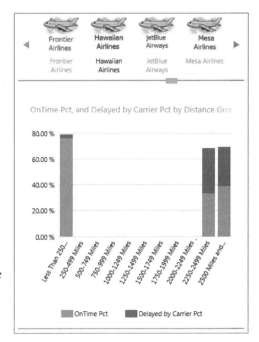

You can also add multiple visualizations side-by-side inside a tiles container. Those nested visualizations are automatically filtered by the selected value in the tile navigation strip. To add a new visualization for on-time flight performance by weekday automatically filtered by airline carrier, follow these steps:

7. Resize the tiles container to make room for a new visualization. Click the empty space of the tiles container.

8. In the field list, expand `Weekdays` and select the `Weekday` field. Then expand `OnTimePerformance2009` and select the `OnTime Pct` field.

FIGURE 13-53

9. Using the ribbon design tools, convert the table into a column chart.

10. Using the Chart Tools Layout, click the Axes drop-down and synchronize the vertical axis.

As you navigate the tiles, you can easily compare flight distance categories and on-time flights by weekday by airline carrier.

Highlighting in Visualizations

Charts can act as filters, using the relationships in the underlying model. This is interactive filtering, meaning that you can select values directly on the chart and have that filter other data regions on a view, as well as within a tile container. If you select one column in a column chart, this automatically does the following:

➤ Filters the values in all the tables and tiles, and bubble charts in the report.

➤ Adds highlighting to bar and column charts. It visually highlights the parts of other bar and column charts that pertain to that value. If values are cumulative, it shows the contribution of the filtered values to the original values. Otherwise, highlighting shows a relative comparison.

Figure 13-54 shows the tile container view created in the previous subsection. Navigate to Hawaiian flights, and then click the column for short-distance flights (less than 250 miles). The chart for on-time flights by weekday is highlighted automatically and shows a relative comparison of the overall averages and the short-distance flight averages.

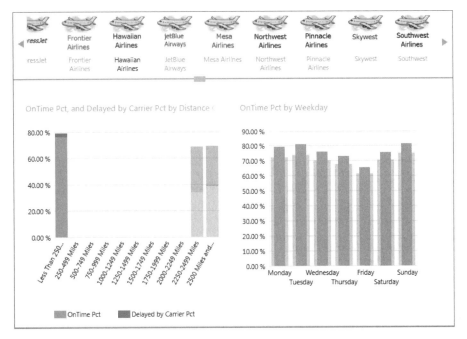

FIGURE 13-54

Matrix

You can convert a table to a matrix, with row and column groups. Add column groups by dragging a field to the Column Groups area of the field well. For example, follow these steps to add a flight delay by originating airport by weekday analysis to your report:

1. Create a new empty view in your report.

2. In the field list, expand `Origin States` and select `OriginStateName`. Then expand `Origins` and select `Origin Code` fields.

3. In the field list, expand `OnTimePerformance2009` and select the `Delay by Carrier Pct` field.

4. Using the ribbon, convert the table into a matrix. In the field list, expand `Weekdays`. Click the down arrow next to the `Weekday` field and select Add to Column Groups, as shown in Figure 13-55.

The resulting matrix visualization shown in Figure 13-56 shows grand totals and subtotals for each group by default. You can change this behavior using the Totals drop-down menu from the ribbon, to show only totals on row groups, or column groups, or not at all.

FIGURE 13-55

OriginStateName	Origin Code	Monday	Tuesday	Wednesday	Thursday	Friday	Saturday	Sunday	Total
Alabama	BHM	9.21 %	5.92 %	7.16 %	9.42 %	9.38 %	7.98 %	9.93 %	**8.44 %**
	DHN	22.22 %	12.68 %	14.90 %	13.73 %	18.63 %	10.69 %	8.87 %	**14.68 %**
	HSV	6.40 %	4.98 %	5.60 %	5.99 %	6.97 %	8.12 %	8.21 %	**6.52 %**
	MGM	13.89 %	8.79 %	10.44 %	11.83 %	13.96 %	10.20 %	13.78 %	**11.88 %**
	MOB	9.19 %	6.12 %	6.20 %	7.74 %	7.48 %	6.15 %	7.90 %	**7.31 %**
	Total	**9.35 %**	**6.20 %**	**7.18 %**	**8.67 %**	**9.20 %**	**8.05 %**	**9.53 %**	**8.32 %**
Alaska	ADK				5.77 %			1.92 %	**3.85 %**
	ADQ	4.81 %	7.69 %	4.35 %	6.82 %	10.34 %	16.98 %	8.65 %	**7.91 %**
	AKN	18.18 %	27.27 %	9.09 %	36.36 %	45.45 %	45.45 %	54.55 %	**33.77 %**

FIGURE 13-56

Slicers

Slicers are another kind of filter that filter everything in the current view. Power View slicers look very similar to slicers in PowerPivot for Excel. You create a single-column table from any field and convert it into a slicer. If the table has more than one column, the slicer icon in the ribbon is disabled.

Each distinct value in the slicer acts as a button to select the value. As you hover the mouse cursor over a slicer area, an icon appears in the top-right corner to clear (reset) the filter. You can create multiple slicers per view, as well as dependent slicers (based on relationships in the underlying model). For example, if you create two slicers, one for Product Categories and another for Products, when you click a category in the former, it filters the latter to show only products in that category. The filtering effects of all slicers are combined.

Figure 13-57 shows three slicers bound to independent fields, with the icon and tooltip for clearing the airline slicer shown when you hover the mouse cursor over the slicer area. Slicers can also be bound to image fields, such as the airline logo in the FAA sample model.

FIGURE 13-57

To select a particular slicer value, just click the value. The data is filtered in the report immediately. You can also select all except a certain set of values by resetting the filter with the button in the top corner and then using Ctrl+click to deselect specific values. This shows overall values excluding the deselect values.

Selected slicer values are saved with the report. When you reopen a report, the selected slicer values are reapplied.

Filters

You learned about filters that affect an entire view in the previous section. You can also set visualization-level filters on tables, matrices, cards, and charts, but not on tile containers or slicers. You can still set filters on the tables, matrices, and charts that are inside a tile container.

Like slicers, filters in the filters area are saved with the report and affect only one view or a specific visualization, not the entire report. Unlike slicers, filters are not shown directly in the view itself, so they do not take up any space in the view.

You can show or hide the filters area in design mode. If you make the filters area visible, it is also shown in reading and full-screen presentation modes. You can view filters for an individual visualization by hovering the mouse cursor over its upper-right corner and then clicking the filter icon, shown in Figure 13-39 in the previous section. This opens the filters area prepopulated with the fields used in the selected visualization.

You can drag additional fields from the field list to the filters area to create further filter conditions. You can use fields that are not in that visualization or anywhere on the view.

Power View provides basic and advanced filters:

➤ **Basic filters** — Numeric fields are automatically visualized as a range between the minimum and maximum value in the underlying data. You drag markers on a slider, or the overall slider, to set value ranges. For nonnumeric fields, the filter visualization shows a list of values. The numbers after each value show how many records have that value, as shown earlier in Figure 13-40. If a field contains more than 500 distinct values, you see a message that not all items are shown. Figure 13-58 shows examples of numeric and nonnumeric filter visualizations.

➤ **Advanced filters** — You can switch to advanced filter mode by clicking the icon shown in Figure 13-59. In advanced mode, you can create more sophisticated filters using conditions such as greater than, contains, and starts with. You can type all or part of a value to include or exclude.

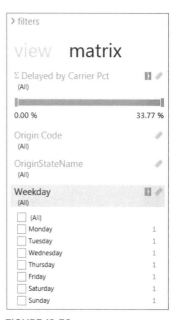

FIGURE 13-58

FIGURE 13-59

Card and Callout Views

You can convert a table to a series of cards that display the data from each row in the table laid out in card format, like an index card. An alternative visualization style, callout, is available for cards. It uses larger font sizes to draw your attention to key indicators on the card.

For example, follow these steps to add card and callout visualizations to your report:

1. Create a new empty view in your report.

2. In the field list, click Airlines. This adds a table to the view, with two fields shown by default. In addition, select the Flight Count field.

Default fields for tables are specified in the semantic model. You can define default fields in PowerPivot for Excel using the ribbon's Advanced tab, as shown in Figure 13-60.

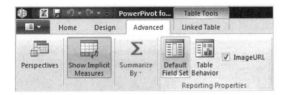

FIGURE 13-60

3. Convert the table into cards using the visualization ribbon, as shown in Figure 13-61.

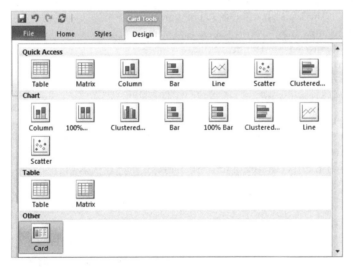

FIGURE 13-61

4. In the field list, expand `OnTimePerformance2009` and visualize several metrics on each card by selecting the following fields:

➤ `EarlyArrival Count`

➤ `Late Arrival Count`

➤ `Cancelled`

➤ `OnTime Pct`

➤ `Delayed by Carrier Pct`

➤ `Weather Delay Pct`

Figure 13-62 shows the resulting card visualization.

5. Select the card visualization on the view, create a copy (using the keyboard or the ribbon menu), and paste. The copied card is automatically positioned into an area with free space. Because a callout style uses larger font sizes, remove the fields for `EarlyArrival Count`, `Late Arrival Count`, and `Delayed by Carrier Pct` from the Fields list in the field well.

6. Click the Style drop-down in the ribbon to convert the card layout into a callout layout, as shown in Figure 13-63. Figure 13-64 shows the resulting callout visualization.

FIGURE 13-62

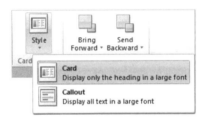

FIGURE 13-63

FIGURE 13-64

Zooming in Charts

Column and bar charts can show numeric, date, or nonnumeric values on the x-axis. If the list of distinct nonnumeric values is too long, the horizontal chart axis enables scrolling.

If the horizontal axis of a column or bar chart has too many distinct values (more than 1,000), Power View automatically retrieves a representative sample of the data instead of the full set. This gives you an idea of the characteristics of the full value range while still providing fast performance. You can then narrow down the range of values using filters and slicers.

For numeric and date values, the chart axis enables zooming, as shown in Figures 13-65 and 13-66. The first chart shows the percentage of flights delayed by weather throughout the entire year. The second chart shows the same data zoomed to the time period of November and December. You can zoom by dragging the markers on of the horizontal axis to narrow the time window. You can scroll through the entire date range by dragging the slider.

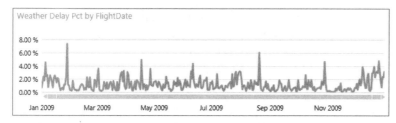

FIGURE 13-65

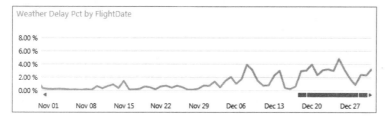

FIGURE 13-66

To create the chart shown, follow these steps:

1. Create a new empty view in your report.

2. In the field list, expand `OnTimePerformance2009` and select the `FlightDate` and `Weather Delay Pct` fields.

3. Convert the table into a line chart using the ribbon.

4. Zoom in by dragging the markers on the horizontal axis to narrow the time window. Scroll through the entire date range by dragging the slider.

Scatter and Bubble

Scatter and bubble charts are an effective way to visualize lots of related data in one chart. They help you understand and present patterns and clustering of data values. In scatter charts, the x-axis displays one measure and the y-axis displays another, making it easy to see the relationship between the two values for all the items in the chart. In a bubble chart, a third measure controls the size of the data points.

For this tutorial on scatter, bubble, and animated charts, you will use the `Population Statistics.xlsx` PowerPivot workbook, provided on the Wrox download site for this book. You can follow these steps:

1. Upload `Population Statistics.xlsx` into the PowerPivot Gallery.

2. After you refresh the gallery site in the browser, click the Create Power View Report icon next to the Population Statistics workbook. This launches a new Power View report.

3. In the field list, expand `Population Stats` and select the `Males per 100 Females` field. Notice that the Power View field well shows the Average aggregate function applied by default, as shown in Figure 13-67. The default aggregation for each field is defined in the semantic model, but if you want to, you can change the aggregation function in Power View.

FIGURE 13-67

 When designing a model, you can define the default aggregation function for client tools using PowerPivot for Excel. Select the column in the PowerPivot window, go to the Advanced tab, and choose the function from the Summarize By drop-down, as shown in Figure 13-68.

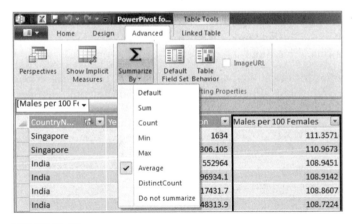

FIGURE 13-68

4. Convert the table into a scatter chart using the ribbon.

5. Add the following additional fields from `Population Stats` by clicking them:

➤ `CountryName` (because it is a nonnumeric field, Power View automatically groups by country name)

➤ `MedianAge` (the chart maps it to the y-axis)

➤ `TotalPopulation` (the chart maps it to the bubble size)

Figure 13-69 shows the resulting chart. It visualizes effectively that the median age of the population of Germany and Japan is fairly old, whereas India and China have a young average population. It also shows that the Russian Federation has a large percentage of females.

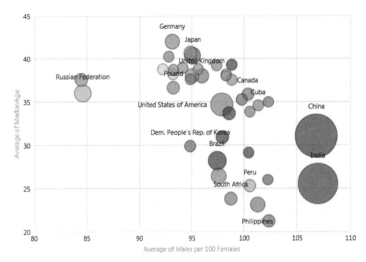

Average of Males per 100 Females, Average of MedianAge, and Average of TotalPopulation by Co

FIGURE 13-69

Animated Timeline Charts

Timeline charts are an effective way to visualize change over time. You can add a time dimension to scatter and bubble charts with a play axis. The field used for the play axis in Power View can be of any data type; it is not restricted to a time dimension.

The Population Statistics model contains historical population data, as well as future projections for various countries. Continuing from the bubble chart created in the previous section, follow these steps:

6. In the field list, click the down arrow next to the Year field and select Add as Play Axis, as shown in Figure 13-70.

7. Hover the mouse cursor over the bubble chart until the filter icon appears in the top-right corner. Click the filter icon to narrow down the list of countries you are interested in. For example, select the following country for the CountryName filter on the chart: Austria, Brazil, Canada, China, France, Germany, India, Japan, Russian Federation, United Kingdom, United States of America.

FIGURE 13-70

The bubble chart shows a timeline axis, with the range of available values in the data. By default the timeline is positioned at the last value (last frame of animation), as shown in Figure 13-71.

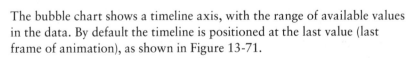

FIGURE 13-71

You can drag the play axis marker to a particular location, such as 2010, as shown in Figure 13-72. As you change the play axis position, the watermark text of the chart updates and shows the current value.

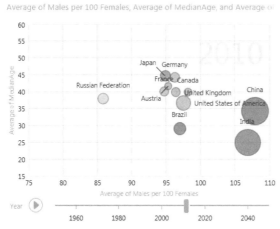

FIGURE 13-72

When you click the play button, the bubbles travel and adjust in size to show how the values change based on the timeline. You can pause at any point to investigate the data in more detail.

When you click a bubble on the chart, you see its history in the trail the bubble follows over time. For example, Figure 13-73 shows the trend for Germany, which following World War II had an imbalance in the ratio of males to females and also had a young population. The average age of the population has increased over time due to recovery and high living standards.

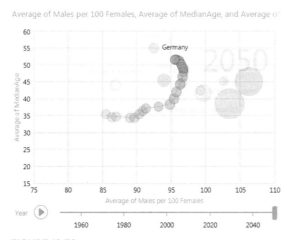

FIGURE 13-73

Figure 13-74 shows the trend for the Russian Federation. After World War II, Russia's male population began to increase. In the 1990s, a demographic crisis began to impact Russian males that coincided with the dissolution of the Soviet Union and the fall of the Berlin Wall. The cause of this problem has been debated, but one theory points to a rise in alcoholism following that time period.

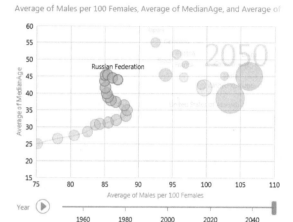

FIGURE 13-74

Refreshing Data in a Power View Report

If Power View is connected to a BI semantic model in Direct Query mode, you see real-time data from the underlying relational database. However, if the database is not optimized or is very large, those queries may not finish with subsecond response times. While a long-running request is in progress, the Refresh button in the top-left corner (Quick Access Toolbar) of Power View temporarily changes to a Cancel button. When you click it, Power View is immediately responsive afterwards.

You can refresh the data in a Power View report at any point without refreshing the page by clicking the Refresh button on the Power View Quick Access Toolbar. The toolbar contains buttons for save, undo, redo, and refresh/cancel, as shown in Figure 13-75.

FIGURE 13-75

 If you click the Refresh button in your browser, and then click Leave this page, you lose whatever changes you have made to the report since you last saved it.

Presenting and Exporting in Power View

A Power View report is always in a presentation-ready state. You can browse your data and present it at the same time, because you are working with real data. Power View offers reading and full-screen presentation modes. Furthermore, you can export an interactive version of the report to PowerPoint.

You built a fairly comprehensive set of analyses in the previous sections about FAA flight and population statistics data as Power View reports. Now it is time to present your findings.

For this section, you can either use the reports you built in the previous section or upload the pre-built `Flight Delay Analysis.rdlx` sample report to your SharePoint site.

If you decide to upload the pre-built report, you need to set the data source connection before you can run the report. Otherwise, you are going to get a connection error. After uploading the report to a SharePoint document library, click the drop-down menu for the RDLX report and select Manage Data Sources. On the data source page, click EntityDataSource. On the data source settings, specify the connection string to point to the location of the FAA database, and click OK.

Reading and Presentation Modes

Reading and full-screen presentation modes hide the ribbon and other design tools to provide more room for the visualizations. The report is still fully interactive, with filtering, sorting, and highlighting capabilities.

If you open an existing report by clicking an RDLX document in SharePoint, the report is opened in reading mode. If you are in design mode, you can switch to reading mode using the ribbon.

Figure 13-76 shows the Flight Delay Analysis report in reading mode. You can navigate between views using the keyboard (left and right arrow keys, Page Up/Down) or using the navigation buttons in the bottom-right corner of the reading mode screen.

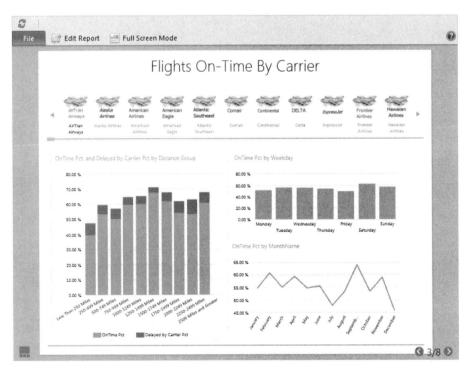

FIGURE 13-76

If you click the preview icon in the bottom-left corner of the reading mode screen, a navigation panel appears at the bottom of the browser window, as shown in Figure 13-77. You can navigate between views by scrolling and clicking preview images.

FIGURE 13-77

Full-screen presentation utilizes the entire screen, with no browser frame, as shown in Figure 13-78. Full-screen presentation mode has identical interactivity (filtering, sorting, highlighting).

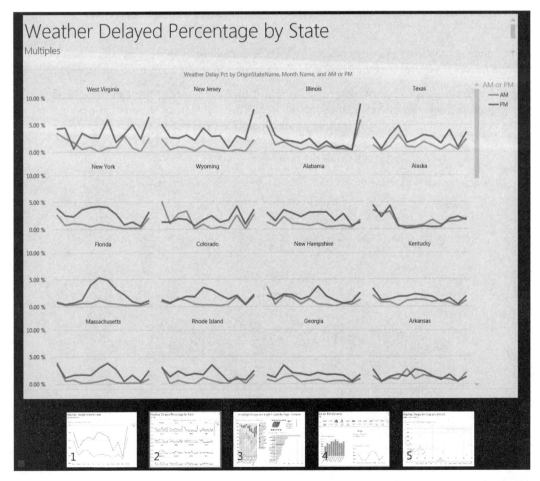

FIGURE 13-78

If the filter pane is visible in design mode, it is also available in reading mode and presentation mode.

Printing Views

You can print a Power View report from design or reading mode by selecting File ⇨ Print. Power View prints one view at a time — the current view. The view always prints in landscape orientation, regardless of settings in the Print dialog box. It prints exactly what you see in the view. For example, Power View prints the selected tile in a tile container, the filters area if it is expanded, or the current frame of a scatter or bubble chart with a play axis.

PowerPoint Export and Interactivity

Power View supports PowerPoint export. No add-ons are required; it works out of the box with PowerPoint 2007 and newer.

You can export an interactive version of your Power View report to PowerPoint by selecting File ⇨ Export to PowerPoint, as shown in Figure 13-79. Each view in Power View becomes a separate PowerPoint slide.

FIGURE 13-79

Interacting with Power View reports exported to PowerPoint is similar to interacting with views in Power View reading and full-screen modes. In PowerPoint's slide show and reading view modes, you can click to activate the view and then utilize full Power View presentation interactivity while in PowerPoint.

You can export a Power View report to PowerPoint by following these steps:

1. In Power View, select File ⇨ Export to PowerPoint, as shown in Figure 13-79.

2. Save the new PowerPoint presentation. You can save the PowerPoint file anywhere locally or back into the SharePoint site.

Access to the original Power View report on a SharePoint server is required for enabling interactivity of the views inside a PowerPoint presentation. If you open a saved PowerPoint file with Power View contents, and you do not have access to the original Power View report on a SharePoint server, you can only see the placeholder images in all PowerPoint modes (normal, slide show, and reading view), and the Power View views are not interactive.

3. If you have not yet saved the Power View report, you are prompted to save it now. You cannot export a Power View report to PowerPoint without saving it first.

4. To generate the PowerPoint export, Power View navigates through each view and captures a higher-resolution thumbnail image. After the export phase is complete, save the PowerPoint PPTX presentation file, and open the saved presentation in PowerPoint. PowerPoint opens in normal view. A static image of each view is centered on a separate slide, as shown in Figure 13-80.

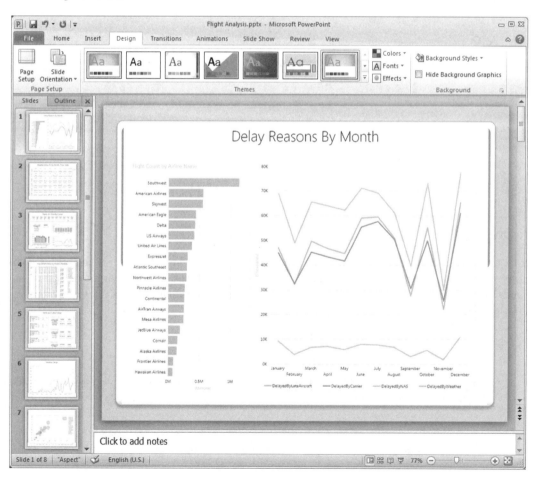

FIGURE 13-80

5. In PowerPoint, click Enable Editing. You can modify the PowerPoint presentation as you would any other, with styles and other enhancements. Note that these do not affect the Power View views, because they remain opaque areas on the slide. The font and size of text in the Power View views also remains unaffected.

6. In the lower-right corner, click the Reading View or Slide Show button.

7. To interact with the visualizations in PowerPoint slide show or reading view mode, in the lower-right corner of the slide, click "click to interact" (shown in Figure 13-81) to load the live Power View report from the SharePoint server.

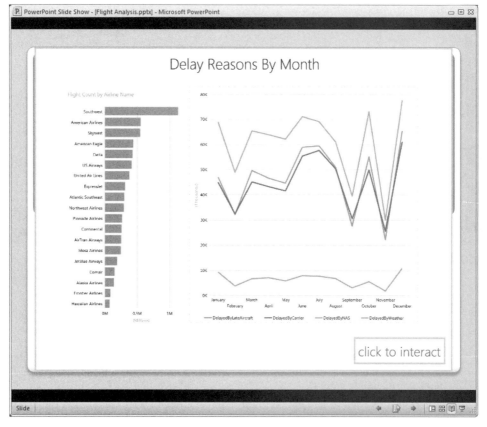

FIGURE 13-81

8. As soon as the report is live, you can utilize all interactivity options of Power View presentation mode inside PowerPoint, such as filtering, shown in Figure 13-82.

If you have chosen not to save preview images with the Power View report, when the PowerPoint presentation opens, you see placeholder images.

When you update and save the original Power View report in Power View, the next time you view the PowerPoint presentation in slide show or reading view mode, you see the updates to the Power View views.

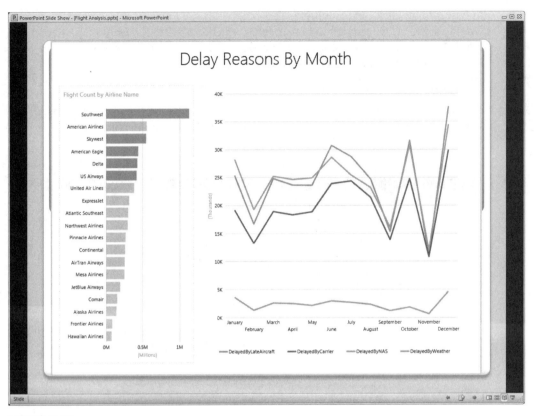

FIGURE 13-82

Tips and Tricks for Power View

This section describes tips and tricks and gives answers to frequently asked questions.

➤ **Grayed-out fields in the field list** — Sometimes a field is grayed out in the fields section of the field list when a visualization is selected. If so, this means a relationship is not defined between the fields already in the visualization and the field in the fields section of the field list. Relationships need to be defined in the tabular model, either using PowerPivot for Excel, as shown in Chapter 9, or in SQL Server Data Tools.

➤ **Grayed-out icons in the ribbon** — Power View's ribbon is context-sensitive based on the visualization selected in the current view. When an icon in the ribbon is grayed out, this means that the action is unavailable for the currently selected visualization on the view. For example, if a table has no measures, all the chart icons are disabled on the Design tab. A chart needs at least one measure.

➤ **What settings are controlled and configured in the model?**

➤ Which fields are visible in the field list.

➤ Data types and data formats.

➤ Whether a numeric field is a measure or nonmeasure by default.

➤ Whether the sort order for a field that is used as a nonmeasure is controlled by the sort order of a different field. For example, sorting for a `Month Name` field might be controlled by a `Month Number` field so that the months are in chronological rather than alphabetical order.

➤ In a card visualization, which text field appears prominently as the title (the Default Label defined in Table Behavior in PowerPivot for Excel).

➤ In a card visualization, which image field appears prominently on the left (the Default Image defined in Table Behavior in PowerPivot for Excel).

➤ Whether fields with potentially duplicate values, such as customer names, are grouped by the field or by the related key field. For example, you cannot group on binary image fields. Power View implicitly groups on the unique identifier defined for that table.

➤ Whether the aggregate function for a measure can be changed in the report.

➤ For external images, whether the image URL or the image itself displays in the report (determined by the field's ImageURL setting on the Advanced tab in PowerPivot).

➤ **Show all rows or columns, even if they have no data (outer join)** — Sometimes you want to see all the rows in a table, even if some of them have no values (this is called an outer join). For example, say you have a table of regions, cities, stores, and sales totals. Maybe you want to see all the stores in a region, even if some have no sales, or all the cities, even if some cities have no stores.

You might also want to see all the columns in a matrix, even if some have no data. For example, you could have a column for each year, and you want to see all the years, even those with no values.

You can control the setting for each field independently. Click the drop-down arrow next to the field name in the Values box in the layout section of the field list. Then click Show items with no data, as shown in Figure 13-83.

FIGURE 13-83

CONFIGURING DATA SOURCE CONNECTIONS

This section explains several scenarios for data connection and authentication configurations for Power View. Power View is a thin web client that launches in the browser, which always connects to an artifact in SharePoint to open an existing report, or create a new report from a BI semantic model, as shown in Figure 13-84. Power View uses the Reporting Services service application to resolve and make actual data connections, as shown in Figure 13-85.

Icon and FileType	Description
PowerPivot workbook (**XLSX**)	The PowerPivot workbook model is loaded and hosted by the PowerPivot service in SharePoint. If a PowerPivot workbook is published in the PowerPivot Gallery, as shown in Figure 13-25, a new Power View report can be created directly from the workbook.
BI Semantic Model (**BISM**) connection file	A BISM connection file points to a specific model that can be either a workbook or a database on an Analysis Services server. The BISM connection file effectively provides a redirect for the Analysis Services data provider when the connection is opened initially. A BISM connection can be used by Power View as well as other BI applications such as Excel.
Report Data Source (**RSDS**)	A Report Data Source stores a full connection string and can be configured to store credentials with optional impersonation, as well as pass-through security. RSDS is a data source connection type used by Reporting Services clients only, such as Power View and Report Builder.
Power View report (**RDLX**)	A published Power View report. Clicking an RDLX file in SharePoint opens the report in Power View presentation mode.

FIGURE 13-84

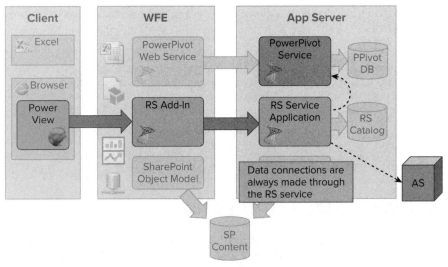

FIGURE 13-85

As explained in the previous section, you can create a connection to a BI semantic model in multiple ways. How you connect to a tabular model depends on how it is published or deployed.

Connecting to PowerPivot Workbooks

If a PowerPivot workbook is published in a PowerPivot Gallery, a business user can easily create a new Power View report using the workbook as its data source by selecting Create Power View Report, as shown in Figure 13-86.

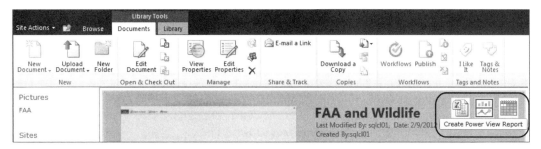

FIGURE 13-86

The connection string for using a PowerPivot workbook as data source has the following format:
`Data Source=http://`*SharePointSite*`/PowerPivot%20Gallery/`*WorkbookName*`.xlsx`

From a technical perspective, when a connection to a PowerPivot workbook is opened, Reporting Services uses the Analysis Services data provider to connect to the model through the PowerPivot service in SharePoint, as shown in Figure 13-87. The PowerPivot service checks whether the requested workbook is already loaded in its server instance. If needed, it loads the PowerPivot workbook on-the-fly from SharePoint as a new Analysis Services PowerPivot database.

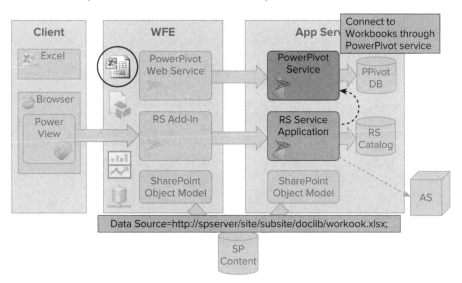

FIGURE 13-87

The PowerPivot service verifies that the Power View user has permission to read the workbook and denies the connection otherwise.

Connecting to a BISM Connection File

A BI semantic model connection file (.bism) connects Excel or Power View reports to BI semantic model data on a server or a workbook published in a SharePoint farm. There are similarities in how an Office data connection (.odc) file and a .bism connection file are defined and used.

A BI semantic model connection is created and accessed via SharePoint. A BI semantic model connection provides an HTTP endpoint to a database. It simplifies tabular model access for business users who routinely use documents on a SharePoint site. They need to know only the location of the BI semantic model connection file or its URL to access tabular-model databases.

BI semantic model connection files provide quick launch commands to open a new Excel workbook or options for editing the connection file. If Reporting Services is installed, you also see a command to create a Power View report, as shown in Figure 13-88. The default click action for a .bism connection file is to create a new Power View report from the model connection.

From a technical perspective, when a Power View report is created from a .bism file in SharePoint, the Reporting Services service application provides a connection string pointing to the location of the .bism file, as shown in Figure 13-89. The Analysis Services data provider looks up the contents of the .bism file to connect and redirect to the actual model that the .bism points to.

FIGURE 13-88

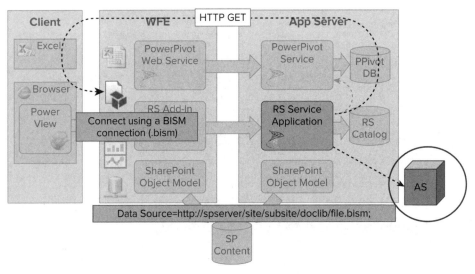

FIGURE 13-89

If the .bism file points to a workbook, the data provider communicates with the PowerPivot service. The equivalent sequence of loading the workbook as a database and verifying user permissions is performed as explained in the preceding section about connecting to PowerPivot workbooks.

If the .bism file points to an external Analysis Services server, the data provider attempts to establish a connection with that server. The server performs user authentication based on the actual end user who connects using the .bism file. Users who connect to tabular databases must have membership in a database role that specifies read access. Roles are defined when the model is authored with SQL Server Data Tools, or, for deployed models, by using SQL Server Management Studio.

Connecting to an RSDS

Report Data Sources (RSDS) were introduced in the initial version of SQL Server Reporting Services. A report server uses credentials to connect to external data sources that provide content to reports. Similar to .bism connection files, an RSDS simplifies tabular model access for business users who routinely use documents on a SharePoint site. They need to know only the location of the RSDS to access the model.

An RSDS provides many authentication configuration options. You can specify credentials that use Windows Authentication, database authentication, no authentication, or custom authentication. When sending a connection request over the network, the report server impersonates either a user account (and optionally sets the original user as execution context after the connection is successfully opened) or the unattended execution account.

Similar to .bism connection files, an RSDS connects Power View reports to BI semantic model data on a server or a workbook published in a SharePoint farm. An RSDS provides additional authentication configurations not available through .bism, as explained in detail in the next section.

An RSDS connection is created and accessed via SharePoint. It provides a quick launch command on its context menu to create a new Power View report, as shown in Figure 13-90. Note that the default click action on an RSDS connection is to edit connection settings. Although .bism connection files are used primarily for Power View (and hence the default click action creates a new Power View report from the model connection), RSDS serves significantly broader usage scenarios.

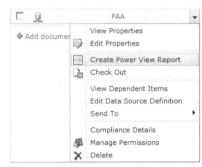

FIGURE 13-90

From a technical perspective, when a Power View report is created from an RSDS in SharePoint, first the Reporting Services service application looks up the RSDS configuration settings in its catalog database. Then it performs authentication and impersonation as specified. Finally, it invokes the Analysis Services data provider to open the data connection to the PowerPivot workbook or a model database deployed on an Analysis Server. See Figure 13-91.

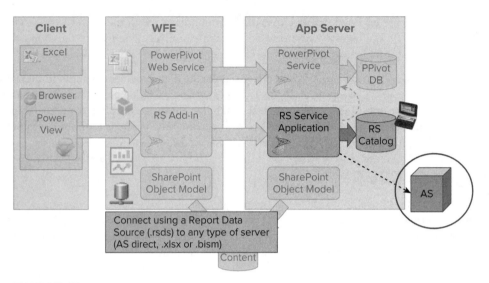

FIGURE 13-91

Authentication Scenarios

When connecting to a PowerPivot workbook published within the SharePoint farm, the tabular model inside the workbook is published on-the-fly to PowerPivot for SharePoint. As covered earlier, PowerPivot for SharePoint is a dedicated Analysis Services server in tabular mode running inside the SharePoint farm. Because workbooks are published on demand (and automatically unloaded later when they are no longer used), significant latency can occur when connecting to a model in a PowerPivot workbook initially. Deploying a PowerPivot workbook to a stand-alone Analysis Server makes it available as a permanent database on that server.

The authentication model for PowerPivot workbooks in SharePoint is based on the claims configuration for the SharePoint site with the PowerPivot workbook. Authorization for model data access in PowerPivot for SharePoint is based on whether the user has permissions to view and read the PowerPivot workbook. If you have read permissions, you can read all the data residing in the workbook.

In summary, authentication scenarios for PowerPivot workbooks published in a SharePoint farm are fairly straightforward. However, a stand-alone Analysis Server offers many additional capabilities for BI semantic models that you may want to leverage in an enterprise deployment:

➤ Role-based security in the model

➤ Scalability and control of load balancing when using dedicated servers

➤ Partitioning of model data

➤ DirectQuery, which allows you to run queries against the model directly against a SQL Server database, providing up-to-date data and security enforced in the underlying relational database

However, connecting to stand-alone Analysis Services is not as simple. Typically you have multiple-machine deployments. This means that several hops are necessary between the following:

➤ A client application (for example, Power View running in the browser of a business user)

➤ A SharePoint web front end

➤ SharePoint services (for example, Reporting Services performing data connections and processing on behalf of Power View)

➤ The Analysis Services server hosting the model database

You may need to consider the following factors:

➤ **Analysis Services only supports Windows authentication.**

    ➤ Is Analysis Services running on the same machine as your SharePoint deployment? Frequently that is not the case.

    ➤ Is Analysis Services even running on the same domain?

    ➤ Is Kerberos delegation enabled?

    ➤ Do business users have read permission on the databases deployed on the Analysis Server?

    ➤ Is row-level security enabled?

➤ **SharePoint Claims-Based Identity** — SharePoint 2010 supports two modes in which a client can authenticate with the platform: Classic mode and Claims mode. Reporting Services 2012 is fully integrated with both modes, including all types of SharePoint claims authentication.

Windows identities generally are valid only for making a connection to one additional machine on behalf of the user (NTLM protocol), but not multiple machine hops. The Kerberos protocol is a more secure protocol for Windows integrated authentication that supports ticketing authentication. A Kerberos authentication server grants a ticket in response to a client computer authentication request if the request contains valid user credentials and a valid Service Principal Name (SPN). The client computer then uses the ticket to access network resources.

Support for claims authentication is a new feature in SharePoint 2010 and is built on Windows Identity Foundation. In a claims model, SharePoint Server accepts one or more claims about an authenticating client to identify and authorize the client. The claims come in the form of Security Assertion Markup Language (SAML) tokens and are facts about the client stated by a trusted authority. For example, a claim could state, "Robert is a member of the Enterprise Admins group for the domain Contoso.com." If this claim came from a provider trusted by SharePoint Server, the platform could use this information to authenticate Robert and to authorize him to access SharePoint Server resources. The types of claims supported for incoming authentication are Windows claims, forms-based authentication (FBA) claims, and SAML claims.

The Reporting Services 2012 web front-end component is claims-enabled to perform appropriate claims authentication. It communicates the claims token(s) to the Reporting Services service application. Using that approach, the end user's identity can flow from a client application such as Power View running in the browser to the SSRS service application, even in a multiple-machine SharePoint farm scenario. The challenge to make successful model data connections is about connecting to a stand-alone SSAS server outside the SharePoint farm, because Analysis Services supports only Windows authentication.

Comparison and Trade-offs

Table 13-1 compares the available authentication configuration options. Subsequent sections cover each of the four options in detail — specifically, how to use BISM connection files and RSDS in each situation.

TABLE 13-1

CRITERION	KERBEROS (BISM, RSDS)	BISM AND RS SERVICE ACCOUNT	RSDS AND STORED CREDENTIALS	RSDS AND EFFECTIVE USER
Easy to set up and configure	No	Yes	Yes	Yes
Enables row-level security based on the end user	Yes	Yes	No	Yes
Manages user permissions on...	SSAS	SSAS	RSDS	SSAS
Supports non-Windows users	No	No	Yes	No
Additional network hops (DirectQuery mode)	Yes	No	No	No
Clients supported	Power View and Excel	Power View and Excel	Power View only	Power View only

Kerberos Delegation with BISM or RSDS

If the client authenticates with the WFE service by using Kerberos authentication (on a SharePoint site configured for Windows Classic authentication), Kerberos Delegation can be used to pass the client's identity to the back-end system. Kerberos does not work in combination with SharePoint sites configured for claims authentication.

As shown in Figure 13-92, using a BISM connection file or an RSDS configured as "integrated security," the end user's Windows identity can flow from Power View to the Reporting Services service application and connect as the end user's Windows identity to Analysis Services.

Permissions are directly managed in the model on the Analysis Services server. The drawback of Kerberos Delegation is that it is often complex to set up and configure correctly. You can find more information about Kerberos authentication in SharePoint 2010 in the documentation at `http://technet.microsoft.com/en-us/library/gg502594.aspx`.

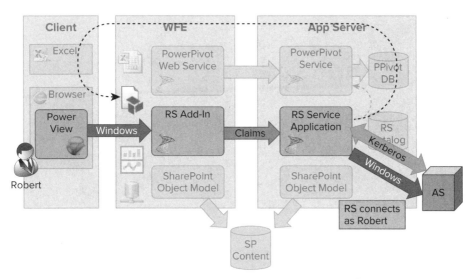

FIGURE 13-92

BISM Connection and RS Service Account

If Kerberos is not configured, the Analysis Services data provider still attempts to make a Windows integrated security connection to the Analysis Server outside the SharePoint farm.

If that first connection attempt fails due to too many network hops, in case of a BISM connection file, the Analysis Services data provider automatically makes a second attempt using the process account that hosts the data provider by applying EffectiveUserName=[client Windows identity] on the connection.

The data provider runs inside the Reporting Services service application process, so if the RS service account is an administrator on the Analysis Server, this second connection attempt succeeds. The connection is opened as an Analysis Server administrator, with an explicit security context applied of the EffectiveUserName specified. EffectiveUserName is an AS data provider capability similar to SetUser in Transact-SQL.

Consequently, although the database connection was initially opened as an AS administrator, it effectively connects as the original end user. Commands executed on the opened connections are constrained to the permissions of that (lower-privileged) user, as shown in Figure 13-93.

Permissions are still directly managed in the model on the Analysis Services server. Configuring the Reporting Services service account as a Windows user who is also an administrator on a stand-alone Analysis Server may be a good alternative if configuring Kerberos Delegation is not an option.

RSDS and Stored Windows Credentials

If you need to support non-Windows Classic authentication — that is, claims authentication — this approach is the only option that enables Power View to run with models published to a stand-alone Analysis Server.

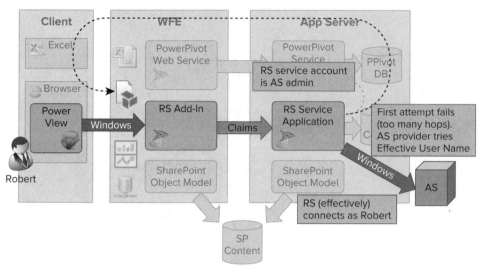

FIGURE 13-93

Figure 13-94 shows the RSDS configuration settings page. When configured as shown, it instructs the Reporting Services service application to impersonate the specified stored credentials as Windows identity, and then it opens the connection to Analysis Services with that Windows user. You can limit the use of the RSDS impersonated connection by setting read permissions in SharePoint on the RSDS file.

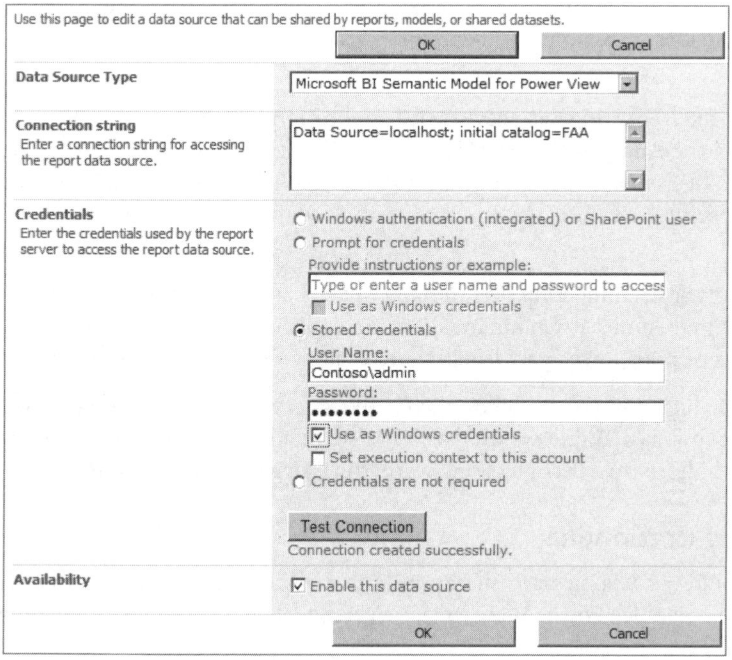

FIGURE 13-94

This approach enables you to control permissions in SharePoint on the RSDS file. You can enable model access to Power View users without needing to give users read permissions on the back-end Analysis Server. Setting up an RSDS with stored Windows credentials for impersonation is easy. However, it provides the same data view to all users, because it is always the stored user identity that connects to the Analysis Services database, as shown in Figure 13-95.

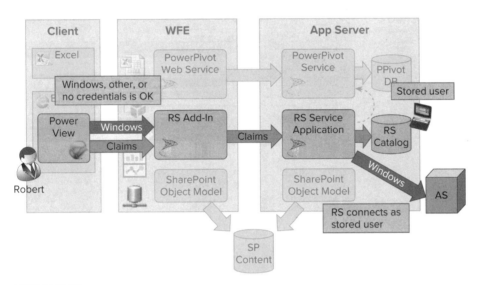

FIGURE 13-95

RSDS with Impersonation and EffectiveUser

This approach is similar to using a BISM connection file with the RS service account configured as an administrator on the Analysis Server, enabling you to flow the actual end user to the back-end database via the EffectiveUserName feature of the data provider.

The difference in this approach with using an RSDS is that you can chose administrator account settings per the RSDS you create in SharePoint. This also enables you to separate the identity of the RS service application from a set of AS back-end servers on which you may want to host BI semantic models. Doing this provides further isolation from a security point of view.

Figure 13-96 shows an example of the RSDS configuration settings page. When it is configured as shown, the following things happen:

➤ The Reporting Services service application impersonates the specified stored credentials as a Windows identity.

➤ The connection to Analysis Services is opened with that Windows user. The impersonated user needs to be an administrator on the Analysis Server.

➤ After the connection is opened, the data provider applies the security context of the EffectiveUserName explicitly specified by Reporting Services based on the SharePoint-authenticated Power View user.

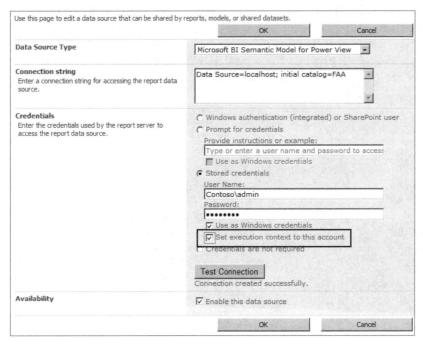

Use this page to edit a data source that can be shared by reports, models, or shared datasets.

| OK | Cancel |

Data Source Type
Microsoft BI Semantic Model for Power View

Connection string
Enter a connection string for accessing the report data source.
Data Source=localhost; initial catalog=FAA

Credentials
Enter the credentials used by the report server to access the report data source.

○ Windows authentication (integrated) or SharePoint user
○ Prompt for credentials
　Provide instructions or example:
　Type or enter a user name and password to access
　☐ Use as Windows credentials
● Stored credentials
　User Name:
　Contoso\admin
　Password:
　••••••••
　☑ Use as Windows credentials
　☑ Set execution context to this account
○ Credentials are not required

Test Connection
Connection created successfully.

Availability
☑ Enable this data source

| OK | Cancel |

FIGURE 13-96

This approach enables you to control permissions in SharePoint on the RSDS file and, in addition, in Analysis Services as the end user identity flows through to the model database, as shown in Figure 13-97.

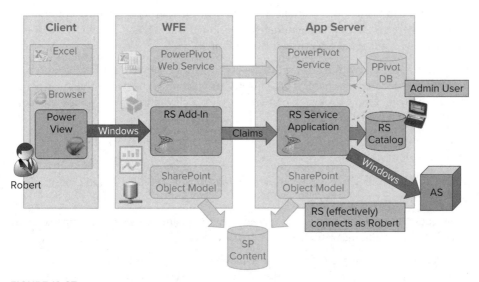

FIGURE 13-97

ANALYSIS SERVICES TABULAR

Analysis Services in general provides analytical and data mining capabilities. As you learned in Chapter 9, an Analysis Services 2012 server instance can be configured for the following two modes:

➤ Multidimensional and Data Mining mode

➤ Tabular mode

Tabular mode of Analysis Services, by default, caches data in the so-called VertiPaq store, but it can also be configured for DirectQuery, which translates and generates on-the-fly to the underlying SQL Server database store. Analysis Services Tabular Mode provides the VertiPaq store as a stand-alone server, without requiring SharePoint.

The VertiPaq store is an in-memory database. Unlike traditional relational database management systems, which use disk storage (hard drives, solid-state drives) and store data by rows, an in-memory database utilizes main memory (RAM) to store data. It frequently stores data by columns.

RAM is still a few orders of magnitude faster than disk-based storage, and RAM has become relatively cheap in recent years, although it is still costly compared to disk storage. It is not uncommon today for a mainstream laptop to come with 4 to 8 GB of RAM preinstalled and for a regular desktop machine to have 16 GB of RAM.

The VertiPaq engine used in tabular mode is a column-oriented data store and uses high data compression. Depending on the nature of the data, it achieves a compression of factor 10 on average. The VertiPaq engine is optimized for performing calculations over the raw, compressed data held in main memory and achieves very high performance.

Unlike PowerPivot for Excel and PowerPivot for SharePoint, which have a dataset size limit of 2 GB of compressed data, Analysis Services in tabular mode does not have any size limit.

Installing Analysis Services Tabular

Follow these steps to install a new server instance of Analysis Services in tabular mode:

1. Launch SQL Server 2012 `setup.exe` in administrator mode.

2. On the SQL Server Installation Center screen, click Installation, and select "New installation or add features to an existing installation."

3. Click OK after passing Setup Support rules.

4. On the Installation Type page, select "Perform a new installation of SQL Server 2012."

5. On the Product Key page, specify the product key and click Next. You can also try Evaluation Edition or Developer Edition for evaluation purposes.

6. Review the license terms, and check the "I accept the license terms" checkbox to accept the license terms. Click Next.

7. In the Setup Support Files dialog, click Install.

8. When the installation of setup support files is complete, click Next.

9. On the Setup Role page, select SQL Server Feature Installation, as shown in Figure 13-98. Click Next.

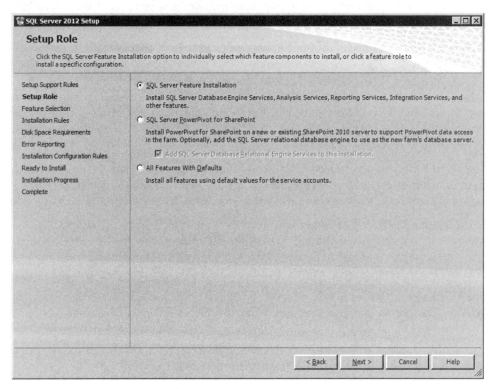

FIGURE 13-98

10. On the Feature Selection page, select Analysis Services and Shared Features such as SQL Server Data Tools and Management Tools, as shown in Figure 13-99. Click Next.

11. On the Installation Rules page, click Next after the installation-rules check has been completed successfully and passed.

12. On the Instance Configuration page, select Default Instance. Alternatively, you can specify a named instance. Click Next.

13. On the Disk Space Requirements page, verify that you have sufficient disk capacity to install the feature, and then click Next.

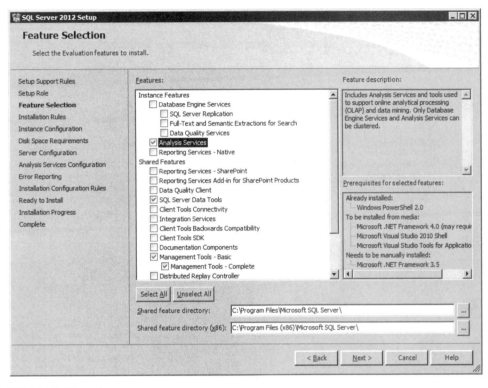

FIGURE 13-99

14. On the Server Configuration page, specify account information, as shown in Figure 13-100. Click Next.

15. On the Analysis Services Configuration page, select Tabular Mode, as shown in Figure 13-101. Click Add Current User to grant your user-account administrative permissions. On the same page, add additional Windows user accounts that also require administrative permissions for connecting with SQL Server Management Studio to administer the Analysis Server. Click Next.

16. Click Next on each of the remaining pages until you get to the Ready to Install page. Click Install.

17. Click Close when the installation of files is complete.

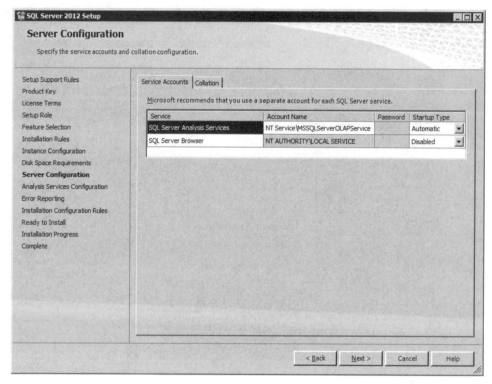

FIGURE 13-100

Deploying a PowerPivot Workbook to Analysis Services Tabular

Follow these steps to upload a PowerPivot workbook as a new database in an Analysis Services server in tabular mode:

1. Select All Programs ➪ Microsoft SQL Server 2012. Launch SQL Server Management Studio as administrator by right-clicking the entry and selecting Run as administrator.

2. In SQL Server Management Studio, connect to the Analysis Services instance installed in the preceding section.

3. After connecting, right-click Databases and select Restore from PowerPivot, as shown in Figure 13-102.

4. In the Restore from PowerPivot dialog, specify the location of your workbook as a backup file, and specify a database name, as shown in Figure 13-103. Click OK.

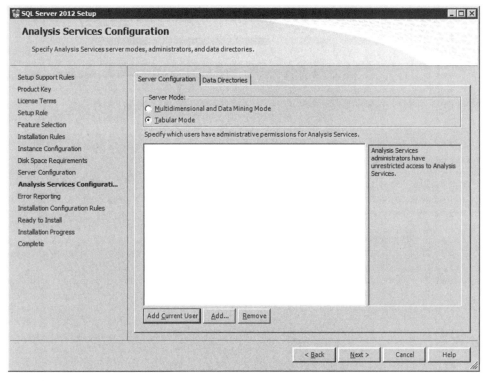

FIGURE 13-101

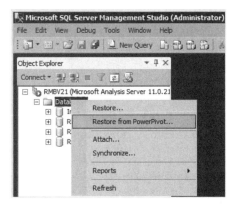

FIGURE 13-102

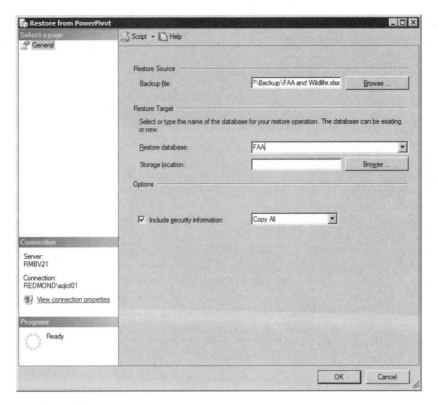

FIGURE 13-103

SUMMARY

In this chapter you have learned about the architectural components of Power View and Reporting Services in SharePoint integrated mode.

You deployed the large FAA PowerPivot sample workbook. You learned about connection files that make it easy for end users to connect to models without needing to know connection strings or credentials.

In the main part of the chapter you learned about analyzing and visualizing BI semantic models with Power View, and creating exciting presentations in the process. This included exporting to PowerPoint and showing interactive Power View visualizations inside PowerPoint.

Finally, you walked through several advanced data-source connection configuration scenarios, depending on the authentication requirements in your SharePoint environment. You learned about the capabilities and trade-offs of the available connection configuration options.

Special thanks to Bob Meyers and Sean Boon. Bob helped with the figures for describing authentication scenarios, and Sean helped mash up public FAA and other data for the sample model database.

Resources

➤ BI Semantic Model design in depth: see *Professional Microsoft SQL Server 2012 Analysis Services with MDX and DAX* (Wrox, 2012).

➤ Installing Reporting Services SharePoint Mode Report Server for Power View and Data Alerting: `http://msdn.microsoft.com/en-us/library/cc281311(v=SQL.110).aspx`

➤ Deployment checklist: Reporting Services, Power View, and PowerPivot for SharePoint: `http://msdn.microsoft.com/en-us/library/hh231687(SQL.110).aspx`

➤ Kerberos authentication in SharePoint 2010: `http://technet.microsoft.com/en-us/library/gg502594.aspx`

➤ For more information about claims authentication, see "A Guide to Claims-based Identity and Access Control": `http://go.microsoft.com/fwlink/p/?LinkID=187911`

14

Report Builder Solution Strategies

Since Reporting Services 2008, Report Builder has become the primary method for report designers to create standard RDL-based reports. As you know, two report design tools are targeted to serve different report design audiences, but they share a lot of the same functionality and capabilities. In short, SQL Server Data Tools (SSDT) is primarily for IT professionals and developer teams to collaborate and design report solutions. Report Builder is for business-focused report designers to create individual reports using published resources on the server. However, both tools support basic and advanced report design capabilities. One doesn't replace the other, and one isn't necessarily better than the other. It depends on the needs and the person performing the task.

Figure 14-1 shows the major feature differences and similarities between the Report Builder and SSDT design tools.

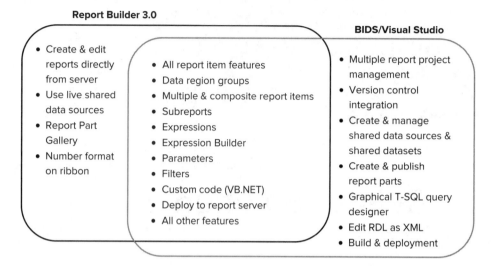

FIGURE 14-1

As you can see, these design tools share core capabilities, making them suited to mainstream report design. Many professional designers don't have a strong preference. Some who do simply prefer to use the tool to which they are accustomed. Figure 14-2 shows the tasks and roles that are best suited for each design tool.

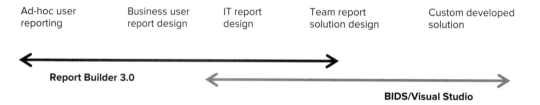

FIGURE 14-2

For purely ad hoc and self-service user report design, Report Builder is more appropriate because of its simplicity and straightforward interface. Experience has proven that nontechnical users get lost in the complexity of the Visual Studio shell as a business user tool. The concepts of managing solutions and projects in SSDT are cumbersome and seem unnecessary for users who just want to create a report. Report Builder is streamlined to eliminate some of the "report development" tasks. For example, to use a shared data source, you don't need to define a separate embedded, named data source to reference the external, named data source. I've had students struggle with this concept for the duration of a week-long class. By contrast, the Report Builder design experience is simple and sleek.

At the opposite end of the spectrum, for team development, the Visual Studio-based SSDT provides integrated version control and report project management capabilities. IT professionals use SSDT to design and deploy shared objects used by business users in self-service reporting scenarios. These include shared data sources, shared datasets, and report parts.

REPORT BUILDER AND SEMANTIC MODEL HISTORY

If you've used earlier versions of Reporting Services, or if you've grown up with the product like I have, you probably know that a little history has brought us to this point in the product's evolution. The details aren't important, but a few points are notable. Figure 14-3 shows the product time line and the various incarnations of self-service reporting tools and semantic data models.

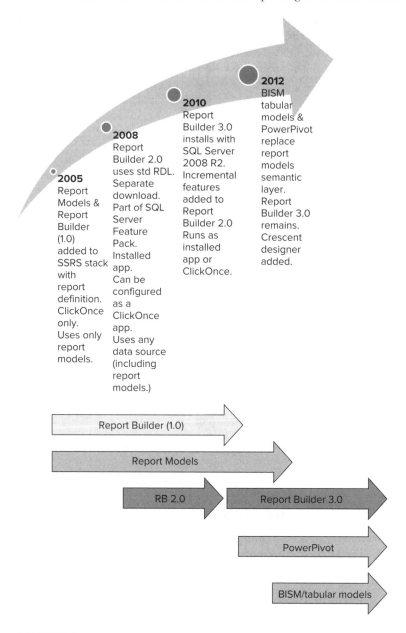

2012
BISM tabular models & PowerPivot replace report models semantic layer. Report Builder 3.0 remains. Crescent designer added.

2010
Report Builder 3.0 installs with SQL Server 2008 R2. Incremental features added to Report Builder 2.0 Runs as installed app or ClickOnce.

2008
Report Builder 2.0 uses std RDL. Separate download. Part of SQL Server Feature Pack. Installed app. Can be configured as a ClickOnce app. Uses any data source (including report models.)

2005
Report Models & Report Builder (1.0) added to SSRS stack with report definition. ClickOnce only. Uses only report models.

Report Builder (1.0)

Report Models

RB 2.0

Report Builder 3.0

PowerPivot

BISM/tabular models

FIGURE 14-3

The 2005 version of Reporting Services included a self-service reporting and data browsing tool called Report Builder. This should not be confused with the first generation of the report designer we have today that has the same name — first called Report Builder 2.0 and now Report Builder 3.0. Although the general purpose is the same, the architecture and design of these applications are vastly different.

The application now called Report Builder 1.0 consumed data through a semantic object layer known as the Report Model. This offered some useful capabilities, but also had some limitations and was not enterprise class by most standards. It was a first step toward a better solution, and many businesses found some good value for limited ad hoc reporting. This newest release of the SQL Server product platform is a welcome replacement for Report Models and Report Builder 1.0. The new Tabular BI Semantic Model architecture promises to deliver a solid foundation for ad hoc reporting that is simple, secure, and scalable. Report Builder 3.0 is the most flexible design tool for creating reports that can consume all standard data sources and data surfaced through semantic models, which now includes OLAP cubes and tabular models.

PLANNING A SELF-SERVICE REPORTING ENVIRONMENT

As the information technology and business leader in an organization, you cannot simply turn the user community loose with a set of design tools to use as they please. We've seen what happens when businesses run without data governance. Heck, I've stepped into organizations with thousands of Access databases, Excel workbooks, and reports strewn throughout the network file system, with no understanding of ownership or where reliable data resided. This is clearly not the right answer.

You Need a Plan

A manageable self-service reporting solution begins with a concise plan, well-defined processes, and a clear understanding of who owns what and where reports will reside. Part of that plan should encompass tracking the ownership and ongoing status of each report. At regular intervals, say once a month or once a quarter, the status of new or evolving reports should be revisited. Some user reports may be considered for migration to IT-supported business reports. Some may be considered for consolidation, to have their features added to an existing report. Other reports may be dismissed as one-off, unsupported, or legacy reports to be deleted or archived.

If you perform these reviews on a regular, scheduled cycle, nothing falls through the cracks. The information technology group has a clear understanding of the reports they support and those that are the responsibility of business units, leaders, and individual users.

Design Approaches and Usage Scenarios

Before you over-engineer the solution, you need to understand what business users will do with these reports they create. If I've learned anything from years of consulting with many different companies, it's that it is important to have a process in place to manage IT assets such as reports and BI dashboards. Too much process can be a hindrance to getting business done and performing other important tasks. That balance will be different for each organization, but some general principles apply to all. Seek to understand what users need to accomplish with their self-service reporting solution. From a user reporting perspective, these scenarios may include the following:

➤ **A report created for personal use.** This report may be used by the person who created it at some point in the future, or that person may be done with it after the first use. Because it is a user-owned report, others in the organization will not use it to make critical business decisions based on the information it presents.

➤ **A report or set of reports to be used by a business unit or small group.** These ad hoc reports are used to help a small group of business users perform a task but they understand that they own these reports and are responsible for the information they provide.

➤ **A report created by a business user to be migrated to production.** After the design is reviewed by an IT professional, this report may be validated and migrated to a production report, or redesigned and then used and supported by the whole organization. These reports are often viewed as prototypes or proofs of concept to be rebuilt from scratch to company IT standards.

➤ **Production reports designed and created by IT for company use.** This is the traditional approach to IT solutions. Users or business unit leaders submit a request, a Business Analyst gathers and documents requirements, and then IT developers create the solution that is vigorously tested before being deployed to production. Some critical reports may fall into this category, but this doesn't provide the freedom and flexibility required by most organizations.

Allowing business users to own some of the day-to-day report creation can free IT developer resources to build more complex and critical reporting solutions. Since many experienced business users may know their data better than IT pros, who better to do the initial design and prototyping than those who will use the reports? Complex and mission-critical solutions should be developed using IT project standards and development methodology. Using the prototyping approach, certain trained and educated users design proof-of-concept reports that can be reviewed and analyzed to help establish the business and technical requirements. IT developers then redesign the reports from the prototypes and agreed-upon requirements.

Define Ownership

A classic problem in most any business environment is that information tends to move from place to place and person to person. Without a set of governance rules, people gather the information they need to perform their jobs and store it in whatever form works best for them. Over time, people may share their Excel workbooks and other documents with others, and some of these may become de facto standard sources for others. The problem is that the latest version may be in someone's local folder or inbox. In many cases, multiple copies are changed and updated with new information. Local reports work much the same way. If each doesn't have an owner and a home, people will continue to build on their own copies.

The most significant fault in unmanaged business reporting environments is that the administrators don't know who created certain reports, or who is responsible for the reports they have. Over the years, the number of reports grows, with no traceability to the person who requested that a report be created, who designed it, or who last updated it. In part, this problem is aided by Reporting Services' report catalog logging, but having the network ID of the person who originally deployed a report may not be a comprehensive solution. That person may no longer own the report and may not even work for the company anymore.

When called in to consolidate a set of reports, our IT project sponsors commonly say, "We don't know who these reports belong to or how they are used. What do we do?" My response has been, "Make a backup and then delete them from the servers. I'm sure you'll hear from the owners eventually." That's probably not the best solution, but I can assure you it works.

Report ownership really has two components. The first is the person who created, or is responsible for maintaining, a report. The second is the business entity that uses a report — and that may be responsible for the ongoing business and data requirements. For the first question, ownership may simply fall into the hands of the business entity that created or assumes responsibility for the report. Here are a few possible scenarios:

➤ A single user created a report, and he or she assumes full responsibility for the information it presents.

➤ A business unit or department owns the report. The users within that business entity will use the report for their own needs, and it won't be shared outside that group.

➤ The business enterprise owns the report. The design was conducted in accordance with IT and business standards. The data access method, query, and data have been validated and approved by IT and the business.

Ideally, we would like all reports to be well-designed and reliable, but if we are to allow business users to create their own reports, they should be suspect until formally validated or redesigned by IT. Until that happens, they should be deployed to an isolated location and branded so that any user understands who the owner is and the conditions of its use. If the CEO is handed a copy of Martha's personal report, she should know to validate any information it contains before making a critical business decision. If she is looking at an IT-sanctioned report, she should know, with confidence, that the information is accurate and reliable.

Every report should have a clear owner and sponsor. If IT owns the report server, they should have a clear and tangible record for each report, including the following:

➤ Who requested that the report be created and defined the business requirements?

➤ Who designed and developed the report?

➤ Who tested and validated the design?

➤ Have the queries and data access methods been validated to be accurate and efficient?

➤ Does the report meet corporate security requirements?

➤ Who should be able to run and get data through the report?

➤ What data should or should not be accessible through this report to specific users or members of AD groups?

Data Governance

Laying down rules often does no good unless people have reasonable alternatives to find what they need and to perform their jobs. Therefore, the first step toward governing the source and storage media for important information should be to provide a convenient and reasonable way to get to it. Enterprise data should be stored in enterprise databases. Department-level documents and reports should be stored in a designated location accessible to that group. Only after a foundation for collaboration exists can we mandate the rules for common use.

When users design their own reports, they should connect to the same data sources using the same methods as others, and then consume the data using a standard approach. Business data entities, such as a product catalog, customer contact list, or employee directory, should be queried from a central location. Or copies should be derived from a central store and then updated at regular intervals. Only when report data is obtained from an authorized source are reports reliable and consistent. This may be achieved by surfacing the appropriate data through an enterprise data warehouse, OLAP cubes, and semantic data models.

Data Source Access and Security

All users who will do their own reporting must be able to connect to enterprise data sources. But this doesn't mean that all users must have access to sensitive information. By employing user-level access and managing Active Directory group membership, users may be granted access to only the data they should be permitted to read.

Certain reporting capabilities, such as subscriptions and alerting, require report data to be accessed when the user is not online to be authenticated. In these cases, a shared data source should be created with stored credentials and minimal access to data records for a group of users. When reports and queries are executed at scheduled intervals, these results are sent to the user via e-mail, a file share, or are made available in cached result sets.

The use of shared data sources with stored credentials is common in Reporting Services solutions and can be adequately secure. Care should be taken to return only necessary data for the report. Access to the reports should be secured in addition to securing access to the database. In some cases, it may be necessary to manage two sets of shared data sources. One provides fine-grained access to certain data for interactive users, and the other supports these unattended reporting situations.

Create and deploy these shared data sources to a central location on your report server or SharePoint site. By default, a folder named Data Sources is created on the report server. In a SharePoint integrated site, add or use a document library set aside for shared data sources. Since you may use the SharePoint site to host other BI reports and content such as Excel Services reports, PerformancePoint, and Power View reports, you can designate one data source library for all the different data source content types. If the site is created using the Business Intelligence Center site template, a library called Data Connections is created and may be used for this purpose.

User Education

As soon as the report infrastructure is prepared and a plan is in place for your organization's self-service reporting strategy, train your users on the essentials. Start with a pilot user group to help iron out the rough spots, and then show them how to launch Report Builder, search the gallery, and add report parts. Then show them how to use shared datasets and select and use a shared data source (in that order).

With some preparation and planning, many business users can design reports without possessing query language or advanced report design skills. Depending on the sophistication of the need, users might have to acquire only basic skills. Using reports parts, they simply drag and drop pluggable parts onto the report body and then run the report. Using shared datasets, they need not write queries; they just add data regions and bind and group fields.

Optimizing the Report Builder User Experience

If you leave users to figure out how to design reports on their own, they will probably fail. Out of the box, Reporting Services doesn't lend itself to self-exploration, because it contains many features and capabilities that will confuse users if they try it on their own. But with a little guidance, this can be a good experience for the users. Guided, users can learn the basics and then learn more advanced features when they're ready.

Conducting User Training

Start small, keep it simple, and help your users understand the basic, essential tasks to design simple reports. Don't teach these users to write queries and use expressions. For advanced users, you can schedule a second-level training session after they have mastered the basics. In your first training session, teach your users to do the following:

➤ Navigate to the Report Manager or SharePoint site

➤ Launch Report Builder

➤ Choose the report type to create

➤ Choose the data source

➤ Assemble a dashboard from the report part gallery or design the report using wizards and drag-and-drop tools

➤ Browse data in the report

➤ Save the report to a folder or library

Folder and Library Management

One of the easiest ways to segregate user reports from enterprise reports is to designate a location for each. Users and IT report designers are granted permissions to deploy to appropriate libraries or folders. In a large-scale environment, these may be separate servers. In a smaller solution, they could be separate folders or document libraries on the same server or site.

Report Branding

After a report has been printed or exported to a file, it should also be identifiable. Using a template, brand these reports so that they will be recognizable as user-created or enterprise-standard reports. This could be as simple as a brief textbox in the report header or a designated image or logo. Figure 14-4 is a simplified example of a simple label in the report header.

FIGURE 14-4

Formal reports can have a "mark of approval" logo that lets people know at a glance that they are looking at a tested and trusted report. One of my customers took this advice and created three report templates to meet their business needs. Each template had an image in the report header to mark the report with the corporate report conformance level. Here's a summary of their approach:

➤ **Level 1** — Sourced from corporate BI data, but created by anyone without IT controls.

➤ **Level 2** — Sourced from BI data and query/report logic reviewed by a BI team member.

➤ Level 3 — Sourced from BI data, query/report logic reviewed by a BI team member, and validated/approved by the business data stewards for the data on the report.

Data Source and Query Options

Reporting Services has the flexibility to connect to a variety of data sources and to use different database objects. Too many choices are confusing, though. Standardize on a data access method and then teach users to work with a set of database objects. Most IT shops have established standards for connecting users to their databases and making data available through various objects. It's important that you establish and enforce these standards before turning your users loose on corporate data. In brief, your options are to encapsulate data using these objects:

➤ Relational database views

➤ Relational database stored procedures

➤ OLAP database cubes and perspectives

➤ Semantic data model

If your users will be reporting directly on a relational database, (preferably a data warehouse and not operational transactional schemas), you can provide access through views, stored procedures, or a semantic model.

If you provide access through a view, this simplifies data access by providing a layer of abstraction from multiple table relationships and join operations. Views don't provide parameterization. Users must still write a SELECT statement and a WHERE clause to query this data.

A stored procedure used to select and return data from multiple tables can have parameters built into its design. To use a stored procedure for a report, users need only select it from a list of procedures for the database specified in the report data source. No SELECT clause is necessary, and parameters in the stored procedure are automatically used to derive report parameters by the report designer. There are some minor limitations, such as how multivalue parameters must be handled. But for a relational data source, stored procedures can simplify the user report design experience and provide a simple and efficient way to query data at the source.

Using Shared Data Sources

Report Builder requires shared data sources for deployment. Create a data source for each database or semantic model, and deploy it to the shared data sources folder or library on the server. For all interactive reports that will be run while the user is logged into his or her desktop computer, you can use Windows Integrated security and pass through the user's security credentials. The databases and database servers need to be configured to allow access to a role, Windows, or Active Directory group to which all the report users have membership.

A network administrator can create a group for the report users and add each user to the group. For SQL Server, create a login for the group, and then map the SQL Server login to the db_datareader role for the database that a report queries data from. For Analysis Services, create a role for the OLAP database, and add the group to the role with Read permission granted for the cube, dimensions, and members.

Using a BI Semantic Model

Using a semantic model to provide data for a report can simplify user report design even further. The term *semantic model* or *semantic data layer* is used in a generic sense to describe a technology that simplifies and abstracts a set of data from the underlying data source.

In SQL Server 2012 the term BI Semantic Model actually refers to either an Analysis Services OLAP database or a Tabular Model created using the Analysis Services Tabular project type in SSDT. Here, I use the term to describe a tabular model, but we can also use it to encompass an SSAS OLAP (cube) database (now called a multidimensional database). Both OLAP/multidimensional databases and tabular models are stored using the Analysis Services storage engine, and the security model is the same for both types. A role is defined in the database with a set of permissions, and then one or more Windows users or groups are added to the role.

To grant access to an Analysis Services Tabular model, define a role with Read permissions, and then add the appropriate Windows or AD group to the role.

Designing and Deploying Report Parts

Report parts are fragments of a report, complete with a data source, dataset, and parameters, that can be reused in another report. A report part may be a single data region, such as a table or chart, or it may be a combination of report items and data regions, such as a complete dashboard. Report parts are published to a folder or library on the report server from any report using SSDT. This is considered to be an IT activity and should be part of the preparation effort to support user report design. Figure 14-5 shows the Project Properties dialog in SSDT. In a SharePoint integrated solution, the server address is set to the SharePoint root-site address. Like all of the target deployment folder properties (data sources, datasets, and reports), the report part folder is set to the full path to the library used for report parts.

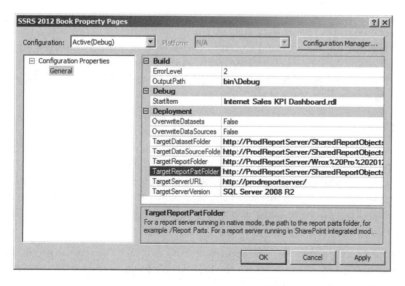

FIGURE 14-5

Figure 14-6 shows the Options dialog in Report Builder. In a SharePoint integrated solution, the server address is set to the SharePoint root-site address, and the report part folder is set to a relative path to the library used for report parts. Pay close attention to this, because the address formats are different between the two tools.

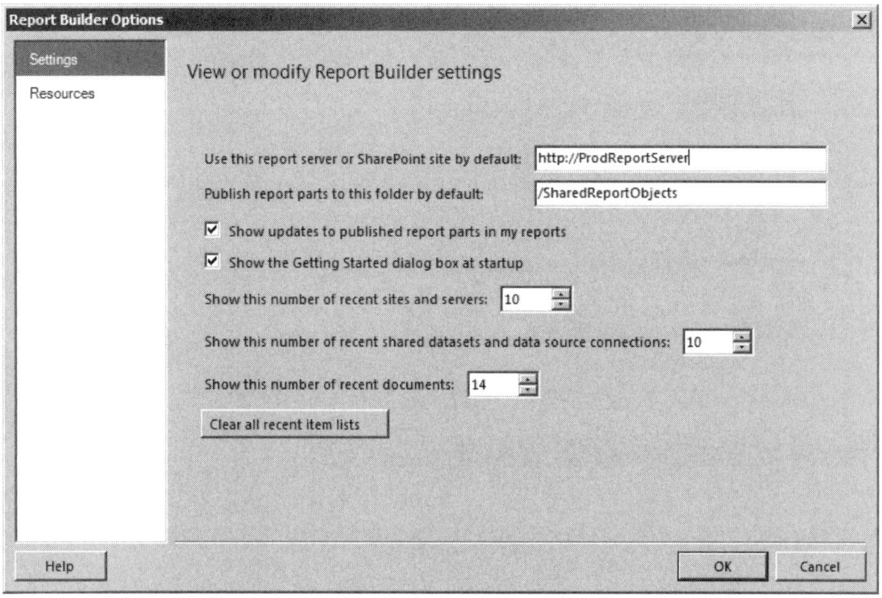

FIGURE 14-6

Report parts may be published from either SSDT or Report Builder. Publish report parts to a designated library, and give each report part an appropriate searchable name.

In SSDT, the report part names are specified in the Publish Report Parts dialog, which is accessible from the report. The selected report parts are then published to the server when the report is deployed. In Report Builder, choose Publish Report Parts from the Report Builder button menu, as shown in Figure 14-7.

In either SSDT or Report Builder, the Publish Report Parts dialog (see Figure 14-8) is used to select the report-design objects you want to deploy, and to rename these objects as report parts. When a data region is added to a report, we commonly don't worry about giving it a friendly name. But if you choose to publish a table or chart as a report part, you need to give it a more recognizable name than Table3 or Chart1. Remember that when naming report parts, eventually several report parts may be deployed. The user will need to know not only what type of report item a part represents, but also exactly what it does. Names should be descriptive, making it easy to discern how they consume or visually present a set of data. A good name might be something like Sales Amount by Sales Territory Country Chart.

FIGURE 14-7

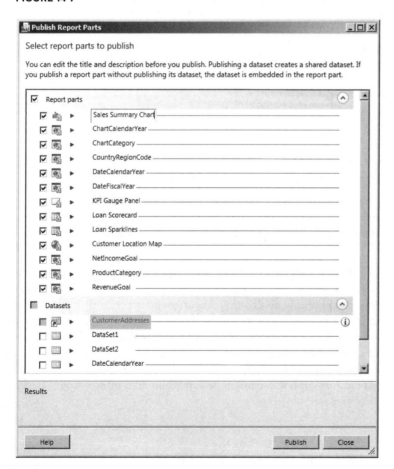

FIGURE 14-8

All the dependent objects that the report part needs to function are included on this list. If you uncheck any of these objects, they are still added to the report, but they are not made available to add individually. You typically don't need to select the datasets, data sources, and parameters when deploying report parts.

Using Report Parts

In Report Builder, users choose to insert a report part and then search the gallery. If these report parts are used without modification, a user can simply add them to a report and then run the report without having any report design skills beyond the basics.

When a developer updates and republishes existing report parts, users are given the option to update their reports. In this case, a report opened in Report Builder displays a Report Part update notification. If the user chooses to allow an update to take place, the affected report parts are replaced with the new components on the server.

Using Shared Datasets

Shared datasets allow for more advanced and granular report design without the need for users to write queries and consume data directly from data sources. A shared dataset is designed by an IT developer and is deployed to the report server in the same way that shared data sources and report parts are deployed and used. When designing a new report, a report user can choose a shared dataset from the server catalog and then design standard report data regions as they would with a dataset of their own design.

This requires greater aptitude than using report parts, but it also mitigates common mistakes made in query design and simplifies data access for common users. Users can have more flexibility to use advanced report design techniques without having to deal with the complexities of using SQL and MDX. Shared datasets can have associated parameters, filters, and calculated field definitions that users simply utilize rather than design themselves. Each deployed dataset can be configured with caching options to speed up report execution and minimize redundant database queries.

Shared datasets should be tested thoroughly before they are deployed and generally should not be modified after they have been used.

USER REPORT MIGRATION STRATEGIES

For reports that will serve as prototypes or the starting point for IT-supported business reports, you should consider a formal process. This can be part of the scheduled user report review cycle, or it can be performed for specific reports to let users assist with the design process and proof of concept. Figure 14-9 shows the phases of this process.

Report Migration Phases

Review

A user-designed report helps IT analysts and developers understand how they want to consume data. If the report is proposed to IT acceptance, it should be reviewed for security, effective query design, and proper use of report design techniques. If the report meets these standards, it may be tested and then promoted to the production IT-supported report server or library for general use by the business. It should be branded so that business users can identify it as a reliable source of business data.

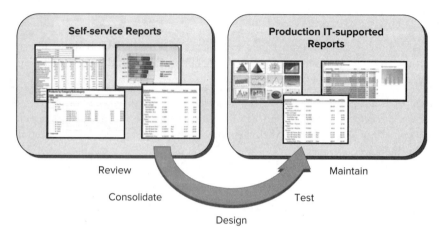

FIGURE 14-9

Consolidate

When new reports are introduced, in many cases they may have functionality that duplicates other reports. It's common for new reports to simply be a variation of an existing design that may be sorted, grouped, or filtered a little differently. Using common report design techniques, you can modify existing reports to use parameters and expressions to dynamically sort, group, and filter data. In many organizations, existing user-designed reports can be consolidated to drastically reduce the number of reports that IT must support. For example, I've seen cases where 800 reports were reduced to about 100 by retiring unused reports and consolidating redundant reports with those having more interactive features.

Don't wait until you have hundreds of out-of-control reports. Make this a regular effort in your periodic review.

Design

When reports are created as prototypes, treat them as examples and not as the starting point for a production report. There is great value in throwing away exemplary designs. Only keep a report that was designed from the beginning according to corporate IT project standards. Otherwise, you'll be money ahead by learning from it as a proof of concept, tossing it out, and starting over.

Test

Every report should go through the same testing and quality assurance process as custom software. Generally, report development cycles are shorter, and testing need not be a long and expensive ordeal. However, critical business reports should be tested by an objective team, separate from developers and report designers. Each report should be tested by a technical professional for security conformance, query, and report.

Maintain

As new requirements are introduced, the entire process may be repeated to decide if features should be added to existing reports, or if new reports should be added to the solution. Database servers may be added or moved, and shared data sources should be updated to reflect these changes. As new features are contemplated or reports are considered for consolidation, you should think about the trade-offs involved with report execution, query efficiency, and reduced functionality. Meeting multiple requirements using a single report must be weighed against the increased cost of maintaining multiple reports. The overall goal is to strike a balance between having reports that are simple to maintain and reducing the overall number of reports by combining features through more advanced design.

SUMMARY

This chapter has presented a set of guidelines for planning, designing, and maintaining a solution using Report Builder to enable your business users to design their own reports. Implementing a successful self-service report strategy requires planning, purposeful execution, and ongoing maintenance.

You learned that it's critical to define and understand the ownership of reports. When users own a report's requirements and design, they must accept responsibility for the data it presents and the business decisions. As IT professionals or business leaders, we must manage user access to important data and tools that provide these capabilities. Data sources should be governed by the business, and users should be trained to use only reliable data sources.

User reports and business standard reports that have been accepted and signed off on should be stored in separate locations and branded separately. Report design features such as shared data sources, shared datasets, and report parts make it easier to guide users and provide convenient tools for them to use the right data in the right way to gain insight with business information.

Finally, self-service report design is a partnership between users and IT professionals. Some user-designed reports may be used simply to browse information and for casual observations. Other reports may be used to help IT professionals better understand user reporting requirements and data use patterns. A user report may serve as a proof of concept that can be used to evolve a solution or to redesign properly developed report solutions using efficient design patterns and industry best practices.

PART V
Solution Patterns

15

Managing Report Projects

The first decision facing a report solution developer is how to best structure his or her work in a manner that is both consistent and logical. This becomes particularly important when you are working as part of a project team, with each team member responsible for delivering a part of the overall solution requirements.

This chapter looks at ways in which you can organize your report development to support the full deployment life cycle, from requirements to production implementation.

SOLUTIONS AND PROJECTS

What is a solution?

In its most basic form, a solution can be thought of as simply a collection of related projects. When you create a new project using the File menu in the Visual Studio environment, a solution is created automatically in the location you specify in the New Project dialog box, as shown in Figure 15-1. When creating a project for the first time, you can create a directory on your computer or network hard drive to contain the solutions and projects you create. You also can save your solution to your source control system as it is created. You'll read more about that later.

FIGURE 15-1

As you have learned, Reporting Services and Report Model projects are examples of the types of projects you can create. But you also can create SQL Server Integration Services (SSIS), Analysis Services, database, and even programming (C# .NET, VB.NET) projects.

Before you start developing a Reporting Services solution, you are faced with several important questions:

➤ Should the Reporting Services project be created in its own solution or be added to an existing solution containing other project types? Adding it to an existing project has the advantage of providing a seamless development environment, where the impact of changes to one area of development can be more readily applied to another. The disadvantage of placing multiple projects into a solution is that it can make the solution unwieldy and slower to open. It can also affect version control if several people make changes to the solution (see the section "Version Control").

➤ How do you intend to separate reports that have been deployed to production from reports on which you are currently working and/or that have been deployed to your test environment? The following section discusses your options when addressing this question.

Project Structure

As with any software development project, each component or report should progress through a series of design and development phases. These may include prototyping or proof-of-concept, design, testing, and deployment. You have a couple different ways to keep reports organized: multiple environments, or multiple logical folders and/or projects for each phase.

Multiple Reporting Environments

The multiple-environment approach involves maintaining multiple reporting environments that reflect the phases of design and development. The most common scenario is to have a development report server, a test/QA server, and, finally, the production environment. This is more involved, requiring a well-defined report promotion and deployment path. It also requires that multiple server environments be set up.

The idea is to keep the report development in the development sandbox environment. As report development is complete, the report can be deployed to the next stage — testing. In the testing/ quality assurance (QA) environment, analysts can verify the report's integrity and validate report data and layout. After the report has gone through testing and validation, it can be marked ready for production and go through any formalized promotion processes, such as change control. Visual Studio/SSDT can be used with an integrated version control solution, such as Team Foundation Server or a number of third-party versioning applications, to manage the development ownership, archival, and check-in/check-out process for report project files.

Although SSDT is typically the tool of choice for IT developers in these formalized project settings; Report Builder, utilizing the features of SharePoint, can also be used in a similar manner. If you have well-established processes in place for managing project asset check-in/check-out and versioning through SharePoint, Report Builder is a viable alternative. With Reporting Services configured in SharePoint integrated mode, designate different document libraries to manage collections of reports. You can then use the versioning and work flow features of SharePoint to manage report definition files.

If you don't already have a standard, or you're not using SSRS in integrated mode, and you need to manage multiple reports through a proper development, QA, and production life cycle, use SSDT for report design. Using the Configuration Manager, you can define a configuration for each deployment target: one for the development report server and data sources, another for QA, and still another for production. Select the development configuration, and then use the project properties to set your report server deployment.

Multiple Logical Folders and Projects

When following the multiple-folder approach, you might find it helpful to create separate projects and folders and then graduate reports from one project to another as they are verified and pass testing criteria. For each of the Visual Studio projects, within a master solution, create duplicate shared data sources. You can drag and drop reports from one project into another. Note that when you do this, the report definition is not physically deleted from the original report folder, so you may need to clean up the report definition file using Windows Explorer.

For each report project, set the `TargetFolder` property of a deployment folder to a name that corresponds to the project name (such as Prototype Phase, Design Phase, Test Phase, and Completed Reports).

Finally, remember one last thing about what will happen on practically every report project. In the beginning, your sponsor will tell you what reports and features they want, and you'll work with them to capture all the requirements in detail. Things generally will go pretty smoothly until they begin testing and you come up on a deadline. In the eleventh hour, users will start asking for things, and your sponsor will request changes.

You'll learn of some minor misunderstandings you may have had about the early requirements, and this will prompt even more changes. Some last-minute changes are inevitable in any project, but when a change is requested, it must be in writing. Whether they are requested in handwritten form, in a document, or in an e-mail message, save these requests. You should be able to trace every new request back to an earlier requirement or understand that it is a new requirement. If users request changes, have the project sponsor approve them. In the end, managing these changes will go a long way toward ensuring the success of your report project.

Report-Naming Conventions

One of the important decisions faced by a reporting solution developer is how to name the reports being produced. Many developers find it useful to include a number in the report name as a shorthand way to refer to a report. For example, this would enable report users to ask questions about "Report four" rather than the "Consolidated income and reconciled expenses" report.

You also need to consider whether you will include the name of the report in the report heading so that any confusion between a report's name and its title can be cleared up. Using `=Replace(Globals!ReportName, ".rdl", "")` as the expression for the report title ensures that the title and report name are the same.

Shared Datasets and Data Sources

Another significant challenge facing a report developer is whether to create and deploy a shared dataset or to use a dataset embedded in each report. As with many things in a development project, this question has no right or wrong answer. Shared datasets have a number of advantages:

➤ They allow the report writer to focus on addressing the report requirements rather than spending time working out the best way to retrieve data from the data store. Data retrieval queries can be written by staff with a closer appreciation of the most efficient ways to access the data.

➤ You can deploy enhancements to the query used retrieve the required data to multiple reports without needing to change their definition.

Shared datasets have some disadvantages as well:

➤ They can result in more data being retrieved than is strictly necessary to run a given report.

➤ Changes to the query used to retrieve the required data may result in a given report no longer operating or in returning data that was not part of the report definition.

If you are considering extensive use of shared datasets, you need to follow a couple of best practices:

➤ Make sure that you have a system for rolling back changes to a report and/or shared dataset. It might also be necessary to employ a deployment methodology whereby multiple versions of the same dataset can be deployed to eliminate the unintended consequence of changes on reports that will not be upgraded.

➤ Make sure you have a strong test regime to ensure that all reports are tested when a change to a shared dataset is deployed.

Key Success Factors

Reporting projects have a much better chance of being successful when the business requirements are well defined and clearly communicated. In particular:

➤ Report specifications should be documented using a standard format for all reports.

➤ Report specifications are a "living, breathing" document that will evolve as the report goes through its life cycle.

➤ Report layout should be mocked up and included in the specifications to capture the stakeholder's vision.

➤ Report designers must understand the source data. In cases in which the designer is unfamiliar with the database design and business data, specific queries or stored procedures should be defined and prepared before report design.

➤ Whenever possible, the details of database objects and their relationships should be abstracted into a stored objects or semantic view.

➤ The database schema should be frozen before work begins.

➤ Accurate samples or real data should be available to support the design and testing of all reports.

➤ Report designers should update report specifications to reflect any layout, data, and business rule changes that might have occurred during development, and to include further relevant details to assist in future maintenance.

These may seem like lofty goals. The fact is that often you may be unable to control all these factors. Experience will help you figure out where to draw the line between situations in which you should work in less-than-ideal conditions and situations in which you should insist that these conditions be met before you begin work. In any case, be sure to clearly communicate your concerns and the associated risks.

Solution Scope

You should understand the scope of the solution before report work begins. If you lack a clear understanding of all the solution's related components, the project can easily spin out of control, with more work being started than finished.

Here are some common examples of solution scope challenges:

➤ Report performance problems prompt database schema changes or the construction of denormalized fact tables containing duplicate data.

➤ Realizing that changing transactional data doesn't support reporting scenarios, you redesign the database while in production.

➤ Database and report features are added as you go, not according to a predefined plan, causing each report to take on different behavior and features.

➤ Report designers and users brainstorm new features during the report development and subsequently define new requirements.

When a data warehouse, data mart, or semantic model is unavailable and outside the scope of the report project, you may consider using an operational data store (ODS). An ODS reflects transactional data closer to real time, as opposed to the historical volumes in a data warehouse. It has gone through some data cleansing and integrity checking to create more accurate reports.

If these kinds of issues aren't mitigated and managed, even simple projects may be doomed before they start. Ideally, a report designer should be on the receiving side of business requirements and should help clarify the details, rather than making up new requirements as the project moves along. In most cases, the report designer should rely on the business analyst/information worker as the subject-matter expert on the data in context, allowing for a separation of concerns and better-defined tasks.

Report Specifications

The perfect, universal report requirements template doesn't exist, because business environments, data sources, and reporting scenarios differ wherever you go. Working for a large consulting firm, at the request of our project methodology development team, I wrote a report specification template. It was simple and flexible, but the content writers turned it into something rigid and unusable. That's how such things often evolve when we try to make them comprehensive and prescriptive.

I'm often asked what is the best mock-up diagramming or prototyping tool for Reporting Services. In the end, a report requirements template should serve as a checklist used to define each report. It should include a diagram of the report indicating the layout and function of each section or data region, and it should cover these areas:

➤ **Data sources** (server, authentication method, principles)

➤ **Database objects and fields** (tables, joins, views, stored procedures, cubes, dimensions, attributes, measures, KPIs)

➤ **Data regions** (table, matrix, list)

➤ **Groups and group levels**

➤ **Fields and aggregate functions** (Sum, Average, Count, Distinct Count)

➤ **Visualizations** (chart, gauge, map, scorecard, sparkline, indicator, bar)

➤ **Interactions and actions** (drill-down, drill-through, dynamically hidden/displayed and filtered regions)

➤ **Security levels and permissions to access the report and the underlying data sources**

Work with your users and project sponsor to design a report specification template that addresses your unique business needs. Some reports may query data from multiple tables, and users may not be familiar enough with the data structures to specify column names and keys for joins. In this case, you may need to involve a database expert to help with these requirements. Other reports may get their data from existing views or stored procedures, making this part of the process much easier.

Report Template

As soon as you have developed a template that satisfies your business requirements, you can deploy it to the local development environment by copying the .rdl file to the following location:

```
C:\Program Files (x86)\Microsoft Visual Studio 10.0\Common7\IDE
\PrivateAssemblies\ProjectItems\ReportProject
```

> *Consider setting the attributes of your template files to read-only to prevent accidental overwriting.*

> *Note that the directory name quoted here contains a version number that is relevant to the current version of Reporting Services. This is subject to change in future releases, so it's important to find out the folder name for the release you are using.*

You might find that if the project sponsor and users are unfamiliar with the data structures, you are left to make assumptions about how the tables should be joined and queried. In these cases, the report specification becomes more of a checklist and a forum to validate assumptions and to answer questions. This also lengthens the report's development cycle, because you have the onus of learning the details of the data model. Remember that the key to success is effective communication. On larger projects or when reporting on more complex databases, you may need to separate the report's business requirements from the technical specification, perhaps by using two separate documents to gather these requirements. In any case, the key is to involve users and business stakeholders in obtaining buy-off and validating the results.

Development Phases

As with any software development project, each component or report should progress through a series of design and development phases. These may include prototyping or proof-of-concept, design, testing, and deployment. You have a couple different ways to keep reports organized: multiple environments or multiple logical folders and/or projects for each phase.

Multiple Reporting Environments

The multiple-environment approach involves maintaining several reporting environments that reflect the phases of design and development. The most common scenario is to have a development report server, a test/QA server, and, finally, the production environment. This is more involved, requiring a well-defined report promotion and deployment path. It also requires that multiple server environments be set up.

The idea is to keep the report development in the development sandbox environment, and as report development is complete, the report can be deployed to the next stage—testing. In the test/QA environment, analysts can verify the report's integrity and validate report data and layout. As soon as the report has gone through testing and validation, it can be marked ready for production and go through any formalized promotion processes, such as change control and so on. SQL Server Data Tools (SSDT) is based on the development foundation of Visual Studio 2010 and can be used with an integrated version control solution, such as Team Foundation Server, to manage the development ownership, archival, and check-in/check-out process for report project files.

Although SSDT typically is the tool of choice for IT developers in these formalized project settings, Report Builder, utilizing the features of SharePoint, can be used in a similar manner. If you have well-established processes in place for managing project asset check-in/check-out and versioning through SharePoint, Report Builder is a viable alternative. With Reporting Services configured in SharePoint Integrated mode, you can designate different document libraries to manage collections of reports. You can then use SharePoint's versioning and workflow features to manage report definition files.

If you don't already have a standard or you're not using SSRS in integrated mode, and you need to manage multiple reports through a proper development, QA, and production life cycle, use SSDT for report design. Using the Configuration Manager, you can define a configuration for each deployment target—one for the development report server and data sources, another for QA, and another for production. Select the development configuration, and then use the project properties to set your report server deployment.

Multiple Logical Folders and Projects

When following the multiple folder approach, you might find it helpful to create separate projects and folders and then graduate reports from one project to another, as they are verified and pass testing criteria. For each Visual Studio project, within a master solution, create duplicate shared data sources. You can drag and drop reports from one project to another and then remove the previous report using the Solution Explorer. When you right-click the old report and choose the Remove option, the second Remove option leaves the file in the project folder and removes the entry from the project file. Because a new copy is created in the destination project, you should choose the Delete option so that you maintain only one copy of the report definition file.

For each report project, set the `TargetFolder` property of a deployment folder to a name that corresponds to the project name (such as Prototype Phase, Design Phase, Test Phase, and Completed Reports).

Finally, you should remember one last thing about what will happen on practically every report project. In the beginning, your sponsor will tell you what reports and features they want, and you'll work with them to capture all the requirements in detail. Things will generally go pretty smoothly until they begin testing and you come up on a deadline. In the eleventh hour, users will start asking for things, and your sponsor will request changes.

You'll learn of some minor misunderstandings you had about the early requirements, and this will prompt even more changes. Some last-minute changes are inevitable in any project, but when a change is requested, it must be in writing. Whether in handwritten form, in a document, or in an e-mail message, keep and save these requests. You should be able to trace every new request back to an earlier requirement or obtain a clear understanding that it is a new requirement. If users request changes, you should have the project sponsor approve them. In the end, managing these changes will go a long way toward ensuring the success of your report project.

VERSION CONTROL

One of the key issues that must be addressed when you are working as part of a team is how to ensure that you do not overwrite another developer's changes and that the changes you make are not overwritten by someone else.

The purpose of this section is to outline the major characteristics of version control in a report development project and to show how these can be implemented and used in an SSDT environment.

Why Use Version Control?

For most development projects, the use of version control is a given because it is the only method of ensuring that multiple developers can work on the same project without overwriting each other's work. It is worth pointing out that a number of administrative and process costs are associated with maintaining a version control system, so it is worth considering what we are getting for this cost.

Here are some of the benefits of version control systems:

➤ They ensure that a backup is made of each object as and when it is checked in to the server. This means that any data loss caused by a corruption of the developer's code is limited to the version on which the developer is actively working. If you ensure that the check-in policy states that all code must be checked in no later than the end of the current business day, this significantly reduces the cost of rework after any failures.

➤ They allow a change to be associated with a documented task or bug and therefore encourage developers to ensure that these are documented before work commences.

➤ If used in conjunction with a build process, they ensure that only tested versions of code are deployed to production.

➤ They provide a history of changes to code that helps when trying to distinguish stable reports from volatile ones and obtain some metrics on the cost of development.

Setting Up Version Control

Version control systems normally operate by introducing a new menu structure into the Visual Studio/SSDT environment that is used to establish a connection between your project and the version control server. For example, Team Foundation Server has a Connect to Team Foundation Server option on the Tools menu. If you know the URL for your project's server, you can use this menu to establish a connection to your project's code repository on the server. Whenever you open the project, a connection to the version control server is established, so it may be necessary to reenter your username and/or password whenever you open the project. If the server is unavailable when you open the project, normally you have a choice to "Go offline" or "Disable source control for this session." In this case, any changes you make are synchronized with the server the next time you go online. Note that the Visual Studio/SSDT environment normally remembers that the project was opened offline and continues to work disconnected from the server until you select File ➪ Source Control ➪ Go online.

Getting the Latest Version

One of the first things you should do when working in a version-controlled environment is ensure that you have the latest version of the report in your local workspace before you make any changes. Many version-control systems allow more than one developer to work on the same thing at the same time. You find out that someone has changed your report only when you try to check it back in. When this happens, normally you have at least three alternatives. You can save your local version, use the server version, or merge the two. When this happens, it is good corporate citizenship not to elect to overwrite the server version until you are absolutely certain that the person who changed the report agrees to lose the changes he or she has made.

Viewing a Report's History

You can obtain a history of changes to a report by right-clicking it and selecting View change history. This displays a window showing the following information for each change:

- ➤ The date of the change.

- ➤ Who made the change.

- ➤ Any comments the developer made when the report was checked in.

- ➤ A list of work items (bug reports, tasks) associated with the change. You see this by double-clicking the change.

Restoring a Previous Version of a Report

You can restore a previous version of a report by right-clicking it and selecting Get Specific Version. The default version is always the latest version, but you can search for the required version using a date, change number, or label. Note that doing so copies the nominated version to your local workspace only. So if you want the version you selected to be the latest version, you need to check it back in again.

Setting Check-out and Check-in Policies

Most version-control systems allow the user to specify the policy to employ when checking in and/or checking out reports or code. For example, you might want to set a policy that states that no two developers can work on the same project at the same time or that a report must be reviewed by another developer before it is checked in.

For example, to prevent two developers from checking out the same report in a Team Foundation Server environment, select Team ➪ Team Project Settings ➪ Source Control and uncheck the "Enable Multiple check out" check box.

Applying Labels

You apply a label to a version of a report when you want to be able to find it again using the label you supply. You add a label to a report by right-clicking the project and selecting Apply Label. You then select the report and version combination to which the label is to applied, supply a label value and an optional comment, and click OK. You can add more than one report to a label by clicking Add.

SYNCHRONIZING CONTENT

When you have completed the development of your report, the next challenge will be to deploy your report to a server environment to allow it to be seen and/or reviewed by your co-workers or business users. This section deals with how to build and deploy either an individual report or a suite of reports to a server environment.

Deploying an Individual Report

Deploying a single report is straightforward; you just right-click the report and select Deploy. Note that the report goes through a build process that checks that the report is valid before it is deployed. If there are no build or deployment errors (see the section "Checking for Build Errors"), a message in the output window tells you that the report has deployed successfully.

Deploying a Suite of Reports

To save time, instead of deploying each report in your project individually, you might choose to deploy all of them at the same time. You can do this in one of two ways:

➤ Right-click the project name and choose Deploy.

➤ Click the first report you want to deploy, hold down the Shift key, click the last report you want to deploy, right-click, and choose Deploy.

Each report you select will go through the same build and deploy process, but this time, a message in the output window tells you how many of the reports were built and deployed successfully.

Checking for Build Errors

Most common errors in reports are displayed in the report preview pane when you preview the report. However, you might also be notified of an error or warning on your report on the Error tab of the SSDT environment. If the Error tab does not appear, you can display it by selecting View ⇨ Error List.

Excluding a Report from a Deployment

As noted, you can remove an individual report from an individual deployment by just not clicking it before you select the Deploy option. You can unclick a report by holding down the Ctrl key and clicking the report you want to exclude after the reports you want to include have been highlighted.

But what if you want a report to be excluded on a more permanent basis? You could just delete the report, but this would remove any record of it, which would also remove its history.

Another alternative is to right-click the report and select Exclude From Project. This removes the report from the project without deleting it from either your local workspace or the version control server. If in the future you want to reinclude the report, you can add it back to the project by right-clicking it, selecting Add ➪ Existing item, and navigating to the report definition file (.rdl) in your local workspace.

MANAGING SERVER CONTENT

This section deals with how you manage your report content (reports, datasets, and data sources) on a report server that has been installed in either a native mode or SharePoint configuration. In a development environment, you will probably not need to know a great deal about managing reports on the server, because you will be modifying content directly using the Visual Studio/SSDT. However, you might not have the required access to perform a direct deployment in either the test or production environment, so you may need to know how these can be managed on the server. You might also want to check that the way your report has been configured in your Visual Studio/SSDT environment matches the way it has been deployed to the server.

Checking the Deployment Location

The first thing you need to know before you manage content on your Reporting Services server is the server's location. You can discover this by selecting Project ➪ Properties in the Visual Studio/SSDT environment. You see the window shown in Figure 15-2. Here are the things you need to review on this screen:

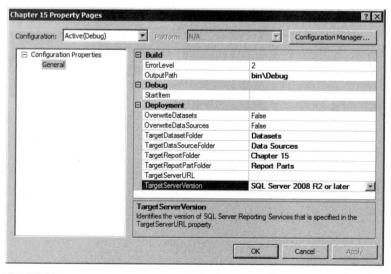

FIGURE 15-2

➤ The configuration determines the rest of the settings. In Figure 15-2, the Debug configuration is being used. As a report developer, you can set up a configuration for each of the environments (development, test, and production, for example). You can change these settings automatically by selecting the required configuration from this drop-down menu.

➤ If the `OverwriteDatasets` or `OverwriteDataSources` setting is set to true, a dataset/data source is overwritten on the server when a report is displayed that uses the setting. If it is set to false, you are warned in the output window that the dataset/data source is not being changed.

➤ You see the `TargetDatasetFolder`, `TargetDataSourceFolder`, `TargetReportFolder`, and `TargetReportPartFolder` object types. Creating a folder for each of these types is a good way to organize them on the server for ease of access and to allow them to be properly secured. Figure 15-2 shows the defaults for these settings. Note that the report folder defaults to the name of your project.

➤ The target server URL is one of the signs that a report is being deployed in native rather than SharePoint mode. If the report is deployed in native mode, you see a URL similar to the one shown in Figure 15-2. If the reports are deployed to SharePoint, you are likely to see a port number following the server name, as in `http://ProductionServer:7777`.

Managing Content in Native Mode

When your report server was set up, it was decided whether your reports would be deployed to a SharePoint environment. Reporting Services ships with a "native" mode deployment option for customers who do not have (or do not want) a SharePoint site. This section deals with the content management options in default (native) mode for Reporting Services.

Managing Data Sources

In native mode, data sources are stored in a folder you can view from the Reports URL. This is normally `http://ServerName/Reports`, but it is best to check where it is deployed in your environment by examining the settings by selecting Project ⇨ *Projectname* Properties from SSDT. The folder name is located in the `TargetDataSourceFolder` row of this screen.

You can manage the following from the server:

➤ Whether the report can be viewed by visitors to the report site when in tiled mode. This is the default view used by Reporting Services in native mode. The alternative view is Details view, which displays reports as a list.

➤ Enabling/disabling the data source.

➤ The type of the data source, such as whether the data is stored in an XML file or a SQL Server database.

➤ The folder in which the data source is stored.

➤ The description that appears next to the data source.

➤ The credentials used to run the report.

➤ The connection string used to connect to the data source.

➤ The data-driven subscriptions applied to this data source.

➤ The list of reports, datasets, and data models that depend on the data source. If required, any of these can be deleted from the Dependent Items tab.

➤ The list of users who can view or overwrite this data source on the server.

Note that any changes you make on the server will be overridden by the settings in your project each time a report is deployed if the `OverwriteDataSources` project property is set to true.

To manage a data source, select it from the Reports URL and click the down arrow that appears to the right of the data source name when you hover the mouse cursor over the data source. Just make sure that you click the Apply button after you make your changes. If you have trouble applying the changes, you might have to run your browser using local administrator privileges by right-clicking the icon and selecting "Run as administrator."

Another interesting thing you can manage on the server is to create a data model from your data source. This will be generated in the folder you nominate. You can download and open it from the SSDT environment by selecting Open ➪ Existing Project and selecting the downloaded project.

Managing Data Sets

In native mode, datasets are also stored in a folder that can be viewed from the Reports URL. You can check this location in the same way as for data sources but in the `TargetDataSetFolder` row of the properties screen.

The things you can manage on the server for a dataset include the things you can manage for a dataset, except that you can't disable a dataset.

You can additionally set the timeout in seconds for a dataset to respond to a request from a report, and set up and manage dataset caching. This is a way of enhancing a report's performance by using a cached copy of the dataset rather than looking up the data from the data source. This cache can be refreshed after a specified interval or on a schedule. If you elect to have the cache refreshed on a schedule, a SQL Agent job will be created for you when you click Apply on the Caching options.

Note that any changes you make on the server will be overridden by the settings in your project each time a report is deployed if the `OverwriteDataSets` project property is set to true.

Managing Reports

In native mode, reports are also stored either in a folder or on the home screen of the Reports URL. The things you can manage on the server include most of the things you can manage on a dataset. You also can manage some additional items:

➤ Create a linked report with a predefined set of parameters.

➤ Create a scheduled and/or data-driven subscription to the report. This can be used to automatically distribute copies of the report to a predefined set of recipients via the file system or e-mail.

➤ Create a snapshot of the report either manually or at given intervals.

Managing Content in SharePoint

All the things you can manage in native mode can also be managed from your SharePoint site. You access the SharePoint report management menu, shown in Figure 15-3, in the same way as you access the native mode menu. Just select the blue down arrow instead of the yellow one.

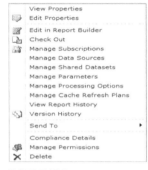

FIGURE 15-3

Here are some additional options:

➤ Edit in Report Builder. Report Builder is a user-friendly tool for developing reports that looks more like an Office product than a developer product. You get only a subset of the facilities that are available to you from the Visual Studio/SSDT environment, but in many cases this is all you need. If you do not have a copy of Report Builder installed on your local computer, one is automatically downloaded from your server.

➤ Manage Parameters is useful in cases where your report uses default values for parameters and you need to check what those default values are. You should not assume that the values in your development environment match those in SharePoint, even immediately after a report is deployed. It is always best to check.

➤ Send To can be used to download a copy of the report, copy it to a new location, or e-mail it to someone as a link.

 If you are making changes directly on your reporting server, be sure that these changes are reflected in your local reporting development workspace. Failure to do so may result in any changes being overwritten the next time the project or report is deployed.

GETTING STARTED WITH AZURE REPORTING

Among the many capabilities offered through Azure, Microsoft's cloud-based services, you can host your reports online without the need to install and configure an on-premises report server. Azure Reporting allows standard Reporting Services reports, hosted in one of many data centers located throughout the world, to access data stored in a SQL Server Azure database instance. Reports are deployed, managed, and accessed over secure channels on the Internet.

You can easily establish a report server in the cloud using the SQL Server Azure platform. You set up an Azure report server by navigating to the SQL Azure portal (`https://windows.azure.com/default.aspx`), logging on, and selecting Reporting from the menu on the left. You need to use a Windows Live ID to sign in, which you can create if you haven't done so before. Figure 15-4 shows the Windows Azure Platform portal.

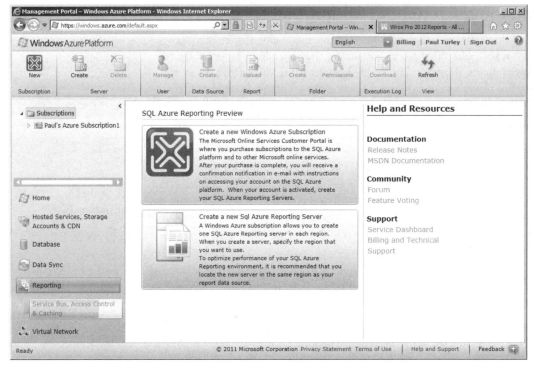

FIGURE 15-4

Use the New Subscription option in the ribbon bar to set up a subscription. You are prompted for your contact and billing information. Azure is a paid service, but one of the advantages is that you need to pay only for what you use. Of course, you should carefully read the billing and subscription agreement before you provide payment information.

When you select Create a new SQL Azure Reporting Server from the middle pane, a popup window asks you to agree with the terms and conditions, as shown in Figure 15-5. After you have read and understood these, check "I agree to the Terms of Use statement above" and click Next.

You are asked to nominate a subscription and a region to use to create the report server. You can select the subscription you want to use from the Subscription drop-down menu. If your company has more than one active subscription, you might need to find out from your systems administration staff which one to use before proceeding. The next window, shown in Figure 15-6, prompts you for the Azure data center region. The choice of region is an important one. Ideally, you want to select the region that hosts the SQL Azure database(s) on which you will be reporting.

The next window, shown in Figure 15-7, prompts you to set up an administrator account to be used to administer your report server. This account will have full access to your server, so it is important to think of a strong password or passphrase you can remember without writing it down.

Note that the password must be at least eight characters long and contain at least three of the following types of characters: uppercase, lowercase, numbers and nonalphabetic characters (such as @, #, and !). You are prompted to correct the entered password if it does not meet these criteria.

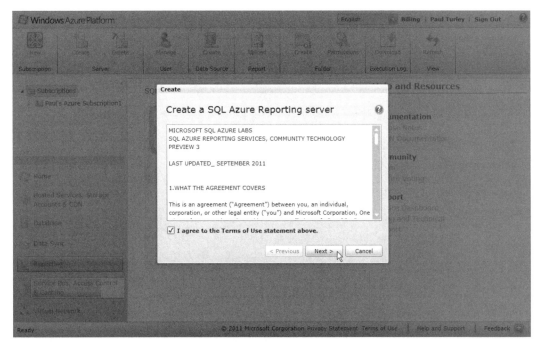

FIGURE 15-5

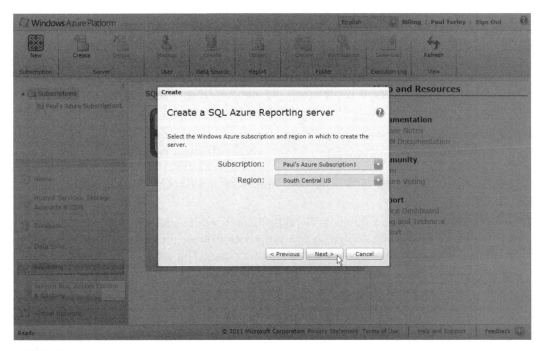

FIGURE 15-6

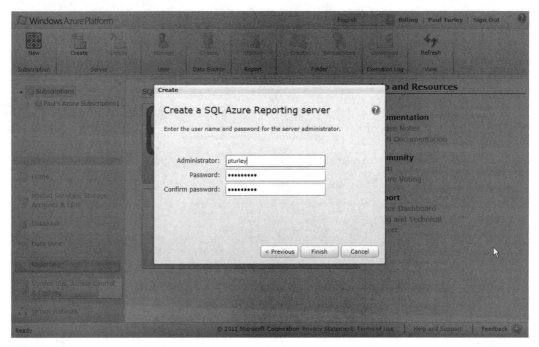

FIGURE 15-7

After you have entered these details, click Finish; your report server is provisioned. When this is complete, you are returned to the page shown in Figure 15-8. To navigate to your new report server, click the Link button next to Web service URL on the Server Home page. You can reach this page by clicking the server name under the Subscriptions folder in the pane on the left. If you can't see the Subscriptions folder, click Reporting in the bottom half of the pane on the left. Note that the server name appears as a random sequence of letters and numbers. If your subscription has many servers, you might have to click each one to find the server you just created.

For production use, you need to create additional users. To do this, click the Manage icon from your server home page. You are prompted to enter the user details and decide what level of access to give them. Note that the rules that apply to the administrator account password also apply to all other users. Therefore, you need to think of a password with at least eight letters, numbers, and perhaps nonalphabetic characters.

To deploy reports to your new Azure server, copy the web service URL listed on your Server Home page to the Target Server URL of your project properties. You are prompted to enter the credentials of a Content Manager or Publisher when you deploy a report. You can also upload (and download) reports using your Server Home page.

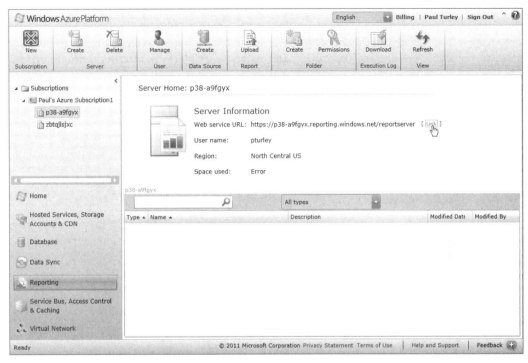

FIGURE 15-8

Deploying and Executing Reports

The rest is easy and similar to working with an on-premises report server. After you select the report server and navigate to that link in your web browser, copy the URL to the clipboard. Use it for the `TargetServerURL` project property in BIDS or as the Save As destination path in Report Builder. The report server URL starts with your server name. The following is a sample Azure report server URL for a server named rzbiymk19i:

```
https://rzbiymk19i.reporting.windows.net/ReportServer
```

As far as the report design tools are concerned, deploying to your Azure report server is no different from deploying to a report server on your corporate network. When you deploy or save a report, you are prompted to enter the username and password for a Windows Azure subscription user. For testing, you can use the administrator account you established in Figure 15-7.

When a user runs a report, his or her experience should be the same as with a report hosted on-premises. One minor difference is that Azure Reporting doesn't use the Report Manager interface.

Your options for user report delivery are to provide a page or individual hyperlinks to your users who connect them directly to each report, to use the ReportViewer control to visualize reports in a custom application, or to use the simple pages generated when users navigate directly to the Azure report server. These options are likely to expand as the Azure platform offering continues to mature.

SUMMARY

This chapter has considered some of the decisions you face when organizing your report projects. We looked at ways to work with version control systems to ensure that you have a full record of any changes, and can work efficiently as part of a team. We also considered report deployment and showed how you can use the report server in either native or SharePoint mode to manage your reports after they have been deployed.

Hopefully, you now have enough information to make informed choices about how to structure your report development in a way that supports rather than inhibits the report development life cycle.

16

Report Solutions, Patterns, and Recipes

WHAT'S IN THIS CHAPTER?

➤ Designing super reports

➤ Report specifications and requirements

➤ Development phases

➤ Report recipes

➤ Dashboard solutions

➤ Designing a KPI scorecard

➤ Designing an interactive sparkline report

➤ Maps with navigation

➤ Using report parts

➤ Dynamic colors

➤ Tables with dynamic columns

Anyone who does a lot of advanced report design work can appreciate the fact that Reporting Services can be used to build highly customized reports to meet the demands of complex business requirements. Features and properties have been added in each product version to improve these capabilities. Some objects have dozens of properties, many of which are used only for very specific needs and to solve specific problems.

The concept of the report recipe was born from a series of conference presentations I've given at the PASS Global Summit over the past few years. The topic of advanced report design led to discussions about practical design patterns and different ways that one more capable report could be created to replace many simple reports. Through the use of some well-established design techniques, we've learned to create fewer, more complex and adaptable reports rather than one report for each user request or individual requirement.

Let's face it — a lot of reporting environments aren't meticulously planned. In most organizations, different people create reports to surface information from various data sources. Over time, the reports grow and evolve. To some degree this situation is inevitable, but that doesn't mean we must sit back and watch it turn into chaos. In Chapter 14, we discussed an approach to conducting regular user report reviews with consideration for consolidation and redesign. This concept isn't exclusively for migrating user reports to those under IT control. We can take a similar approach with reports developed in more formal settings that may have become redundant or obsolete. The process is much the same: assign ownership and schedule regular reviews, comparing similar reports slated for consolidation or retirement.

SUPER REPORTS

When a set of business requirements are presented for development, they are translated into a set of report capabilities and features. When a set of similar requirements is presented with considerable overlap, this may be an opportunity to combine them into a cohesive set of features. A super report combines features to present each set of business users with only the capabilities and information they need.

How can we design one report to present different information for different users? We can offer each set of users different report behaviors by enabling elements of the report under different conditions. This is all possible by using the skills and techniques discussed in earlier chapters. These features may be combined to take the user's reporting experience to a whole new level.

Figure 16-1 shows the interdependencies between basic report design elements.

Through examples, you'll learn to combine these techniques and features to create more capable, advanced, and useful reports.

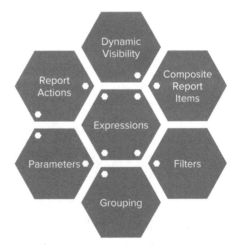

FIGURE 16-1

Working with the Strengths and Limitations of the Architecture

Before I continue, I want to be clear about something: I love this product. I have found Reporting Services to be extremely powerful, flexible, and capable of solving most business problems I've encountered in about nine years of using it. Given a challenge, I can usually find a way to tackle it with Reporting Services. In learning about the product team's vision and long-term goals for Reporting Services' features and capabilities, we've gained insight into the mechanics of the product's components and why they behave as they do. Without fully understanding the design goals in constructing the architecture of this product, it's easy for a report designer to ask questions such as Why does it work that way? and Why did it do that? Reporting Services has some limitations that may not make sense to the casual user. I've found that most advanced capabilities that I want to include in reports can be implemented, but not necessarily using my chosen technique. As I've run up against limitations and have discussed these with the product architects and product managers, the answers are often in the vein of "That feature wasn't designed to work that way. You can accomplish the same thing by using this other feature or technique." My goal is to share these techniques and capabilities with you.

One of the chief goals of this product is to render reports in a variety of presentation formats using server-side components. In doing so, a report rendered to a specific format may not take advantage of all the capabilities offered by that format, a client tool, or markup language. For example, reports rendered to HTML don't offer all the advanced behavior you might implement in a custom-built web page with cascading style sheets and JavaScript. If you designed a report in Microsoft Excel, you might design the workbook with formulas used to recalculate the spreadsheet rather than using literal values for summaries and totals. The general approach is that Reporting Services renders using methods to address the commonality of all these formats. There's always room for more features and advanced functionality. Some of these may be added to the product in later versions, because this makes sense for mass consumption. Because of the modular architecture of Reporting Services, certain features can be added through custom programming extensions. This topic is covered extensively in Chapter 22.

A common scenario I find in the business community is when experienced Excel users (usually financial analysts) ask for reports to be rendered to an Excel workbook containing formulas, data sources, pivot tables, and other advanced Excel capabilities. Don't misunderstand me when I say that extensively formatted reports can be exported to Excel with a great deal of precision. However, it stands to reason that if Excel users want to use advanced capabilities in Excel, they should use Excel as their reporting tool rather than Reporting Services.

It's not easy to define the limits of most products. For some reason, the specifications and documentation for most products don't contain a list of things they can't do — at least not in bold type. I've had very little success going to a large software vendor and saying, "Tell me what your product *can't* do." Wouldn't it be nice if, when you shop for a car or house, the salespeople list the comparative shortcomings of their product? It would make the process so much easier. For this discussion, that is where I'd like to start. Table 16-1 details some of the more recognizable limitations of the Reporting Services architecture. This is by no means a complete list, nor is it a list of bugs and issues. It's simply a guideline of design constraints to be aware of when taking reports to the next level. I also describe some common alternatives to implement desired functionality.

TABLE 16-1

AREA	LIMITATION	ALTERNATIVES
Data presentation	In the report body or a group section, all fields must be aggregated, even if the dataset returns only one row.	Use an aggregate function even if your query returns one row or if all rows for the field return the same value. Typically, you should use the FIRST() function for character and date data and the SUM() function for numeric data.

continues

TABLE 16-1 *(continued)*

AREA	LIMITATION	ALTERNATIVES
Formatting	Conditional formatting expressions can be complicated and difficult to maintain, especially when nesting Boolean logic and when same expression is repeated for multiple report items and fields.	Write a Visual Basic function in the Report Properties Code window, and call the function as an expression for each report item. For example: `=Code.MyFunction(Fields!MyField.Value)` In certain cases, you might also be able to leverage the newly introduced `Report` and `Group` variables to hold certain values.

	Aggregate functions don't return 0 for summaries on NULL values. Our users want to see 0s.	Use a Visual Basic function to return a 0 in place of a NULL value. For example:
		
		`=IIF(IsNothing(SUM(Fields!MyField.Value)), 0, SUM(Fields!MyField.Value))`
		
		Or, pass values to a Visual Basic function to convert NULL, empty string, or no value to a 0 or another value. For example:
		
		`=Code.NullToZero (Fields!MyField.Value)`

	Some highly formatted reports don't export well to Excel.	Often, only data regions that translate to a grid layout export neatly to Excel. If you need more visual report styles to export to Excel, design two alternate data regions: one optimized for browsing, and the other for Excel. Use the built-in Render Format Name field in an expression on the `Hidden` property to conditionally hide each data region, depending on the render format. For example:
		
		`=(Global!RenderFormat.Name="Excel")`
		or
		`=NOT(Global!RenderFormat.Name="Excel")`

	Grouped column headers can't be hidden using expressions.	Only data columns can be hidden; group header columns cannot. Rather than using group header columns, add the group header fields to the data columns collection (by dragging the field to the right side of the double dash group/data column separator). Then set the cell `HideDuplicates` property to the dataset name. To conditionally hide a column, right-click the column header, choose Column Visibility, and set an expression for the `Hidden` property. For example, if you want to hide the column for the Tax Amount field if the dataset doesn't return that column, use this expression: `=(Fields!TaxAmt.IsMissing)`

AREA	LIMITATION	ALTERNATIVES
Rendering	HTML rendering doesn't support some table design formatting. For example, narrow columns used for spacing and borders are padded with extra space.	This is a characteristic of HTML rendering and is not considered a bug. If reports require more exact tolerances, users should be instructed to use printer-friendly rendering formats such as PDF and TIFF.
	Using images in place of borders causes extra vertical and horizontal padding and column misalignment.	Most rendering formats were not designed to use images in place of borders. Images placed in table cells typically are padded. Report design is a little different from web design, and some of the techniques may not work. Reports should be tested in all common rendering formats when using image borders.
	Reports don't support events like Access does. I want to count pages, rows, groups, and report item values.	Reporting Services supports the concept of on-demand processing and `Report` and `Group` variables. These variables are set once and can be retrieved from within their scope. With the combination of these new variable types and some custom code, you can re-create those counts.
Actions	Code variables aren't tracked across multiple "postings" of an interactive report. I need to keep track of values that are modified by code as my user interacts with a report.	You can use report parameters and set the action of the interactive item to "post" to the same report, passing the changed value in the parameter collection.

REPORT RECIPES: BUILDING ON BASIC SKILLS

A recipe is a design pattern based on the design components and basic skills acquired by creating simple reports. Many of the following examples are based on solutions created for clients and demonstrate some of the learning and best practices acquired from many years of field experience. To implement these solutions, you need to apply the skills you learned in the previous chapters.

To illustrate a complete, working solution, I will step through the process to create a series of reports. Each self-contained report will be published as a report part that you will use to assemble a dashboard. Each of these examples will show you how to use a different technique and design pattern.

I won't show you every little step, but I will use techniques and skills that have been demonstrated in earlier chapters. As you follow along, go back and review the appropriate instructions.

Dashboard Solution Data Sources and Datasets

In preparation for creating all the report parts of a complete dashboard, you will create data sources and datasets to be shared and used in each report. Use SSDT to create the following shared data sources and deploy them to the report server. In Native mode, by default the designer deploys these to a folder named Data Sources. In SharePoint Integrated mode, you must create and specify a document library for shared data sources.

DATA SOURCE	TYPE	DATABASE
AdventureWorksDW_WroxSSRS2012	SQL Server	AdventureWorksDW_WroxSSRS2012
AdventureWorks_WroxSSRS2012	SQL Server	AdventureWorks_WroxSSRS2012
AdventureWorks_AS	Analysis Services	Adventure Works DW Multidimensional_WroxSSRS2012

KPI Scorecard

A scorecard is a standard in the business community for displaying the status of metrics and key performance indicators. A typical scorecard is a table report with optional row groups and drill down to allow users to progressively discover more details.

Our scorecard report will show product gross margin summaries by fiscal years and the months within each year for selected product categories. Figure 16-2 shows the finished report with the first fiscal group expanded to reveal the details for each month. The calculations and business logic for the Gross Profit Margin KPI are encapsulated in the cube. The purpose of the report is to simply surface these values.

We'll start with a shared data source for the Adventure Works DW Multidimensional_ WroxSSRS2012 database in Analysis Services. Create a new dataset using this data source and use the graphical query builder to design the query shown in Figure 16-3.

1. Expand the Date dimension and then drag the Fiscal hierarchy to the data grid.

2. Expand KPIs and drag the Product Gross Profit Margin KPI to the rightmost column in the grid to add the Value, Goal, Status, and Trend columns.

3. Close the Query Designer and Dataset Properties dialog.

4. Add a new table data region to the report body in preparation to complete the following steps. Figure 16-4 shows the table's groups in the finished report so you can see where I'm heading with this.

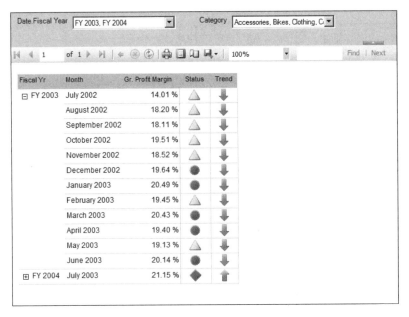

FIGURE 16-2

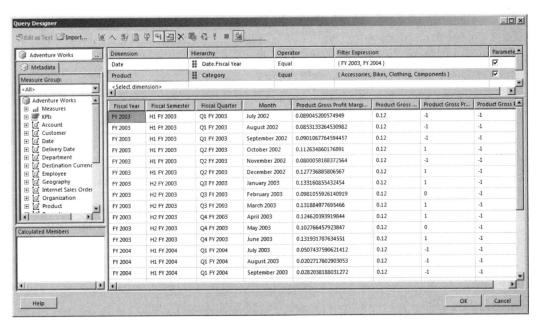

FIGURE 16-3

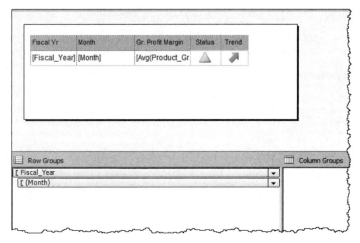

FIGURE 16-4

5. With the table selected, drag the Fiscal Year field from the Report Data pane to the Row Groups pane above the details group.

6. Edit the details group, add a group expression, and select the Month field.

7. Drag the Gross Profit Margin Value, Status, and Trend fields to separate detail columns.

8. Change the expressions for each of these cells to use the AVG function instead of the SUM function. Figure 16-5 shows the report in design view at this stage.

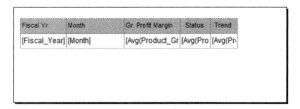

FIGURE 16-5

If you are using Report Builder to design the report, use the Insert ribbon. If you are using SSDT, use the Toolbox, shown in Figure 16-6.

9. Drag an Indicator to the Status cell in the details row of the table. The Select Indicator Type dialog opens.

10. Select an appropriate 3-state KPI indicator. I prefer the red, yellow and green state indicators that use the diamond, triangle and circle shapes.

11. Click OK to close this dialog. These icons, shown in Figure 16-6, correspond to the state field values –1, 0, and 1, respectively.

12. Drag another indicator to the Trend detail cell, and select a five-state trend directional arrow set. The icons shown in Figure 16-7 correspond to the trend state values −2, −1, 0, 1, and 2, respectively.

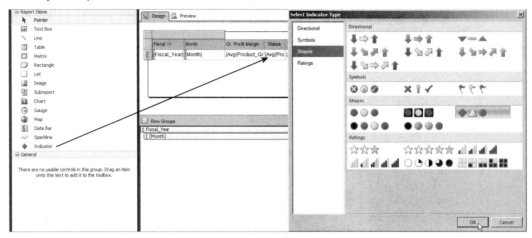

FIGURE 16-6

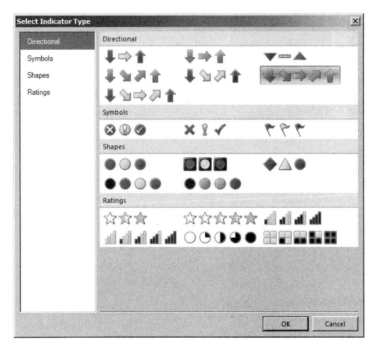

FIGURE 16-7

13. Configure the details group to hide and toggle visibility, using the Fiscal_Year textbox as a toggle item.

For a refresher on creating a drill-down table, refer to the section "Creating Drill-Down Reports and Dynamic Visibility" in Chapter 5.

Deploying a Report Part

You want each of the reports you design in this series of exercises to be published as report parts so that users can use them to assemble their own ad hoc reports. First you'll configure the design environment, and then you'll deploy the first report part. Then you'll repeat the deployment process for subsequent reports.

If you are using Report Builder, use the Report Builder menu to access the Options dialog. The first box should contain the URL for your Report server or SharePoint site. In Native mode, typically this is in the format `http://<report server name>/ReportServer`. The example shown in Figure 16-8 is the root address for a SharePoint site with Reporting Services configured in SharePoint Integrated mode.

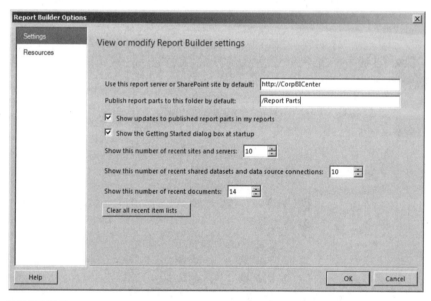

FIGURE 16-8

If you are using SSDT, open the Project Properties. You can access this dialog by right-clicking the project name in Solution Explorer.

Note that the TargetServerURL is the URL address of the report server in Native mode and the SharePoint site address in SharePoint Integrated mode, terminated with a slash. All the other addresses are for folders or SharePoint document libraries. In Native mode, these are only the folder names without the full address. In Integrated mode, use the full path for each library. Any named folders or libraries that do not exist are created when reports are deployed. In Figure 16-9, report parts are deployed to a library named Report Parts in the root SharePoint site.

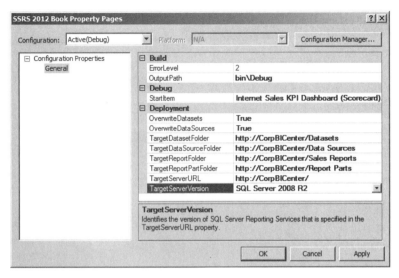

FIGURE 16-9

Publish the table as a report part. In SSDT, use the Report menu to access the Publish Report Parts dialog. In Report Builder, it's on the Report Builder menu.

 There are a few notable differences between the settings in Report Builder and SSDT when using Reporting Services in SharePoint Integrated mode. In the SSDT Project Property Pages dialog, all the SharePoint addresses are fully qualified URLs. In the Report Builder options, the report parts address is only the name of a document library, preceded by a forward slash. Do not use the full address. In the case of both tools, the target server is the URL for the report server in SSRS Native mode. It is the address of the SharePoint site when SSRS is in Integrated mode.

1. In Report Builder, select Start ➪ Publish Report Parts. You are prompted to specify a target. Select the Report Parts library, modify the report part object names (see Figure 16-10), and deploy the parts. In SSDT, select Report ➪ Publish Report Parts.

2. Uncheck all items except the Tablix.

3. Change the name to Gross Profit Margin Scorecard, and then click OK to accept these changes.

4. If you are using SSDT, right-click and deploy the report in the Solution Explorer. In Report Builder, just follow the prompts to complete the report part deployment.

This report part now is available to report Builder users in the report Parts Gallery. You'll use it in a later exercise.

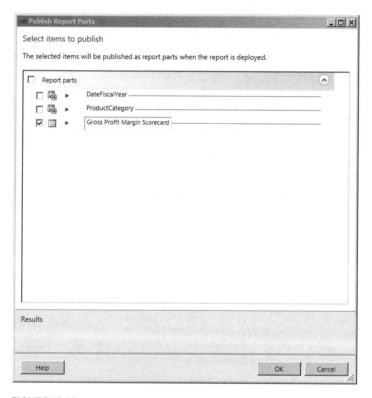

FIGURE 16-10

Interactive Sparkline and Chart

This report will include a grouped table that contains an embedded sparkline. The report also includes a separate line chart. On any row representing the summary of product category sales for a year, the user can click the sparkline or row label to see a detailed view of the same data in the chart. Figure 16-11 shows the finished report in design view.

1. Start by creating a new report. Give it any name you like. I've named mine Trend Sparkline and Detail.

2. Add a data source and dataset to connect to the Adventure Works cube in the Adventure Works DW Multidimensional_WroxSSRS2012 Analysis Services sample database.

3. Use the query designer to create the query shown in Figure 16-12.

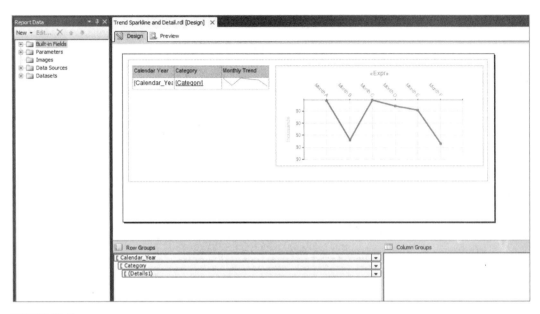

FIGURE 16-11

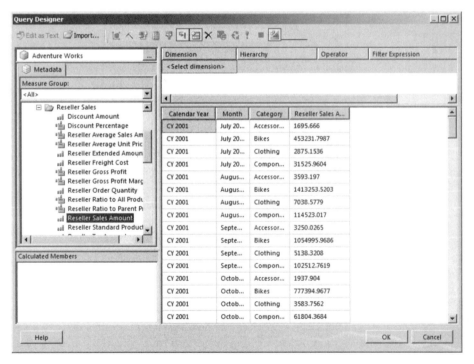

FIGURE 16-12

For reference, the MDX for the generated query should be similar to the following script. (Line breaks and indents have been added to aid readability.) If you prefer, you can switch the query designer to text mode and type this script:

```
SELECT NON EMPTY { [Measures].[Reseller Sales Amount] } ON COLUMNS
    , NON EMPTY { ([Date].[Calendar].[Month].ALLMEMBERS *
      [Product].[Category].[Category].ALLMEMBERS ) }
      DIMENSION PROPERTIES MEMBER_CAPTION, MEMBER_UNIQUE_NAME ON ROWS
FROM [Adventure Works]
    CELL PROPERTIES VALUE, BACK_COLOR, FORE_COLOR, FORMATTED_VALUE, FORMAT_STRING
    , FONT_NAME, FONT_SIZE, FONT_FLAGS
```

4. Add two parameters named `ChartCalendarYear` and `ChartCategory`. You can leave all the default properties and settings for the parameters. However, check the "Allow null value" box on the General page for each parameter, as shown in Figure 16-13.

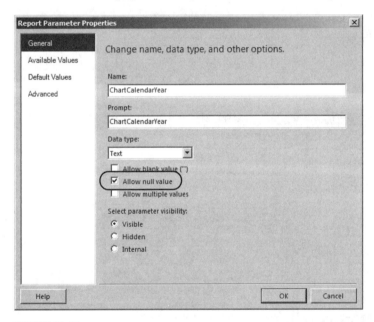

FIGURE 16-13

5. Add a rectangle to the report body. This will be used as a container to define a single report part. Resize the rectangle large enough to contain a table and large line chart.

6. Within the rectangle, add a table.

7. Click the table and create groups based on the Calendar Year and Category fields. Either remove the details group or add a group expression to it using the Category field.

8. Add a line type sparkline to the detail cell, and then click the sparkline to show the Chart Data window.

9. Add the Reseller_Sales_Amount to define the series value for the sparkline.

10. Add the Month field to define the category group, as shown in Figure 16-14.

11. Edit the category group expression so that it uses the `UniqueName` property rather than the Value of the Month field. You need to use the Expression Editor to make this change.

12. In the expression, backspace over the Value, and type or choose `UniqueName` from the property list. Close the Expression Editor and save the change.

The Category Group Properties dialog should look similar to Figure 16-15.

Next, you will use a chart to show the same values as one of the selected sparklines in detail.

13. Add a line chart next to the table.

14. Use the same category group and series value as the sparkline.

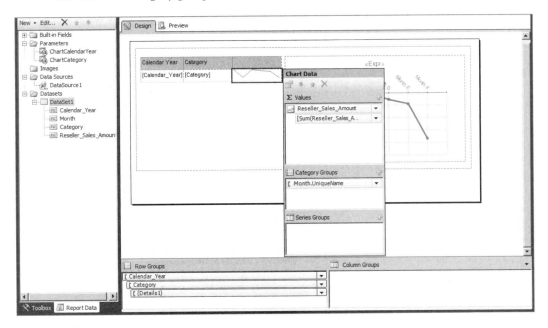

FIGURE 16-14

15. Format the chart to your liking.

In Figure 16-16, I've added some additional adornments and properties that are optional for this exercise. You're welcome to dress it up as you see fit.

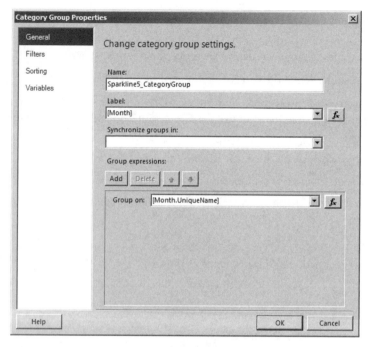

FIGURE 16-15

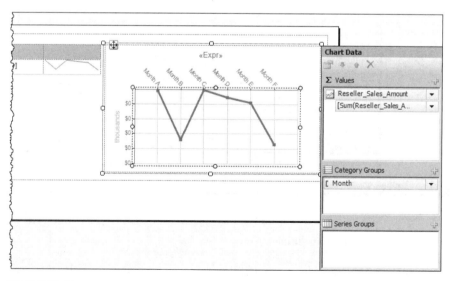

FIGURE 16-16

16. Edit the chart properties and add the two filter expressions shown in Figure 16-17. The chart is filtered to restrict records matching the `ChartCalendarYear` and `ChartCategory` parameters.

17. For each filter expression, use the Expression drop-down list to select the field. Then use the expression builder button to the right of the Value box to open the expression editor and build an expression using the appropriate parameter. For each Value expression, close the editor and save the expression.

Do the following to create the report action used to pass these parameters and filter the chart:

18. Click to select the sparkline again.

19. Edit the series by selecting Series Properties, as shown in Figure 16-18.

20. In the Series Properties dialog, use the Actions page to set a report action. Select the "Go to report" radio button.

21. Select (or type) the name of the report you are designing. This causes the same report to be executed when the user clicks this report item.

22. Add two items to the list of parameters for the report action.

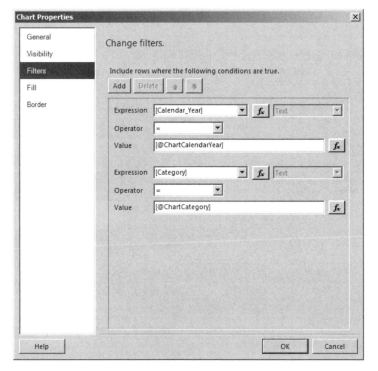

FIGURE 16-17

23. Select or type the name of each parameter. Parameter names are case-sensitive. For each parameter, select the corresponding field, as shown in Figure 16-19.

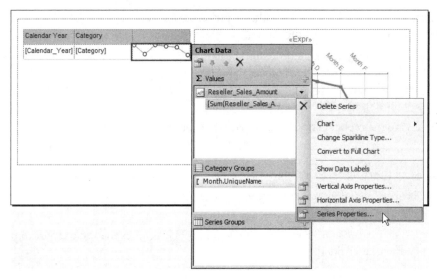

FIGURE 16-18

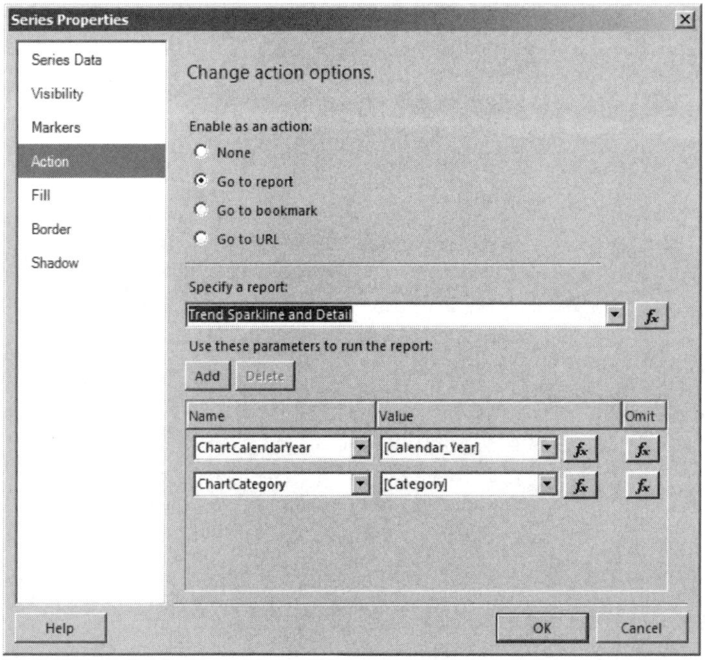

FIGURE 16-19

24. Test and make sure that the drill-through action works as expected. Hover the mouse pointer over the series line until the pointer changes to a hyperlink pointer. When you click the series line, the report should rerender, showing a chart with data that matches the sparkline.

25. After testing, replace the report name with an expression. Use the built-in fields list to use the ReportName (=Globals!ReportName). This will come in handy later, when you use this as a report part and the report name changes.

26. Optionally, repeat the same process, adding an action to the Category textbox in the second group header.

Because it can be difficult to use a small sparkline as a drill-through link, the textbox is a good alternative.

Figure 16-20 shows the report in the designer preview. When you hover the mouse pointer over the sparkline or the Category text, the hyperlink pointer is displayed. (I always tell my students that the web browser will give you the finger if it's working.)

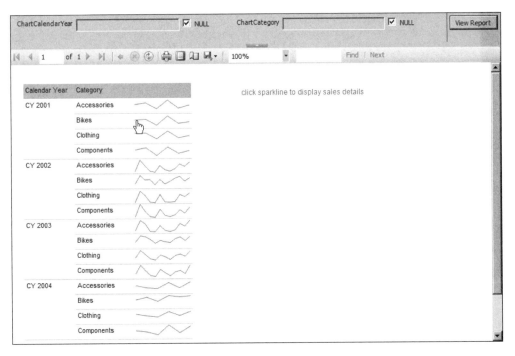

FIGURE 16-20

27. Click the link for the sparkline or text for the year and category you want to see.

The report should rerender and display a filtered chart. The chart line should show the same trend as the sparkline, with the added axis details. If you click a different row, you should see a different chart trend line for each, as shown in Figure 16-21.

Finally, publish the rectangle as a report part. In SSDT, use the Report menu to access the Publish Report Parts dialog. In Report Builder, it's on the Report Builder menu.

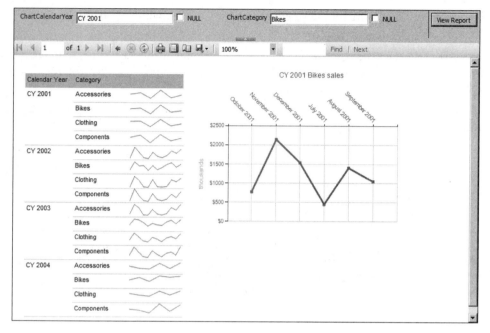

FIGURE 16-21

28. Give the rectangle a report part name, "Sparkline and Chart," as shown in Figure 16-22, and then deploy the report.

The Sparkline and Chart report part is now available for a user to add to a dashboard report in Report Builder from the Report Parts Gallery.

Map with Navigation and Zoom

The Map report item can help you visualize geographic and spatial data. A map may get its data from an external file (in a standard format such as TIGER/LINE or ESRI), from spatial shapes or point objects stored in a SQL Server database, from SQL Server functions used to calculate or derive geospatial objects, or from an external source such as the Bing Maps web service. A single map may be assembled from data and metadata obtained from any combination of these sources. In the following example, you will create a map report consisting of the following elements:

➤ Geographic boundaries in a polygon layer

➤ Geographic polygon objects colored using grouped aggregate values

➤ Locations stored as SQL Server geographic points

➤ A tile layer showing imagery from Bing Maps

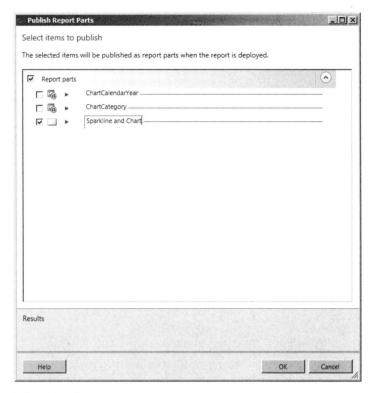

FIGURE 16-22

Let's get started! You will need to have an Internet connection in order to use the Bing Maps layer in this report.

1. Create a new report. (I have called my report "Customer US Map".)

2. Show the Properties window. (In Report Builder, the Properties window is enabled from the View ribbon.)

3. Add a data source connecting to your instance of the Adventure Works operational database (AdventureWorks_WroxSSRS2012).

4. Create a dataset using the following query. A script is provided in the sample code book downloads so that you don't have to type this long query script:

```
select TOP 1000
    c.AccountNumber
    ,p.FirstName + ' ' + p.LastName CustomerName
    ,a.AddressLine1
    ,a.City
```

```
        ,a.PostalCode
        ,a.SpatialLocation
        ,at.Name AddressTypeName
        ,s.StateProvinceCode
        ,s.Name StateProvinceName
        ,cr.CountryRegionCode
        ,cr.Name CountryRegionName
from
        Sales.Customer c inner join Person.Person p
          on c.PersonID = p.BusinessEntityID
        inner join Person.BusinessEntity b
          on p.BusinessEntityID = b.BusinessEntityID
        inner join Person.BusinessEntityAddress ba
          on b.BusinessEntityID = ba.BusinessEntityID
        inner join Person.Address a on ba.AddressID = a.AddressID
        inner join Person.AddressType at
          on ba.AddressTypeID = at.AddressTypeID
        inner join Person.StateProvince s
          on a.StateProvinceID = s.StateProvinceID
        inner join Person.CountryRegion cr
          on s.CountryRegionCode = cr.CountryRegionCode
where
        @CountryRegionCode is null or (s.CountryRegionCode = @CountryRegionCode)
```

5. Add a Map report item to the report body using the option to run the map wizard.

The Map Wizard (or map layer wizard) is necessary only to define the type of map and some initial properties. You will build most of this report using the designer, not the wizard.

6. In the first page of the map wizard, leave the default option to use map shape data from the map gallery.

The map gallery is a set of report files installed with the product that include maps of the United States. You may obtain additional map shape files for different geographies from many online resources and fee-based services. For additional information about spatial map files and data sources, refer to the following resources:

➤ SQL Server 2008 R2 Map Tips: How To Import Shapefiles Into SQL Server and Aggregate Spatial Data (http://blogs.msdn.com/b/seanboon/archive/2009/11/17/sql-server-2008-r2-map-tips-how-to-import-shapefiles-into-sql-server-and-aggregate-spatial-data.aspx)

➤ Visualizing Spatial Data (http://msdn.microsoft.com/en-us/magazine/ee335706.aspx)

7. Use the USA by State Inset map gallery selection, shown in Figure 16-23, and click Next.

8. On the second wizard page, check the box to add a Bing Maps layer, and then click Next. This adds a tile layer to the map to stream live map imagery from the Bing Map service when the user or report server has the necessary Internet connectivity. (This depends on whether the report is viewed in the designer or deployed to the report server.)

9. Accept the default, Basic Map, and click Next.

10. Select a theme, and then click Finish to complete the wizard.

11. In the report designer, click to select and then delete each of the three default scales and legends on the map.

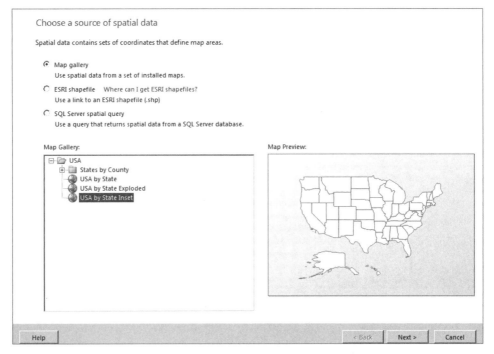

FIGURE 16-23

12. Click the map. This should select the Map Viewport object in the Properties window. Click again to show the Map Layers window to the right of the view port designer, as shown in Figure 16-24.

13. Use the second toolbar drop-down button to add a point layer.

The map port now has three layers:

➤   The polygon layer is used to display geographic shapes that the map wizard imported from the U.S. map gallery file. This content is now embedded in the report file.

➤   The tile layer visualizes bitmap content from the Bing Map web service when the report is executed.

➤   The point layer is used to plot shapes on the map using geospatial coordinates stored in the database.

In the Map Data window, each of these layers can be shown or hidden to make the design effort easier. To focus on each layer, I hide the other layers so that I can easily see the results of my work. After all the layers are designed, I make them all visible before deploying the report.

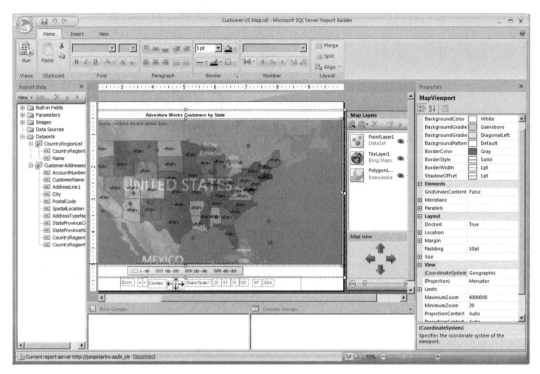

FIGURE 16-24

Geographic Shape Colors

Polygon shapes typically are used to visualize geographic boundaries, such as the U.S. states in our example. Each polygon is bound to data using key/value pairs. Several properties may be used to visualize data-bound values in the form of center point markers that may be sized, colored, or labeled to express relative or proportional values. You will use the background color of each state to show the relative number of customers in that state.

1. Choose the polygon layer in the Map Layers window. Make sure you have the polygon layer selected by checking the title in the Properties window.

2. In the Properties window, choose the dataset you created earlier in the drop-down list for the DatasetName property.

3. Select the Group property, and then click the ellipsis button (...) to open the Group Properties dialog.

4. Add a group expression, and then select the StateProvinceName field. Close the Group Properties window to accept the changes.

5. Select the BindingFieldPairs property, and click the ellipsis to open the MapBindingFieldPair Collection Editor, shown in Figure 16-25.

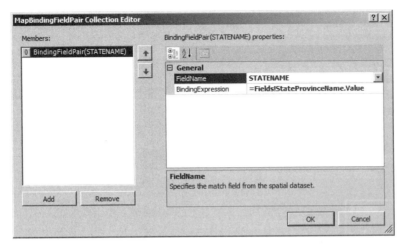

FIGURE 16-25

6. Add a binding field collection member.

7. For the `FieldName` property, select the `STATENAME` polygon identifier.

8. For the `BindingExpression` property, select the `StateProvinceName` dataset field.

9. Compare your selections to Figure 16-25, and then close the dialog window to accept the changes.

Do the following to set the background color:

10. In the Properties window for the polygon layer, expand the `CenterPointRules` property group.

11. Expand the `ColorRule` group.

12. From the (DataValue) property list, select the expression used to return the count of the `AccountNumber` field. This expression should read as follows:

```
=Count(Fields!AccountNumber.Value)
```

You set several color rule properties to make minor changes to the colors, legend, and labeling for each state. I encourage you to play with these to create a style that works best for you. You can spend a lot of time tweaking many properties in an effort to get it just right.

We'll add a label to display the customer count for each state.

13. Expand the `PolygonTemplate` group.

14. From the `Label` property list, select the same expression you used for the `ColorRule` data value to show the count of account numbers in each state.

15. Preview the report. You should see a map of the United States with various states filled in with different colors, as shown in Figure 16-26.

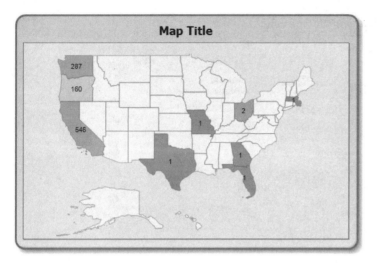

FIGURE 16-26

This example uses a default color rule where the range of grouped values is evaluated, and then a set of colors in a standard palette is applied. You can apply different color rules or use expressions to apply colors to represent grouped values in a variety of different ways.

Adding Spatial Point Markers

You can use a lot of very creative features with point markers using the many properties organized into various groups. However, the appropriate choice of properties may not seem very intuitive until you've had a chance to work with these features for a while. It's easy to get lost and spend hours on trial-and-error design, trying to find the right property settings.

If you want the marker shape, size, or color to be consistent for all points, use the properties in the `PointTemplate` group. If you want to vary the shape, size, or color based on different values, use the corresponding properties in each subgroup under the `PointRules` group. Use `ColorRule` to apply color ranges and stock or custom color palettes, `MarkerRule` to change the shapes of markers (which can include using custom graphics and icons), and `SizeRule` to vary the marker sizes based on data vales. These properties are disabled by default; you will leave them that way for this exercise.

1. Return to design view, and select the map to view the Map Data window as you did before.

2. Select the point layer, and view the Properties window.

3. Set the `DataSetName` property, using the drop-down list, to the name of the dataset you created earlier.

4. Expand the `SpatialData` group, change the Type to `Dataset`, and select the dataset you created earlier from the `DataSetName` property drop-down list.

5. For the `SpatialField` property, choose the `SpatialLocation` field. This field in the database contains a geospatial point value that the map view port can use to plot a point on the map.

6. Select the `FieldBindingPairs` property and click the ellipsis to open the MapBindingFieldPair Collection Editor.

7. If a binding pair member exists in the Members list, edit it. Otherwise, click Add.

8. Set the `FieldName` property to AccountNumber.

9. For the `BindingExpression` property, use the drop-down list to select = Fields!AccuntNumber.Value.

10. Close the editor dialog.

11. Expand the `PointRules` property group.

12. Expand the `ColorRule` group.

13. Set (Enabled) to `True`.

14. Set (Type) to `Custom`.

15. Use the (`CustomColors`) collection to add a single color. Click the ellipsis to add Lime to the `MapColor` collection.

16. Expand the `MarkerRule` group, and select the `Markers` collection property.

17. Enable the `MarkerRule`.

18. Click the ellipsis to open the Marker Collection dialog.

19. Remove all the default marker shapes, but leave a single diamond marker in the collection. Then close and accept the changes.

20. Use the `PointTemplate` properties group to set the marker's Size to 8pt.

21. Select the `ToolTip` property, and then use the Expression Builder to concatenate a list of fields to be displayed in the tooltip for each marker, which represents a customer's location. For example, I've added the following expression:

```
=Fields!CustomerName.Value & vbCrLf
& Fields!AddressTypeName.Value & ":"
& vbCrLf & Fields!AddressLine1.Value & vbCrLf & Fields!City.Value & ", "
& Fields!StateProvinceCode.Value
```

Again, you can use several properties to make visual adjustments; this can be time-consuming. When you have a working baseline map report, you can return to the designer and experiment with these properties.

22. Preview the report. You should see a working map report with colored and labeled states, and lime green diamond markers showing the location of the top 1,000 customers.

Zoom, Pan, and Tilt

I have one more set of features to add. I'll cover this topic at a high level to keep things simple.

Three useful properties help you change the view of the map and zoom it in and out. The zoom feature typically is useful only when you have included a tile layer with Bing Map content or if you are using more detailed geographic shapes than I'm using in this report.

In my finished version of this map report, I have added textboxes and images with report actions that act as pan, tilt, and zoom controls for the map. As I've demonstrated with some earlier report, a report action may be used to re-execute the same report, sending parameter values that modify content and behavior using expressions. In the advanced map report scenario, these "controls" are used to add or subtract values for these map properties to let the user reposition the map view. If you want to see the more advanced version, take a look at the finished report in the book downloads.

1. Add three numeric parameters to the report named CenterX, CenterY, and ZoomLevel. Make them all Float types.

2. In the designer, click the map. In the Properties window, expand the Viewport group and then expand the View subgroup. Note the current values of the CenterX, CenterY, and Zoom properties.

3. For each of the corresponding parameters, add the value for the corresponding property as the default value for that parameter.

My finished report, shown in Figure 16-27, has been dressed up some, but the basic features are the same.

FIGURE 16-27

I've added images and textboxes to manipulate the parameters that were added. I've also added links to move and zoom the map to a few selected metropolitan areas to show the customer locations in greater detail. The view shown in Figure 16-28 shows the map report after the SF textbox is clicked. The report action on this textbox passes the coordinates for the San Francisco Bay area.

To view the additional features of this report, open the Customer US Map report in the book download samples.

FIGURE 16-28

As before, publish the map as a report part. In the Publish Report Parts dialog, uncheck all the components except the map, and change the name to Customer US Map. Then publish it using the same steps as in the previous two examples.

Using Report Parts to Assemble a Dashboard

We've published three report parts to the server. These are now available for business users to create their own dashboard reports. Of course, you can control access to report parts, just like any other objects on the report server or SharePoint libraries. An authorized business user will require very little instruction to help with the following steps.

Now, take off your advanced report designer hat and assume the role of a business user. As such, you know little or nothing about things such as data sources, queries, SQL, MDX, or any of those other techie terms that our friends and family outside of IT are pretty clueless about.

1. If you are using SharePoint 2010 in Integrated mode, do the following:

    a. Navigate to a library designated for reports (with the Report Builder report content type enabled).

    b. Select the Documents tab under Library Tools.

    c. Use the New Document drop-down button on the Documents ribbon to select Report Builder Report, as shown in Figure 16-29.

2. If you are using Reporting Services in Native mode, navigate to a folder in Report Manager. Click the Report Builder button on the toolbar, as shown in Figure 16-30.

3. Report Builder opens and prompts you for a report style and design wizard. Choose the Blank Report option.

4. Click the report title, and enter some text for the title. I've titled my report "Sales Dashboard."

5. Click the Insert tab, and then click the leftmost button on the ribbon, labeled Report Parts. This shows the Report Part Gallery on the right side of the design area, as shown in Figure 16-31.

6. In the Report Part Gallery pane, click the search button without entering any search text. This shows all the report parts in the default library. Of course, you can also enter text to search for specific items.

7. Locate the Gross Profit Margin Scorecard, and drag it to the report body to the left, just under the report title.

8. Drag the Sparkline and Chart report part below the first item.

9. Drag the Customer US Map report part to the next available area below these two items.

Figure 16-32 shows the completed report in design view. Note that all of the dependent objects — parameters, data sources, and datasets — have been added to the report with no additional effort from the user designing the report. As a user, all you need to do is save and run the report.

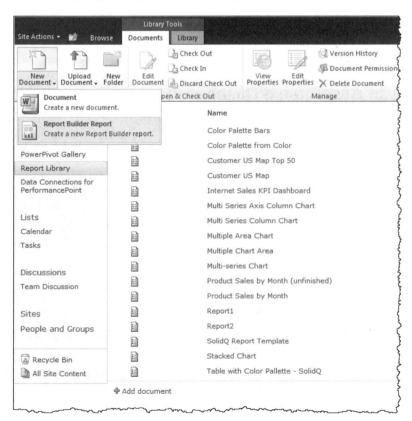

FIGURE 16-29

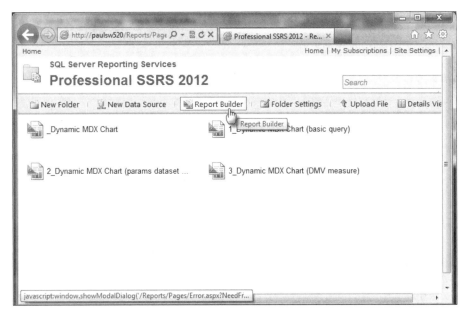

FIGURE 16-30

FIGURE 16-31

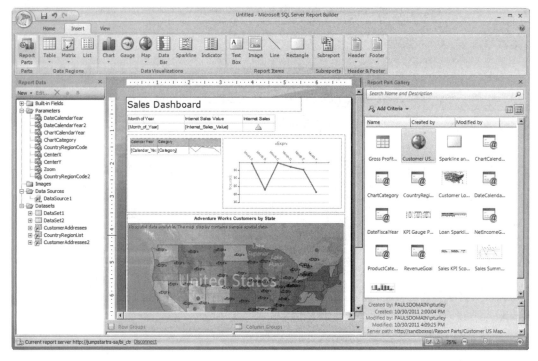

FIGURE 16-32

If you switch back to design view, you can drag around each report part to arrange them any way you like. Savvy users can use this as a starting point to modify the design. Nontechnical business users can use this technique to assemble completely functional reports and composite dashboards without needing technical design skills.

Dynamic Colors and Themes

This is one of my favorite tricks. For years I struggled with selecting and using matching colors to style my reports. Depending on how plain or artistic I think a report should be, I use coordinated colors for the report background, title text, report and page headers and footers, group headers and footers, borders and contrasting text, chart lines, and bars and gauge properties. In some cases, report styling can take many hours. After you're finished, if you're unhappy with the result, you can start over.

Typically we invest most of our time and effort into the functional report design. We want to make sure that the dataset query is written efficiently, and that the numbers and other values on the report are accurate and easy for users to understand. The last thing on our minds is the aesthetic style of a report and the colors that we will ultimately use for header fills, borders, and fonts. These decisions usually are made at the last minute, after all the design work and testing are complete.

I usually try to use colors that match an organization's corporate standards — perhaps the company logo. Some companies have a well-defined color palette and are meticulous about making sure that all their intranet, portal, and report content has the same look and feel. Others may not have stringent guidelines about such things as colors and report layout.

A common problem with mixing different colors in a report is that what looks good at design time may be problematic when printed on a black-and-white printer or viewed by color-challenged users. Even computer monitors and digital projectors translate colors differently. When was the last time you watched a PowerPoint presentation and the presenter apologized for projecting text over a colored background that "looked good on my monitor when I created the deck"? Color is actually a complicated business. Many career professionals concern themselves with the subtleties of color matching and the appropriate use of color in marketing and presentations. There are many books and resources on this topic, but most report designers don't have the time or patience to read them.

If you're not a seasoned graphic artist, you should appreciate the following solution: Using different shades of a single color to build a palette gives you several different matching color fills. People can easily discern eight or more shades of a color that not only will look good together but also will translate to an accurate grayscale for printing and color-blind users.

Here's an example to make the point. This book is printed in black and white, so you have the benefit of being a colorblind reader. Figure 16-33 shows two color scales. The one on the left is red mixed with white on a graduated scale in steps of 20%. The box at the top of the scale is pure red, and the next one down is 20% more white, and so on. The right side starts with red, and then each box below it adds 20% black.

Now let's do the same thing with green. Figure 16-34 shows similar scales, starting with pure green at the top and then mixing it with white and black in the same proportions. It looks the same, doesn't it?

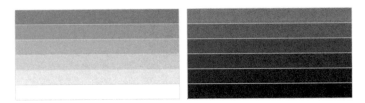

FIGURE 16-33

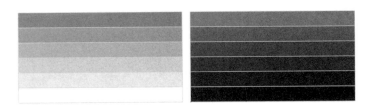

FIGURE 16-34

The scales shown in the previous figures are two tables bound to a dataset that returns the values 0, 20, 40, 60, 80, and 100. These values are passed to a function that mixes a base color with a percentage of white or black to produce any shade I want. The base color can be passed into the report in a parameter, making it easy to restyle the entire report with no rework.

How does this work? It's actually a simple mathematical calculation, because all digital colors are really just a mixture of red, green, and blue, each on a scale from 0 to 255. The RGB value for red is 255,0,0; green is 0,255,0; and purple is 255,0,255.

The `BackgroundColor` property of the textboxes is set using a custom function that that takes three arguments: a string representing the RGB color base color, a percentage, and the word White or Black to indicate the scale. Equal proportions of the red, green, and blue values are mixed to produce a shade of that base color. Any object in the report can be colored in this manner using a simple expression like this:

```
=Code.RGBToHexPalette("255,0,255", 40, "White")
```

The following function can be embedded in each report, as I've done here, or it can be compiled into a .NET assembly and reference by several reports and called as an object method:

```
' Creates colors in different shades within the same color palette,
' mixing each RGB value in the same proportion in percentage to either
' black or white color scale.
' Paul Turley
'
' Enter 3 arguments:
' Comma-separated string for the RGB value of the color as "RRR,GGG,BBB"
' Percentage as a whole integer (0 to 100)
' "Black" or "White" to indicate the color scale range.
' 0 percent will return either black or white.
Function RGBToHexPalette(ByVal PaletteRGB As String, ByVal PalettePct As _
    Integer, ByVal PaletteScale As String) As String

    Dim sNumString As String()
    Dim InR As Integer, InG As Integer, InB As Integer
    Dim OutR As Byte, OutG As Byte, OutB As Byte

    sNumString = Split(PaletteRGB, ",")
    InR = CInt(sNumString(0))
    InG = CInt(sNumString(1))
    InB = CInt(sNumString(2))

    Select Case PaletteScale
       Case "Black"
       OutR = InR * PalettePct / 100
       OutG = InG * PalettePct / 100
       OutB = InB * PalettePct / 100
    Case "White"
       OutR = (((100 - PalettePct) / 100) * (255 - InR)) + InR
       OutG = (((100 - PalettePct) / 100) * (255 - InG)) + InG
       OutB = (((100 - PalettePct) / 100) * (255 - InB)) + InB
    End Select
       Return "#" & Right("0" & Hex(OutR), 2) & Right("0" & _
       Hex(OutG), 2) & Right("0" & Hex(OutB), 2)
End Function
```

Several examples of this technique are included in the sample reports provided in the book downloads.

Table Report with Dynamic Columns

Over time, similar reports may be designed from variations of common queries and datasets. Creating one report to meet all these requirements can minimize development time and maintenance overhead. By evaluating existing reports and making modifications, future requirements can be met without creating yet another report. Parameters and expressions may be used to dynamically sort and group data. By hiding and showing table columns, a report can accommodate different queries that return similar but different sets of fields.

The following sample report contains a table data region that displays different columns when presented with different query results. In this scenario, three different sets of requirements are identified:

> Requirement set 1:
>
> > Group on: `Category`, `Subcategory`
> >
> > Aggregate: `SalesAmt`, `TaxAmt`, `FreightAmt`
>
> Requirement set 2:
>
> > Group on: `Category`, `Subcategory`
> >
> > Aggregate: `SalesAmt`, `FreightAmt`
>
> Requirement set 3:
>
> > Group on: `Category`, `Product`
> >
> > Aggregate: `SalesAmt`, `TaxAmt`

Three separate queries can be presented to a report using expressions and parameters using a few different techniques. A parameter can return an entire SELECT statement to an expression, the query can be modified in an expression, or a custom code function or conditional logic may be used to change the name of a stored procedure or view stored in the database. For this example to be portable, my report uses a parameter to pass in one of three separate SELECT statements.

As you can see, there are six possible fields in various combinations. Normally a query would be written to return the specific fields, a table data region would be added to the report, and then groups would be designed for only the two fields defined for that report. When the group fields (say, Category and Subcategory) are dragged into the Row Groups pane in the report designer, two groups are defined, and two group columns are added in the table's group header area.

Designing the Report

We start with a query that returns all six columns. When this query is executed the first time, the report designer adds all six fields to the dataset fields collection in the report definition:

```
SELECT
    c.EnglishProductCategoryName Category
  , s.EnglishProductSubcategoryName Subcategory
  , p.EnglishProductName Product
  , SUM(f.SalesAmount) SalesAmt
  , SUM(f.TaxAmt) TaxAmt
  , SUM(f.Freight) FreightAmt
```

```
FROM
    DimProductCategory c
    INNER JOIN DimProductSubcategory s
    ON c.ProductCategoryKey = s.ProductCategoryKey
    INNER JOIN DimProduct p
    ON s.ProductSubcategoryKey = p.ProductSubcategoryKey
    INNER JOIN FactInternetSales f
    ON p.ProductKey = f.ProductKey
GROUP BY
    c.EnglishProductCategoryName
    , s.EnglishProductSubcategoryName
    , p.EnglishProductName
```

Next, add a table to the report body, select the table, and then drag the first three fields to the Row Groups pane. Drag the three measure fields (the `SalesAmt`, `TaxAmt`, and `FreightAmt` numeric fields that should be summed at the group levels) into the three data cells to the right of the groups. Then set the `Format` to `Currency` for these cells.

This is a pretty typical table report design so far, as shown in Figure 16-35.

Here's where we change things up a bit. You cannot hide group header columns. If you look carefully at the table in design view, you'll see a double-dashed line separating the group header column cells from the data cells (between `Product` and `SalesAmt`). This indicates that the *static* cells on the left will render one cell per distinct group value and the *dynamic* cells on the right will render one cell per value on detail rows. If any total row headers or footers are added to the design, or if the groups are set up to drill down, the dynamic cells also return aggregate totals for their respective group ranges. By definition, this is the difference in behavior for static and dynamic cells.

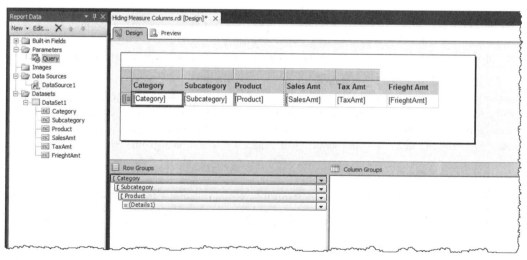

FIGURE 16-35

Problem: A column of static cells cannot be hidden.

Solution: Group header values don't have to use static cells.

Drag and drop the three group fields (`Category`, `Subcategory`, and `Product`) into new cells on the right side of the double-dashed separator line, and then delete the three original group header columns. A dialog box asks if you want to remove the groups or just the columns, as shown in Figure 16-36. You want to delete the columns and leave the groups intact.

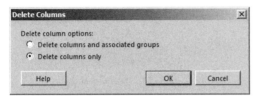

FIGURE 16-36

At this point the table repeats the nondistinct group field values. You can fix this by setting the textboxes in these cells to hide duplicate values within their respective groups. For each cell, I use the drop-down list in the `HideDuplicates` property to select the name of that field's group. If you run the report, it looks like a grouped table with nonrepeating header columns.

Add a parameter to the report named `pQuery`, and add three available values. Each value is a complete `SELECT` statement that returns a different combination of the same fields.

Available value 1: Label: Sales, Tax and Freight by Subcategory:

```
SELECT
    c.EnglishProductCategoryName Category
  , s.EnglishProductSubcategoryName Subcategory
  , SUM(f.SalesAmount) SalesAmt
  , SUM(f.TaxAmt) TaxAmt
  , SUM(f.Freight) FreightAmt
FROM
    DimProductCategory c
    INNER JOIN DimProductSubcategory s
    ON c.ProductCategoryKey = s.ProductCategoryKey
    INNER JOIN DimProduct p
    ON s.ProductSubcategoryKey = p.ProductSubcategoryKey
    INNER JOIN FactInternetSales f
    ON p.ProductKey = f.ProductKey
GROUP BY
    c.EnglishProductCategoryName
  , s.EnglishProductSubcategoryName
```

Available value 2: Label: Sales and Freight by Subcategory:

```
SELECT
    c.EnglishProductCategoryName Category
  , s.EnglishProductSubcategoryName Subcategory
  , SUM(f.SalesAmount) SalesAmt
  , SUM(f.Freight) FreightAmt
FROM
    DimProductCategory c
    INNER JOIN DimProductSubcategory s
    ON c.ProductCategoryKey = s.ProductCategoryKey
    INNER JOIN DimProduct p
```

```
        ON s.ProductSubcategoryKey = p.ProductSubcategoryKey
        INNER JOIN FactInternetSales f
        ON p.ProductKey = f.ProductKey
    GROUP BY
        c.EnglishProductCategoryName
      , s.EnglishProductSubcategoryName
```

Available value 3: Label: Sales, Tax and Freight by Product:

```
    SELECT
        c.EnglishProductCategoryName Category
      , p.EnglishProductName Product
      , SUM(f.SalesAmount) SalesAmt
      , SUM(f.TaxAmt) TaxAmt
    FROM
        DimProductCategory c
        INNER JOIN DimProductSubcategory s
        ON c.ProductCategoryKey = s.ProductCategoryKey
        INNER JOIN DimProduct p
        ON s.ProductSubcategoryKey = p.ProductSubcategoryKey
        INNER JOIN FactInternetSales f
        ON p.ProductKey = f.ProductKey
    GROUP BY
        c.EnglishProductCategoryName
      , p.EnglishProductName
```

As you can see, each of these queries returns a different combination of fields. But each one was present in the original query that was used to create the fields that are still part of the report definition.

We can feed a selected query string to the dataset by using an expression in place of the query. Open the dataset properties, and use the expression builder. Delete all the query text, and replace it with this simple expression:

```
=Parameters!pQuery.Value
```

1. Click the table in the designer. This shows the row and column selection handles. For each column, repeat the following steps:

2. Right-click the column header and choose Column Visibility.

3. In the Column Visibility dialog, select the radio button labeled "Show or hide based on an expression."

4. Use the expression builder to create an expression that hides the column if that column is missing from the dataset result set:

```
=Parameters!pQuery.Value
```

That's it! Switching to the preview shows that you now have a report that is completely flexible. Figure 16-37 shows a view of the report with two of three group headers and two of three detail columns. The Subcategory and Freight amount columns are nowhere to be found.

FIGURE 16-37

Selecting any one of the three parameters causes the report to show only the columns returned by the corresponding query.

SUMMARY

We just finished the extended tour of advanced report design solution patterns. You may not use every one of these designs in your professional reports to meet the immediate needs of your business. However, I'll bet you'll find similar applications that the same or similar techniques will address.

We started with a high-level discussion of report solution requirement gathering, and you learned that report design solutions are successful when you can clearly define the scope and purpose of a request. Reports are best designed from a detailed, written specification from the business owner. We designed a reporting solution in phases that include planning, design, implementation, testing and validation. Advanced reports should be deployed to a test server for inspection and testing before they are migrated to production servers for the entire business to use.

You designed three separate reports that were designed to be deployed as report parts. After completing the KPI scorecard, Interactive Sparkline and Chart and the Map reports; you assembled the report parts to create a master dashboard report, complete with datasets, parameters and interactive actions.

This chapter has given you some valuable tools that you can take with you to help you create the right report solutions for your business and users. Download and use the samples to practice these techniques and then go out and solve some tough data problems with high-value report designs.

PART VI
Administering Reporting Services

17

Content Management

WHAT'S IN THIS CHAPTER?

➤ Using Report Manager

➤ Content management activities

➤ Item-level security

➤ Content management automation

As discussed in Chapter 2, reports are made available through a three-phase process of authoring, management, and delivery called the reporting life cycle.

Much of the material in the preceding chapters focused on the authoring phase of the life cycle. This chapter marks the book's transition to focusing on the management and delivery phases. The goal of this and the subsequent chapters is to show you how to effectively put content you have spent hours, days, or even weeks developing into the hands of your users. Even if you're focused primarily on report authoring, you are encouraged to understand this material.

In this chapter, you explore the management of Reporting Services content. Reporting Services content includes reports, report models, shared data sources, and report resources as well as the folder structure within which these are maintained. Shared schedules, used by reports for subscriptions, history, and snapshots, are also addressed in this chapter even though these items are maintained at the site level, outside the folder structure.

In Native mode, Reporting Services content management is performed primarily through the Report Manager application. Scripts executed through the RS utility provide an alternative means of performing these tasks.

In SharePoint Integrated mode, content management activities are performed in a similar manner but through the SharePoint site or through the ReportServer web services endpoint. In this mode, Report Manager and the RS utility are unavailable.

USING REPORT MANAGER

Report Manager is the primary content management tool for Reporting Services installations running in Native mode. The application provides an easy-to-use graphical interface to navigate the Reporting Services site. Through Report Manager, various items can be accessed or even altered, assuming you have the appropriate permissions.

For default installations, Report Manager is accessed through the following URL:

```
http://<servername>/reports
```

If you've installed Reporting Services as a named instance, the URL you will use has this form:

```
http://<servername>/reports_<instancename>
```

If you are unable to connect to Report Manager, verify with your administrator that the application has not been explicitly disabled or that its URL reservation is not configured for an alternative address.

When you first connect to Report Manager, you see the Contents page of the Home folder, as shown in Figure 17-1. A number of Report Manager's basic features are on display.

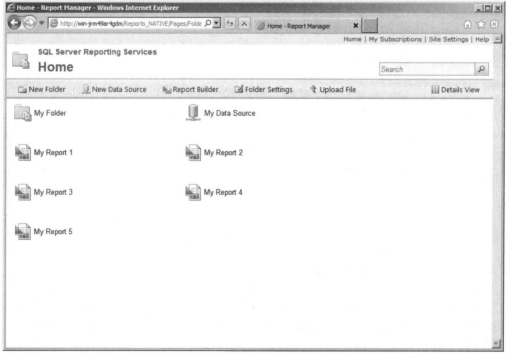

FIGURE 17-1

At the top of the page is the header. The header provides navigational assistance and access to site-level functionality. On the main page you see a list of reports, folders, and data sources contained in the current Report Manager environment.

By clicking an item on the page, you can navigate to that item. For example, if you click a report, the report loads for you to view. If you click a folder, you enter that folder. Clicking the Home link always takes you back to the Home page.

On the right side of the header, you will notice a series of links. Which links appear depend on your rights on the system. Table 17-1 lists potentially available links.

TABLE 17-1

LINK	DESCRIPTION
Home	Takes you to the Content page of the Home folder.
My Subscriptions	Takes you to the My Subscriptions site-level page. This page displays all the subscriptions on the site that you own.
Site Settings	Provides access to the Site Settings pages. From these pages you can modify general site-level settings, site-level security, and shared schedules.
Help	Opens a separate browser window displaying the Report Manager Help and Support pages.

Just below these links is a Search box. When you enter text in the box and click the button to its right, Report Manager performs a case-insensitive search for items with names and descriptions matching the text you entered. The search, as presented through Report Manager, does not support wildcards or Boolean operators.

Below the header is the page body. The header varies little across the site, but the page body varies significantly based on the type of item being accessed. The type of item and its characteristics identify the Report Manager page. Each type of item in Reporting Services supports one or more Report Manager pages.

You access a page by first selecting a particular item. That item's default page is presented. Other pages are accessible through tabs.

Figure 17-2 shows the Properties page of the My Folder folder. You access this page by selecting the My Folder folder from the Home page and then clicking the Folder Settings button.

Back on the Home page, the Details View link in the gray bar above the list provides a more detailed view of the items on the page. In Figure 17-3 the page has been reloaded, with content displayed in a tabular format. Also notice that more options are available through the gray bar.

The gray bar gives you access to various actions throughout the Report Manager application. Notice in Figure 17-3 that the Delete and Move buttons are disabled. Many buttons on the gray bar are disabled until one or more items on the page are selected. You select an item by clicking the checkbox to its left. You can select all items by checking the checkbox in the table heading.

Report Manager frequently displays information using columns and rows as shown in Figure 17-3. The topmost row identifies field names, and the rows below represent individual items. Each column is a data field such as Type, Name, Description, Last Run, Modified Date, and Modified By as shown in Figure 17-3.

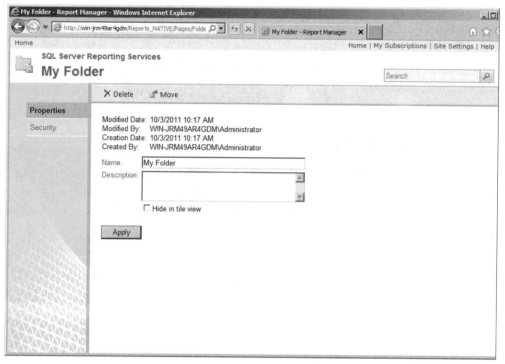

FIGURE 17-2

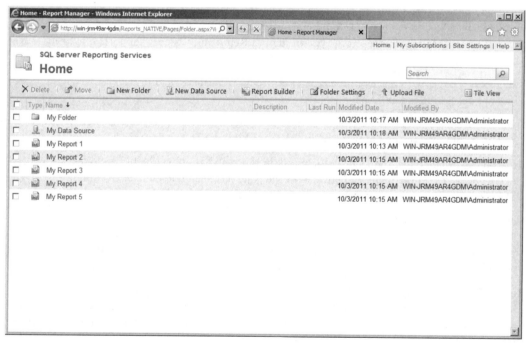

FIGURE 17-3

Many tables allow you to sort their contents by clicking individual fields. Not all fields are sortable, but you can easily identify which ones are by placing the cursor just above a field name and watching the cursor change to indicate that a link is present.

CONTENT MANAGEMENT ACTIVITIES

Now that you are familiar with Report Manager basics, it's time to look at the management of various Reporting Services items through the application. If you skipped the preceding section, please review it quickly so that you are familiar with the terminology used here.

The following sections explore the management of these items:

➤   Folders

➤   Shared data sources

➤   Report models

➤   Reports

➤   Report resources

➤   Shared schedules

Folders

Most Reporting Services items are housed within a folder hierarchy. This provides a simple, familiar structure for organizing content.

The folder hierarchy is a virtual structure; in other words, you will not find it recreated on a Reporting Services server's drives. Instead, the structure exists as a set of self-referencing records in the ReportServer database.

The default page for the Home folder and every folder in Reporting Services is the Contents page. On the Contents page, items within the folder including any child folders are presented in a list.

The items on the Contents page are identified by name, an optional description, and an icon denoting the item's type, such as Folder, Report, Linked Report, Report Model, Shared Data Source, Resource, Standard Subscriptions, or Data-Driven Subscriptions.

The gray bar at the top of the folder Contents page list presents buttons for creating new folders and shared data sources and uploading items to the folder. You will explore creating new shared data sources and uploading items later in this chapter. Of interest now is the New Folder button.

Clicking the New Folder button takes you to the New Folder page, as shown in Figure 17-4. On this page, you enter a name and description for your new folder. Selecting the "Hide in tile view" option makes the folder hidden in its parent folder's list view.

Clicking OK submits the request to create the new folder. If a folder or other item with the same name already exists under the parent folder, an error message is presented. If the request is successful, you are taken back to the Contents page from which you originally clicked the New Folder button, as shown in Figure 17-5.

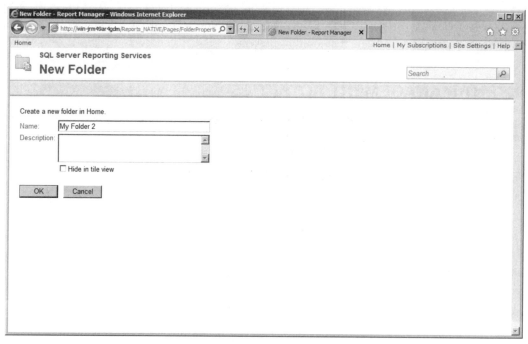

FIGURE 17-4

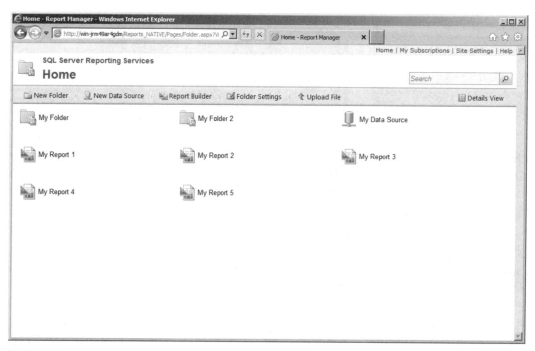

FIGURE 17-5

If the folder is configured to be hidden in list view, you need to switch to the parent folder's detail view to see the new folder. To switch to detail view, click the Details View button in the gray bar.

 To switch back to list view, click the Tile View button in the detail view's gray bar.

In detail view, all the folder's contents are displayed in a tabular format, as discussed in the preceding section. The table supports Edit, Type, Name, Description, Last Run, Modified Date, and Modified By fields, with all but the Edit selection checkbox being sortable.

Clicking an individual item's Name field takes you to that item's Properties page. Clicking an item's Type icon or name takes you to that item's default page. For reports and reporting resources, the default page is the View page. For folders, the default page is the Contents page in list mode. For all other items, the default page is the Properties page.

Selecting one or more items enables the Delete and Move buttons in the gray bar. The Delete button confirms and then drops the items you have selected. The Move button takes you to Move Items page, which requires you to select where in the site's folder structure the items are to be moved. If you are deleting or moving a folder, the operation succeeds only if you have the required permissions on each item it contains.

Now that you know how to create, alter, and remove folders, what kind of folder structure should you build for your site? There are a variety of reasoned opinions on this subject, providing guidance on naming conventions, standard folder locations, and the balance of the breadth and width of the site's hierarchy.

However you ultimately decide to organize your site, we recommend that it be driven by a set of guidelines adopted before site construction. In developing those guidelines, we further recommend that you keep the end-user experience at the forefront of your thought process and consider the maintenance and security implications of your scheme. (Security is discussed later in this chapter.) You should review the guidelines with administrators, report developers, and end-user representatives not only to obtain support but also to begin the process of educating those who will be working with the guidelines.

Shared Data Sources

Shared data sources hold connection information in a secure manner, allowing this information to be centrally administered while being shared among reports and report models throughout the site.

Report authors often create shared data sources as part of the report development process. In SQL Server Data Tools (SSDT), you can add these to the Report Server project by right-clicking the Shared Data Sources folder in the Solution Explorer, selecting Add New Data Source, and providing the required information in the Shared Data Source dialog. The shared data source item is deployed to the site folder identified by the project's `TargetDataSourceFolder` property. You can access this property by right-clicking the project in Solution Explorer and selecting Properties.

To create a shared data source item without the help of a report-authoring tool, open Report Manager and navigate to the folder within which the item will be housed. Click the New Data Source button on the gray bar of the folder's Contents page. In the resulting New Data Source page, shown in Figure 17-6, enter a name and description for the new item. Set the options that control whether the item is displayed in its parent folder's Contents page list view and/or enabled for use on the site. Then select the registered data extension to be used, and enter an appropriate connection string. Which data extension you select determines the syntax of the connection string.

 It is important to note that Report Manager does not automatically verify the connection. To test the connection, click the Test Connection button on the creation screen.

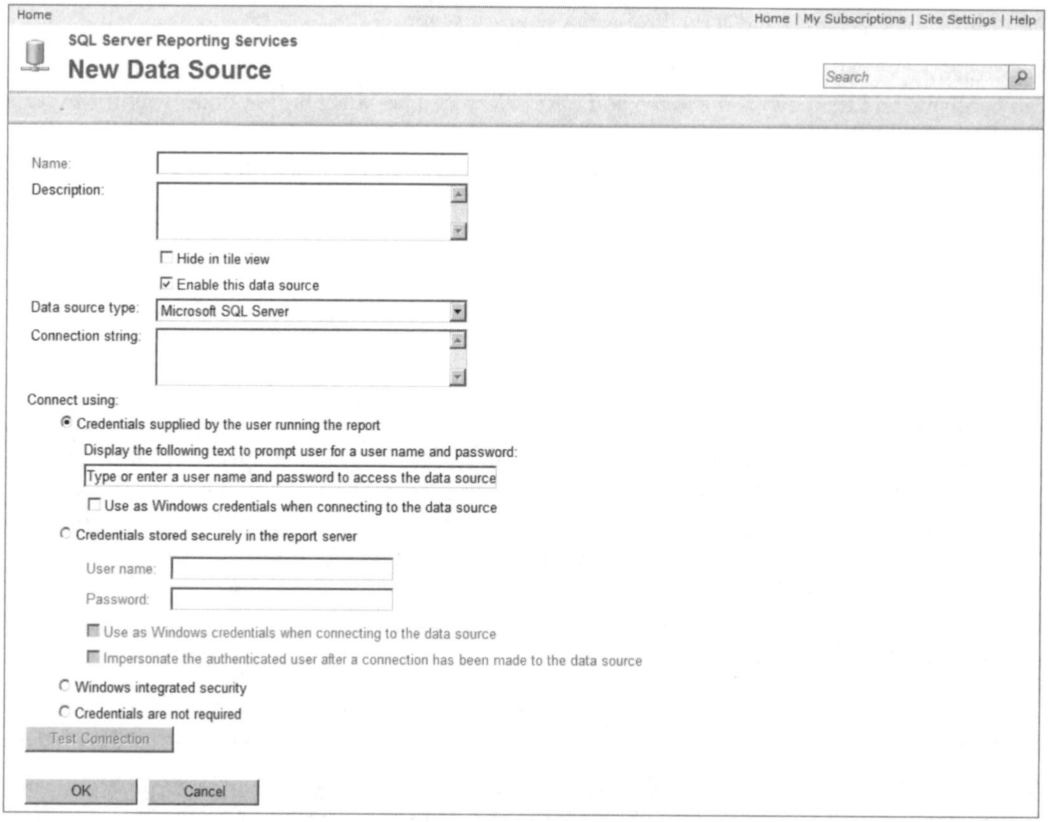

Home   Home | My Subscriptions | Site Settings | Help

SQL Server Reporting Services
New Data Source

Search

Name:
Description:

☐ Hide in tile view
☑ Enable this data source

Data source type: Microsoft SQL Server

Connection string:

Connect using:
  ◉ Credentials supplied by the user running the report
     Display the following text to prompt user for a user name and password:
     Type or enter a user name and password to access the data source
     ☐ Use as Windows credentials when connecting to the data source
  ○ Credentials stored securely in the report server
     User name:
     Password:
     ☐ Use as Windows credentials when connecting to the data source
     ☐ Impersonate the authenticated user after a connection has been made to the data source
  ○ Windows integrated security
  ○ Credentials are not required
  Test Connection

  OK   Cancel

FIGURE 17-6

Below the connection string, set the security context to be used when establishing the connection. You have four basic options, a couple of which support one or more variations.

The "Credentials supplied by the user running the report" option allows you to configure a prompt to be presented to the user. The check box associated with this option instructs Reporting Services whether to treat these as Windows user credentials.

The "Credentials stored securely in the report server" option allows you to enter a username/password combination that will be encrypted and stored in the primary Reporting Services application database. Again, you have the option to have Reporting Services treat these as Windows or source-specific credentials. The associated "Impersonate the authenticated user after a connection has been made to the data source" option allows database-user impersonation to be employed after the connection has been established. This option provides support for the use of SETUSER functionality within SQL Server.

The "Windows integrated security" option allows the user to be impersonated when making the connection to the external data source. For this feature to work, the external data source must be local to the Reporting Services server, or Kerberos must be enabled on the domain.

In addition, Reporting Services must have support for integrated security enabled for this option to be employed.

The final option, "Credentials are not required," instructs Reporting Services to use the Unattended Execution Account when establishing the connection. This account is not enabled by default and is not recommended for use against most data sources. Whether or not the Unattended Execution Account is enabled, the "Credentials are not required" option is provided. If you attempt to leverage a data source with this option set and the unattended execution account not enabled, you receive an error indicating an invalid data source credential setting. The unattended execution account is covered in more detail in Chapter 19.

Clicking OK creates the data source item. Clicking the new shared data source item takes you to its Properties page.

On the Properties page, you can move, rename, or delete the data source. Moving or renaming a shared data source does not impact the Reporting Services items that refer to it. Deleting a shared data source breaks the reports, report models, and subscriptions that depend on it. To view items that refer to the shared data source before deleting it, click the shared data source's Dependent Items and Subscriptions tabs on the left. If the shared data source is deleted, the listed items are broken until they are pointed to a new data source.

The shared data source Properties page also has a Generate Model button, as discussed in the next section.

Report Models

Report models provide the data layer for ad hoc reporting. They record metadata about the structures of an external data source in a manner that makes interaction with these easier for less-technical users. In Reporting Services 2012, report models support SQL Server, Analysis Services, and Oracle (9.2.0.3 or later) data sources. Chapter 18 has more information about report models.

A report model is typically constructed through a report model project in SSDT. As an alternative to using SSDT to construct a report model, you can assemble one from within Report Manager. To do this, locate a SQL Server, Analysis Services, or Oracle shared data source on the site. On the shared data source's Properties page, verify that the data source uses stored credentials or Windows Integrated security. Then click the Generate Model button at the top of the screen to open the New Model page, shown in Figure 17-7. Enter a name and description for your model. If you want to place the model somewhere else on the site, use the Change Location button to set an alternative location.

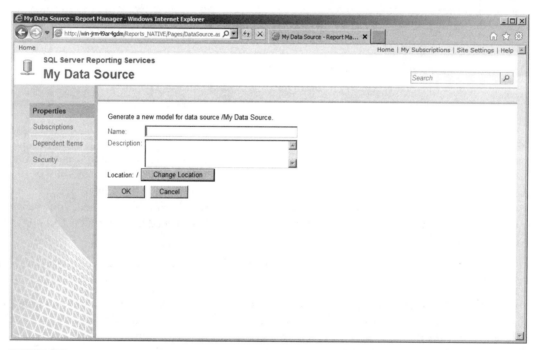

FIGURE 17-7

Clicking OK starts the model generation process. Depending on the data source used, model generation can be an intensive process, taking quite a bit of time. When it is done, you see the new report model's Properties page.

From here you can edit the report model's properties and perform basic item management. Before deleting a report model, be sure to review the Dependent Items and Subscriptions pages to identify which Reporting Services items will be impacted by this operation.

The model's Properties page also provides functionality to regenerate the model. You need to regenerate the model when structural changes have occurred in the external data source that need to be reflected in the model. Like model generation, model regeneration can take quite a bit of time.

If a report model is in use when you attempt to regenerate it, an error occurs. To prevent this, locate the shared data source used by the model and disable it from its Properties page. Reenable it as soon as model regeneration is complete.

The Properties page also provides access to the model definition. Clicking the Edit link returns an SMDL file that you can add to a SSDT Report Model project for modification. SSDT separates the data source view and model definition components, so you need to redeploy the model from SSDT after making changes to it.

In addition to the Properties page, Report Manager provides Data Sources Properties, Clickthrough Reports Properties, Model Item Security Properties, and Security Properties pages to help you manage report models.

The Data Sources Properties page allows you to select the data source used by the report model. As mentioned, report models are limited to SQL Server, Analysis Services, and Oracle 9.2.0.3 (or later) and must use stored credentials or Windows integrated security.

The Clickthrough Properties page allows you to replace the pages Report Builder generates when users click interactive data elements in reports based on report models. Through this interface you can specify which custom reports are used when one or multiple elements are engaged.

The Model Item Security Properties page allows you to specify a finer level of access to data provided through the report model. By enabling the "Secure individual model items independently for this model" option, you can select which model elements inherit permissions from their parent items and which grant read access to a custom list of groups and users. Books Online provides much more information on the use of this feature.

Reports

Reports present data to end users in an easy-to-consume manner. They consist of a set of instructions encoded in Report Definition Language (RDL) that is processed by Reporting Services to retrieve data from one or more sources and present this data in various report elements.

The Report Designer interface accessed through a Report Server project in SSDT is commonly used to assemble reports. The Report Server project's `TargetReportFolder` property defines where on the Reporting Services site the report will be deposited when the project is deployed. To access this property, right-click the project in the Solution Explorer window and select Properties.

As an alternative to using SSDT (or another report authoring tool) to deploy a report to the site, you can use Report Manager's file upload functionality. To do this, open the folder within which you want to place the report, and click the Upload File button on the gray bar of the folder's Contents page. Through the resulting Upload File page, shown in Figure 17-8, identify the RDL file for the report and set the basic report properties. Click OK to upload the file. The file now appears as an item in the folder's list and/or detail views, depending on how it is configured.

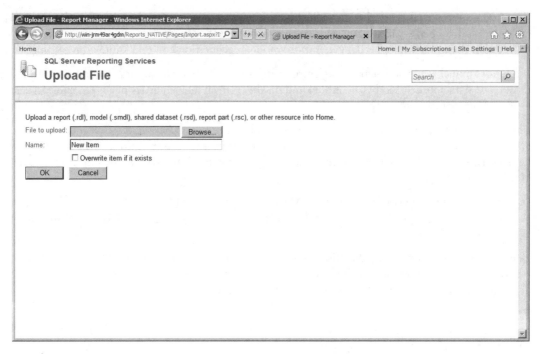

FIGURE 17-8

Clicking a report item takes you to its View page, which presents an HTML rendered version of the report. It's a good idea to review your report here after publication to identify any discrepancies between the published report and how it was presented in Preview mode of your report authoring tool.

Hovering the mouse cursor over the report displays a context menu that allows you to perform other actions on the report, as shown in Figure 17-9:

- ➤ Moving the report
- ➤ Deleting the report
- ➤ Subscribing to the report
- ➤ Creating a linked report
- ➤ Viewing the report's history
- ➤ Managing security
- ➤ Managing the report's properties
- ➤ Downloading a copy of the report
- ➤ Editing the report in Report Builder

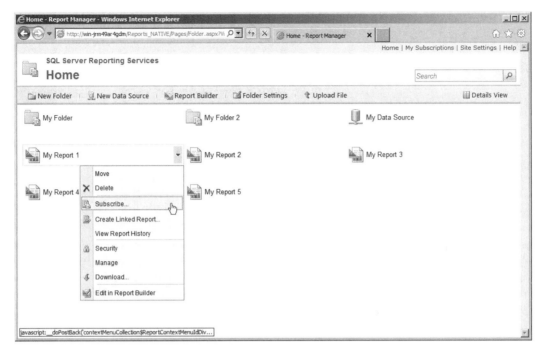

FIGURE 17-9

The Delete and Move buttons do just what you would expect. Deleting a report removes any subscriptions and history for it and makes orphans of any linked reports built from it.

You can subscribe to the report, which provides you with updates via e-mail or to a shared file location. Using this functionality you can choose to run the report at a specific time or select a shared schedule that is already set up.

Clicking the Subscriptions tab opens the report's Subscriptions page. On this page, existing subscriptions associated with the report are presented in a sortable table.

Clicking the New Subscription button allows you to set up a new standard subscription. On the New Subscription page, you specify the subscription delivery mechanism for the report, which then determines which additional information is needed. Table 17-2 lists the settings for e-mail and file share subscription delivery.

Below the delivery method options are the subscription processing options. These determine whether the subscription is delivered based on a subscription-specific or shared schedule. If the report includes parameters, values for these are entered in the Report Parameter Values section at the bottom of the New Subscription page. Clicking OK creates the new subscription.

TABLE 17-2

DELIVERY METHOD	SETTING	DESCRIPTION
E-mail	To	A semicolon-delimited list of e-mail addresses to which the report will be delivered. These addresses will be listed on the To line of the e-mail message.
	Cc	A semicolon-delimited list of e-mail addresses to which the report will be delivered. These addresses will be listed on the Cc line of the e-mail message.
	Bcc	A semicolon-delimited list of e-mail addresses to which the report will be delivered. These addresses will not be listed in the e-mail message.
	Reply-To	The e-mail address to which replies should be directed.
	Subject	The subject line of the e-mail message. The default subject line includes two variables that will be replaced with appropriate values at the time of execution.
	Include Report	Indicates whether the report should be rendered and included in the e-mail message.
	Render Format	Specifies the format to which the report should be rendered if it is to be included in the e-mail message. If you specify Web Archive, the report is embedded in the message body. For any other format, the report is included as an attachment.
	Include Link	Indicates whether a link to the report on the Reporting Services site should be included in the e-mail message.
	Priority	Indicates the flag to be used for the message's importance.
	Comment	A message to be included in the body of the e-mail message.

DELIVERY METHOD	SETTING	DESCRIPTION
Windows file share	File Name	The name of the file to deliver. You can supply an extension or select the "Add a file extension when a file is created" option to add an extension based on the rendering format you select.
	Path	The UNC path of the folder to which the file will be delivered.
	Render Format	A rendering format selected from a drop-down list of those available on the site.
	Credentials Used to Access the File Share	The username/password combination used as credentials when accessing the file share specified in the Path setting.
	Overwrite Options	One of three options indicating how to respond to the existence of a file with the name identified in the File Name setting. Options allow the file to be overwritten; the subscription to fail if the file exists; or the file to be written to the share but under a name with a sequential, numeric value appended.

Clicking the New Data-Driven Subscription button from the report Subscriptions page opens the Create Data-Driven Subscription Step 1 page. On this page, you give the subscription a name and identify its delivery type. All subscribers to this data-driven subscription will use this delivery method.

The Step 1 page requires you to specify the data source through which subscription data will be retrieved. You can use a shared data source or elect to create a subscription-specific data source. The data source is then either selected or configured on the Step 2 page.

On the Step 3 page, you enter a query that retrieves the information required by the subscription, along with a time-out. What information is required depends on how you intend to map fields to various options in the next step. A list of delivery method settings and report parameters is provided toward the middle of the page to assist you in developing your query.

Just below these lists, you can specify the query time-out and use the Validate button to test your query against the data source. Clicking the Next button automatically validates the query before taking you to the Step 4 page.

On the Step 4 page, you map delivery method settings to fields returned by your query. Alternatively, you can map these settings to constants or, in some cases, elect to provide no value.

If the report contains parameters, clicking the Next button takes you to the Step 5 page, where you map parameters in the report to fields in the query. Again, you can also map a parameter to a constant or elect to provide no value if appropriate.

Clicking Next takes you to the Step 6 page. Here you specify whether a subscription-specific or shared schedule will be used to control the timing of subscription delivery. You can also elect to have the subscription delivered whenever data for the snapshot associated with the report is updated. If you choose to use a subscription-specific schedule, you click Next to be taken to the Step 7 page, where this schedule is defined. Otherwise, you click the Finish button on the Step 6 page to complete the setup of the data-driven subscription.

> *You may notice that the context menu takes you to the report management page. Depending on which menu item you choose, you land on a specific tab of the management page. You can also access any of the context menu functionality from the management page by clicking the tabs on the left, as shown in Figure 17-10. In general, you have a number of ways to access the same pages. For example, the context menu item for creating a new linked report takes you to the same page as clicking the Create Linked Report button from the report's Properties tab.*

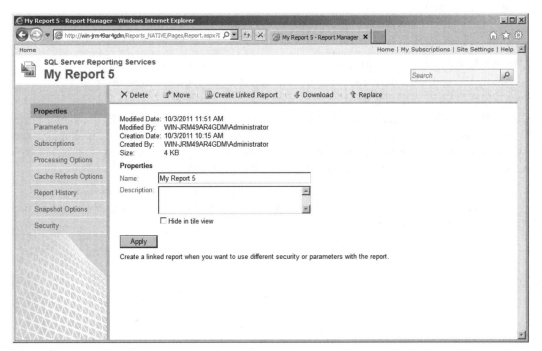

FIGURE 17-10

The Create Linked Report context menu item takes you to the New Linked Report page, as shown in Figure 17-11. You can think of a linked report as a kind of shortcut to a standard report, except that you can configure the linked report's properties differently from those of the report it references. This includes setting alternative processing options, cache refresh options, snapshot options, and security options. In addition, if the report has parameters or uses a shared data source, you also see pages to configure those.

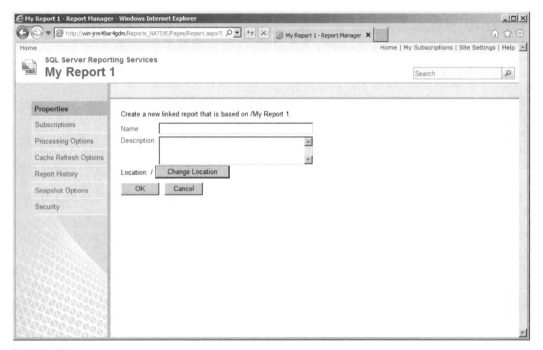

FIGURE 17-11

The View Report History context menu item takes you to a page that shows you the report's history, such as the most recent snapshots and subscriptions. In addition, you can use this page to create a new snapshot of the report.

 For a report to support history, its data sources must use stored credentials, and all parameters must have been assigned default values.

The Security functionality allows you to manage the report's security, including assigning roles to users or groups. By default the report's security is inherited from the parent container. You can break this inheritance to create item-level security, or you can restore this inheritance for an item with unique security settings.

If a report, linked or otherwise, has parameters, a Parameters Properties page is available on the left for that report's management page. On this page, you can set the default value, nullability, visibility, and prompt settings for each report parameter. These settings can be different from those specified during the report authoring phase.

If a report uses a data source, the Data Sources Properties page is available on the left. On this page, you can configure the report-specific and shared data sources that a report uses. You can also swap out report-specific and shared data sources in use by the report.

The Processing Options tab is used to configure a report's use of the Reporting Services caching features. By default, the "Do not cache temporary copies of this report" option is selected, which means that neither report execution caching nor snapshots are employed. (Session caching, discussed in Chapter 2 and configured at the site level, is still in effect.)

Selecting either of the "Cache a temporary copy of the report" suboptions enables report execution caching. With either of these options set, a copy of the report is cached when the report is run unless a valid cached copy already exists. That cached copy is held in the `ReportServerTempDB` database to fulfill subsequent requests until the cache expires. The first of the two "Cache a temporary copy of the report" options instructs Reporting Services to expire the cached copy after a fixed number of minutes. The second option instructs Reporting Services to expire the cached copy at a fixed point in time. This allows you to set a report-specific schedule or use a shared schedule.

The set of suboptions under the "Render this report from a report execution snapshot" option instruct Reporting Services to create and render the report from a snapshot. The snapshot is a scheduled execution of the report. Snapshots eliminate the potentially long run times experienced by the first user of a report when a cached copy has expired. You can specify a report-specific or shared schedule for the timing of the snapshot and can elect to run the snapshot immediately following its configuration. The snapshot remains valid until the next snapshot is executed.

 To leverage either report execution caching or snapshots, the report must use data sources with cached credentials. The reason is discussed in Chapter 2.

The bottom of the Processing Options page contains settings affecting report execution time-out. The default for a report is to use the system-level setting (which is set to a default value of 1800 seconds). The "Do not timeout report execution" option specifies that the report will not use a time-out. The "Limit report execution to the following number of seconds" option allows you to specify a report-specific time-out, overriding the system-level setting.

It is generally recommended that you use an execution time-out, whether system- or report-specific. The time-out should be sufficient for data to be retrieved and the report to be fully rendered. If you find you must set long time-outs for your report, consider using caching or snapshots as well as subscription features unless you want your users to stare at their screens, waiting for the report to render.

The Cache Refresh Options tab allows you to create a caching plan if one does not exist. When creating a new plan, you are required to set default parameters, if any exist, and specify a time or schedule for refreshing the cached report. Since report parameters require a default value with caching, this can limit your ability to use snapshots as an execution option. However, the well-thought-out use of dataset filters can allow you to make wider use of a report snapshot.

The Snapshot Options tab allows you to manage the snapshots for this particular report. The "Store all report execution snapshots in history" option stores all snapshots configured in the Execution Properties page as part of the report history. The "Use the following schedule to add snapshots to report history" option allows you to configure an alternative schedule for recording snapshots to history.

Storing the report history can start to add up within the ReportServer database. The History Properties page provides a set of options to limit the number of historical snapshots maintained for a report. The "Use default setting" option instructs Reporting Services to retain history for this report according to the site-level history setting. This setting has a default value of 10 days. The other two options override the site-level setting with a report-specific value, allowing you to keep history indefinitely or for simply an alternative number of days.

To actually see historical snapshots for a report, navigate to the Report History page by clicking the report's Report History tab. Report snapshots recorded to history are presented here in a detailed, tabular view. You can sort the table by the When Run and Size field headers.

Clicking an entry's When Run value opens a new window showing the report rendered using data from this snapshot. You can remove a snapshot from the history by clicking the checkbox to the far left of an item and then clicking the Delete button in the gray bar above the table. The New Snapshot button is presented in the gray bar if the "Allow report history to be created manually" option is set on the History Properties page. This button generates an on-demand report snapshot for inclusion in the report history.

Report Resources

Resources are files referenced by a report. Image files are the most commonly used reporting resources, but HTML, XML, XSLT, text, PDF, and Microsoft Office files are often employed as well. Reporting Services does not restrict what kind of resource a report can leverage, so the possibilities are endless. That said, there are practical limitations to what may be used as a reporting resource.

Reporting Services is simply a way to store and return the binary image of a resource file. The consuming application, whether the Reporting Services report processor or a custom report processing extension, must understand how to consume the resource item for it to be incorporated into the report. Otherwise, your only option is to provide a link to the resource and depend on the report-viewing tool, typically a web browser, to handle the binary image for you.

In addition, the binary image of the resource file is stored in an Image data type field in the ReportServer database. This imposes a 2 GB limitation on the file size. If you exceed this limit, an error is returned as you attempt to upload it to the site.

To upload a resource to Reporting Services, open the parent folder's Contents page and click the Upload File button. Locate the file to upload, and click the OK button. After it is uploaded, you should see the item displayed within the folder.

Clicking the item takes you to the resource's View page. If your web browser can render a resource, such as a JPEG or GIF file, the item is displayed within the body of the Report Manager page. If your web browser cannot render a resource, such as a TIFF file, the browser prompts you to save the file to your local system.

Clicking a resource's Properties tab takes you to the resource item's General Properties page. Through this page you can perform basic maintenance on the item.

Shared Schedules

Shared schedules allow you to define and administer schedules in a centralized manner for use throughout the site.

Shared schedules are managed at the site level, outside the folder structure. To access these, click the Site Settings link in the upper-right corner of the Report Manager header. Move to the Schedules page to see a tabular representation of Shared Schedules on the system.

The table on the Schedules page shows Name, Schedule (description), Creator, Last Run, Next Run, and Status fields, all of which can be used to sort the table's contents. Selecting one or more items in the table enables the Delete, Pause, and Resume buttons within the gray bar.

Clicking the New Schedule button in the gray bar on this page takes you to the New/Edit Schedule page. This page allows you to enter a name for the schedule and set its frequency of execution. You can also set a date range during which this schedule is executed, as shown in Figure 17-12.

Clicking the OK button submits the request to create the schedule. Behind the scenes, Reporting Services attempts to create a scheduled job through SQL Agent. If the SQL Agent Windows service is not started, you receive an error message.

Back on the Schedules page, clicking a schedule item's name or schedule value takes you back to the New/Edit Schedule page, where you can edit the item's configuration. Before making changes, it is a good idea to review the schedule's Reports page to identify reports dependent on it.

Shared schedules can also be created and managed through SQL Server Management Studio. Open SQL Server Management Studio, connect to the Reporting Services instance, and locate the Shared Schedules folder under the instance icon. You can right-click the Shared Schedules folder to create or delete a shared schedule. You can also right-click an individual schedule to delete it or access its properties page. The properties page provides access to the same properties presented through Report Manager.

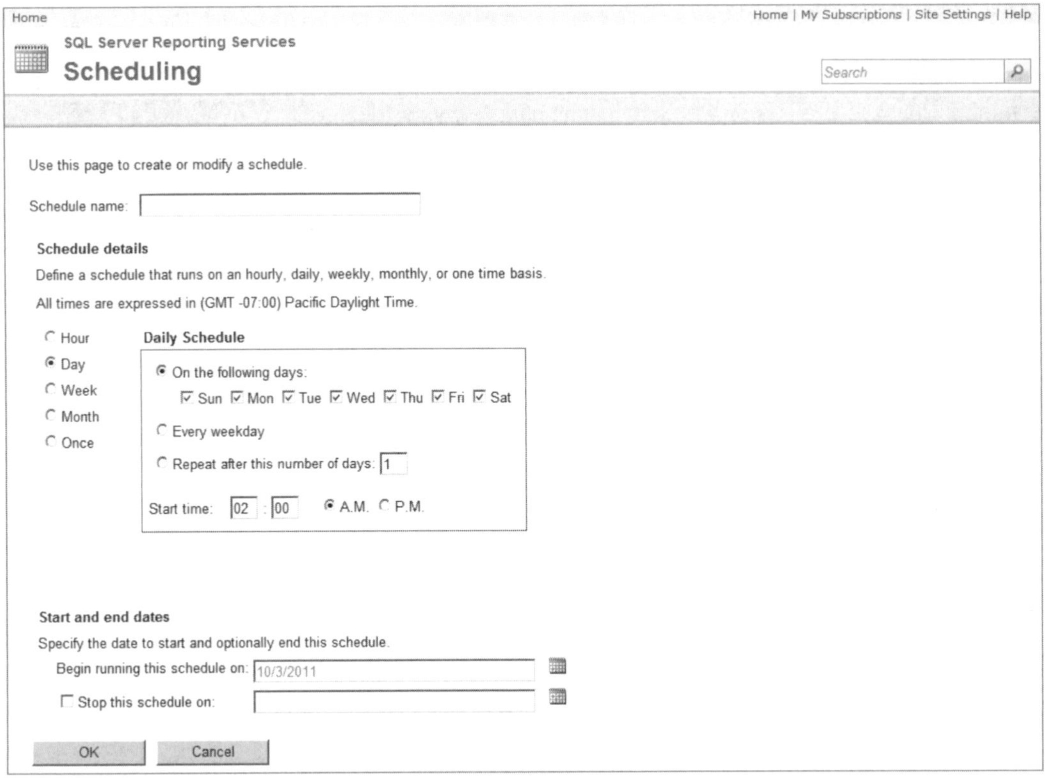

FIGURE 17-12

ITEM-LEVEL SECURITY

To perform an action against a Reporting Services item, you must have been granted the permissions to do so. Reporting Services supports a fixed set of permissions associated with each type of item, as shown in Table 17-3.

Explicitly assigning the right combinations of permissions required to perform an action on the site would be challenging. To simplify things, Reporting Services organizes these permissions into a more condensed set of item-level tasks. These tasks more naturally align with the kinds of activities users need to perform. Table 17-4 lists the task-to-permission mappings. Although it's important to understand these permissions as the underlying mechanism behind item-level security, Reporting Services does not expose these permissions and does not allow tasks to be created or altered.

TABLE 17-3

ITEM	PERMISSIONS
Report	Create Any Subscription
	Create Link
	Create Report History
	Create Subscription
	Delete Any Subscription
	Delete Report History
	Delete Subscription
	Delete Update Properties
	Execute Read Policy
	List Report History
	Read Any Subscription
	Read Content
	Read Data Sources
	Read Properties
	Read Report Definition
	Read Report Definitions
	Read Security Policies
	Read Subscription
	Update Any Subscription
	Update Data Sources
	Update Parameters
	Update Policy
	Update Report Definition
	Update Security Policies
	Update Subscription
Report Model	Delete Update Content
	Delete Update Properties
	Read Content
	Read Data Sources
	Read Model Item Authorization Policies
	Read Properties
	Update Data Sources
	Update Model Item Authorization Policies

ITEM	PERMISSIONS
Shared Data Source	Delete Update Content
	Read Properties
	Read Security Policies
	Update Properties
	Update Security Policies
Reporting Resource	Delete Update Content
	Read Content
	Read Properties
	Read Security Policies
	Update Properties
	Update Security Policies
Folder	Create Data Source
	Create Folder
	Create Model
	Create Report
	Create Resource
	Delete Update Properties
	Execute and View
	List Report History
	Read Properties
	Read Security Policies
	Update Security Policies

TABLE 17-4

ITEM	TASK	PERMISSIONS
Folder	Manage data sources	Create Data Source
	Manage folders	Create Folder
		Delete Update Properties
		Read Properties
	Manage models	Create Model
	Manage reports	Create Report
	Manage resources	Create Resource
	Set security for individual items	Read Security Policies
		Update Security Policies
	View folders	Read Properties
		Execute and View
		List Report History

continues

TABLE 17-4 *(continued)*

ITEM	TASK	PERMISSIONS
Reports	Consume reports	Read Content Read Report Definitions Read Properties
	Create linked reports	Create Link Read Properties
	Manage all subscriptions	Read Properties Read Any Subscription Create Any Subscription Delete Any Subscription Update Any Subscription
	Manage individual subscriptions	Read Properties Create Subscription Delete Subscription Read Subscription Update Subscription
	Manage individual subscriptions	Read Properties Create Subscription Delete Subscription Read Subscription Update Subscription
	Manage report history	Read Properties Create Report History Delete Report History Execute Read Policy Update Policy List Report History
	Manage reports	Read Properties Delete Update Properties Update Parameters Read Data Sources Update Data Sources Read Report Definition Update Report Definition Execute Read Policy Update Policy
	View reports	Read Content Read Properties
	Set security for individual items	Read Security Policies Update Security Policies

ITEM	TASK	PERMISSIONS
Data Sources	Manage data sources	Update Properties
		Delete Update Content
		Read Properties
	View data sources	Read Content
		Read Properties
	Set security for individual items	Read Security Policies
		Update Security Policies
Models	Manage models	Read Properties
		Read Content
		Delete Update Content
		Read Data Sources
		Update Data Sources
		Read Model Item Authorization Policies
		Update Model Item Authorization Policies
		Delete Update Properties
	View models	Read Properties
		Read Content
		Read Data Sources
Resources	Set security for individual items	Read Security Policies
		Update Security Policies
	Manage resources	Update Properties
		Delete Update Content
		Read Properties
	View resources	Read Content
		Read Properties

Take a moment to consider the users of a particular section of your Reporting Services site, such as a folder. Some users will simply need to browse the folder's contents. Others may need to both browse and publish items to the folder. A few may even need the rights to manage the folder's security. These users can be described as having one or more roles within this portion of the site. Each of those roles requires a set of rights for its members to perform their expected tasks. This is the basic model for applying item-level security in Reporting Services.

In Reporting Services, roles are defined at the site level and are assigned tasks, as described earlier. Reporting Services comes with five preconfigured item-level roles, as described in Table 17-5.

TABLE 17-5

ROLE	DESCRIPTION	TASKS
Browser	Run reports and navigate through the folder structure.	View reports View resources View folders View models Manage individual subscriptions
Content Manager	Define a folder structure for storing reports and other items, set security at the item level, and view and manage the items stored by the server.	Consume reports Create linked reports Manage all subscriptions Manage data sources Manage folders Manage models Manage individual subscriptions Manage report history Manage reports Manage resources Set security policies for items View data sources View reports View models View resources View folders
Report Builder	Build and edit reports in Report Builder.	Consume reports View reports View resources View folders View models Manage individual subscriptions
Publisher	Publish content to a report server.	Create linked reports Manage data sources Manage folders Manage reports Manage models Manage resources

ROLE	DESCRIPTION	TASKS
My Reports	Build reports for personal use or store reports in a user-owned folder.	Create linked reports Manage folders Manage data sources

To modify the tasks assigned to these roles, open SQL Server Management Studio and connect to the Reporting Services instance. In the Object Explorer pane, expand the Security folder and its Roles subfolder. The Reporting Services item-level roles are listed, as shown in Figure 17-13.

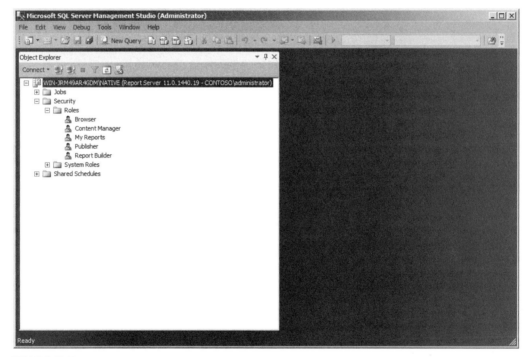

FIGURE 17-13

Right-click a role and select Properties to open its User Role Properties dialog. Here you may change the role's description and tasks assigned to it. Clicking OK saves your changes.

To create a new role, right-click the Roles subfolder in the SQL Server Management Studio Object Explorer pane and select New Role. In the resulting New User Role dialog, provide the name, description, and task assignments for this role. Click OK to create the role.

To drop a role, right-click it and select Delete. You are asked to confirm this action before the role is dropped. You can drop both custom and predefined Reporting Services roles.

Because roles are simply named sets of tasks (which themselves are nothing more than named sets of permissions), item-level security is implemented by linking users with one or more roles for a given Reporting Services item.

In Report Manager, you implement this "linking" by first navigating to an item and engaging its Security page from the context menu for an item, such as a report. Note that you need to break the inheritance from the parent to manage item-level security. Clicking the New Role Assignment button takes you to the New Role Assignment page, as shown in Figure 17-14.

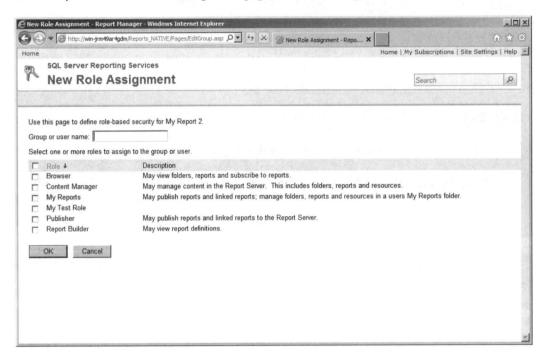

FIGURE 17-14

Here, you enter the account name for the user or group to which you want to assign this access and then select one or more of the roles as appropriate. Clicking OK submits the assignment to Reporting Services.

Creating item-user-role assignments for every item on the site would get old quickly. So, instead, Reporting Services uses inheritance for item-level security. When a user is assigned to one or more roles on a folder, this assignment is inherited by that folder's child items. If these child items include folders, the inheritance cascades down the folder hierarchy.

Inheritance makes administering security much easier, but you may need to break inheritance to assign permissions on an item appropriately. To do this, navigate to the item's Security page in Report Manager. When inheritance is in place, you see an Edit Item Security button. Clicking this button causes a warning about breaking inheritance to appear. After you click OK, the item has separate security from the parent, and you can edit security for the item, as shown in Figure 17-15.

After inheritance is broken, you will notice that the New Role Assignment button is available, allowing you to create user-role assignments for this item.

Also notice that the user-role assignments that would have been inherited from this folder's parent are preassigned to this item. Selecting the checkbox for any unnecessary assignments and clicking the Delete button on the gray bar removes these.

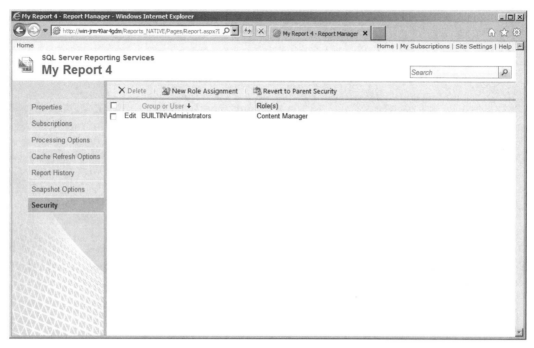

FIGURE 17-15

Finally, if you want to reset this item's security to use inheritance, again click the Revert to Parent Security button in the gray bar. The item reverts to inherited security, and any noninherited assignments are dropped.

CONTENT MANAGEMENT AUTOMATION

Content management consists of many repetitive actions. Performing these manually can be time-consuming and can risk introducing errors. Scripts allow these frequently performed actions to be automated. If implemented correctly, scripts can produce significant time savings and minimize the risks associated with changes to your environment. To support automation through scripts, Reporting Services comes with the rs.exe command-line application, also known as the RS utility.

The RS Utility

The RS utility, rs.exe, allows scripts to be run against local and remote instances of Reporting Services. The application is typically located in the *drive*:\Program Files (x86)\Microsoft SQL Server\110\Tools\Binn folder. It is responsible for creating an environment within which a Reporting Services script can be executed.

As part of this responsibility, the RS utility handles communications with an instance of the Reporting Services web service. It also handles the declaration and instantiation of variables supplied through the command-line call. These features allow flexible scripts to be developed with relative ease.

The following is a simple call to the RS utility. Note the use of the -i parameter to identify the Reporting Services script. The script file is a simple text file with an RSS file extension. The contents of the text file is Visual Basic .NET code.

The RSS script file that contains Visual Basic .NET code is written against a proxy based on Web Service Description Language (WSDL). The WSDL defines the Reporting Services SOAP API. RSS Scripts are covered in the next section. However, if you want to learn more about writing scripts for rs.exe, *check out the MSDN guidance at* http://msdn.microsoft.com/en-us/library/ms154561(v=SQL.110).aspx *or search for "Reporting Services Script File" using your favorite search engine. Make sure you select SQL Server 2012 when you find the MSDN article as previous versions provide examples to endpoints that are deprecated.*

Also note the identification of the web service URL with the -s parameter. In this example, the script is pointed to the web service presented by the local, default instance of Reporting Services.

```
rs.exe -i "c:\my scripts\my script.rss" -s http://localhost/reportserver
```

The connection to the web service is established using the current user's identity. To specify an alternative identity, a username/password combination can be specified with the -u and -p parameters. In the next example, the connection is made through the fictional MyDomain\SomeUser account, which has a password of pass@word:

```
rs.exe -i "c:\my scripts\my script.rss" -s http://localhost/reportserver
-u MyDomain\SomeUser -p pass@word
```

In Native mode, the Reporting Services web service presents an endpoint with the name ReportService2010.

In past versions of SQL Server, the web service endpoints were broken down into different endpoints depending on the type of install. These were called ReportService2005, which was designed for Reporting Services in Native mode, and ReportService2006, which was designed for Reporting Services in SharePoint Integrated mode. These endpoints are deprecated in SQL Server 2012 and have been combined into a new endpoint called ReportService2010. The previous endpoints are deprecated but still available for backward compatibility. It is important to note however, that when using the rs.exe *utility without the* -e *flag you are actually using the ReportService2005 endpoint. This seems contradictory, but I imagine it was designed this way for backward compatibility.*

Access to the ReportService endpoints in previous releases of Reporting Services is available using the -e *flag. Note that the Reporting Services 2000 endpoint is deprecated and no longer available.*

As mentioned at the start of this section, the RS utility declares and instantiates variables on behalf of the script. Variables are specified with the -v parameter followed by one or more variable/value combinations. Variable/value combinations are separated by an equals sign. Values containing spaces should be enclosed in double quotes. These quotation marks are not part of the variable's value. Here is a sample call to the utility with three variables that illustrates these concepts:

```
rs.exe -i "c:\my scripts\my script.rss" -s http://localhost/reportserver
-v VarA=1 VarB=apple VarC="keeps the doctor away"
```

Table 17-6 is a complete list of parameters that the rs.exe command-line utility supports.

TABLE 17-6

PARAMETER	DESCRIPTION
-i	Identifies the script file to execute.
-s	Identifies the URL of the Reporting Services web service.
-u	Supplies the username used to log in to the Reporting Services site.
-p	Supplies the password associated with the username used to log in to the Reporting Services site.
-e	Identifies which Reporting Services web service endpoint to employ:
	Mgmt2010: Used in SQL Server 2012 to customize report processing and rendering. This endpoint can be used in either mode of Reporting Services.
	Mgmt2006: Used in previous versions of SQL Server to manage objects when Reporting Services is installed in Native mode.
	Mgmt2005: Used in previous versions of SQL Server to manage objects when Reporting Services is installed in Integrated mode.
	Exec2005: Used in previous versions of SQL Server to customize report processing and rendering. This endpoint can be used in either mode of Reporting Services.
-l	Specifies the number of seconds before the connection with Reporting Services times out. The default is 60 seconds. A value of 0 indicates an infinite connection time-out.
-b	Indicates that the script should be executed as a batch.
-v	Provides variables and values to pass to the script.
-t	Instructs the utility to include trace information in error messages.

Reporting Services Scripts

Reporting Services scripts are implemented in VB.NET. Only a few namespaces are supported, making the scripts fairly limited but still powerful enough to handle most content-management tasks. Supported namespaces include System, System.Diagnostics, System.IO, System.Web.Services, and System.Xml.

Every script must contain a Sub Main code block. This serves as the script's entry point. The Sub Main block does not have to be the first or only code block in the script. This allows you to move code to additional subroutines and functions you declare in the script.

Within the script, the Reporting Services web service is engaged through the rs object. You do not need to declare this object. The RS utility handles the details of setting up a web reference to a particular endpoint presented by a specific instance of the Reporting Services web service. More details are provided in the preceding section.

The requirement for the script developer is to call the appropriate classes and methods exposed by this endpoint through the rs object. To understand the classes and methods available for each endpoint, refer to the documentation available through Books Online.

Variables specified at the command line are automatically declared and initialized for use within the script. Variables in the script are aligned with those at the command line using a case-insensitive name match. If a variable is not declared in the script or does not match a variable supplied from the command line, you receive an undeclared variable error. All variables passed from the command line are passed in as strings.

The following code sample is a simple demonstration of these concepts. The script consists of a single code block, Sub Main. The ReportService2010 endpoint is accessed through the rs object to recursively read the site's contents starting from a folder identified by the MyFolder variable. The MyFolder variable is passed in from the command line.

```
Sub Main

    'Write the starting folder to the screen
    Console.WriteLine("The starting folder is " + MyFolder)

    'Open the Output File
    Dim OutputFile As New IO.StreamWriter( _
                        "c:\my scripts\contents.txt", False)

    'Obtain an array of Catalog Items
    Dim Contents As CatalogItem() = rs.ListChildren(MyFolder, True)

    'Loop through Array of CatalogItems
    For i As Int32 = 0 To Contents.GetUpperBound(0)

        'Write CatalogItem Type & Path to Output File w/ Pipe Delimiter
        OutputFile.Write(Contents(i).Type.ToString)
        OutputFile.Write("|")
        OutputFile.WriteLine(Contents(i).Path)
    Next

    'Close Output File
    OutputFile.Close()

End Sub
```

This script is saved to a file named `List Contents.RSS` located in the `C:\my scripts` folder and is executed against the local Reporting Services instance through the following command-line call:

```
rs.exe -i "c:\my scripts\list contents.rss" -s http://localhost/reportserver
-v MyFolder="/"
```

The `"/"` value represents the Home folder in the Reporting Services folder hierarchy.

This is a simple script. It is presented in this form simply to demonstrate the basics of Reporting Services script development. More information about building applications for Reporting Services using the web services can be found at the following URL or by searching for the text "Building Applications Using the Web Service and the .NET Framework":

```
http://msdn.microsoft.com/en-us/library/ms154699(v=SQL.110).aspx
```

 A detailed explanation of the Report Server Web Service Endpoints architecture including how the scripting components fit in is available on MSDN at the following location:

```
http://msdn.microsoft.com/en-us/library/ms152787(v=SQL.110).aspx
```

SUMMARY

In this chapter, you explored various aspects of Report Manager. You saw how Report Manager works and how it is used to manage Reporting Services content. You learned that Report Manager is available only when Reporting Services is installed in Native mode. You looked at how security works in Report Manager, including item-level security. You also looked at some of the endpoints that are available when scripting and automating tasks.

This chapter covered the following topics:

➤ Managing reports using Report Manager

➤ Viewing reports, models, and other content in Report Manager

➤ Configuring the Report Manager environment

➤ Automating reporting services with the RS utility

➤ Configuring Report Manager, including caching, schedules, and subscriptions

18

Integrating Reports with SharePoint

WHAT'S IN THIS CHAPTER?

➤ Leveraging the Report Viewer web part to create seamless reports

➤ Exploring a reporting library with the Report Explorer web part

➤ Tuning the Report Viewer web part for Integrated mode

➤ Publishing reports to SharePoint

➤ Managing reports in SharePoint

➤ Working with report models from SharePoint

This chapter explores the integration of SQL Server 2012 Reporting Services with SharePoint. In recent years, SharePoint has become a web-portal centerpiece for collaboration and information sharing. As a result, Microsoft has tightly integrated its reporting solution with SharePoint.

Integrating SQL Server 2012 Reporting Services and SharePoint allows a user to navigate to his or her intranet portal and have instant access to company information as well as personalized business reports and key performance indicators (KPIs). The reports can be embedded directly into web portal pages for seamless integration for the user.

SQL Server 2012 Reporting Services can be installed in either Native mode or SharePoint Integrated mode. In Native mode, a user interacts with Reporting Services using two web parts (Report Explorer and Report Viewer). In Integrated mode, SharePoint takes over all the duties of the Report Manager. It also adds SharePoint document management values such as a consistent and friendly user experience, versioning, security trimming, alerts, enterprise search, and, when properly configured, the meeting of regulatory compliance requirements.

NATIVE MODE WEB PARTS

A fundamental SharePoint concept is the web part. Web parts can be thought of as modular elements containing functionality that is added to the user interface. Typically, web parts display specific information and can be moved around the web page. For example, SharePoint comes with web parts that can display images and list files. They have a consistent format, with a customizable title bar and a web part drop-down menu available in the upper-right corner.

To interact with Reporting Services in Native mode, you need to install the SQL Server Reporting Services web parts on each server in the SharePoint environment. After that, you add them to a SharePoint page and configure them just as you would any other web part in SharePoint.

Native Mode Web Parts Installation

Chapter 2 discussed in detail the installation of SQL Server 2012 Reporting Services in Native mode. The web parts installation file, RSWebParts.cab, was installed on the reporting server when Reporting Services was installed. By default it is located here:

```
C:\Program Files (x86)\Microsoft SQL Server\110\Tools\Reporting Services\SharePoint
```

 For the RSWebParts.cab *file to show up, the Native Reporting Services feature must be selected during the installation of SQL Server. If the* RSWebParts. cab *file is not present, you can add the feature by rerunning the SQL Server installation and choosing to add functionality to the existing instance instead of installing a completely new instance. After the Native Reporting Services feature is added, the* RSWebParts.cab *file will be available at the file system location just given.*

If you are not integrating with a SharePoint environment on the same server on which you have installed SSRS 2012, you need to copy this installation file from the Reporting Services computer to the SharePoint computer. As soon as the file is on the SharePoint server, it must be installed. Install the web parts by navigating to the BIN directory of the SharePoint installation and executing the following commands from a command prompt:

```
C:\>cd "C:\Program Files\Common Files\Microsoft Shared\web server extensions\14\
BIN"

C:\Program Files\Common Files\Microsoft Shared\web server extensions\14\BIN>
stsadm.exe -o addwppack -filename "C:\RSWebParts.cab" -globalinstall

Operation completed successfully.


C:\Program Files\Common Files\Microsoft Shared\web server extensions\14\BIN>
```

Be sure that you are on the computer running SharePoint. In this example, the RSWebParts.cab file has been copied to the root C:\ directory.

After installing the web parts on the SharePoint server, you can use them by adding them to any site in the farm, just as you would any other web part, as shown in Figure 18-1.

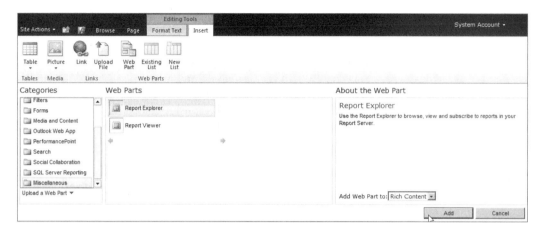

FIGURE 18-1

Report Viewer

The Report Viewer web part (for Native mode) is used to display reports in the SharePoint environment.

 A Report Viewer web part was also designed for viewing reports when SSRS is installed in Integrated mode. Even though the web parts are both called Report Viewer, they are specifically designed for different installation types. One Report Viewer is used to view reports when SSRS is installed in Native mode, and the other is used to view reports when SSRS is installed in Integrated mode.

You can interact with reports as you would in Report Manager, using links within the report and DHTML functionality to collapse report sections. For drill-down reports, the target report displays in the same Report Viewer web part. Drill-through reports, however, are rendered in a new browser window. Depending on the report's layout and the size of the web part on the page, only a portion of the report may be visible. You'll need to use the scroll bars to view the rest of the report. As with all SharePoint web parts, you can change the size of the Report Viewer web part on the page in the Tool pane. The Tool pane is a configuration window that lets you set property values for web parts displayed on the SharePoint page, as shown in Figure 18-2.

You can either connect the Report Viewer web part to the Report Explorer web part or use it by itself. If it's connected, clicking a link in the Report Explorer web part renders the report in the Report Viewer. The Report Explorer web part is covered in the next section. With the Report Viewer by itself, the web part doesn't have the Report Explorer pointing it to a report for rendering.

You have to provide the path to the report manually. You set the report path using the Tool pane. This might not seem very user-friendly, but it has a purpose.

After the report path has been set, the Report Viewer can display the report without user-initiated input or action. This functionality allows report developers to develop KPI dashboard pages. The reports contained in these dashboard pages could run on a schedule and automatically update. Executives could have these dashboards on their start page so that whenever they open Internet Explorer, they see the current metrics for their organization without having to interact with the report.

Another use I have seen for the Report Viewer is in manufacturing. Developers develop a specific report for a particular group. Monitors are then placed in key areas, and the workers can simply look at the monitor to see key information for their specific tasks.

The Report Viewer web part shows up under the Miscellaneous category when you go to add the web part to a SharePoint page. Simply select the Report Viewer web part to add it to the page.

After you have added the Report Viewer web part to a page, you can configure it by clicking the Modify Shared Web Part item under the web part drop-down menu (the small arrow in the upper-right corner of the web part). This brings up the Tool pane described a moment ago (refer to Figure 18-2).

Report parameters are displayed at the top of the web part content area. This parameters section expands to display the report parameters, with the standard Report Manager toolbar below it. Using the toolbar, you can export reports to an XML file with report data, a comma-separated values (CSV) file, an Acrobat PDF file, a MIME-encoded Hypertext Markup Language web archive, a Microsoft Excel file, a TIFF image, or a Microsoft Word document, as shown in Figure 18-3.

Report Explorer

The Report Explorer web part provides a miniature version of the Report Manager web application described in Chapter 17. The Report Explorer web part allows a user to navigate the content in the Report Server hierarchy. Clicking a report link in the Report Explorer displays the report. The report can be displayed in two ways: connected or stand-alone. When connected to a Report Viewer web part, the report renders in that web part. When standing alone, the report is rendered in a new browser window. Which mode you choose typically depends on how much screen real estate you have available. When connected, the selected report is passed to the Report Viewer web part for rendering.

FIGURE 18-2

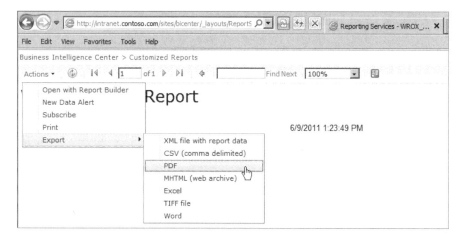

FIGURE 18-3

Like Report Manager, the Report Explorer web part has a Details view. In this view, you can create or edit a subscription to a report. If no icons are showing up, you likely have not configured the e-mail settings in the Reporting Services configuration utility. As soon as e-mail settings are configured, an e-mail icon shows up in the subscriptions column for reports for which you have subscription access.

The Report Explorer web part also provides bread-crumb-trail navigation and columns that can be sorted. In Report Explorer, however, only folders, reports, and resources are displayed. You don't have access to data sources from Report Explorer.

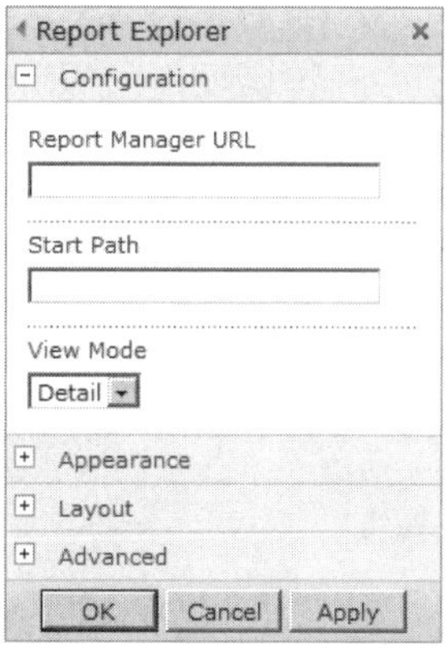

After you have added the Report Explorer web part to a page, you can configure it by clicking the Modify Shared Web Part item under the web part drop-down menu (the small down arrow in the upper-right corner of the web part). Figure 18-4 shows the configuration window for the Report Explorer.

You can also launch Report Builder from within the Report Explorer web part, as shown in Figure 18-5. The Report Builder is a click-once application that is downloaded to your computer from the host computer. Report Builder was covered in detail in Chapter 4.

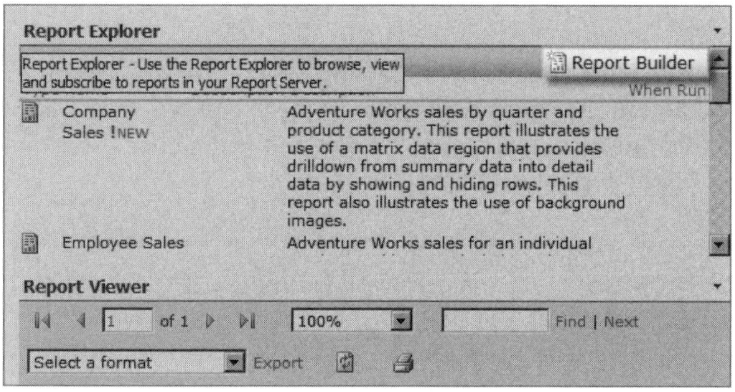

FIGURE 18-4

FIGURE 18-5

PUBLISHING REPORTS TO SHAREPOINT

Reports can be published to a SharePoint library in a number of ways. Since a report is just another document type, such as a Word document, it can be uploaded to the report library just like any other document. The same is true of data connection types.

After the Reporting Services add-in for SharePoint has been installed on either a SharePoint Foundation or SharePoint Server installation, the farm "knows" about these new content types. You can manually create a Reports and Data Connections library in any site, and publish your reports and data connections to these libraries.

SharePoint Foundation and SharePoint Server Standard Edition

Publishing reports in SharePoint Foundation and SharePoint Server Standard Edition is nearly identical. The key difference between these editions is that SharePoint Server Standard Edition adds functionality to the SharePoint environment, such as audiences. It is not until SharePoint Server Enterprise Edition that major features related to reporting are introduced — namely, the Business Intelligence Center Site template. The Enterprise features are explored later in the chapter.

You can publish reports in SharePoint Foundation and SharePoint Server Standard Edition by manually uploading reports and setting data connections. Or you can use Visual Studio SQL Server Data Tools (SSDT) to publish reports and data connections directly to SharePoint libraries.

 Note that in previous versions of SQL Server the SSDT tool was called Business Intelligence Development Studio (BIDS). You might see the tools still sometimes referred to as BIDS, but the product is actually now SQL Server Data Tools (SSDT), which is the terminology used throughout this book. You install SSDT from the SQL Server media.

After the SharePoint environment has been integrated with SQL Server 2012 Reporting Services, a number of report content types are made available. The following steps walk through creating libraries that use these content types and then publishing the sample reports from within the SSDT environment.

The reports and data connections can be published directly to the same library, or to separate libraries dedicated to reports or data connections. In the following example, you will create a library to hold only reports and a library to hold only data connections. You will then publish the sample reports and data connections to these respective libraries.

 Before beginning, ensure that the Report Server Integration feature is activated for the Site Collection.

1. You start with a SharePoint site that was created using the Blank template. The first step is to create the report-specific SharePoint library. Choose Site Actions ⇨ More Options to go to the SharePoint creation screen.

2. From the Create menu, click the Document Library button. Note that you can narrow down the list of items you can create using the refiners on the left side of the Create page. Choosing the Library refiner shows you only the Library items you can create.

3. Click the Document Library button, and then click the More Options button to bring up the More Options screen. If you clicked the Create button at this point, the library would be created with default values. The More Options button allows you to customize the default values. Clicking the More Options button brings up the form used to create the library. This library will be used for reports, so fill in the name My Reports and also choose None for the Document Template, as shown in Figure 18-6.

FIGURE 18-6

4. At this point you have a document library, but it is not associated with the Reporting Services report content type. To change the content type associated with this library, open the Document Library Settings by choosing Library Settings from the Library tab of the newly created My Reports library.

5. By default, the management of content types is turned off in a document library. Click the Advanced Settings link, and then select Yes for "Allow management of content types?", as shown in Figure 18-7. Click OK to save the setting.

Content Types	Allow management of content types?
Specify whether to allow the management of content types on this document library. Each content type will appear on the new button and can have a unique set of columns, workflows and other behaviors.	⦿ Yes ○ No

FIGURE 18-7

6. Now that content type management is allowed, a new section called Content Types appears on the Document Library Settings page. The default content type is Document. Click this link to open this content type, and then delete it from the library by clicking the Delete This Content Type link under the Settings section. Click OK to confirm the deletion.

7. Click Add From Existing Site Content Types under the Content Types section in the Library settings page. Click the drop-down, and choose SQL Server Reporting Services Content Types to display the content types that were added with the Reporting Services add-in for SharePoint. You can choose from three content types: Report Builder Report, Report Builder Model, and Report Data Source. For this library, you only want to store reports, so add the Report Builder Report content type, as shown in Figure 18-8, and then click OK.

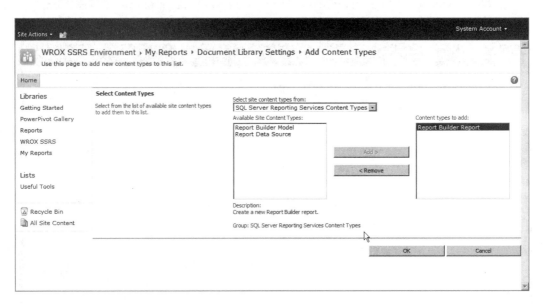

FIGURE 18-8

8. The Content Types section on the library settings page should now include the Report Builder Report content type. At this point the library is ready to hold Reporting Services reports.

9. Repeat Steps 1 through 8 to create a Data Sources library to store the shared data connections. Name the new library My Connections, and choose the content type Report Data Source. You also use this same procedure to add the Report Model content type to a library.

You now have a library to hold reports and a library to hold data connections on your blank SharePoint page, as shown in Figure 18-9. You can also have reports and data sources in the same directory, but functionally it is easier to manage reports and data connections in separate libraries.

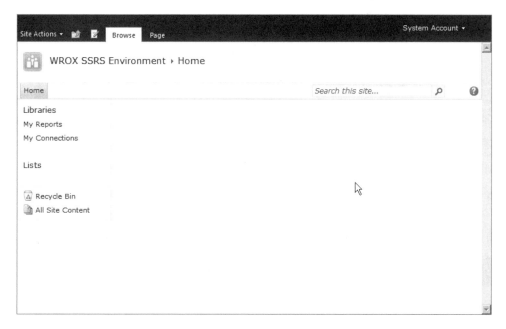

FIGURE 18-9

Now that you have a Reports and Data Connections library to hold the Reporting Services content, you can fire up SSDT and open the sample Reporting Services project.

> *You can access links to all SQL Server reporting samples at the book's website:* http://www.wrox.com.

Once you have downloaded the sample reporting project from the Wrox website you can unzip it to extract all of the sample files to your computer.

Double-click the solution file, SSRS 2012 Book.sln, to fire up SSDT and load the sample solution, as shown in Figure 18-10. If you do not have SSDT installed, you can go back and install it from the SQL Server installation media.

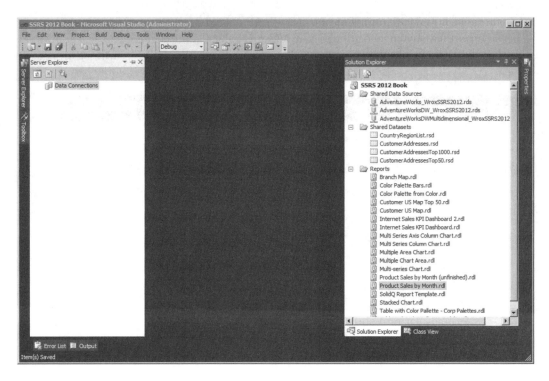

FIGURE 18-10

 A major cause of frustration in previous versions of SQL Server was the inability of SSDT to work with the most recent version of Visual Studio. SQL Server 2012 ships with SSDT based on Visual Studio 2010.

Now that the solution is open, you are ready to publish the reports and data connections contained within it to the newly created Reports and Data Connections libraries. Right-click the SSRS 2012 Book solution and choose Properties, as shown in Figure 18-11.

The properties window is displayed with the `TargetDataSourceFolder`, `TargetReportFolder`, and `TargetServerURL` properties. As the name suggests, the `TargetDataSourceFolder` property corresponds to the Data Connections library you created earlier, and the `TargetReportFolder` property corresponds to the Reports library. The `TargetServerURL` property is the URL of the blank SharePoint site that contains your libraries. Fill in these fields with values that match your environment.

FIGURE 18-11

The format is `http://<server>:port/<site>/<library>`. If you are using the default site, you would have something like `http://<server>/<library>`. Table 18-1 shows an example of my environment. Note that I created the blank site as a subsite of the ssrs2012book site.

TABLE 18-1

PROPERTY NAME	VALUE
TargetDataSourceFolder	http://prossrs2012/ssrs2012book/My%20 Connections
TargetReportFolder	http://prossrs2012/ssrs2012book/My%20 Reports
TargetServerURL	http://prossrs2012/ssrs2012book

When the settings are correct, click OK to save them. Right-click the SSRS 2012 Book project in the Solution Explorer and choose Deploy.

As soon as the solution has been deployed, you can go back to the My Reports folder and see all the reports in the SharePoint library, as shown in Figure 18-12. You can click a report to view it. The report now contains all the content management features SharePoint has to offer.

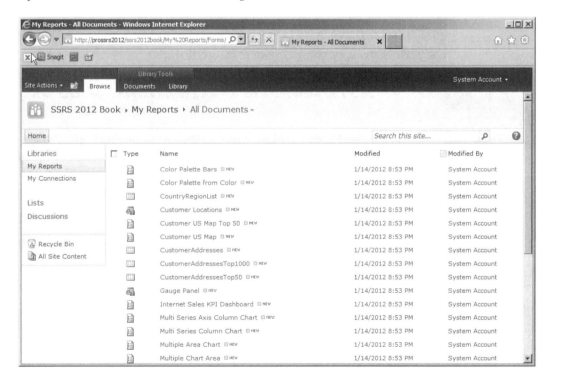

FIGURE 18-12

If for some reason the report is not displayed when you click it within the SharePoint Reports library, you must ensure that it is using the correct data source. Click the down arrow next to the report to drop down the SharePoint-specific menu, and choose Manage Data Sources. Ensure that the connection string in the data source that it is using is correct. Also, ensure that you have installed the sample databases from the http://www.wrox.com website for this book.

SharePoint Server Enterprise Edition

SharePoint Server Enterprise Edition adds a number of Reporting Services integration features. One feature allows you to enable the Reporting Services content types and a site template called Business Intelligence Center. The Report Server Integration feature allows you to activate the Reporting Services content types for a particular site. The Business Intelligence Center provides a site geared toward business intelligence with a library that already has the SSRS content types enabled, a library for data connections, and a preconfigured PerformancePoint list.

 To see the Business Intelligence Center site template, you must have activated the PerformancePoint Services site features.

You can create a Business Intelligence Center site by selecting the Business Intelligence Center site template from the SharePoint create screen, as shown in Figure 18-13.

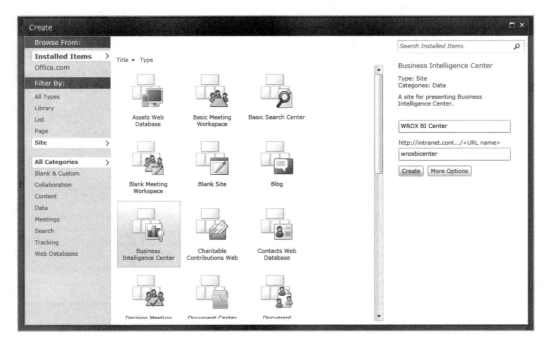

FIGURE 18-13

The Business Intelligence Center site template takes the work out of creating Report and Data Connection libraries manually, as you did in the preceding section, by embedding a library called Customized Reports directly in the template. The Customized Reports library already has the SSRS content types enabled, which you can see by clicking the New Document button drop-down, as shown in Figure 18-14.

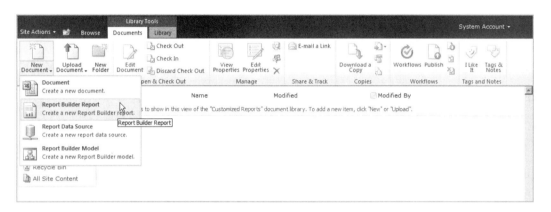

FIGURE 18-14

Publishing reports to the Business Intelligence Center is very similar to publishing reports to a SharePoint Foundation or SharePoint Server Standard Edition site, although the manual configuration has been taken out of the equation. To publish reports to the Business Intelligence Center, you simply need to supply the Reports library, Data Connections library, and site location to the Properties window of the Visual Studio project. You can access these properties by right-clicking the project name in the Solution Explorer section of Visual Studio and choosing Properties. The values take the format of `http://<servername>/<site>/<library>`. Table 18-2 shows my lab environment values. The name of the server running SharePoint Server Enterprise Edition is `prossrs2012`. The name of the default library that contains the content types for the reports and data connections is called `AnalyticsReports`.

TABLE 18-2

PROPERTY NAME	VALUE
`TargetDataSourceFolder`	`http://prossrs2012/sites/bicenter/AnalyticsReports`
`TargetReportFolder`	`http://prossrs2012/sites/bicenter/AnalyticsReports`
`TargetServerURL`	`http://prossrs2012/sites/bicenter`

If any of the features are not showing up for a newly created site, be sure that the Office SharePoint Server Enterprise Site Collection features and the Report Server Integration feature are activated. These features generally are activated for the default web application when the Reporting Services add-in is installed. If a new web application is created, it must be activated for the Report Library content type to appear under Library on the Create screen. You can activate these features by going to Site Actions ⇨ Site Setting and then navigating to Site Actions ⇨ Manage Site Features.

REPORT MANAGEMENT

Chapter 17 described in detail how to manage reports using Report Manager when SQL Server 2012 Reporting Services is installed in Native mode. In Integrated mode Report Manager is no longer available. All report management functionality is performed from within the SharePoint environment. Every report has a context menu associated with it for management. You can access the menu by hovering the mouse pointer over a report until a down arrow appears to the right of the report name, as shown in Figure 18-15. When this arrow appears, click it to reveal the context menu for that report.

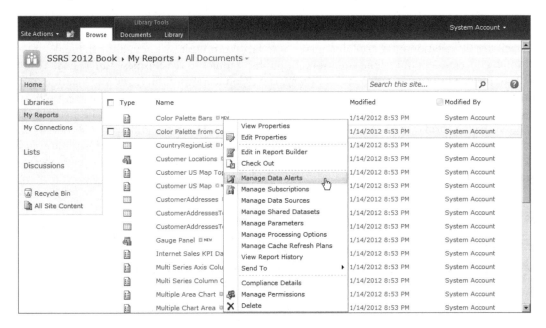

FIGURE 18-15

The following tables outline the Reporting Services-specific options contained in the context menu for the Report Builder Report, Report Builder Model, and Report Data Source content types, respectively. If a user does not have access to any particular menu, that menu item does not show up for that user. SharePoint utilizes security trimming so that users see only the items for which they have the appropriate permissions.

Table 18-3 outlines the Report Builder Report context menu items.

TABLE 18-3

ITEM NAME	DESCRIPTION
Edit in Report Builder	Opens the Report in Report Builder for editing.
Manage Data Alerts	Lets you set alerts on data in the reports. For example, a user might want to know when profitability in this report reaches a negative number.
Manage Subscriptions	Opens the subscription management screen, which lets you add a subscription to the report, add a data-driven subscription to the report, or delete the report.
Manage Data Sources	Opens the data source management screen, which lists the report's data sources, and lets you change the data source's Content Type and Data Source Link.
Manage Shared Datasets	A shared dataset is a query that can be used across multiple reports. This allows multiple reports to maintain a consistent set of data.
Manage Parameters	Opens a screen that lets you manage the parameters contained in the report.
Manage Processing Options	Opens a screen that lets you manage report processing. The screen includes Data Refresh Options, Processing Time-Out Options, History Snapshot Options, and History Snapshot Limits.
Manage Cache Refresh Plans	A cache lets you preload data for a report or shared dataset. Using the Cache Refresh Plans page, you can create and manage caching plans for the report.
View Report History	Displays a history of the report.

 Notice that the context menu also contains items that every item in a SharePoint library contains, such as the ability to view or edit the properties and check in and check out the document.

Figure 18-16 and Table 18-4 describe the Report Builder Model context menu items.

TABLE 18-4

ITEM NAME	DESCRIPTION
Load in Report Builder	Loads the Model into Report Builder.
View Dependent Items	Opens a screen that lists the reports that depend on this model.
Manage Data Sources	Opens the data source management screen, which lists the report's data sources and lets you change the data source's Content Type and Data Source Link.
Manage Clickthrough Reports	Opens a screen that lets you manage Clickthrough reports. Clickthrough reports contain detailed information and are accessed by clicking data items in a main Report Builder report.
Manage Model Item Security	Opens a screen that lets you manage security for specific portions of the model.
Regenerate Model	Regenerates the model from the data source.

Figure 18-17 and Table 18-5 describe the Report Data Source context menu items.

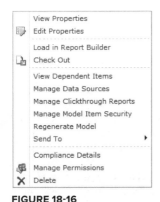

FIGURE 18-16

FIGURE 18-17

INTEGRATED MODE WEB PARTS

Traditionally, Reporting Services included two SharePoint web parts: the Report Explorer, for navigating through the report server content, and the Report Viewer, for viewing rendered reports. Beginning with the release of Service Pack 2 for SQL Server 2005 Reporting Services, a new way of running Reporting Services with SharePoint was born. The new method installed Reporting Services in a mode called SharePoint Integrated mode. This mode has been refined and upgraded with the release of SQL Server 2012 Reporting Services. Integrated mode introduces an additional web part, which is designed to display reports when SSRS is installed in Integrated mode. This web part is called the Report Viewer web part, which is the same name as the web part designed to display reports when SSRS is installed in Native mode. Don't get them confused, however. These are two separate web parts and are not interchangeable. Whether you want to integrate with SSRS in Native mode or Integrated mode, it will dictate which Report Viewer web part you will use.

TABLE 18-5

ITEM NAME	DESCRIPTION
Create Power View Report	Lets you create a Power View report based on the Report Data Source. Power View was covered in Chapter 13.
View Dependent Items	Lists all the items that use this data source.
Edit Data Source Definition	Opens a screen that lets you manage the Data Source. The screen includes sections for setting the Data Source type, Connection String, Credentials, and Availability of the Data Source. The Data Source Types include the following: Microsoft SQL Server Microsoft SQL Azure OLE DB Microsoft SQL Server Analysis Services Oracle ODBC XML Microsoft SharePoint List SAP NetWeaver BI Hyperion Essbase Microsoft Business Intelligence Semantic Model

The previous sections discussed publishing reports to SharePoint and managing reports in Integrated mode. Now the reports live in SharePoint, and you can view them simply by clicking them in a document library. Nevertheless, you might still want to present them on a nice dashboard or entry page that users will view instead of navigating to the report library.

The Report Viewer web part can be used much like how it is used when it is integrated with Reporting Services in Native mode. The SQL Server Reporting Services Report Viewer web part, however, is designed to interact with a Reporting Services instance running in Integrated mode. The web part is listed under the SQL Server Reporting category, as shown in Figure 18-18.

FIGURE 18-18

The SQL Server Reporting Services Report Viewer web part can be set up to display a single defined report, or it can receive its report information from a web part based on user interaction. The following example walks through setting up a Reports library web part that feeds a report to the viewer based on the report selected:

1. Add the SQL Server Reporting Services Report Viewer web part to the SharePoint page by clicking Site Actions ➪ Edit Page to place the page in Edit view.

2. Add the viewer web part to the left side of the page so that the user can view the report that he or she selects. Click Add a Web Part to the Top Left Zone. Select the SQL Server Reporting Services Report Viewer Web Part, which is located in the SQL Server Reporting category.

3. Now you need a web part from which the user will select the report he or she wants to view. For this you can use any library that contains reports. In this example we will use the My Reports library. Remember that any library has an associated web part in the web part gallery. You will find this web part under the Lists and Libraries category. Add the My Reports web part to the page.

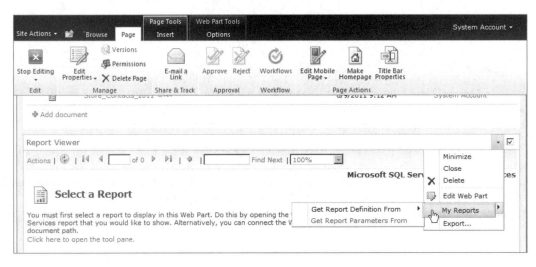

FIGURE 18-19

4. Now that both web parts are on the page, you need to configure them. In the top-right corner of the Report Viewer web part, select Edit ➪ Connections ➪ Get Report Definition From ➪ My Reports, as shown in Figure 18-19.

5. Save the page and exit edit mode by clicking the Stop Editing button on the ribbon. Now when a report is selected in the web part on the top, the report is displayed in the viewer web part on the bottom. The size of the web parts and formatting on the screen can all be formatted to fit your organization's look and feel.

NATIVE MODE VERSUS INTEGRATED MODE

Determining the best type of integration depends on many variables surrounding the SharePoint farm and the level of integration you want between the farm and the Reporting Services instance. The content in Table 18-6 comes mostly from SQL Server 2012 Books Online (BOL). I feel that it is important enough to include similar content here as well.

Although sometimes a client chooses to use Native mode integration, I have increasingly seen most environments take advantage of the tight integration that Integrated mode provides. As an Enterprise Content Management (ECM) system, SharePoint is quickly becoming unmatched because of its ease of use and close integration with the Microsoft Office suite. For organizations that are already running a SharePoint environment, there are very few reasons not to take advantage of the SharePoint ECM environment, with all its features, for reporting needs as well. Users are becoming hyperconnected to the data in their organization, and soon they will *expect* to see all their personal KPIs on their intranet start page.

TABLE 18-6

	NATIVE MODE	INTEGRATED MODE
Integration	The Report Explorer and Report Viewer web parts provide access to the report server and let you view reports. But all management is done on the report server using the standard Report Manager application.	Viewing and managing reports is integrated into the existing web portal environment. A standard SharePoint library is used to store and manage all reports and data connections. The SharePoint server farm becomes the main front-end mechanism for Reporting Services. The actual report server becomes a back-end system. A single web part is used to display reports. It is easily integrated with other web parts and customized to fit the overall page design. The free Reporting Services SharePoint add-in provides Reporting Services-specific application pages to the SharePoint farm.
Content	Content is stored exclusively on the report server.	Content is stored in a SharePoint library on the farm. Content also exists on Report Server, but only for performance reasons. All content is managed through the SharePoint portal.

continues

TABLE 18-6 *(continued)*

Security	The report server controls all security for content and is configured through the Report Manager web application. The Report Manager web application is completely separate from SharePoint.	SharePoint manages and controls all security. Security is integrated with the existing SharePoint farm environment.
Content Creation	Content is created using Report Manager or the Reporting Services client tools. Report Builder can be launched from Report Manager.	Content is created using the Reporting Services client tools or directly from within a SharePoint site and published to SharePoint libraries. Within a SharePoint site a user can generate report models, launch Report Builder, launch Power View, and publish and view the resulting reports.
Installation and Configuration	Copy web parts from Report Server to SharePoint servers, install web parts on SharePoint servers, add web parts to SharePoint sites, and configure web parts.	Download and install the SQL Server Reporting Services SharePoint add-in on SharePoint servers and configure the Reporting Services service application in SharePoint Central Administration.
Limitations	Must maintain separate security policies. Security in SharePoint is completely separate from security on the Reporting Services server (Report Manager). Requires separate Reporting Services tools for managing the reporting environment on the Reporting Services server. Does not include all the content-management features that SharePoint has to offer.	The Report Manager application is not supported. Programmatic batch operations and job management are not supported.

REPORT MODELS

In Chapter 12 you learned about report models. You can generate report models from within the SharePoint environment by adding the Report Model content type to a document library and then creating a new item with that content type. Adding the Reporting Services content types to a document library was discussed earlier in the chapter.

A required field in the creation of a Report Model is a Report Data Source. You can create a Report Data Source by adding the content type to a library and then selecting it from the Add Document drop-down menu. Adding content types was discussed earlier in the chapter. As soon as the content types are available, you can select Add Document from the drop-down menu on the SharePoint ribbon when viewing the document library.

A report model can be built from many data sources, including the following:

- Microsoft SQL Server
- Microsoft SQL Azure
- OLE DB
- Microsoft SQL Server Analysis Services
- Oracle
- ODBC
- XML
- Microsoft SharePoint List
- SAP NetWeaver BI
- Hyperion Essbase
- Microsoft Business Intelligence Semantic Model

SUMMARY

Organizations have come to rely on SharePoint for their intranet, extranet, and Internet web sites. Integrating SQL Server 2012 Reporting Services and SharePoint is a natural fit and provides an attractive solution for delivering reports to end users throughout the organization.

This chapter covered the following topics:

- An introduction to SharePoint web parts
- SharePoint integration with SQL Server Reporting Services in Native mode, including the installation and usage of the Report Viewer and Report Explorer web parts
- SharePoint integration with SQL Server Reporting Services in Integrated mode, including publishing reports (SharePoint Foundation and SharePoint Server), and the SQL Server Reporting Services Report Viewer for Integrated Mode
- A comparison of Reporting Services integration with SQL Server in Native mode versus Integrated mode
- Managing reports using the SharePoint interface — in particular, the drop-down context menu for each report, connection, and model item

19

Native Mode Server Administration

WHAT'S IN THIS CHAPTER?

➤ Security

➤ Account management and system-level roles

➤ Surface area management

➤ Backup and recovery

➤ Application databases

➤ Encryption keys

➤ Configuration files

➤ Monitoring and logging

➤ Performance counters and server management reports

➤ Memory management

➤ URL reservations

➤ E-mail delivery

➤ Managing rendering extensions

With any mission-critical service, it's important to properly configure and administer your report server. If you have Reporting Services configured in Native mode and not integrated into SharePoint, you will use tools that are specific to Reporting Services.

This chapter addresses the administration tasks for a report server configured in Native mode. It does not apply to SharePoint Integrated mode. Some significant architectural changes took place in SQL Server 2012 with respect to SharePoint integration. In earlier product versions, the service configuration was managed using the same tools, regardless of which mode the server was configured in, with some additional integration settings in SharePoint. In the 2012 version, this all changed. Now the integrated report server is managed completely within the SharePoint Central Administrator and other SharePoint user interfaces. The Reporting Services Configuration Manager and configuration files are no longer used in that case. Reporting Services no longer runs as a Windows Service in Integrated mode. That version of the core report server is now managed as a SharePoint service application and is managed entirely in SharePoint. By contrast, although SSRS has been enhanced with newer features, little has changed for the Native mode configuration since SSRS 2008.

An administration plan should address the following general concerns:

➤ Security

➤ Backup and recovery

➤ Monitoring

➤ Configuration

This chapter explores these topics as they relate to Reporting Services in Native mode. This gives you the basic knowledge you need to engage users, developers, and IT administrators in developing a plan tailored to your organization's specific needs.

SECURITY

Properly securing your Reporting Services environment requires you to find the right balance between risk, availability, and supportability. Following good network, system, and facilities management practices goes a long way toward securing your installation. Specific to Reporting Services, you should consider how to best approach the following:

➤ Account management

➤ System-level roles

➤ Surface area management

Account Management

Reporting Services must interact with various resources. To access these resources, Reporting Services must present its requests as originating from a specific, valid user. Reporting Services stores credentials, typically username and password combinations, for the following three accounts, each of which is used to handle specific interactions with resources:

➤ The service account

➤ The application database account

➤ The unattended execution account

Whenever possible, it is recommended that you use Windows domain user accounts as the source of the credentials for these three application accounts. This allows you to leverage Windows' security infrastructure for credential management.

In addition, it is recommended that you employ accounts dedicated for use in these roles. Reuse of credentials can make long-term management of these accounts more difficult and can lead to unintended resource access. This can also lead to the accumulation of permissions associated with an account. An account used for one of these roles should have no more permissions than those required for it to successfully complete its operations.

Finally, you should limit the number of trusted individuals who have knowledge of these credentials. As individuals move out of roles requiring them to have this knowledge (or leave the organization), these accounts should be updated to maintain a secure environment. If Windows accounts are used (as just recommended), you can prevent inappropriate use by prohibiting their use for interactive log-ins to Windows systems.

The Service Account

During installation you are asked to specify the account under which the Reporting Services Windows service operates. This is called the *service account*. Through this account, the Reporting Services Windows service accesses various system resources. If your installation runs in SharePoint Integrated mode, this is the account that Reporting Services also uses to access the SharePoint databases.

The Reporting Services service account can be one of three built-in accounts or a Windows user account that you define, as described in Table 19-1.

TABLE 19-1

ACCOUNT	DETAILS
Local System	A built-in account that behaves as a member of the local Administrators group. When accessing resources on the network, it uses the computer's credentials. It is not recommended that you use this for the service account.
Local Service	A built-in account that behaves as a member of the local Users group. It accesses resources on the network with no credentials.
Network Service	A built-in account that behaves as a member of the local Users group. When accessing resources on the network, it uses the computer's credentials. It is no longer recommended that you use this for the service account.
User Account	Allows you to enter the credentials of a local or domain Windows user account. If a local account is used, access to network resources is with no credentials. If a domain account is used, access to network resources is through the domain account. This is the recommended account type for the service account.

The service account requires permissions to specific resources on the system on which the Reporting Services Windows service runs. Instead of granting these rights to the service account itself, the service account obtains them through membership in a local group created by the SQL Server setup application during installation. This group is named SQLServerReportServerUser$*ComputerName*$ MSRS11.*InstanceName*. MSSQLSERVER is used as the instance name for the default instance.

There is no need to directly alter membership to this group when making changes to the service account. Instead, you are strongly encouraged to make any changes to the service account using the Service Account page of the Reporting Services Configuration Manager, shown in Figure 19-1. The tool handles the details of managing membership to this group, updating the Windows service, adjusting encryption keys, altering URL reservations, and granting access to the Reporting Services application databases (if the service account is used as the application database account). All these tasks must be performed with a change in the service account.

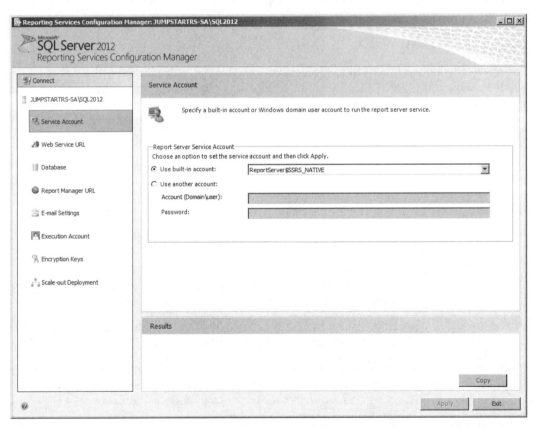

FIGURE 19-1

Finally, if you are running in SharePoint Integrated mode and you switch the service account, make sure that the account has appropriate access to the SharePoint databases. To do this, open SharePoint Central Administration. In the Reporting Services section, click "Grant database access," and enter the Reporting Services service account information in the resulting dialog. After this change is saved, it is recommended that you restart the SharePoint Services service to ensure that the appropriate credentials are being used.

The Application Database Account

Reporting Services depends on content stored in its application databases. These databases are hosted by a local or remote instance of SQL Server. To connect to its databases, Reporting Services must maintain connection string data along with valid credentials for establishing a connection. The credentials are called the *application database account*.

You have three options for the application database account. You can specify a SQL Server authenticated username and password, provide the credentials for a valid Windows user account, or elect to have Reporting Services simply use its service account when establishing the connection.

The SQL Server Authenticated User option requires the SQL Server instance hosting the application databases to support both Windows and SQL Server authentication. By default, SQL Server is configured for Windows (Integrated) authentication only, because SQL Server authentication is considered less secure. It is recommended that you employ the SQL Server Authenticated User option only in special circumstances, such as when Windows user accounts cannot be authenticated.

The application database account is set during installation and can be modified later using the Reporting Services Configuration Manager, as shown in Figure 19-2. If you installed using a default configuration, the application database account was automatically set to use the service account.

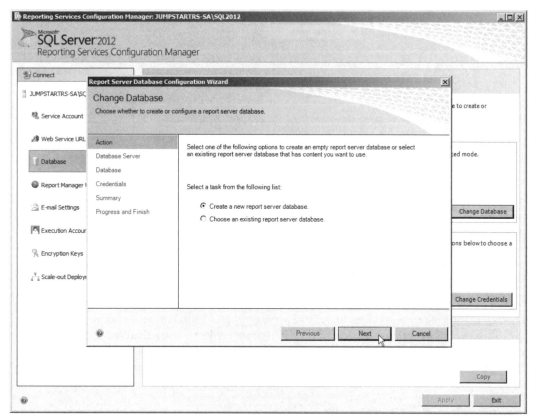

FIGURE 19-2

If you use the service account or Windows user option, a login is created within SQL Server mapped to this Windows account. (If you use the SQL Server Authenticated User option, you need to create a login in advance.) The login is then granted access to the two Reporting Services application databases as well as the master and msdb system databases. Within each database, the account is mapped to a collection of roles that provide it the rights it needs to handle Reporting Services' database operations, including the creation and management of jobs through a SQL Agent. Table 19-2 lists the database roles to which the application database account is mapped.

TABLE 19-2

DATABASE	ROLES
Master	public
	RSExecRole
Msdb	public
	RSExecRole
	SQLAgentOperatorRole
	SQLAgentReaderRole
	SQLAgentUserRole
ReportServer	db_owner
	public
	RSExecRole
ReportServerTempDB	db_owner
	public
	RSExecRole

It is important to note that if you change the application database account used by Reporting Services to connect to its application databases, the Reporting Services Configuration Manager does not remove the previous application database account from the SQL Server instance. Instead, a valid login is left within the instance of SQL Server Database Engine, retaining its membership in the database roles listed in Table 19-2. If you change the application database account, you should follow up by removing the prior login from these roles or from the SQL Server instance.

The Unattended Execution Account

Reports might need to access files on remote servers or data sources that do not require authentication. To access these resources, you can specify that no credentials are required as part of the datasource definition. When you do so, you are instructing Reporting Services to use the credentials it has cached for the *unattended execution account* (also known as the *unattended report processing account* or simply the *execution account*) when accessing the resource.

By default, the unattended execution account is disabled and should remain so unless a specific need is recognized that cannot be addressed by other reasonable means. To enable the account and configure its credentials, access the Execution Account page within the Configuration Manager and provide the required credentials, as shown in Figure 19-3.

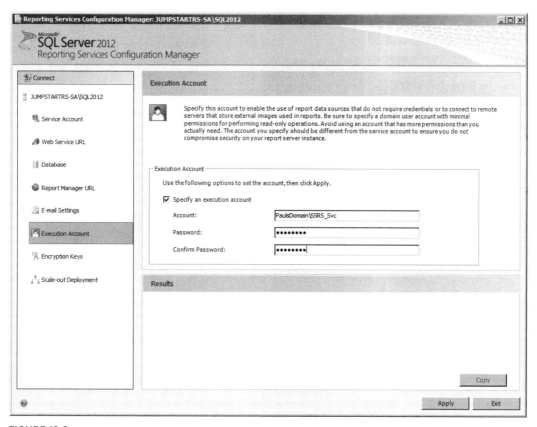

FIGURE 19-3

System-Level Roles

System-level roles give members the rights to perform tasks across the Reporting Services site. Reporting Services comes preconfigured with two system-level roles: System User and System Administrator. The System User role allows users to retrieve information about the site and to execute reports in Report Builder that have not yet been published to the site. The System Administrator role gives administrators the rights required to manage the site, including the rights to create additional roles. Table 19-3 describes the specific system-level tasks assigned to these roles.

TABLE 19-3

TASK	DESCRIPTION	SYSTEM ADMINISTRATOR	SYSTEM USER
Execute report definitions	Start execution from the report definition without publishing it to the Report Server	Yes	Yes
Generate events	Lets an application generate events within the Report Server namespace	No	No
Manage jobs	View and cancel running jobs	Yes	No
Manage Report Server properties	View and modify properties that apply to the Report Server and to items managed by the Report Server	Yes	No
Manage roles	Create, view, modify, and delete role definitions	Yes	No
Manage shared schedules	Create, view, modify, and delete shared schedules used to run reports or refresh a report	Yes	No
Manage Report Server security	View and modify system-wide role assignments	Yes	No
View Report Server properties	View properties that apply to the Report Server	No	Yes
View shared schedules	View a predefined schedule that has been made available for general use	No	Yes

You can create additional site-level roles using SQL Server Management Studio. Doing so allows you to permit site-level tasks to be performed by others without granting them System Administrator rights. The process of creating these roles, assigning tasks, and granting membership is nearly identical to the creation of item-level roles. The only difference is that system-level roles are created through the System Roles folder instead of the Roles folder within SQL Server Management Studio, as shown in Figure 19-4.

By default, the BUILTIN\Administrators group is assigned to both the System Administrator system-level role and the Content Manager item-level role within the Home folder. You are encouraged to alter this so that a more appropriate user account or group is assigned these permissions. If you decide to leave the BUILTIN\Administrators group in these roles, carefully consider who is allowed administrative rights on your servers.

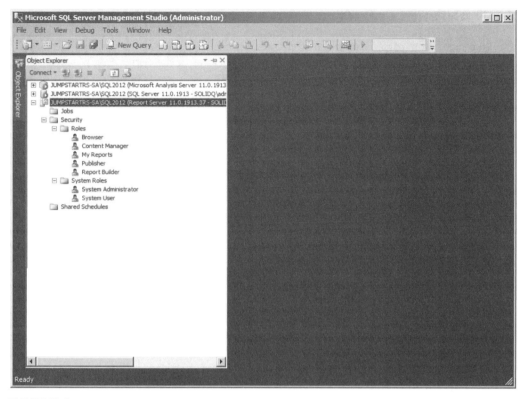

FIGURE 19-4

Surface Area Management

A feature that is not enabled is one that cannot be exploited. This is the general principle behind *surface area management*.

Reporting Services comes with several features disabled. These include the execution account, e-mail delivery, and My Reports. Still other features are enabled by default but are not necessarily required within your Reporting Services environment. These include Report Builder, Report Manager, the use of Windows Integrated security to access report data sources, and scheduling and delivery functionality. Carefully consider which Reporting Services features are truly required, and disable any that are not needed. Books Online provides documentation on disabling each of these features.

BACKUP AND RECOVERY

Although redundant hardware solutions offer considerable protection against many types of failure, they do not shield you from every eventuality. Regular backups of the critical components of your Reporting Services environment are required to better ensure its recoverability.

Of course, simply making backups is not enough. Your backups must be properly managed to ensure their availability following a failure event. This typically involves secured, off-site storage and the development of retention schedules so that you have the option to recover to various points in time.

In addition, those responsible for recovery should have experience with the recovery techniques. They should also be well versed in the procedures for accessing the backup media. It's not much fun to attempt a recovery when you do not know how to locate and use the recovery media.

Finally, you should establish policies regarding how communications and decision making will be handled during a recovery event. You want to ensure that all those potentially involved understand these policies. This will help minimize confusion during what can be an already stressful situation.

This section of the chapter reviews the backup and recovery of the following critical components of a Reporting Services environment:

➤ Application databases

➤ Encryption keys

➤ Configuration files

➤ Other items

Application Databases

Reporting Services uses two application databases. The primary database, ReportServer, houses content, whereas the secondary database, ReportServerTempDB, houses cached data. These default names are offered by the Configuration Manager, but can be changed.

 Although the names of the application databases can vary, the secondary application database must always be named the same as the primary, with TempDB appended. For example, if the primary application database is named MyRS, the secondary database associated with it must be named MyRSTempDB. The names of these databases should not be altered after they are created, and the two databases must always exist within the same SQL Server instance.

The primary application database, ReportServer, should be backed up on a regular basis and following any significant content changes. This database operates under the Full recovery model, which allows both data and log backups to be performed. If properly managed, the combination of data and log backups allows for point-in-time recovery of the ReportServer database.

The secondary application database, ReportServerTempDB, does not actually require a backup. If you need to recover it, you can create a new database appropriately named within the SQL Server instance housing the ReportServer database. Within this new database, execute the `CatalogTempDB.sql` script found within the *drive*:\Program Files\Microsoft SQL Server\MSRS11 *.instancename*\Reporting Services\ReportServer folder. The script re-creates the database objects required by Reporting Services. Be sure to run this from within the ReportServerTempDB database you just created.

If you decide to back up ReportServerTempDB, it is important to note that it operates under the Simple recovery model. This model allows for data backups but not log backups. Ideally, both databases should be backed up and restored as a set to maintain server consistency. However, a current backup of this database is not always critical, because it manages only temporary cached report execution information.

 Books Online includes a script for the backup and recovery of the ReportServer and ReportServerTempDB databases to another server. This script uses the COPY_ONLY *backup option and modifies the recovery model used with ReportServerTempDB. It is important to note that this script is provided in the context of performing a database migration, not a standard backup-and-recovery operation. Be sure to work with your database administrators to develop a backup-and-recovery plan that is tailored to the needs of your environment and that you have tested prior to promoting an environment to production status.*

If you recover a backup of ReportServerTempDB, be sure to purge its contents following recovery. The following statement can be used to perform this task. After the database is purged, it is recommended that you restart the Reporting Services service.

```
exec ReportServerTempDB.sys.sp_MSforeachtable
     @command1='truncate table #',
     @replacechar='#'
```

If you need to recover your application databases to another SQL Server instance, it is important to preserve the databases' original names. If Reporting Services uses a SQL Server authenticated account to connect to its application databases, you need to re-create that login in the new SQL Server instance. Following the restoration of the databases, you need to reassociate the user account in your application databases with the re-created login. This script demonstrates one technique for performing this task:

```
exec ReportServer.dbo.sp_change_users_login
     @Action = ' Update_One',
     @UserNamePattern = 'MyDbAccount',
     @LoginName = 'MyDbAccount'

exec ReportServerTempDB.dbo.sp_change_users_login
     @Action = 'Update_One',
     @UserNamePattern = 'MyDbAccount',
     @LoginName = 'MyDbAccount'
```

As soon as the database user and login are properly associated, launch the Reporting Services Configuration Manager against your Reporting Services instance, and locate the Database page, as shown in Figure 19-5.

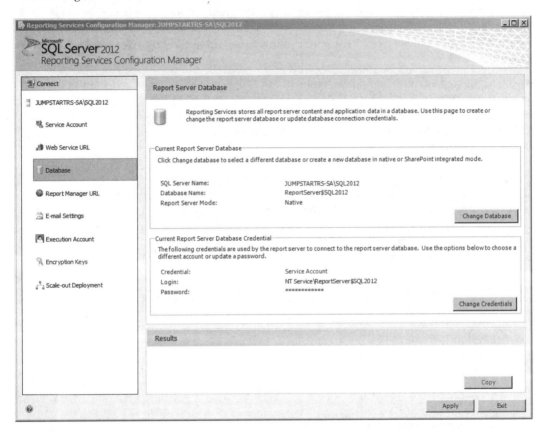

FIGURE 19-5

From this page, click the Change Database button. In the resulting dialog, enter the information required to connect to the primary application database at its new location. Restarting Reporting Services from the Reporting Service Configuration Manager completes the process.

Encryption Keys

Reporting Services protects the sensitive information it stores through encryption based on a *symmetric key* generated during initialization. The symmetric key, per its definition, is used in both encryption and decryption operations. To prevent unauthorized decryption of sensitive data, the symmetric key itself must be protected. This is accomplished by encrypting the symmetric key using an asymmetric key pair generated by the operating system.

Although this protects the symmetric key, also called the *encryption key*, it increases the system's administrative complexity. Certain operations invalidate the asymmetric key pair. Unless handled properly, these operations cause Reporting Services to lose its ability to decrypt the symmetric key, leaving its sensitive data inaccessible. These operations include the following:

➤ Resetting the service account's password

➤ Changing the Reporting Services Windows service account

➤ Changing the server's name

➤ Changing the name of the Reporting Services instance

If you need to perform these operations, it is critical that you follow the steps outlined in this chapter and in Books Online. If the precise steps required by these operations are not followed, the symmetric key can no longer be decrypted. Your options then are to either recover the key from a backup or delete it. Deleting the key, as described in a moment, is extremely disruptive to your site.

To back up the encryption key, use either the Encryption Keys page of the Reporting Services Configuration Manager, shown in Figure 19-6, or the `rskeymgmt` command-line utility with the `-e` parameter:

```
rskeymgmt.exe -e -i MSSQLSERVER -f c:\backups\rs_2012_11_04.snk -p p@ssw0rd
```

With either approach, you need to provide a name for the backup file, along with a password to protect its contents.

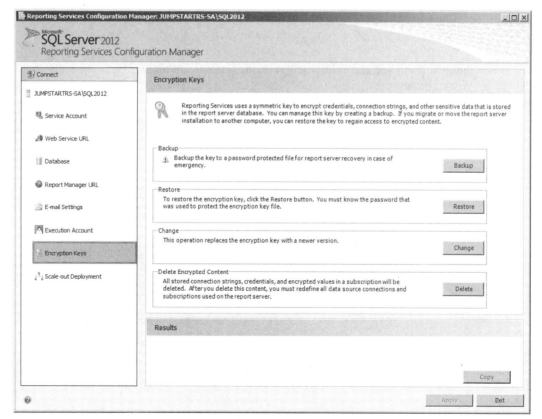

FIGURE 19-6

The -i parameter is used to specify the name of the Reporting Services instance on the local system. The default instance is identified with the MSSQLSERVER *keyword.*

It is recommended that you back up the encryption key when the server is first initialized, when the service account is changed, or whenever the key is deleted or re-created. Although it is password-protected, the backup file should be secured to prevent unauthorized access to sensitive information.

If you suspect that the encryption key has been compromised, you can re-create it using the Reporting Services Configuration Manager or the rskeymgmt command-line utility with the -s parameter:

```
rskeymgmt.exe -s -i MSSQLSERVER
```

This operation can be time-consuming, so you might want to restrict user access to the Reporting Services instance until you're finished.

If your Reporting Services instance is part of a scale-out deployment, you need to reinitialize the other instances in the environment with the newly created key per the instructions provided in Books Online.

To recover the encryption key, use either the Reporting Services Configuration Manager or the rskeymgmt command-line utility with the -a parameter. Both approaches require you to identify the backup file and supply its password:

```
rskeymgmt.exe -a -i MSSQLSERVER -f c:\backups\rs_2012_11_04.snk -p p@ssw0rd
```

Deleting the encryption key is considered an operation of last resort. After doing so, you need to re-create all shared and report-specific connection strings containing it and reactivate all subscriptions. As before, this operation can be performed using the Reporting Services Configuration Manager or the rskeymgmt command-line utility, this time with the -d parameter:

```
rskeymgmt.exe -d -i MSSQLSERVER
```

If your Reporting Services instance is part of a scale-out deployment, you need to delete the key on each instance in the environment. Refer to Books Online for instructions on completing this operation.

Configuration Files

Several configuration files affect Reporting Services. To fully recover your installation, you need backups of these files. Reporting Services itself does not provide a mechanism for this. However, you can use any number of file backup techniques to safeguard these files. Table 19-4 describes the configuration files you will want to back up and their default locations.

TABLE 19-4

CONFIGURATION FILE	DEFAULT LOCATION
ReportingServicesService.exe .config	*drive*:\Program Files\Microsoft SQL Server\MSRS11.*instancename*\ Reporting Services\ReportServer\Bin
RSReportServer.config	*drive*:\Program Files\Microsoft SQL Server\MSRS11.*instancename*\ Reporting Services\ReportServer
RSSrvPolicy.config	*drive*:\Program Files\Microsoft SQL Server\MSRS11.*instancename*\ Reporting Services\ReportServer
RSMgrPolicy.config	*drive*:\Program Files\Microsoft SQL Server\MSRS11.*instancename*\ Reporting Services\ReportManager
Web.config	*drive*:\Program Files\Microsoft SQL Server\MSRS11.*instancename*\ Reporting Services\ReportServer
Web.config	*drive*:\Program Files\Microsoft SQL Server\MSRS11.*instancename*\ Reporting Services\ReportManager
Machine.config	*drive*:\Windows\Microsoft.NET\Framework*version*\CONFIG

Other Items

Your backup-and-recovery plan should consider any custom scripts or components in use by your installation. In addition, you will want to make sure that purchased components, installation media, service packs, and hotfixes are available during a recovery event. If you have created a database to house execution log data (discussed later), you may want to back this up as well.

MONITORING

Effective monitoring should allow you to quickly identify or even anticipate problems within your environment. Reporting Services provides various features to support this activity. Reporting Services can be used as a tool to present this data to administrators in an easier-to-consume manner.

This section explores the use of:

➤ Setup logs

➤ Windows application event logs

➤   Trace logs

➤   Execution log

➤   Performance counters

➤   Server management reports

Setup Logs

During installation, the setup application creates a series of text-based log files that record messages and statistics generated as part of the process. By default, these are located in subfolders of the *drive*:\Program Files\Microsoft SQL Server\110\Setup Bootstrap\LOG folder. These subfolders are named using the convention *YYYYMMDD_nnnn*, where *YYYY*, *MM*, and *DD* represent the year, month, and day of the installation. The *nnnn* portion of the name represents an incrementing four-digit number, the highest value of which identifies the most recent installation attempt.

The contents of these folders are a bit overwhelming but worth exploring if you experience errors during an installation attempt. To review the summary status of the most recent installation attempt, simply direct your attention to the `Summary.txt` file within the *drive*:\Program Files\ Microsoft SQL Server\110\Setup Bootstrap\LOG folder.

Windows Application Event Logs

Reporting Services writes critical error, warning, and informational messages to the *Windows application event log*. These messages are identified as originating from the Report Server, Report Manager, and Scheduling and Delivery Processor event sources.

The complete list of Reporting Services event log messages is documented in Books Online. Administrators will want to familiarize themselves with this list and periodically review the Windows Application event log for these and other critical messages. You can view the Windows event logs using the operating system's Event Viewer applet.

Trace Logs

The *trace logs* are a great source of information about activity taking place within the Reporting Services Windows service. You can locate these files in the *drive*:\Program Files\Microsoft SQL Server\MSRS11.*instancename*\Reporting Services\LogFiles folder. The logs are by default named *ReportServerService__MM_DD_YYYY_hh_mm_ss*, where *MM*, *DD*, *YYYY*, *hh*, *mm*, and *ss* represent the month, day, year, hour, minute, and second, respectively, that the file was created. You can view each of these files using a simple text editor.

By default, Reporting Services is configured to write exceptions, warnings, restart, and status messages to the trace log files. Log files are retained for a configurable number of days. A new log file is created at the beginning of the day, when the Reporting Services Windows service is started, or when the file reaches a configurable maximum size. The configuration settings affecting the trace logs are found within the `RStrace` section of the `ReportingServicesService.exe.config` file, typically located in the drive:\Program Files\Microsoft SQL Server\MSRS11.instancename\ Reporting Services\ReportServer\Bin folder. The RStrace settings are described in Table 19-5, along with their defaults.

TABLE 19-5

SETTING	DEFAULT	DESCRIPTION
`FileName`	`ReportServerService_`	The first part of the filename. A string indicating the date and time the file was created, along with a .log extension, is appended to produce the full filename.
`FileSizeLimitMb`	32	The maximum size of the trace file in megabytes (MB). A value <u>less than or equal to</u> 0 is treated as 1.
`KeepFilesForDays`	14	The number of days to retain a trace file. A value <u>less than or equal to</u> 0 is treated as 1.
`TraceListeners`	`debugwindow, file`	A comma-delimited list of one or more trace log output targets. Valid values within the list include `debugwindow`, `file`, and `stdout`.
`TraceFileMode`	`Unique` (default)	A value indicating that each trace file should contain data for a single day. Do not modify this setting.
`DefaultTraceSwitch`	3	The default trace level for any component identified in the `Components` setting but for which no trace switch is provided. Here are the values: 0 — Disabled 1 — Exceptions and restarts 2 — Exceptions, restarts, and warnings 3 — Exceptions, restarts, warnings, and status messages 4 — Verbose mode

continues

TABLE 19-5 *(continued)*

SETTING	DEFAULT	DESCRIPTION
Components	All:3	A comma-delimited list of components and their associated trace levels determining the information to be included in the trace.
		These components represent activities that can produce trace messages. Here are the valid components:
		`RunningJobs` — Report and subscription execution
		`SemanticQueryEngine` — Report model usage `SemanticModelGenerator` — Report model generation
		`All` — Any of the components, except `http`, not otherwise specified
		`http` — HTTP requests received by Reporting Services
		The type of message written for each specified component is controlled by a trace level. The levels are as follows:
		0 — Disabled
		1 — Exceptions and restarts
		2 — Exceptions, restarts, and warnings
		3 — Exceptions, restarts, warnings, and status messages
		4 — Verbose mode

The `http` component identified in this table was introduced in SQL Server 2008 Reporting Services. It remains unchanged in the current product version. It instructs Reporting Services to record HTTP requests to a separate trace log file in the traditional W3C extended log format.

The `http` component is not covered by the `All` component. Therefore, the default `Components` setting of `All:3` leaves HTTP logging disabled. To enable HTTP logging, append the `http` component to the `Components` list with a trace level of 4. Any other trace level for the `http` component leaves it disabled.

The HTTP trace log files are stored in the same folder as the traditional trace files. Trace configuration settings such as `FileSizeLimitMb` and `KeepFilesForDays` serve double duty, affecting the management of both the traditional and HTTP trace log files.

Two HTTP trace log-specific settings, `HttpTraceFileName` and `HttpTraceSwitches`, are manually added to the `ReportingServicesService.exe.config` file to override the default HTTP trace log filename and data format, respectively. If the `HttpTraceSwitches` setting is not specified, the fields identified as defaults in Table 19-6 are recorded to the HTTP trace logs.

TABLE 19-6

FIELD	DESCRIPTION	DEFAULT
Date	The date of the event	No
Time	The time of the event	No
ActivityID	The activity identifier	Yes
SourceActivityID	The source activity identifier	Yes
ClientIp	The IP address of the client accessing the Report Server	Yes
UserName	The name of the user who accessed the Report Server	No
ServerPort	The port number used for the connection	No
Host	The content of the host header	No
Method	The action or SOAP method called from the client	Yes
UriStem	The resource accessed	Yes
UriQuery	The query used to access the resource	No
ProtocolStatus	The HTTP status code	Yes
BytesSent	The number of bytes sent by the server	No
BytesReceived	The number of bytes received by the server	No
TimeTaken	The time (in milliseconds) from the instant that HTTP.SYS returns request data until the server finishes the last send, excluding network transmission time	No
ProtocolVersion	The protocol version used by the client	No
UserAgent	The browser type used by the client	No
CookieReceived	The content of the cookie received by the server	No
CookieSent	The content of the cookie sent by the server	No
Referrer	The previous site visited by the client	No

The following sample shows the RSTrace section of the ReportingServicesService.exe. config file with both traditional and HTTP logging enabled and the HttpTraceFileName and HttpTraceSwitches settings explicitly configured. Note the Components setting with the http component specified with a trace level of 4:

```
<RStrace>
    <add name="FileName" value="ReportServerService_" />
    <add name="FileSizeLimitMb" value="32" />
    <add name="KeepFilesForDays" value="14" />
    <add name="Prefix" value="tid, time" />
```

```
        <add name="TraceListeners" value="debugwindow, file" />
        <add name="TraceFileMode" value="unique" />
        <add name="HttpTraceFileName" value="RS_HTTP_" />
        <add name="HttpTraceSwitches" value="Date,Time,ActivityID,
            SourceActivityID,ClientIp,UserName,Method,
            UriStem,UriQuery,ProtocolStatus,BytesSent,
            BytesReceived,TimeTaken" />
        <add name="Components" value="runningjobs:3,all:2,http:4" />
    </RStrace>
```

 When you modify the configuration file, it's important to make a backup in case a problem arises with your changes. Also, be aware that setting names are case-sensitive, although the values do not appear to be.

Execution Logs

Reporting Services stores quite a bit of data about the execution of reports in a collection of tables in the ReportServer database. Collectively, these tables are called the *execution log*.

To make this data accessible, Reporting Services provides a SQL Server Integration Services (SSIS) package named RSExecutionLog_Update.dtsx with the Reporting Services samples from Microsoft, available at http://msftrsprodsamples.codeplex.com. The package extracts execution log data from the ReportServer database into a secondary database. If you have installed these samples, you can typically find this package at *drive*:\Program Files\Microsoft SQL Server\110\ Samples\Reporting Services\Report Samples\Server Management Sample Reports\Execution Log Sample Reports.

The package refers to a SQL Server database named RSExecutionLog, which you need to create. After you have created the RSExecutionLog database, you need to create the table structures it will use to hold your data. The Createtables.sql script provided in the same folder as the SSIS package handles this task for you. When executing this script, be sure that you are using the RSExecutionLog database, because the script itself does not contain a USE statement.

After the database is created, verify that the Connection Managers within the SSIS package point to it. With this done, you can extract data from the ReportServer database to the RSExecutionLog database for review and analysis.

The volume of data associated with the execution logs can get quite large. Reporting Services is configured by default to retain execution log data for 60 days. You can alter this setting through SQL Server Management Studio by connecting to the Reporting Services instance, right-clicking the instance object, and selecting Properties from the context menu. In the Server Properties dialog, shown in Figure 19-7, navigate to the Logging page. Here you can change the number of days that the data is retained or disable execution logging.

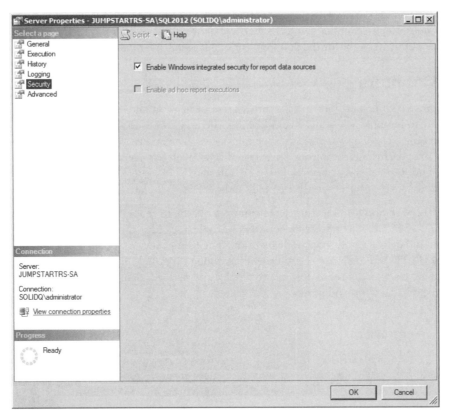

FIGURE 19-7

The RSExecutionLog database does not have a built-in data cleanup mechanism. The `Cleanup.sql` script provided in the same folder as the SSIS package can be used to purge old data from the RSExecutionLog database. The script uses a hard-coded date of January 1, 2004 as the cutoff point for data expiration. The following code sample shows a section of the `Cleanup.sql` script modified to drop data older than 180 days (about six months) from the current date and time:

```
/*
Change this constant for the earliest data
Everything earlier will be deleted
*/
DECLARE @EarliestTimeStart datetime
/* ORIGINAL CODE
SET @EarliestTimeStart = '2004-01-01 00:00:00'
                        -- ** Always use ODBC cannonical form **
                        -- i.e. yyyy-mm-dd hh:mi:ss(24h)SET
*/
-- NEW CODE
SET @EarliestTimeStart = DATEADD(dd, -180, GETDATE())
```

To consume the execution log data, the Reporting Services samples come with three predefined reports: Execution Status Codes, Report Summary, and Execution Summary. They are pretty self-explanatory. They can be used as a starting point for the development of a larger array of administrative reports.

Performance Counters

Windows performance counters provide insight into system utilization and stability. Administrators have long used these to monitor a system's overall health, identify trends that may lead to problems, and verify the effect of changes on various system components. To support this activity, Reporting Services provides three performance objects: SQL Server 2012 Web Service, SQL Server 2012 Windows Service, and ReportServer Service. There are alternative versions of the web service and Windows service counters for SharePoint Integrated mode.

The SQL Server 2012 Web Service object presents counters related to report processing. The SQL Server 2012 Windows Service object presents counters related to scheduled operations, such as subscription execution and delivery and snapshot execution. The ReportServer Service object presents counters related to HTTP- and memory-related events. Although focused on different subject areas, many of the counters presented by these objects are named and defined identically. Table 19-7 lists the counters and the objects with which they are associated.

TABLE 19-7

COUNTER	DESCRIPTION	SQL SERVER 2012 WEB SERVICE	SQL SERVER 2012 WINDOWS SERVICE	REPORT SERVER SERVICE
Active Connections	Number of connections active against the server	No	Yes	Yes
Active Sessions	Number of active sessions	Yes	Yes	No
Bytes Received/Sec	Rate of bytes received per second	No	Yes	Yes
Bytes Received Total	Number of bytes received	No	Yes	Yes
Bytes Sent/Sec	Rate of bytes sent per second	No	No	Yes
Bytes Sent Total	Number of bytes sent	No	No	Yes
Cache Hits/Sec	Number of Report Server cache hits per second	Yes	Yes	No
Cache Hits/Sec (semantic models)	Number of times per second that models can be retrieved from the cache	Yes	Yes	No

COUNTER	DESCRIPTION	SQL SERVER 2012 WEB SERVICE	SQL SERVER 2012 WINDOWS SERVICE	REPORT SERVER SERVICE
Cache Misses/Sec	Number of times per second that reports cannot be retrieved from the cache	Yes	Yes	No
Cache Misses/Sec (semantic models)	Number of times per second that models cannot be retrieved from the cache	Yes	Yes	No
Errors/Sec	Number of errors that occur during the execution of HTTP requests (error codes 400s and 500s) per second	No	No	Yes
Errors Total	Total number of errors that occur during the execution of HTTP requests (error codes 400s and 500s)	No	No	Yes
First Session Requests/Sec	Number of new user sessions that are started per second	Yes	Yes	No
Logon Attempts/Sec	Rate of logon attempts	No	No	Yes
Logon Attempts Total	Number of logon attempts for RSWindows authentication types	No	No	Yes
Logon Successes/ Sec	Rate of successful logons	No	No	Yes
Logon Successes Total	Number of successful logons for RSWindows authentication types	No	No	Yes
Memory Cache Hits/ Sec	Number of times per second that reports can be retrieved from the in-memory cache	Yes	Yes	No
Memory Cache Miss/ Sec	Number of times per second that reports cannot be retrieved from the in-memory cache	Yes	Yes	No

continues

TABLE 19-7 *(continued)*

COUNTER	DESCRIPTION	SQL SERVER 2012 WEB SERVICE	SQL SERVER 2012 WINDOWS SERVICE	REPORT SERVER SERVICE
Memory Pressure State	A number from 1 to 5 indicating the server's current memory state: 1 — No pressure 2 — Low pressure 3 — Medium pressure 4 — High pressure 5 — Exceeded pressure	No	No	Yes
Memory Shrink Amount	Number of bytes the server asked to shrink	No	No	Yes
Memory Shrink Notifications/Sec	Number of shrink notifications the server issued in the last second	No	No	Yes
Next Session Requests/Sec	Number of requests per second for reports that are open in an existing session	Yes	Yes	No
Report Requests	Number of active report requests	Yes	Yes	No
Reports Executed/Sec	Number of reports executed per second	Yes	Yes	No
Requests Disconnected	Number of requests that have been disconnected because of a communication failure	No	Yes	Yes
Requests Executing	Number of requests currently executing	No	No	Yes
Requests Not Authorized	Number of requests failing with HTTP 401 error code	No	Yes	Yes
Requests Rejected	Total number of requests not executed because of insufficient server resources	No	Yes	Yes
Requests/Sec	Number of requests per second	Yes	Yes	Yes

COUNTER	DESCRIPTION	SQL SERVER 2012 WEB SERVICE	SQL SERVER 2012 WINDOWS SERVICE	REPORT SERVER SERVICE
Requests Total	The total number of requests received by the Report Server service since service startup	No	No	Yes
Tasks Queued	Represents the number of tasks that are waiting for a thread to become available for processing	No	Yes	Yes
Total Cache Hits	Total number of Report Server cache hits	Yes	Yes	No
Total Cache Hits (semantic models)	Total number of cache hits made in the model cache	Yes	Yes	No
Total Cache Misses	Total number of cache misses	Yes	Yes	No
Total Cache Misses (semantic models)	Total number of cache misses made in the model cache	Yes	Yes	No
Total Memory Cache Hits	Total number of cache hits made in the in-memory cache	Yes	Yes	No
Total Memory Cache Misses	Total number of cache misses made in the in-memory cache	Yes	Yes	No
Total Processing Failures	Total number of processing failures	Yes	Yes	No
Total Rejected Threads	Total number of rejected threads as a result of thread pressure	Yes	Yes	No
Total Reports Executed	Total number of reports executed	Yes	Yes	No
Total Requests	Total number of requests being processed	Yes	Yes	No

Together, these three objects present 72 counters with which you can monitor an installation. It is not advised that you monitor each one. Instead, consider using high-level statistics such as Active Sessions, Requests/Sec, Reports Executed/Sec, and First Session Requests/Sec for your day-to-day monitoring. As specific needs arise, you will want to incorporate additional counters until those needs are addressed.

In addition to the Reporting Services performance counters, you might consider monitoring the Reporting Services Windows service from the operating system's perspective. Windows provides a Process performance object through which a number of performance counters are provided. Table 19-8 describes a few of the more commonly monitored counters under this object.

TABLE 19-8

COUNTER	DESCRIPTION
% Processor Time	The percentage of elapsed time that all process threads used the processor to execute instructions
Page Faults/sec	The rate at which page faults by the threads executing in this process are occurring
Virtual Bytes	The current size, in bytes, of the virtual address space the process is using

Finally, you will want to keep tabs on a few counters that indicate the overall health of the systems on which Reporting Services resides. Commonly monitored performance counters in this category include those listed in Table 19-9.

TABLE 19-9

OBJECT	COUNTER	DESCRIPTION
Processor	% Processor Time	The primary indicator of processor activity. Displays the average percentage of busy time observed during the sample interval.
System	Processor Queue Length	The number of threads in the processor queue.
Memory	Pages/sec	The rate at which pages are read from or written to disk to resolve hard page faults. This counter is a primary indicator of the kinds of faults that cause system-wide delays.
Logical Disk	% Free Space	The percentage of total usable free space on the selected logical disk drive.
Physical Disk	Avg. Disk Queue Length	The average number of both read and write requests that were queued for the selected disk during the sample interval.
Network Interface	Current Bandwidth	An estimate of the current bandwidth of the network interface in bits per second (BPS). For interfaces that do not vary in bandwidth or for those where no accurate estimation can be made, this value is the nominal bandwidth.
Network Interface	Bytes Total/sec	The rate at which bytes are sent and received over each network adapter, including framing characters. Network Interface\Bytes Total/sec is a sum of Network Interface\Bytes Received/sec and Network Interface\Bytes Sent/sec.

Server Management Reports

As previously mentioned, the Reporting Services samples come with three reports for reviewing the extracted execution log data. Two other sample reports are provided with the Reporting Services tasks to give administrators insight into database structures. Collectively, these are known as the *server management reports*.

The server management reports are not intended to address all your administrative needs. Instead, they illustrate how Reporting Services can be used as a tool supporting its own administration and management. It is not hard to imagine a number of additional administrative reports providing deeper insight into the execution log data. With a bit of effort, data sources such as the performance counters, trace logs, and Windows Application event logs can also be integrated and made accessible for reporting.

The possibilities for server management reporting are endless. With some up-front investment to consolidate data sources, you can leverage Reporting Services functionality to reduce your environment's overall administrative burden.

CONFIGURATION

Reporting Services supports several configurable features and options to meet your organization's precise needs. Books Online documents many of these, and still others can be identified with a little exploration. The following sections explore a few of the more frequently configured Reporting Services elements:

➤ Memory management

➤ URL reservations

➤ E-mail delivery

➤ Rendering extensions

➤ My Reports

Memory Management

The following four settings in the `RSReportServer.config` configuration file, typically located in the *drive*:\Program Files\Microsoft SQL Server\MSRS11.*instancename*\Reporting Services\ReportServer folder, determine how Reporting Services manages its memory:

➤ `WorkingSetMinimum`

➤ `WorkingSetMaximum`

➤ `MemorySafetyMargin`

➤ `MemoryThreshold`

The `WorkingSetMinimum` and `WorkingSetMaximum` settings determine the range of memory that Reporting Services may use. By default, these settings are not recorded in the configuration file.

Instead, Reporting Services assumes values of 60 percent and 100 percent of the system's physical memory, respectively.

To override these defaults, you can add the settings to the configuration file under the same parent as MemorySafetyMargin and MemoryThreshold. The values associated with the WorkingSetMinimum and WorkingSetMaximum settings represent absolute kilobytes of memory. If you are running multiple memory-intensive applications on your Reporting Services server, you should consider implementing these settings to avoid memory contention.

Within the range of memory available to it, Reporting Services implements a state-based memory management model. The MemorySafetyMargin setting, defaulted to 80 percent of the WorkingSetMaximum, defines the boundary between the low and medium memory pressure states. The MemoryThreshold setting, defaulted to 90 percent of the WorkingSetMaximum, defines boundary between the medium and high memory pressure states.

Within each memory pressure state, Reporting Services grants and takes back memory for report requests differently. For systems experiencing consistent loads, operating in the low and medium states is ideal. The default settings for MemorySafetyMargin and MemoryThreshold favor these states.

For systems experiencing spikes in memory utilization, such as might occur if several large reports are processed simultaneously, the medium and even high memory states may allow for greater concurrency, although reports may be rendered a bit more slowly. If this better matches your system's usage pattern, you might want to lower the MemorySafetyMargin and MemoryThreshold settings to more quickly move into these memory states.

URL Reservations

If you performed a Files Only installation of Reporting Services, you must configure URL reservations for the Reporting Services Web service and Report Manager. *URL reservations* tell the operating system's HTTP.SYS driver where to direct requests intended for Reporting Services. URL reservations minimally consist of a virtual directory, an IP address, and a TCP port.

Advanced configuration options enable you to associate an SSL certificate with the URL reservation. This is addressed in Books Online.

The virtual directory identifies the application to which communications will be targeted. Report Manager typically uses the reports virtual directory, whereas the Web service typically uses the reportserver virtual directory.

Named instances typically use the reports_instancename *and* reportserver_instancename *virtual directories for Report Manager and the Web service, respectively.*

The URL reservation's IP address identifies which IP addresses in use by the server the Reporting Services application will be associated with. The URL reservation typically is configured to be associated with all IP addresses in use on the server. But you can configure it to be associated with a specific IP address, including the loopback address, or to work with any IP addresses not explicitly reserved by other applications. This latter option is not recommended in most situations.

Finally, the URL reservation is tied to a TCP port. Typically, HTTP communications take place over TCP port 80. You may have multiple applications on a server listening on the same TCP port, so long as the overall URL reservation is unique on the server. If you specify a TCP port other than 80 (or 433 if you are using HTTPS communications), you need to include the port number in the URL whenever you communicate with Report Manager or the Web service.

> *If you are running Reporting Services on 32-bit Windows XP (SP2), TCP ports cannot be shared between URL reservations. Therefore, it is suggested that you use TCP port 8080 on this system for HTTP communications with Reporting Services. For more information on this topic, see Books Online.*

To configure a URL reservation for the Reporting Services Web service, access the Web Service URL page of the Reporting Services Configuration Manager, as shown in Figure 19-8. On this page, enter the virtual directory, IP address, and TCP port for the Web Service's URL reservation. After the changes are applied, you are presented with the Web services URL, which you can click to test.

FIGURE 19-8

To configure a URL reservation for the Report Manager application, access the Report Manager URL page of the Reporting Services Configuration Manager, as shown in Figure 19-9. The Report Manager URL reservation leverages the IP address and TCP port settings of the Web service's reservation. Enter the Report Manager's virtual directory, apply the changes, and click the provided URL to test the changes.

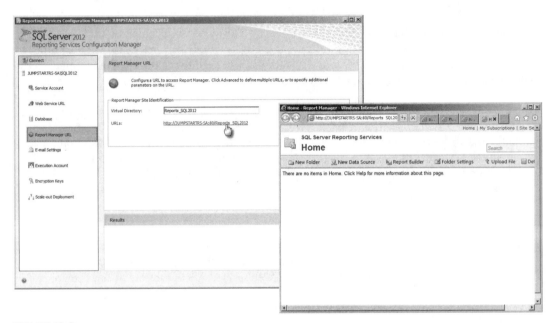

FIGURE 19-9

This has been a high-level discussion of URL reservations. Advanced options are available that require deeper knowledge of networking concepts. If you're familiar with these topics, you should have no problem understanding the interfaces and configuring Reporting Services appropriately. If you need to configure the Reporting Services URL reservations differently from what is discussed here, it is recommended that you engage your network support staff to explore your options.

E-mail Delivery

E-mail delivery of reports is a powerful feature of Reporting Services for driving report consumption. It also provides opportunities for overuse and abuse, and raises the environment's administrative overhead. Because of this fact and the potential complexity of its configuration, the feature is disabled by default.

To enable e-mail delivery, you simply configure the e-mail delivery extension. Books Online documents several variations on its configuration, but most systems use what is described as the "minimum configuration."

The *minimum configuration* requires the name or IP address of a remote SMTP server (or gateway) and a valid e-mail account on the SMTP server. This information is entered into the E-mail Settings page of the Reporting Services Configuration Manager, as shown in Figure 19-10, to enable the delivery extension.

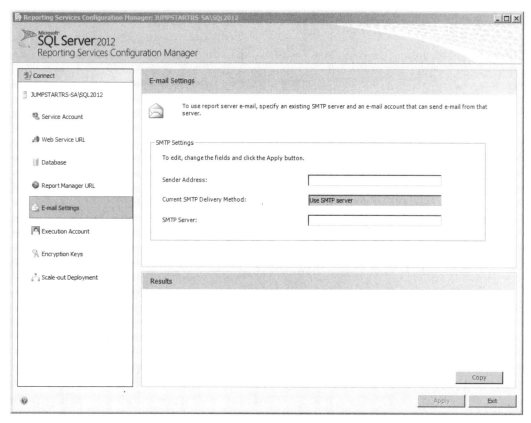

FIGURE 19-10

Communication with the SMTP server occurs through the Reporting Services service account. The service account requires SendAs rights with the SMTP server to send e-mail through the configured e-mail account.

If this is not set properly, or if any other problems prevent Reporting Services from sending e-mail through the SMTP server, error messages are displayed in the Windows application event log, as well as in the status message associated with e-mail-based subscriptions in Report Manager. However, problems with e-mail delivery downstream from the SMTP server are not reflected in Reporting Services. For this reason, it is recommended that you test your e-mail configuration by setting up a test subscription to a monitored e-mail account and verify end-to-end delivery of the subscription message.

After configuration, users assigned the "Manage individual subscriptions" or "Manage all subscriptions" tasks are given the option to use e-mail delivery (and any other enabled delivery options) when setting up subscriptions. Reporting Services does not provide a mechanism to secure the e-mail delivery option separately from other delivery mechanisms.

After it is enabled, you can disable e-mail delivery by simply removing the settings recorded in the Reporting Services Configuration Manager. Be aware that although this disables e-mail delivery, subscriptions already configured to use this delivery mechanism will continue to run as is and fail until they are disabled or reconfigured to use another delivery mechanism. For this reason, it is suggested that you disable e-mail delivery in phases.

In the first phase, prevent the creation of new e-mail-based subscriptions by commenting out the appropriate Extension entry within the `DeliveryUI` section of the `RSReportServer.config` file. This removes e-mail delivery as an option in Report Manager. The following code sample illustrates this modification:

```
<DeliveryUI>
    <!-- Extension Name="Report Server Email"
Type="Microsoft.ReportingServices.EmailDeliveryProvider
        .EmailDeliveryProviderControl,
        ReportingServicesEmailDeliveryProvider">
        <Configuration>
          <RSEmailDPConfiguration>
            <DefaultRenderingExtension>MHTML</DefaultRenderingExtension>
          </RSEmailDPConfiguration>
        </Configuration>
    </Extension -->
    <Extension Name="Report Server FileShare"
Type="Microsoft.ReportingServices.FileShareDeliveryProvider.FileShareUIControl,
    ReportingServicesFileShareDeliveryProvider">
            <DefaultDeliveryExtension>True</DefaultDeliveryExtension>
    </Extension>
</DeliveryUI>
```

It is important to note that although this removes e-mail delivery as an option in Report Manager, it does not prevent applications from creating new e-mail-based subscriptions through the Web services interface. If applications use this interface to create subscriptions, work with the application owners to disable this feature.

The second phase of disabling e-mail delivery involves reconfiguring any subscriptions that use e-mail delivery. Work with content owners to determine appropriate alternatives as part of this work. When migration is completed, you can then safely proceed with disabling e-mail delivery.

Rendering Extensions

Reporting Services comes preconfigured to render reports to a number of formats. The formats available are determined by the rendering extensions installed on the server and configured in the Render section of the `RSReportServer.config` file. Here is a sample entry for the Image rendering extension:

```
<Extension Name="IMAGE"
Type="Microsoft.ReportingServices.Rendering.ImageRenderer.ImageRenderer,
    Microsoft.ReportingServices.ImageRendering"/>
```

Each rendering extension entry minimally consists of name and type attributes. These identify the extension within the configuration file. The value associated with the `Name` attribute serves as a unique identifier for the extension within the configuration file. The `Type` attribute associates the entry with a particular rendering extension.

The name of the extension displayed to end users is the rendering extension's default display name, unless an OverrideNames setting is entered into the configuration file. The OverrideNames setting is recorded with the extension:

```
<Extension Name="IMAGE"
Type="Microsoft.ReportingServices.Rendering.ImageRenderer.ImageRenderer,
    Microsoft.ReportingServices.ImageRendering">
    <OverrideNames>
        <Name Language="en-US">TIFF</Name>
    </OverrideNames>
</Extension>
```

In this example, the default name of the Image rendering extension, TIFF File, is overridden with the shortened name of TIFF.

It is important to note that the Language attribute associated with the OverrideNames setting should match the language settings of the Reporting Services server. If the wrong or no language is specified, the OverrideNames entry is ignored, and the rendering extension's default name is used.

As mentioned in Chapter 2, rendering extensions can support various formats. In addition, aspects of how each extension renders to a particular format are configurable. To override the default rendering settings of a particular rendering extension, you can add DeviceInfo settings to an extension's entry in the configuration file. In addition, more than one entry for a rendering extension, typically with a different set of DeviceInfo settings, can be recorded in the configuration file so long as each extension entry is identified with a unique name attribute.

The following example illustrates this using the Image rendering extension. In this example, the Image rendering extension is registered twice. In the first entry, the Image rendering extension is configured for its default settings, allowing TIFF images to be produced. In the second entry, the Image rendering extension is configured to produce BMP images.

```
<Extension Name="IMAGE"
Type="Microsoft.ReportingServices.Rendering.ImageRenderer.ImageRenderer,
    Microsoft.ReportingServices.ImageRendering"/>
<Extension Name="BMP"
Type="Microsoft.ReportingServices.Rendering.ImageRenderer.ImageRenderer,
    Microsoft.ReportingServices.ImageRendering">
    <OverrideNames>
        <Name Language="en-US">BMP</Name>
    </OverrideNames>
    <Configuration>
        <DeviceInfo>
            <OutputFormat>BMP</OutputFormat>
            <PageHeight>11in</PageHeight>
            <PageWidth>8.5in</PageWidth>
        </DeviceInfo>
    </Configuration>
</Extension>
```

DeviceInfo settings are rendering-extension-specific. Books Online documents these settings for each of the default rendering extensions. It is important to note that without configuring device info settings in the RSReportServer.config file, you can still supply device info settings when accessing a report through URL access or Web services calls to control report rendering for a specific request.

In addition, URL access is the only mechanism allowing device info settings for the CSV rendering extension to be set, resulting in a tab-delimited file.

Finally, you should disable the Extension entry for any rendering extensions you do not intend to use by commenting it out in the RSReportServer.config file. However, if you simply want to prevent a file format from being used with a particular subscription delivery option, you should add its name to the ExcludedRenderFormats section under the appropriate delivery extension within the RSReportServer.config file. In the following example, the extensions with Name attributes set to HTMLOWC, NULL, RGDI, and IMAGE are excluded from use with File Share delivery:

```
<Extensions>
    <Delivery>
        <Extension Name="Report Server FileShare"
Type="Microsoft.ReportingServices.FileShareDeliveryProvider.FileShareProvider,
        ReportingServicesFileShareDeliveryProvider">
            <MaxRetries>3</MaxRetries>
            <SecondsBeforeRetry>900</SecondsBeforeRetry>
            <Configuration>
                <FileShareConfiguration>
                    <ExcludedRenderFormats>
                        <RenderingExtension>HTMLOWC</RenderingExtension>
                        <RenderingExtension>NULL</RenderingExtension>
                        <RenderingExtension>RGDI</RenderingExtension>
                        <RenderingExtension>IMAGE</RenderingExtension>
                    </ExcludedRenderFormats>
                </FileShareConfiguration>
            </Configuration>
        </Extension>
    ...
    </Delivery>

    ...
</Extensions>
```

My Reports

The My Reports feature gives users a personal folder in Reporting Services within which they can manage and view their own content. This is a powerful feature for users, but it can quickly get out of hand. The critical concern is that users are, by default, assigned elevated rights within their My Reports folder. These rights allow them to store content on the site with no mechanism to restrict the type or size of that content.

By default, the My Reports feature is disabled. If it's enabled, a My Reports folder is presented to each user in his or her home directory. This folder is actually a link to a user-specific folder created by Reporting Services within the Users Folders folder. Only System Administrators have direct access to the Users Folders folder.

Within his or her My Reports folder, a user is a member of a preset role. By default, this is the My Reports role, which has the following tasks assigned to it:

➤ Create linked reports

➤ View reports

➤ Manage reports

- ➤ View resources

- ➤ View folders

- ➤ Manage folders

- ➤ Manage report history

- ➤ Manage individual subscriptions

- ➤ View data resources

- ➤ Manage data sources

These tasks, discussed in the preceding chapter, provide elevated rights within this space. You might consider removing some of these tasks from the My Reports role or creating an alternative role with lesser privileges. Then you can use that as the default role assignment for the My Reports feature.

To enable the My Reports feature, open SQL Server Management Studio, and connect to the Reporting Services instance. Right-click the instance object and select Properties to launch the Server Properties dialog. Within the default General page of this dialog, shown in Figure 19-11, use the checkbox next to the "Enable a My Reports folder for each user" option to toggle this feature on and off. If this is enabled, you can assign a role to each user within his or her My Reports folder through the drop-down just below the checkbox.

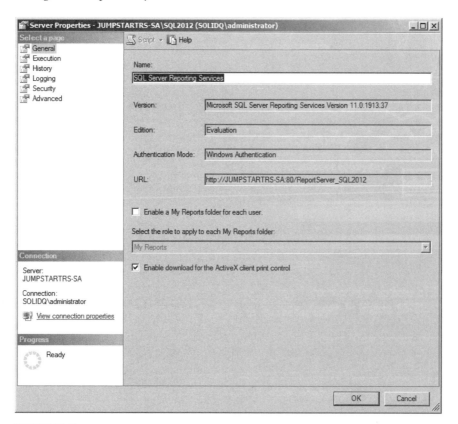

FIGURE 19-11

If you decide to enable this feature, closely monitor the consumption of space by users, and work with them to understand the feature's appropriate use. If you decide to disable the feature after having made it available, users will no longer be able to access their My Reports folder. However, the content of these folders remains within the system. Any subscriptions and snapshots associated with reports in these folders continue to run. To properly clean up the My Reports folders, you need to work with your users to migrate or drop their content.

SUMMARY

In this chapter, you have explored elements of Reporting Services with the goal of developing a comprehensive administrative program. Although there are recommended best practices, there is no one right approach. It is important to understand your options and then work with your users, developers, and administrators to develop a program tailored to your specific needs. After it is in place, it is important to follow through on the actions specified, and to be on the lookout for threats and changes in needs that may require adjustments to your routines and practices.

PART VII
Reporting Services Custom Programming

20

Integrating Reports into Custom Applications

WHAT'S IN THIS CHAPTER?

➤ Leveraging URL access and Web services to render reports

➤ Building a custom Windows Forms application to enter parameters and render reports

➤ Integrating report viewer controls in Windows and web form applications

➤ Rendering reports from within your web applications as HTML or as other downloadable formats such as PDF

➤ Creating custom parameter input interfaces for Reporting Services

Reporting Services was designed to be a flexible reporting technology that can be easily integrated into a variety of scenarios. Many reporting needs will never expand beyond the out-of-the-box functionality provided by Reporting Services. However, if the requirement arises, Reporting Services includes endless opportunities for integration with custom-built applications, as well as SharePoint.

Within a SharePoint portal, Reporting Services leverages the framework to deliver reports via Report Libraries. However, many organizations maintain a custom corporate reporting portal instead of SharePoint. In these situations, developers might need a way to display numerous reports in a Web environment. Reporting Services can also be embedded into line-of-business applications. Developers might want to use Reporting Services to create invoices or purchase orders directly from their applications. Some organizations may decide that the default Report Manager is not robust enough for their needs. In this situation, a custom reporting management application can be built that replaces and expands on the functionality of the out-of-the-box Report Manager.

All these issues can be solved with the features available in Reporting Services. This chapter looks at the following three methods of rendering reports from Reporting Services:

➤   Using URLs to access reports via HTTP

➤   Using the Reporting Services Web service to programmatically render reports

➤   Using the `ReportViewer` controls to embed reports

URL access allows you to quickly incorporate Reporting Services reports in custom applications such as web sites and portals, and even Windows applications. Programmatic rendering lets you create custom interfaces. Developers can do anything from implementing their own security architecture around Reporting Services to creating their own input parameter interface. The code samples and exercises in this chapter are designed for an intermediate or skilled developer and will not go into the details of how to create and setup projects within Visual Studio.

In this chapter, you will learn about the following:

➤   The syntax and structure for accessing Reporting Services through the URL

➤   The reporting items that can be accessed through the URL

➤   The parameter options that can be passed to the URL to control report output

➤   Creating a Windows application that renders reports to the filesystem

➤   Creating a web application that returns rendered reports to the browser

➤   Easily embedding reports in a Windows application using controls

URL ACCESS

Reporting Services' primary means of accessing reports is through HTTP requests. These requests can be made through URLs in a web browser or a custom application. By passing parameters in the URL, you can specify the report item, set the output format, and perform various other tasks. In the next few sections, you will look at the features available through URL requests, URL syntax, passing parameters, and setting the output format.

URL Syntax

The basic URL syntax is as follows:

```
protocol://server/virtualroot?[/pathinfo]&prefix:param=value
[&prefix:param=value] . . . n]
```

The parameters in the syntax are as follows:

➤   `Protocol` specifies the URL's protocol, such as HTTP or HTTPS (if an SSL certificate is applied to the Report Server).

➤   `Server` specifies the name of the Report Server you want to access. This can also include a fully qualified domain name. To access your local machine, you can either type the machine name or use the `localhost` alias.

➤ `Virtualroot` specifies the IIS virtual directory you specified during setup. When installing Reporting Services, you must enter two virtual directories: one for the Report Manager and one for the Report Server (for URL and Web services). By default, the virtual directory you would access is `reportserver`.

➤ `Pathinfo` specifies the full path to the item you want to access within the Report Server database. To access the root of the Report Server, you can simply place a single forward slash (`/`).

After you have listed the path, you can pass various parameters. These parameters depend on the type of object you are referencing. Reports have a number of parameters to specify properties such as the rendering format. Each parameter is separated by an ampersand (`&`) and contains a `name=value` pair for the parameter.

You can retrieve the list of items under the Professional SQL Reporting Services folder using this URL:

```
http://localhost/reportserver?/Professional SQL Reporting Services
        &rs:Command=ListChildren
```

 Note that some of the examples in this chapter take up two lines simply because they are too long to fit on one line.

Now that you're familiar with the basic URL syntax, let's see how it is implemented in each of the Reporting Services objects.

Accessing Reporting Services Objects

URL requests are not limited to reports. You can access various Reporting Services items, including:

➤ Folders

➤ Data sources

➤ Resources (such as images)

➤ Reports

The following sections describe accessing each of these items. You will go through sample URLs and look at items provided in the sample databases and reports that accompany this book.

 The sample databases and reports for this book can be downloaded from the book's site at www.wrox.com.

Folders

Accessing folders will be your starting point for looking at URL requests. Here is the simplest URL request you can make:

```
http://localhost/reports
```

That URL is redirected to the default Home page in Report Manager. With this request, you can see a listing of all reports, data sources, resources, and folders in the root directory of the Report Server, as shown in Figure 20-1. To access another server, simply replace `localhost` with the server's name.

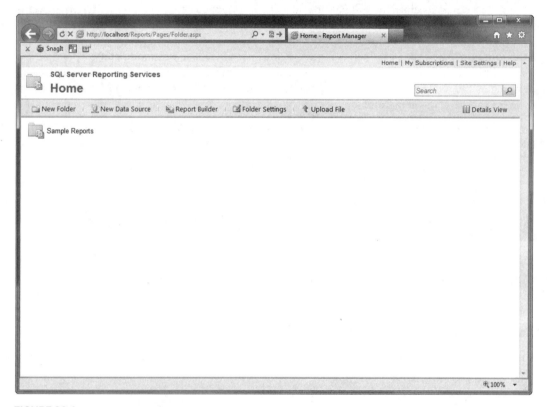

FIGURE 20-1

To see how folder URL requests work, simply enter the Report Server's URL:

```
http://localhost/reportserver
```

A list of directories hosted by the Report Server is displayed. Clicking the Sample Reports link gives you the following URL, as shown in Figure 20-2:

```
http://localhost/ReportServer?/Sample Reports&rs:Command=ListChildren
```

This URL contains the following items:

➤ **Path to the report** — `/Sample Reports` (the browser escapes the URL accordingly)

➤ **Command to list the directory's contents** — `rs:Command=ListChildren`

You'll take a closer look at the URL parameters in the section "Reporting Services URL Parameters."

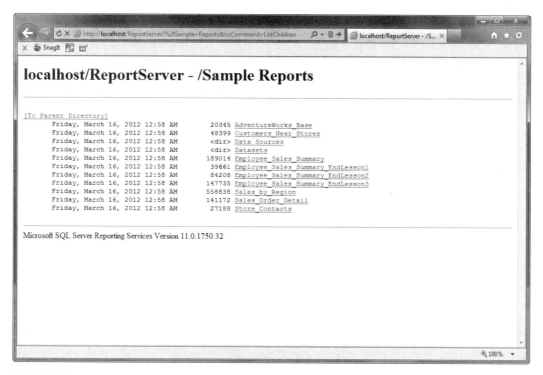

FIGURE 20-2

Data Sources

Through URL requests, you can also view the contents of data sources. Let's examine the Data Sources folder inside the Sample Reports folder. You can access the Data Sources folder by either clicking it from the parent folder or entering the following URL:

```
http://localhost/reportserver?/Sample Reports/Data Sources&rs:Command=ListChildren
```

You see the listing of items, as shown in Figure 20-3.

If you have deployed the sample reports, you will notice that one of the items listed is AdventureWorksWroxSSRS2012. You can tell that this item is a data source by the <ds> tag next to the item name. If you follow the AdventureWorksWroxSSRS2012 link, you can view the contents of that data source. Figure 20-4 shows the data source contents.

Here's the URL used to view the AdventureWorksWroxSSRS2012 data source:

```
http://localhost/reportserver?/Sample Reports/Data Sources/
AdventureWorksWroxSSRS2012&rs:Command=GetDataSourceContents
```

This URL contains the following items:

➤ **Path to the data source** — /Sample Reports/Data Sources/
AdventureWorksWroxSSRS2012

➤ **Command to view the data source content** — rs:Command=GetDataSourceContents

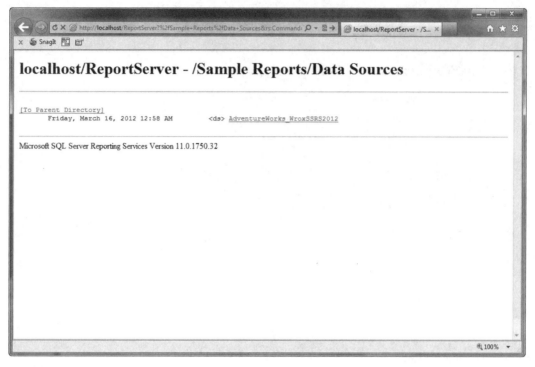

FIGURE 20-3

FIGURE 20-4

Viewing the data source enables you to quickly see how your data source is configured. Notice that this information is returned in XML format, making it easy to work with. If you have your own reporting application that shares a single connection, you could use this URL to dynamically load this data source information. This information could then be used to make other database connections in your application.

Resources

Resources are items used within your reports, such as images or additional resources that have been added to a Report Server folder, such as Word and Excel documents. You can use URLs to access resources stored on the Report Server. Depending on the type of resources you reference, either you will be prompted to open or save a file, such as a Word or Excel document, or the resource will be rendered directly in the browser. The `GetResourceContents` command can be used in the URL to reference the resource. For example, if an image is stored in a directory called Images, the URL to the directory and the command `GetResourceContents` can be used to reference that resource:

```
http://localhost/Reportserver?/Images/MyImage.jpg&rs:Command=GetResourceContents
```

The URL contains the following contents:

➤ **Path to the resource** — `/Images/MyImage.jpg`

➤ **Command to retrieve the resource content** — `rs:Command=GetResourceContents`

You can use this information in other applications. If you want to reference the image from a web page, you could simply set the `src` attribute of an image tag (`<img>`) to reference the earlier URL.

Resources can also be incredibly handy for storing documents. In your reporting solution, you might want to store readme files to accompany your reports. You can store these documents as resources on the Report Server and then apply different properties to them, such as security. Your application could then point to the resource URL to allow downloading of the document. Keep in mind, however, that these resources are stored in the Report Server database along with the report definitions. As such, you should carefully plan for storage if you intend to store several large files, or use an external server to serve up such resources.

Reports

The most important objects you can access through the URL are your reports. This section covers the syntax for accessing reports. The next section discusses the various parameters you can pass to change things such as report parameters, output formats, and other items.

The basic syntax for accessing a report is very similar to accessing all your other resources. You should first specify a path to the report and then provide the commands for its output. Here's the basic URL for accessing the Sales By Region report:

```
http://localhost/ReportServer?/Sample Reports/Sales_by_Region&rs:Command=Render
```

View the Sales report, as shown in Figure 20-5.

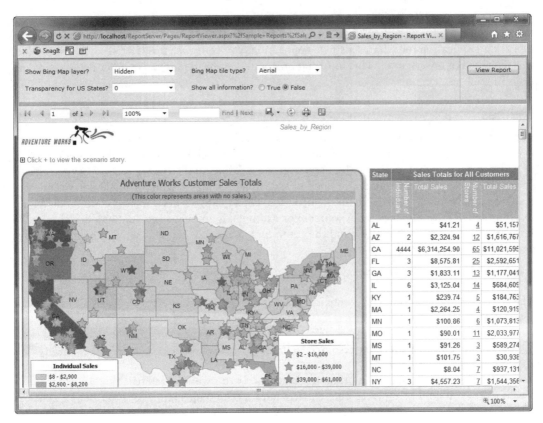

FIGURE 20-5

The URL contains the following contents:

➤ **Path to the resource** — /Sample Reports/Sales_by_region

➤ **Command to retrieve the resource content** — rs:Command=Render

You will also notice that the link URL changes to a ReportViewer.aspx page via redirection (notice the browser address bar in Figure 20-5) when requesting a report. The report server takes the user to a page that has a report viewer configured for the requested report.

Using URLs is the easiest and most convenient way to embed Reporting Services reports into custom applications. A custom application can point to the desired report either by creating a simple hyperlink or by using an HTML rendering object such as the WebBrowser component to render the report within a Windows client application. A special Windows Forms control designed for viewing reports is covered in the section "Programmatic Rendering."

The following section looks at the parameters that can be passed through the URL, including setting report parameters and output format.

Reporting Services URL Parameters

Now that you have seen the basics of obtaining items from your Report Server using URLs, let's take a look at passing some parameters. The next few sections move through how parameters are passed to Reporting Services and what values are available for these parameters. The majority of the parameter functionality focuses on report rendering, but some items also apply to your data source, resources, and folder.

Parameter Prefixes

The first thing you need to consider is the different parameter prefixes in Reporting Services. Reporting Services has five main parameter prefixes: rs, rc, rv, dsp, and dsu. The following sections describe these prefixes in detail.

rs Prefix

In the earlier examples, you saw the parameter rs:Command, which contains the prefix rs. The rs prefix is used to send commands to the Report Server. The following URL shows an example of the rs prefix being used to call the Command parameter and pass the ListChildren argument to it:

```
http://localhost/reportserver?/Sample Reports&rs:Command=ListChildren
```

rc Prefix

The second main parameter prefix in Reporting Services is rc. It provides device-information settings based on the report's output format. For example, if you are outputting your report as HTML, you can control the HTML viewer. You can use this prefix to pass parameters that do things such as hide toolbars or control the initial state of toggle items. The following URL calls the Employee Sales Summary report and turns off the parameter inputs:

```
http://localhost/ReportServer?/Sample Reports/
Employee_Sales_Summary&rs:Command=Render&rc:Parameters=False
```

rv Prefix

The rv prefix was introduced with SQL Server 2008. It is used to pass parameters to reports that are stored in a SharePoint document library. In such a library, a SharePoint Report Viewer Web Part is used to display a report, so the rv prefix should be used for these reports.

dsu and dsp Prefixes

Parameter prefixes can also be used to send database credentials. Use the dsu prefix to pass the data source username, and use the dsp prefix to pass the data source password. In any Reporting Services report, you can incorporate multiple data sources. So, you need a way to specify which data source the credentials should be passed to. That's where the prefixes come in. The full syntax to use these prefixes is as follows:

```
[dsu | dsp]:datasourcename=value
```

For example, to pass the username guest with a password guestPass to your AdventureWorksWroxSSRS2012 data source, you would use the following URL parameters:

```
&dsu:AdventureWorksWroxSSRS2012=guest&dsp:AdventureWorksWroxSSRS2012=guestPass
```

Be aware that these credentials are submitted as clear text over HTTP. You can encrypt the HTTP Request (which contains the URL parameters) using a Secure Sockets Layer (SSL) certificate on your web server and making the URL request over HTTPS. This prevents the information from being sent unencrypted, but it does not prevent the end user from viewing the credentials you pass. Make sure that you consider these factors in your reporting solution architecture.

Now that you have seen the different parameter prefixes in Reporting Services, we'll move on to the available parameters that can be used with the rv, rs, and rc prefixes.

Parameters

First, let's examine the new SharePoint endpoint parameter that can be used with reports that are hosted in a SharePoint Integrated mode Report Server configuration. This chapter does not go into detail about SharePoint integration, but let's look at the parameters that can be used with the rv prefix. Table 20-1 describes the four available values.

TABLE 20-1

PARAMETER	DESCRIPTION
Toolbar	Modifies the toolbar display of the SharePoint Report Viewer Web Part. The default value, Full, displays the entire toolbar. The Navigation value displays only the page navigation in the toolbar. The None value removes the toolbar.
HeaderArea	Modifies the header area of the SharePoint Report Viewer Web Part. The default value, Full, displays the complete header. The BreadCrumbsOnly value displays only bread crumbs in the header. A value of None removes the header from view.
DocMapAreaWidth	Displays the width of the parameter area of the SharePoint Report Viewer Web Part. The value should be a nonnegative number and defined in pixels.
AsyncRender	Tells the SharePoint Report Viewer Web Part whether to render the report asynchronously. The value must be a Boolean flag of True or False, with True meaning that the report will render asynchronously. If this parameter is not specified, the default value of True is used.

Now that you have seen the different rv parameters, let's examine the rs parameters. Table 20-2 describes the four available values.

TABLE 20-2

PARAMETER	DESCRIBES
Command	Sends instructions to the Report Server about the item being retrieved. Available values return the report item and set session time-out values.
Format	Specifies the target output format when rendering reports. Any rendering format available on the Report Server can be passed using this parameter.

PARAMETER	DESCRIBES
ParameterLanguage	Passes a language in the URL that is different from the language specified in the browser. If this parameter is not specified, the default is to use the browser culture value.
Snapshot	Retrieves historical report snapshots. Once a report has been stored in snapshot history, it is assigned a time/date stamp to uniquely identify it. Passing this time/date stamp returns the appropriate report snapshot.

Now that you have seen the different rs parameters, let's take a look at some of their available values.

Command Parameter

The Command parameter is the main parameter with which you set the output of a given report item. It can also be used to reset a user's session information, which guarantees that a report is not rendered from the session cache. Table 20-3 describes the possible values that can be passed to the Command parameter.

TABLE 20-3

VALUE	DESCRIPTION
GetComponent Definition	Returns a published report item's XML definition. You must have Read Contents permission on the report item to use this command value.
GetDataSource Contents	Returns data source information in an XML format. You use this parameter on shared data sources.
GetResourceContents	Returns the binary of your Reporting Services resources, such as images, via the URL.
GetSharedDataset Definition	Returns shared dataset information in an XML format. You must have Read Report Definition permission on the shared dataset to use this command value.
ListChildren	Used in combination with a Reporting Services folder. This lets you view all the items in a given folder.
Render	Allows you to render the report using the URL. Probably the most frequently used command.
ResetSessionTimeout	Can be used to refresh a user's session cache. Because Reporting Services typically works via HTTP, it is crucial for the server to maintain state information about the user. However, if you want to ensure that a report is executed each time the user views a report, this state information needs to be refreshed. Use this parameter to reset the user's session and remove any session cache information.

Format Parameter

The Format parameter is the main parameter for controlling the report output. The available values for this parameter are determined by the different rendering extensions installed on your Report Server. Table 20-4 shows the output formats available with the default installation of Reporting Services.

TABLE 20-4

VALUE	OUTPUT
WEB FORMATS	
HTML3.2	HTML version 3.2 output. Used for older browsers.
HTML4.0	HTML version 4.0. This format is supported by newer browsers, such as Internet Explorer 4.0 and above.
MHTML	MHTML standard output. This output format is used to send HTML documents in e-mail. Using this format embeds all resources, such as images, into the MHTML document instead of referencing external URLs.
PRINT FORMATS	
IMAGE	Allows you to render your reports to several different graphical device interfaces (GDIs), such as BMP, PNG, GIF, and TIFF.
PDF	Portable Document Format (PDF) can be used to view and print documents.
DATA FORMATS	
WORD	Word output. Users can use this format to output a report into a standard Microsoft Word document format.
EXCEL	Excel output. Users can use this format to further manipulate report data.
CSV	Comma-separated value (CSV) format. CSV is a standard data format that can be read by a wide variety of applications.
XML	Extensible Markup Language (XML) format. XML has become a standard data format, used by many different applications.
CONTROL FORMAT	
NULL	The NULL provider allows you to execute reports without rendering. This can be useful when you work with reports that have cached instances. You can use the NULL format to execute the report for the first time and then store the cached instance.

When you set the rendering formats via the URL, either the report is rendered directly in the browser, or you are prompted to save the output file. Let's take a look at rendering the Sales By Region report in PDF format. Enter the following URL using the rs:Format=PDF parameter:

```
http://localhost/ReportServer?/Sample Reports/
Sales_by_Region&rs:Command=Render&rs:Format=PDF
```

Figure 20-6 shows the output.

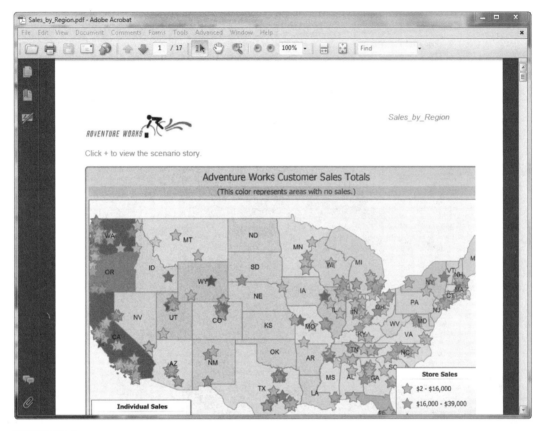

FIGURE 20-6

Note that the browser prompts you to save/open the rendered report PDF. This can be easily incorporated into your own custom applications or portals. You can simply give your users a link containing the rs:Format parameter and automatically output the correct format.

Setting Device Information

Now that you have seen the various output formats available in Reporting Services, you need to see the different device information settings for the various formats. The Format parameter enables you to specify the type of format you want, but each format has specific settings that can be useful to you. For example, if you specify the IMAGE format, you get an output in TIFF. What if you wanted a bitmap or JPEG image? To output in a different image format, you just specify device information when passing the URL. You can output the Sales by Region report in JPEG format using the following URL (Figure 20-7 shows the output):

```
http://localhost/ReportServer?/Sample Reports/
Sales_by_Region&rs:Command=Render&rs:Format=IMAGE&rc:OutputFormat=JPEG
```

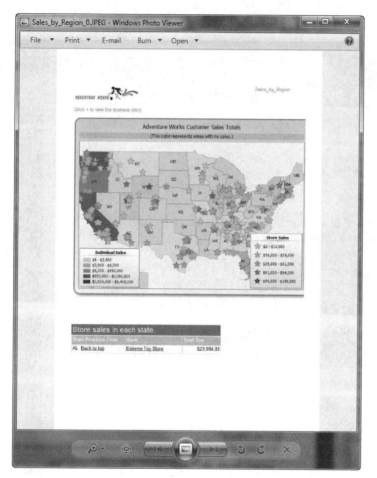

FIGURE 20-7

Notice that the file type sent back to you is a JPEG image. You can use numerous device information settings for each of the rendering extensions. Each device information setting is prefixed using `rc`. The following syntax can be used to pass device information:

```
http://server/virtualroot?/pathinfo&rs:Format=format&rc:param=value
[&rc:param=value...n]
```

Now that you have seen the different output formats and commands you can pass to Reporting Services, let's discuss passing information to your individual reports.

Passing Report Information Through the URL

The previous sections illustrated how a URL can be used to control report rendering. The next section describes how a URL can be used to control report execution. It first explains how to pass report parameters. These are the parameters that you define while authoring your report. Then you'll see how historical snapshots of reports can be rendered using the URL.

Report Parameters

Many of your reports have parameters to control all kinds of behavior. You can use parameters to alter your query, filter and group datasets and tables, and even change the appearance of your reports. In some cases (although it isn't recommended), parameters can be used to insert data into SQL tables via the executing query. Reporting Services allows you to pass this information directly via a URL request. In the previous section, you read about the parameter prefixes and the available values that can be sent to Reporting Services. With report parameters, you simply need to remove the prefix and call the parameter name directly.

In this example, the Employee Sales Summary report accepts six parameters: Report Month, Report Year, Employee, a Boolean flag to show all information and another flag to expand table rows, and a Category quotas list. You might want to allow your users to update these parameters through a custom interface you define. When you call the report, you need to provide the parameter values in the URL, as shown here:

```
http://localhost/ReportServer?/Sample Reports/Employee_Sales_Summary
   &rs:Command=Render
   &EmployeeID=283
   &ReportMonth=11
   &ReportYear=2007
   &ShowAll=false
   &ExpandAllTableRows=false
   &CategoryQuota=1000
   &CategoryQuota=70000
   &CategoryQuota=2500
   &CategoryQuota=20000
```

 Note that the values come from the AdventureWorks_WroxSSRS2012 database. You can see a list of all the employees and their IDs by using this SQL command:

```
SELECT BusinessEntityID, FirstName, LastName
FROM Person.Person
ORDER BY LastName ASC
```

Figure 20-8 shows calling the report with an `EmployeeID` of 283, which is David Campbell.

Notice that when the parameters in your URL are passed, the HTML viewer updates to reflect the values. The parameter name you use in the URL is defined in the report definition. Since your Report Parameter is called `EmployeeID`, that name is used in your URL.

You also might have noticed from the URL that the parameter `CategoryQuota` is repeated with different values. This is because that parameter is configured to allow multiple values and is rendered in the Report Viewer page as a multivalue drop-down list.

Although you can use URL access to submit multi-value parameters to your report, there is a hard limit on the size of a permitted URL within browsers, IIS, and even ASP.NET during an HTTP GET request. As a rule of thumb, it is best to restrict URLs to around 2,000 characters if using GET. This restriction does not apply when using HTTP POST and a form with key-value pairs for each of the parameters.

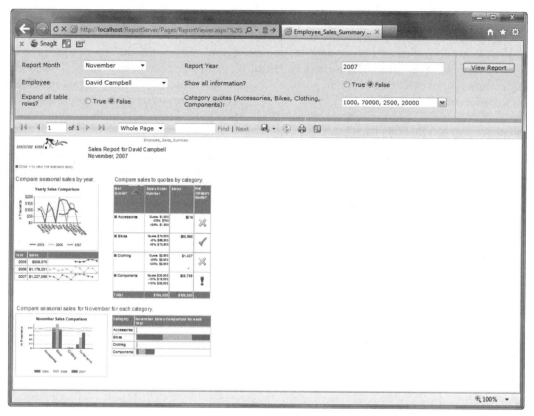

FIGURE 20-8

It is also worth mentioning that if a parameter is configured to allow null values, you can provide the following syntax to pass null from the URL:

```
parameterName:isnull=true
```

Now that you have seen how to pass report parameters to the URL Access of Reporting Services, let's look at passing snapshot IDs to render historical execution snapshots.

Rendering Snapshot History

One of the major features of Reporting Services is the ability to create execution snapshots of reports. Say you have a report in which the data updates on a monthly basis. After the data is updated, it does not change for another month. A perfect example of this is monthly financial statements. If your data changes only once a month, there is no reason to query your database every time you need a report. Therefore, you can use execution snapshots to store this information after the query has been executed. Similar to a monthly report, what should happen when your data updates from, say, January to February? You don't want to lose the January snapshot as soon as the February information is available. That is where historical snapshots come into play. When you create the February snapshot, you add January to the snapshot history, and so on for each subsequent month.

Now that you have execution snapshots stored in history, you need some way to access them. Reporting Services gives you an easy way to do so. As you have seen, each report has a report path that can be used to render the report. To render a historical snapshot, you simply need to add a parameter for the historical snapshot ID along with the `rs` prefix.

The syntax to pass your snapshot ID is as follows:

```
http://server/virtualroot?[/pathinfo]&rs:Snapshot=snapshotid
```

The snapshot ID of your historical snapshot is the date and time stamp of when the report was added to the history, formatted according to the ISO 8601 standard YYYY-MM-DDTHH:MM:SS. For example:

```
http://localhost/ReportServer?/Sample Reports/
Employee_Sales_Summary&rs:Snapshot=2011-05-31T23:59:21
```

URL Rendering Summary

Through URL rendering, you have seen the various commands that can be passed to Reporting Services and that can be used to control the report item display, the format to use, and snapshot information using the `rs` prefix. After you have created your commands for the Report Server, you can pass parameters specific to the output format. Using the `rc` prefix and the device information parameters, you can specify things such as encoding and which items to display in the HTML viewer. After you have specified the report item, you need to know how to output it. You can pass parameters to your report by simply passing the parameter name and value combination.

The next section covers the second part of rendering Reporting Service reports. You can use URLs for simple web applications and web portals, but sometimes you need finer control over report access and rendering. To achieve this, you use the Reporting Service Web service to programmatically render your reports.

PROGRAMMATIC RENDERING

Reports may be integrated into custom Windows Forms and web applications in several ways:

➤ Link to a report in a web browser window using a URL rendering request.

➤ An HTTP form via GET or POST to the Report Server URL.

➤ Replace web page content with a report by using SOAP Web Service rendering to write binary content to the web `HttpResponse` object.

➤ Use SOAP Web Service rendering to write report content to a file.

➤ Embed a report in an area of a web page by setting the source of an HTML frame or an `IFrame` tag.

➤ Use the Microsoft `ReportViewer` control in a Windows Forms or Web Forms .NET application.

➤ Use the Microsoft `ReportViewer` control in a WPF application by wrapping it inside a `WindowsFormsHost`.

Rendering using a URL is handy and easy to implement in many situations, but it does have its limitations. When rendering from the URL, you have to make sure that you use the security infrastructure provided with Reporting Services. For some applications, such as public web sites, you might want to implement your own security layer. In that case, rendering from the URL does not provide the functionality you need. This section describes rendering reports using the Reporting Services Web service.

You'll connect to the Reporting Services Web service, return a list of available reports, retrieve their parameters, and render the report. Let's look at three implementations of programmatic rendering. The first uses a Windows Forms application to render reports to a file. This will help you understand the basic principles without a lot of interface work. The second implementation demonstrates rendering through an ASP.NET page. You'll see some of the items you need to consider when working through a web application. Last, you'll read about how the `ReportViewer` control can embed reports in Windows and Web Forms applications for viewing.

Common Scenarios

Before you look at the actual programming code for rendering reports, it is important to understand a couple of scenarios in which it is reasonable to write your own rendering code. These scenarios commonly are experienced while working with clients. They do not represent the only scenarios in which you would write your own rendering code, but they do illustrate how and when custom code can be used. Let's consider each of these scenarios.

Custom Security

One of the biggest questions around Reporting Services involves how to use Reporting Services without its standard security infrastructure. Reporting Services requires you to connect to reports using a Windows identity, also known as Windows Integrated Authentication. In many organizations, this is just not possible (as is the case with a public Internet reporting solution). They have mixed environments or untrusted domains that do not allow for identification to the Report Server. Some clients also have large-scale authentication and authorization infrastructures already implemented.

You can still use Reporting Services in these situations. Using your own security infrastructure involves creating both authentication and authorization code in your environment. After you have determined that a user can access a report, a Windows identity that you define can be used to connect to reports. To hide this security implementation, the Reporting Services Web service can be used, and the Report Server can be abstracted and behind a firewall. You can render reports directly to a browser or file without passing the original user identity to the Report Server.

When you execute reports by passing a default set of credentials via the Web service proxy, you are running what is known as a "trusted subsystem." Your application's configuration maintains the credentials for the Windows Identity that can access reports on the Report Server.

Server-Side Parameters

Although URL rendering is by far the easiest way to incorporate Reporting Services in your applications, it does have some limitations. When you send information via a URL, it is easy for a user to change that URL or see what you pass. If you are shrewd enough, you might try to obscure the URL parameters by using an HTTP POST instead of GET. However, this is easily circumvented with the use of browser developer tools (Firebug, Internet Explorer Developer Tools) or an HTTP proxy such as Fiddler.

By using the Reporting Services Web service, you can easily hide the details of how you retrieve report information within your code. Parameters are passed through code instead of the URL. This gives you complete control over how that information is retrieved without exposing it to the users. The next section describes your first rendering application.

Rendering Through Windows

This section covers the mechanics of rendering using the Reporting Services Web service. You will build a simple Windows application that returns a list of reports from the Report Server. As soon as you have the list of reports, you use the Web service to return a list of report parameters. After entering any report parameters, you render the report to a file. These steps illustrate the main components of rendering through program code.

Building the Application Interface

First you need to build your application interface. Let's start by building a simple Windows form. For this example, I've added labels, textboxes, and buttons for basic functionality. Figure 20-9 shows the form's design view.

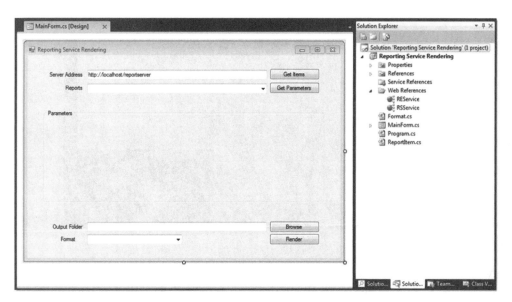

FIGURE 20-9

This form allows you to query a given Report Server to return a list of reports. After it returns the reports, you can use it to access a list of parameters for the reports. Finally, you need to render the report to a given folder location.

Setting Up the Web Services

Before you can begin rendering reports, you need to set up a reference to the Reporting Services and Report Execution Web services. After you create your web references, you can start to develop the application. The next few figures show you how to create references to the Web services. Start by adding the web references to your project.

Open the Solution Explorer. Right-click the References folder and select Add Service Reference, as shown in Figure 20-10. In the bottom-left corner, click the Advanced button to open the Service Reference Settings dialog box, which is shown in Figure 20-11. Make sure the checkbox "Generate asynchronous operations" is checked. We'll leverage the asynchronous Web service capabilities to provide a more responsive UI. Click the Add Web Reference button at the bottom left to open the Add Web Reference dialog.

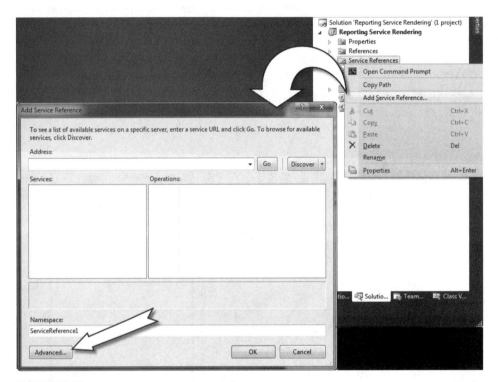

FIGURE 20-10

In the Add Web Reference dialog, shown in Figure 20-12, enter the location of the Web service in the URL box. This URL depends on the Report Server name and the installed location of the Report Server virtual directory. By default, the Report Server virtual directory is located under the root at /ReportServer. For the default virtual directory on a local machine, enter the following URL:

```
http://localhost/ReportServer/ReportService2010.asmx
```

The old endpoints, `ReportService2005.asmx` *(Native mode) and* `ReportService 2006.asmx` *(SharePoint Integrated mode), were deprecated in version 2008 R2. The newer endpoint ReportService2010 was introduced to include functionalities from both endpoints, as well as to offer additional management features.*

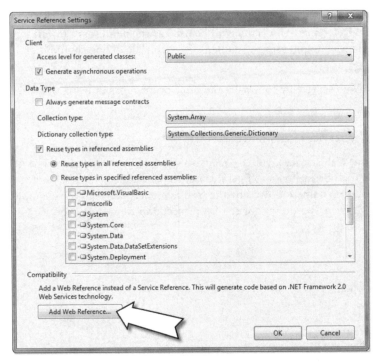

FIGURE 20-11

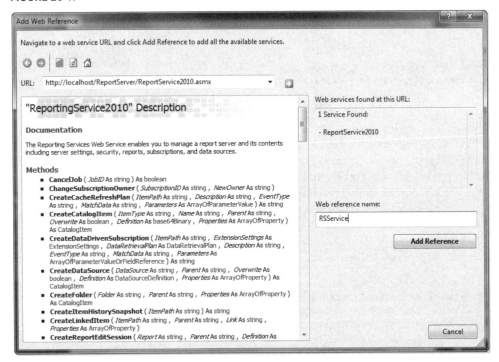

FIGURE 20-12

After you enter the URL, press Enter to view a description of the Web service. Enter a name for the new web reference and click Add Reference. This name will be used as the namespace for all types defined by the proxy assembly. This example uses the name RSService. The dialog should look like Figure 20-12 when filled in.

Now add the Report Execution Web service by following the same procedure but using this URL:

```
http://localhost/ReportServer/ReportExecution2005.asmx
```

In the example, we name this Web service reference REService.

Now that you have referenced the Web services, you are ready to start writing your code. The first thing you can do is add a using (C#) or Imports (VB) statement to your code. The first part of the using statement is the application name followed by the web reference name. In the example, the project is called Reporting_Service_Rendering for the C# project and Reporting_Service_Rendering_VB for the Visual Basic project.

Available for download on Wrox.com

C#

```csharp
using System;
using System.Collections.Generic;
using System.IO;
using System.Linq;
using System.Windows.Forms;
using Reporting_Service_Rendering.RSService;
using Reporting_Service_Rendering.REService;
```

code snippet \Reporting Service Rendering\Reporting Service Rendering\MainForm.cs

Available for download on Wrox.com

VB

```vb
Imports Reporting_Service_Rendering_VB.RSService
Imports Reporting_Service_Rendering_VB.REService
```

code snippet \Reporting Service Rendering\Reporting Service Rendering VB\MainForm.vb

After you have added the using or Imports statement, you need to create an instance of the ReportingService2010 and ReportExecutionService objects. These are the main objects that will be used to retrieve a list of reports and their associated parameters and then render the report. At the top of the Windows Forms class code for the MainForm, create the declarations shown in the following sections. The class declaration is included for clarity.

Available for download on Wrox.com

C#

```csharp
public partial class MainForm : Form
{
        ReportingService2010 _rs = new ReportingService2010();
        ReportExecutionService _rsExec = new ReportExecutionService();
        bool _reportHasParameters = false;
        const string _REPORT_SERVICE_ENDPOINT = "ReportService2010.asmx";
        const string _REPORT_EXECUTION_ENDPOINT = "ReportExecution2005.asmx";
```

code snippet \Reporting Service Rendering\Reporting Service Rendering\MainForm.cs

```vb
Public Class MainForm
    Private _rs As New ReportingService2010
    Private _rsExec As New ReportExecutionService
    Private _reportHasParameters As Boolean = False
    Private Const _REPORT_SERVICE_ENDPOINT As String = "ReportService2010.asmx"
    Private Const _REPORT_EXECUTION_ENDPOINT As String = "ReportExecution2005.asmx"
```

code snippet \Reporting Service Rendering\Reporting Service Rendering VB\MainForm.vb

Next, you need to set the security credentials that these objects will use. In your code, pass the credentials of the currently logged-on user. If you already have your own custom authentication and authorization method in place, you could pass a system identification that you define instead of the current user.

Open the `Form Load` event in the Windows Form. This is a suitable place for setting the credentials. Inside this event, set the `ReportingService2010` and `ReportExecutionService` objects' `Credentials` property to `System.Net.CredentialCache.DefaultCredentials`. This gives the Web services the credentials of the currently logged-on user (Windows Integrated Authentication).

C#

```csharp
_rs.Credentials = System.Net.CredentialCache.DefaultCredentials;
_rsExec.Credentials = System.Net.CredentialCache.DefaultCredentials;
```

VB

```vb
_rs.Credentials = System.Net.CredentialCache.DefaultCredentials
_rsExec.Credentials = System.Net.CredentialCache.DefaultCredentials
```

The final piece you need to add to the `Form Load` event is the code to populate your drop-down list. This code adds all the format names to the list, along with an appropriate extension for each. Begin by adding a new class file to your project to create a small class that helps you populate the drop-down. To add a new class, click ➪ Project ➪ Add class (or use the shortcut SHIFT + ALT + C):

```csharp
internal class Format
{
    public Format(string name, string extension)
    {
        Name = name;
        Extension = extension;
    }

    public string Name { get; private set; }
    public string Extension { get; private set; }

    public static IList<Format> GetFormatsList()
    {
        List<Format> formats = new List<Format>{
```

```
new Format("EXCEL", ".xlsx"),
new Format("WORD", ".docx"),
new Format("HTML3.2", ".html"),
new Format("HTML4.0", ".html"),
new Format("XML", ".xml"),
new Format("CSV", ".csv"),
new Format("PDF", ".pdf"),
new Format("IMAGE", ".tif")
};

        return formats;
    }
}
```

code snippet \Reporting Service Rendering\Reporting Service Rendering\Format.cs

VB

Available for
download on
Wrox.com

```
Friend Class Format

    Public Sub New(ByVal name As String, ByVal extension As String)
        Me.Name = name
        Me.Extension = extension
    End Sub

    Public Property Name As String
    Public Property Extension As String

    Public Shared Function GetFormatsList() As IList(Of Format)

        Dim formats As New List(Of Format) From {
            New Format("EXCEL", ".xlsx"),
            New Format("WORD", ".docx"),
            New Format("HTML3.2", ".html"),
            New Format("HTML4.0", ".html"),
            New Format("XML", ".xml"),
            New Format("CSV", ".csv"),
            New Format("PDF", ".pdf"),
            New Format("IMAGE", ".tif")
        }

        Return formats

    End Function

End Class
```

code snippet \Reporting Service Rendering\Reporting Service Rendering VB\Format.vb

With this class, you can finish your `Form Load` event code. Add the few last lines of code to populate your format combo box:

C#

```csharp
private void MainForm_Load(object sender, EventArgs e)
{
    _rs.Credentials = System.Net.CredentialCache.DefaultCredentials;
    _rsExec.Credentials = System.Net.CredentialCache.DefaultCredentials;

    reportFormatComboBox.DataSource = Format.GetFormatsList();
    reportFormatComboBox.DisplayMember = "Name";
    reportFormatComboBox.ValueMember = "Name";
}
```

code snippet \Reporting Service Rendering\Reporting Service Rendering\MainForm.cs

VB

```vb
Private Sub MainForm_Load(sender As System.Object, _
e As System.EventArgs) Handles MyBase.Load
    _rs.Credentials = System.Net.CredentialCache.DefaultCredentials
    _rsExec.Credentials = System.Net.CredentialCache.DefaultCredentials

    reportFormatComboBox.DataSource = Format.GetFormatsList()
    reportFormatComboBox.DisplayMember = "Name"
    reportFormatComboBox.ValueMember = "Name"
End Sub
```

code snippet \Reporting Service Rendering\Reporting Service Rendering VB\MainForm.vb

You have now created an instance of the `ReportingService2010` object, passed the logged-on user's credentials to it, and populated the format drop-down list. The next section discusses connecting to the Report Server and retrieving a list of available reports.

Retrieving Report Information

Now that you have set up the Reporting Services Web service, you need to retrieve your list of reports. To do this, specify the Report Server that you want to query, and then call the `ListChildren` method of the `ReportingService2010` object. `ListChildren` returns a list of all items, including data sources, resources, and reports. After you have retrieved the list, you need to pull out only report items. Finally, you add the report items to the drop-down.

As pointed out earlier, you ensure that your web-reference proxy was generated with asynchronous operations. When you create a web reference using the Visual Studio IDE, it generates both the synchronous and asynchronous operations. Due to the nature of this application — a Windows form UI — it is best practice to ensure that calls to the Report Services are performed on a different thread than the UI thread. This prevents the UI thread from being blocked while the Web service operation completes, providing a much better user experience.

The asynchronous pattern may seem a bit complex or overwhelming at first, but in essence all it does is register an event handler that invokes a delegate function (the "callback") when the asynchronous operation is completed. In other words, you fire a call to the operation and return from the method. The execution happens on a background thread that waits for the event notification when the operation completes and invokes the callback function.

In addition to the asynchronous operations, you can always call the synchronous methods directly without having to worry about delegates and events. This is fine in scenarios such as server-side code, where there's no user interface to be concerned with.

Let's start by setting the URL to your Report Server. Open the click event of the Get Items button to start your code. You'll keep your UI event handlers pretty lean and perform the bulk of operations in separate methods. Remember that _rs is your private object reference to the Web service, as defined at the top of the class definition. Also, this event handler will need to call a function that loads the reports list box, which will be implemented later on. So for now, just use a "TODO:" comment as a placeholder and reminder.

C#

```csharp
private void btnGetItems_Click(object sender, EventArgs e)
{
    GetItems();
}
private void GetItems()
{
    if (!String.IsNullOrEmpty(txtServer.Text))
    {
        _rs.Url = String.Format("{0}/{1}", txtServer.Text.TrimEnd('/'),
        _REPORT_SERVICE_ENDPOINT);

        _rs.ListChildrenCompleted += new
        ListChildrenCompletedEventHandler((sender, e) =>
        {
            if (e.Error == null && e.Result != null)
                // TODO: Load the list box with e.Result
            else
                MessageBox.Show(e.Error.ToString());
        });

        _rs.ListChildrenAsync("/", true, Guid.NewGuid ());
    }
    else
    {
        MessageBox.Show("Enter a server string first.. " +
"Example: http://localhost/reportserver");
    }
}
```

code snippet \Reporting Service Rendering\Reporting Service Rendering\MainForm.cs

VB

```vb
Private Sub btnGetItems_Click(sender As System.Object, e As System.EventArgs)_
    Handles btnGetItems.Click
    GetItems()
End Sub
```

```
Private Sub GetItems()
    If (Not String.IsNullOrEmpty(Me.txtServer.Text)) Then

        _rs.Url = String.Format("{0}/{1}", txtServer.Text.TrimEnd("/"),
        _REPORT_SERVICE_ENDPOINT)

        AddHandler _rs.ListChildrenCompleted, Sub(sender As Object, args As
        RSService.ListChildrenCompletedEventArgs)
          If (IsNothing(args.Error) AndAlso Not IsNothing(args.Result)) Then
             'TODO: Load the list box with args.Result
          Else
             MessageBox.Show(args.Error.ToString())
          End If
        End Sub

        _rs.ListChildrenAsync("/", True, Guid.NewGuid ())

    Else
        MessageBox.Show("Enter a server string first... Example:
        http://localhost/reportserver")
    End If

End Sub
```

code snippet \Reporting Service Rendering\Reporting Service Rendering VB\MainForm.vb

The preceding code uses the server location specified in the Server Address textbox (txtServer) concatenated with the reference to the Reporting Services Web Service URL endpoint.

As soon as the URL for the Web service is set, you can get the list of reports. Create an array of CatalogItem objects, and then call the ListChildren or ListChildrenAsync method. These methods take two parameters in their synchronous form: the folder path on the Report Server and a Boolean value indicating whether to recurse through the directory. The asynchronous flavor adds a third parameter that allows you to provide the unique state object. This is required to prevent errors when multiple asynchronous operations are outstanding. To ensure uniqueness, you create an instance of type System.Guid In the code above, you already implemented the asynchronous version. For completeness, here is how both the synchronous and asynchronous code look like when calling the ListChildren web service method:

SYNCHRONOUS C#

```
CatalogItem[] items;
items = _rs.ListChildren("/", true);
```

SYNCHRONOUS VB

```
Dim items() As CatalogItem
items = _rs.ListChildren("/", True)
```

ASYNCHRONOUS C#

```
_rs.ListChildrenCompleted +=
    new ListChildrenCompletedEventHandler((sender, e) =>
```

```
        {
            if (e.Error == null && e.Result != null)
                // TODO: Load the list box using e.Result
            else
                MessageBox.Show(e.Error.ToString());
        });

    _rs.ListChildrenAsync("/", true, Guid.NewGuid());
```

ASYNCHRONOUS VB

```
    AddHandler _rs.ListChildrenCompleted, Sub(sender As Object, args As _
    RSService.ListChildrenCompletedEventArgs)
        If (IsNothing(args.Error) AndAlso Not IsNothing(args.Result)) Then
            ' TODO: Load the list box using args.Result
        Else
            MessageBox.Show(args.Error.ToString())
        End If
    End Sub

    _rs.ListChildrenAsync("/", True, Guid.NewGuid ())
```

As soon as the operation returns with an array of Report Items, the last step is to loop through the resulting array and add each item to a drop-down list (ComboBox). Similar to how the formats were loaded, create a class to help data-bind the report items. Let's take a look at the code for this class:

C#

```
internal class ReportItem
{
    public ReportItem(string name, string path)
    {
        Name = name;
        Path = path;
    }

    public string Name { get; private set; }
    public string Path { get; private set; }
}
```

code snippet \Reporting Service Rendering\Reporting Service Rendering\ReportItem.cs

VB

```
Friend Class ReportItem
    Private _name As String
    Private _path As String

    Public Sub New(ByVal name As String, ByVal path As String)
        _name = name
        _path = path
    End Sub

    Public ReadOnly Property Name() As String
```

```
            Get
                Return _name
            End Get
        End Property

        Public ReadOnly Property Path() As String
            Get
                Return _path
            End Get
        End Property
    End Class
```

code snippet \Reporting Service Rendering\Reporting Service Rendering VB\ReportItem.vb

Using the `ReportItem` class just created, you can add the report catalog items to the combo box. In the `MainForm` class, you'll implement a new method that does just that. The following code is for the `LoadReportsBox` method, which is invoked by the asynchronous delegate-callback method to the `ListItemsAsync` operation (where you had originally put a "TODO:" comment line to load the list box):

C#

```csharp
private void LoadReportsBox(CatalogItem[] items)
{
    reportsComboBox.Items.Clear();

    foreach (var item in items)
    {
        if (item.TypeName == "Report")
        {
            reportsComboBox.Items.Add(new ReportItem(item.Name, item.Path));
        }
    }

    reportsComboBox.DisplayMember = "Name";
    reportsComboBox.ValueMember = "Path";
    reportsComboBox.DroppedDown = true;
}
```

code snippet \Reporting Service Rendering\Reporting Service Rendering\MainForm.cs

VB

```vb
Private Sub LoadReportsBox(ByVal items As RSService.CatalogItem())
    'populate report combo box
    reportsComboBox.Items.Clear()
    For Each item As RSService.CatalogItem In items
        If (item.TypeName = "Report") Then
            reportsComboBox.Items.Add(New ReportItem(item.Name, item.Path))
        End If
    Next

    reportsComboBox.DisplayMember = "Name"
```

```
        reportsComboBox.ValueMember = "Path"
        reportsComboBox.DroppedDown = True
    End Sub
```

code snippet \Reporting Service Rendering\Reporting Service Rendering VB\MainForm.vb

Don't forget to replace the TODO comment line inside GetItems with the invocation of
LoadReportsBox. The Result property of the callback argument object should contain the
CatalogItem array expected by LoadReportsBox:

C#

```
rs.ListChildrenCompleted +=
    new ListChildrenCompletedEventHandler((sender, e) =>
    {
        if (e.Error == null && e.Result != null)
            LoadReportsBox(e.Result);
        else
            MessageBox.Show(e.Error.ToString());
    });
```

code snippet \Reporting Service Rendering\Reporting Service Rendering\MainForm.cs

VB

```
AddHandler _rs.ListChildrenCompleted, Sub(sender As Object, args As
RSService.ListChildrenCompletedEventArgs)
    If (IsNothing(args.Error) AndAlso Not IsNothing(args.Result)) Then
        LoadReportsBox(args.Result)
    Else
        MessageBox.Show(args.Error.ToString())
    End If
End Sub
```

code snippet \Reporting Service Rendering\Reporting Service Rendering VB\MainForm.vb

You now can open your form and return a list of report items. The next section describes retrieving
the parameters for a report.

Retrieving Report Parameters

The next area of programmatic rendering consists of retrieving a list of parameters for your report.
This bit of code can be used in various scenarios. The parameter interface that is provided by
Reporting Services works well for simple parameters. However, it does not handle many things,
such as advanced validation based on business rules, or even fancier input interfaces such as dials
and sliders. Being able to return a list of parameters allows you to create your own dynamic
user interface.

In the following example, you will create a simple list of parameters. For each parameter, you will
dynamically add a label control and either a textbox, checkbox, or date/time picker to your form,

based on the parameter type. The following line of code is the first thing you should do within the `GetParameters` method, which is called from the respective button-click event handler. This line of code identifies the report that is selected in your report drop-down list.

C#

```
ReportItem reportItem = (ReportItem)reportsComboBox.SelectedItem;
```

VB

```
Dim reportItem As ReportItem = DirectCast(reportsComboBox.SelectedItem, ReportItem)
```

This creates a new `ReportItem` variable using the selected item of your combo box. The `ReportItem` class created in the preceding section contains a `Name` and a `Path` property. You can use this `Path` property to retrieve your list of parameters.

To return your list of parameters, call the `GetItemParameters` method of the `ReportingService2010` object. This method has two purposes. It returns a list of parameters and can validate parameters against the available values defined when creating the report. Here are the arguments for the `GetItemParameters` method:

➤ `ItemPath` is the path to the report for which you want to retrieve parameters.

➤ `HistoryID` is the ID used to identify any historical snapshots of your report.

➤ `ForRendering` is a Boolean argument that can be used to retrieve the parameters that were set when the report was executed. For example, you might create a snapshot of your report or receive it in an e-mail subscription. In both cases, the report is executed before the user views it. By setting the `ForRendering` property to `true`, you can retrieve these values and use them in your own custom interface.

➤ `Values` is an array of `ParameterValue` objects that can be used to validate the values assigned to a parameter. This can be useful to guarantee that the parameter values you pass to your report match the parameter values the report definition accepts.

➤ `Credentials` are the database credentials to use when validating your query-based parameters in case you have to execute a query to populate available values.

➤ `userState` (async only) is an optional parameter that is available only in the asynchronous version of the operation. It provides a unique state object to prevent errors when multiple asynchronous operations are outstanding. Typically, a new GUID is used for this parameter.

Because you are not working with historical reports or validating values in this exercise, a number of the properties will not be set. The following code can be used to call the `GetItemParameters` method synchronously:

C#

```
ItemParameter[] parameters;
parameters = _rs.GetItemParameters(reportItem.Path, null, false, null, null);
```

VB

```
Dim parameters() As ItemParameter
parameters = _rs.GetItemParameters(reportItem.Path, Nothing, False, _
                    Nothing, Nothing)
```

Since you are using the asynchronous pattern in this sample exercise, here is how to use the asynchronous version, calling the `GetItemParameterAsync` method. The following code should be implemented inside of a private method named `GetParameters`. This method, in turn, is invoked by the "Get Parameters" button click event handler:

Available for download on Wrox.com

ASYNCHRONOUS C#

```
_rs.GetItemParametersCompleted +=
new GetItemParametersCompletedEventHandler((sender, args) =>
{
    if (args.Error == null && args.Result != null)
        LoadParametersGroupBox(args.Result);
    else
        MessageBox.Show(args.Error.ToString());
});
_rs.GetItemParametersAsync(reportItem.Path,
null, false, null, null, Guid.NewGuid());
```

code snippet \Reporting Service Rendering\Reporting Service Rendering\MainForm.cs

Available for download on Wrox.com

ASYNCHRONOUS VB

```
AddHandler _rs.GetItemParametersCompleted, _
    Sub(sender As Object, args As RSService.GetItemParametersCompletedEventArgs)
        If (args.Error Is Nothing AndAlso Not args.Result Is Nothing) Then
                LoadParametersGroupBox(args.Result)
        Else
                MessageBox.Show(args.Error.ToString())
        End If
    End Sub

_rs.GetItemParametersAsync(reportItem.Path, Nothing, False, Nothing, _
Nothing, Guid.NewGuid())
```

code snippet \Reporting Service Rendering\Reporting Service Rendering VB\MainForm.vb

The last task is to create a user interface for your parameters. The `ReportParameter` objects returned by Reporting Services contain information useful for creating a custom interface. Some of the key properties include the parameter data type, prompt, and valid values. All of these can be used to define your own interface. Finish your code by simply adding a label and either a textbox, checkbox, or date/time picker to your form for each `ReportParameter`.

Following is the code for the `LoadParametersGroupBox` method, which is invoked inside the callback delegate upon successful execution of the web operation. Also, the logic to build the appropriate control type based on parameter type was refactored into a separate method, as shown in the method named `GetParameterControl`:

```csharp
private void LoadParametersGroupBox(ItemParameter[] parameters)
{
    // Let everyone know this report has parameters.
    _reportHasParameters = (parameters.Length > 0);

    //add the parameters to the parameter list UI
    int left = 10;
    int top = 20;
    paramInfoGroupBox.Controls.Clear();

    foreach (var parameter in parameters)
    {
        Label label = new Label
        {
            Text = parameter.Prompt,
            Left = left,
            Top = top
        };

        paramInfoGroupBox.Controls.Add(label);
        paramInfoGroupBox.Controls.Add(
            GetParameterControl(parameter, left, top));
        top += 25;
    }
}

private Control GetParameterControl(ItemParameter parameter, int left, int top)
{
    Control parameterControl;
    switch (parameter.ParameterTypeName)
    {
        case "Boolean":
            parameterControl = new CheckBox
            {
                Checked = parameter.DefaultValues != null ?
                Boolean.Parse(parameter.DefaultValues[0]) : false
            };
            break;
        case "DateTime":
            parameterControl = new DateTimePicker
            {
                Text = parameter.DefaultValues != null ?
                parameter.DefaultValues[0] : String.Empty
            };
            break;
        default:
            //there are other types, such as float and int,
            //and you can also retrieve default values and
            //populate as dropdown, but
            //it's beyond scope of this exercise
            parameterControl = new TextBox
            {
                Text = parameter.DefaultValues != null ?
```

```
                    parameter.DefaultValues[0] : string.Empty
            };
            break;
    }
    parameterControl.Name = parameter.Name;
    parameterControl.Left = left + 150;
    parameterControl.Top = top;

    return parameterControl;
}
```

```
Private Sub LoadParametersGroupBox(ByVal parameters As ItemParameter())
    'let everyone know this report has parameters
    _reportHasParameters = (parameters.Length > 0)

    'add the parameters to the parameter list UI
    Dim left As Integer = 10
    Dim top As Integer = 20

    paramInfoGroupBox.Controls.Clear()

    For Each parameter As ItemParameter In parameters
        Dim label As New Label With
        {
            .Text = parameter.Prompt,
            .Left = left,
            .Top = top
        }
        paramInfoGroupBox.Controls.Add(label)
        paramInfoGroupBox.Controls.Add( _
            GetParameterControl(parameter, left, top))
        top += 25
    Next
End Sub

Private Function GetParameterControl(ByVal parameter As ItemParameter, _
                                     ByVal left As Integer, _
                                     ByVal top As Integer) As Control
    Dim parameterControl As Control

    Select Case parameter.ParameterTypeName
        Case "Boolean"
            parameterControl = New CheckBox With {
                .Checked = If(parameter.DefaultValues IsNot Nothing, _
                            Boolean.Parse(parameter.DefaultValues(0)), False)
            }
        Case "DateTime"
            parameterControl = New DateTimePicker With {
                .Text = If(parameter.DefaultValues IsNot Nothing, _
```

```
                         parameter.DefaultValues(0), String.Empty)
              }
      Case Else
          'there are other types, like float and int,
          'and you can also retrieve default values and populate as a drop-down
          'but it's beyond the scope of this exercise
          parameterControl = New TextBox With {
              .Text = If(parameter.DefaultValues IsNot Nothing, _
                         parameter.DefaultValues(0), String.Empty)
          }
  End Select

  parameterControl.Name = parameter.Name
  parameterControl.Left = left + 150
  parameterControl.Top = top

  Return parameterControl
End Function
```

code snippet \Reporting Service Rendering\Reporting Service Rendering VB\MainForm.vb

Now that you have retrieved your list of reports and built a parameter list, we'll discuss rendering and outputting the report to a file.

Rendering a Report to a File on the Filesystem

This section describes rendering a report to a file on the filesystem. Using the `ReportExecution2005` Web service, you can retrieve a byte array that contains the final report. This byte array can be used in a variety of ways. This example writes the byte array to a file by using the filesystem object. Another example in a later section writes the byte array to the HTTP `Response` object.

You set up the `ReportExecution2005` Web service in the previous sections, so now you can use it to render a report to a file on the filesystem. In `btnRender_Click` you call a new method, `RenderReport`, which sets the URL by concatenating the server text the user entered with the `ReportExecution2005.asmx` string.

C#

```
_rsExec.Url = String.Format("{0}/{1}",
    txtServer.Text.TrimEnd('/'), "ReportExecution2005.asmx");
```

VB

```
_rsExec.Url = String.Format("{0}/{1}", _
    txtServer.Text.TrimEnd("/"), "ReportExecution2005.asmx")
```

Next, you need to set a string argument that will be used for the report's path.

Before you get into the rendering code, let's look at the `Render` method that is contained within the `ReportExecutionService` object of the `ReportExecution2005` Web service. Table 20-5 shows the different parameters.

TABLE 20-5

PARAMETER	DATA TYPE	DESCRIPTION
Format	String	The report's output format.
DeviceInfo	String	Information used by a specified rendering format, such as specifying the image type (GIF, JPEG) with the IMAGE format.
Extension (out)	String	The file extension of the rendered report.
MimeType (out)	String	Output returned from Reporting Services containing the MIME type of the underlying report. Useful when rendering a report to the Web. The MIME type can be passed to the Response object to ensure that the browser correctly handles the document returned.
Encoding (out)	String	The encoding used to render the report.
Warnings (out)	Warning Array	The output of any warning returned from Reporting Services during report processing.
StreamIDs (out)	String Array	The output of the stream IDs that can be used with the RenderStream method.

The Render method returns an array of bytes that represents the rendered report. The array can then be used just like any other byte array, such as writing it to a file on the filesystem or sending it over a TCP connection.

The parameters of the Render method are similar to the values that can be passed using URL rendering.

Now that you have seen the basics of the Render method, let's examine the code you need to write for your Render button click event. The first thing you must do in your code is retrieve the selected report and output format. Use the Format and ReportItem classes created earlier to retrieve the selected items in your drop-downs.

C#

```csharp
Format selectedFormat = (Format)reportFormatComboBox.SelectedItem;
ReportItem reportItem = (ReportItem)reportsComboBox.SelectedItem;
```

VB

```vb
Dim selectedFormat As Format = _
    DirectCast(reportFormatComboBox.SelectedItem, Format)
Dim reportItem As ReportItem = _
    DirectCast(reportsComboBox.SelectedItem, ReportItem)
```

You need to retrieve the input parameters the user specified. Then you must create a new function that loops through the controls you created earlier to retrieve their values and return an array of ParameterValue objects.

C#

```csharp
private REService.ParameterValue[] GetReportExecutionParameters()
{
    var controlList = new List<Control>();

    //get the values from the parameter controls that are not labels
    controlList.AddRange(paramInfoGroupBox.Controls
        .OfType<Control>()
        .Where(c => c.GetType() != typeof(Label)));

    //add the control information to parameter info objects
    var parameterValues = new List<REService.ParameterValue>();
    foreach (var control in controlList)
    {
        parameterValues.Add(new REService.ParameterValue
        {
            Name = control.Name,
            Value = (control is CheckBox) ?
            ((CheckBox)control).Checked.ToString() : control.Text
        });
    }

    return parameterValues.ToArray();
}
```

code snippet \Reporting Service Rendering\Reporting Service Rendering\MainForm.cs

VB

```vbnet
Private Function GetReportExecutionParameters() As REService.ParameterValue()
    Dim controlList = New List(Of Control)()

    'get the values from the parameter controls that are not labels
    controlList.AddRange(paramInfoGroupBox.Controls.OfType(Of Control)() _
                        .Where(Function(c) c.[GetType]() <> GetType(Label)))

    'add the control information to parameter info objects
    Dim parameterValues = New List(Of REService.ParameterValue)()
    For Each ctrl As Control In controlList
        parameterValues.Add(New REService.ParameterValue() With {
          .Name = ctrl.Name,
          .Value = If((TypeOf ctrl Is CheckBox), _
                    DirectCast(ctrl, CheckBox).Checked.ToString(), ctrl.Text)
        })
    Next

    Return parameterValues.ToArray()
End Function
```

code snippet \Reporting Service Rendering\Reporting Service Rendering VB\MainForm.vb

You can now use the `GetReportExecutionParameters` function to build an array of input parameters. You can add the following code to your `RenderReport` method to retrieve the input parameters:

C#

```
REService.ParameterValue[] parameters = GetReportExecutionParameters();
```

VB

```
Dim parameters As REService.ParameterValue() = GetReportExecutionParameters()
```

Now that you have your list of input parameters, you are almost ready to call the `Render` method. For this, you need to declare variables that will be used for the output parameters `HistoryID`, `DeviceInfo`, `Encoding`, `MimeType`, `Extension`, `Warnings`, and `StreamIDs`. Not all of these variables are needed, because they are set to `null` and are not used. However, they have been declared here to show the syntax of the `Render` method. The final variable you need for the `Render` method is an array of bytes. This byte array can then be written to the filesystem.

Available for download on Wrox.com

C#

```
byte[] result = null;
string historyID = null;
string devInfo = null;
string encoding;
string mimeType;
string extension;
REService.Warning[] warnings = null;
string[] streamIDs = null;

// Load the report, set the parameters and then render.
_rsExec.LoadReport(reportItem.Path, historyID);
_rsExec.SetExecutionParameters(parameters, "en-us");
result = _rsExec.Render(selectedFormat.Name, devInfo,
    out extension,
    out encoding,
    out mimeType,
    out warnings,
    out streamIDs);
```

code snippet \Reporting Service Rendering\Reporting Service Rendering\MainForm.cs

Available for download on Wrox.com

VB

```
Dim result As Byte() = Nothing
Dim historyID As String = Nothing
Dim devInfo As String = Nothing
Dim encoding As String
Dim mimeType As String
Dim extension As String
Dim warnings As REService.Warning() = Nothing
Dim streamIDs As String() = Nothing

' Load the report, set the parameters and then render.
```

```
_rsExec.LoadReport(reportItem.Path, historyID)
_rsExec.SetExecutionParameters(parameters, "en-us")
result = _rsExec.Render(selectedFormat.Name, devInfo, extension, _
                        encoding, mimeType, warnings, streamIDs)
```

code snippet \Reporting Service Rendering\Reporting Service Rendering VB\MainForm.vb

Finally, you need to take the byte array returned from the Render method and write it to the filesystem. Use the output path specified in the output textbox, along with the report name and format file extension, to open a file stream. Following is the entire RenderReport method, along with the final piece of code for writing the file to the filesystem:

C#

```
private void RenderReport()
{
    _rsExec.Url = String.Format("{0}/{1}",
        txtServer.Text.TrimEnd('/'),
        "ReportExecution2005.asmx");

    Format selectedFormat = (Format)reportFormatComboBox.SelectedItem;
    ReportItem reportItem = (ReportItem)reportsComboBox.SelectedItem;

    REService.ParameterValue[] parameters = GetReportExecutionParameters();

    byte[] result = null;
    string historyID = null;
    string devInfo = null;
    string encoding;
    string mimeType;
    string extension;
    REService.Warning[] warnings = null;
    string[] streamIDs = null;

    // Make sure the report either has parameters
    // that are set or has no parameters.
    if ((_reportHasParameters && parameters.Length != 0) || !_reportHasParameters)
    {
        _rsExec.LoadReport(reportItem.Path, historyID);
        _rsExec.SetExecutionParameters(parameters, "en-us");
        result = _rsExec.Render(selectedFormat.Name,
            devInfo,
            out extension,
            out encoding,
            out mimeType,
            out warnings,
            out streamIDs);

        // Make sure there is an output path then
        // output the file to the file system.
        if (txtOutputFolder.Text != "")
        {
            string fullOutputPath = txtOutputFolder.Text + "\\" +
```

```
                    reportItem.Name + selectedFormat.Extension;
                    FileStream stream = File.Create(fullOutputPath, result.Length);
                    stream.Write(result, 0, result.Length);
                    stream.Close();
                    MessageBox.Show("Report Rendered to: " + fullOutputPath);
                }
                else
                {
                    MessageBox.Show("Choose a folder first");
                }
            }
            else
            {
                MessageBox.Show("Click Get Parameters button and then set values.");
            }
        }
```

code snippet \Reporting Service Rendering\Reporting Service Rendering\MainForm.cs

VB

Available for
download on
Wrox.com

```
Private Sub RenderReport()
    _rsExec.Url = String.Format("{0}/{1}", txtServer.Text.TrimEnd("/"), _
    "ReportExecution2005.asmx")

    Dim selectedFormat As Format =
    DirectCast(Me.reportFormatComboBox.SelectedItem, Format)
    Dim reportItem As ReportItem =
    DirectCast(Me.reportsComboBox.SelectedItem, ReportItem)

    Dim parameters As REService.ParameterValue() = GetReportExecutionParameters()

    Dim result As Byte() = Nothing
    Dim historyID As String = Nothing
    Dim devInfo As String = Nothing
    Dim encoding As String
    Dim mimeType As String
    Dim extension As String
    Dim warnings As REService.Warning() = Nothing
    Dim streamIDs As String() = Nothing

    ' Make sure the report either has parameters that are set or has no parameters.
    If ((_reportHasParameters AndAlso Not parameters.Length = 0) OrElse Not _
    _reportHasParameters) Then

        _rsExec.LoadReport(reportItem.Path, historyID)
        _rsExec.SetExecutionParameters(parameters, "en-us")
        result = _rsExec.Render(selectedFormat.Name, devInfo, extension, _
                                encoding, mimeType, warnings, streamIDs)

        ' Make sure there is an output path then output the file to the file
        system.
        If (Not txtOutputFolder.Text = "") Then
            Dim fullOutputPath As String = txtOutputFolder.Text & "\" & _
```

```
                                        reportItem.Name &
                                        selectedFormat.Extension
            Dim stream As System.IO.FileStream = _
              System.IO.File.Create(fullOutputPath, result.Length)
            stream.Write(result, 0, result.Length)
            stream.Close()
            MessageBox.Show("Report Rendered to: " & fullOutputPath)
        Else
            MessageBox.Show("Choose a folder first")
        End If
    Else
        MessageBox.Show("Click Get Parameters button and then set values.")
    End If
End Sub
```

code snippet \Reporting Service Rendering\Reporting Service Rendering VB\MainForm.vb

Now that you have completed the code for rendering the application, let's try it. You need to build and run the project. When the form opens, enter your server information in the Server Address text-box, and click the Get Items button, as shown in Figure 20-13.

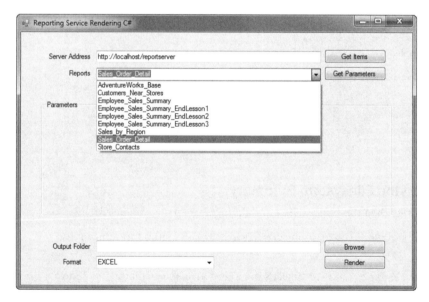

FIGURE 20-13

Select a report that takes parameters (the example uses the Sales Order Detail sample report), click the Get Parameters button, and then fill in the parameters, as shown in Figure 20-14.

Finally, select an output folder and the rendering format PDF. After specifying these items, you can click the Render button to render your report. When the rendering is complete, you see a message box saying that the file has been written to the specified location, as shown in Figure 20-15. You can now open your saved file using a PDF reader such as Adobe Reader.

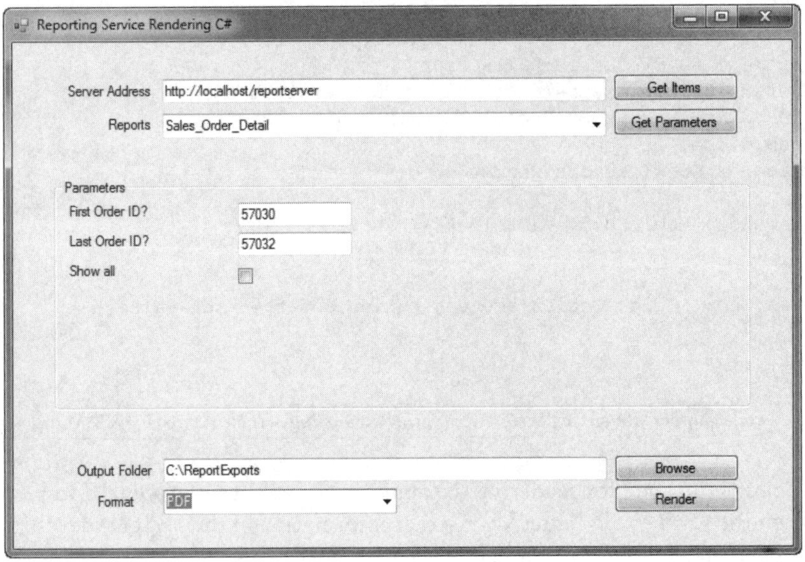

FIGURE 20-14

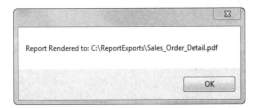

FIGURE 20-15

Rendering a Report to the Filesystem Summary

In this section, you have learned the basic steps of rendering a report to the filesystem:

➤ Using the `ReportingService2010` object's `ListChildren` method to return a list of reports

➤ Using the `ReportingService2010` object's `GetItemParameters` method to return a list of report parameters

➤ Using the `Render` method of the `ReportExecutionService` object to output your report in a given format

These basic steps can be used in numerous applications to render a report. Using these methods, users can create their own custom list of reports and customer-report parameter pages and output the report using the returned byte array. In the next section, you will use some of these steps to render a report to the Web via the `Response` object.

Rendering to the Web

In the preceding section, you saw the mechanics of rendering to a filesystem. However, most of today's applications are written for the Web. Along with URL requests, you can use Reporting Services Web services to render reports programmatically to the Web.

While doing this, most of your steps will be identical to rendering to the filesystem; you simply change the interface. Using the `ListChildren` method, developers can easily bind a list of reports to an ASP.NET GridView or create a tree view of available reports. Likewise, developers could use the `GetItemParameters` method to create their own web-based parameter interface.

Because you have seen both the `ListChildren` and `GetItemParameters` methods, in this section you will work more with the specifics of developing ASP.NET applications. You'll see what kinds of changes you can make to the `web.config` file to pass credential information to Reporting Services. Then you will look at the mechanics of rendering to the ASP.NET `HttpResponse` object.

Using Integrated Windows Authentication

Every security model has two main components: authentication and authorization. In Reporting Services, you can use Windows Integrated Authentication within an ASP.NET application to authenticate users. Before you start this example, you need to ensure that your application is configured to use Integrated Windows Authentication.

When deploying an ASP.NET web application to leverage Windows Authentication, you need to open IIS and change some settings of the virtual directory for your web site. Make sure that Anonymous Access has been turned off and that Integrated Windows Authentication has been turned on in IIS. Also, if you are not impersonating users in your web application, you will want to configure the application pool identity for your web site with a service account and password that has access to the Reporting Services catalog.

Using Integrated Windows Authentication in an ASP.NET web application is the easiest way to take advantage of the security features in Reporting Services. Using this method allows developers to concentrate on other areas of an application without having to build their own authentication mechanism. It also lets you take full advantage of the Reporting Services role-based security model.

In addition to updating the target IIS web-server settings for your web site to use Integrated Windows Authentication, you have to make some modifications to your ASP.NET web application.

While developing for ASP.NET, you can leverage the Visual Studio Development Server to quickly debug your application. The only caveat is that the web application will run under the identity of the user account that started the Visual Studio `devenv.exe` process. In most cases, this will be your own user account, so you must be sure to grant yourself permissions in the Reporting Services catalog accordingly.

For this demonstration, you will need to create a new ASP.NET Web Application using your .NET language of choice (e.g. C# or VB).

Modifying the web.config File

In the web application created for this demonstration, you want to pass the user's security credentials to the Reporting Services Web service. To accomplish this, you have to allow your ASP.NET
application to impersonate the currently logged-on user. Setting up impersonation requires adding
the following line of code to the `web.config` file. Place this line after the authentication element in
the file:

```
<identity impersonate="true" />
```

If your `web.config` file does not contain an authentication element, you must first add this element
with the appropriate mode attribute for Windows authentication, and place the identity element
inside of it:

```
<authentication mode="Windows" />
<identity impersonate="true" />
```

Configuring ASP.NET 2.0 in IIS 6 and Older Versions

The sample code with this exercise uses the ASP.NET Web Application project template and targets
.NET 4. However, you can still write and build similar code that targets the ASP.NET 2.0 runtime
and runs on IIS 6.0 to consume SSRS Web services.

As with any standard ASP.NET 2.0 web application, you can take a few steps to ensure that you can
run your ASP.NET 2.0 web application on IIS 6.0.

Make sure that, in the properties for the web site in IIS, on the ASP.NET page, ASP.NET 2.0 is
selected as the target version.

Confirm that ASP.NET 2.0 is listed as "Allowed" under the Web Service Extension list. If ASP.NET
2.0 is not listed, you can install it using the following `aspnet_regiis` command to configure the
ISAPI correctly:

```
C:\WINDOWS\Microsoft.NET\Framework\v2.0.50727>aspnet_regiis /i
Start installing ASP.NET (2.0.50727).
........................
Finished installing ASP.NET (2.0.50727).

C:\WINDOWS\Microsoft.NET\Framework\v2.0.50727>
```

Setting Up the Report Execution Web Service

The example needs only Rendering functionality, so you will use only the Report Execution Web
service. However, you generally need to also interact with the `ReportingService2010.asmx` Web
service, as discussed in the previous section.

For this example, we've added a web reference to `http://localhost/reportserver/reportex-
ecution2005.asmx` and named it `REService`.

Rendering to the Response Object

Now that you have set up Windows Integrated Authentication, modified the `web.config` file, and
optionally configured ASP.NET 2.0, you're ready to write some code. In this simple application, you

will have one page that takes in a report path and format from the URL. You'll use this information to call the Render method of the Report Execution Web service object and write that information back to the response stream.

This example uses one ASP.NET page called Render.aspx. Place your code sample in the page's Page_Load event. This would be a logical approach when developing an application around Reporting Services. It allows you to have one point of entry to the Report Server. The page could then be referenced from other areas of an application. For the entry page, you will use a simple Default.aspx page that has the path and format as a textbox and drop-down box. The Default.aspx page passes the Format and Path parameters to the Render.aspx page on a button event. Although the input for this example is simple, a more robust example could be built using the same technique that was shown in the previous section.

Let's add some code to the page's Page_Load event to retrieve the report path and format from the HTTP Request object:

C#

```csharp
string path = Request.Params["Path"];
string format = Request.Params["Format"];
```

VB

```vb
Dim path As String = Request.Params("Path")
Dim format As String = Request.Params("Format")
```

Now that you have the report path and format, you can start setting up the ReportExecutionService object. This is an instance of the Web Service reference, similar to what you did in the Windows Forms application. You will create an instance of the ReportExecutionService object and then set the credentials to the credentials of the currently logged-on user.

C#

```csharp
//create the ReportExecutionService object
ReportExecutionService _rsExec = new ReportExecutionService();

//set the credentials to be passed to reporting services
_rsExec.Credentials = System.Net.CredentialCache.DefaultCredentials;
```

VB

```vb
'create the ReportingService object
Dim _rsExec As New ReportExecutionService

'set the credentials to be passed to Reporting Services
_rsExec.Credentials = System.Net.CredentialCache.DefaultCredentials
```

As soon as the ReportingService object has been created and your credentials are set, you can render the report. You will create variables to pass any report parameters (none in this example) and capture the report's encoding, MIME type, parameters used, warnings, and stream IDs. The key output parameter, through which you'll render your report, is the MIME type. This parameter tells the HTTP `Response` object which type of document is being passed back. The following code renders your report to the web application. Notice that it is identical to the code used in the Windows Forms application.

C#

```csharp
ParameterValue[] parameters = new ParameterValue[0];

byte[] result = null;
string historyID = null;
string devInfo = null;
string encoding;
string mimeType;
string extension;
REService.Warning[] warnings = null;
string[] streamIDs = null;

_rsExec.LoadReport(path, historyID);
_rsExec.SetExecutionParameters(parameters, "en-us");
result = _rsExec.Render(format, devInfo, out extension,
            out encoding, out mimeType, out warnings, out streamIDs);
```

code snippet \Web Rendering\Web Service Rendering \Render.aspx.cs

VB

```vb
Dim parameters As ParameterValue()
Dim result() As Byte
Dim historyID As String
Dim devInfo As String
Dim encoding As String
Dim mimeType As String
Dim extension As String
Dim warnings() As Warning
Dim streamIDs() As String

_rsExec.LoadReport(path, historyID)
_rsExec.SetExecutionParameters(parameters, "en-us")
result = _rsExec.Render(format, devInfo, extension, encoding, _
            mimeType, warnings, streamIDs)
```

code snippet \Web Rendering\Web Service Rendering VB \Render.aspx.vb

The `Render` method of the `ReportExecutionService` object returns a byte array that can be used in several ways. For the Web, you write this information directly back to the HTTP `Response` object. Before you write back the data, however, you need to set some information about the report — namely, a filename. To do this, you use the name of the report followed by an extension that you determine using the value returned in the extension variable.

Now construct the filename using the following code. The code uses the information returned from the `Render` method.

C#

```csharp
string reportName = path.Substring(path.LastIndexOf("/") + 1);
string fileName = reportName + "." + extension;
```

VB

```vb
Dim reportName As String = path.Substring(path.LastIndexOf("/") + 1)
Dim fileName As String = reportName & "." & extension
```

Finally, you need to put it all together by writing the data and file information back to the `HttpResponse` object. Do the following:

1. Clear any information that is already in the response buffer.

2. Set the content type of the response equal to the MIME type of your rendered report.

3. Attach your filename information to the response if your report is in a format other than HTML.

4. Use the `BinaryWrite` method to write the rendered report byte array directly to the `Response` object.

The following is the completed code for the `Page_Load` event:

C#

```csharp
protected void Page_Load(object sender, EventArgs e)
{
    if (!Request.Params.HasKeys())
        Response.Redirect("~/Default.aspx");

    //get the path and output format from the query string
    string path = Request.Params["Path"];
    string format = Request.Params["Format"];

    var _rsExec = new ReportExecutionService();
    _rsExec.Credentials = System.Net.CredentialCache.DefaultCredentials;

    // Prepare report parameter.
    // The GetParameters method could be implemented as was shown in
    // the previous section on rendering to the file system.
    ParameterValue[] parameters = new ParameterValue[0];

    // Variables used to render the report.
    byte[] result = null;
    string historyID = null;
    string devInfo = null;
    string encoding;
    string mimeType;
    string extension;
    REService.Warning[] warnings = null;
    string[] streamIDs = null;

    // Load the report, set the parameters and then render.
```

```
_rsExec.LoadReport(path, historyID);
_rsExec.SetExecutionParameters(parameters, "en-us");
result = _rsExec.Render(format, devInfo, out extension, out encoding,
        out mimeType, out warnings, out streamIDs);

string reportName = path.Substring(path.LastIndexOf("/") + 1);
string fileName = reportName + "." + extension;

//Write the report back to the Response object.
Response.Clear();
Response.ContentType = mimeType;

//Add the file name to the response if it is not a web browser format.
if (mimeType != "text/html")
    Response.AddHeader("Content-Disposition", "attachment; filename=" +
                        fileName);

Response.BinaryWrite(result);
}
```

code snippet \Web Rendering\Web Service Rendering\Render.aspx.cs

```
Protected Sub Page_Load(ByVal sender As Object, ByVal e As System.EventArgs)
 Handles Me.Load

    Dim path As String = Request.Params("Path")
    Dim format As String = Request.Params("Format")

    'create the ReportingService object
    Dim _rsExec As New ReportExecutionService

    'set the credentials to be passed to Reporting Services
    _rsExec.Credentials = System.Net.CredentialCache.DefaultCredentials

    'prepare report parameters
    Dim parameters(0) As ParameterValue

    'variables used to render the report
    Dim result() As Byte
    Dim historyID As String
    Dim devInfo As String
    Dim encoding As String
    Dim mimeType As String
    Dim extension As String
    Dim warnings() As Warning
    Dim streamIDs() As String

    _rsExec.LoadReport(path, historyID)
    _rsExec.SetExecutionParameters(parameters, "en-us")
    result = _rsExec.Render(format, devInfo, extension, encoding, _
            mimeType, warnings, streamIDs)
```

```vb
    Dim reportName As String = path.Substring(path.LastIndexOf("/") + 1)
    Dim fileName As String = reportName & "." & extension

    'write the report back to the Response object
    Response.Clear()
    Response.ContentType = mimeType
    'add the file name to the response if it is not a web browser format
    If mimeType <> "text/html" Then
        Response.AddHeader("Content-Disposition", "attachment; " _
                           & "filename=" & fileName)
    End If
    Response.BinaryWrite(result)

End Sub
```

code snippet \Web Rendering\Web Service Rendering VB \Render.aspx.vb

This example demonstrates some of the key pieces of code you can use to render reports to the Web. You first need to set the application's security context by configuring Windows Integrated Authentication and allowing impersonation from your application (or provide credentials for the application pool that can access the Report Server). Next, you retrieve a report from Reporting Services by specifying the report path and format. Finally, you use the rendered report data along with its associated MIME type to render the report using the HTTP `Response` object.

Now that the code for your web application is complete, let's take a look at using your `Render.aspx` page. You can use a simple query string to render your report. Here's a sample query string that renders the Employee List report from the Professional Reporting Services sample reports in HTML 4.0 format:

```
http://localhost/Render.aspx?Path=%2fSample+Reports%2fEmployee_Sales_Summary&Format
=HTML4.0
```

This URL does the following:

➤ It calls the `Render.aspx` page from your C# project.

➤ It passes in the required parameters: the path (`/Sample Reports/Employee_Sales_Summary`) and the Format (HTML 4.0).

Notice that when you enter HTML 4.0 as the output format, the report data is rendered directly in the browser. In your code, the MIME type of your HTTP `Response` is `text/html` in this scenario. When the browser receives the response, it recognizes the MIME type and renders it directly to the browser.

 Depending on your security settings, IE asks if you want to save the HTML page or open it. You can click Open to view the report in the browser.

Let's take a quick look at rendering in a format that does not go directly to the browser. Use the following URL to render the same Employee List report, but in EXCEL format:

```
http://localhost/Render.aspx?Path=%Sample+Reports%2fEmployee_Sales_Summary&Format=
EXCEL
```

Figure 20-16 shows the result.

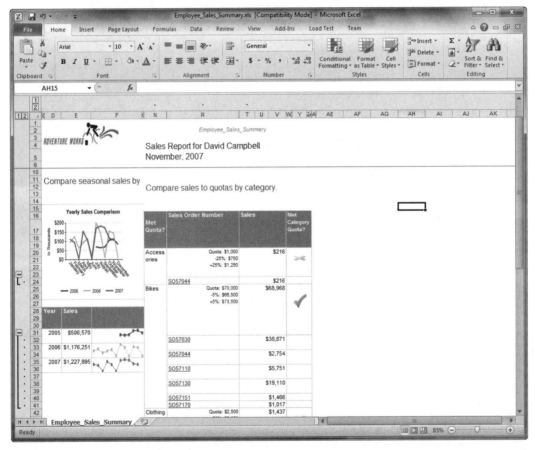

FIGURE 20-16

Notice this time that when you set the format to EXCEL, you are prompted to save to the filesystem. In this case, the MIME type needs to be set to application/vnd.ms-excel. You also need to add header information to the HttpResponse object that contains the filename Employee_Sales_Summary.xls. The MIME type notifies Internet Explorer that you are sending a file, and the added header gives it the appropriate filename.

In this section, you have seen some of the base mechanics of rendering a report using an ASP.NET application. To start, you need to pass the currently logged-on user's credentials (or the credential of the application pool). This is accomplished by setting the application's virtual directory to use Windows Integrated Authentication and then modifying the web.config file for the application to use impersonation. In the code, you need to call the Report Execution Web service to retrieve the report along with content information such as MIME type. As soon as you have the binary report data, you can write that information directly back to the `HttpResponse` object.

USING THE REPORTVIEWER CONTROL

Many improvements have been made in Visual Studio 2010 for working with Reporting Services reports in your custom applications. For starters, an out-of-the-box Reports Application project is listed in the New Project list, as shown in Figure 20-17.

FIGURE 20-17

When the Reports Application project template is selected, it creates a new Windows Forms application project with a form containing the Report Viewer control and a Report RDLC file. It also automatically starts the Report Wizard, as shown in Figure 20-18.

The Report Wizard walks you through creating a data source, selecting an existing data source, saving the connection information to the configuration file, choosing the database objects you want to report on, and then creating a report based on those objects.

The Reports Application project is a great starting point, but the `ReportViewer` control can also be added to any custom application. In Visual Studio, the control is automatically made available under a grouping in the toolbox called Reporting, as shown in Figure 20-19.

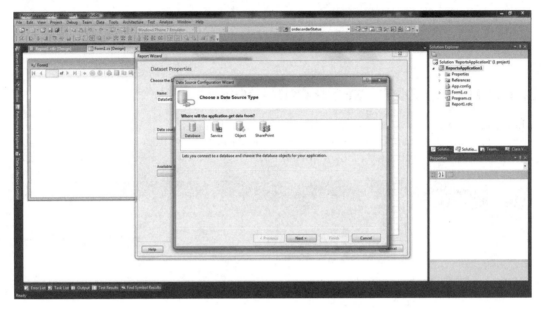

FIGURE 20-18

The `ReportViewer` control is by far the most flexible and, in most cases, the easiest technique for adding a report to your .NET application. Two separate but similar controls are available — .NET Windows Forms and ASP.NET Web Forms applications. All the user-interface attributes you have seen in the Report Manager and Designer Preview tab can be managed using properties of the control and can be set at design time in the Properties window, or at run time using program code. You can even dynamically create an instance of the control, set its properties programmatically, and render a report without adding it to a form in the designer.

The `ReportViewer` controls are client-side controls that do not need a SQL Server instance to be used. Their only dependency is the .NET Framework 3.5.

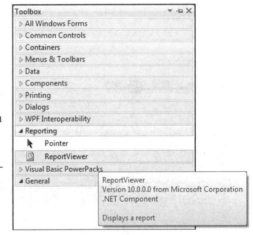

FIGURE 20-19

The source data used by the controls can come from any data source, not just SQL Server. The `ReportViewer` controls themselves don't know where the data comes from. Your application brings in the data from whichever source you choose and makes it available to the `ReportViewer` controls in the form of an `IEnumerable` collection, such as ADO.NET `DataTables`, `IQueryable` objects, or custom collections. The `ReportViewer` controls don't even know how to connect to databases or execute queries. By requiring the host application to supply the data, you can use the `ReportViewer` controls with any data source, including relational, nonrelational, and nondatabase data sources.

Two different report execution scenarios are supported in both types of the ReportViewer control:

➤ Remote mode

➤ Local mode

In Remote mode, standard RDL reports are deployed and executed on the Report Server and then are viewed in the control as you would expect. This is similar to the approach used by the Report Manager's ReportViewer.aspx page when accessing reports as HTML via URL access.

In Local mode, the ReportViewer control acts as a mini report-hosting engine that allows reports to execute in your application without needing a connection to the Report Server. In fact, the control hosts a complete version of the SSRS processing and rendering engine, which makes this possible. However, this requires a different version of the report definition file that has been retrofitted for client-side execution. The file is an RDLC file, where the C stands for client-side processing.

 The version of the ReportViewer *control that ships with Visual Studio 2010 supports the RDL 2005 and 2008 schemas while in local processing mode. However, when executing server reports in Remote mode, it does not support the SSRS 2005 version of the Report Server. Also, for reports created with the RDL 2010 schema, the report processing and rendering are done on the server. Therefore, you can leverage the latest features, such as maps, sparklines, KPI indicators, and report parts (introduced in 2008 R2), from within the report viewer.*

Both RDL and RDLC formats have the same base XML schema, but the latter allows some of its XML elements to contain empty values. RDLC also ignores the <Query> element of the RDL schema. Actually, the <Query> element is included in the XML file only if the file began its life as an RDL format and was later manually converted to an RDLC. When client-side processing files are created using the Visual Studio wizards, the generated file will already have omitted unnecessary elements. RDLC files may also contain design-time information that the ReportViewer control uses to generate data-binding code.

You can create an RDLC report by manually converting an RDL report into RDLC by using the Report Creation Wizard, by using the Add New Item dialog in Visual Studio, or by generating the RDLC programmatically.

The last option opens a world of opportunities for custom applications. You can create a custom user interface to allow users to generate new reports on the fly by interacting with your own business/domain data model and then serialize your in-memory report to XML based on the RDL schema. As soon as you have the XML, you can simply provide it to the Report Viewer control, along with the data, during execution. In fact, this is similar to how the Report Designer works inside Visual Studio, except that it adds the missing XML elements related to data querying and saves the serialized XML to a file on disk.

Embedding a Server-Side Report in a Windows Application

In the following exercise you view a server-side report in a Windows Forms application using the `ReportViewer` control in Remote mode. The properties and methods of the Web Forms version of the control are nearly identical, making your code transportable between Windows and Web application projects. You will start by just viewing a report in your custom application and then move on to working with the report's parameters in your code.

As you know, the report rendering interface can generate several toolbar options and parameter prompts when rendering a server report. You can either use these default UI elements or replace them with your own. When you start working with the report parameters, you hide the default prompts and force the user to enter the parameters through your custom application. This gives you much control over how the user interacts with the report and allows you to introduce robust parameter validation according to your business requirements.

To get started, open up Visual Studio, and select File ➪ New ➪ Project. Select the Windows Forms Application project template for either C# or VB. This will create a new project with a blank Windows Form and the required references.

The example uses the Sales_By_Region report used throughout the chapter. First, you will add a form to your Visual Studio Windows Application project. Drag and drop the `ReportViewer` control onto the form. Resize and anchor it to meet your needs.

The first thing to notice about the `ReportViewer` control is the drop-down Context menu used to configure the control's most important aspects. The drop-down allows you to choose a specific report or choose a report from a Report Server. You can also set the Report Server URL and the report path, as well as kick off the Report Wizard to design a new report and dock the report in the current container.

Set the Report Server property to the local report server, and then set the report path to the Sales_By_Region report. You can do this quickly by clicking the smart tag button to the right of the report viewer control (the little arrow) to open the common tasks dialog, as shown in Figure 20-20.

The `ReportPath` property is the report location in the Report Server catalog. In this case, we've selected a report on the local server to display in the `ReportViewer` control. The location of the Report Server is set using the `ReportServerUrl` property. The `ReportPath` and `ReportServerUrl` properties can also be accessed under the `ServerReport` grouping in the Properties pane of the Visual Studio IDE when the control has focus in the designer.

Because you'll use the Report Server for processing, set the `ProcessingMode` property to Remote. This will cause the Report Server to query and retrieve source data that will be used in the report. In Remote mode, the `ReportViewer` controls display reports that are hosted on a SQL Server Reporting Services server. The source data for those reports can come from any appropriate data source, not just SQL Server. This behavior is normal report processing behavior — specific not to the viewer controls, but rather to the Reporting Services platform.

You are now ready to run the custom application and view the report in a Windows Form, as shown in Figure 20-21.

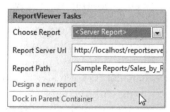

FIGURE 20-20

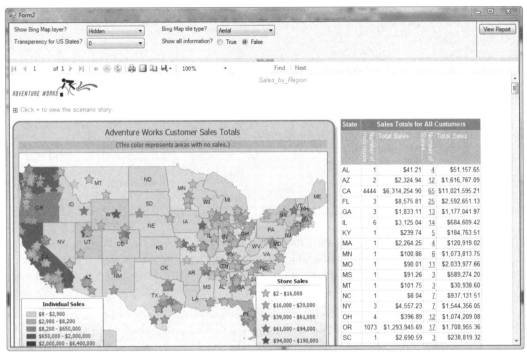

FIGURE 20-21

You have seen a simple example of running a report in a custom application; however, you might also want to add functionality to control the parameters that the users see and select. For example, let's introduce a slider (TrackBar) that controls the opacity parameter for the Bing Maps layer of this report to replace the standard drop-down values.

Since the available list of values for the opacity parameter is a nonlinear set of six values (0, 10, 25, 35, 50, 75), you must create an array that maps these values to an indexer to correspond to the slider's ticks. Let's add this array as a private member to our form. Then we can load it with values in the form constructor. The following code is from the code-behind for the Form1 class (partial class):

C#

Available for
download on
Wrox.com

```csharp
private int[] _trackBarValues = new int[6];
public Form1()
{
    InitializeComponent();
    _trackBarValues[0] = 0;
    _trackBarValues[1] = 10;
    _trackBarValues[2] = 25;
    _trackBarValues[3] = 35;
    _trackBarValues[4] = 50;
    _trackBarValues[5] = 75;
}
```

code snippet \WroxReportViewer\WroxReportViewer\Form1.cs

VB

```vb
Private _trackBarValues As Integer() = New Integer(5) {}
Public Sub New()
    ' This call is required by the designer.
    InitializeComponent()

    _trackBarValues(0) = 0
    _trackBarValues(1) = 10
    _trackBarValues(2) = 25
    _trackBarValues(3) = 35
    _trackBarValues(4) = 50
    _trackBarValues(5) = 75
End Sub
```

code snippet \WroxReportViewer\WroxReportViewerVB\Form1.vb

Next, we'll add our new controls to the form, above the report viewer control, to collect parameter input from the user. We'll need to add a label and combo box (name it `ShowMapLayerComboBox`) for the parameter `ShowBingMaps` and specify the values `Hidden` and `Visible` as the items for the combo box by entering these values in the Items property of the combo box.

Now, add another label and a TrackBar control, located in the All Windows Forms toolbox group, to the form to correspond to the `USStatesTransparency` parameter, which controls the opacity level of the Bing Map layer when it is visible. For the TrackBar, be sure to set the properties `TickFrequency` to 1, `Minimum` to 0, and `Maximum` to 5. This ensures that we have a total of only six ticks on the slider to map to the number of available values for this report parameter. In addition, we'll set the `Enabled` property to false so that the slider is enabled only when the user chooses to set the Bing Maps layer parameter to visible.

Finally, we'll add a new button to the form, give it the text "View Report," and create an empty click-event handler method by double-clicking it. We'll add code in there later.

Your form design surface should look like Figure 20-22.

Now we need to edit the `Form Load` event and remove the line of code that automatically refreshes the ReportViewer control. Because we first will give the users a chance to select parameters, we don't want the report to run when the form opens. Also, we'll add the following line of code to preselect the first item in the combo box:

C#

```csharp
private void Form1_Load(object sender, EventArgs e)
{
    this.ShowMapLayerComboBox.SelectedIndex = 0;
}
```

VB

```vb
Private Sub Form1_Load(sender As Object, e As EventArgs) Handles MyBase.Load
    Me.ShowMapLayerComboBox.SelectedIndex = 0
End Sub
```

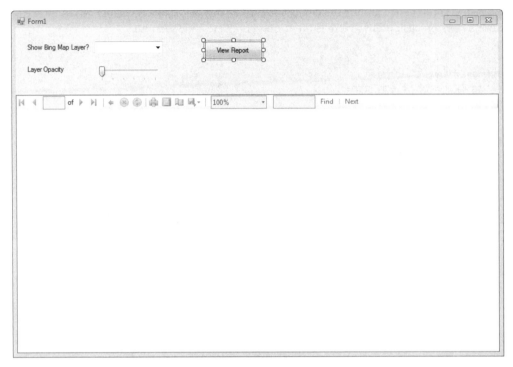

FIGURE 20-22

With every property of the `ReportViewer` control (except the parameters that we are providing via our user interface) set using the Properties window, the only necessary code is to set our two parameters and execute the report.

Parameters are managed as an array of `ReportParameter` objects. Since we are overriding two of the required parameters, we'll create an array of two elements. Each element is populated by passing the parameter name and value to each `ReportParameter` constructor.

To use the `ReportParameter` object, you need to either add the following using/`Imports` statement to your code or instantiate the object using the full `Microsoft.Reporting.WinForms` namespace. Adding the using/`Imports` statement provides for much cleaner and easier-to-read code, so add the following statements to your form's code-behind file:

C#

```
using Microsoft.Reporting.WinForms;
```

VB

```
Imports Microsoft.Reporting.WinForms
```

The report parameters are populated by passing the array to the `SetParameters` method of the `ServerReport` object.

Finally, the `ReportViewer`'s `RefreshReport` method causes report execution to begin.

The last two event handlers are for the combo box, to enable or disable the slider based on the selection, and the button click event. Here is the form's complete code section:

C#

```csharp
using System;
using System.Windows.Forms;
using Microsoft.Reporting.WinForms;

namespace WroxReportViewer
{
    public partial class Form1 : Form
    {
        private int[] _trackBarValues = new int[6];
        public Form1()
        {
            InitializeComponent();
            _trackBarValues[0] = 0;
            _trackBarValues[1] = 10;
            _trackBarValues[2] = 25;
            _trackBarValues[3] = 35;
            _trackBarValues[4] = 50;
            _trackBarValues[5] = 75;
        }

        private void Form1_Load(object sender, EventArgs e)
        {
            this.ShowMapLayerComboBox.SelectedIndex = 0;
        }

        private void ShowMapLayerComboBox_SelectedIndexChanged(object sender,
        EventArgs e)
        {
            this.trackBar1.Enabled =
                (sender as ComboBox).SelectedItem.ToString()
                    .Equals("visible", StringComparison.OrdinalIgnoreCase);
        }

        private void button1_Click(object sender, EventArgs e)
        {
            ReportParameter[] parameters = new ReportParameter[2];

            parameters[0] = new  ReportParameter("ShowBingMaps",
            this.ShowMapLayerComboBox.SelectedItem.ToString());

            parameters[1] = new ReportParameter("USStatesTransparency",
            _trackBarValues[this.trackBar1.Value].ToString());

            reportViewer1.ServerReport.SetParameters(parameters);
            reportViewer1.ShowParameterPrompts = false;
            reportViewer1.ShowPromptAreaButton = false;
            reportViewer1.RefreshReport();
        }
    }
}
```

code snippet \WroxReportViewer\WroxReportViewer\Form1.cs

```vb
Imports System
Imports Microsoft.Reporting.WinForms

Public Class Form1
    Private _trackBarValues As Integer() = New Integer(5) {}
    Public Sub New()
        ' This call is required by the designer.
        InitializeComponent()

        _trackBarValues(0) = 0
        _trackBarValues(1) = 10
        _trackBarValues(2) = 25
        _trackBarValues(3) = 35
        _trackBarValues(4) = 50
        _trackBarValues(5) = 75
    End Sub
    Private Sub Form1_Load(sender As Object, e As EventArgs) Handles MyBase.Load
        Me.ShowMapLayerComboBox.SelectedIndex = 0
    End Sub

    Private Sub ShowMapLayerComboBox_SelectedIndexChanged(sender As Object, e
    As EventArgs) Handles ShowMapLayerComboBox.SelectedIndexChanged
        Me.trackBar1.Enabled = DirectCast(sender,
        ComboBox).SelectedItem.ToString().Equals("visible",
        StringComparison.OrdinalIgnoreCase)
    End Sub

    Private Sub button1_Click(sender As Object, e As EventArgs) _
      Handles button1.Click
        Dim parameters As ReportParameter() = New ReportParameter(1) {}
        parameters(0) = New ReportParameter("ShowBingMaps",
        Me.ShowMapLayerComboBox.SelectedItem.ToString())
        parameters(1) = New ReportParameter("USStatesTransparency",
        _trackBarValues(Me.trackBar1.Value).ToString())

        ReportViewer1.ServerReport.SetParameters(parameters)
        ReportViewer1.ShowParameterPrompts = False
        ReportViewer1.ShowPromptAreaButton = False
        ReportViewer1.RefreshReport()
    End Sub
End Class
```

code snippet \WroxReportViewer\WroxReportViewerVB\Form1.vb

Figure 20-23 shows the result. The report is displayed in the `ReportViewer` control embedded on the form. The standard report parameter bar and prompts are not displayed in the top of the viewer because they were suppressed using the related `ReportViewer` properties.

The `ReportViewer` controls provide an easy-to-implement way to embed reports in your custom web and Windows applications. They also give you complete control over the code for the rest of the application to provide users with an all-around solution. There's an in-between option in which reports can be made available to users without going through the Report Manager application. That in-between option is SharePoint, which is discussed in Chapter 18.

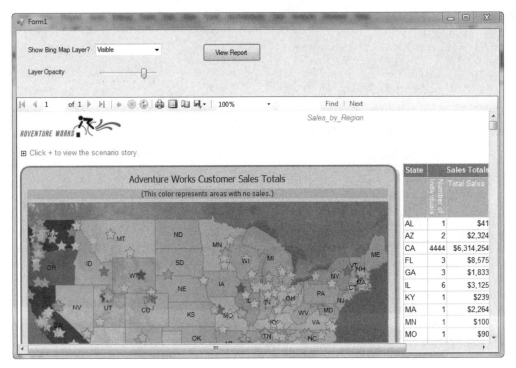

FIGURE 20-23

SUMMARY

This chapter showed you three ways to render reports from Reporting Services. The first part of the chapter focused on rendering reports via URL requests. The second part looked at rendering reports programmatically through the Reporting Services Web services. In the last part, you used the `ReportViewer` control to easily embed reports in a Windows Forms application.

URL rendering gives you a quick way to add Reporting Services reports to your own applications. You can add Reporting Services reports to custom portals or create your own custom report links in other applications.

Rendering reports directly through an ASP.NET application can be helpful. It allows developers to create their own interface for items such as parameters using well-known UI constructs in HTML. A key point to remember is that Report Manager uses the same Reporting Services Web services used in the examples in this chapter. Therefore, anything you can do from the Report Manager can also be done through your own code. This adds an incredible amount of flexibility for developers of custom applications.

This chapter has shown you how to do the following:

➤   Use simple URL query strings to access reports

➤   Programmatically work with the Reporting Service and Report Execution Service APIs

- ➤ Embed reports into custom Windows and web applications
- ➤ Work with the `ReportViewer` control in Visual Studio

Because the Reporting Services APIs are implemented as Web services, you can call them from various types of applications, including .NET Windows applications, ASP.NET web applications, and .NET console applications. You can even use these Web services from Visual Basic 6.0, VBA applications using Microsoft's SOAP library, or essentially any application that can send a properly formatted SOAP request to the Report Server. This flexibility lets you create a number of applications, including those that use custom security or pass parameter information stored in other application databases.

21

Using Embedded and Referenced Code

WHAT'S IN THIS CHAPTER?

➤ Building advanced expressions

➤ Using custom code to extend formatting

➤ Using custom code to apply business logic

The real power behind Reporting Services is its ability to creatively use data groups and combinations of report items. Calculations and conditional formatting may be added by using simple to intermediate programming code. Whether you are an application developer or a report designer, this chapter contains important information to help you design reports to meet your users' requirements and to raise the bar with compelling report features.

Perhaps we've put the cart before the horse with regard to expressions. In previous examples, you typed expression text without receiving an explanation. This couldn't be avoided, because using expressions is central to doing a lot of interesting things in Reporting Services. But we've just gotten started!

Any textbox bound to a dataset field or built-in field actually contains an expression. But in an effort to simplify the design interface, expressions are no longer displayed in the Report Designer as they were prior to the 2008 version of Reporting Services. Perhaps this might make life less hectic for entry-level report designers, but the rest of us have to be mindful that what we see in the Designer is not exactly what's going on behind the report design surface.

You'll recall that you can build simple composite expressions in a textbox by dragging items from the Report Data pane into a textbox. For example, if you want to display the page number and total number of report pages in the report footer, insert a textbox into the report footer and do the following:

1. Drag the `PageNumber` built-in field from the Report Data pane into the textbox.

2. Place the cursor at the end of this text, press the spacebar, type the word **of**, press the space bar, and then drag the `TotalPages` built-in field to the end of the text.

This produces an expression that appears like this in the Report Designer:

```
[&PageNumber] of [&TotalPages]
```

If you have worked with versions of Reporting Services prior to 2012, you will notice an improvement in the user experience. After the cursor leaves the textbox, the Report Designer no longer displays the following non-descriptive label in gray:

<<Expr>>

You get to see the expression that was typed in the textbox. Now let's get to the bottom of this. What value is really stored in this textbox? Unfortunately, if the expression is created by using the designer (instead of the Expression Builder), you no longer can right-click and choose Expression to find out. Instead, these types of expressions are built as "text runs" inside a paragraph defined for the textbox. To see what is really going on under the covers, you would need to open the RDL file using a text editor such as Notepad. You will find an XML snippet as follows:

```xml
<Paragraphs>
    <Paragraph>
        <TextRuns>
            <TextRun>
                <Value>=Globals!TotalPages</Value>
                <Style />
            </TextRun>
            <TextRun>
                <Value> of </Value>
                <Style />
            </TextRun>
            <TextRun>
                <Value>=Globals!PageNumber</Value>
                <Style />
            </TextRun>
        </TextRuns>
        <Style />
    </Paragraph>
</Paragraphs>
```

However, if you prefer to build your expressions in a more "programmatic" way, you can always use the Expression Builder dialog and type in the following:

```
=Globals!PageNumber & " of " & Globals!TotalPages
```

Don't worry; the next section explains the detailed steps to accomplish this task. This type of expression built by hand-coding in the Expression Builder is stored slightly differently in the RDL file:

```xml
<Paragraphs>
    <Paragraph>
        <TextRuns>
```

```
                    <TextRun>
                        <Value>
                            =Globals!PageNumber &amp; " of " &amp; Globals!TotalPages
                        </Value>
                        <Style />
                    </TextRun>
                </TextRuns>
                <Style />
            </Paragraph>
        </Paragraphs>
```

Notice that the RDL generated is slightly less verbose and contains only one `TextRun` element, which holds the expression you typed in the Expression Builder. If you've worked with previous versions of Reporting Services, this will look familiar. It's the same Visual Basic expression code that Reporting Services has used all along.

A little history behind this may be worth pointing out. You'll recall that Reporting Services was originally designed to be an application developer-centric tool, used by programmers in Microsoft Visual Studio. As time went on and the product matured, the powers that be at Microsoft took a good hard look at Reporting Services and realized that the industry was asking for a more information worker-centric reporting tool. Several incremental steps have helped Reporting Services become this dual-identity product that appeals to both programmers and business users. The downside is that, in places, the product can be a bit schizophrenic. In addition to the Designer's drag-and-drop expressions and the Expression Editor's expression syntax differences, the built-in fields in the Report Data pane are referred to as members of the Globals collection within true report expressions. The term built-in fields is just a friendly term, not a syntax convention.

USING THE EXPRESSION BUILDER

You've already used a few expressions in the basic report design work you've done so far. Any field reference is an expression. In the Group Properties dialog, you used a field expression. In the previous example, we used an expression to show the page number and total pages so that it reads "X of Y" when the report is rendered. Expressions are used to create a dynamic value based on a variety of built-in fields, dataset fields, and programming functions. Expressions can be used to set most property values based on a variety of conditions, parameters, field values, and calculations. Let's take a quick look at common methods to build simple expressions. We'll explain the previous example, only this time in the Expression Builder.

To display the page number and page count, right-click the textbox and select Expression, and then use the Expression window to create the expression. You can use two methods to add expressions to the expression text area. One method is to select items from the category tree and member list and double-click an item to add to the expression. The other method is to simply type text into the expression text area. This uses the IntelliSense Auto List Members feature to provide drop-down lists for known items and properties.

1. Begin by typing `="Page" &` in the Expression box, and then click the Built-in Fields item in object tree view. All related members are listed in the adjacent list box.

2. Double-click the `PageNumber` item in the list.

3. Place the cursor at the end of the text, and type the text `& " of " &`. Then select and insert the `TotalPages` field.

The finished expression should read as follows:

```
="Page " & Globals!PageNumber & " of " & Globals!TotalPages
```

The Expression window (also called the Expression Builder) should appear, as shown in Figure 21-1.

FIGURE 21-1

The term globals (or built-in fields) applies to a set of variables built in to the Reporting Services namespace that provide useful information such as page numbers, report name, and path. A list of available global variables, fields, and parameters can be found in the Expression Builder.

You'll see this dialog again. In fact, you probably will use it often. In the Properties window, you can set many property values by using the drop-down list to select the item labeled <Expression . . . >. In the custom Properties dialog for each report item, the Expression dialog is invoked using the button labeled *fx* adjacent to each property value.

In previous chapters, you learned how parameter values are passed into a query to limit or alter the result set. Parameters may also be used within the report to modify display characteristics by dynamically changing item properties. For example, we can affect grouping expressions of data regions based on values in parameter variables. A report's parameters collection is publicly accessible from the expression window and can be included as part of expressions.

CALCULATED FIELDS

Custom fields can be added to any report and can include expressions, calculations, and text manipulation. This might be similar in functionality to alias columns in a query or view, but the calculation or expression is performed on the Report Server after data has been retrieved from the database. Calculated field expressions can also use Reporting Services global variables, custom code, and functions that may be unavailable in a SQL expression.

Let's start with a basic report that displays product details. You will replace a simple expression previously used in a textbox with a calculated field. Figure 21-2 shows a textbox used to calculate the profit margin for each product by subtracting the StandardCost field from the ListPrice. The Expression dialog is shown for this textbox.

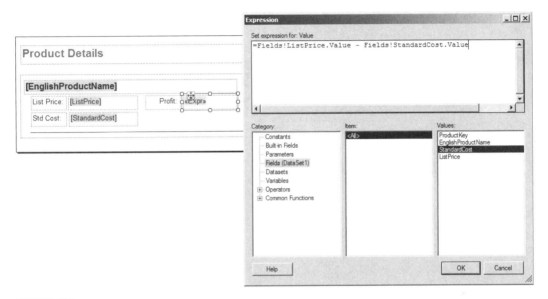

FIGURE 21-2

Rather than performing the calculation on the textbox, let's add a calculated field to the dataset definition so that this calculation can be reused by other objects in the report.

Use the Report Data pane in the Report Designer to select the dataset you want to use. Right-click the dataset and choose Add Calculated Field, as shown in Figure 21-3.

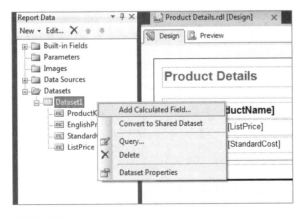

FIGURE 21-3

The Dataset Properties dialog opens, as shown in Figure 21-4. On the Fields page, click the Add button to add a new item to the Fields collection. Type the new field name, and then click the expression button (*fx*) next to the Field Source box on this new row.

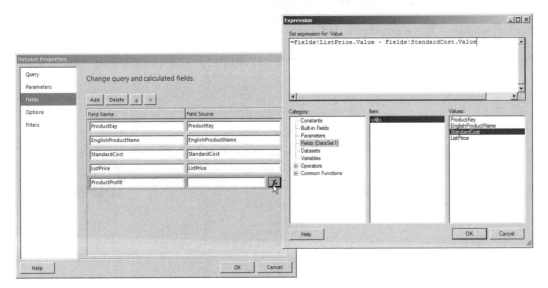

FIGURE 21-4

When the Expression dialog opens, simply type or build the same expression as before. Verify the results with Figure 21-4, and then click OK on both of these dialogs to save the newly calculated field to the dataset.

Using the calculated field is no different from using any other field derived from the dataset query. Just drag and drop the new field from the Report Data pane to the textbox on the report. Note the `Profit` field reference in the textbox, as shown in Figure 21-5.

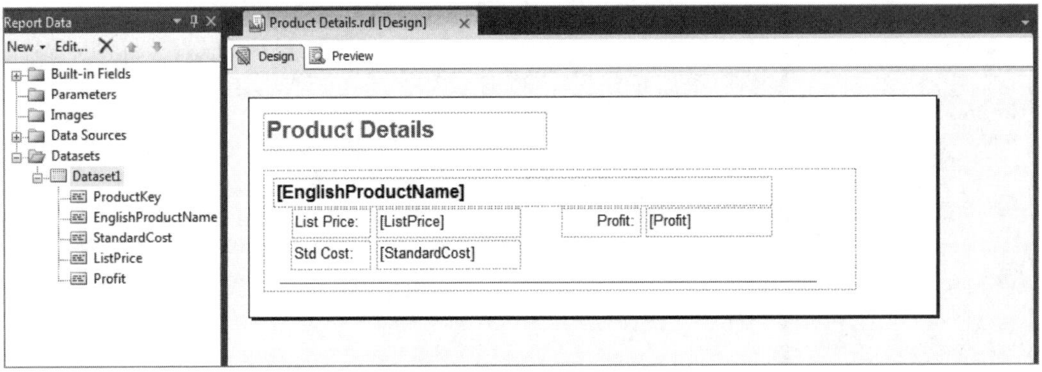

FIGURE 21-5

You can use the expression button to invoke the Expression Builder to use any functionality available within the design environment in addition to the database fields exposed by the dataset query. These calculations will be performed on the Report Server rather than on the database server.

CONDITIONAL EXPRESSIONS

You've seen some simple examples of using expressions to set item values and properties. Let's look at one more example of a conditional expression, and then we'll discuss using program code to handle more complex situations. We'll create a simple Product Inventory report that uses conditional formatting. The table in this report returns a list of products with current inventory values. The Product table in the AdventureWorks_WroxSSRS2012 database contains a `ReorderPoint` value that informs stock managers when they need to reorder products. If the inventory count falls below this value, you can set the inventory quantity to appear in red next to the name. Using a conditional expression in this manner is similar to using conditional formatting in Excel.

The following example uses a dataset with this SQL expression:

```
SELECT      Product.Name, Product.ReorderPoint,
            ProductInventory.Quantity, Product.ListPrice
FROM        Production.ProductInventory
INNER JOIN Production.Product
            ON ProductInventory.ProductID = Product.ProductID
ORDER BY    Product.Name
```

The table bound to this dataset has four columns: `Name`, `ReorderPoint`, `Quantity`, and `ListPrice`. On the Quantity textbox in the table's detail row, the `Color` property is set to an expression containing conditional logic instead of being set to a value. You can use the Expression Builder or just type this expression into the Properties window under the `Color` property:

```
=IIF(Fields!Quantity.Value < Fields!ReorderPoint.Value, "Red", "Black")
```

We've done the same thing with the `Font > FontWeight` property so that if the inventory quantity for a product is below the reorder point value, the quantity is displayed in both red and bold text.

Preview the report to check the results; they should look like Figure 21-6.

IIF() IS YOUR FRIEND

Even if you're not a programmer, learning a few simple Visual Basic commands and functions will prove valuable and will likely meet most of your needs. The most common and useful function you're likely to use in simple expressions is `IIF` (immediate if). As you saw in the previous example, the `IIF()` function takes three arguments. The first is a Boolean expression that returns either `True` or `False`. If the expression is `True`, the value passed into the second argument is returned. Otherwise (if the first expression is `False`), the third argument value is returned. Take another look at the expression used in the previous example:

```
=IIF(Fields!Quantity.Value < Fields!ReorderPoint.Value, "Red", "Black")
```

If the expression `Fields!Quantity.Value < Fields!ReorderPoint.Value` yields a `True` result (where `Quantity` is less than `ReorderPoint`), the value `"Red"` is returned. Otherwise, the value returned is `"Black"`.

Product Inventory / Reorder

Name	Reorder Point	Quantity
Adjustable Race	750	408
Adjustable Race	750	324
Adjustable Race	750	353
All-Purpose Bike Stand	3	144
AWC Logo Cap	3	288
BB Ball Bearing	600	585
BB Ball Bearing	600	443
BB Ball Bearing	600	324
Bearing Ball	750	427
Bearing Ball	750	318
Bearing Ball	750	364
Bike Wash - Dissolver	3	36
Blade	600	532
Blade	600	388
Blade	600	441
Cable Lock	3	252
Chain	375	236
Chain	375	192

FIGURE 21-6

In cases where an expression may return more than two states, IIF() functions can be nested to form multiple branches of logic. In this example, three different conditions are tested:

```
=IIF( Fields!Quantity.Value < Fields!ReorderPoint.Value, "Red",
IIF(Fields!ListPrice.Value > 100, "Blue", "Black" ))
```

Let's analyze the logic. If Quantity is not less than ReorderPoint, the third IIF() function argument is invoked. This contains a second IIF() function, which tests the ListPrice field value. If the value is greater than 100, the value "Blue" is returned; otherwise, the return value is "Black". According to the definition of this function, the second argument is the TruePart value, and the third argument is the FalsePart value. This means that the value in the second position is returned if the expression evaluates to True, and the value in the third position is returned if it is False.

Since IIF() *is a function, it evaluates* all *its parameters/arguments. In other words, even if the condition expression evaluates to true, the code in the false part also executes. But the function doesn't return it, and vice versa. This is significant, because you might have code that throws* NullReference *exceptions on either true or false parts when the condition does not favor that outcome. The best way to circumvent this behavior is to write a custom code function embedded in the report that contains a true Visual Basic (VB)* If/Then/Else *statement and returns the expected outcome. Then you can call this embedded code function from the Expression Builder. This topic is covered in the following section.*

Beyond the simplest nested functions, expressions can be difficult to write and maintain. In addition to decision structures, you can use common functions to format the output, parse strings, and convert data types. Count the opening and closing parentheses to make sure that they match. This is yet another example of where writing this code in a Visual Basic class library or forms project is helpful because of the built-in code-completion and integrated debugging tools. Consider using these other functions in place of nested IIF() functions.

The SWITCH() function accepts an unlimited number of expression and value pairs. The last argument accepts a value that is returned if none of the expressions resolves to True. You can use this in place of the previous nested IIF() example:

```
=SWITCH( Fields!Quantity.Value < Fields!ReorderPoint.Value, "Red",
    Fields!ListPrice.Value > 100, "Blue", 1=1, "Black" )
```

 A completed version of the sample report containing this modification is named Conditional Formatting 2.

Unlike the IIF() function, the SWITCH() function has no FalsePart value. Each expression and return value is passed as a pair. The first expression in the list that evaluates to True causes the function to stop processing and return a value. This is why we included the expression 1=1. Because this expression always evaluates to True, it becomes the catchall expression that returns "Black" if no other expressions are True.

Visual Basic supports many of the old-style VBScript and VB 6.0 functions, as well as newer overload method calls. In short, this means that there may be more than one way to perform the same action. Table 21-1 describes a few other Visual Basic functions that may prove useful in basic report expressions.

TABLE 21-1

FUNCTION	DESCRIPTION	EXAMPLE
FORMAT()	Returns a string value formatted using a regular expression format code or pattern. Similar to the Format property but can be concatenated with other string values.	=FORMAT(Fields!TheDate .Value, "mm/d/yy")
MID() LEFT() RIGHT()	Returns a specified number of characters from a specified position (if using MID()) and for a specific length. You can also use the .SUBSTRING() method.	=MID(Fields!TheString .Value, 3, 5) =LEFT(Fields!TheString .Value, 5) = Fields!TheString .Value.SUBSTRING(2, 5)

continues

TABLE 21-1 *(continued)*

FUNCTION	DESCRIPTION	EXAMPLE
INSTR()	Returns an integer for the first character position of one string within another string. Often used with MID() or SUBSTRING() to parse strings.	=INSTR(Fields!TheString.Value, ",")
CSTR()	Converts any value to a string type. Consider using the newer ToString() method.	=CSTR(Fields!TheNumber.Value) =Fields!TheNumber.Value.ToString()
CDATE() CINT() CDEC() ...	A type-conversion function similar to CSTR(). Converts any compatible value to an explicit data type. Consider using the newer CTYPE() function to convert to an explicit type.	=CDATE(Fields!TheString.Value) =CTYPE(Fields!TheString.Value, Date)
ISNOTHING()	Tests an expression for a null value. May be nested within an IIF() to convert nulls to another value.	=ISNOTHING(Fields!TheDate.Value) =IIF(ISNOTHING(Fields!TheDate.Value), "n/a", Fields!TheDate.Value)
CHOOSE()	Returns one of a list of values based on a provided integer index value (1, 2, 3, and so on).	=CHOOSE(Parameters!FontSize.Value, "8pt", "10pt", "12pt", "14pt")

Hundreds of Visual Basic functions can be used in some form, so this list is just a starting point. For additional assistance, view the Online Help index in Visual Studio, under Functions [Visual Basic]. This information is also available in the public MSDN library at http://msdn.microsoft.com.

USING CUSTOM CODE

When you need to process more-complex expressions, it may be difficult to build all the logic into one expression. In such cases, you can write your own function to handle different conditions and call it from a property expression.

You can take two approaches to managing custom code. One is to write a block of code to define functions that are embedded in the report definition. This technique is simple, but the code will be available to only that report. The second technique is to write a custom class library compiled to an external .NET assembly and reference this from any report on your Report Server. This approach has the advantage of sharing a central repository of code, which makes updates to the code easier to manage. It also gives you the freedom to use any .NET language (C#, VB). The downside of this approach is that the configuration and initial deployment are a bit tedious.

Using Custom Code in a Report

A report can contain embedded Visual Basic .NET code that defines a function you can call from property expressions. The Code Editor window is simple; it doesn't include any IntelliSense, editing, or formatting capabilities. For this reason, you might want to write the code in a separate, temporary Visual Studio project of type "VB class library," to test and debug before you place it into the report. When you are ready to add code, open the Report Properties dialog. You can do this from the Report menu. The other method is to use the Report Designer right-click menu. Right-click the Report Designer outside of the report body and select Properties. On the Properties window, switch to the Code tab, and write or paste your code in the Custom Code box.

The following example starts with a new report. Here is the code, along with the expressions you will need to create a simple example report on your own. The following Visual Basic function accepts a phone number or social security number (SSN) in a variety of formats and outputs a standard U.S. phone number and properly formatted SSN. The Value argument accepts the value, and the Format argument accepts the value Phone or SSN. You use it only with phone numbers, so you can omit the SSN branch if you like.

```
'****************************************************************
'    Returns properly formatted Phone Number or SSN
'    based on format arg & length of text arg
'****************************************************************
Public Function CustomFormat(ByVal text as String, ByVal format as String) as_
String
      Select Case format
      Case "Phone"
          Select Case text.Length
          Case 7
              Return text.SubString(0, 3) & "-" & text.SubString(3, 4)
          Case 10
              Return "(" & text.SubString(0, 3) & ") " _
                    & text.SubString(3, 3) _
                    & "-" & text.SubString(6, 4)
          Case 12
              Return "(" & text.SubString(0, 3) & ") " _
                    & text.SubString(4, 3) & "-" & text.SubString(8, 4)
          Case Else
              Return text
          End Select
      Case "SSN"
          If text.Length = 9 Then
              Return text.SubString(0, 3) & "-" _
                    & text.SubString(3, 2) & "-" & text.SubString(5, 4)
          Else
              Return text
          End If
      Case Else
          Return text
      End Select
End Function
```

The dataset in this report gets its data from the Vendor and related tables in the AdventureWorks_ WroxSSRS2012 database and returns three columns: FirstName, LastName, and Phone. The SQL expression used to retrieve this information is as follows:

```
SELECT      FirstName, LastName, PhoneNumber
FROM        Purchasing.vVendorWithContacts
```

These three columns are used in a table bound to the dataset. The Value property of the Phone column uses an expression that calls the custom function preceded by a reference to the Code object:

```
=Code.CustomFormat(Fields!PhoneNumber.Value, "Phone")
```

Figure 21-7 shows the report in design layout view.

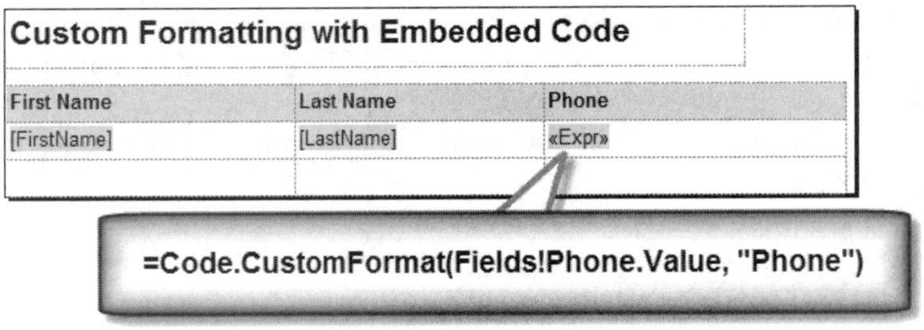

FIGURE 21-7

Using a Custom Assembly

Rather than embedding code directly into each report, you can use a custom assembly as a central repository of reusable code to extend the functionality of multiple reports. In Reporting Services, custom assembly support is enabled by default. However, the code in the assembly has restricted access to system resources due to Code Access Security policies (as discussed in the next section). If you intend for the assembly to interact with the filesystem or perform data access, you need to modify some configuration settings to grant the appropriate level of access to your code. We'll discuss these conditions after a simple walk-through to create an assembly that won't require any special settings. For this discussion, you should have a basic understanding of .NET and how to create and build libraries using Visual Studio.

To begin, open Visual Studio, then from the File ⇨ New Project menu, create a class library project. You can write this code in any .NET language, because it will be compiled into an assembly that uses a low level intermediate language (IL), common to .NET. The methods you create can be either static or instanced. It's easier to use static methods so that you don't have to manage the instancing and life of each object. This simply means that you will declare public functions in your class using the static keyword in C# or the Shared keyword in Visual Basic. Using the same code logic as in the previous example, the Visual Basic class code would look like this:

```
Public Class Report_Formats
    '****************************************************************
    '    Returns properly formatted Phone Number or SSN
    '    based on format arg & length of text arg
    '****************************************************************
```

```
Public Function CustomFormat(ByVal text as String, ByVal format as String) _
   As    String
      Select Case format
      Case "Phone"
         Select Case text.Length
         Case 7
            Return text.SubString(0, 3) & "-" & text.SubString(3, 4)
         Case 10
            Return "(" & text.SubString(0, 3) & ") " _
                   & text.SubString(3, 3) _
                   & "-" & text.SubString(6, 4)
         Case 12
            Return "(" & text.SubString(0, 3) & ") " _
                   & text.SubString(4, 3) & "-" & text.SubString(8, 4)
         Case Else
            Return text
         End Select
      Case "SSN"
         If text.Length = 9 Then
            Return text.SubString(0, 3) & "-" _
                   & text.SubString(3, 2) & "-" & text.SubString(5, 4)
         Else
            Return text
         End If
      Case Else
         Return text
      End Select
   End Function
End Class
```

In order to test the external assembly code from a Visual Studio IDE report preview window, you must build the class library project in Debug configuration and then copy the output DLL assembly to the IDE's `PrivateAssemblies` folder. The default path to this folder is `C:\Program Files \Microsoft Visual Studio 10.0\Common7\IDE\PrivateAssemblies`. Once the assembly is copied, you will need to open a new instance of Visual Studio in order for it to load the assembly in memory.

In the Report Properties dialog (this is where you entered the code in the previous topic example), select the References page, as shown in Figure 21-8. Add the reference by browsing to the assembly file. The reference line shows metadata from the assembly, including the version number.

To use a custom method in an expression, reference the namespace, class, and method using standard code syntax. The expression for the `CustomFormat` method should look like this:

```
=Reporting_Component.Report_Formats.CustomFormat(Fields!Phone.Value, "Phone")
```

The report should look exactly like it did in the previous example.

After debugging and testing the code, you are ready to deploy it to the Report Server. Save and build the class library project in Release configuration, and then copy the assembly (DLL) file to the `ReportServer\bin` folder. The default path to this folder is `C:\Program Files\Microsoft SQL Server\MSRS11.MSSQLSERVER\Reporting Services\ReportServer\bin`.

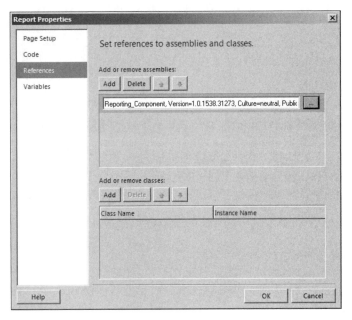

FIGURE 21-8

Custom Assembly Security

When you use a custom assembly deployed to your Report Server, the assembly must run with the appropriate level of security access. This feature, Code Access Security (CAS), is a common challenge for all server-side .NET applications running prior to .NET 4. A thorough discussion of this topic is beyond the scope of this book. If you are a seasoned developer, these should be familiar topics. If you are not, you should consult a .NET application developer to help configure your custom assemblies.

In short, the steps to deploy and configure an assembly to run on your Report Server are not much different from any other remotely deployed component. The permissions depend on the resources the assembly uses. For example, a component that interacts with the local filesystem or that consumes features of another component or database connections requires privileges to do so. The following are some of the more common steps to make custom assemblies more accessible:

1. Build the assembly with a strong name. Use the `SN.exe` command-line utility to create a strongly named key pair, and then reference the generated key file within the `AssemblyInfo` class file in the class library project.

2. Register the assembly in the Global Assembly Cache (GAC) on the Report Server. Not only does this elevate the assembly's trustworthiness, it also provides downward version compatibility control.

3. You can apply the `AllowPartiallyTrustedCallers` assembly attribute to allow the Reporting Services engine to call into this code.

4. You can explicitly enable nondefault security permissions for the assembly using policy configuration files. Two files are used to manage these permissions. The `rssrvpolicy.config` file controls assembly permissions for the development and preview environment. The `rspreviewpolicy.config` file controls permissions on the Report Server.

For additional assistance with specific security considerations and configuration details, use SQL Server 2012 Books Online to look up the topic "Using Reporting Services Security Policy Files."

Errors, Warnings, and Debugging Code

When you preview or try to deploy a report, all the expressions and embedded code in the report are cranked through the .NET Common Language Runtime debugger and native code compiler. If no errors are found, an assembly is built on the Report Server. This means that when reports execute, all the expression and program code actually runs from compiled binaries rather than from the Visual Basic source code.

Errors are listed in the IDE task window if this process fails. The Report Designer has a quirk that can be a bit confusing until you get used to it. Along with errors that prevent code compilation and report deployment, another set of information shows up in this list. Some conditions may cause Reporting Services to be less than ecstatic about your code, but not unhappy enough to prevent it from compiling. These are called warnings, and they appear on the task list below any errors. The confusing thing is that Visual Studio displays this window only when errors occur, unless you have it pinned and always visible. This means that you can build a big, elaborate report that runs perfectly until you make one small mistake in the code. When you try to preview this report, you might suddenly see 30 issues on the task list. These may include "can't deploy shared datasource..." and "textbox42 has a `BackgroundColor` set to ... which is invalid." If this happens, don't get excited; this is just how the Designer works. Those warnings were there all along. Visual Basic just didn't put the list in front of you until you committed a serious infraction. Start at the top of the list, and work your way down until you see an error description that makes sense. Double-click this line. In most cases, doing so takes you to the properties for the offending report item, allowing you to make the correction and move on.

When you test reports in the Visual Studio Report Designer, your custom assembly is loaded into memory when it is first invoked and cannot be unloaded until you exit Visual Studio. This means that if you make code changes and redeploy the assembly, these changes may be unavailable to the report unless you restart the Visual Studio process (`devenv.exe`). The best way to work around this issue is to deploy your report to your local Report/Web Server and test it using the Report Manager.

SUMMARY

Expanding on the basic design concepts and building blocks you learned about in the previous chapters, in this chapter you raised the bar and created more powerful and compelling reports using custom expressions and code techniques.

Expressions and custom programming take report design to new heights by allowing a single report to deliver more functionality, behaving more like a multifunction business application than a traditional report.

By leveraging the .NET framework and its runtime, you can create highly specialized code modules that can do everything from simple string manipulations to complex mathematical and statistical calculations. You can even load data from files in the file system or make web calls to other servers. The possibilities are endless when you have such a powerful feature to leverage from inside your reports.

22

Extending Reporting Services

WHAT'S IN THIS CHAPTER?

➤ Leveraging extensibility options

➤ Reasons for extending SQL Server Reporting Services

➤ Creating custom extensions

➤ Installing custom extensions

As you learned in previous chapters, Reporting Services is a robust and scalable product for enterprise report processing. In addition, Microsoft has created Reporting Services using a modular extensible architecture that allows users to customize, extend, and expand the product to support their enterprise business intelligence (BI) reporting needs. This chapter introduces you to most of the areas within Reporting Services that allow customization and explains some of the reasons that you might want to extend the product. The basic requirements for implementing each type of extension are discussed, followed by a detailed example of creating and deploying a data processing extension.

Reporting Services currently supports extending its behavior in the following areas:

➤ **Data Processing Extensions (DPEs)** — Custom DPEs enable you to access any type of data using a consistent programming model. This option is for you if you cannot access your data using one of the currently supported providers (Analysis Services, Hyperion Essbase, ODBC, OLE DB, Oracle, Report Model, SAP BI NetWeaver Business Intelligence, SQL Server, Teradata, SQL Azure, Parallel Data Warehouse, SharePoint List, and XML). Microsoft has also released a Feature Pack for SQL Server that provides customized extensions, such as SAP Relational DB and DB2, in addition to the ones built into the product.

➤ **Delivery extensions** — Chapter 17, "Content Management," discussed subscribing to a report. During this process, one of the required options is the method of delivery. Do you want the report sent to your cell phone in image format, or perhaps delivered to a file share for your perusal at a later date? The ability to extend SSRS with delivery extensions allows you to choose.

Delivery extensions allow you to deliver reports to users or groups of users according to a schedule. E-mail, network file shares, and SharePoint content are the delivery mechanisms currently built into the product. There is also a delivery extension that preloads the cache with pre-rendered parameterized reports. This extension, known as the "null delivery" extension, is not exposed to users, but rather it is leveraged by administrators of data-driven subscriptions. Creating a delivery extension is really a two-part process. You must create the extension itself, as well as a UI tool to manage the extension if you want it to be usable from the SSRS Report Manager. The difficulty in creating a delivery extension is primarily a function of the delivery mechanism.

➤ **Rendering extensions** — These control the type of document/media that gets created when a report is processed. Theoretically, you could have Reporting Services create any type of media given the ability to extend the product in this area. Microsoft provides the following rendering extensions out of the box:

➤ **HTML** — The HTML extension generates HTML 4.0. Support for HTML 3.2 has been discontinued in this version of Reporting Services.

➤ **Excel** — The new Excel extension creates Excel 2007-2010 compatible files using the Open XML Office format (XLSX). The older Excel rendering extension, which generates XLS files compatible with Excel 97 and later, using the Binary Interchange File Format (BIFF), is still available but is hidden by default via the `RSReportServer.config` file.

➤ **Word** — The new Word rendering extension creates Word 2007-2010 compatible files using the Open XML Office format (DOCX). The older Word rendering extension, which generates DOC files compatible with Word 97 and later, is still available but has been hidden by default via the `RSReportServer.config` file.

➤ **Image** — The Image extension allows you to export reports as images in the BMP, EMF, GIF, JPEG, PNG, TIFF (default), and WMF formats.

➤ **PDF** — This extension allows the generation of reports in the Adobe PDF format.

➤ **CSV** — Comma-separated values emit the data fields separated by commas as plain text files. The first row of the CSV results contains the Field names for the data.

➤ **XML** — This extension renders the report in XML format and allows for optional transformations to manipulate the output of the rendered markup.

➤ **Security extensions** — These allow you to authenticate and authorize users and groups into a Report Server. In its first release, Reporting Services supported only Integrated Windows Security for report access. This was a pretty big problem for some enterprise players. Most companies have heterogeneous networks with multiple operating systems and products. In a perfect world, all our networks, applications, and resources would support some form of "single sign-on," or at least would allow us to build this ourselves. If Microsoft wanted SQL Server to be a key part of an Enterprise Business Intelligence platform, it had to play nicely with others. Microsoft fixed this problem in Service Pack 1 for SQL Server 2000 and made it a part of SQL Server 2005. The release contained fully documented security extension interfaces and an example using ASP.NET forms-based authentication. You may implement your custom security model using SSRS, but only one security extension can be used per Reporting Services instance.

➤ **Report Processing Extensions (Custom Report Items)** — This extension type came with the 2005 release of Reporting Services. It enabled the creation of custom report items that were processed by the report processing engine. This enables us to extend the RDL standard to include functionality not natively supported by the RDL, such as custom MapPoint maps and horizontal lists. Developers can also extend current report items to provide alternative versions that better fit their needs.

➤ **Report definition customization extensions** — This extension type, which was introduced with the 2008 release, provides a hook into the preprocessing of the report definition. You can plug in custom code that can modify the report definition stream before it gets processed. This is handy, for example, if you need to modify the report's layout based on a culture, locale, or user identity that is specified with the report request. Note that you are not guaranteed where or when in the request pipeline the customization will occur, but you *are* guaranteed that it will always happen before the processing of the report definition takes place. For this extension, a new interface was included and is required to be implemented:

```
IReportDefinitionCustomizationExtension
```

EXTENSION THROUGH INTERFACES

Reporting Services uses common interfaces or "extension points" to allow expanding the product in a standard way. Enforcing the requirement that RS extension objects must implement certain interfaces allows Reporting Services to interact with different object types without knowledge of their specific implementation. This is a common object-oriented programming technique used to abstract the design from the implementation.

 For an in-depth study of this topic, look at Chapter 3, "Creational Patterns," *of* Design Patterns: Elements of Reusable Object-Oriented Software, *by Erich Gamma, Richard Helm, Ralph Johnson, John M. Vlissides, and Grady Booch (Addison-Wesley, 1994).*

What Is an Interface?

Most C/C++ developers are intimately familiar with *interfaces*. Seasoned .NET developers know about interfaces because we use them to interact with FCLs (Framework Class Libraries) and to program to contracts for loosely coupled code. In fact, Reporting Services itself is exposed to developers through a web service interface. To provide complete coverage of extending Reporting Services, a definition and an explanation of interfaces are required.

So what is an interface? An *interface* is a predefined code construct that forms a contract between software components and defines how they communicate. The interface provides an abstraction layer of its entity to the outside.

That sounds great, but what does it mean? It simply means that to adhere to the contract defined by an interface, all extension components must contain certain methods, properties, and so on.

In Reporting Services specifically, it means that every extension component must contain certain methods defined by the IExtension interface. Other interface implementations may be required as well, depending on the type of extension you are trying to create.

Interface Language Differences

There are differences in how VB.NET and C# require interface methods to be declared. C# supports "implicit" interface definitions. If the method names and signatures match those of an interface that the class implements, the class methods are automatically mapped to their associated interface definitions. We chose System.IDisposable for this example because many of the classes you will create are required to implement it.

C#

```
public class TestClass : System.IDisposable
{
  //this method is automatically mapped to IDisposable.Dispose
  public void Dispose()
  {
      //write some code to dispose of non-memory resources
  }
}
```

VB.NET requires explicit interface implementation. To be mapped correctly, VB.NET requires that you specify that the method is implementing a certain interface. This is done with the Implements keyword:

VB.NET

```
Public Class TestClass
    Implements IDisposable

    Public Sub Dispose() Implements IDisposable.Dispose
          'write some code to dispose of non-memory resources
    End Sub
End Class
```

Visual Studio provides code refactoring features that assist with interface implementation — specifically, a feature called Interface AutoComplete. When you indicate that a class should implement a certain interface, Visual Studio can generate wrapper methods for all the properties, methods, and so on that are required for that interface, as shown in Figure 22-1. This saves a huge amount of typing and is a great productivity enhancement when you're creating objects designed to "plug in to" an existing framework.

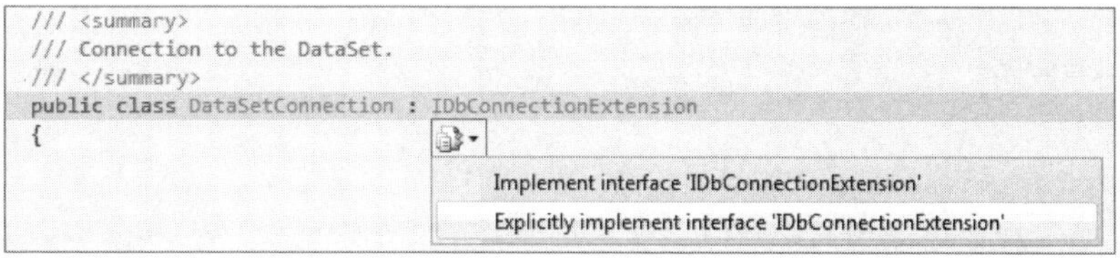

```
/// <summary>
/// Connection to the DataSet.
/// </summary>
public class DataSetConnection : IDbConnectionExtension
{
```

Implement interface 'IDbConnectionExtension'

Explicitly implement interface 'IDbConnectionExtension'

FIGURE 22-1

Microsoft is also attempting to build "best practices" into Visual Studio. Although the two examples just shown are technically correct in that they implement IDisposable, they do not implement the IDisposable design pattern shown in the .NET Framework SDK. Allowing Visual Studio to do the heavy lifting creates a more feature-complete implementation that includes consideration for cascading object chains and explicit release of memory and nonmemory resources. Visual Studio would create code similar to the following for IDisposable. We did take liberties with the comments to make it easier to read.

C#

```
public class TestDispose : System.IDisposable
{
    private bool disposed = false;

    //IDisposable
    private void Dispose(bool disposing)
    {
        if (! this.disposed)
        {
            if (disposing)
            {
                // TODO: put code to dispose of managed resources here
            }
            // TODO: put code to free unmanaged resources here
        }
        this.disposed = true;
    }

    //IDisposable Support
    //Don't change
    public void IDisposable.Dispose()
    {
        // Don't change. Put cleanup code
        // in Dispose(bool) above.
        Dispose(true);
        GC.SuppressFinalize(this);
    }

    // Don't change
    protected void Finalize()
    {
        Dispose(false);
        base.Finalize();
    }

}
```

VB.NET

```
Public Class TestDispose
    Implements System.IDisposable

    Private disposed As Boolean = False

    'IDisposable
    Private Overloads Sub Dispose(ByVal disposing As Boolean)
        If Not Me.disposed Then
            If disposing Then
                ' TODO: put code to dispose of managed resources here
            End If
            ' TODO: put code to free unmanaged resources here
        End If
        Me.disposed = True
    End Sub

    'IDisposable Support
    'Don't change
    Public Overloads Sub Dispose() Implements IDisposable.Dispose
        ' Don't change. Put cleanup code
        ' in Dispose(ByVal disposing As Boolean) above.
        Dispose(True)
        GC.SuppressFinalize(Me)
    End Sub

    ' Don't change
    Protected Overrides Sub Finalize()
        Dispose(False)
        MyBase.Finalize()
    End Sub

End Class
```

You will be using this Interface AutoComplete feature for the remainder of this chapter. Extensions for Reporting Services must be compiled using the .NET Framework 3.5, so you will need to use Visual Studio 2008 or higher to target that version of the .NET Framework. (The code samples for this chapter were created using Visual Studio 2010 Service Pack 1 [SP1].) The generated code for IDisposable is suitable for demonstration purposes, so we won't repeat this code for each object; we'll simply indicate that it is required.

A Detailed Look at Data Processing Extensions

Reporting Services allows you to access data from traditional data sources such as relational databases using the existing .NET data providers. The following providers are supported as part of the .NET Framework supplied by Microsoft:

➤ ODBC

➤ OLE DB

➤ SqlClient

DPEs are components that allow you to access data for use within Reporting Services. If that implies a ".NET data provider" to you, congratulations are in order. These two types of data access objects are very similar and are based on a common set of interface definitions. If you have already built a custom .NET data provider, you may use that provider with Reporting Services with no modification. However, you also can extend your existing provider to offer additional functionality.

To begin, we need to discuss the similarities and differences between a standard .NET data provider and a Reporting Services DPE. Let's start with some architectural information about data providers in general and then dive into the details of creating a custom DPE. The .NET Framework has a data access object model named ADO.NET, as shown in Figure 22-2.

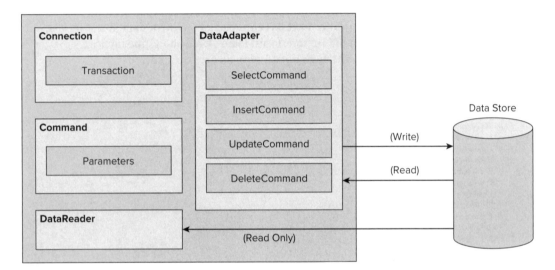

FIGURE 22-2

Ever since Service Pack 1 of SSRS on SQL Server 2000, it has been possible to customize and extend the security model of Reporting Services. This required adding a few things to the object model.

Here are the basic steps for working with a data source:

1. Connect to a data source.

2. Issue a command to manipulate data.

3. Retrieve the results of your query.

These actions map directly to the objects just described, although a `DataAdapter` implementation is not needed because Reporting Services only reads the data.

Table 22-1 lists the objects that are normally created in a DPE and describes their responsibilities.

TABLE 22-1

OBJECT	DESCRIPTION
Connection	Establishes a connection to a specific data source.
Command	Executes a command against a data source. Exposes a `Parameterscollection` and can execute within the scope of a transaction.
DataReader	Provides access to data using a forward-only, Read Only stream.
DataAdapter	Retrieves data and resolves updates with the data source. This object is not required for a DPE because SSRS only needs to read the data to create reports.

Each of these objects contains implementation-specific code needed to create a connection, issue commands, or read and update data. Microsoft has enforced a consistent data access mechanism by basing these objects on a set of standard interfaces. Figure 22-3 shows the interfaces that may be implemented when creating a DPE, although not all of them are required.

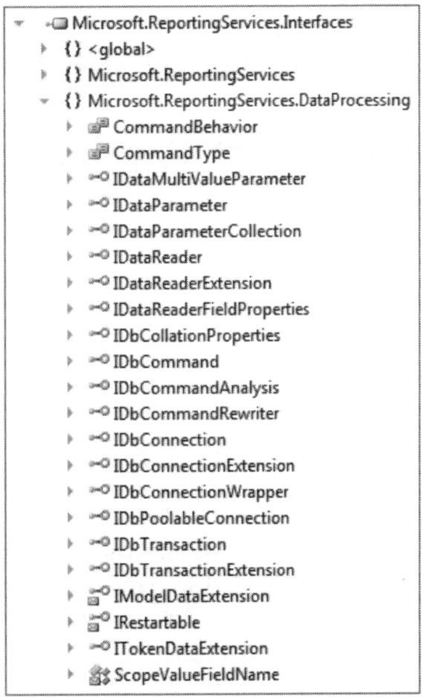

FIGURE 22-3

You may build a minimalist `DataExtension` by implementing the required interfaces listed in Table 22-2 and add additional behavior by implementing the optional interfaces listed in Table 22-3.

TABLE 22-2

REQUIRED INTERFACE	DESCRIPTION
IDataParameter	Methods to support passing parameters to a `Command` object
IDataParameterCollection	Collection of parameters

REQUIRED INTERFACE	DESCRIPTION
IDataReader	Methods used to read a forward-only, Read Only data stream
IDbCommand	Represents query command methods to be executed against a data source
IDbConnection	Unique session with a data source
IExtension	Reporting Services-specific interface that supports localization and is implemented by all SSRS extensions

TABLE 22-3

OPTIONAL INTERFACE	DESCRIPTION
IDataReaderExtension	Provides Resultset-specific aggregation information
IDbCommandAnalysis	Analysis Services-specific extension
IDbConnectionExtension	Unique session with a data source
IDbTransaction	Local transaction (nondistributed)
IDbTransactionExtension	Reporting Services-specific interface that supports localization and is implemented by all SSRS extensions

CREATING A CUSTOM DATA PROCESSING EXTENSION

Creating a full-blown data provider is no trivial task. The goal of this walk-through is to familiarize you with the .NET data access mechanism, as well as help you create and install a custom Reporting Services DPE. Our implementation is simplified in that it does not support transactions or the use of parameters, and many of the methods are empty unless code is explicitly required. All the images shown were created using the Visual Studio 2010 IDE. The code snippets are given in both C# and VB unless there is a reason to do otherwise.

The Scenario

The first release of Reporting Services (with SQL Server 2000) lacked support for consuming existing ADO.NET DataSet objects. After the release of Service Pack 1, the Books Online documentation contained a sample extension that used some of the dataset's intrinsic properties to allow you to query a DataSet object and limit the resulting rows based on certain criteria. The only problem was that you couldn't do complex filtering or limit the columns that a query returned.

In SQL Server 2005, Reporting Services gained a new DPE — the XML data extension. This enabled reports to retrieve data from XML content, which could be located in a file, hosted on a web or file server, or even better, from web services. This new extension provided an XPATH-like syntax for the command text, giving it greater flexibility for searching through data within the

XML as well as supporting schemata and namespaces. This DPE has remained largely unchanged through to the current SQL Server 2012 release.

Interestingly, many companies have data stores that never really talk to each other directly, and remain isolated. These companies usually have requirements to query those data sources and create reports that join all that data. SSRS does not provide an explicit mechanism to federate data across multiple servers, besides SQL Server's Linked Server features. If linked servers are just not an option for you, you are left to come up with a creative solution for the situation.

The XML data extension may be useful in this scenario. You can set up a web service that does the dirty work of joining data from multiple tables in memory using ADO.NET. Then all that SSRS needs to provide to the web method is a collection of command texts to be executed, such as SQL statements or stored procedure names, and the relationship details, such as key columns and types of joins. Once the web service has executed the commands and joined the data tables in memory, it returns the XML dataset ready for SSRS to consume.

In our example, we'll provide a similar but more simplistic extension that shows the fundamental pieces required to implement the Reporting Services Interfaces and consume data from an XML dataset file. The ADO.NET `DataSet` type contains a method that allows it to read in the data from XML and build the internal data table that Reporting Services will consume.

Creating and Setting Up the Project

Let's start by creating our project. Launch Visual Studio, and create the project by choosing File ➪ New Project. Change the name of the project to DataSetDataExtension. Use the Class Library template with the language of your choice and, if you are using Visual Studio 2010, make sure you target the .NET Framework 3.5. After your project is created, you need to set up your environment to help you work. The Visual Basic IDE tends to hide some things from you, so you will make some changes to help our C# brethren follow along. The first thing you want to do is show all your references. The default behavior of VB.NET is to hide them. Choose Project ➪ Show All Files. The Explorer tab should now show all your project references.

Next, you need to add the references to the required Reporting Services DLL file. The `Microsoft` `.ReportingServices.DataProcessing` namespace is needed to implement the DPE interfaces, and the `Microsoft.ReportingServices.Interfaces` namespace is needed to implement the `IExtension` interface. Both of these namespaces are defined in the same assembly file, `Microsoft` `.ReportingServices.Interfaces.dll`.

The extensions and their dependencies are located in a subdirectory below the installation directory of SQL Server itself. We will call the SQL Server installation path `<InstallPath>`. You need the following directory for the SSRS extensions DLL:

```
<InstallPath>\MSRS11.MSSQLSERVER\Reporting Services\ReportServer\bin
```

 On my machine, this directory is `C:\Program Files\Microsoft SQL Server\` `MSRS11.MSSQLSERVER\Reporting Services\ReportServer\bin.`

Choose Project ⇨ Add Reference. Select the Browse tab, find the appropriate directory, and add the reference. Your Solution Explorer window should now look something like that shown in Figure 22-4.

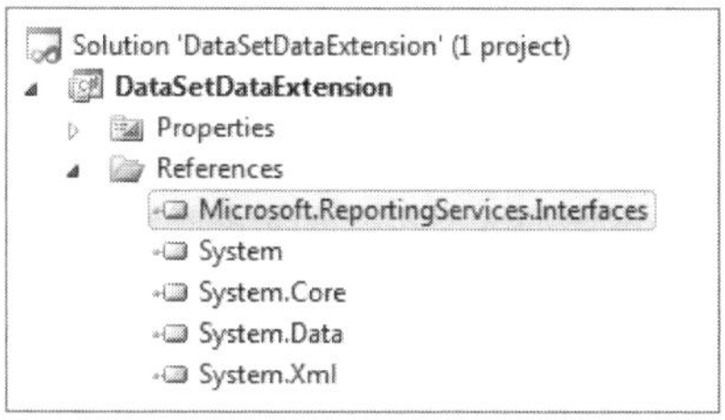

FIGURE 22-4

Change the name of the project assembly to reflect your custom namespace for the project. Choose Project ⇨ Properties. At this point, you can either fill in the root namespace for your components or put it in your code. The sample code contains the namespaces directly. This was another way to avoid IDE problems, as shown in Figure 22-5.

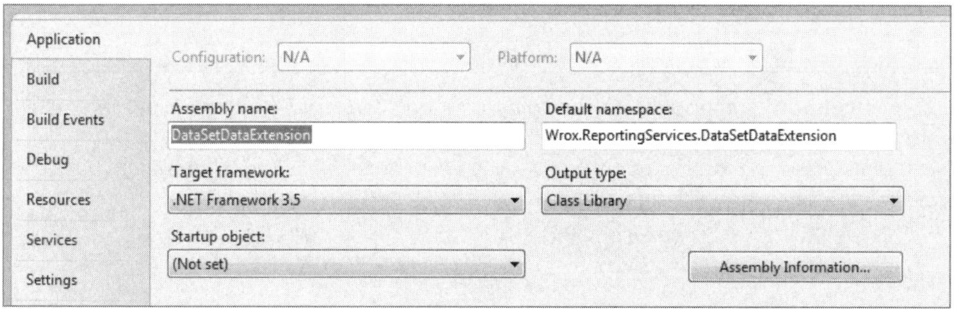

FIGURE 22-5

Most of the classes created for this project have common requirements. Several of them have empty, default constructors, and all of them require the use of some common namespaces. The code shown next is a skeleton of how each class should look after you create it. Replace the *ClassName* with the name of the class you are working on. This will allow you to concentrate on only the differences between the objects that will be created in your data extension project.

In this example, you will work with `DataSet` objects that are defined in the `System.Data` namespace. To support the SSRS interface requirements, you should include the `Microsoft .ReportingServices.DataProcessing` namespace at the top of your classes. This is the namespace where the interface `IExtension` is defined. Because the common data interfaces are defined in both ADO.NET and SSRS namespaces, you should fully qualify one of them to avoid name collisions and ambiguous reference errors. For the sake of saving keystrokes, we will fully qualify `System.Data` object types instead of the SSRS one when we use it. This namespace, however, is not needed in the `DataSetParameter` and `DataSetParameterCollection` classes.

C#

```csharp
using System;
using Microsoft.ReportingServices.DataProcessing;
using System.Data;

namespace Wrox.ReportingServices.DataSetDataExtension
{
    public class DataSetClassName
    {
    }
}
```

VB.NET

```vbnet
Imports System
Imports Microsoft.ReportingServices.DataProcessing
Imports System.Data

Namespace Wrox.ReportingServices.DataSetDataExtension
    Public Class DataSetClassName

    End Class
End Namespace
```

> *You can also use namespace aliases to avoid name collisions between types in
> the ADO.NET and SSRS namespaces. The following snippet shows how you
> can alias the* `Microsoft.ReportingServices.DataProcessing` *namespace to a
> shorter name:*
>
> **C#**
>
> ```csharp
> using RSDataProc =
>     Microsoft.ReportingServices.DataProcessing;
> ```
>
> **VB.NET**
>
> ```vbnet
> Imports RSDataProc =
>     Microsoft.ReportingServices.DataProcessing;
> ```

Creating the DataSetConnection Object

The `DataSetConnection` object is responsible for connecting to the data source and providing a
mechanism for accessing both the DPE-specific `Transaction` and `Command` objects. These responsibilities are enforced through the `IDbConnection` interface. The `DataSetConnection` object is
the extension entry point and will be the first object in the extension that will deal with Reporting
Services. As such, it also is required to implement the `IExtension` interface, as discussed earlier.

Because the `DataSetConnection` object is usually responsible for connecting to an unmanaged resource, it is required to implement `IDisposable`. The aggregate interface for all these others is `IDbConnectionExtension`, which is what you will implement. Figure 22-6 shows a diagram created with the Visual Studio class designer. Having the class designer within Visual Studio makes it easier to implement and understand the relationships between objects in a complex system.

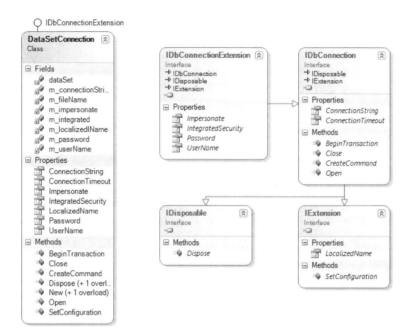

FIGURE 22-6

To add the `DataSetConnection` class to the project, choose Project ➪ Add Class. Change the name of the class to `DataSetConnection`. Open the file and indicate that the class should implement the `IDbConnectionExtension` interface, as just discussed. Visual Studio creates all the wrapper methods for you. Because you will be doing file I/O and using regular expressions to parse your `ConnectionString` property, you need to add those namespaces to this class:

C#

```csharp
using System;
using System.IO;
using System.Text.RegularExpressions;
using Microsoft.ReportingServices.DataProcessing;
```

VB.NET

```vbnet
Imports System
Imports System.IO
Imports System.Text.RegularExpressions
Imports Microsoft.ReportingServices.DataProcessing
```

Variable Declarations

To maintain state for your connection object, you need to declare some member variables. The `m_connectionString` variable will hold the connection string that will be used to connect to the data source. The `m_localizedName` variable should hold a localized name of the current extension used to list the extension as a data source option in the user interface of tools such as Visual Studio Report Designer or SQL Management Studio. The `m_fileName` variable will hold the path to the `DataSet` object persisted (serialized) as XML.

C#

```csharp
private string m_userName;
private string m_password;
private bool m_integrated;
private string m_impersonate;
private string m_connectionString = String.Empty;
private string m_localizedName = "DataSet Data Source";
private string m_fileName;

internal System.Data.DataSet dataSet;
```

code snippet \DataSetDataExtensionCS\DataSetDataExtension\DataSetConnection.cs

VB.NET

```vbnet
Private m_impersonate As String
Private m_integrated As Boolean
Private m_password As String
Private m_userName As String
Private m_connectionString As String = String.Empty
Private m_localizedName As String = "DataSet Data Source"
Private m_fileName As String

Friend dataSet As System.Data.DataSet = Nothing
```

code snippet \DataSetDataExtensionVB\DataSetDataExtension\DataSetConnection.vb

Constructors

The `DataSetConnection` object has an empty default constructor. It also has an overloaded constructor that allows the developer to create the object and initialize the connection string in one line of code.

C#

```csharp
public DataSetConnection(string connectionString)
{
        this.m_connectionString = connectionString;
}
```

code snippet \DataSetDataExtensionCS\DataSetDataExtension\DataSetConnection.cs

VB.NET

```vbnet
Public Sub New(ByVal connectionString As String)
     Me.m_connectionString = connectionString
End Sub
```

code snippet \DataSetDataExtensionVB\DataSetDataExtension\DataSetConnection.vb

Implementing IDbConnectionExtension

`IDbConnectionExtension` adds support for extending the SSRS security model, which is used to authenticate and authorize the connection to the data source. The interface definition is shown next. Notice the unusual use of `WriteOnly` properties.

C#

```csharp
public interface IDbConnectionExtension : IDbConnection, IDisposable, IExtension
{
    // Properties
    string Impersonate { set; }
    bool IntegratedSecurity {get; set; }

    string Password { set; }
    string UserName { set; }
}
```

VB.NET

```vbnet
Public Interface IDbConnectionExtension
     Implements IDbConnection, IDisposable, IExtension

     ' Properties
     WriteOnly Property Impersonate As String
     Property IntegratedSecurity As Boolean
     WriteOnly Property Password As String
     WriteOnly Property UserName As String
End Interface
```

Impersonate Property

Windows supports the concept of impersonation, in which a process of execution can "assume" the identity of a set of assigned security credentials. The `Impersonate` property lets you assign a string representing the user account whose security context the process should run under.

C#

```csharp
public string Impersonate
{
     set { m_impersonate = value; }
}
```

code snippet \DataSetDataExtensionCS\DataSetDataExtension\DataSetConnection.cs

VB.NET

```vb.net
Public WriteOnly Property Impersonate() As String
    Implements IDbConnectionExtension.Impersonate
        Set(ByVal value As String)
            m_impersonate = value
        End Set
End Property
```

code snippet \DataSetDataExtensionVB\DataSetDataExtension\DataSetConnection.vb

IntegratedSecurity Property

The `IntegratedSecurity` property indicates whether you want the extension to run using
Windows security for both authentication (identifying the user) and authorization (denying/granting
a user permission to perform certain actions).

C#

```csharp
public bool IntegratedSecurity
{
    get{ return m_integrated;}
    set {m_integrated = value;}
}
```

code snippet \DataSetDataExtensionCS\DataSetDataExtension\DataSetConnection.cs

VB.NET

```vb.net
Public Property IntegratedSecurity() As Boolean
    Implements IDbConnectionExtension.IntegratedSecurity
        Get
            Return m_integrated
        End Get
        Set(ByVal value As Boolean)
            m_integrated = value
        End Set
End Property
```

code snippet \DataSetDataExtensionVB\DataSetDataExtension\DataSetConnection.vb

UserName and Password Properties

The `UserName` and `Password` properties are used during the Reporting Services authentication process. The `UserName`/`Password` pair is authenticated against either the Windows credential store or
some custom store you provide. Next, a principal object that implements `IPrincipal` is created and
assigned to the current thread of execution. That object contains the user's identity and role membership information and is used to authorize user access to system resources (the data source). Good
security practice dictates that this information be available for the shortest time possible — thus the
use of Write Only properties.

C#

```
public string Password
{
        set { m_password = value; }
}

public string UserName
{
        set { m_userName = value; }
}
```

code snippet \DataSetDataExtensionCS\DataSetDataExtension\DataSetConnection.cs

VB.NET

```
Public WriteOnly Property Password() As String
 Implements IDbConnectionExtension.Password
        Set(ByVal value As String)
                m_password = value
        End Set
End Property

Public WriteOnly Property UserName() As String
 Implements IDbConnectionExtension.UserName
        Set(ByVal value As String)
                m_userName = value
        End Set
End Property
```

code snippet \DataSetDataExtensionVB\DataSetDataExtension\DataSetConnection.vb

Implementing IDbConnection

The IDbConnection interface is the standard mechanism that data providers use to control the use of the DataSetConnection object. These properties and methods help you change the connection settings, open and close the connection, and associate the connection with a valid transaction. Your connection object does not support transactions because of its Read Only nature and because, in this DPE example, you are working against a filesystem, which is not a resource manager. Here is the definition of the IDbConnection interface:

C#

```
public interface IDbConnection : IDisposable, IExtension
{
        IDbTransaction BeginTransaction();
        IDbCommand CreateCommand();
        void Open();
        void Close();
        string ConnectionString { get; set; }
        int ConnectionTimeout { get; }
}
```

VB.NET

```
Public Interface IDbConnection
    Inherits IDisposable, IExtension
      Function BeginTransaction() As IDbTransaction
      Function CreateCommand() As IDbCommand
      Sub Open()
      Sub Close()
      Property ConnectionString() As String
      Property ConnectionTimeout() As Integer
End Interface
```

After adding the `DataSetConnection` class to your project, you will need to implement the `IExtension` interface as shown here:

C#

```
public string LocalizedName
{
    get
    {
        return m_localizedName;
    }
}
public void SetConfiguration(string configuration) {}
```

code snippet \DataSetDataExtensionCS\DataSetDataExtension\DataSetConnection.cs

VB.NET

```
Public ReadOnly Property LocalizedName() As String Implements
IDbConnection.LocalizedName
    Get
        Return m_localizedlName
    End Get
End Property

Public Sub SetConfiguration(ByVal configuration As String) Implements
IDbConnection.SetConfiguration
End Sub
```

code snippet \DataSetDataExtensionVB\DataSetDataExtension\DataSetConnection.vb

Because the `IDbConnection` interface implements `IDisposable`, we must provide an implementation for its `Dispose()` method:

C#

```
public void Dispose()
{
    Dispose(true);
    GC.SuppressFinalize(this);
}

protected virtual void Dispose(bool disposing)
```

```
    {
        if (disposing)
        {
            this.Close();
        }
    }
```

```
Public Sub Dispose() Implements IDisposable.Dispose
    Dispose(True)
    GC.SuppressFinalize(Me)
End Sub

Protected Overridable Sub Dispose(ByVal disposing As Boolean)
    If disposing Then
        Me.Close()
    End If
End Sub
```

Begin Transaction Method

The BeginTransaction method is primarily responsible for initiating a new transaction and returning a reference to a valid, implementation-specific Transaction object. The filesystem, which is our data store, does not support transactions, but the interface requires this method. You need to ensure that the developer who will use your object in code knows this. You do so by throwing a NotSupportedException.

```
public IDbTransaction BeginTransaction()
{
    // this example does not support transactions
    throw new NotSupportedException("Transactions not supported");
}
```

```
Public Function BeginTransaction() As IDbTransaction _
    Implements IDbConnection.BeginTransaction
        ' example does not support transactions
        Throw New NotSupportedException("Transactions not supported")
End Function
```

CreateCommand Method

The `CreateCommand` function is responsible for creating and returning a reference to a valid implementation-specific `Command` object. The method uses an overloaded constructor of your custom `Command` object to pass that object a reference to the current connection. Also, notice that it will create and return a new instance of the `DataSetCommand` type, which you will be creating later on.

```csharp
public IDbCommand CreateCommand()
{
    // Return a new instance of the implementation-specific command object
    return new DataSetCommand(this);
}
```

code snippet \DataSetDataExtensionCS\DataSetDataExtension\DataSetConnection.cs

```vbnet
Public Function CreateCommand() As IDbCommand _
    Implements IDbConnection.CreateCommand
        ' Return a new instance of the implementation-specific command object
        Return New DataSetCommand(Me)
End Function
```

code snippet \DataSetDataExtensionVB\DataSetDataExtension\DataSetConnection.vb

Open Method

In a full data provider implementation, the `Open` method is used to make a data source-specific connection. This sample implementation uses the `Open` method to create an instance of a generic dataset object from ADO.NET and fills it from the XML file provided in our `ConnectionString` property.

```csharp
public void Open()
{
    this.dataSet = new System.Data.DataSet();
    this.dataSet.ReadXml(this.m_fileName);
}
```

code snippet \DataSetDataExtensionCS\DataSetDataExtension\DataSetConnection.cs

```vbnet
Public Sub Open() Implements IDbConnection.Open
        Me.dataSet = New System.Data.DataSet
        Me.dataSet.ReadXml(Me.m_fileName)
End Sub
```

code snippet \DataSetDataExtensionVB\DataSetDataExtension\DataSetConnection.vb

Close Method

The `Close` method is used to close your data source-specific connection. You will use the `Close` method to release the `DataSet` object you have in memory.

C#

Available for
download on
Wrox.com

```csharp
public void Close()
{
        this.dataSet = null;
}
```

code snippet \DataSetDataExtensionCS\DataSetDataExtension\DataSetConnection.cs

VB.NET

Available for
download on
Wrox.com

```vbnet
Public Sub Close() Implements IDbConnection.Close
        Me.dataSet = Nothing
End Sub
```

code snippet \DataSetDataExtensionVB\DataSetDataExtension\DataSetConnection.vb

ConnectionString Property

The `ConnectionString` property allows you to set the connection string through code. This property uses a private variable to store the current connection string, which provides the information needed to connect to the data source. Most developers are familiar with this property because of its frequent use in both traditional ADO and ADO.NET. In this DPE example, the `ConnectionString` property is used to indicate the XML dataset file that you will parse for data. The user of your DPE should input the path to the file he or she wants to parse into the connection string textbox of the Report Designer's Dataset dialog or the shared data source's Properties page. You will store the connection string value in the private member variable `m_connectionString`.

C#

Available for
download on
Wrox.com

```csharp
public string ConnectionString
{
        get {return m_connectionString;}
        set {m_connectionString = value;}
}
```

code snippet \DataSetDataExtensionCS\DataSetDataExtension\DataSetConnection.cs

VB.NET

Available for
download on
Wrox.com

```vbnet
Public Property ConnectionString() As String _
    Implements IDbConnection.ConnectionString
        Get
                Return m_connectionString
        End Get
        Set(ByVal Value As String)
```

```
        m_connectionString = Value
    End Set
End Property
```

code snippet \DataSetDataExtensionVB\DataSetDataExtension\DataSetConnection.vb

You want to enforce that the value passed into the ConnectionString property meets your criteria for supplying the information needed to connect to the data source. You want to enforce that the string is in this format:

```
FileName=c:\FileName.xml
```

The easiest way to validate the string format is to use regular expressions. You need to modify the default Set accessor of the ConnectionString property to reflect this change. First, you will execute the static/shared Match method of the Regex class.

> *You are passing in an expression that basically says "Parse the connection string and make matches on character arrays that are preceded by FileName= and are not composed of beginning-of-line characters or semicolons."*

All that is left is to test to see if the filename is valid and, if so, assign it to your private filename variable. Your code should resemble the following:

C#

Available for download on Wrox.com

```csharp
set
{
    this.m_connectionString = value;

    Match m = Regex.Match(value, "FileName=([^;]+)",RegexOptions.IgnoreCase);
    if (!m.Success)
    {
        string msg = "\"FileName=<filename>\" must be present in the connection"+
                    "string and point to a valid DataSet xml file";
        throw (new ArgumentException(msg, "ConnectionString"));
    }

    string filename = m.Groups[1].Captures[0].ToString();
    if (!File.Exists(filename))
    {
        string msg = "Incorrect file name, or file does not exist";
        throw (new ArgumentException(msg, "ConnectionString"));
    }

    this.m_fileName = filename;
}
```

code snippet \DataSetDataExtensionCS\DataSetDataExtension\DataSetConnection.cs

VB.NET

```vb.net
Set(ByVal Value As String)
    Me.m_connectionString = Value

    Dim m As Match = Regex.Match(Value, "FileName=([^;]+)",
                    RegexOptions.IgnoreCase)
    If Not m.Success Then
        Dim msg As String = "'FileName=<filename>' must be present string " &
                    "and point to a valid DataSet xml file"
        Throw (New ArgumentException(msg, "ConnectionString"))
    End If
    If Not File.Exists(m.Groups(1).Captures(0).ToString) Then
        Throw (New ArgumentException("Incorrect FileName", "ConnectionString"))
    End If
    Me.m_fileName = m.Groups(1).Captures(0).ToString
End Set
```

code snippet \DataSetDataExtensionVB\DataSetDataExtension\DataSetConnection.vb

ConnectionTimeout Property

The ConnectionTimeout property allows you to set the connection's time-out property. This is used to control how long the interval for connecting to the source should be before an error is thrown. Your sample class does not actually use this value, but it is implemented for consistency and because of interface requirements. Returning a value of 0 indicates that there is an infinite time-out period.

C#

```csharp
public int ConnectionTimeout
{
    get
    {
        // Returns the connection time-out value.
        // Zero indicates an indefinite time-out period.
        return 0;
    }
}
```

code snippet \DataSetDataExtensionCS\DataSetDataExtension\DataSetConnection.cs

VB.NET

```vb.net
Public ReadOnly Property ConnectionTimeout() As Integer _
    Implements IDbConnection.ConnectionTimeout
    Get
        ' Returns the connection time-out value.
        ' Zero indicates an indefinite time-out period.
        Return 0
    End Get
End Property
```

code snippet \DataSetDataExtensionVB\DataSetDataExtension\DataSetConnection.vb

Creating the DataSetParameter Class

The DataSetParameter class is not needed until the command class is created, but because of that dependency, you do need to create it. The parameter object is used to send parameters to the command object that can be used to execute commands against the data source. Despite the fact that this class is not used to perform any work, the interface requirements of the command class force you to create it. This class also has interface requirements; it is required to support the IDataParameter interface defined in the Reporting Services DPE assembly.

To add the DataSetParameter class to the project, choose Project ⇨ Add Class, and change the name to DataSetParameter.

Declarations

The following declarations are used internally to hold the parameter's value and name. The name is stored in a string variable called m_parameterName. Because the value variable might contain any type of value, m_parameterValue is declared as an Object type.

C#

Available for download on Wrox.com

```
String m_parameterName = string.Empty;
Object m_parameterValue;
```

code snippet \DataSetDataExtensionCS\DataSetDataExtension\DataSetParameter.cs

VB.NET

Available for download on Wrox.com

```
Dim m_parameterName As String
Dim m_parameterValue As Object
```

code snippet \DataSetDataExtensionVB\DataSetDataExtension\DataSetParameter.vb

Implementing IDataParameter

The IDataParameter interface enforces that your custom parameter class allows a programmer to get and set the name and value of the current parameter.

C#

```
public interface IDataParameter
    {
        string ParameterName { get; set; }
        object Value { get; set; }
    }
```

VB.NET

```
Public Interface IDataParameter
    Property ParameterName() As String
    Property Value() As Object
End Interface
```

Begin by adding a `using` (C#) or `Imports` (VB) statement to include the `Microsoft.ReportingServices.DataProcessing` namespace in the `DataSetParameter` class file. Modify the class code to force the `DataSetParameter` class to implement `IDataParameter` using the Interface AutoComplete technique discussed at the beginning of the chapter. Your code should resemble the following. The wrappers for all your interface methods should have been created automatically and surrounded by region tags. Here is what your parameter class definition should look like:

C#

Available for
download on
Wrox.com

```csharp
namespace Wrox.ReportingServices.DataSetDataExtension
{
    public class DataSetParameter : IDataParameter
    {
        string m_parameterName = string.Empty;
        object m_parameterValue;
```

code snippet \DataSetDataExtensionCS\DataSetDataExtension\DataSetParameter.cs

VB.NET

Available for
download on
Wrox.com

```vb
Namespace Wrox.ReportingServices.DataSetDataExtension
    Public Class DataSetParameter
        Implements IDataParameter

        Private m_parameterName As String = String.Empty
        Private m_parameterValue As Object = Nothing
```

code snippet \DataSetDataExtensionVB\DataSetDataExtension\DataSetParameter.vb

ParameterName Property

The `ParameterName` property is used to store the parameter's name in a string variable called `m_parameterName`. This field is typically used to map to parameters in stored procedures but is unused in this implementation.

C#

Available for
download on
Wrox.com

```csharp
public string ParameterName
{
    get { return m_parameterName; }
    set { m_parameterName = value; }
}
```

code snippet \DataSetDataExtensionCS\DataSetDataExtension\DataSetParameter.cs

VB.NET

Available for
download on
Wrox.com

```vb
Public Property ParameterName() As String Implements IDataParameter.ParameterName
    Get
        Return m_parameterName
    End Get
```

```
        Set(ByVal Value As String)
            m_parameterName = value
        End Set
    End Property
```

Value Property

The `Value` property is similar to the name just created in that it is not actually used in this example. The value is stored in an object variable called `m_value`. You will need to include the `System.Diagnostics` namespace at the top of the class file, via the `using` (C#) or `Imports` (VB) keyword, in order to use the `Debug.WriteLine()` method.

C#

```csharp
public object Value
{

    get
    {
        Debug.WriteLine(string.Format("Getting parameter [{0}] value: [{1}]",
        this.m_parameterName, this.m_parameterValue.ToString()));
        return (this.m_parameterValue);
    }
    set
    {
        Debug.WriteLine(string.Format("Setting parameter [{0}] value: [{1}]",
        this.m_parameterName, this.m_parameterValue.ToString()));
        this.m_parameterValue = value;
    )}
```

VB.NET

```vbnet
Public Property Value() As Object _
    Implements IDataParameter.Value

Get
    Debug.WriteLine(String.Format("Getting parameter [{0}] value: [{1}]", _
    Me.m_parameterName, _
    Me.m_parameterValue.ToString))
    Return (Me.m_parameterValue)
End Get
Set(ByVal Value As Object)
    Debug.WriteLine(String.Format("Setting parameter [{0}] value: [{1}]", _
    Me.m_parameterName, _
    Me.m_parameterValue.ToString))
    Me.m_parameterValue = Value
End SetEnd Property
```

Creating the DataSetParameterCollection Class

The `DataSetParameterCollection` class is simply a collection of parameter objects. Although you could have created a custom collection class that implements all the required methods, an easier route exists. The `IDataParameterCollection` interface is basically a subset of the `IList<T>` interface that is used to define other generic collections in the .NET Framework. By using an available object, you significantly reduce the required coding effort. In our example, `T` is the type `IDataParameter`, which is implemented by our custom `DataSetParameter` class.

To add the `DataSetParameterCollection` class to the project, choose Project ➪ Add Class. Change the name of the class to `DataSetParameterCollection`.

There is no need to create custom constructors or member variables for use in your collection class. This is because you can use the internal variables and constructors that exist inside the `List<T>` base class that this class inherits from. The properties that you create will be mapped directly to properties and methods that exist in the `List<T>` class.

Namespaces

The `DataSetParameterCollection` class uses the standard namespaces just discussed. An additional namespace is needed because of the use of `List<T>`. You must add the `System.Collections.Generic` namespace and a private variable for our internal collection.

C#

Available for download on Wrox.com

```
using System;
using Microsoft.ReportingServices.DataProcessing;
using System.Collections.Generic;
```

code snippet \DataSetDataExtensionCS\DataSetDataExtension\DataSetParameterCollection.cs

VB.NET

Available for download on Wrox.com

```
Imports System
Imports Microsoft.ReportingServices.DataProcessing

Imports System.Collections.Generic
```

code snippet \DataSetDataExtensionVB\DataSetDataExtension\DataSetParameterCollection.vb

Implementing IDataParameterCollection

We have created the `DataSetParameterCollection` class by using an object wrapper around an `IList<T>` generic collection. Generics are a feature available starting with .NET 2.0 and later versions, so our example will not compile or run within earlier versions of the .NET Framework run time. The `IDataParameterCollection` interface defines a custom `Add` method and provides methods to access the members of this collection through the `IEnumerable` interface. The `List<T>` base class implements this interface. Your class will use the internal `List<IDataParameter>` class properties and methods to service its needs. You will need to include the `System.Collections` namespace at the top of the class file, via the `using` (C#) or `Imports` (VB) keyword, in order to use the `IEnumerable` interface.

C#

```csharp
public interface IDataParameterCollection : IEnumerable
{
    int Add(IDataParameter parameter);
}
```

VB.NET

```vbnet
Public Interface IDataParameterCollection
    Inherits IEnumerable
    Function Add(ByVal parameter As IDataParameter) As Integer
End Interface
```

Here's the modified code in C#:

```csharp
namespace Wrox.ReportingServices.DataSetDataExtension
{

    public class DataSetParameterCollection : IDataParameterCollection
    {
        List<IDataParameter> paramList;
        public DataSetParameterCollection()
        {
            paramList = new List<IDataParameter>();
        }

        public IEnumerator GetEnumerator()
        {
            return paramList.GetEnumerator();
        }
```

code snippet \DataSetDataExtensionCS\DataSetDataExtension\DataSetParameterCollection.cs

Here's the modified code in VB.NET:

```vbnet
Namespace Wrox.ReportingServices.DataSetDataExtension

    Public Class DataSetParameterCollection

        Implements IDataParameterCollection
        Private paramList As List(Of IDataParameter)

        Public Sub New()
            paramList = New List(Of IDataParameter)
        End Sub

        Public Function GetEnumerator() As IEnumerator _
            Implements IEnumerable.GetEnumerator
            Return (paramList.GetEnumerator)
        End Function
```

code snippet \DataSetDataExtensionVB\DataSetDataExtension\DataSetParameterCollection.vb

Since most of the functionality of the `DataSetParameterCollection` class exists through the `paramList` reference, all that needs to be done is to create the wrapper `Add` method required by the `IDataParameter` interface. The internal collection uses this method to add parameters to an instance of the collection object.

C#

```csharp
public int Add(IDataParameter parameter)
{
    paramList.Add(parameter);
    return paramList.IndexOf(parameter);
}
```

code snippet \DataSetDataExtensionCS\DataSetDataExtension\DataSetParameterCollection.cs

VB.NET

```vbnet
Public Overloads Function Add(ByVal parameter As IDataParameter) As Integer _
        Implements IDataParameterCollection.Add

        paramList.Add(parameter)
        Return paramList.IndexOf(parameter)

End Function
```

code snippet \DataSetDataExtensionVB\DataSetDataExtension\DataSetParameterCollection.vb

Creating the DataSetCommand Class

The `command` object is responsible for sending commands to the data source. This is enforced by making the object implement the `IDbCommand` interface, which supplies a standard mechanism for passing in commands to be executed against the data source. It also supplies parameters that might be needed in the process of executing these commands. Finally, it defines a property that allows the developer to associate the command with a `Transaction` object. Your implementation is simplified in that it does not support transactions or parameters.

In your implementation, this class is where the majority of the work is done. You need to process the command text to know what data the user wants. You must validate that this text conforms to your requirements, and then you need to create the internal data reference that will supply the data for the data reader object to process. You will use some of the built-in behaviors of the `System.Data.DataSet` class to satisfy your needs.

To add the `DataSetCommand` class to the project, choose Project ➪ Add Class. Change the name of the class to `DataSetCommand`. Use the Interface AutoComplete feature to have Visual Studio create the wrappers for the methods you will implement. Most of the functionality that exists in this extension will live in this class. You will need to include the `Microsoft.ReportingServices.DataProcessing` namespace at the top of the class file, via the `using` (C#) or `Imports` (VB) keyword, in order to use the `Debug.WriteLine()` method.

Variable Declarations

Because most of our work is done in this class, it makes sense that most of our code is also in it. First, you need to create variables to hold your property data. This class actually will be a wrapper around some of the built-in `DataSet` functionality, so you will need reference variables for the dataset objects as well as other variables used for text parsing and the like. To avoid being repetitive, we'll discuss the variables in more depth where they are used. You will need to include the `System.Text.RegularExpressions` namespace at the top of the class file, via the `using` (C#) or `Imports` (VB) keyword, in order to use the regular expression-specific types.

C#

Available for
download on
Wrox.com

```csharp
//member variables
int m_commandTimeOut = 0;
string m_commandText = string.Empty;
DataSetConnection m_connection;
DataSetParameterCollection m_parameters;

//dataset variables
string tableName = string.Empty;
System.Data.DataSet dataSet = null;
internal System.Data.DataView dataView = null;

//regex variables
MatchCollection keywordMatches = null;
Match fieldMatch = null;

//regex used for getting keywords
Regex keywordSplit = new Regex(@"(Select|From|Where| Order[ \s] +By)",
    RegexOptions.IgnoreCase | RegexOptions.Multiline
    | RegexOptions.IgnorePatternWhitespace | RegexOptions.Compiled);

// regex used for splitting out fields
Regex fieldSplit = new Regex(@"([^ ,\s]+)",
    RegexOptions.IgnoreCase | RegexOptions.Multiline
    | RegexOptions.Compiled | RegexOptions.IgnorePatternWhitespace);

//internal constants
const int SELECT_POSITION = 0;
const int FROM_POSITION = 1;
const string TEMPTABLE_NAME = "TempTable";

//these variables can change
int keyWordCount = 0;
int wherePosition = 2;
int orderPosition = 3;

bool filtering = false;
bool sorting = false;
bool useDefaultTable = false;
```

code snippet \DataSetDataExtensionCS\DataSetDataExtension\DataSetCommand.cs

VB.NET

```vbnet
'property variables
Private m_cmdTimeOut As Integer = 0
Private m_commandText As String = String.Empty
Private m_connection As DataSetConnection
Private m_parameters As DataSetParameterCollection = Nothing

'dataset variables
Private tableName As String = String.Empty
Private dataSet As FCLData.DataSet
Friend dataView As FCLData.DataView

'regex variables
Private keywordMatches As MatchCollection
Private fieldMatch As Match
Private tableMatch As Match
Private keywordSplit As Regex = New Regex("(Select|From|Where| Order[ \s] +By)",_
        RegexOptions.IgnoreCase Or RegexOptions.Multiline Or _
        RegexOptions.IgnorePatternWhitespace Or RegexOptions.Compiled)
Private fieldSplit As Regex = New Regex("([^ ,\s]+)", RegexOptions.IgnoreCase Or _
        RegexOptions.Multiline Or RegexOptions.Compiled Or _
        RegexOptions.IgnorePatternWhitespace)

'constants
Private tempTableName As String = "TempTable"
Private selectPosition As Integer = 0
Private fromPosition As Integer = 1
Private wherePosition As Integer = 2
Private orderPosition As Integer = 3

'internal variables

Private keyWordCount As Integer = 0
Private filtering As Boolean = False
Private sorting As Boolean = False
Private useDefaultTable As Boolean = False
```

code snippet \DataSetDataExtensionVB\DataSetDataExtension\DataSetCommand.vb

Constructors

You want the users of your processing extension to be forced to create the Command object either through the CreateCommand method of the IDbConnection interface, or by passing in a valid DataSetConnection object as a parameter. The purpose is to ensure that you have access to the underlying DataSet object created and parsed in the connection process. You can do this by deleting or not providing an empty default constructor. This prevents the developer from creating the DataSetCommand object without the correct initialization. In the constructor, you want to get a reference to the DataSet that you opened from the filesystem in your connection object.

C#

```csharp
internal DataSetCommand(DataSetConnection conn)
{
        this.m_connection = conn;
        this.dataSet = this.m_connection.dataSet;
```

```
            this.m_parameters = new DataSetParameterCollection();
    }
```

code snippet \DataSetDataExtensionCS\DataSetDataExtension\DataSetCommand.cs

VB.NET

```
    Friend Sub New(ByVal conn As DataSetConnection)

        Me.m_connection = conn
        Me.dataSet = Me.m_connection.dataSet
        Me.m_parameters = New DataSetParameterCollection
    End Sub
```

code snippet \DataSetDataExtensionVB\DataSetDataExtension\DataSetCommand.vb

Implementing IDbCommand

The required interface for all Command objects is called IDbCommand. It consists of methods that allow the developer to pass commands and parameters to the Command object. The most interesting method in our implementation is the CommandText method, where you will parse the command string provided by the user and return the appropriate data.

C#

```
    public interface IDbCommand : IDisposable
    {
        void Cancel();
        IDataReader ExecuteReader(CommandBehavior behavior);
        string CommandText { get; set; }
        int CommandTimeout { get; set; }
        CommandType CommandType { get; set; }
        IDataParameter CreateParameter();
        IDataParameterCollection Parameters { get; }
        IDbTransaction Transaction { get; set; }
    }
```

VB.NET

```
    Public Interface IDbCommand
        Inherits IDisposable
        Sub Cancel()
        Function ExecuteReader(ByVal behavior As CommandBehavior) As IDataReader
        Property CommandText() As String
        Property CommandTimeout() As Integer
        Property CommandType() As CommandType
        Function CreateParameter() As IDataParameter
        Property Parameters() As IDataParameterCollection
        Property Transaction() As IDbTransaction
    End Interface
```

Now that you have created the method wrappers and all the variables you need to work, you can begin implementing your IDbCommand methods.

Cancel Method

The `Cancel` method is typically used to cancel a method that has been queued. Most implementations of data providers are multithreaded and support the issue of multiple commands against the data store. You created this method only to support the `IDbCommand` interface requirements. You should inform the developer of your lack of support by throwing a `NotSupportedException`. You will need to include the `System.Diagnostics` namespace at the top of the class file, via the `using` (C#) or `Imports` (VB) keyword, in order to use the `Debug.WriteLine()` method.

C#

```csharp
public void Cancel()
{
    Debug.WriteLine("IDBCommand.Cancel");
    throw (new NotSupportedException("IDBCommand.Cancel currently not supported"));}
```

code snippet \DataSetDataExtensionCS\DataSetDataExtension\DataSetCommand.cs

VB.NET

```vbnet
Public Sub Cancel() _
        Implements IDbCommand.Cancel

    Debug.WriteLine("IDBCommand.Cancel")
    Throw New NotSupportedException("IDBCommand.Cancel currently not supported")
End Sub
```

code snippet \DataSetDataExtensionVB\DataSetDataExtension\DataSetCommand.vb

ExecuteReader Method

The `ExecuteReader` method returns an extension-specific reader object to the caller so that it can loop through and read the data. The `DataSetCommand` object creates an instance of your custom reader object by executing this method. A reference to your custom data reader is then returned. Your implementation actually builds a temporary table with a schema built based on the query issued by the user. You don't want to fill this temporary table unless the user actually requests the data, so you are checking to see if it is a schema-only command.

You are also checking to see if the users indicated that they want all the fields available from the data source. If that is the case, you use a view of the default `DataTable`, which already contains all the data. Notice that you will return a new `DataSetDataReader`, which you will create later in the chapter.

C#

```csharp
public IDataReader ExecuteReader (CommandBehavior behavior)
{
    if(!(behavior == CommandBehavior.SchemaOnly) && !useDefaultTable)
    {
        FillView();
    }
    return (IDataReader) new DataSetDataReader(this);
```

```csharp
    }

    private void FillView()
    {
        System.Data.DataRow tempRow = null;
        string[] tempArray = null;
        int count;

        count = this.dataSet.Tables[TEMPTABLE_NAME].Columns.Count;
        tempArray = new string[count];

        foreach (System.Data.DataRow row in this.dataSet.Tables[this.tableName].Rows)
        {
            tempRow = this.dataSet.Tables[TEMPTABLE_NAME].NewRow();

            foreach (System.Data.DataColumn col in this.dataSet.Tables[TEMPTABLE_NAME]
             .Columns)
            {
                tempArray[col.Ordinal] = row[col.ColumnName].ToString();
            }

            tempRow.ItemArray = tempArray;
            this.dataSet.Tables[TEMPTABLE_NAME].Rows.Add(tempRow);
        }

        // go ahead and clean up the array instead of waiting for the GC
        tempArray = null;
    }
```

code snippet \DataSetDataExtensionCS\DataSetDataExtension\DataSetCommand.cs

VB.NET

```vbnet
Public Function ExecuteReader(ByVal behavior As CommandBehavior) As IDataReader _
    Implements IDbCommand.ExecuteReader
    If Not (behavior = CommandBehavior.SchemaOnly) AndAlso Not useDefaultTable Then
            FillView()
    End If
    Return CType(New DataSetDataReader(Me), IDataReader)
End Function

Private Sub FillView()
    Dim tempRow As System.Data.DataRow = Nothing
    Dim tempArray As String() = Nothing
    Dim count As Integer
    count = Me.dataSet.Tables(tempTableName).Columns.Count
    tempArray = New String(count - 1) {}
    For Each row As System.Data.DataRow In Me.dataSet.Tables(Me.tableName).Rows
            tempRow = Me.dataSet.Tables(tempTableName).NewRow
            For Each col As System.Data.DataColumn In _
Me.dataSet.Tables(tempTableName).Columns
                    tempArray(col.Ordinal) = row(col.ColumnName).ToString
            Next
            tempRow.ItemArray = tempArray
```

```
                        Me.dataSet.Tables(tempTableName).Rows.Add(tempRow)
            Next
        End Sub
```

code snippet \DataSetDataExtensionVB\DataSetDataExtension\DataSetCommand.vb

CommandText Property

Reporting Services does not manually create a separate Command object. It uses the CreateCommand method of the IDbConnection interface to return an implementation-specific Command object. We will use the CommandText property to help us build the data schema that we will return, as well as fill our data source for use of Reporting Services. This method has been broken into methods reflecting the actual work being done and to facilitate this discussion. Notice the ValidateCommandText method. It is the entry point for your text-parsing and table-building process and you will create it later in the chapter. You will need to include the System.Diagnostics namespace at the top of the class file, via the using (C#) or Imports (VB) keyword, in order to use the Debug.WriteLine() method.

C#

Available for
download on
Wrox.com

```csharp
public string CommandText
    {
        get
        {
            Debug.WriteLine("IDBCommand.CommandText: Get Value =" +
            this.m_commandText);
            return this.m_commandText;
        }
        set
        {
            Debug.WriteLine("IDBCommand.CommandText: Set Value =" + value);
            ValidateCommandText(value);
            this.m_commandText = value;
        }
    }
```

code snippet \DataSetDataExtensionVB\DataSetDataExtension\DataSetCommand.vb

VB.NET

Available for
download on
Wrox.com

```vbnet
Public Property CommandText() As String Implements IDbCommand.CommandText
    Get
        Debug.WriteLine("IDBCommand.CommandText: Get Value =" &
        Me.m_commandText)
Return (Me.m_commandText)
    End Get
    Set(ByVal value As String)
        Debug.WriteLine("IDBCommand.CommandText: Get Value =" &
        Me.m_commandText)
        ValidateCommandText(value)
        Me.m_commandText = value
```

```
        End Set
    End Property
```

code snippet \DataSetDataExtensionVB\DataSetDataExtension\DataSetCommand.vb

The `ValidateCommandText` method is used to parse the command text to ensure that it meets the requirements for the extension. The first step is to apply the `keywordSplit` regular expression that was defined in the member variable section. The regular expression is `(Select|From|Where|Order[`
`\s] +By)`, which could be translated into English as follows: "Match the keywords `Select`, `From`, `Where`, and `Order`, where each is followed by the word `By`, but allow spaces and nonvisible characters between them." After you have parsed the statement, you can make some basic assumptions based on the number of matches. At a minimum, you require that the user tell you the Field names and the table name that he or she wants to pull the information from. This means that you must have a `Select` keyword, followed by a Field List, and a `From` keyword, followed by a table name. Thus, the minimum keyword count is 2. If you have a keyword count greater than 2, you know that the user has given you either a filtering criterion such as `Where userID = 3` or a sort criterion such as `Order by lastname ASC`. You can find out which by checking the value in the third position. If that value is a `Where` clause, you can assume that the user wants filtering. If it is not, assume that sorting is the order of the day. If the count is 4, you know that both filtering and sorting are needed. The `ValidateCommandText` method will also call other `Validate` methods which are discussed and implemented in the following paragraphs.

C#

```csharp
private void ValidateCommandText(string cmdText)
{
    keywordMatches = keywordSplit.Matches(cmdText);
    keyWordCount = keywordMatches.Count;
    switch (keyWordCount)
    {
        case 4:
            sorting = true;
            filtering = true;
            break;
        case 3:
            if (keywordMatches [keyWordCount - 1]
                .ToString()
                .ToUpper() == "WHERE")
                filtering = true;
            else
            {
                sorting = true;
                orderPosition = 2;
            }
            break;
        case 2:
            break;
        default:
            string msg = "Command Text should start with 'select <fields> " +
                         "from <tablename>'";
            throw new ArgumentException(msg);
```

```
    }

    ValidateTableName(cmdText);
    ValidateFieldNames(cmdText);

    if (filtering)
    {
        ValidateFiltering(cmdText);
    }

    if (sorting)
    {
        ValidateSorting(cmdText);
    }
}
```

code snippet \DataSetDataExtensionCS\DataSetDataExtension\DataSetCommand.cs

VB.NET

Available for download on Wrox.com

```
Private Sub ValidateCommandText(ByVal cmdText As String)
    keywordMatches = keywordSplit.Matches(cmdText)
    keyWordCount = keywordMatches.Count
    Select Case keyWordCount
        Case 4
            sorting = True
            filtering = True
            ' break
        Case 3
            If keywordMatches (keyWordCount - 1).ToString.ToUpper = _
                "WHERE" Then
                filtering = True
            Else
                sorting = True
            End If
        Case Else
            Dim msg As String = "Command Text should start with 'select " & _
                                "<fields> from <tablename>'"
            Throw (New ArgumentException(msg))
    End Select
    ValidateTableName(cmdText)
    ValidateFieldNames(cmdText)

    If filtering Then
        ValidateFiltering(cmdText)
    End If

    If sorting Then
        ValidateSorting(cmdText)
    End If
End Sub
```

code snippet \DataSetDataExtensionVB\DataSetDataExtension\DataSetCommand.vb

The next step in the process is validating that the table name and Field names provided by the user are valid. You have created methods specifically for this purpose. Shown next is the `ValidateTableName` method. In the member declaration section, constant values were created, indicating the assumed positions of the keywords within the command text. The table name must immediately follow the `From` keyword. You then use that keyword's position to locate the table name. Next, you check to see if your internal `DataSet` contains this table. If so, the table name is valid; otherwise, it is invalid.

C#

```csharp
private void ValidateTableName(string cmdText)
{
    //Get tablename
    //get 1st match starting at end of from
    fieldMatch = fieldSplit.Match(cmdText,
                    (keywordMatches [FROM_POSITION].Index)
        + keywordMatches [FROM_POSITION].Length + 1);
    if(fieldMatch.Success)
    {
        if(this.dataSet.Tables.Contains(fieldMatch.Value))
        {
            this.tableName = fieldMatch.Value;
        }
        else
        {
            throw new ArgumentException("Invalid Table Name");
        }
    }
}
```

code snippet \DataSetDataExtensionVB\DataSetDataExtension\DataSetCommand.vb

VB.NET

```vbnet
Private Sub ValidateTableName(ByVal cmdText As String)
    fieldMatch = fieldSplit.Match(cmdText, _
    (keywordMatches (FROM_POSITION).Index) + _
        keywordMatches (FROM_POSITION).Length + 1)
    If fieldMatch.Success Then
        If Me.dataSet.Tables.Contains(fieldMatch.Value) Then
            Me.tableName = fieldMatch.Value
        Else
            Throw New ArgumentException("Invalid Table Name")
        End If
    End If
End Sub
```

code snippet \DataSetDataExtensionVB\DataSetDataExtension\DataSetCommand.vb

The next step is to validate the Field names. You also want users to be able to use the * character to indicate that they want all the fields without having to list them individually. This is standard SQL syntax. You need to parse all the text between the `Select` statement and the `From` statement. You do this using the constant values created earlier to signify character position and a regular expression to pull out exactly what you are interested in.

The `fieldSplit` regular expression looks like `([^ ,\s]+)`. In English, this reads as follows: "Match all character groups that do not contain spaces, commas, and nonvisible white space and that have spaces at the end." If the first field is an asterisk, you know that the user wants all fields. This means that you do not have to build a temporary table to reflect the schema and that you can use the table she requested in the `From` portion of the text. If the first field is not an asterisk, you must build a temporary table reflecting the schema of the data you will return. To avoid problems with a user changing the fields, and the temp table previously existing, you will simply test for its existence each time and remove it if you must.

Next, you check to see whether the Field names exist in your main table by testing to see whether the column names exist. If they do, the column is valid, and you add a column with this name to your new temp table. You continue to do this as long as the Field names are valid. If an invalid field is submitted, you throw an exception to make the user aware of her mistake.

C#

```csharp
public void ValidateFieldNames(string cmdText)
{
    //get fieldnames
    //get first match starting at the last character of the Select
    // with a length from that position to the from
    fieldMatch = fieldSplit.Match(cmdText,
    (keywordMatches [SELECT_POSITION].Index +
        keywordMatches [SELECT_POSITION].Length + 1),
    (keywordMatches [FROM_POSITION].Index -
        (keywordMatches [SELECT_POSITION].Index +
            keywordMatches [SELECT_POSITION].Length + 1)));

    if (fieldMatch.Value == "*")  // all fields, use default view
    {
        this.dataView = this.dataSet.Tables[this.tableName].DefaultView;
        this.useDefaultTable = true;
    }
    else   //custom fields :  must build table/view
    {
        //don't use default table
        this.useDefaultTable = false;

        //remove table if exists - add new
        if (this.dataSet.Tables.Contains(TEMPTABLE_NAME))
        {
            this.dataSet.Tables.Remove(TEMPTABLE_NAME);
        }

        System.Data.DataTable table = new System.Data.DataTable(TEMPTABLE_NAME);

        //loop through column matches
        while (fieldMatch.Success)
        {
```

```
            if (this.dataSet.Tables[this.tableName]
                    .Columns.Contains(fieldMatch.Value))
            {
                System.Data.DataColumn col = this.dataSet.Tables[this.tableName]
                    .Columns[fieldMatch.Value];
                table.Columns.Add(
                    new System.Data.DataColumn(col.ColumnName, col.DataType));
                fieldMatch = fieldMatch.NextMatch();
            }
            else
            {
                throw new ArgumentException("Invalid column name");
            }
        }

        //add temptable to internal dataset and set view to tempView;
        this.dataSet.Tables.Add(table);
        this.dataView = new System.Data.DataView(table);
    }
}
```

code snippet \DataSetDataExtensionCS\DataSetDataExtension\DataSetCommand.cs

VB.NET

```
Private Sub ValidateFieldNames(ByVal cmdText As String)
    fieldMatch = fieldSplit.Match(cmdText, _
(keywordMatches (selectPosition).Index + _
keywordMatches (selectPosition).Length + 1), _
(keywordMatches (fromPosition).Index -  keywordMatches (selectPosition).Index _
 + keywordMatches (selectPosition)
.Length + 1)))

    If fieldMatch.Value = "*" Then
        Me.dataView = Me.dataSet.Tables(Me.tableName).DefaultView
        Me.useDefaultTable = True
    Else
        Me.useDefaultTable = False
        If Me.dataSet.Tables.Contains(Me.tempTableName) Then
            Me.dataSet.Tables.Remove(Me.tempTableName)
        End If
        Dim table As DataTable = New DataTable(Me.tempTableName)
        While fieldMatch.Success
            If Me.dataSet.Tables(Me.tableName).Columns _
                                    .Contains(fieldMatch.Value) Then
                Dim col As DataColumn = dataSet.Tables(tableName) _
                                    .Columns(fieldMatch.Value)
                table.Columns.Add(New DataColumn(col.ColumnName, col.DataType))
                fieldMatch = fieldMatch.NextMatch
            Else
                Throw New ArgumentException("Invalid column name")
            End If
        End While
        Me.dataSet.Tables.Add(table)
```

```vb
            Me.dataView = New System.Data.DataView(table)
        End If
    End Sub
```

Assuming that the table name is valid and that all the requested fields are valid, you will use the temp table you have built to satisfy data access requirements. The only thing left to do is add the new table to the existing dataset.

You have now validated all the parts of your query except the filtering and sorting criteria. In the CommandText method, you test whether filtering and sorting are enabled based on your keyword count. If they are enabled, you execute a method that uses the internal behavior of the DataSet class to do the work. In the ValidateFiltering() method, you need to parse the text based on the keyword count. You need to either grab all the text after the Where clause or, if an order clause exists, stop there.

```csharp
public void ValidateFiltering(string cmdText)
{
    if(filtering)
    {
        int startPos =0;
        int length =0;

        startPos = keywordMatches [wherePosition].Index +
            keywordMatches [wherePosition].Length + 1;
        if(keyWordCount == 3)  //no "order by" - Search from Where till  end
        {
            length = cmdText.Length-startPos;
        }
        else // "order by" exists -  search from where  position to "order by"
        {
            length =  keywordMatches [orderPosition].Index - startPos;
        }

        this.dataView.RowFilter = cmdText.Substring(startPos,length);
    }
}
```

```vbnet
Private Sub ValidateFiltering(ByVal cmdText As String)
    If filtering Then
        Dim startPos As Integer = 0
        Dim length As Integer = 0
        startPos = (keywordMatches (wherePosition).Index + _
          keywordMatches (wherePosition).Length + 1)
        If keyWordCount = 3 Then
```

```
                length = cmdText.Length - startPos
        Else
                length = keywordMatches (orderPosition).Index - startPos
        End If

        Me.dataView.RowFilter = cmdText.Substring(startPos, length)
    End If
End Sub
```

code snippet \DataSetDataExtensionVB\DataSetDataExtension\DataSetCommand.vb

After you parse the text, you will use the `DataView.RowFilter` property to filter the results. Simply apply the string you extracted to the `RowFilter`, and the `DataView` class takes care of the rest. The same technique is applied to get ordering.

C#

```csharp
public void ValidateSorting(string cmdText)
{
    if(sorting)
    {
        int startPos =0;
        int length =0;

        //start from end of 'Order by' clause
        startPos = keywordMatches [orderPosition].Index +
            keywordMatches [orderPosition].Length + 1;
        length =  cmdText.Length - startPos;

        this.dataView.Sort = cmdText.Substring(startPos,length);
    }
}
```

code snippet \DataSetDataExtensionCS\DataSetDataExtension\DataSetCommand.cs

VB.NET

```vbnet
Private Sub ValidateSorting(ByVal cmdText As String)
    If sorting Then
        Dim startPos As Integer = 0
        Dim length As Integer = 0
        startPos = (keywordMatches (orderPosition).Index + _
            keywordMatches (orderPosition).Length + 1)
        length = cmdText.Length - startPos

        Me.dataView.Sort = cmdText.Substring(startPos, length)
    End If
End Sub
```

code snippet \DataSetDataExtensionVB\DataSetDataExtension\DataSetCommand.vb

CommandTimeout Property

The `CommandTimeout` property specifies how long the `Command` object should wait for the results of an executed command before throwing an exception. You do not actually use this value, but it must be implemented because of interface requirements. Just return a 0 value to indicate that time-outs are not supported.

C#

```csharp
public int CommandTimeout
    {
        get
        {
            Debug.WriteLine("IDBCommand.CommandTimeout: Get");
            return this.m_commandTimeOut;
        }
        set
        {
            Debug.WriteLine("IDBCommand.CommandTimeout: Set");
            //throw new NotImplementedException("Timeouts not supported");
        }
    }
```

code snippet \DataSetDataExtensionCS\DataSetDataExtension\DataSetCommand.cs

VB.NET

```vbnet
Public Property CommandTimeout() As Integer Implements IDbCommand.CommandTimeout
        Get
            Debug.WriteLine("IDBCommand.CommandTimeout: Get")
            Return Me.m_cmdTimeOut
        End Get
        Set(ByVal value As Integer)
            Debug.WriteLine("IDBCommand.CommandTimeout: Set")
        End Set
    End Property
```

code snippet \DataSetDataExtensionVB\DataSetDataExtension\DataSetCommand.vb

CommandType Property

Most DPEs allow the developer to pass in a command as text, or they can pass in a fully initialized `Command` object for the `Execute` reader method to examine and use. The `DataSetCommand` class accepts only text; any other type will cause your component to throw a `NotSupported` exception.

C#

```csharp
public CommandType CommandType
    {
        // supports only a text commandType
        get { return CommandType.Text; }
```

```
            set { if (value != CommandType.Text) throw new NotSupportedException(); }
        }
```

VB.NET

```
Public Property CommandType() As CommandType _
        Implements IDbCommand.CommandType
            Get
                Return CommandType.Text
            End Get
            Set(ByVal Value As CommandType)
                If Value <> CommandType.Text Then
                    Throw New NotSupportedException
                End If
            End Set
        End Property
```

CreateParameter Method

The `CreateParameter` method returns an extension-specific parameter to the `Command` object. The method must be supported because of the interface requirements, although it is not actually used. The `DataSetParameter` object is a simple class that implements another interface called `IDataParameter`, which allows it to be returned as an object of the interface type.

C#

```
public IDataParameter CreateParameter()
{
    //return DataSetParameter
    return new DataSetParameter();
}
```

VB.NET

```
Public Function CreateParameter() As IDataParameter _
        Implements IDbCommand.CreateParameter
            Return New DataSetParameter
End Function
```

Parameters Property

The `Parameters` property returns a collection that implements the `IDataParameterCollection` interface. Your custom collection class is `DataSetParameterCollection` and satisfies these requirements. The `Parameters` property allows the developer to index into the `Parameters` collection to `set` or `get` the parameter values.

C#

```csharp
public IDataParameterCollection Parameters
{
    get
    {
        return this.m_parameters;
    }
}
```

code snippet \DataSetDataExtensionCS\DataSetDataExtension\DataSetCommand.cs

VB.NET

```vbnet
Public ReadOnly Property Parameters() As IDataParameterCollection _
        Implements IDbCommand.Parameters
            Get
                Return Me.m_parameters
            End Get
End Property
```

code snippet \DataSetDataExtensionVB\DataSetDataExtension\DataSetCommand.vb

Creating the DataSetDataReader Object

The data reader in our implementation does nothing more than read properties of our internal `DataView`. The data reader's behavior is enforced by the `IDataReader` interface, which supplies methods to indicate the number, names, and types of the fields that will be read. It also allows the object to actually access the data.

To add the `DataSetDataReader` class to the project, choose Project ➪ Add Class. Change the name of the class to `DataSetDataReader`. After adding the class, add the custom namespace, and edit the class definition.

Declarations

The members of the `DataSetDataReader` class hold all the information that you will use to build the properties it supports. The `currentRow` variable is used to store the value of the current row as the data is being read from your data file. The `dataView` variable holds a reference to the current view of data from the `DataSetCommand` that is passed in via the constructor. Finally, the `dataSet-Command` variable holds a reference to the command that is passed in via the constructor.

C#

```csharp
System.Data.DataView dataView;
DataSetCommand dataSetCommand = null;
int currentRow = -1;
```

code snippet \DataSetDataExtensionCS\DataSetDataExtension\DataSetDataReader.cs

VB.NET

```vb
Private dataView As System.Data.DataView = Nothing
Private dataSetCommand As dataSetCommand = Nothing
Private currentRow As Integer = -1
```

code snippet \DataSetDataExtensionVB\DataSetDataExtension\DataSetDataReader.vb

Implementing IDataReader

The IDataReader interface exposed by Reporting Services enforces consistency in working with data. It provides properties and methods that allow you to examine the data and its types as well as the Read method that actually does the dirty work. Below is the definition of this interface, which shows all methods and properties that will need implementation:

C#

```csharp
public interface IDataReader : IDisposable
{
    Type GetFieldType(int fieldIndex);
    string GetName(int fieldIndex);
    int GetOrdinal(string fieldName);
    object GetValue(int fieldIndex);
    bool Read();
    int FieldCount { get; }
}
```

VB.NET

```vb
Public Interface IDataReader
    Inherits IDisposable
    Function GetFieldType(ByVal fieldIndex As Integer) As Type
    Function GetName(ByVal fieldIndex As Integer) As String
    Function GetOrdinal(ByVal fieldName As String) As Integer
    Function GetValue(ByVal fieldIndex As Integer) As Object
    Function Read() As Boolean
    Property FieldCount() As Integer
End Interface
```

You need to modify your class definition to force the custom DataSetDataReader class to support (implement) the interface requirements.

C#

```csharp
namespace Wrox.ReportingServices.DataSetDataExtension
{

    public class DataSetDataReader : IDataReader
    {
        internal DataSetDataReader(DataSetCommand command)
        {
            //set member variables based upon command object
            this.dataSetCommand = command;
            this.dataView = command.dataView;
```

```
    }

    public void Dispose() {}
```

```
Namespace Wrox.ReportingServices.DataSetDataExtension
    Public Class DataSetDataReader
        Implements IDataReader

        Friend Sub New(ByVal command As dataSetCommand)
            Me.dataSetCommand = command
            Me.dataView = command.dataView
        End Sub

        Public Sub Dispose() Implements IDisposable.Dispose
        End Sub
```

GetFieldType Method

The `GetFieldType` method returns the type of data at a particular position within the stream that is being read. This data is used to allow the developer to store the data being read in the correct data type upon retrieval from the data reader.

```
public Type GetFieldType (int fieldIndex)
{
    return this.dataView.Table.Columns[fieldIndex].DataType;
}
```

```
Public Function GetFieldType(ByVal fieldIndex As Integer) As Type _
    Implements IDataReader.GetFieldType
        Return Me.dataView.Table.Columns(fieldIndex).DataType
End Function
```

GetName Method

The `GetName` method allows the developer to retrieve a data field from the `DataReader` object by passing in the name of the field to be read.

C#

```csharp
public string GetName(int fieldIndex)
{
        return this.dataView.Table.Columns[fieldIndex].ColumnName;
}
```

code snippet \DataSetDataExtensionCS\DataSetDataExtension\DataSetDataReader.cs

VB.NET

```vbnet
Public Function GetName(ByVal fieldIndex As Integer) As String _
    Implements IDataReader.GetName
        Return Me.dataView.Table.Columns(fieldIndex).ColumnName
End Function
```

code snippet \DataSetDataExtensionVB\DataSetDataExtension\DataSetDataReader.vb

GetOrdinal Method

The GetOrdinal method allows the developer to index the data based on its position within the DataReader stream.

C#

```csharp
public int GetOrdinal(string fieldName)
{
        return this.dataView.Table.Columns[fieldName].Ordinal;
}
```

code snippet \DataSetDataExtensionCS\DataSetDataExtension\DataSetDataReader.cs

VB.NET

```vbnet
Public Function GetOrdinal(ByVal fieldName As String) As Integer _
    Implements IDataReader.GetOrdinal
        Return Me.dataView.Table.Columns(fieldName).Ordinal
End Function
```

code snippet \DataSetDataExtensionVB\DataSetDataExtension\DataSetDataReader.vb

GetValue Method

The GetValue method retrieves the actual value from the data stream. All of these methods are typically used together. The developer pulls the type information from the stream, creates variables of the correct type to hold this data, and gets the data's values using the GetValue function.

C#

```csharp
public object GetValue(int fieldIndex)
{
```

```
            return this.dataView[this.currentRow][fieldIndex];
    }
```

code snippet \DataSetDataExtensionCS\DataSetDataExtension\DataSetDataReader.cs

VB.NET

Available for
download on
Wrox.com

```
Public Function GetValue(ByVal fieldIndex As Integer) As Object _
    Implements IDataReader.GetValue
        Return Me.dataView(Me.currentRow)(fieldIndex)
End Function
```

code snippet \DataSetDataExtensionVB\DataSetDataExtension\DataSetDataReader.vb

Read Method

The `Read` method is the workhorse of the `DataSetDataReader` class. The function loops through the current `DataView`. If a line is read successfully, this is indicated to the user of your extension by incrementing the row count variable `currentRow` and by returning a `Boolean` value. As long as `true` is returned, data is read successfully. `false` is returned when the internal `view` hits the end of the result set. Notice that we use a thread-safe increment function available in the .NET Framework to ensure that the current row variable is safely locked during the increment operation and won't yield a race condition.

C#

Available for
download on
Wrox.com

```
public bool Read()
{
    System.Threading.Interlocked.Increment(ref this.currentRow);
    if (this.currentRow >= this.dataView.Count)
    {
        return false;
    }
    return true;
}
```

code snippet \DataSetDataExtensionCS\DataSetDataExtension\DataSetDataReader.cs

VB.NET

Available for
download on
Wrox.com

```
Public Function Read() As Boolean Implements IDataReader.Read
    System.Threading.Interlocked.Increment(Me.currentRow)
    If Me.currentRow >= Me.dataView.Count Then
        Return False
    End If
    Return True
End Function
```

code snippet \DataSetDataExtensionVB\DataSetDataExtension\DataSetDataReader.vb

FieldCount Property

The `FieldCount` property returns the number of fields or columns available in each row of data that the `Read` method returns.

C#

```csharp
public int FieldCount
{
    // Return the count of the number of columns,
    get { return this.dataView.Table.Columns.Count; }
}
```

code snippet \DataSetDataExtensionVB\DataSetDataExtension\DataSetDataReader.vb

VB.NET

```vbnet
Public ReadOnly Property FieldCount() As Integer Implements IDataReader.FieldCount
    Get
        Return Me.dataView.Table.Columns.Count
    End Get
End Property
```

code snippet \DataSetDataExtensionVB\DataSetDataExtension\DataSetDataReader.vb

Installing the DataSetDataProcessing Extension

After creating your custom DPE, you must install it to enable access. The installation process has two steps:

1. Install and configure the extension.

2. Configure extension security.

This particular extension is used by both the Reporting Server and the Report Designer itself, which requires us to install it in two locations. It must be installed on the report server and the workstation used to design the reports (using SSDT/Visual Studio).

Server Installation

Reporting Services has a standard location where extensions should be installed. This location is a subdirectory below the installation directory of SQL Server itself. We refer to the SQL Server installation path as `InstallPath`. On my machine, this directory is `C:\Program Files\Microsoft SQL Server\`.

Depending on the different SQL Server products you have installed on the machine, the subdirectories under `InstallPath` may vary. The naming convention for the `Reporting Services` subdirectory is `MSRS11.MSSQLSERVER`, where `MSRS11` represents the product and version name (Microsoft Reporting Services version 11).

The directory into which you will install the extension is the bin directory of the report server: `InstallPath\MSRS11.MSSQLSERVER\Reporting Services\ReportServer\bin`. Copy your custom DPE assembly into this directory. The extension is now in the correct location, but you need to inform the Report Server of its presence. You do so by editing the configuration file that Reporting Services uses for its settings. This file is called RSReportServer.config and is located in the parent directory. Open this file and look for the <Data> section. Within this section, you should see entries similar to the following:

```
<Data>
    <Permissions>
        <PermissionSet class="System.Security.NamedPermissionSet" version="1"
                    Unrestricted="true" Name="FullTrust"
                    Description="Allows full access to all resources"/>
    </Permissions>
    <Extension Name="SQL"
        Type="Microsoft.ReportingServices.DataExtensions.SqlConnectionWrapper,
            Microsoft.ReportingServices.DataExtensions"/>
    <Extension Name="OLEDB"
      Type="Microsoft.ReportingServices.DataExtensions.OleDbConnectionWrapper,
            Microsoft.ReportingServices.DataExtensions"/>
    <Extension Name="ORACLE"
        Type="Microsoft.ReportingServices.DataExtensions.OracleClient
         ConnectionWrapper,Microsoft.ReportingServices.DataExtensions"/>
    <Extension Name="ODBC"
        Type="Microsoft.ReportingServices.DataExtensions.OdbcConnection
            Wrapper,Microsoft.ReportingServices.DataExtensions"/>
    <Extension Name="DATASET"
        Type="Wrox.ReportingServices.DataSetDataExtension.DataSetConnection,
            Wrox.ReportingServices.DataSetDataExtension"/>
</Data>
```

Add the DataSet entry shown in the highlighted code snippet. The Name tag is the unique name you want users to see when they select your extension. The Type element contains the entry point class for your extension (the first object created and the one that is required to implement the IExtension interface), followed by the fully qualified name of your extension.

Save the file. Reporting Services will now recognize your extension, but you must change the Code Access Security (CAS) policy to give the extension the permissions it needs to do its job. CAS is a constraint security model used by the .NET Framework to restrict which system resources and operations that code can access and perform, regardless of the caller.

Server Security Configuration

The security policy file is located in the same directory as the server configuration file. Simply locate the file called rssrvpolicy.config, which contains the security policy information for SSRS. Make an entry that looks similar to the following, replacing <INSTALLPATH> with the appropriate installation path of the SQL Server Reporting Services instance on the server:

```
</CodeGroup>
<CodeGroup   class="UnionCodeGroup"
  version="1"
  PermissionSetName="FullTrust"
  Name="WroxSRS"
  Description="Code group for Wrox DataSet data processing extension">
```

```
        <IMembershipCondition class="UrlMembershipCondition"
            version="1"

    Url="<INSTALLPATH>\Reporting Services\ReportServer\bin\
    DataSetDataExtension.dll" />
    </CodeGroup>
```

This `CodeGroup` policy specifies that we grant `FullTrust` to our assembly to execute its code. As a best practice, though, you should grant only the permission set required by your code to execute appropriately, thus reducing the possible attack surface.

WorkStation Installation

The next task is installing the extension on your development machine so that you can use it in the Report Designer within SSDT/Visual Studio. The process for installing the extension into the Report Designer is much the same as that for the server, with the exception of the filenames and locations. This is also done by copying the file to a specific directory of your development machine and making an entry in the configuration file so that the designer is aware of the extension.

Copy your extension to the `C:\Program Files(x86)\Microsoft Visual Studio 10.0\Common7\` `IDE\`PrivateAssemblies directory. All the files needed for workstation configuration are located here. The designer's configuration file is called `RSReportDesigner.config`. Insert the same information that you inserted at the server-side extension at the end of the `<Data>` section in this file.

```
<Data>
    <Extension Name="ODBC"
        Type="Microsoft.ReportingServices.DataExtensions.OdbcConnection
        Wrapper, Microsoft.ReportingServices.DataExtensions"/>
    <Extension Name="DATASET"
        Type="Wrox.ReportingServices.DataSetDataExtension.DataSetConnection,
        Wrox.ReportingServices.DataSetDataExtension"/>
</Data>
```

This file has an additional requirement. You must also tell Visual Studio what designer to use with your extension. We chose not to implement a custom designer class but to use the Generic Query Designer provided by Microsoft instead. Your query is based on SQL, so this works well. Make an entry in the `<Designer>` section that immediately follows the `<Data>` section:

```
<Extension Name="DATASET"
    Type="Microsoft.ReportingServices.QueryDesigners.GenericQueryDesigner,
            Microsoft.ReportingServices.QueryDesigners"/>
```

WorkStation Security Configuration

The next step is to set up the security policy so that the extension will run in the designer correctly. The required file is called `rspreviewpolicy.config`. Add an entry resembling the following to this file, replacing `<InstallPath>` with your actual Visual Studio installation path:

```
<CodeGroup class="UnionCodeGroup" version="1"
    PermissionSetName="FullTrust"
    Name="WroxSRS"
    Description="Code group for my DataSet data processing extension">
      <IMembershipCondition class="UrlMembershipCondition"
```

```
            version="1"
      Url="<InstallPath>\Common7\IDE\PrivateAssemblies\DataSetDataExtension.dll" />
</CodeGroup>
```

Testing DataSetDataExtension

To test the `DataSetDataExtension` extension, you must create a report that uses the custom extension. You must also create a `DataSet` file to contain your data or use the one provided in the sample code. The code is generic enough that you can use it against any serialized dataset. The file included in the example is just a `SELECT * FROM DimCustomer` run against the AdventureWorksDW_WroxSSRS2012 database and persisted from a dataset object.

Add a new project to your existing solution. Create the project by choosing File ⇨ Add Project ⇨ New Project. If the development environment is set up correctly, you will see the Business Intelligence template folder. Choose the Report Server Project template. Change the project's name to TestReport, and click OK. This launches the Report Designer with a blank report. Click the link on the Designer canvas to add a new data source and dataset for the report. The Data Source Properties page appears, as shown in Figure 22-7. Leave the default data source name, and click the Type drop-down box. Your new `DataSetDataExtension` should now be available as `DATASET`. Using a `FileName` attribute, enter the physical path to your serialized dataset into the Connection String textbox. When you are done, the result should resemble Figure 22-7.

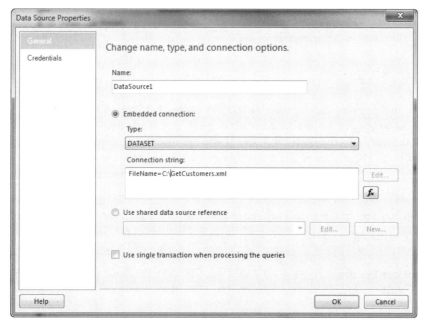

FIGURE 22-7

Next, you need to indicate the credentials you want to use. Click the Credentials menu on the left side of the Data Source Properties page; the Credentials window appears, as shown in Figure 22-8.

Instruct the data source to "Use Windows Authentication (integrated security)" by selecting the radio button.

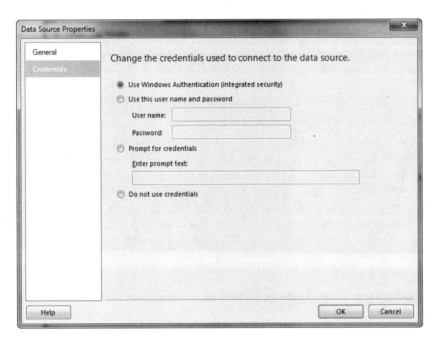

FIGURE 22-8

After you have set both the type and connection strings, you are ready to set up the basic data query. The dataset we used included a table called DimCustomer that we want to query. Enter SELECT * FROM DimCustomer into the Query window if you are using the sample provided, or some statement that works on your specific data. The query should resemble the text shown in Figure 22-9.

Finish setting up the data source and dataset by clicking OK. Now you can drag and drop a new Table item from the toolbox onto the report body. Then select three fields from the dataset, represented in the Report Data window, and put them into the detail section of the Tablix. The resulting report is shown in Figure 22-10.

Next, you need to see if our extension actually returns data. Click the Preview tab. The resulting data should resemble Figure 22-11.

Now you know that your extension works. You can experiment with the field-limiting/filtering and field-sorting functionality by right-clicking the Dataset name in the Report Data window and selecting Edit Query. This brings up the Query Designer, shown in Figure 22-12, where you can enter more advanced queries and test the results.

FIGURE 22-9

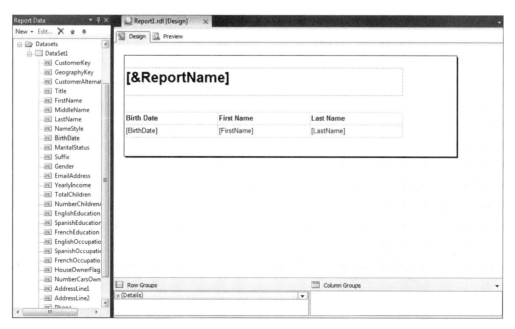

FIGURE 22-10

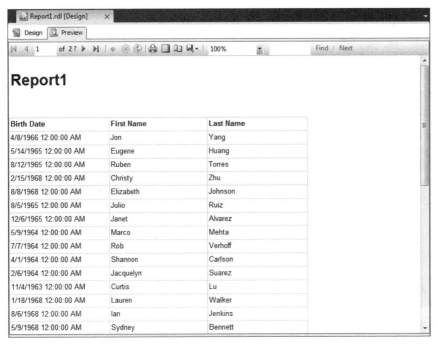

FIGURE 22-11

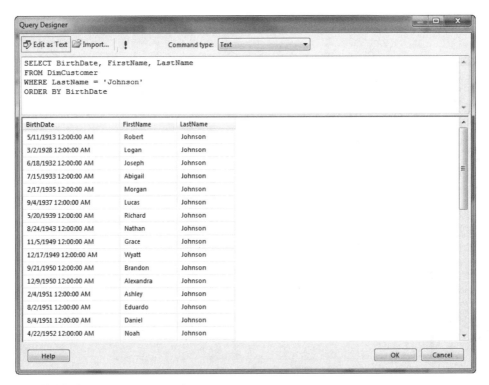

FIGURE 22-12

Another option for testing the custom data extension is to open a new instance of Visual Studio and load the extension project. Add a breakpoint on a line of code that you want to step into, and then select Debug ⇨ Attach to process.

In the Attach to Process window, select the process for the Visual Studio instance that has the Report Designer open to the test report consuming the data extension.

Finally, click the Attach button. Visual Studio attaches the project code to the Report Designer. To step into the breakpoint, just preview the report in the Report Designer. As soon as Reporting Services hits the line of code with the breakpoint, you are taken to the code view, where you can use all the debugging features of the Visual Studio IDE.

SUMMARY

In this chapter, you learned about the extensibility of Reporting Services and the areas that currently support customization, including the following topics:

➤   Which extensibility options are available

➤   Reasons for extending SQL Server Reporting Services

➤   How to create custom data processing extensions

➤   How to install custom extensions

Along with the extensibility options available in SQL Server Reporting Services, you also learned about some of the business opportunities created. Microsoft has created a flexible, powerful reporting solution that allows you to modify its behavior by implementing the interfaces required by the particular extension type. This functionality has created a third-party market for tools and has allowed enterprise developers to create custom solutions for their businesses' unique needs.

Also discussed were the data access methods that the .NET Framework uses — specifically, how to create a custom Data Processing Extension to work with nonrelational data. The example given was simple and cannot stand alone as an application, but it can easily be extended to provide additional functionality, such as support for parameters. The primary purpose of the example was to familiarize you with the requirements for creating and installing an extension. This type of extension was chosen because it is used on the server for report processing, and on the developer machine for report creation.

PART VIII
Appendixes

▶ **APPENDIX A:** T-SQL Command Syntax Reference

▶ **APPENDIX B:** T-SQL System Variables and Functions

▶ **APPENDIX C:** MDX Reference

T-SQL Command Syntax Reference

SQL Server 2012 recognizes up to four parts of object names. This convention is the same in SQL Server 2005, 2008, and 2008 R2. Depending on the context of an expression, some parts may or may not be necessary when referencing an object. When a script runs on a different server or when you are using a different database, related object names may be required. Note that versions of SQL Server since 2005 recognize the schema name in the third position, whereas SQL Server 2000 and earlier versions recognized the object owner name in the third position. Table A-1 summarizes the valid syntax for referencing database objects.

TABLE A-1

OBJECT REFERENCE	USE AND CONTEXT
`object`	Used in the context of the local database, on the same server. `object` is part of the dbo schema. There are no duplicate object names.
`schema.object`	Used in the context of the local database, on the same server. Duplicate object names that have schema names (and, subsequently, different owners) are permitted. Also uses a standard convention for clarity.
`database..object`	Used in the context of the same or different database on the same server. If you haven't specified the owner or schema, assumes the dbo schema.
`database.schema.object`	A three-part name fully describes an object on the same server, in the same or a different database.
`server.database.schema.object`	A four-part name is valid in the context of a remote server or the local server, in the local or a different database, and for any schema.

continues

TABLE A-1 *(continued)*

OBJECT REFERENCE	USE AND CONTEXT
`server.database..` `object`	The database owner or schema in the third position can be omitted to use the default dbo schema.
`server..schema.object`	The database name can be omitted to use the default database on that server. This is not a typical practice.
`server ... object`	Omitting the database and owner or schema name causes the default database and the default dbo schema to be used. This is valid syntax but not a typical practice.

T-SQL COMMANDS, CLAUSES, AND PREDICATES

The following sections describe the core components of the T-SQL language. The version that introduces newer syntax features is noted.

WITH

Introduced in SQL Server 2005, this technique may be used to define an alias for the result set returned by a SELECT expression.

```
WITH MyCTE

AS
( SELECT * FROM Production.Product WHERE ListPrice < 1000 )
SELECT * FROM MyCTE
```

Optionally, column aliases can be defined in parentheses following the Common Table Expression (CTE) name:

```
WITH MyCTE ( ID, ProdNumber, ProdName, Price )
AS
( SELECT
    ProductID
  , ProductNumber
  , Name
  , ListPrice
  FROM Production.Product WHERE ListPrice < 1000
)
SELECT * FROM MyCTE
```

SELECT

➤ To return all columns from a table or view:

```
SELECT * FROM table_name
```

➤ To return specific columns from a table or view:

```
SELECT Column1, Column2, Column3 FROM table_name
```

➤ Column alias techniques:

```
SELECT Column1 AS Col1, Column2 AS Col2 FROM table_name
SELECT Column1 Col1, Column2 Col2 FROM table_name
SELECT Col1 = Column1, Col2 = Column2 FROM table_name
```

➤ To return literal values:

```
SELECT 'Some literal value'
SELECT 'Some value' AS Col1, 123 AS Col2
```

➤ To return an expression value:

```
SELECT (1 + 2) * 3
```

➤ To return the result of a function call:

```
SELECT CONVERT( varchar(20), GETDATE(), 101 )
```

SELECT TOP

➤ To return a fixed number of rows:

```
SELECT TOP 10 * FROM table_name ORDER BY Column1
SELECT TOP 10 Column1, Column2 FROM table_name ORDER BY Column2
```

➤ To return a fixed number of rows with the ties for last position:

```
SELECT TOP 10 WITH TIES Column1, Column2 FROM table_name ORDER BY Column2
```

➤ To return a percentage of all available rows:

```
SELECT TOP 25 PERCENT * FROM table_name ORDER BY Column2
SELECT TOP 25 PERCENT Column1, Column2 FROM table_name ORDER BY Column2
```

➤ To substitute a variable or expression for a top values number:

```
DECLARE @TopNumber Int
SET @TopNumber = 15
SELECT TOP (@TopNumber) * FROM table_name ORDER BY Column2
```

➤ To return top values based on an expression:

```
SELECT TOP (SELECT a_column_value FROM some_table) * FROM another_table
```

SELECT INTO

➤ To create and populate a table from a result set:

```
SELECT Column1, Column2 INTO
new_table_name FROM existing_table_or_view_name
```

FROM

➤   Single table query:

```
SELECT * FROM table_name
```

➤   Multitable join query:

```
SELECT *
FROM table1.key_column INNER JOIN table2 ON table1.key_column = table2.key_column
```

➤   Derived table:

```
SELECT DerTbl.Column1, DerTbl.Column2
FROM
    ( SELECT Column1, Column2 FROM some_table ... ) AS DerTbl
```

WHERE

➤   Exact match:

```
SELECT ... FROM ...
WHERE Column1 = 'A literal value'
```

➤   Not NULL:

```
SELECT ... FROM ...
WHERE Column1 IS NOT NULL
```

➤   Any trailing characters:

```
SELECT ... FROM ...
WHERE Column1 LIKE 'ABC%'
```

➤   Any leading characters:

```
SELECT ... FROM ...
WHERE Column1 LIKE '%XYZ'
```

➤   Any leading or trailing characters:

```
SELECT ... FROM ...
WHERE Column1 LIKE '%MNOP%'
```

➤   Placeholder wildcard:

```
SELECT ... FROM ...
WHERE Column1 LIKE '_BC_EF'
```

➤   Criteria using parentheses to designate order:

```
SELECT ... FROM ...
WHERE
    (Column1 LIKE 'ABC%' AND Column2 LIKE '%XYZ')
    OR
    Column3 = '123'
```

GROUP BY

All nonaggregated columns in the SELECT list must be included in the GROUP BY list:

```
SELECT COUNT(Column1), Column2, Column3
FROM ... WHERE ...
GROUP BY Column2, Column3
```

➤ Designating order:

```
SELECT COUNT(Column1), Column2, Column3
FROM ... WHERE ...
GROUP BY Column2, Column3
ORDER BY Column2 DESC, Column3 ASC
```

WITH ROLLUP

➤ Legacy method to implement a rollup subtotal break:

 Note that the ROLLUP *and* CUBE *operators cause SQL Server to return a non-two-dimensional result set that is not supported by many APIs and client interfaces.*

```
SELECT Column1, Column2, SUM(Column3)
FROM table_name
GROUP BY Column1, Column2
WITH ROLLUP
```

This syntax is still supported in SQL Server 2012, but the newer BY ROLLUP syntax, introduced in SQL Server 2008, is preferred.

BY ROLLUP

This syntax was introduced in SQL Server 2008 for implementing a rollup subtotal break:

```
SELECT Column1, Column2, SUM(Column3)
FROM table_name
GROUP BY ROLLUP(Column1, Column2)
```

WITH CUBE

➤ Legacy method to implement a cube subtotal break:

```
SELECT Column1, Column2, SUM(Column3)
FROM table_name
GROUP BY Column1, Column2
WITH CUBE
```

This syntax is still supported in SQL Server 2012, but the newer BY CUBE syntax, introduced in SQL Server 2008, is preferred.

BY CUBE

This syntax was introduced in SQL Server 2008 for implementing a cube subtotal break:

```
SELECT Column1, Column2, SUM(Column3)
FROM table_name
GROUP BY CUBE(Column1, Column2)
```

HAVING

➤ To filter results based on values available after the aggregations and groupings are performed:

```
SELECT COUNT(Column1), Column2, Column3
FROM ... WHERE ...
GROUP BY Column2, Column3
HAVING COUNT(Column1) > 5
```

UNION

➤ To combine multiple results with the same column count:

```
SELECT Column1, Column2 FROM table1_name
UNION
SELECT Column1, Column2 FROM table2_name
```

➤ To combine literal values and query results:

```
SELECT -1 AS Column1, 'A literal value' AS Column2
UNION
SELECT Column1, Column2 FROM table1_name
```

➤ To include nondistinct selection (UNION performs SELECT DISTINCT by default):

```
SELECT Column1, Column2 FROM table1_name
UNION ALL
SELECT Column1, Column2 FROM table2_name
```

EXCEPT and INTERSECT

➤ To select the differences (EXCEPT) or common values (INTERSECT) between two queries:

```
SELECT * FROM TableA EXCEPT SELECT * FROM TableB
SELECT * FROM TableA INTERSECT SELECT * FROM TableB
```

ORDER BY

➤ To order a result set by one or more column values:

```
SELECT * FROM table_name ORDER BY Column1
SELECT * FROM table_name ORDER BY Column1 DESC, Column2 ASC
```

The default order is ascending. If ordering by more than one column, each column can have a different order.

COMPUTE and COMPUTE BY Clauses

➤ To generate totals that are appended to the end of an aggregate query result set:

```
SELECT Column1, Column2, Column3
FROM table_name
ORDER BY Column1, Column2
COMPUTE SUM(Column3)
```

The COMPUTE and COMPUTE BY clauses are not very useful in applications because the aggregated results are not in relational form and cannot be used in a dataset.

As of SQL Server 2008, the CUBE and ROLLUP operators are appended to the COMPUTE BY clause (see WITH CUBE, BY CUBE, WITH ROLLUP, and BY ROLLUP).

FOR Clause

The FOR clause is used with either the XML or BROWSE option in a SELECT statement. However, the BROWSE and XML options are unrelated. FOR XML specifies that the result set is returned in XML format. FOR BROWSE is used when accessing data through the DB-Library so that rows can be browsed and updated one row at a time in an optimistic locking environment. The FOR BROWSE option has several requirements. For more information, consult SQL Server Books Online, under the topic "Browse Mode."

```
SELECT * FROM table_name FOR XML {XML Option}
SELECT * FROM table_name FOR BROWSE
```

OPTION Clause

The OPTION clause is used in a SELECT statement to provide a query hint that will override the query optimizer and specify an index or specific join mechanism to be used along with other hint options.

CASE

➤ To evaluate one or more expressions and return one or more specified values based on the evaluated expression:

```
SELECT expression = CASE Column
WHEN value THEN resultant_value
WHEN value2 THEN resultant_value2
...
ELSE alternate_value
END
FROM table
SELECT value =
        CASE
        WHEN column IS NULL THEN value
```

```
        WHEN column {expression true} THEN different_value
        WHEN column {expression true} and price {expression true} THEN other_value
        ELSE different_value
        END,
        column2
FROM table
```

INSERT

➤ To add a new row to a table:

```
INSERT table (column list)
VALUES
(column values)
INSERT table
SELECT columns FROM source expression
INSERT table
EXEC stored_procedure
```

The following is the multitable INSERT syntax introduced in SQL Server 2008:

```
INSERT table (column list)
VALUES
(column values),
(column values),
(column values)
```

> *Note that column values are comma-separated and must appear in the same order as in the column list or as they are defined in the table.*

UPDATE

➤ To update selected columns in a table:

```
UPDATE table SET column1 = expression1, column2 = expression2
WHERE filter_expression
```

➤ To update a table based on the contents of another table:

```
UPDATE table SET column1 = expression
FROM table INNER JOIN table2
ON table.column = table2.column
WHERE table.column = table2.column
```

DELETE

➤ To delete selected rows from a table:

```
DELETE table
WHERE filter_expression
```

➤ To delete rows from a table based on the contents of a different table:

```
DELETE table
FROM table INNER JOIN table2
ON table.column = table2.column
WHERE column = filter_expression
```

DECLARE @local_variable

This creates a named object that temporarily holds a value with the data type defined in the declaration statement. Local variables only have scope within the calling batch or stored procedure. The value of a local variable can be set with either a SET or SELECT operation. SELECT is more efficient than SET and has the advantage of populating multiple variables in a single operation, but the SELECT operation cannot be confined with any data retrieval operation.

```
DECLARE @local_variable AS int
SET @local_variable = integer_expression
DECLARE @local_variable1 AS int, @local_variable2 AS varchar(55)
SELECT @local_variable1 = integer_column_expression, @local_variable2 =
character_column_expression FROM table
```

SET

The SET operator has many functions, from setting the value of a variable to setting a database or connection property. The SET operator is divided into the categories shown in Table A-2.

TABLE A-2

CATEGORY	ALTERS THE CURRENT SESSION SETTINGS FOR
Date and time	Handling date and time data
Locking	Handling SQL Server locking
Miscellaneous	Miscellaneous SQL Server functionality
Query execution	Query execution and processing
SQL-92 settings	Using the SQL-92 default settings
Statistics	Displaying statistics information
Transactions	Handling SQL Server transactions

LIKE

LIKE is a pattern-matching operator for comparing strings or partial strings.

➤ To compare a string value where the compared string is anywhere in the string:

```
SELECT * FROM table WHERE column1 LIKE '%string%'
```

➤ To compare a string value where the compared string is at the beginning of the string:

```
SELECT * FROM table WHERE column1 LIKE 'string%'
```

➤ To compare a string value where the compared string is at the end of the string:

```
SELECT * FROM table WHERE column1 LIKE '%string'
```

➤ To compare a string value where a specific character or character range is in the string:

```
SELECT * FROM table WHERE column1 LIKE '[a-c]'
SELECT * FROM table WHERE column1 LIKE '[B-H]olden'
```

➤ To compare a string value where a specific character or character range is not in the string:

```
SELECT * FROM table WHERE column1 LIKE '[M^c]%' -Begins with M but not Mc
```

ALTER TABLE

➤ To alter a table's structure by adding or removing table objects such as columns, constraints, and partitions, or by enabling and disabling triggers:

```
ALTER TABLE table_name ADD new_column int NULL;
ALTER TABLE table_name ADD CONSTRAINT new_check CHECK (check expression) ;
ALTER TABLE table_name DROP COLUMN existing_column;
ALTER TABLE table_name ENABLE TRIGGER trigger_name;
ALTER TABLE table_name DISABLE TRIGGER trigger_name;
```

PIVOT Operator

➤ To cause a normalized columnar set to be transformed and restructured with repeating column values according to a predefined column list specification:

```
SELECT Column3, [Col2_List_Val1], [Col2_List_Val2], [Col2_List_Val3]... FROM
(
    SELECT
        Column1  -- Value to aggregate as measure value in pivot cells
        , Column2  -- Value for column headers as column list
        , Column3  -- Value for row headers
    FROM source_table_name
)   AS Source
PIVOT
(
    Sum(Column1) FOR Column2
        IN ([Col2_List_Val1], [Col2_List_Val2], [Col2_List_Val3]...)
)   AS pvt
```

UNPIVOT Operator

➤ To cause a pivoted result set to be transformed into a normalized, columnar table structure:

```
SELECT
 Column3, Column2, Column1  -- columns same as pivot source above
```

```
FROM
 (
    SELECT
      Column1
    , [Col2_List_Val1], [Col2_List_Val2], [Col2_List_Val3]... FROM
      FROM pivot_source_table_name
 ) AS pvt
UNPIVOT
 (
      Column1 FOR Column2
        IN ([Col2_List_Val1], [Col2_List_Val2], [Col2_List_Val3]...)
 )
 AS unpvt
```

CREATE DATABASE

➤   To create a database and all associated files:

```
CREATE DATABASE new_database
ON (
    NAME = 'logical_name',
    FILENAME = 'physical_file_location',
    SIZE = initial_size_in_MB,
    MAXSIZE = max_size_in_MB, --If no MAXSIZE specified unlimited growth is assumed
    FILEGROWTH = percentage_OR_space_in_MB)
LOG ON
( NAME = 'logical_log_name',
    FILENAME = 'physical_file_location',
    SIZE = initial_size_in_MB,
    MAXSIZE = max_size_in_MB, --If no MAXSIZE specified unlimited growth is assumed
    FILEGROWTH = percentage_OR_space_in_MB)
COLLATE database_collation
```

CREATE DEFAULT

➤   To create a database-wide default value that can then be bound to columns in any table to provide a default value:

```
CREATE DEFAULT default_name AS default_value
--bind the default to a table column
sp_bindefault default_name, 'table.column'
```

CREATE PROCEDURE

➤   To create a new stored procedure:

```
CREATE PROCEDURE proc_name @variable variable_data_type ...n
AS
...procedure code
```

or

```
CREATE PROC proc_name @variable variable_data_type ...n
AS
...procedure code
```

CREATE RULE

➤ To create a database-wide rule, much like a check constraint, that can then be bound to individual columns in tables throughout the database:

```
CREATE RULE rule_name AS rule_expression
--bind the rule to a table column
sp_bindrule rule_name, 'table.column'
```

CREATE TABLE

➤ To create a new table:

```
CREATE TABLE table_name (
Column1 data_type nullability column_option,
Column2 data_type nullability column_option,
Column3 data_type nullability column_option,
--Column_option = Collation, IDENTITY, KEY...
```

➤ To create a new partitioned table:

```
CREATE TABLE partitioned_table_name (Column1 int, Column2 char(10))
Column1 data_type nullability column_option,
Column2 data_type nullability column_option,
Column3 data_type nullability column_option
ON partition_scheme_name (column)
```

CREATE TRIGGER

➤ To create a new trigger on a table that fires *after* a DML event:

```
CREATE TRIGGER trigger_name
ON table_name FOR dml_action -INSERT, UPDATE or DELETE
AS
...trigger_code
```

➤ To create a new trigger on a table that fires *instead of* a DML event:

```
CREATE TRIGGER trigger_name
ON view_or_table_name INSTEAD OF dml_action -INSERT, UPDATE or DELETE
AS
...trigger_code
```

CREATE VIEW

➤ To create a new view:

```
CREATE VIEW view_name
AS
...Select Statement
```

CREATE SCHEMA

➤ To create a new database schema with the option of specifying a non-dbo owner with the AUTHORIZATION clause:

```
CREATE SCHEMA schema_name AUTHORIZATION user_name
```

CREATE PARTITION FUNCTION

➤ To create a partition function to use when physically partitioning tables and indexes:

```
CREATE PARTITION FUNCTION partition_function_name ( input_parameter_type )
AS RANGE LEFT -- or RIGHT
FOR VALUES (value1, value2, value3, ...n)
```

CREATE PARTITION SCHEME

➤ To create a partition scheme to use when physically partitioning tables and indexes:

```
CREATE PARTITION SCHEME partition_scheme_name
AS PARTITION partition_function_name
TO (filegroup1, filegroup2, filegroup3, ...n)
```

SCRIPT COMMENT CONVENTIONS

➤ Inline comment:

```
SELECT ProductID, Name AS ProductName   -- Comment text
```

➤ Single-line comment:

```
/* Comment text */
```

or

```
-- Comment text
```

➤ Comment block:

```
/***************************************************
    spProductUpdateByCategory
    Created by Paul Turley, 5-21-11
    nospam@sqlreportservices.com
    Updates product price info for a category
    Revisions:
    3-24-12 - Fixed bug that formatted C:
              drive if wrong type was passed in.
 ***************************************************/
```

RESERVED WORDS

By convention, reserved words should not be used as names of objects. Reserved words typically are easy to see in SQL Server Management Studio, which changes the color of reserved words to blue. If the object names are delimited with double quotes or square brackets, which they often are if you are using a graphical tool to create queries, they may not show up as being color-coded.

The keywords shown in Table A-3 have significant meaning within T-SQL and should be avoided in object names and expressions. If any of these words must be used in a SQL expression, they must be contained within square brackets ([ ]).

TABLE A-3

ABLESAMPLE	EXIT	PROC
ADD	EXTERNAL	PROCEDURE
ALL	FETCH	PUBLIC
ALTER	FILE	RAISERROR
AND	FILLFACTOR	READ
ANY	FOR	READTEXT
AS	FOREIGN	RECONFIGURE
ASC	FREETEXT	REFERENCES
AUTHORIZATION	FREETEXTTABLE	REPLICATION
BACKUP	FROM	RESTORE
BEGIN	FULL	RESTRICT
BETWEEN	FUNCTION	RETURN
BREAK	GOTO	REVERT
BROWSE	GRANT	REVOKE
BULK	GROUP	RIGHT
BY	HAVING	ROLLBACK
CASCADE	HOLDLOCK	ROWCOUNT
CASE	IDENTITY	ROWGUIDCOL
CHECK	IDENTITY_INSERT	RULE
CHECKPOINT	IDENTITYCOL	SAVE
CLOSE	IF	SCHEMA

CLUSTERED	IN	SECURITYAUDIT
COALESCE	INDEX	SELECT
COLLATE	INNER	SEMANTICKEYPHRASETABLE
COLUMN	INSERT	SEMANTICSIMILARITYDETAILSTABLE
COMMIT	INTERSECT	SEMANTICSIMILARITYTABLE
COMPUTE	INTO	SESSION_USER
CONSTRAINT	IS	SET
CONTAINS	JOIN	SETUSER
CONTAINSTABLE	KEY	SHUTDOWN
CONTINUE	KILL	SOME
CONVERT	LEFT	STATISTICS
CREATE	LIKE	SYSTEM_USER
CROSS	LINENO	TABLE
CURRENT	LOAD	TEXTSIZE
CURRENT_DATE	MERGE	THEN
CURRENT_TIME	NATIONAL	TO
CURRENT_TIMESTAMP	NOCHECK	TOP
CURRENT_USER	NONCLUSTERED	TRAN
CURSOR	NOT	TRANSACTION
DATABASE	NULL	TRIGGER
DBCC	NULLIF	TRUNCATE
DEALLOCATE	OF	TRY_CONVERT
DECLARE	OFF	TSEQUAL
DEFAULT	OFFSETS	UNION
DELETE	ON	UNIQUE
DENY	OPEN	UNPIVOT
DESC	OPENDATASOURCE	UPDATE
DISK	OPENQUERY	UPDATETEXT
DISTINCT	OPENROWSET	USE

continues

TABLE A-3 *(continued)*

DISTRIBUTED	OPENXML	USER
DOUBLE	OPTION	VALUES
DROP	OR	VARYING
DUMP	ORDER	VIEW
ELSE	OUTER	WAITFOR
END	OVER	WHEN
ERRLVL	PERCENT	WHERE
ESCAPE	PIVOT	WHILE
EXCEPT	PLAN	

ODBC Reserved Words

Although the ODBC keywords listed in Table A-4 are not strictly prohibited, as a best practice to prevent driver inconsistencies, they should be avoided.

TABLE A-4

ABSOLUTE	EXEC	OVERLAPS
ACTION	EXECUTE	PAD
ADA	EXISTS	PARTIAL
ADD	EXTERNAL	PASCAL
ALL	EXTRACT	POSITION
ALLOCATE	FALSE	PRECISION
ALTER	FETCH	PREPARE
AND	FIRST	PRESERVE
ANY	FLOAT	PRIMARY
ARE	FOR	PRIOR
AS	FOREIGN	PRIVILEGES
ASC	FORTRAN	PROCEDURE
ASSERTION	FOUND	PUBLIC
AT	FROM	READ

AUTHORIZATION	FULL	REAL
AVG	GET	REFERENCES
BEGIN	GLOBAL	RELATIVE
BETWEEN	GO	RESTRICT
BIT	GOTO	REVOKE
BIT_LENGTH	GRANT	RIGHT
BOTH	GROUP	ROLLBACK
BY	HAVING	ROWS
CASCADE	HOUR	SCHEMA
CASCADED	IDENTITY	SCROLL
CASE	IMMEDIATE	SECOND
CAST	IN	SECTION
CATALOG	INCLUDE	SELECT
CHAR	INDEX	SESSION
CHAR_LENGTH	INDICATOR	SESSION_USER
CHARACTER	INITIALLY	SET
CHARACTER_LENGTH	INNER	SIZE
CHECK	INPUT	SMALLINT
CLOSE	INSENSITIVE	SOME
COALESCE	INSERT	SPACE
COLLATE	INT	SQL
COLLATION	INTEGER	SQLCA
COLUMN	INTERSECT	SQLCODE
COMMIT	INTERVAL	SQLERROR
CONNECT	INTO	SQLSTATE
CONNECTION	IS	SQLWARNING
CONSTRAINT	ISOLATION	SUBSTRING
CONSTRAINTS	JOIN	SUM
CONTINUE	KEY	SYSTEM_USER

continues

TABLE A-4 *(continued)*

CONVERT	LANGUAGE	TABLE
CORRESPONDING	LAST	TEMPORARY
COUNT	LEADING	THEN
CREATE	LEFT	TIME
CROSS	LEVEL	TIMESTAMP
CURRENT	LIKE	TIMEZONE_HOUR
CURRENT_DATE	LOCAL	TIMEZONE_MINUTE
CURRENT_TIME	LOWER	TO
CURRENT_TIMESTAMP	MATCH	TRAILING
CURRENT_USER	MAX	TRANSACTION
CURSOR	MIN	TRANSLATE
DATE	MINUTE	TRANSLATION
DAY	MODULE	TRIM
DEALLOCATE	MONTH	TRUE
DEC	NAMES	UNION
DECIMAL	NATIONAL	UNIQUE
DECLARE	NATURAL	UNKNOWN
DEFAULT	NCHAR	UPDATE
DEFERRABLE	NEXT	UPPER
DEFERRED	NO	USAGE
DELETE	NONE	USER
DESC	NOT	USING
DESCRIBE	NULL	VALUE
DESCRIPTOR	NULLIF	VALUES
DIAGNOSTICS	NUMERIC	VARCHAR
DISCONNECT	OCTET_LENGTH	VARYING
DISTINCT	OF	VIEW
DOMAIN	ON	WHEN

DOUBLE	ONLY	WHENEVER
DROP	OPEN	WHERE
ELSE	OPTION	WITH
END	OR	WORK
END-EXEC	ORDER	WRITE
ESCAPE	OUTER	YEAR
EXCEPT	OUTPUT	ZONE
EXCEPTION		

Future Reserved Words

Table A-5 contains keywords that may be reserved in future editions of SQL Server.

TABLE A-5

ABSOLUTE	HOST	RELATIVE
ACTION	HOUR	RELEASE
ADMIN	IGNORE	RESULT
AFTER	IMMEDIATE	RETURNS
AGGREGATE	INDICATOR	ROLE
ALIAS	INITIALIZE	ROLLUP
ALLOCATE	INITIALLY	ROUTINE
ARE	INOUT	ROW
ARRAY	INPUT	ROWS
ASENSITIVE	INT	SAVEPOINT
ASSERTION	INTEGER	SCROLL
ASYMMETRIC	INTERSECTION	SCOPE
AT	INTERVAL	SEARCH
ATOMIC	ISOLATION	SECOND
BEFORE	ITERATE	SECTION
BINARY	LANGUAGE	SENSITIVE

continues

TABLE A-5 *(continued)*

BIT	LARGE	SEQUENCE
BLOB	LAST	SESSION
BOOLEAN	LATERAL	SETS
BOTH	LEADING	SIMILAR
BREADTH	LESS	SIZE
CALL	LEVEL	SMALLINT
CALLED	LIKE_REGEX	SPACE
CARDINALITY	LIMIT	SPECIFIC
CASCADED	LN	SPECIFICTYPE
CAST	LOCAL	SQL
CATALOG	LOCALTIME	SQLEXCEPTION
CHAR	LOCALTIMESTAMP	SQLSTATE
CHARACTER	LOCATOR	SQLWARNING
CLASS	MAP	START
CLOB	MATCH	STATE
COLLATION	MEMBER	STATEMENT
COLLECT	METHOD	STATIC
COMPLETION	MINUTE	STDDEV_POP
CONDITION	MOD	STDDEV_SAMP
CONNECT	MODIFIES	STRUCTURE
CONNECTION	MODIFY	SUBMULTISET
CONSTRAINTS	MODULE	SUBSTRING_REGEX
CONSTRUCTOR	MONTH	SYMMETRIC
CORR	MULTISET	SYSTEM
CORRESPONDING	NAMES	TEMPORARY
COVAR_POP	NATURAL	TERMINATE
COVAR_SAMP	NCHAR	THAN
CUBE	NCLOB	TIME

CUME_DIST	NEW	TIMESTAMP
CURRENT_CATALOG	NEXT	TIMEZONE_HOUR
CURRENT_DEFAULT_TRANSFORM_GROUP	NO	TIMEZONE_MINUTE
CURRENT_PATH	NONE	TRAILING
CURRENT_ROLE	NORMALIZE	TRANSLATE_REGEX
CURRENT_SCHEMA	NUMERIC	TRANSLATION
CURRENT_TRANSFORM_GROUP_FOR_TYPE	OBJECT	TREAT
CYCLE	OCCURRENCES_REGEX	TRUE
DATA	OLD	UESCAPE
DATE	ONLY	UNDER
DAY	OPERATION	UNKNOWN
DEC	ORDINALITY	UNNEST
DECIMAL	OUT	USAGE
DEFERRABLE	OUTPUT	USING
DEFERRED	OVERLAY	VALUE
DEPTH	PAD	VAR_POP
DEREF	PARAMETER	VAR_SAMP
DESCRIBE	PARAMETERS	VARCHAR
DESCRIPTOR	PARTIAL	VARIABLE
DESTROY	PARTITION	WHENEVER
DESTRUCTOR	PATH	WIDTH_BUCKET
DETERMINISTIC	PERCENT_RANK	WINDOW
DICTIONARY	PERCENTILE_CONT	WITHIN
DIAGNOSTICS	PERCENTILE_DISC	WITHOUT
DISCONNECT	POSITION_REGEX	WORK
DOMAIN	POSTFIX	WRITE
DYNAMIC	PREFIX	XMLAGG
EACH	PREORDER	XMLATTRIBUTES
ELEMENT	PREPARE	XMLBINARY

continues

TABLE A-5 *(continued)*

END-EXEC	PRESERVE	XMLCAST
EQUALS	PRIOR	XMLCOMMENT
EVERY	PRIVILEGES	XMLCONCAT
EXCEPTION	RANGE	XMLDOCUMENT
FALSE	READS	XMLELEMENT
FILTER	REAL	XMLEXISTS
FIRST	RECURSIVE	XMLFOREST
FLOAT	REF	XMLITERATE
FOUND	REFERENCING	XMLNAMESPACES
FREE	REGR_AVGX	XMLPARSE
FULLTEXTTABLE	REGR_AVGY	XMLPI
FUSION	REGR_COUNT	XMLQUERY
GENERAL	REGR_INTERCEPT	XMLSERIALIZE
GET	REGR_R2	XMLTABLE
GLOBAL	REGR_SLOPE	XMLTEXT
GO	REGR_SXX	XMLVALIDATE
GROUPING	REGR_SXY	YEAR
HOLD	REGR_SYY	ZONE

B

T-SQL System Variables and Functions

The terms "variable" and "function" are often used interchangeably. SQL Server Books Online documents some variables as though they were functions. However, it is important to note that variables are used in expressions to obtain a value, whereas functions process specific business logic and may return a value. Many functions accept input arguments.

This appendix applies to SQL Server 2008, 2008 R2, and 2012. It is a reference of common T-SQL objects provided as a convenient guide to many functions and variables that may be useful in report queries. It is by no means meant to be a comprehensive reference. For complete details and examples of usage, consult Books Online.

SYSTEM GLOBAL VARIABLES

The system-supplied global variables are organized into the following categories:

➤ Configuration

➤ Cursor

➤ System

➤ System statistics

Configuration

VARIABLE	RETURN TYPE	DESCRIPTION
@@DATEFIRST	tinyint	The system setting for the first day of the week: 1 = Monday 2 = Tuesday 3 = Wednesday 4 = Thursday 5 = Friday 6 = Saturday 7 = Sunday The U.S. default is 7.
@@DBTS	varbinary	The last assigned unique TimeStamp value.
@@LANGID	smallint	The current language ID for the server: 0 = U.S. English 1 = German 2 = French and so on.
@@LANGUAGE	nvarchar	The current language string for the server. Returns the language name in the native language form (us_english, Deutsch, Français, Dansk, Español, Italiano, and so on).
@@LOCK_TIMEOUT	int	Locks the time-out setting for the current session in milliseconds (ms).
@@MAX_CONNECTIONS	int	The maximum concurrent connections setting for the server.
@@MAX_PRECISION	tinyint	The maximum precision setting for the decimal and numeric types. The default is 38 significant digits (the total to the left and right of the decimal point).
@@MICROSOFTVERSION	int	An internal tracking number used by product development and support groups at Microsoft.
@@NESTLEVEL	int	The current number of nested stored procedure or trigger calls. This may be used to limit cascading and/or recursive calls prior to reaching the system limit of 32 recursive calls.

VARIABLE	RETURN TYPE	DESCRIPTION
@@OPTIONS	int	The set of query-processing options for the current user session. Multiple options are combined mathematically using bitwise addition (such as `If SELECT @@OPTIONS & (512 + 8192) > 0...`). Any combination of option values can be added to determine whether all these options are enabled. Option values: 1 = DISABLE_DEF_CNST_CHK 2 = IMPLICIT_TRANSACTIONS 4 = CURSOR_CLOSE_ON_COMMIT 8 = ANSI_WARNINGS 16 = ANSI_PADDING 32 = ANSI_NULLS 64 = ARITHABORT 128 = ARITHIGNORE 256 = QUOTED_IDENTIFIER 512 = NOCOUNT 1024 = ANSI_NULL_DFLT_ON 2048 = ANSI_NULL_DFLT_OFF 4096 = CONCAT_NULL_YIELDS_NULL 8192 = NUMERIC_ROUNDABORT 16384 = XACT_ABORT
@@REMSERVER	nvarchar	The name of the remote server if executing remote procedures.
@@SERVERNAME	nvarchar	The name of the current server.
@@SERVICENAME	nvarchar	The name of the Windows service for the current SQL Server instance.
@@SPID	int	The process/session ID assigned to the current user's connection.
@@TEXTSIZE	int	The current value of the `TEXTSIZE` option for a query returning data from a `text`, `ntext`, or `image` type. The default setting is `4,096` (4 KB).
@@VERSION	nvarchar	A text string with detailed information about the current version of SQL Server. This includes the major version, build number, service pack, and copyright information.

Cursor

VARIABLE	RETURN TYPE	DESCRIPTION
@@CURSOR_ROWS	int	The row count for the currently open cursor. Used for explicit cursor processing following an OPEN command. If an asynchronous cursor is opened, the row count is unknown, and this variable returns -1.
@@FETCH_STATUS	int	Used as a flag to indicate whether the open cursor has navigated past the last row (EOF). Status values: 0 = Normal fetch operation -1 = Fetch past last row or unsuccessful -2 = Fetched row has been removed

System

VARIABLE	RETURN TYPE	DESCRIPTION
@@ERROR	int	The value of the most recent error within the current user session. Error numbers (from the sysmessages table) are used to determine the status of an error condition.
@@IDENTITY	numeric	The value of the most recently generated identity value. This is typically the result of an identity column insert.
@@ROWCOUNT	int	The number of rows affected by, or returned by, the last operation.
@@TRANCOUNT	int	The number of currently active transactions. Used to determine the number of nested transactions. The maximum number of nested transactions is 11.

System Statistics

VARIABLE	RETURN TYPE	DESCRIPTION
@@CONNECTIONS	int	The total connects that have been opened or attempted since the SQL Server service was last started.
@@CPU_BUSY	int	The total time in milliseconds that the server has not been idle since the SQL Server service was last started.
@@IDLE	int	The total time in milliseconds that the server has been idle since the SQL Server service was last started.

VARIABLE	RETURN TYPE	DESCRIPTION
@@IO_BUSY	int	The total time in milliseconds that the server has performed physical disk I/O operations since the SQL Server service was last started.
@@PACK_RECEIVED	int	The total number of network packets received by the server since the SQL Server service was last started.
@@PACK_SENT	int	The total number of network packets sent by the server since the SQL Server service was last started.
@@PACKET_ERRORS	int	The total number of network packet errors that have occurred since the SQL Server service was last started.
@@TIMETICKS	int	The number of milliseconds per CPU tick. Each tick takes 1/32nd of a second.
@@TOTAL_ERRORS	int	The total number of disk read/write errors that have occurred, while performing physical disk I/O, since the SQL Server service was last started.
@@TOTAL_READ	int	The total number of physical disk reads that have occurred since the SQL Server service was last started.
@@TOTAL_WRITE	int	The total number of physical disk writes that have occurred since the SQL Server service was last started.

SYSTEM FUNCTIONS

The system functions are organized into the following categories:

➤ Aggregation

➤ Checksum

➤ Conversion

➤ Cryptographic

➤ Cursor

➤ Date and time

➤ Error handling

➤ Image/text

➤ Mathematical

➤ Metadata

➤ Ranking

➤ Rowset

➤   Security

➤   String manipulation

➤   System

➤   System statistics

Aggregation

FUNCTION	RETURN TYPE	DESCRIPTION
AVG()	(numeric — depends on input)	Calculates the arithmetic average for a range of column values. Internally, this function counts rows and calculates the sum for all non-null values in the column and then divides the sum by the count. Returns the same `numeric` data type as the column.
COUNT()	int	Counts all non-null values for a column. The row count is returned using COUNT(*) regardless of null values.
COUNT_BIG()	bigint	The same as COUNT(), but returns a `bigint` type rather than an `int` type.
GROUPING()	int	Used in conjunction with ROLLUP and CUBE operations in a GROUP BY query. This function returns 0 to indicate that it is on a detail row and 1 to indicate a summary row.
MAX()	(numeric or date — depends on input)	Returns the largest value in a range of column values.
MIN()	(numeric or date — depends on input)	Returns the smallest value in a range of column values.
STDEV()	float	Calculates the standard deviation for a range of non-null column values.
STDEVP()	float	Calculates the standard deviation over a population for a range of non-null column values.
SUM()	(numeric — depends on input)	Calculates the arithmetic sum for a range of non-null column values. If all values are NULL, it returns NULL.

FUNCTION	RETURN TYPE	DESCRIPTION
VAR()	float	Calculates the statistical variance for a range of non-null column values. If all values are NULL, it returns NULL.
VARP()	float	Calculates the statistical variance over a population for a range of non-null column values. If all values are NULL, it returns NULL.

Checksum

FUNCTION	RETURN TYPE	DESCRIPTION
BINARY_ CHECKSUM()	int	Calculates a checksum value for a row or range of column values. This function accepts a single column name, a comma-delimited list of columns, or * to use the entire row. Accepts columns of all types except text, ntext, image, cursor, and sql_variant. The returned value itself is meaningless but consistently yields the same result for a column or row unless a value changes. String comparisons are case-sensitive.
CHECKSUM()	int	Calculates a checksum value for a row or range of column values. This function accepts a single column name, a comma-delimited list of columns, or * to use the entire row. Accepts columns of all types except text, ntext, image, cursor, and sql_variant. The returned value itself is meaningless but consistently yields the same result for a column or row unless a value changes. String comparisons are case-insensitive.
CHECKSUM_AGG()	int	Calculates a single checksum value for a range of int type column values. When applied to the result of the CHECKSUM() or BINARY_CHECKSUM() functions, returns a scalar (single value) checksum value for the entire range of values. Can be used to detect value changes over a table or range of column values.

Conversion

FUNCTION	RETURN TYPE	DESCRIPTION
`CAST()`	Returns a specified type.	Converts a value into a specified data type. `CAST(the_value AS the_type)`

`CONVERT()`	Returns a specified type.	Converts (and optionally formats) a value into a specified data type. Formatting can be applied to `numeric` and `date` types.
		`CONVERT(the_type, the_value)`
		or
		`CONVERT(the_type, the_value, format_number)`

Cryptographic

FUNCTION	RETURN TYPE	DESCRIPTION
`AsymKey_ID()`	`int`	Returns the ID of an asymmetric key.
`Cert_ID`	`int`	Returns the ID of a certificate.
`CertProperty()`	`sql_variant`	Returns the value of a specified certificate property.
`DecryptByAsmKey()`	`varbinary`	Decrypts data with an asymmetric key.
`DecryptByCert()`	`varbinary`	Decrypts data with a certificate's private key.
`DecryptByKey()`	`varbinary`	Decrypts data using a symmetric key.
`DecryptByKeyAutoCert()`	`varbinary`	Decrypts by using a symmetric key that is automatically decrypted with a certificate.
`DecryptByPassPrase()`	`varbinary`	Decrypts data that was encrypted with a passphrase.
`EncryptByAsmKey()`	`varbinary`	Encrypts data with an asymmetric key.
`EncryptByCert()`	`varbinary`	Encrypts data with a certificate's public key.
`EncryptByKey()`	`varbinary`	Encrypts a string of text using a unique identifier key.
`EncryptByPassPhrase()`	`varbinary`	Encrypts a string of text using a passphrase.

FUNCTION	RETURN TYPE	DESCRIPTION
Key_GUID()	uniqueidentifier	Returns the global unique identifier of a named encryption key.
Key_ID()	int	Returns the integer ID of a named symmetric key.
SignByAsymKey()	varbinary	Applies a digital signature generated by an asymmetrical key to a block of plain text.
SignByCert()	varbinary	Applies a digital signature generated by a certificate key to a block of plain text.
VerifySignedByAsmKey()	int	Verifies that text signed by an asymmetrical key has not been altered.
VerifySignedByCert()	int	Verifies that text signed by a certificate has not been altered.

Cursor

FUNCTION	RETURN TYPE	DESCRIPTION
CURSOR_STATUS()	smallint	Returns the status of a previously opened cursor. 1 = Open and populated 0 = Contains no records −1 = Closed −2 = No cursor or deallocated −3 = Doesn't exist

Date and Time

FUNCTION	RETURN TYPE	DESCRIPTION
CURRENT_TIMESTAMP()	datetime	Returns the current date and time. Is synonymous with the GETDATE() function. It exists for ANSI-SQL compliance.
DATEADD()	datetime or smalldatetime (depending on input type)	Returns a date value (datetime or smalldatetime) from a date value added by *X* number of date interval units. Units may be Year, Quarter, Month, DayOfYear, Day, Hour, Minute, Second, or Millisecond.

continues

(continued)

FUNCTION	RETURN TYPE	DESCRIPTION
DATEDIFF()	int	Returns an integer representing the difference between two date values (datetime or smalldatetime) in specified date interval units. Units may be Year, Quarter, Month, DayOfYear, Day, Hour, Minute, Second, or Millisecond.
DATENAME()	nvarchar	Similar to DATEPART(). Returns a character string representing the specified datepart for a date value. The datepart parameter is the same as the DATEDIFF() interval and includes Year, Quarter, Month, DayOfYear, Day, Hour, Minute, Second, or Millisecond.
DATEPART()	int	Similar to DATENAME(). However, it returns the integer value representing the specified datepart for a date value. The datepart parameter is the same as the DATEDIFF() interval and includes Year, Quarter, Month, DayOfYear, Day, Hour, Minute, Second, or Millisecond.
DAY()	int	Returns the day date part for a date as an integer.
GETDATE()	datetime	Returns the current date and time value.
GETUTCDATE()	datetime	Returns the current date and time value for the Universal Time Zone (UTC), based on the server's time zone settings. UTC is the same as Greenwich Mean Time (GMT).
ISDATE()	int	Returns a flag to indicate whether a specified value is, or is capable of being converted into, a date value.
MONTH()	int	Returns the month part for a date as an integer.
SWITCHOFFSET()	datetimeoffset (Date)	Returns and/or modifies the UTC offset for a time zone.

FUNCTION	RETURN TYPE	DESCRIPTION
SYSDATETIME()	datetime	Returns the current database system time stamp.
SYSDATETIMEOFFSET()	datetimeoffset (Date)	Returns the current database time offset.
SYSUTCDATETIME()	datetime2	Returns the current database system UTC time stamp.
TODATETIMEOFFSET()	datetimeoffset	Modifies the time zone offset for a date and time.
YEAR()	int	Returns the year part for a date as an integer.

Error Handling

FUNCTION	RETURN TYPE	DESCRIPTION
ERROR_LINE()	int	Returns the line number of the last error when called in a CATCH block.
ERROR_MESSAGE()	nvarchar	Returns the full error text for the last error when called in a CATCH block.
ERROR_NUMBER()	int	Returns the system- or user-defined error number for the last error when called in a CATCH block.
ERROR_PROCEDURE()	nvarchar	Returns the name of the stored procedure or function that raised the last error when called in a CATCH block.
ERROR_SEVERITY()	int	Returns the system- or user-defined severity value for the last error when called in a CATCH block.
ERROR_STATE()	int	Returns the state number for the last error when called in a CATCH block.
XACT_STATE()	smallint	Tests the commitability of the current transaction within a CATCH block. Returns –1 if the transaction is uncommittable.

Image/Text

FUNCTION	RETURN TYPE	DESCRIPTION
PATINDEX()	bigint or int (depending on input type)	Returns the character index (first position) for a character string pattern occurring within another character string. Similar to CHARINDEX() but supports wildcards. Returns bigint for varchar(max) and nvarchar(max) type strings; otherwise, returns int.
TEXTPTR()	varbinary	Returns a varbinary text pointer handle to be used with the READTEXT(), WRITETEXT(), and UPDATETEXT() functions. Used to perform special operations on text, ntext, and image type column data.
TEXTVALID()	int	Verifies a varbinary text pointer value, obtained from the TEXTPTR() function.

Mathematical

FUNCTION	RETURN TYPE	DESCRIPTION
ABS()	(numeric — same type as input)	Returns the absolute value for a numeric value.
ACOS()	float	Computes the arccosine (an angle) in radians.
ASIN()	float	Computes the arcsine (an angle) in radians.
ATAN()	float	Computes the arctangent (an angle) in radians.
ATN2()	float	Computes the arctangent of two values in radians.
CEILING()	(numeric — same type as input)	Returns the smallest integer value that is greater than or equal to a number.
COS()	float	Computes the cosine of an angle in radians.

FUNCTION	RETURN TYPE	DESCRIPTION
COT()	float	Computes the cotangent of an angle in radians.
DEGREES()	(numeric — same type as input)	Converts an angle from radians into degrees.
EXP()	float	Returns the natural logarithm raised to a specified exponent. The result is in exponential form.
FLOOR()	(numeric — same type as input)	Returns the largest integer value that is less than or equal to a number.
LOG()	float	Calculates the natural logarithm of a number using base-2 (binary) numbering.
LOG10()	float	Calculates the natural logarithm of a number using base-10 numbering.
PI()	float	Returns the value of pi.
POWER()	float	Raises a value to a specified exponent as FLOAT(*the_value*, *the_exponent*).
RADIANS()	(numeric — same type as input)	Converts an angle from degrees into radians.
RAND()	float	Returns a fractional number based on a randomizing algorithm. Accepts an optional seed value.
ROUND()	(numeric — same type as input)	Rounds a fractional value to a specified precision.
SIGN()	float	Returns -1 or 1 depending on whether a single argument value is negative or positive.
SIN()	float	Computes the sine of an angle in radians.
SQRT()	float	Returns the square root of a value.
SQUARE()	float	Returns the square (n^2) of a value.
TAN()	float	Computes the tangent of an angle in radians.

Metadata

FUNCTION	RETURN TYPE	DESCRIPTION
ASSEMBLYPROPERTY()	sql_variant	Returns descriptive information about a specified assembly property.
COL_LENGTH()	int	Returns the length of a column from the column name.
COL_NAME()	sysname (nvarchar)	Returns the name of a column from the object ID.
COLUMNPROPERTY()	int	Returns a flag to indicate the state of a column property.
DATABASEPROPERTY()	int	This function is maintained for backward compatibility with older SQL Server versions. Returns a flag to indicate the state of a database property.
DATABASEPROPERTYEX()	sqlvariant	Returns a numeric flag or string to indicate the state of a database property.
DB_ID()	smallint	Returns the database ID from the database name.
DB_NAME()	nvarchar	Returns the database name from the database ID.
FILE_ID()	smallint	Returns the file ID from the filename.
FILEGROUP_ID()	int	Returns the ID for a file group name.
FILEGROUP_NAME()	nvarchar(128)	Returns the file group name for a file group ID.
FILEGROUPPROPERTY()	int	Returns a specified file group property value for a file group name and property name.
FILEPROPERTY()	int	Returns a specified file property value for a filename and property name.
FILE_NAME()	nvarchar	Returns the filename from the file ID.
fn_listextendedproperty()	table	Returns a table object populated with extended property names and their settings.
FULLTEXTCATALOGPROPERTY()	int	Returns a flag to indicate the state of a full-text catalog property.

FUNCTION	RETURN TYPE	DESCRIPTION
FULLTEXTSERVICEPROPERTY()	int	Returns a flag to indicate the state of a full-text service property.
INDEX_COL()	nvarchar	Returns the name of a column contained in a specified index, by table, index, and column ID.
INDEXKEY_PROPERTY()	int	Returns a flag to indicate the state of an index key property.
INDEXPROPERTY()	int	Returns a flag indicating the state of an index property.
OBJECT_ID()	int	Returns an object ID from the object name.
OBJECT_NAME()	nchar	Returns an object name from the object ID.
OBJECTPROPERTY()	int	Returns property information from several different types of objects. It is advisable to use a function designed to query specific object types, if possible. Returns a flag indicating the state of an object property.
OBJECTPROPERTYEX()	sql_variant	Similar to OBJECTPROPERTY() but returns descriptive property values.
SCHEMA_ID()	int	Returns the schema ID for a schema name.
SCHEMA_NAME()	sysname (nvarchar)	Returns the schema name for a schema ID.
SQL_VARIANT_PROPERTY()	sql_variant	Returns the base data type and other information about a sql_variant value.
TYPE_ID()	int	Returns the ID for a specified data type name.
TYPE_NAME()	sysname	Returns the data type name of a specified type ID.
TYPEPROPERTY()	int	Returns information about data type properties.

Ranking

FUNCTION	RETURN TYPE	DESCRIPTION
DENSE_RANK()	bigint	Returns a running incremental value based on an ORDER BY clause passed into the function. Doesn't preserve the ordinal position of the row in the list if there are ties.
NTILE(*n*)	bigint	Returns an evenly distributed ranking value, dividing the result into a finite number of ranked groups.
RANK()	bigint	Returns a running incremental value based on an ORDER BY clause passed into the function. Preserves the ordinal position of the row in the list with duplicate values for ties followed by subsequent skips.
ROW_NUMBER()	bigint	Returns a running incremental value based on an ORDER BY clause passed into the function.

Rowset

FUNCTION	RETURN TYPE	DESCRIPTION
CONTAINSTABLE()	table	Returns a table object that can be used in a join operation. Each row in this table contains a Key column value, which is the primary key value for qualifying rows of the queried table. This key value is useful for joining the resulting table object back to the physical table to obtain column values. Two arguments are passed: the name of the indexed table and a search string containing words to be matched.
FREETEXTTABLE()	table	Similar to CONTAINSTABLE(), but the search condition can match inexact phrasing rather than exact words.
OPENDATASOURCE()	table	Used to open an ad hoc connection to a remote OLE DB data source and return a table reference to a database object. Arguments include the name of a registered OLE DB provider, a connection string, and the four-part name of a database object.

FUNCTION	RETURN TYPE	DESCRIPTION
OPENQUERY()	table	Used to reference an existing linked server and return the results of a query. Arguments include the name of the linked server and a query string.
OPENROWSET()	table	Used to connect to a remote OLE DB data source and return the results of a query. Arguments include the name of a registered OLE DB provider, a connection string, and a query string.
OPENXML()	table	Transforms an XML document string into a rowset table. The table structure conforms to the standard "edge" table format. The `sp_xml_preparedocument` system stored procedure must be called first to obtain a document handle ID, which is then passed to this function, along with the document text.

Security

FUNCTION	RETURN TYPE	DESCRIPTION
fn_trace_geteventinfo()	table	Returns a `table` type populated with event information for a specified trace ID.
fn_trace_getfilterinfo()	table	Returns a `table` type populated with information about filters applied to a trace, for a specified trace ID.
fn_trace_getinfo()	table	Returns a `table` type populated with trace information for a specified trace ID.
fn_trace_gettable()	table	Returns a `table` type populated with file information for a specified trace ID.
HAS_DBACCESS()	int	Returns a flag indicating whether the current user has access to a specified database.
IS_MEMBER()	int	Returns a flag indicating whether the current user is a member of a Windows group or SQL Server role.

continues

(continued)

FUNCTION	RETURN TYPE	DESCRIPTION
IS_SRVROLEMEMBER()	int	Returns a flag indicating whether the current user is a member of a database server role.
ORIGINAL_LOGIN()	sysname (varchar)	Returns the first user or login name for the first system login in the current session context.
SUSER_SID()	varbinary	Returns the security ID for a specified username.
SUSER_SNAME()	nvarchar	Returns the username for a specified security ID.
USER_ID()	int	Returns a username for a specified user ID.

String Manipulation

FUNCTION	RETURN TYPE	DESCRIPTION
ASCII()	int	Returns the numeric ASCII character value for a standard character.
CHAR()	char	Returns the ASCII character for a numeric ASCII character value.
CHARINDEX()	int	Similar to PATINDEX(), returns the index (character position) of the first occurrence of a character string within another character string.
DIFFERENCE()	int	Returns the numeric difference between two character strings based on the consensus Soundex values.
LEFT()	varchar or nvarchar	Returns the leftmost *X* characters from a character string.
LEN()	int	Returns the length of a character string.
LOWER()	varchar or nvarchar	Converts a character string into all lowercase characters.
LTRIM()	varchar or nvarchar	Removes leading spaces from the left side of a character string.

FUNCTION	RETURN TYPE	DESCRIPTION
NCHAR()	nchar	Like the CHAR() function, returns the Unicode character for a numeric character value.
PATINDEX()	int or bigint	Returns the index (first character position) for the first occurrence of characters matching a specified pattern within another character string. Wildcard characters may be used.
QUOTENAME()	nvarchar	Returns a character string with square brackets around the input value. Used with SQL Server object names so that they can be passed into an expression.
REPLACE()	varchar or nvarchar	Returns a character string with all occurrences of one character or substring replaced with another character or substring.
REPLICATE()	varchar or nvarchar	Returns a character string consisting of a specified number of repeated characters.
REVERSE()	varchar or nvarchar	Returns a character string with all characters in reverse order.
RIGHT()	varchar or nvarchar	Returns a specific number of characters from the rightmost side of a character string.
RTRIM()	varchar or nvarchar	Removes trailing spaces from the right side of a character string.
SOUNDEX()	varchar	Returns a four-character alphanumeric string representing the approximate phonetic value of a word, based on the U.S. Census Soundex algorithm.
SPACE()	char	Returns a character string consisting of a specified number of spaces.
STR()	char	Returns a character string value that represents a converted numeric data type. Three arguments include the value, the overall length, and the number of decimal positions.

continues

(continued)

FUNCTION	RETURN TYPE	DESCRIPTION
STUFF()	Character or binary types, depending on input	Returns a character string with one string placed into another string at a given position and for a specified length.
SUBSTRING()	Character or binary types, depending on input	Returns a portion of a character string from a specified position and for a specified length.
UNICODE()	int	Returns the numeric Unicode character value for a specified character.
UPPER()	varchar or nvarchar	Converts a character string into all upper-case characters.

System

FUNCTION	RETURN TYPE	DESCRIPTION
APP_NAME()	nvarchar	Each session is associated with an application name, passed to the database server by explicit program code or by the driver or data provider.
COALESCE()	Same type as input	Returns the first non-null value from a comma-delimited list of expressions.
COLLATIONPROPERTY()	sql_variant	Returns the value of a specific property for a specified collation. Properties include CodePage, LCID, and ComparisonStyle.
COLUMNS_UPDATED()	varbinary	Used only within an Insert or Update trigger. Returns a bitmap of modified column flags for the current table. Bytes are left-to-right, with the bits in each byte ordered right-to-left, representing the state (0 = unmodified, 1 = modified) of each column.
CURRENT_USER()	sysname (varchar)	Returns the name of the current user. Synonymous with the USER_NAME() function.
DATALENGTH()	int	Returns the number of bytes used to store or handle a value. For ANSI string types, this returns the same value as the LEN() function, but for other data types the value may be different.

FUNCTION	RETURN TYPE	DESCRIPTION
fn_Get_SQL()	table	Returns a table type populated with the full text of a query based on a process handle. This value is stored in the sysprocesses table referencing a SPID. This function was introduced with SQL Server 2000 SP3.
fn_HelpCollations()	table	Returns a table type populated with a list of collations supported by the current version of SQL Server.
fn_ServerSharedDrives()	table	Returns a table type populated with a list of drives shared by the server.
fn_VirtualFileStats()	table	Returns a table type populated with I/O statistics for database files, including log files.
FORMATMESSAGE()	nvarchar	Returns an error message from the sysmessages table for a specified message number and comma-delimited list of parameters.
GETANSINULL()	int	Returns the nullability setting for the database, according to the ANSI_NULL_DFLT_ON and ANSI_NULL_DFLT_OFF database settings.
HOST_ID()	char	Returns the workstation ID for the current session.
HOST_NAME()	nchar	Returns the workstation name for the current session.
IDENT_CURRENT()	sql_variant	Returns the last identity value generated for a specified table regardless of the session and scope.
IDENT_INCR()	numeric	Returns the increment value specified in the creation of the last identity column.
IDENT_SEED()	numeric	Returns the seed value specified in the creation of the last identity column.
IDENTITY()	Same as input	Used in a SELECT ... INTO statement to insert an explicitly generated identity value into a column.
ISNULL()	Same as input	Determines whether a specified value is null and then returns a provided replacement value.

continues

(continued)

FUNCTION	RETURN TYPE	DESCRIPTION
ISNUMERIC()	int	Returns a flag to indicate whether a specified value is, or is capable of being converted into, a numeric value.
NEWID()	uniqueidentifier	Returns a newly generated `uniqueidentifier` type value. This is a 128-bit integer, globally unique value, usually expressed as an alphanumeric hexadecimal representation (such as 89DE6247-C2E2-42DB-8CE8-A787E505D7EA). This type is often used for primary key values in replicated and semi-connected systems.
NULLIF()	Same as input	Returns a NULL value when two specified arguments have equivalent values.
PARSENAME()	nchar	Returns a specific part of a four-part object name.
ROWCOUNT_BIG()	bigint	Like the @@ROWCOUNT variable, returns the number of rows either returned by or modified by the last statement. Returns a `bigint` type.
SCOPE_IDENTITY()	sql_variant	Like the @@IDENTITY variable, returns the last Identity value generated, but is limited to the current session and scope (stored procedure, batch, or module).
SERVERPROPERTY()	sql_variant	Returns a flag indicating the state of a server property. Properties include `Collation`, `Edition`, `EngineEdition`, `InstanceName`, `IsClustered`, `IsFullTextInstalled`, `IsIntegratedSecurityOnly`, `IsSingleUser`, `IsSyncWithBackup`, `LicenseType`, `MachineName`, `NumLicenses`, `ProcessID`, `ProductLevel`, `ProductVersion`, and `ServerName`.
SESSION_USER	nchar	Returns the current username. The function is called without parentheses.

FUNCTION	RETURN TYPE	DESCRIPTION
SESSIONPROPERTY()	sql_variant	Returns a flag indicating the state of a session property. Properties include ANSI_NULLS, ANSI_PADDING, ANSI_WARNINGS, ARITHABORT, CONCAT_NULL_YIELDS_NULL, NUMERIC_ROUNDABORT, and QUOTED_IDENTIFIER.
STATS_DATE()	datetime	Returns the date that statistics for a specified index were last updated.
SYSTEM_USER()	nvarchar	Returns the current username. The function is called without parentheses.
USER_NAME()	nvarchar	Returns the username for a specified user ID.

System Statistics

FUNCTION	RETURN TYPE	DESCRIPTION
sys.dm_io_virtual_file_stats()	table	Returns a table type populated with I/O statistics for database files, including log files.
sys.dm_db_index_operational_stats()	table	Returns current I/O, locking, latching, and access method activity for each table or index in the database.
sys.dm_db_index_physical_stats()	table	Returns size and fragmentation information for the data and indexes of a specified table or view.
sys.dm_db_index_usage_stats()	rowset	Returns counts of different types of index operations and the time each type of operation was last performed.
sys.dm_db_missing_index_columns()	table	Returns information about database table columns that are missing an index.

MDX Reference

This appendix provides information on aspects of the SQL Server 2008, 2008 R2, and 2012 implementations of the Multidimensional Expressions (MDX) language relevant to Reporting Services authors. The material provided here is intended to provide a quick reference, not to be fully instructional. Nor is this material intended to provide an overview of SQL Server Analysis Services. For a complete reference on these topics, refer to *Professional Microsoft SQL Server 2012 Analysis Services with MDX* (Wrox).

OBJECT IDENTIFIERS

All objects within Analysis Services — cubes, cube dimensions, attribute hierarchies, user hierarchies, hierarchy levels, members, and so on — are referenced through an object identifier. An object identifier is a value containing between 1 and 100 characters. The first character of the object identifier must be a letter or underscore. Subsequent characters can be letters, numbers, or underscores. Object identifiers cannot contain spaces or special characters and cannot be a reserved keyword, as discussed in the next section. Identifiers adhering to these rules are called regular identifiers.

An object identifier violating one or more of these rules is known as a delimited identifier. A delimited identifier must be encapsulated by square brackets — known as the object's delimiters — for the identifier to be correctly interpreted. Although required for delimited identifiers, square brackets can also be used with regular identifiers.

RESERVED KEYWORDS

Table C-1 lists reserved keywords within SQL Server 2012 Analysis Services MDX.

TABLE C-1

ABSOLUTE	ERROR	PERIODSTODATE
ACTIONPARAMETERSET	EXCEPT	POST
ADDCALCULATEDMEMBERS	EXCLUDEEMPTY	PREDICT
AFTER	EXTRACT	PREVMEMBER
AGGREGATE	FALSE	PROPERTIES
ALL	FILTER	PROPERTY
ALLMEMBERS	FIRSTCHILD	QTD
ANCESTOR	FIRSTSIBLING	RANK
ANCESTORS	FOR	RECURSIVE
AND	FREEZE	RELATIVE
AS	FROM	ROLLUPCHILDREN
ASC	GENERATE	ROOT
ASCENDANTS	GLOBAL	ROWS
AVERAGE	GROUP	SCOPE
AXIS	GROUPING	SECTIONS
BASC	HEAD	SELECT
BDESC	HIDDEN	SELF
BEFORE	HIERARCHIZE	SELF_AND_AFTER
BEFORE_AND_AFTER	HIERARCHY	SELF_AND_BEFORE
BOTTOMCOUNT	IGNORE	SELF_BEFORE_AFTER
BOTTOMPERCENT	IIF	SESSION
BOTTOMSUM	INCLUDEEMPTY	SET
BY	INDEX	SETTOARRAY
CACHE	INTERSECT	SETTOSTR
CALCULATE	IS	SORT
CALCULATION	ISANCESTOR	STDDEV
CALCULATIONCURRENTPASS	ISEMPTY	STDDEVP
CALCULATIONPASSVALUE	ISGENERATION	STDEV

CALCULATIONS	ISLEAF	STDEVP
CALL	ISSIBLING	STORAGE
CELL	ITEM	STRIPCALCULATEDMEMBERS
CELLFORMULASETLIST	LAG	STRTOMEMBER
CHAPTERS	LASTCHILD	STRTOSET
CHILDREN	LASTPERIODS	STRTOTUPLE
CLEAR	LASTSIBLING	STRTOVAL
CLOSINGPERIOD	LEAD	STRTOVALUE
COALESCEEMPTY	LEAVES	SUBSET
COLUMN	LEVEL	SUM
COLUMNS	LEVELS	TAIL
CORRELATION	LINKMEMBER	THIS
COUNT	LINREGINTERCEPT	TOGGLEDRILLSTATE
COUSIN	LINREGPOINT	TOPCOUNT
COVARIANCE	LINREGR2	TOPPERCENT
COVARIANCEN	LINREGSLOPE	TOPSUM
CREATE	LINREGVARIANCE	TOTALS
CREATEPROPERTYSET	LOOKUPCUBE	TREE
CREATEVIRTUALDIMENSION	MAX	TRUE
CROSSJOIN	MEASURE	TUPLETOSTR
CUBE	MEDIAN	TYPE
CURRENT	MEMBER	UNION
CURRENTCUBE	MEMBERS	UNIQUE
CURRENTMEMBER	MEMBERTOSTR	UNIQUENAME
DEFAULTMEMBER	MIN	UPDATE
DEFAULT_MEMBER	MTD	USE
DESC	NAME	USERNAME
DESCENDANTS	NAMETOSET	USE_EQUAL_ALLOCATION
DESCRIPTION	NEST	USE_WEIGHTED_ALLOCATION

continues

TABLE C-1 *(continued)*

DIMENSION	NEXTMEMBER	USE_WEIGHTED_INCREMENT
DIMENSIONS	NON	VALIDMEASURE
DISTINCT	NONEMPTYCROSSJOIN	VALUE
DISTINCTCOUNT	NOT_RELATED_TO_FACTS	VAR
DRILLDOWNLEVEL	NO_ALLOCATION	VARIANCE
DRILLDOWNLEVELBOTTOM	NO_PROPERTIES	VARIANCEP
DRILLDOWNLEVELTOP	NULL	VARP
DRILLDOWNMEMBER	ON	VISUAL
DRILLDOWNMEMBERBOTTOM	OPENINGPERIOD	VISUALTOTALS
DRILLDOWNMEMBERTOP	OR	WHERE
DRILLUPLEVEL	PAGES	WITH
DRILLUPMEMBER	PARALLELPERIOD	WTD
DROP	PARENT	XOR
EMPTY	PASS	YTD
END		

MEMBER REFERENCES

A *member* is a value within a hierarchy. A member is partially referenced by the dimension, hierarchy, and level to which it belongs. Each of these components must adhere to the rules for object identifiers, as described earlier. Each part of the reference is separated from the others by a period.

The member's key or name value serves as the final part of the member reference. Member names and keys must adhere to the rules for object identifiers. Member keys may have several parts, with each part preceded by the ampersand (&) character.

The following are a couple examples of member references in the forms described. Note the use of square brackets for both regular and delimited identifiers. This is done to standardize the form of the reference.

```
[Date].[Calendar].[Month].[January 2004]
[Date].[Calendar].[Month].&[2004].&[01]
```

Alternatively, you can reference a member according to its lineage within a hierarchy. In this form, a member reference is provided for a member on a higher level in a hierarchy. Appended to this reference are the period-delimited keys or names of descendants forming the lineage of the initial member reference to the member of interest. The final name or key is the member of interest.

The following examples show the members in the preceding example in this form. Note that the `[Date].[Calendar]` hierarchy consists of an (All) level followed by `[Calendar Year].[Calendar Semester].[Calendar Quarter].[Month]` levels. (The hierarchy contains a `[Date]` level below this, but that is not of interest in these examples.)

```
[Date].[Calendar].[Calendar Year].[CY 2004].[H1 CY 2004].[Q1 CY 2004]
    .[January 2004]
[Date].[Calendar].[Calendar Year].&[2004].&[2004]&[1].&[2004]&[1].&[2004]&[1]
```

If unambiguous, the `[Dimension].[Hierarchy].[Level]` part of a member reference can be abbreviated to any of the following forms:

```
[Dimension].[Hierarchy]
[Dimension].[Level]
[Hierarchy].[Level]
[Dimension]
```

The entire `[Dimension].[Hierarchy].[Level]` part of the reference can also be omitted. The following examples illustrate these abbreviated forms:

```
[Date].[Calendar].[January 2004]
[Date].[Month].[January 2004]
[Date].[January 2004]
[Month].[January 2004]
[January 2004]
```

Be careful when using abbreviated member references. If a reference could represent more than one member within a cube, Analysis Services returns the first one encountered. Although data is returned, you might not receive the data you expected.

SETS

Sets represent zero, one, or more members from an attribute or user hierarchy. Sets may be defined through the use of MDX functions, the assembly of members in a comma-delimited list, or a named set.

Within MDX statements, sets are encapsulated by curly braces. The curly braces are optional if the set is not defined as a comma-delimited list of more than one member reference.

The following are examples of valid single-member sets. These sets are equivalent to each other.

```
{[Date].[Calendar].[Month].[January 2004]}
[Date].[Calendar].[Month].[January 2004]
```

The following are examples of valid multimember sets. The last two use the `Children` MDX function. All three sets are equivalent.

```
{[Date].[Calendar].[Month].[January 2004], [Date].[Calendar].[Month]
    .[February 2004], [Date].[Calendar].[Month].[March 2004]}
{[Date].[Calendar].[Q1 CY 2004].Children}
[Date].[Calendar].[Q1 CY 2004].Children
```

Sets may be combined to form multipart sets through a cross-join operation. This is done by first defining basic sets and then combining them using the `CrossJoin` MDX function. You can use the asterisk character (*) as shorthand notation for the `CrossJoin` function. The following examples illustrate the construction of identical multipart sets using these cross-join methods:

```
CrossJoin({[Date].[Calendar].[Q1 CY 2004].Children},
{[Product].[Categories].[Categories].Members})
{[Date].[Calendar].[Q1 CY 2004].Children}
  * {[Product].[Categories].[Categories].Members}
```

Multipart sets can also be constructed through a delimited list of tuples, as illustrated in the following example:

```
{([Date].[Calendar].[Month].[January 2004],[Product].[Category].[Bikes]),
([Date].[Calendar].[Month].[February 2004],[Product].[Category].[Components]),
([Date].[Calendar].[Month].[March 2004],[Product].[Category].[Accessories])}
```

TUPLES

All points within a cube are identified by a coordinate value. The full coordinate value for any point identifies a member from each attribute hierarchy within the cube. This coordinate is known as the *full tuple* (or *complete tuple*) for that point. Partial tuples specify a member value for one or more attributes within the coordinate system. Any attributes not explicitly identified within a partial tuple are supplied by Analysis Services using the following rules:

➤ If the implicitly referenced dimension has a default member, the default member is added to the tuple.

➤ If the implicitly referenced dimension has no default member, the (All) member of the default hierarchy is used.

➤ If the implicitly referenced dimension has no default member, and the default hierarchy has no (All) member, the first member of the topmost level of the default hierarchy is used.

Tuples are encapsulated in parentheses. Parentheses are optional if only a single member reference is used. The following are valid tuple references:

```
([Date].[Calendar].[Month].[January 2004])
[Date].[Calendar].[Month].[January 2004]
([Date].[Calendar].[Month].[January 2004], [Date].[Date].[Date].[January 1, 2004])
([Date].[Calendar].[Month].[January 2004], [Date].[Date].[Date].[January 1, 2004]
    , [Product].[Category].[Category].[Bikes])
```

THE SELECT STATEMENT

The MDX SELECT statement is used to retrieve data from a cube. The statement specifies sets of members along a number of axes. The intersection of members along these axes, coupled with members identified in the statement's optional WHERE clause, form a collection of tuples that identify points within a specified cube or subcube as described in the FROM clause. The values associated with these points, called *cells*, are returned as a *cellset*. Although variations from what is described here exist, this is the basic form of the MDX SELECT statement. The following example illustrates this form:

```
SELECT
    {[Measures].[Sales Amount], [Measures].[Tax Amount]} ON COLUMNS,
    {[Date].[Calendar].[Q1 CY 2004].Children} ON ROWS
FROM [Adventure Works]
WHERE ([Product].[Category].[Category].[Bikes])
```

In addition to the axis definitions and WHERE and FROM clauses, the MDX SELECT statement supports a WITH clause that can be used to specify query-scoped calculated members and named sets. Reporting Services also provides support for parameters within the MDX SELECT statement, although these are not formally part of the statement.

Axis Definitions

The MDX SELECT statement supports the identification of between 0 and 128 axes. Each axis is identified by the formal name of AXIS(n), where n is the numeric identifier of the axis, the first of which is 0. The axis name can be shortened to be just the number of the axis, and no axis can be skipped. The first five axes, the most frequently used, also support aliases, as shown in Table C-2.

TABLE C-2

FORMAL NAME	SHORTENED NAME	ALIAS
AXIS(0)	0	COLUMNS
AXIS(1)	1	ROWS
AXIS(2)	2	PAGES
AXIS(3)	3	SECTIONS
AXIS(4)	4	CHAPTERS

Along each axis, a set is defined. The set may be singular or composed of multiple sets cross-joined to form a multipart set. The set may also be an empty set, specified by an opening and closing curly brace ({}). No hierarchy may be used to supply members in sets along more than one axis.

Within the context of Reporting Services, the MDX SELECT statement defining the cells set to be returned to the report supports up to two axes. Typically, the COLUMNS axis is used to specify members of the Measures dimension, and cross-joined sets are not supported on this axis. These constraints are due to Reporting Services' limitations in converting cell sets into the data table structure it uses internally.

The WHERE Clause

The MDX SELECT statement supports an optional WHERE clause. The WHERE clause, also known as the *slicer*, is used to specify members not otherwise specified within the axis definitions. The members specified in the WHERE clause are incorporated into all tuples defining the cellset to be returned by the SELECT statement.

The WHERE clause typically consists of a single, partial tuple. The members identified within this tuple are from hierarchies not specified along the axis definitions.

Alternatively, the WHERE clause can be composed of a singular or multipart set. The members of the various hierarchies are aggregated so that the WHERE clause continues to function as a tuple. This is not a common use of the WHERE clause.

The FROM Clause

The FROM clause defines the context within which the query is resolved. The context can be defined as a cube or as a nested MDX SELECT statement, also known as a *query-scoped subcube*, which limits the cube space within which a query is resolved.

The following rules govern the effect of query-scoped subcubes on cube space:

➤ If you include the (All) member of a hierarchy, you include every member of that hierarchy.

➤ If you include any member, you include that member's ascendants and descendants.

➤ If you include every member from a level, you include all members from the hierarchy. Members from other hierarchies are excluded if those members do not exist with members from the level (for example, an unbalanced hierarchy such as a city that does not contain customers).

➤ A subcube always contains every (All) member from the cube.

The WITH Clause

The WITH clause is used within an MDX SELECT statement to define query-scoped calculated members and named sets. The WITH clause lets you construct one or more calculated members or named sets within a given query, and calculated members and named sets may reference each other. The order of the declaration of calculated members and named sets within a query is unimportant.

A calculated member is an expression providing instruction for the derivation of a member within a hierarchy. The basic form of a named member is as follows:

```
WITH MEMBER [Dimension].[Hierarchy].[Level].[Member] as
    <expression>
```

where <expression> is a valid MDX expression resolving to a single member or value. The expression defining the calculated member can be followed by a comma and the FORMAT keyword. The FORMAT keyword can be assigned one of the following named formats:

➤ Currency

➤ Percent

➤ Short Date

➤ Short Time

➤ Standard

Alternatively, the FORMAT keyword can be assigned an expression identifying a format. See the Analysis Services Books Online article "FORMAT_STRING Contents" for a complete listing of the rules for defining these expressions.

A named set is an expression evaluating to a set of members, stored or calculated. The basic form of a named set is as follows:

```
WITH SET [Set] as
    <expression>
```

Where <expression> is a valid MDX expression resolving to a single- or multipart set.

When more than one calculated member or named set is defined for a query, the WITH keyword precedes the first calculated member or named set only.

The following example illustrates a SELECT statement using the WITH clause:

```
WITH
    MEMBER [Measures].[Tax Percent] as
        ([Measures].[Tax Amount])/([Measures].[Sales Amount])
        ,FORMAT="Percent"
    SET [Periods Of Interest] as
        {[Date].[Calendar].[Q1 CY 2004].Children}
SELECT
    {
        [Measures].[Sales Amount],
        [Measures].[Tax Amount],
        [Measures].[Tax Percent]
    } ON COLUMNS,
    {[Periods of Interest]} ON ROWS
FROM [Adventure Works]
WHERE ([Product].[Category].[Category].[Bikes])
```

Parameters

The MDX SELECT statement provides support for parameters. However, Reporting Services cannot exploit this syntax. Instead, it provides an alternative, substitution-based mechanism for incorporating parameters.

Reporting Services parameters within MDX SELECT statements are identified by variables preceded by the "at" character (@). At execution, the Reporting Services variable is replaced with a string representing the variable's value. This string is encapsulated by double quotes and is therefore interpreted as a string by Analysis Services. To convert the string value to a member, tuple, or set reference, the SELECT statement uses the STRTOMEMBER, STRTOTUPLE, or STRTOSET MDX function, respectively.

Reporting Services uses the CONSTRAINED keyword with each of these function calls. The CONSTRAINED keyword prohibits the use of MDX functions within the string being evaluated. This is used to prevent injection attacks.

The following illustrates an MDX statement generated by Reporting Services containing a parameter:

```
SELECT
    NON EMPTY {[Measures].[Reseller Sales Amount]} ON COLUMNS
FROM (
        SELECT (STRTOSET(@DateCalendarYear, CONSTRAINED)) ON COLUMNS
        FROM [Adventure Works]
        )
WHERE (
    IIF(
        STRTOSET(@DateCalendarYear, CONSTRAINED).Count = 1,
        STRTOSET(@DateCalendarYear, CONSTRAINED),
        [Date].[Calendar Year].currentmember
        )
    )
CELL PROPERTIES VALUE, BACK_COLOR, FORE_COLOR, FORMATTED_VALUE,
    FORMAT_STRING, FONT_NAME, FONT_SIZE, FONT_FLAGS
```

MDX FUNCTIONS AND KEYWORDS

The following tables provide information on the MDX functions and keywords available for use with Analysis Services through Reporting Services queries. Each table represents a particular category of function or keyword.

Keywords

TABLE C-3

KEYWORD	DESCRIPTION
EXISTING	Forces a specified set to be evaluated within the current context. By default, sets are evaluated within the context of the cube that contains the members of the set. The EXISTING keyword forces a specified set to be evaluated within the current context instead.
NON EMPTY	Eliminates any members along the axis for whom only empty cells are returned.

KPI Functions

TABLE C-4

FUNCTION	SYNTAX	DESCRIPTION
KPICURRENTTIMEMEMBER	KPICURRENTTIMEMEMBER(«String Expression»)	Returns the current time member of the specified key performance indicator (KPI).
KPIGOAL	KPIGOAL(«String Expression»)	Returns the member that calculates the value for the goal portion of the specified KPI.
KPISTATUS	KPISTATUS(«String Expression»)	Returns a normalized value that represents the status portion of the specified KPI.
KPITREND	KPITREND(«String Expression»)	Returns the normalized value that represents the trend portion of the specified KPI.
KPIVALUE	KPIVALUE(«String Expression»)	Returns the member that calculates the value of the specified KPI.
KPIWEIGHT	KPIWEIGHT(«String Expression»)	Returns the weight of the specified KPI.

Metadata Functions

TABLE C-5

FUNCTION	SYNTAX	DESCRIPTION
AXIS	AXIS(«Numeric Expression»)	Returns the set of tuples on a specified axis.
COUNT	«Tuple».COUNT	Returns the number of dimensions in a tuple.
DIMENSIONS.COUNT	DIMENSIONS.COUNT	Returns the number of hierarchies in a cube, including the [Measures].[Measures] hierarchy.

continues

TABLE C-5 *(continued)*

FUNCTION	SYNTAX	DESCRIPTION
HIERARCHY	«Level».HIERARCHY	Returns the hierarchy that contains a specified member or level.
HIERARCHY	«Member».HIERARCHY	Returns the hierarchy that contains a specified member or level.
LEVEL	«Member».LEVEL	Returns the level of a member.
LEVELS	«Hierarchy».LEVELS(«Numeric Expression»)	Returns the level whose position in a dimension or hierarchy is specified by a numeric expression or whose name is specified by a string expression.
LEVELS.COUNT	«Hierarchy».LEVELS.COUNT	Returns the number of levels in a hierarchy.
NAME	«Member».NAME	Returns the name of a dimension, hierarchy, level, or member.
NAME	«Hierarchy».NAME	Returns the name of a dimension, hierarchy, level, or member.
NAME	«Level».NAME(Level)	Returns the name of a dimension, hierarchy, level, or member.
ORDINAL	«Level».ORDINAL	Returns the zero-based ordinal value associated with a level.
UNIQUENAME	«Hierarchy».UNIQUENAME	Returns the unique name of a specified dimension, hierarchy, level, or member.
UNIQUENAME	«Member».UNIQUENAME	Returns the unique name of a specified dimension, hierarchy, level, or member.
UNIQUENAME	«Level».UNIQUENAME	Returns the unique name of a specified dimension, hierarchy, level, or member.

Navigation Functions

TABLE C-6

FUNCTION	SYNTAX	DESCRIPTION
ANCESTOR	ANCESTOR(«Member», «Level»)	Returns the ancestor of a member at a specified level or distance.
ANCESTOR	ANCESTOR(«Member», «Distance»)	Returns the ancestor of a member at a specified level or distance.
ANCESTORS	ANCESTORS(«Member», «Distance»)	Returns a set of all ancestors of a member at a specified level or distance.
ANCESTORS	ANCESTORS(«Member», «Level»)	Returns a set of all ancestors of a member at a specified level or distance.
ASCENDANTS	ASCENDANTS(«Member»)	Returns the set of the ascendants of a specified member, including the member itself.
CHILDREN	«Member».CHILDREN	Returns the children of a specified member.
COUSIN	COUSIN(«Member1», «Member2»)	Returns the child member with the same relative position under a parent member as the specified child member.
CURRENT	«Set».CURRENT	Returns the current tuple from a set during iteration.
CURRENTMEMBER	«Hierarchy».CURRENTMEMBER	Returns the current member along a specified dimension or hierarchy during iteration.
CURRENTORDINAL	«Set».CURRENTORDINAL	Returns the current iteration number within a set during iteration.
DATAMEMBER	«Member».DATAMEMBER	Returns the system-generated data member that is associated with a nonleaf member of a dimension.
DEFAULTMEMBER	«Hierarchy».DEFAULTMEMBER	Returns the default member of a dimension or hierarchy.
FIRSTCHILD	«Member».FIRSTCHILD	Returns the first child of a member.

continues

TABLE C-6 *(continued)*

FUNCTION	SYNTAX	DESCRIPTION
FIRSTSIBLING	«Member».FIRSTSIBLING	Returns the first child of the parent of a member.
ISANCESTOR	ISANCESTOR(«Member1»,«Member2»)	Returns whether a specified member is an ancestor of another specified member.
ISGENERATION	ISGENERATION(«Member»,«Numeric Expression»)	Returns whether a specified member is in a specified generation.
ISLEAF	ISLEAF(«Member»)	Returns whether a specified member is a leaf member.
ISSIBLING	ISSIBLING(«Member1»,«Member2»)	Returns whether a specified member is a sibling of another specified member.
LAG	«Member».LAG(«Numeric Expression»)	Returns the member that is a specified number of positions before a specified member along the member's dimension.
LASTCHILD	«Member».LASTCHILD	Returns the last child of a specified member.
LASTSIBLING	«Member».LASTSIBLING	Returns the last child of the parent of a specified member.
LEAD	«Member».LEAD(«Numeric Expression»)	Returns the member that is a specified number of positions following a specified member along the member's dimension.
LINKMEMBER	LINKMEMBER(«Member», «Hierarchy»)	Returns the member equivalent to a specified member in a specified hierarchy.
LOOKUPCUBE	LOOKUPCUBE(«Cube Name», «Numeric Expression»)	Returns the value of an MDX expression evaluated over another specified cube in the same database.
NEXTMEMBER	«Member».NEXTMEMBER	Returns the next member in the level that contains a specified member.
PARENT	«Member».PARENT	Returns the parent of a member.

FUNCTION	SYNTAX	DESCRIPTION
PREVMEMBER	«Member».PREVMEMBER	Returns the previous member in the level that contains a specified member.
PROPERTIES	«Member».PROPERTIES(«String Expression»[, TYPED])	Returns a string, or a strongly typed value, that contains a member property value.
SIBLINGS	«Member».SIBLINGS	Returns the siblings of a specified member, including the member itself.
UNKNOWNMEMBER	UNKNOWNMEMBER	Returns the unknown member associated with a level or member.

Other Functions

TABLE C-7

FUNCTION	SYNTAX	DESCRIPTION
CALCULATIONCURRENTPASS	CALCULATIONCURRENTPASS	Returns the current calculation pass of a cube for the specified query context.
CALCULATIONPASSVALUE	CALCULATIONPASSVALUE(«Numeric Expression», «Pass Value»[[, «Access Flag»], ALL])	Returns the value of an MDX expression evaluated over the specified calculation pass of a cube.
CUSTOMDATA	CUSTOMDATA	Returns the value of the CustomData property.
ITEM	«Tuple».ITEM(«Numeric Expression»)	Returns a member from a specified tuple.
ITEM	«Set».ITEM(«String Expression»[, «String Expression»...] | «Index»)	Returns a tuple from a set.
PREDICT	PREDICT(«Mining Model Name», «Numeric Expression»)	Returns a value of a numeric expression evaluated over a data mining model.
SETTOARRAY	SETTOARRAY(«Set»[, «Set»...] [, «Numeric Expression»])	Converts one or more sets to an array for use in a user-defined function.

Set Functions

TABLE C-8

FUNCTION	SYNTAX	DESCRIPTION
ADDCALCULATEDMEMBERS	ADDCALCULATEDMEMBERS(«Set»)	Returns a set generated by adding calculated members to a specified set.
ALLMEMBERS	«Level».ALLMEMBERS	Returns a set that contains all members, including calculated members, of the specified dimension, hierarchy, or level.
ALLMEMBERS	«Hierarchy».ALLMEMBERS	Returns a set that contains all members, including calculated members, of the specified dimension, hierarchy, or level.
BOTTOMCOUNT	BOTTOMCOUNT(«Set», «Count»[, «Numeric Expression»])	Sorts a set in ascending order and returns the specified number of tuples with the lowest values.
BOTTOMPERCENT	BOTTOMPERCENT(«Set», «Percentage», «Numeric Expression»)	Sorts a set in ascending order and returns a set of tuples with the lowest values whose cumulative total is equal to or less than a specified percentage.
BOTTOMSUM	BOTTOMSUM(«Set», «Value», «Numeric Expression»)	Sorts a set in ascending order and returns a set of tuples with the lowest values whose total is equal to or less than a specified value.
CROSSJOIN	CROSSJOIN(«Set1», «Set2»)	Returns the cross-product of one or more sets.
DESCENDANTS	DESCENDANTS(«Member»[, «Level»[, «Desc_flags»]])	Returns the set of descendants of a member at a specified level or distance, optionally including or excluding descendants in other levels.

FUNCTION	SYNTAX	DESCRIPTION
DESCENDANTS	DESCENDANTS(«Member», «Distance»[, «Desc_flags»])	Returns the set of descendants of a member at a specified level or distance, optionally including or excluding descendants in other levels.
DISTINCT	DISTINCT(«Set»)	Returns a set, removing duplicate tuples from a specified set.
EXCEPT	EXCEPT(«Set1», «Set2»[, ALL])	Finds the difference between two sets, optionally retaining duplicates.
EXISTING	EXISTING	Forces a specified set to be evaluated within the current context. By default, sets are evaluated within the context of the cube that contains the members of the set. The EXISTING keyword forces a specified set to be evaluated within the current context instead.
EXISTS	EXISTS(«Set1», «Set2»)	Returns the set of members of one set that exist with one or more tuples of one or more other sets.
EXTRACT	EXTRACT(«Set», «Dimension»[, «Dimension»...])	Returns a set of tuples from extracted dimension elements.
FILTER	FILTER(«Set», «Search Condition»)	Returns the set that results from filtering a specified set based on a search condition.
GENERATE	GENERATE(«Set1», «Set2»[, ALL])	Applies a set to each member of another set and then joins the resulting sets by union. Alternatively, this function returns a concatenated string created by evaluating a string expression over a set.

continues

TABLE C-8 *(continued)*

FUNCTION	SYNTAX	DESCRIPTION
HEAD	HEAD(«Set»[, «Numeric Expression»])	Returns the first specified number of elements in a set while retaining duplicates.
HIERARCHIZE	HIERARCHIZE(«Set»[, POST])	Orders the members of a set in a hierarchy.
INTERSECT	INTERSECT(«Set1», «Set2»[, ALL])	Returns the intersection of two input sets, optionally retaining duplicates.
MEASUREGROUPMEASURES	MEASUREGROUPMEASURES(«String Expression»)	Returns a set of measures that belongs to the specified measure group.
MEMBERS	«Hierarchy».MEMBERS	Returns a member specified by a string expression.
MEMBERS	«Level».MEMBERS	Returns a member specified by a string expression.
NONEMPTY	NONEMPTY(«Set1», «Set2»)	Returns the set of tuples that are not empty from a specified set, based on the cross-product of the specified set with a second set.
NONEMPTYCROSSJOIN	NONEMPTYCROSSJOIN(«Set1», «Set2»[, «Set3»...][, «Crossjoin Count»])	Returns the cross-product of one or more sets as a set, excluding empty tuples and tuples without associated fact table data.
ORDER	ORDER(«Set», {«String Expression» | «Numeric Expression»}[, ASC | DESC | BASC | BDESC])	Arranges members of a specified set, optionally preserving or breaking the hierarchy.
STRIPCALCULATEDMEMBERS	STRIPCALCULATEDMEMBERS(«Set»)	Returns a set generated by removing calculated members from a specified set.
SUBSET	SUBSET(«Set», «Start»[, «Count»])	Returns a subset of tuples from a specified set.
TAIL	TAIL(«Set»[, «Count»])	Returns a subset from the end of a set.

FUNCTION	SYNTAX	DESCRIPTION
TOPCOUNT	TOPCOUNT(«Set», «Count»[, «Numeric Expression»])	Sorts a set in descending order and returns the specified number of elements with the highest values.
TOPPERCENT	TOPPERCENT(«Set», «Percentage», «Numeric Expression»)	Sorts a set in descending order and returns a set of tuples with the highest values whose cumulative total is equal to or less than a specified percentage.
TOPSUM	TOPSUM(«Set», «Value», «Numeric Expression»)	Sorts a set and returns the topmost elements whose cumulative total is at least a specified value.
UNION	UNION(«Set1», «Set2»[, ALL])	Returns the union of two sets, optionally retaining duplicates.
UNORDER	UNORDER(«Set»)	Removes any enforced ordering from a specified set.

Statistical Functions

TABLE C-9

FUNCTION	SYNTAX	DESCRIPTION
AGGREGATE	AGGREGATE(«Set»[, «Numeric Expression»])	Returns a scalar value calculated by aggregating either measures or an optionally specified numeric expression over the tuples of a specified set.
AVG	AVG(«Set»[, «Numeric Expression»])	Returns the average value of measures or the average value of an optional numeric expression, evaluated over a specified set.
COALESCEEMPTY	COALESCEEMPTY(«Numeric Expression»[, «Numeric Expression»...])	Coalesces an empty cell value to a number or string and returns the coalesced value.

continues

TABLE C-9 *(continued)*

FUNCTION	SYNTAX	DESCRIPTION
CORRELATION	CORRELATION(«Set», «Numeric Expression»[, «Numeric Expression»])	Returns the correlation coefficient of two series evaluated over a set.
COUNT	«Set».COUNT	Returns the number of cells in a set.
COUNT	COUNT(«Set»[, EXCLUDEEMPTY | INCLUDEEMPTY])	Returns the number of cells in a set. The Count(Set) function includes or excludes empty cells, depending on the syntax used. If the standard syntax is used, empty cells can be excluded or included by using the EXCLUDEEMPTY or INCLUDEEMPTY flags, respectively. If the alternative syntax is used, the function always includes empty cells.
COVARIANCE	COVARIANCE(«Set», «Numeric Expression»[, «Numeric Expression»])	Returns the population covariance of two series evaluated over a set, using the biased population formula.
COVARIANCEN	COVARIANCEN(«Set», «Numeric Expression»[, «Numeric Expression»])	Returns the sample covariance of two series evaluated over a set, using the unbiased population formula.
DISTINCTCOUNT	DISTINCTCOUNT(«Set»)	Returns the number of distinct, nonempty tuples in a set.
LINREGINTERCEPT	LINREGINTERCEPT(«Set», «Numeric Expression»[, «Numeric Expression»])	Calculates the linear regression of a set and returns the value of the intercept in the regression line, $y = ax + b$.
LINREGPOINT	LINREGPOINT(«Numeric Expression», «Set», «Numeric Expression»[, «Numeric Expression»])	Calculates the linear regression of a set and returns the value of y in the regression line, $y = ax + b$.
LINREGR2	LINREGR2(«Set», «Numeric Expression»[, «Numeric Expression»])	Calculates the linear regression of a set and returns the coefficient of determination, R2.

FUNCTION	SYNTAX	DESCRIPTION
LINREGSLOPE	LINREGSLOPE(«Set», «Numeric Expression»[, «Numeric Expression»])	Calculates the linear regression of a set and returns the value of the slope in the regression line, $y = ax + b$.
LINREGVARIANCE	LINREGVARIANCE(«Set», «Numeric Expression»[, «Numeric Expression»])	Calculates the linear regression of a set and returns the variance associated with the regression line, $y = ax + b$.
MAX	MAX(«Set»[, «Numeric Expression»])	Returns the maximum value of a numeric expression that is evaluated over a set.
MEDIAN	MEDIAN(«Set»[, «Numeric Expression»])	Returns the median value of a numeric expression that is evaluated over a set.
MIN	MIN(«Set»[, «Numeric Expression»])	Returns the minimum value of a numeric expression that is evaluated over a set.
RANK	RANK(«Tuple», «Set»)	Returns the one-based rank of a specified tuple in a specified set.
ROLLUPCHILDREN	ROLLUPCHILDREN(«Member», «String Expression»)	Returns a value generated by rolling up the values of the children of a specified member using the specified unary operator.
STDDEV	STDDEV(«Set»[, «Numeric Expression»])	Alias for STDEV.
STDDEVP	STDDEVP(«Set»[, «Numeric Expression»])	Alias for STDEVP.
STDEV	STDEV(«Set»[, «Numeric Expression»])	Returns the sample standard deviation of a numeric expression evaluated over a set, using the unbiased population formula.
STDEVP	STDEVP(«Set»[, «Numeric Expression»])	Returns the population standard deviation of a numeric expression evaluated over a set, using the biased population formula.
SUM	SUM(«Set»[, «Numeric Expression»])	Returns the sum of a numeric expression evaluated over a set.

continues

TABLE C-9 *(continued)*

FUNCTION	SYNTAX	DESCRIPTION
VAR	VAR(«Set»[, «Numeric Expression»])	Returns the sample variance of a numeric expression evaluated over a set, using the unbiased population formula.
VARIANCE	VARIANCE(«Set»[, «Numeric Expression»])	Alias for VAR.
VARIANCEP	VARIANCEP(«Set»[, «Numeric Expression»])	Alias for VARP.
VARP	VARP(«Set»[, «Numeric Expression»])	Returns the population variance of a numeric expression evaluated over a set, using the biased population formula.
VISUALTOTALS	VISUALTOTALS(«Set», «Pattern»)	Returns a set generated by dynamically totaling child members in a specified set, optionally using a pattern for the name of the parent member in the resulting cellset.

String Functions

TABLE C-10

FUNCTION	SYNTAX	DESCRIPTION
GENERATE	GENERATE(«Set», «String Expression»[, «Delimiter»])	Applies a set to each member of another set and then joins the resulting sets by union. Alternatively, this function returns a concatenated string created by evaluating a string expression over a set.
MEMBERTOSTR	MEMBERTOSTR(«Member»)	Returns an MDX-formatted string that corresponds to a specified member.
NAMETOSET	NAMETOSET(«Member Name»)	Returns a set that contains the member specified by an MDX-formatted string.

FUNCTION	SYNTAX	DESCRIPTION
SETTOSTR	SETTOSTR(«Set»)	Returns the set specified by an MDX-formatted string.
STRTOMEMBER	STRTOMEMBER(«String Expression»)	Returns the member specified by an MDX-formatted string.
STRTOSET	STRTOSET(«String Expression»)	Returns the set specified by an MDX-formatted string.
STRTOTUPLE	STRTOTUPLE(«String Expression»)	Returns the tuple specified by an MDX-formatted string.
STRTOVALUE	STRTOVALUE(«String Expression»)	Returns the value specified by an MDX-formatted string.
TUPLETOSTR	TUPLETOSTR(«Tuple»)	Returns an MDX-formatted string that corresponds to the specified tuple.

Time Functions

TABLE C-11

FUNCTION	SYNTAX	DESCRIPTION
CLOSINGPERIOD	CLOSINGPERIOD([«Level»[, «Member»]])	Returns the last sibling among the descendants of a member at a specified level.
LASTPERIODS	LASTPERIODS(«Index»[, «Member»])	Returns a set of members up to and including a specified member.
MTD	MTD([«Member»])	Returns a set of sibling members from the same level as a given member, starting with the first sibling and ending with the given member, as constrained by the Year level in the Time dimension.
OPENINGPERIOD	OPENINGPERIOD([«Level»[, «Member»]])	Returns the first sibling among the descendants of a specified level, optionally at a specified member.

continues

TABLE C-11 *(continued)*

FUNCTION	SYNTAX	DESCRIPTION
PARALLELPERIOD	PARALLELPERIOD([«Level»[, «Numeric Expression»[, «Member»]]])	Returns a member from a prior period in the same relative position as a specified member.
PERIODSTODATE	PERIODSTODATE([«Level»[, «Member»]])	Returns a set of sibling members from the same level as a given member, starting with the first sibling and ending with the given member, as constrained by a specified level in the Time dimension.
QTD	QTD([«Member»])	Returns a set of sibling members from the same level as a given member, starting with the first sibling and ending with the given member, as constrained by the Quarter level in the Time dimension.
WTD	WTD([«Member»])	Returns a set of sibling members from the same level as a given member, starting with the first sibling and ending with the given member, as constrained by the Week level in the Time dimension.
YTD	YTD([«Member»])	Returns a set of sibling members from the same level as a given member, starting with the first sibling and ending with the given member, as constrained by the Year level in the Time dimension.

UI Functions

TABLE C-12

FUNCTION	SYNTAX	DESCRIPTION
DRILLDOWNLEVEL	DRILLDOWNLEVEL(«Set»[, «Level»])	Drills down the members of a set to one level below the lowest level represented in the set, or to one level below an optionally specified level of a member represented in the set.

FUNCTION	SYNTAX	DESCRIPTION
DRILLDOWNLEVEL	DRILLDOWNLEVEL(«Set»[, , «Index»])	Drills down the members of a set to one level below the lowest level represented in the set, or to one level below an optionally specified level of a member represented in the set.
DRILLDOWNLEVELBOTTOM	DRILLDOWNLEVELBOTTOM(«Set», «Count»[, [«Level»][, «Numeric Expression»]])	Drills down the bottommost members of a set, at a specified level, to one level below.
DRILLDOWNLEVELTOP	DRILLDOWNLEVELTOP(«Set», «Count»[, [«Level»][, «Numeric Expression»]])	Drills down the topmost members of a set, at a specified level, to one level below.
DRILLDOWNMEMBER	DRILLDOWNMEMBER(«Set1», «Set2»[, RECURSIVE])	Drills down the members of a specified set that are present in a second specified set. Alternatively, this function drills down on a set of tuples.
DRILLDOWNMEMBERBOTTOM	DRILLDOWNMEMBERBOTTOM(«Set1», «Set2», «Count»[, [«Numeric Expression»] [, RECURSIVE]])	Drills down the members of a specified set that are present in a second specified set, limiting the result set to a specified number of members. Alternatively, this function drills down on a set of tuples.
DRILLDOWNMEMBERTOP	DRILLDOWNMEMBERTOP(«Set1», «Set2», «Count»[, [«Numeric Expression»] [, RECURSIVE]])	Drills down the members of a specified set that are present in a second specified set, limiting the result set to a specified number of members. Alternatively, this function drills down on a set of tuples.
DRILLUPLEVEL	DRILLUPLEVEL(«Set»[, «Level»])	Drills up the members of a set that are below a specified level.

continues

TABLE C-12 *(continued)*

FUNCTION	SYNTAX	DESCRIPTION
DRILLUPMEMBER	DRILLUPMEMBER(«Set1», «Set2»)	Drills up the members of a specified set that are present in a second specified set.
TOGGLEDRILLSTATE	TOGGLEDRILLSTATE(«Set1», «Set2»[, RECURSIVE])	Toggles the drill state of members.

Value Functions

TABLE C-13

FUNCTION	SYNTAX	DESCRIPTION
IIF	IIF(«Logical Expression», «object», «object»)	Returns one of two values determined by a logical test.
IS	IS	Performs a logical comparison on two object expressions.
ISEMPTY	ISEMPTY(«Value Expression»)	Returns whether the evaluated expression is the empty cell value.
MEMBERVALUE	«Member».MEMBERVALUE	Returns the value of a member.
VALIDMEASURE	VALIDMEASURE(«Tuple»)	Returns a valid measure in a virtual cube by forcing inapplicable dimensions to their top level.
VALUE	«Tuple».VALUE	Returns the value of a measure.

INDEX

F

J

K

L